Testing and Assessment in Counseling Practice
Second Edition

Testing and Assessment in Counseling Practice
Second Edition

Edited by

C. Edward Watkins, Jr.
Vicki L. Campbell
University of North Texas

LAWRENCE ERLBAUM ASSOCIATES, PUBLISHERS

2000   Mahwah, New Jersey   London

Lawrence Erlbaum Associates, Inc., Publishers
10 Industrial Avenue
Mahwah, NJ 07430

Cover design by Kathryn Houghtaling Lacey

Library of Congress Cataloging-in-Publication Data

Testing and assessment in counseling practice / edited by
C. Edward Watkins, Jr., Vicki L. Campbell. — 2nd ed.
        p. cm. — (Contemporary topics in vocational
        psychology)
    Includes bibliographical references and index.
ISBN 0-8058-2380-8 (cloth : alk. paper) — ISBN
0-8058-2381-6 (pbk. : alk. paper).
1. Psychological tests. 2. Personality tests. 3. Vocational interest—Testing. 4. Counseling. I. Watkins, C.
Edward. II. Campbell, Vicki Lynn. III. Series
BF176.T423 1999
150' .28'7—dc21

                                        98-38251
                                             CIP

Books published by Lawrence Erlbaum Associates are
printed on acid-free paper, and their bindings are chosen for
strength and durability.

Printed in the United States of America
10 9 8 7 6 5 4 3 2 1

To our respective sources of support
Connie
and
Alan, Keith, and Alex

Contents

Preface to Second Edition

The first edition of this book was published in 1990. Since that time, continuing changes have been occurring in the field of assessment. Such changes led to the need for a second edition. As you will find, some of the tests covered here (e.g., the MMPI) have gone through major revision; others have continued to develop and we felt, for this book to remain viable, those developments, revisions, refinements, and extensions needed to be noted. The same lineup of tests or assessment procedures was kept for this edition.

Preface to First Edition

Testing has long been regarded as an important role of the counselor. Counselors traditionally have provided a variety of testing services, including personality, vocational, intellectual, and aptitude testing. In this book, we hope to consider further the role that tests play in the counseling process. Specifically, the purposes of this book are: (a) to provide important information on tests that are of value to counselors, (b) to provide information on how counselors think about and use tests, and (c) to illustrate how counselors can use different types of test information in counseling.

The book is designed to introduce readers to important theoretical, research, and practical information about the tests included here; it is oriented toward counselors, psychologists, and other mental health and education professionals. The book is suitable for graduate students who want to learn about different types of tests and for professionals who wish to get a comprehensive introduction about a test or tests. This book is appropriate for both master's-level and doctoral-level training courses that teach students about tests and their place in counseling.

In considering the tests covered here, an important point to remember is as follows: The tests were included because they focus more on a "normal" or "relatively normal" clientele. The tests presented in Parts I one and II are suited most appropriately for clients who could be described as psychologically healthy or relatively healthy, nonpathological, and psychiatrically nondisturbed. The clients who use these tests may be mildly to moderately distressed, experiencing some type of developmental issue or concern (e.g., deciding on a career), and in need of facilitative information. For the most, these tests are designed to help individuals who are well-functioning or, functioning adequately in their life roles.

A number of books that focus on using tests with a more pathological or psychologically disturbed clientele are available. However, there seems to be a dearth of books that focus on using tests with a more healthy clientele. Counselors do need to be familiar with psychological disturbance, but they need to know that there are many psychologically nondisturbed clients who can profit from counseling (Watkins & Peterson, 1986). We hope this book will demonstrate how tests can be used effectively for counseling healthy well-functioning clients.

Although we regard the chapters as comprehensive introductions to certain tests, two points about this book are important to keep in mind. First, a basic Pledge of test and measurement concepts (e.g., reliability, validity) is made of the reader. Therefore, to be able to use and understand the information included here, such knowledge is requisite. This book on testing logically follows a basic testing/measurement course or, if used in the course, would logically follow source material (e.g., Anastasi, 1988; Walsh & Betz, 1985) that provides an understanding of basic measurement concepts. Second, although the test chapters are excellent and provide rich information, they are not meant to replace study of the test annuals and other more specific, indepth sources. We believe the material to follow provides the reader with a sound beginning knowledge base, which will then need to be further reinforced and refined by more specific study of the particular tests the counselor wishes to learn.

As indicated previously, each of the test chapters contains a blend of theory, research, and practice material. The theoretical portion provides the conceptual foundations for the test under consideration, whereas the research portion provides information supporting the test and considers directions in which future research efforts should move. The practice material focuses on the different ways in which counselors can use the test and also includes a case ample. We thought it was important to include a case example, to enable the reader to gain a better understanding of how the tests could actually be ed in practice. In developing the case example, we gave the contributors two options: (a) Drawing on a counseling case, present test information and show how to integrate it into the work of counseling; or (b) provided work with the client did not proceed beyond the assessment phase, indicate how to integrate the test information into the counseling process if you were to be seeing this client for counseling. Thus, a major purpose of the book is to show how tests should be used to facilitate the counseling process.

To assist the contributors in developing their chapters, an outline for them to follow was developed. We hoped the outline would provide some continuity within and across chapters and insure that a number of important areas would be addressed. Although we recommended that contributors examine our outline and use it as they deemed appropriate, it was presented more as a tool to use in chapter development rather than a fixed, inflexible format to which everyone had to adhere. So, some continuity can be expected between chapters, but some variation can be expected also.

The idea of using a chapter outline is certainly not unique to our effort here. Previous works that have used a basic outline to organize chapters include Greenburg and Pinsof's (1986) *The Psychotherapeutic Process: A Research Handbook*, Gurman and Kniskern's (1981) *Handbook of Family Therapy*, and Norcross' (1986) *Handbook of Eclectic Psychotherapy*. In each case, the outline seemed useful in rendering the chapter material more effective. We hope our outline, presented at the end of this preface, worked similarly.

The book consists of three parts. Part I presents a model for using tests in counseling and considers five different tests that provide personality, cognitive, and behavioral assessment information. Part II considers various tests and methods that provide vocational assessment information. Part III considers issues and innovative applications in using tests in counseling. The last chapter presents some integrative postulates about the place of tests in counseling.

The decision about which personality and vocational tests to include in the book was given considerable thought and deliberation. In making our decision, three general criteria were used: (a) that the tests be used frequently by counselors; (b) that the tests have a solid history in the counseling profession; and (c) if relatively new in origin, that the tests show much promise for use in counseling. We made our final selection decisions based on test surveys of counselors (Bubenzer, Zimpfer, & Mahrle, 1990; Watkins & Campbell, 1987, 1989; Watkins, Campbell, & McGregor, 1988), readings of the professional literature in counseling, and personal observations about the types of tests counselors use and consider useful in counseling. Although some degree of arbitrariness may have been involved in our decision-making process, we tried to make our decisions in as informed a manner as possible.

Most of the chapters, of course, deal with a specific test. In a case or two (e. g., chap. 6 on cognitive and behavioral assessment), we chose to include assessment material that technically could not be called a "test," but that seemed of much potential value to counselors. In these cases, the word test can be applied loosely to the assessment material. However, for all practical purposes, the best way to refer to such assessment methods is to just call them that: assessment methods.

Like most books, this one is not without its limitations. Perhaps the primary limitation is that, although the chapters that follow contain some highly valuable information on some highly valuable tests, there are other important personality and vocational tests not covered. Also, there are other types of tests beyond the scope of this book (e. g., intellectual, projectives) about which the counselor should have knowledge. Although all books generally have frictions on their scope of content, it seems important to be aware of these frictions and the manner in which they limit the reader's knowledge base. In closing, as we reflect on our development of this book, there are a number of people who deserve thanks. First, we express our appreciation to our respective spouses, Wallene Watkins and Alan Wilson, for the support they provided us regarding this book project and for their continuing support of our careers. Second, we give a hearty thanks to all of the individuals who agreed to provide the chapters that compose this book. Their hard work helped us to bring our idea to realization, and we are indeed appreciative of their efforts. Third, we thank Lawrence Erlbaum for the assistance he provided us from a publishing perspective. Fourth, we express a deeply felt thank you to Sam Osipow for all the assistance and guidance he provided us for this project and for helping us bring it to final form.

—*C. Edward Watkins, Jr.*
Vicki L. Campbell

REFERENCES

Anastasi, A. (1988). *Psychological testing* (6th ed.). New York: Macmillan.

Bubenzer, D. L., Zimpfer, D. G., & Mahrle, C. L. (1990). Standardized individual appraisal in agency and private practice: A survey. *Journal of Mental Health Counseling, 12,* 51–66.

Greenburg, L. S., & Pinsof, W. M. (Eds.). (1986). *The psychotheraputic process: A research handbook.* New York: Guilford Press.

Gurman, A. S., & Kniskern, D. P. (Eds.). (1981). *Handbook of family therapy.* New York: Brunner/Mazel.

Norcross, J. C. (Ed.). (1986). *Handbook of eclectic psychotherapy.* New York: Brunner/ Mazel.

Walsh, W. B., & Betz, N. E. (1985). *Tests and assessment.* Englewood Cliffs, NJ: Prentice-Hall.

Watkins, C. E., Jr., & Campbell, V. L. (1987, September). Counseling psychologists and psychological testing: Practices, applications, and attitudes. In C. E. Watkins, Jr. (Chair), *Contemporary perspectives on and uses of tests in counseling psychology.* Paper presented as part of a symposium Psychological Association, New York.

Watkins, C. E., Jr., & Campbell, V. L. (1989). Personality assessment and counseling psychology. *Journal of Personality Assessment, 53,* 296–307.

Watkins, C. E., Jr., Campbell, V. L., & McGregor, P. (1988). Counseling psychologists' uses of and opinions about psychological tests: A contemporary perspective. *The Counseling Psychologist, 16,* 476–486.

Watkins, C. E., Jr., & Peterson, P. (1986). Psychiatric epidemiology: Its relevance for counselors. *Journal of Counseling and Development, 65,* 57–59.

Chapter Outline for *Testing in Counseling Practice**

I.   Background of the Test
     Aim: To describe the development of the test and place it in historical perspective
     1. What were the primary influences that contributed to the development of the test (e.g., people, experiences, research, books, conferences)?
     2. What were the direct antecedents of the test?
     3. How was the test originally conceptualized?
     4. What type of construction was used in developing the test?

*Several of the questions in this outline were taken or adapted from Norcross (1986).

II. Conceptual Foundations of the Test

Aim: To describe the uses, guiding principles, and current status of the test

1. What are the guiding principles and tenets of the test?
2. What is the basis for electing to use the test in counseling?
3. What are the different ways in which the test can be used in counseling?
4. What major client and/or environmental variables are assessed by the test?
5. At which *unit* levels (e.g., individual, dyadic, system) are assessments made with the test?
6. At which *psychological* levels (e.g., intrapsychic, behavioral) are assessments made with the test?
7. For what populations or types of clients is the test designed?

III. Test Administration and Scoring

Aim: To describe the composition of the test and how the instrument is administered and scored

1. Of what do the test materials consist (e.g., item types, stimuli, booklets, answer sheets, forms, etc.)?
2. How is the test administered (e.g., group, individual, special instructions)?
3. What types of scores result and how are they obtained?
4. Are there alternate scoring systems?
5. What scales or subtests comprise the test and how are they obtained and reported?
6. Are scores presented normatively, and if so, what norm groups are available?

IV. Test Information

Aim: To describe how the tester understands and interprets the test information

1. What constructs do the scales or subtests measure?
2. How is the meaning of particular scores understood or interpreted for the test's scales or subtests?
3. Are there different methods or systems for interpretation?
4. What are the author's views regarding the interpretive process (e.g., involvement of clients, presenting information to clients)?
5. Do different strategies exist for approaching the interpretive process?
6. Are there special issues or cautions related to the interpretive process that need to be described?

V. Case Example
    Aim: To illustrate how the test can be used and interpretive strategies
         can be applied in working with clients who seek counseling
         services
        1. Who is the client (e. g., age, sex, other relevant demographic
           variables, presenting problem)?
        2. What is the setting in which the counseling occurred (e. g.,
           counseling center, mental health center, private practice)?
        3. What prompted you to use the test with this client?
        4. What questions were you (and the client) hoping to have an-
           swered through giving the test?
        5. What results did you obtain from the test and what do they
           mean?
        6. How did you go about integrating the test information into a co-
           hesive picture?
        7. How did you go about interpreting the results to the client?
        8. How were you and the client able to use the test results in coun-
           seling?

VI. Research on the Test
     Aim: To briefly summarize the clinical and empirical research on the
          test
        1. What evidence exists to support the psychometric and techni-
           cal properties of the test?
        2. How does the existing evidence support the test's usefulness in
           counseling practice?
        3. Is there any evidence suggesting that certain cautions or reser-
           vations

VII. Evaluation and Future Directions
     Aim: To conclude by offering some evaluative comments about the
          test and considering its future directions and needs
        1. What are the advantages/disadvantages and strengths/weak-
           nesses that accompany the test (e.g., applied uses of the instru-
           ment, psychometric and technical properties)?
        2. How does the test compare with other instruments that are
           similar in nature?
        3. What is your overall evaluation of the test?
        4. What are the most important issues surrounding the test that
           need to be addressed?
        5. What further work (clinical, research, theoretical) is needed to
           improve the test or its usefulness in counseling?
        6. In what directions (clinical, research, theoretical) do you see
           the test moving in the next decade?

INTRODUCTION

1

A Framework for Using Tests in Counseling

Vicki L. Campbell
University of North Texas

In counseling the test taker "is viewed as the primary user of test results" (AERA, APA, & NCME, 1985, p. 55). Consequently, a defining feature of practice for counselors and counseling psychologists is their use of test results to stimulate client exploration and empower clients to make their own decisions (Gelso & Fretz, 1992; Tittle, 1982). This contrasts with typical forms of assessment, where the practitioner's understanding of clients and their functioning is the major focus. These differences in focus and the goals of testing are significant because they result in different practices. When the client is the primary user of results it is important to integrate testing with the goals of counseling. When assessment and evaluation are the primary focus, the goals of testing may be separate from those of counseling.

Historically, testing and assessment have been important foundations of counseling and applied psychology. Tests have important roles both as tools to facilitate the goals of counseling and for assessment. Yet, in training and in practice the use of tests for evaluative purposes has tended to get the greatest amount of attention (Watkins, 1991; Watkins, Campbell, & McGregor, 1988), and comparatively little has been written about using tests as a counseling tool. Although client involvement with testing has been encouraged by a few authors for some time (e.g., Fischer, 1970, 1985; Goldman, 1971, 1982), recently authors have noted that traditional assessment can benefit from attention to collaborative and therapeutic aspects of testing (Finn, 1996; Lewak, Marks, & Nelson, 1990). This chapter focuses on using testing to its full potential within the counseling process, although the ideas also have application for the use of tests in assessment.

Many authors have pointed out the potential of tests for achieving counseling goals. Testing can enhance short-term treatment, focus on developmental issues, aid problem solving and decision making, and contribute to psychoeducational goals (Duckworth, 1990). Tests can be used to identify client strengths and positive characteristics rather than focusing solely on pathology (Bradley, 1978; Duckworth & Anderson, 1995; Kunce & Anderson, 1976; Myers & McCaulley, 1985). Tests can be used to teach a process of decision making or problem solving, and to empower clients to make their own decisions (Mastie, 1994). Tests can be used to foster self-understanding, development, and self-actualization (Patterson & Watkins, 1982; Zytowski, 1982). Tests can be used to help clients clarify goals and gain a sense of perspective (Hood & Johnson, 1991). Goldman (1972, 1982; Prediger, 1972) believed the most effective use of tests in counseling is to facilitate self-awareness and self-exploration, partly because this use avoids limitations of tests' predictive validity.

From this viewpoint, client activity is an important outcome of using tests, and tests are said to have "exploration validity" if they stimulate client exploration (Tittle, 1978). Outcomes support the usefulness of tests as a counseling tool (Goodyear, 1990), although these methods may be most fully realized in career counseling. For instance, the use of vocational card sorts and interest inventories can encourage self-exploration and exploration of the occupational world (Cooper, 1976; Dolliver & Will, 1977; Randahl, Hansen, & Haverkamp, 1993). Other studies have found that feedback from personality tests can have therapeutic effects (Finn & Tonsager, 1992), and that feedback from marital inventories can result in positive changes in couples' relationships (Worthington et al., 1995).

Ultimately, the usefulness of tests for a client is dependent on the way they are used, not on the tests themselves. Tests can be used to involve clients in self-exploration and learning, and to teach a process of problem solving or decision making. Conversely, test use can consolidate the view of the counselor as an expert, foster dependency, and do little to engage the client (Healy, 1990). Mastie (1994) elaborated on four possible roles for the counselor when using tests. Two describe traditional roles, where test information is used by the counselor to guide clients toward the "right" decision, and test results are used for decision-making purposes by the counselor or agency. She also noted that there may be a "better standard" (p. 32) for test use. Tests can be used to teach an underlying process that clients can use following counseling. In addition, the way tests are used can encourage clients to assume control of their own learning rather than rely upon professional intervention. Mastie believed the latter two ways of using tests will best serve our clients.

There are reasons to believe that test use often does not live up to its potential. Many writers have suggested that counselors are not adequately trained to use tests, particularly in ways that involve clients and are of benefit in the counseling process (Goldman, 1971; Tinsley & Bradley, 1986). Tinsley and Bradley (1986) believed that more emphasis on the counseling skills used to interpret tests is needed, rather than an emphasis on technical aspects of tests. Recent surveys have found that test use and training remain traditional and may not encourage the use of tests as a counseling tool (Watkins et al., 1988). For example, counseling psychologists reported using tests primarily to assess psychopathology, vocational or career issues, and intellectual and ability characteristics, and the tests most frequently used were those that have been traditionally taught in training programs (Watkins et al., 1988). Even in vocational counseling, where test use may be most fully integrated with counseling, the tests used are limited in scope (Watkins, Campbell, & Nieberding, 1994). Practitioners reported that graduate training and previous clinical experience have the greatest effect on their use of tests, yet current training typically focuses on traditional assessment batteries (Watkins et al., 1988; Watkins, Campbell, & Manus, 1990).

Perhaps if practitioners were aware of the potential benefits of testing for the counseling process they would use tests in a greater variety of ways. Examining the outcomes, processes, and dimensions of test use may encourage diversity and imagination in practice. Tests available for use in counseling cover a wide range of content. Although certain types of instruments are typically associated with counseling applications (e.g., vocational testing), many tests provide information that could be useful to clients. Although content is a significant factor when choosing tests, thinking about how the information will be used in counseling may bring equally important factors to light. The potential contributions of testing to the counseling process can guide test selection, along with clearly specified goals and a consideration of the steps involved when using test information.

USES OF TEST INFORMATION

Tests can be used to contribute to the counseling process in a variety of ways. During counseling clients engage in self-exploration, learn about themselves and their environment, and work on decision making and problem solving. Change processes that occur in counseling fall within the categories of support, learning, and action (Lambert, 1986). Testing can contribute to each of these change processes, and a consideration of these contributions may help practitioners expand their use of tests.

Although support is usually thought of as a function of the counseling relationship, clients may also find that test information supports their efforts. Information from tests is a type of feedback, because results are based on the client's responses. Feedback from tests may confirm something a client already knows, and in that way encourage or increase confidence and self-efficacy. Mastie (1994) pointed out that "the 'magic' in our assessments is not that they dig out hidden secrets, but that they confirm the individual's own capacity to deal with the problem" (pp. 37–38). Career interest tests often function in this way. Seeing how test results fit with expressed interests may encourage clients and increase their sense of self-efficacy for career decision making. Similarly, feedback from a personality test can increase a client's confidence in his or her own self-appraisal or coping abilities, or support an individual style.

Information from tests contributes to client learning in a variety of ways. Information about personal characteristics can increase self-awareness and make self-appraisals more accurate. Feedback from tests can reflect and clarify issues for clients. Test results may be a way for clients to confront aspects of themselves that have been out of awareness or are difficult to acknowledge. Tests can give clients information that allows them to compare themselves to others or evaluate aspects of themselves. Normative feedback may help a client take stock of interests or abilities for decision making. Test information can also help clients make comparisons within themselves, for example, the relative importance of values or their preferences for different types of functioning. Qualitative methods can help clients become more aware of their own needs, values, or personal framework (Goldman, 1992). An example is the card sort, which helps clients describe and learn about their own way of thinking about occupations.

Test information can also encourage learning and insight by providing new perspectives. Test instruments often incorporate information from the client into a framework provided by the test. The presentation of a framework or cognitive map of a topic can provide a new perspective on information. "A set of test data adds no *new* information but contributes to the organization of the client's concept of himself in relation to whatever decisions are in focus" (Goldman, 1971, p. 30). The organization of interest inventories, for example, may provide a structure for considering interests and the career decision-making process. A personality inventory may help clients conceptualize aspects of themselves and link those concepts with behaviors, concerns, or future courses of action.

Tests can also be a tool for teaching new ideas. Many instruments are based on a theoretical viewpoint that provides a way of understanding test results. Responding to the questions on the instrument and learning the concepts necessary to make sense of the results can be an introduction to a theoretical view. For example, the Strong Interest Inventory can be used to introduce Holland's theory of occupational types (Harmon, Hansen, Borgen, & Hammer, 1994), the Career Development Inventory (Super, Thompson, Lindeman, Jordaan, & Myers, 1981) can be an introduction to dimensions of Super's model of vocational maturity, and results from the Myers–Briggs Type Indicator familiarize clients with concepts from Jungian theory (Myers & McCaulley, 1985). Theories vary in their focus, and test information may depict a process (e.g., career decision making), or it may be a way to expose clients to new information (e.g., unfamiliar occupations).

Another avenue for learning is the discussion that can be stimulated by the content of tests. The questions or ideas presented in a testing instrument may help clients express themselves, or introduce topics that may be difficult to talk about. The dimensions of a personality inventory or clients' reactions to answering test items may be a starting point for discussions. From this perspective, tests can be a way of giving clients permission to discuss difficult subjects, or a way of presenting the kind of information that is significant to a topic. For example, items that ask questions about decision-making difficulties inform clients that this is an appropriate topic of discussion in career counseling; items that focus on emotional distress may encourage clients to discuss issues of concern. Questions about decision-making difficulties may also help clients express their concerns by adding structure and specific content to a struggle that is vaguely felt.

Finally, test information may encourage action. By increasing clients' self-confidence, by developing a focus on goals, or by providing new perspectives or ideas, test information may encourage movement to the action stage of counseling. Similarly, increasing self-awareness may motivate clients to move to the next step of acting on that awareness. Information from tests may also encourage action more directly. For example, career decision-making instruments may lay out the next step in decision making. Feedback about coping styles may encourage active steps in coping. Information that identifies steps in problem solving can encourage clients to take those steps. Test information also encourages exploration. For example, interest measures may promote exploration of career alternatives, or information about interpersonal style may encourage social exploration.

COUNSELING SKILLS AND TEST USE

Using tests in counseling requires the communication skills and steps important in any type of counseling. Attention to counseling skills when using tests can encourage a collaborative atmosphere and client involvement, and avoid a passive reaction or deferral to the counselor's authority. Decisions are made about how to make use of test information when setting goals, selecting tests, understanding and discussing results, and evaluating the usefulness of testing. Tasks at each stage of the counseling process are important for the optimal use of tests.

At the beginning stages of counseling a good working alliance is crucial to set the stage for the effective use of tests. A supportive atmosphere provides the safety to respond honestly to tests and fully consider questions or feedback that result from testing. Collaboration in regard to the goals and tasks of counseling can assure that testing is not simply an exercise or activity external to counseling, but an integral part of the work in counseling.

Clarification of the goals of testing is an initial step in using tests. "Taking a test" is not a useful goal statement. It doesn't describe the purpose of testing or the information a client hopes to obtain by taking a test. A goal related to testing should state not only what is being measured, but the purpose of measuring it. A useful goal might be to measure aspects of personality style and compare the client's scores to norms for the purpose of checking the client's self-perceptions; another example would be to measure vocational interests for the purpose of learning how the test organizes interests and seeing how the client's interests fit within that framework. Useful goals will label the topics a client wants to explore and also will state how test information may contribute to the client's goal. Putting the anticipated contributions of testing into words is a way to label process goals that will guide the discussion of test results. The functions of test information discussed in the previous section may help frame process goals. For example, clients might take an interest inventory for the purpose of broadening their ideas of potential majors or occupations, or for the purpose of validating choices they have already made. Clients may want to take personality tests to clarify conflicts within themselves, or to compare their own characteristics to those of other people. Framing goals as questions to be explored, in part through the use of test information, can set the stage for the use of test results. Thinking about and labeling the specific purpose of testing prior to discussing results is likely to make for productive applications.

Selecting instruments that can contribute to clients' goals is the second step in using tests. If the purpose of taking a test was clarified in the previous step, then the choice of testing instruments will be simplified. Approaches to testing vary in their views of the extent that clients can be usefully involved in the selection of test instruments. However, if the client is to be optimally involved in the testing process, that involvement will begin with goal setting and the selection of tests (Patterson & Watkins, 1982). If appropriate information is provided by the counselor, clients can be effectively involved in choosing tests. Options can be discussed with clients, with the counselor presenting information concerning possible tests, differences among the instruments, and the contributions that each could make to the client's goals.

The third step in using test information is helping clients explore the meaning of results and relate them to the purpose of counseling. The use of all of the communication skills of counseling is particularly significant at this phase of the testing process. A basic principle is that "test interpretation must not be viewed as a discrete activity but conceptualized as a part of the ongoing counseling process" (Tinsley & Bradley, 1986, p. 462). Traditionally, training in the use of tests has focused on the counselor's understanding or interpretation of test results, without a corresponding emphasis on conveying that information to clients or making use of the information in relation to counseling goals. This may be why interpretations are often "in a 'data dump' fashion and with the counselor maintaining responsibility for interpretations and inferences" (Goodyear, 1990, p. 252). A tentative and questioning approach by the counselor about the meaning of test results is more likely to involve the client and has been found to be more helpful and effective than an absolute interpretation (Jones & Gelso, 1988).

When interpreting test results, Tinsley and Bradley (1986) noted that counselors need to keep clients' goals in mind, keep the precision of the test in mind, minimize defensive reactions, avoid jargon, and encourage feedback. Helping clients understand test results requires some expertise on the part of the counselor to provide information about the structure and content of results. Counseling skills are necessary, though, to encourage the client's active involvement in understanding the results, facilitate an understanding of the personal meanings and applications of results, and integrate information with the goals of counseling. These tasks involve careful listening, and relating test information to goals and issues the client and counselor have discussed earlier. Once again, the clear specification of goals is an important precursor to the successful use of test information. The counselor's role in this process may range from providing technical information, to using basic counseling skills to facilitate the exploration and discussion of test material, to learning about the client's own conceptualization of the meaning of results.

Finally, the client and counselor need to evaluate whether the goals of testing were accomplished. Practitioners may need to think about appropriate criteria to evaluate the effectiveness of test information. In the past tests have been evaluated for their construct or criterion related validity, and test interpretations have been evaluated by whether a client learns or recalls the information presented. However, these may not be particularly meaningful criteria for the effective use of test information within counseling. Several authors have raised questions about traditional forms of test evaluation, suggesting that they may not appropriately evaluate the counseling use of tests (Dolliver, 1967; Goodyear, 1990; Tyler, 1961). Tittle (1978) proposed the evaluation of tests on the basis of their ability to stimulate the exploration of issues and questions, "exploration validity," a concept that may be particularly applicable to the counseling use of tests. This or other forms of validity that address hoped for outcomes of test use in counseling and the relevance and utility of information may encourage a better standard of practice.

REFERENCES

American Educational Research Association, American Psychological Association, and National Council on Measurement in Education. (1985). *Standards for educational and psychological testing.* Washington, DC: American Psychological Association.

Bradley, R. W. (1978). Person-referenced test interpretation: A learning process. *Measurement and Evaluation in Guidance, 10,* 201–210.

Cooper, J. F. (1976). Comparative impact of the SCII and the Vocational Card Sort on career salience and career exploration of women. *Journal of Counseling Psychology, 23,* 348–352.

Dolliver, R. H. (1967). An adaptation of the Tyler Vocational Card Sort. *Personnel and Guidance Journal, 45,* 916–920.

Dolliver, R. H., & Will, J. A. (1977). Ten-year follow-up of the Tyler Vocational Card Sort and the Strong Vocational Interest Blank. *Journal of Counseling Psychology, 24,* 48–54.

Duckworth, J. (1990). The counseling approach to the use of testing. *The Counseling Psychologist, 18,* 198–204.

Duckworth, J. C., & Anderson, W. P. (1995). *MMPI & MMPI-2 interpretation manual for counselors and clinicians* (4th ed.). Bristol, PA: Accelerated Development.

Finn, S. E. (1996). *Using the MMPI-2 as a therapeutic intervention.* Minneapolis: University of Minnesota Press.

Finn, S. E., & Tonsager, M. E. (1992). Therapeutic effects of providing MMPI-2 test feedback to college students awaiting psychotherapy. *Psychological Assessment, 3,* 278–287.

Fischer, C. T. (1970). The testee as co-evaluator. *Journal of Counseling Psychology, 17,* 70–76.

Fischer, C. T. (1985). *Individualizing psychological assessment.* Hillsdale, NJ: Lawrence Erlbaum Associates.

Gelso, C. J., & Fretz, B. R. (1992). *Counseling psychology.* Fort Worth, TX: Harcourt Brace Jovanovich.

Goldman, L. (1971). *Using tests in counseling* (2nd ed.). Santa Monica, CA: Goodyear.

Goldman, L. (1972). Tests and counseling: The marriage that failed. *Measurement and Evaluation in Guidance, 4,* 213–220.

Goldman, L. (1982). Assessment in counseling: A better way. *Measurement and Evaluation in Guidance, 15,* 70–73.

Goldman, L. (1992). Qualitative assessment: An approach for counselors. *Journal of Counseling and Development, 70,* 616–621.

Goodyear, R. K. (1990). Research on the effects of test interpretation: A review. *The Counseling Psychologist, 18,* 240–247.

Harmon, L. W., Hansen, J. C., Borgen, F. H., & Hammer, A. L. (1994). *Strong Interest Inventory applications and technical guide.* Palo Alto, CA: Consulting Psychologists Press.

Healy, C. C. (1990). Reforming career appraisals to meet the needs of clients in the 1990s. *The Counseling Psychologist, 18,* 214–226.

Hood, A. B., & Johnson, R. W. (1991). *Assessment in counseling: A guide to the use of psychological assessment procedures.* Alexandria, VA: American Counseling Association.

Jones, A. S., & Gelso, C. J. (1988). Differential effects of style of interpretation: Another look. *Journal of Counseling Psychology, 35,* 363–369.

Kunce, J., & Anderson, W. P. (1976). Normalizing the MMPI. *Journal of Clinical Psychology, 32,* 776–780.

Lambert, M. J. (1986). Implications of psychotherapy outcome research for eclectic psychother-apy. In J. C. Norcross (Ed.), *Handbook of eclectic psychotherapy* (pp. 436–462). New York: Brunner/Mazel.

Lewak, R. W., Marks, P. A., & Nelson, G. E. (1990). *Therapist guide to the MMPI & MMPI-2: Providing feedback and treatment.* Bristol, PA: Accelerated Development.

Mastie, M. M. (1994). Using assessment instruments in career counseling: Career assessment as compass, credential, process and empowerment. In J. T. Kapes, M. M. Mastie, & E. A. Whitfield (Eds.), *A counselor's guide to career assessment instruments* (pp. 31–40). Alexandria, VA: National Career Development Association.

Myers, I. B., & McCaulley, M. H. (1985). *Manual: A guide to the development and use of the Myers-Briggs Type Indicator.* Palo Alto, CA: Consulting Psychologists Press.

Patterson, C. H., & Watkins, C. E., Jr. (1982). Some essentials of a client-centered approach to assessment. *Measurement and Evaluation in Guidance, 15,* 103–106.

Prediger, D. (Ed.). (1972). Symposium: Tests and counseling—The marriage that failed? *Measurement and Evaluation in Guidance, 5,* 395–429.

Randahl, G. J., Hansen, J. C., & Haverkamp, B. E. (1993). Instrumental behaviors following test administration and interpretation: Exploration validity of the Strong Interest Inventory. *Journal of Counseling and Development, 71,* 435–439.

Super, D. E., Thompson, A. S., Lindeman, R. H., Jordaan, J. P., & Myers, R. A. (1981). *The Career Development Inventory.* Palo Alto, CA: Consulting Psychologists Press.

Tinsley, H. E., & Bradley, R. W. (1986). Test interpretation. *Journal of Counseling and Development, 64,* 462–466.

Tittle, C. K. (1978). Implications of recent developments for future research in career interest measurement. In C. K. Tittle & D. G. Zytowski (Eds.), *Sex fair interest measurement: Research and implications* (pp. 123–128). Washington, DC: National Institute of Education.

Tittle, C. K. (1982). Career guidance: Program evaluation and validity. *Measurement and Evaluation in Guidance, 15,* 22–25.

Tyler, L. E. (1961). Research explorations in the realm of choice. *Journal of Counseling Psychology, 8,* 195–201.

Watkins, C. E., Jr. (1991). What have surveys taught us about the teaching and practice of psychological assessment? *Journal of Personality Assessment, 56,* 426–437.

Watkins, C. E., Jr., Campbell, V. L., & Manus, M. (1990). Is vocational assessment training in counseling psychology programs too restricted? *Counseling Psychology Quarterly, 3,* 295–298.

Watkins, C. E., Jr., Campbell, V. L., & McGregor, P. (1988). Counseling psychologists' uses of and opinions about psychological tests: A contemporary perspective. *The Counseling Psychologist, 16,* 476–486.

Watkins, C. E., Jr., Campbell, V. L., & Nieberding, R. 1994. The practice of vocational assessment by counseling psychologists. *The Counseling Psychologist, 22,* 115–128.

Worthington, E. L., McCullough, M. E., Shortz, J. L., Mindes, E. J., Sandage, S. J., & Chartrand, J. M. (1995). Can couples assessment and feedback improve relationships? Assessment as a brief relationship enrichment procedure. *Journal of Counseling Psychology, 42,* 466–475.

Zytowski, D. G. (1982). Assessment in the counseling process for the 1980s. *Measurement and Evaluation in Guidance, 15,* 15–21.

PERSONALITY, COGNITIVE, AND BEHAVIORAL ASSESSMENT

2

The MMPI–2 in Counseling Practice

James E. DeLamatre
James M. Schuerger
Cleveland State University

BACKGROUND FOR THE TEST

Historical

The Minnesota Multiphasic Personality Inventory–2 (MMPI–2; Butcher, Dahlstrom, Graham, Tellegen, & Kaemmer, 1989) is the direct descendant of the Minnesota Multiphasic Personality Inventory (MMPI; Hathaway & McKinley, 1943). In the late 1930s, Stark Hathaway had been searching for an objective method of measuring treatment outcomes with schizophrenic patients (Cohen, Swerdlik, & Phillips, 1996). He and J. Charley McKinley, MD, had hopes of creating a simple and routine means of diagnosing psychiatric disorders. Their goal was to efficiently place people into diagnostic categories without the limitations of previous psychological tests that made use of rationally constructed content scales.

Previous authors had used the content approach to test construction and had produced tests that were theoretically pleasing but clinically disappointing. The tests were easily biased and often diagnostically inaccurate. Hathaway and McKinley, following the lead of E. K. Strong, decided to use the empirical or criterion keying approach for test construction. Strong had used the the approach in developing the Strong Vocational Interest Blank (Strong, 1927), now the Strong Interest Inventory (Chap. 7). This method initially disregards item content and statistically determines if an item should be included in a scale. Items selected empirically may or may not appear to be theoretically or expressly representative of a psychological characteristic. A key aspect of test development using the empirical approach is the construction of the comparison groups.

For the main MMPI comparison group, Hathaway and McKinley had visitors to the University of Minnesota Hospitals complete a questionnaire with experimental MMPI items. The visitors were mainly rural White blue-collar Minnesota residents. This group of 724 people became the "normal" comparison group for the MMPI, although they were not representative of the entire United States population. The contrasting groups were patients with psychiatric diagnoses who were given the experimental test items so that the authors could compare the patients' answers to those of the "normal" group. The types of people who made up the original comparison groups are presented in Table 2.1 (Welsh & Dahlstrom, 1956). Comparison groups for scales 5 and 0 are somewhat different from the others. The people in the scale 5 group were selected because they had problems with sexual identity. The items in scale 5 were initially written to assess sexual concerns and later refined by group comparison. People in the scale 0 group were selected because they had scored either high or low on a separate test of introversion and extroversion (Greene, 1991).

Hathaway and McKinley's goal of definitively classifying people into diagnostic categories was not realized. Patients often had several elevated scales, did not have the same diagnosis as the criterion group, and did not behave as expected based on the scale elevations. However, MMPI users found that the test produced useful diagnostic information despite the problems. Although the MMPI did not achieve its original intent, its popularity and clinical use steadily increased.

TABLE 2.1
MMPI Criterion Group Samples

Scale		Criterion Group
1. Hs	Hypochondriasis	Patients preoccupied with exaggerated health concerns.
2. D	Depression	Patients who were clinically depressed.
3. Hy	Hysteria	Patients who had a conversion disorder.
4. Pd	Psychopathic Deviate	Patients with an antisocial history such as delinquency.
5. Mf	Masculinity/Femininity	Draftees, airline stewardesses, and male homosexual college students.
6. Pa	Paranoia	Patients with paranoid delusions and suspiciousness.
7. Pt	Psychasthenia	Patients who were anxious, guilt-ridden, or obsessive.
8. Sc	Schizophrenia	Patients diagnosed with schizophrenia.
9. Ma	Hypomania	Patients with expansive mood and excessive energy, most diagnosed as bipolar.
10. Si	Social Introversion	College students with high introversion or extroversion scores on another test.

As the MMPI aged, researchers became increasingly concerned about the use of the original norm group, outdated wording in the questions, and objectionable content. Given new encouragement from the University of Minnesota in the early 1980s, a revision committee was formed and researchers began the task of revising the test (Butcher & Williams, 1992). The restandardization committee had several goals to accomplish while revising the MMPI: (a) to delete problematic items, (b) to keep the clinical and validity scales intact on the new instrument, (c) to develop new scales that addressed areas not covered on the MMPI, (d) to collect a random sample of adults that was representative of the current United States demographics, (e) to develop a similar sample of adolescents, and (f) to collect new clinical data so that the new test could be compared to the old (Butcher & Williams, 1992).

The restandardization committee decided that some MMPI content was inappropriate for adolescents, that the MMPI did not address adolescent developmental problems, and that the existing adolescent norms were no longer adequate. Consequently, others later engineered the Minnesota Multiphasic Personality Inventory–Adolescent version (MMPI–A; Butcher et al., 1992) to assess problems specific to adolescent development. The basic structure of the MMPI–2 is otherwise very similar to the MMPI and interpretation of the main clinical scales is also similar. Due to changes in the norm group and in scaling methods, the clinically significant elevation of 70 on the MMPI is now changed to 65 on the MMPI–2.

Conceptual

A distinguishing feature of the MMPI is the scale construction method already described. As noted elsewhere in this book, there are many methods of constructing a personality questionnaire: the domain-sampling method used for Cattell's Sixteen Personality Questionnaire (16PF; Chap. 4); creating scales for their expected utility and ease of understanding, as with the California Psychological Inventory (CPI; Chap. 3); or writing items based on a particular psychological theory, as with the Meyers–Briggs Type Inventory (MBTI; Chap. 5). The approach used with the MMPI, in contrast with these others, was starkly empirical. On a scale based on the responses of persons diagnosed with depression, an item was used only if it differentiated those persons from persons in the "normal" group. It didn't make any difference if the item made psychological sense, because the purpose of the scale was not to measure some concept—the purpose of the scale was to diagnose. For this reason, the main scales of the MMPI, the clinical scales, do not represent pure concepts and cannot be interpreted as such. The items in a particular scale are heterogeneous in content. For example, not all the items on the Pa (paranoia) scale have to do with obvious symptoms of paranoia.

The nature of the original clinical scales is revealed to some degree by the discussion of Table 2.1, and extended in Table 2.5, discussed later. In addition, many researchers contributed scales for the MMPI and MMPI–2, and today there are, in addition to the clinical scales, many other scales in common use. For example, the Validity Scales are intended to assess the degree of confidence with which a counselor can begin interpreting the instrument. A second category is the Content Scales, of two kinds: subscales to aid in the interpretation of the clinical scales, and broad content scales, which are meant as alternative arrangements of the main body of items. Finally, there is a large corpus of supplementary scales with special purposes created from the original items. Each of these is considered in the Interpretation section.

ADMINISTRATION AND SCORING

Prior to administering the MMPI, the counselor needs to consider the client's abilities. The client should be able to read and comprehend at an eighth-grade level. Problems that may prevent comprehension are poor reading skills, disability, learning disabilities, head injuries, low intellectual ability, psychosis, and severely restricted life experiences (Butcher et al., 1989). Cultural background may also affect how clients approach the testing. Some cultures will be more suspicious of any assessment method and the implications of test scores. Others may not understand the purpose of the testing or be offended by items that ask about very personal issues. Graham (1993) and Greene (1991) provided additional information on some of the cultural differences found in MMPI–2 profiles.

The counselor should take time to introduce the test to the client and allay any fears the person may have. It is important to reassure the client that the results of the test are confidential. The counselor should arrange the testing area so that it is quiet, well lit, and has a minimum of distractions. The arrangement should guarantee confidentiality and allow the client access to help or supervision from the test administrator. The setting should communicate to the clients that their efforts will be worthwhile and respected. Allowing the test to be taken without supervision compromises the security of the test items and jeopardizes the standard conditions for taking the test. Final responsibility for test administration, scoring, interpretation, security, and record keeping lies with the person trained in testing.

The counselor will need some basic materials to use the MMPI–2: the administration manual, the questionnaire, an answer sheet, and a scoring mechanism. The questionnaires are available in a reusable soft-cover booklet written in English or Spanish, a hardcover lap book, and on audio cassettes. The materials are distributed by National Computer Systems (NCS) in Minneapolis, MN. Answer sheets are purchased to match one of several scoring options.

Answer sheets may be scored by purchasing the standard hand-scoring templates and profile sheets, by main-in, or on one's own personal computer. If scoring is done by computer, NCS has several report options that contain combinations of (1) the 10 clinical and three validity scales, (2) the supplementary, content, Harris–Lingoes, and subtle–obvious scales, and (3) the critical item, a profile plotted using the original MMPI norms. Interpretive reports comment on test-taking attitude, symptom patterns, relationship issues, treatment considerations, addiction issues, and occupational issues for high-stress and high-risk occupations. In addition to the NCS service, computerized reports are available from Caldwell (1996), Greene, Brown, and Kovan (1996), Marks, Lewak, and Nelson (1996), and Rainwater (1995).

If scoring is done by hand, MMPI–2 raw scores are converted to T-scores by consulting tables in the manual. Exceptions are the F-K index, MAC–R, and K correction scores, which are calculated using raw scores. The basic 13 clinical scales can be scored using only the first 370 items, which means that some incomplete answer sheets will still be useful. The content and supplementary scales require a completed answer sheet. Scales 1, 2, 3, 4, 6, 7, 8, and 9 make use of new uniform T-scores that are equalized across percentile ranks. Scales 5 and 0 continue to make use of linear T-scores with slightly different distributions of scores. More detailed explanation of the new normalized T-scores is available in the manual. For all the scales, the clinically significant elevation is 65, as opposed to 70 on the MMPI. About 5% of the population will score above T65 on the MMPI–2.

The primary norm group available for the MMPI–2 is the national census-matched adult sample presented in the administration manual. It consists of the test protocols from 1,138 men and 1,462 women from seven different states, and a small percentage from the military. The sample demographics are similar to the U.S. demographics from the 1980 Census including appropriate percentages of Asians, African Americans, Hispanics, and Native Americans. The participants' ages range from 18 to 84 years, with slightly more people being in the 20 to 39 age range. People in the sample have more education than is average for the United States.

INTERPRETATION

Counselors find the MMPI–2 useful because it assesses many aspects of personality and particularly of psychopathology. It addresses many facets of the personality domain and gives the counselor a glimpse into the client's world view. Scales can be interpreted in terms of strengths, weaknesses, and occupational comfort. It can be a rich source of feedback information that the counselor can use to help clients understand themselves (Lewak,

Marks, & Nelson, 1990). The feedback can be tailored to the counselor's theoretical orientation because the MMPI–2 was not designed around a particular theory or conceptualization of people's problems.

MMPI–2 interpreters should have at least a basic knowledge of psychological test construction concepts such as reliability, validity, standardization, and standard score equivalence, and specific training on the MMPI–2. They should be thoroughly familiar with any scales they choose to use including how the scale was constructed, the characteristics of the people in the original norm group, and the basic interpretation issues for the scale. To aid in interpretation, there numerous sources of information on using the MMPI–2 with various populations. The MMPI–2 manual provides means and standard deviations for both males and females by sampling sites, and a comparison with previous norms (Butcher et al., 1989). Some couples were also included in the sample to add the ability to assess dyadic issues. Graham (1993) and Greene (1991) provided summaries of the research on the MMPI–2 with various cultural groups. Duckworth and Anderson (1995) provided interpretive data for using the MMPI–2 with college and outpatient practice populations. Greene and Nichols (1995) developed additional interpretations for psychiatric populations.

Organization of MMPI–2 Information

One way to organize the MMPI–2 scales is presented in Table 2.2, adapted from Schuerger, Watterson, and Croom (1994) and influenced by Lanyon (1978). Table 2.2 presents the scales in a conceptual framework similar to

TABLE 2.2
Conceptual Organization of Main MMPI–2 Variables

Validity Scales Affecting All Scale Interpretations

? L F K VRIN TRIN Fb F-K

							Treatment Considerations	
		Main Problem Areas						
							Other Problem Areas	*Treatment Response*
Discomfort			*Social Non-Conformity*		*Alienation*	*Non-Pathology*		
Neuroticism		*Somatization*						
2	7	1	3	4	5	6	8	5	0	HEA	TRT
D	Pt	Hs	Hy	Pd	Ma	Pa	Sc	Mf	Si	FAM	
										WRK	

Note: HEA = Health Concerns; FAM = Family Problems; WRK = Work Interference; TRT = Negative Treatment Indicators.

the order of the interpretation process presented later. The first level contains the validity scales. These scales influence interpretation of all the other scales. Very high scores on the validity scales bring into question the accuracy of the profile, the person's motivation, or the person's ability to understand the test questions.

The next level contains the main problem areas organized into three broad areas—Discomfort, Social Nonconformity, and Alienation—and one section for the nonpathology scales. The Discomfort (section A) area encompasses painful problems that the person may feel intensely and consider to be a major focus in treatment. The problems in this area often motivate the person to seek therapy. The Social Nonconformity (section B) area contains problems that may or may not disturb the person, but always affect other people. Because problems in this area often infringe on the rights of others, the person may have been encouraged by someone else to seek therapy. The Alienation (section C) area contains scales that assess problems in affiliating with people that are often accompanied by odd thought patterns or behaviors. High scores in these areas also indicate the person is uncomfortable because their world view is an obstacle to intimacy and leaves them feeling alone and misunderstood. The two nonpathological scales assess normal personality characteristics related to the client's style. The personality scales will give the therapist clues about the person's typical approach toward other people. It may be important for the therapist to adapt his or her therapeutic style accordingly.

The Treatment Considerations area contains scales that assess issues likely to be prominent in treatment. One should consider them when planning interventions. The Other Problems area scales do not fit neatly into the Main Problem Areas, but may be prominent for the client. The Treatment Response section features scales that are known to be related to success in therapy.

Other organizational schemes are available, including that by Greene and Nichols (1995) mentioned earlier. These authors originated a Structural Summary that divides the MMPI–2 scales into six broad functional categories, each with smaller content areas, thereby providing a conceptual framework for the interpretation. These conceptual and complex organizational schemes include consideration of the various content scales and scales for special purposes, as well as of the 10 clinical scales. The method outlined next includes only the validity scales and 10 clinical scales: L, F, K; 1, 2, 3, 4, 5, 6, 7, 8, 9, 0. It is a strategy for interpretation of the MMPI or MMPI–2, adapted from Graham (1993):

1. Consider the context of the assessment, including the age, gender, ethnicity, and status of the client, the purpose of the assessment, and who will use the information—client, counselor, or some institution.

2. Examine the answer sheet for missing items, patterned responses, faint marks, crossed out marks, extremely neat marks, and so on.
3. Go over the validity scales to see if it is safe to use the standard rules in interpreting the MMPI.
4. Evaluate the overall level of distress by averaging the eight clinical scores or counting the number of scores outside of the normal range (above 70 for MMPI, above 65 for MMPI–2).
5. Develop inferences about probable behavior and attitudes by reviewing the clinical scores and combinations of scores in the following order: two-point code if there is one; peaks of the pathology scales (1, 2, 3, 4, 6, 7, 8, 9); the nonpathological scales, 5 and 0.
6. Apply the information to specific questions or issues that are the focus of the assessment.

This basic strategy is illustrated in the case example that follows. First it is helpful to consider the main scale categories in a bit more detail.

Validity Scales: Test-Taking Approach

The person's test-taking approach is determined by the context of the testing and the client's conscious and unconscious beliefs about the situation. Clients can skew their answers to appear either virtuous or disturbed. Clinicians often refer to these approaches as "faking good" and "faking bad." For example, the person may consciously lean toward virtue if he or she is taking the inventory as part of an employment application. Other people "fake good" when it allows them to avoid negative self-evaluation. People who have something to gain from their illness may consciously or unconsciously agree to more complaints. Some people "faking bad" intentionally may be seeking to avoid punishment or gain access to treatment. Others unconsciously distort their responses to avoid responsibilities or to ensure that they will receive help. Random profiles may also appear very elevated. Random profiles are generated by people who have responded unpredictably because of confusion, poor reading ability, or mistakes they made in filling out the answer sheet. Those readers interested may refer to other sources for a more complete discussion of test-taking attitudes on the MMPI–2 (Butcher et al., 1989; Butcher & Williams, 1992; Duckworth & Anderson, 1995; Graham, 1993; Greene, 1991; Pope, Butcher, & Seelen, 1993). The counselor can estimate which test-taking approach, if any, is operating by consulting the validity scales.

These scales, presented in Table 2.3, help the clinician decide whether to alter the interpretation of the MMPI–2 profile because of suspected distortion (invalidity). They are concerned with the "validity" of an individual profile, not of the test generally. It is commonly believed that the profile

TABLE 2.3
Validity Scales

Scale and T-Score Level	Interpretation Issues
? >30	The Cannot Say scale indicates the number of omitted answers. Omissions may be due to confusion, poor reading ability, indecision, or poor cooperation. If the omissions occur only in the last half of the test, you can score and interpret the 3 validity and 10 clinical scales. Omissions in the first half may lower the scores or make the profile uninterpretable.
L	The Lie scale consists of questions that ask about unlikely virtues.
<50	Willing to admit to minor faults. Often seen as socially responsive, relaxed, and independent.
50–60	Strikes a balance between admitting and denying minor faults. The normal test-taking attitude.
61–70	May be attempting to give a good impression, deny faults, or avoid being vulnerable or exposed. Sometimes described as moralistic and rigid.
>70	Unwilling to admit to minor personal shortcomings. Sometimes described as being naive, unsophisticated, or lacking in insight. Often unaware of effect on others and have poor stress tolerance. May have been confused or given random answers.
F	The Infrequency scale consists of items in the first half of the test that indicate distress. Most of these were endorsed by less than 10% of the norm group.
<55	Is reporting few symptoms. Denying psychological problems and turmoil. Generally well functioning, or has presented as having no problems.
56–69	A moderate elevation. May have presented very honestly and have concerns limited to a single area. Could be unconventional or have uncommon religious, social, or political beliefs.
70–89	Is experiencing a lot of stress and may be asking for help. May have unusual political or religious beliefs, or be struggling with identity problems. Sometimes described as moody, complex, restless, opinionated, or unstable.
>90	May have intentionally wanted to appear as disturbed as possible, perhaps to escape some noxious consequences, or to have exaggerated symptoms to get sympathy. May be very psychologically disturbed or out of touch with reality. May not read well, may have given random answers (VRIN and TRIN can help decide), or may have answered true to all the questions.
K	The Defensiveness scale is used to correct for a person's tendency to deny problems. The items were selected because they differentiated profiles generated by nonpatients from normal looking profiles generated by psychiatric inpatients. People with higher intelligence and education score a bit higher.
<40	May be feeling very bad, confused, or asking for help. Often judge themselves as being emotionally inferior to others. Sometimes described as cynical, critical, or having low self-esteem. A person who deliberately "fakes bad" or responds true to every question will also have very low scores.
41–55	Scores in this range are essentially normal, and the client is likely to strike a balance between guarding and revealing personal information.
56–65	May have a tendency to blame others and be unwilling to admit to problems. Often seen as independent, adaptive, and self-controlled.
>65	The higher the score, the more defensive. May use denial excessively, have little personal insight, need to always appear in control, and be unable to admit to weaknesses.

(Continued)

TABLE 2.3
(Continued)

Scale and T-Score Level	Interpretation Issues
Fb	The Back F scale is made up of rarely endorsed items from the last half of the test. It is interpreted the same as the F scale. It can be used to decide if a person became tired or distracted later in the test. If Fb is high and F is not, the first 13 scales may be useful but the content and supplementary scales may be inaccurate.
VRIN >79	The Variable Response Inconsistency scale increases when a person has answered inconsistently to item pairs with similar or opposite content. It can be used to supplement the F scale in determining if the answers are random because the person was careless when taking the test.
TRIN >79	The True Response Inconsistency scale consists of pairs of items with opposite content, so that the same answer to both items increases the score. All true or all false answers create higher scores, and show that the person had a tendency to bias their answers in that direction.
F-K >+11 Raw	The F minus K index is calculated by subtracting raw scores. If the index is greater than 11, the person has presented very negatively. This may be because of "faking bad" or exaggerating symptoms, or because of severe pathology.
<−11 Raw	When F-K is negative, the person has presented defensively and may be attempting to appear very virtuous. This indication of "faking good" is less reliable than the F-K "faking bad" index.

provides the least information if the person was confused or filled out the answer sheet incorrectly, and that it provides the most information when the person read, understood, and responded honestly to each and every question. Table 2.3 provides common interpretations to the MMPI–2 validity scales adapted from various sources (Butcher et al., 1989; Butcher & Williams, 1992; Duckworth & Anderson, 1995; Graham, 1993; Greene, 1991; Lewak et al., 1990; Meyer & Deitsch, 1996).

Two-Point Codes

Early in the MMPI's development, it became apparent that the sheer number of scales made interpretation difficult. Test users observed that certain scale combinations seemed indicative of specific behavioral sets, and they began to interpret profiles in terms of the highest two- and three-point combinations of the 10 major clinical scales. To aid clinicians in making quick and accurate interpretations of MMPI profiles, authors developed systems of interpretation based on the behavioral correlates of the two and three highest MMPI scale elevations (Gilberstadt & Duker, 1965; Marks & Seeman, 1963). For example, if scales 4 and 9 were the highest of the clinical scores, the person would have a 4–9 code and might be expected to disre-

TABLE 2.4
MMPI-2 Two-Point Code Descriptions

Discomfort Code	Descriptive Adjectives	Behaviors and Issues
1–2	Passive, rigid, tense, high-strung, inhibited, unhappy, distractible, irritable.	Unhappily preoccupied with physical ailments such as headaches, fatigue, and stomach distress. Poor insight. Possible alcohol abuse.
1–3	Tired, passive, nervous, needy, immature, social, responsible, achiever, conventional.	Vague medical complaints with no physical cause (as above), especially if scale 2 is low. Resists psychological explanations. Expects answers and drops out of treatment if dependency needs are not met.
2–3	Sad, depressed, worried, passive, insecure, self-doubting, fragile, inadequate, selfish, superficial.	Bottled up anger. Lack of assertiveness. Low motivation in therapy. Can tolerate a lot of unhappiness.
2–7	Nervous, ruminating, pessimistic, brooding, depressed, insecure, compulsive, responsible, successful, dependable.	High expectations of achievement. Feels guilty when falling short of goals. Anxiety disorders are common. Stays in therapy. Relaxation training can be helpful.
2–9	Self-centered, anxious, somatic, impulsive, antagonistic.	Sets self up for failure. Flees depressive feelings through activity.
2–0	Depressed, shy, introverted, passive, indecisive, inferior.	Lacks social skills and becomes isolated. Remains in therapy. Low motivation for change.
1–2–3	Despondent, lethargic, fatigued, tense, nervous, dependent, irritable, complaining.	Somatic complaints with no physical cause. Poor insight. Won't take risks. Stress management sometimes helpful.

Social Non-Conformity Code	Descriptive Adjectives	Behaviors and Issues
1–4	Grouchy, anxious, indecisive, unfocused, rebellious, social.	Extroverted but poor skills with the opposite sex. Relationship difficulties. Alcohol problems.
2–4	Insincere, impulsive, resentful, inadequate, manipulative, introverted, energetic, social.	Legal trouble often involving substance abuse. After acting out, they feel bad but do it again anyway.
3–4	Angry, impulsive, hostile, overcontrolled, appears calm.	Demands attention. Sensitive to slights. Overcontrolled anger with periods of violent acting out. Poor insight. Poor prognosis for change.

(Continued)

TABLE 2.4

(Continued)

Social Non-Conformity Code	Descriptive Adjectives	Behaviors and Issues
4–5	Immature, passive, unconventional, rebellious.	Unresolved dependency and dominance issues. Low frustration tolerance but usually adequate control.
4–6	Tense, irritable, angry, suspicious, sullen, demanding, self-indulgent.	Long history of poor social adaptation. Evades admission of problems. Poor prognosis in therapy.
4–7	Insecure, tense, exhausted, impulsive, anxious, inferior, resentful.	Vacillates between being acting out and feeling guilty about it. Therapist thinks that change is occurring. Needs work on behavior changes.
4–8	Inadequate, inferior, insecure, odd, suspicious, resentful, impulsive.	Low self-esteem. Sets self up for failure. Substance abuse. Poor social skills. Sexual concerns and acting out.
4–9	Extroverted, energetic, engaging, irritable, caustic, angry, impulsive, distrustful.	Disregards the rules. Seeks stimulation. Superficial interpersonal relationships. Lack of empathy. Legal troubles. Substance abuse. Poor prognosis for change.

Alienation Code	Descriptive Adjectives	Behaviors and Issues
1–8	Abrasive, unhappy, confused, inadequate, hostile.	Intense somatic preoccupation that may be almost delusional. Bottled up feelings. Poor modulation of affect.
2–8	Sad, dependent, withdrawn, confused, tense, agitated, suspicious, apathetic, distant.	Very depressed and may have suicidal issues. Resistant to change. Has a sense of being hurt at an early age.
3–6	Defiant, anxious, hostile, suspicious, rigid, self-centered, pollyanna-ish.	Strong feelings of hostility toward the family. Doesn't recognize own anger. Expresses anger indirectly.
3–8	Self-centered, dependent, apathetic, hostile, anxious, confused, odd, needy.	Unusual or disturbed thinking. Poor insight. Regresses to immature behavior. Responds to supportive relationship.

(Continued)

TABLE 2.4

(Continued)

Alienation Code	Descriptive Adjectives	Behaviors and Issues
6–8	Insecure, inferior, suspicious, moody, bizarre, indecisive, tense.	Easily overwhelmed. Low self-esteem. Low confidence. Externally rationalized anger. Disrupted thought process. Uses fantasy to escape.
6–9	Anxious, overly sensitive, suspicious, excitable, irritable, agitated.	Withdraws into fantasy when stressed. Overreacts to stress. Disordered or disorganized thought process.
7–8	Withdrawn, anxious, agitated, dependent, inadequate, labile ruminative, confused.	Poor social adjustment. Severe emotional turmoil. Sense of being damaged. Bizarre behavior or thought disturbance.
8–9	Self-centered, demanding, labile, confused, inferior, vague, fearful, pressured.	Periods of intense excitement and confusion interfere with functioning. Help with self-esteem, goals, and modulating activity can be useful.
2–7–8	Depressed, despondent, hopeless, tense, anxious, insecure, shy, withdrawn, odd.	Disrupted or disorganized thought process. Suicidal thoughts. Poor social skills. Bizarre thoughts or interests.

gard rules. Most of the available code type interpretive data is based on the original norms for the MMPI code types, so it is best to interpret only well-differentiated profile code types above T65 on MMPI–2. Edwards, Morrison, and Weissman (1993) found that congruence between MMPI and MMPI–2 code types increased from 58% to 83% when the high points were at least 5 points higher than other scales.

Space limitations prevent us from including here extensive information on the two-point codes (Table 2.4). The codes are organized according to the same broad headings used in Table 2.2. For additional information regarding code type characteristics, the reader is referred to one of the many fine works from which the information is derived (Butcher & Williams, 1992; Duckworth & Anderson, 1995; Graham, 1993; Greene, 1991; Lewak et al., 1990; Meyer & Deitsch, 1996; Schuerger et al., 1994).

Individual Scales

MMPI–2 clinical scale interpretive data are presented in Table 2.5. In the first row of each section, the first column contains the scale number and abbreviation, the second column provides a brief description of what is

TABLE 2.5
MMPI–2 Clinical Scales Interpretation

Scale and T-Score Level	Associated Characteristics	Possible Counseling Issues
1–Hs	The Hypochondriasis scale indicates concern with physical symptoms and fear of bodily harm.	High scores are generally interpreted the opposite of low scores.
<40	Denies aches and pains, sees self as healthy, may ignore symptoms, seen by others as alert, capable, and responsible.	May appear very moralistic and have trouble with closeness. Some people will disregard illness symptoms.
40–58	No special health concerns, realistic, insightful.	People with scores in this range will usually be able to think about their symptoms but not overemphasize them.
59–65	Medical problems, complaining, irritable.	May be overconcerned with health and loss of functioning.
>65	Pessimistic, selfish, unhappy, not insightful, gastric complaints, seen as dull, whining, defeatist.	May complain about health problems to avoid experiencing emotions. May ignore the effects of stress, not see the need for help, or sabotage therapy.
2–D	The Depression scale measures depressive symptoms and psychic energy.	Other scales may alter the interpretation of this scale as it is often part of a high point code. It also changes rapidly with mood.
<40	Relaxed, confident, energetic, cheerful, witty, uninhibited, optimistic, outgoing.	May make other people angry or have trouble with authority. If an employment evaluation, may deny problems.
40–57	Comfortable, well adjusted emotionally.	May not see a need to remain in therapy because of discomfort.
58–65	Has situational stress, dissatisfied, discouraged, moody, pessimistic.	Discomfort may be transient due to a current problem. May need support and problem solving.
>65	Depressed, tired, guilt-ridden, low self-regard and confidence, sleep problems, trouble concentrating, difficulty with decisions, anhedonia, may have thoughts of death; above T75, the mood is pervasive, and the person is overwhelmed.	Often will seek help, but not seek supportive social contact. Planning social contact, group therapy, cognitive therapy, and exercise are possible interventions. Often discounts therapy gains. At higher elevations medication may be helpful as low energy and pessimism make it difficult to engage in therapy.
3–Hy	The Hysteria scale indicates awareness of problems and vulnerabilities, and social comfort.	May admit to a problem and deny being concerned about it. This scale should be interpreted in relation to scales 1 and 2. Scores tend to increase a bit with education and social class.
<41	Logical, caustic, tough, isolated, constricted, few interests.	May be distant, unfriendly, lack trust, and have difficulty forming therapeutic alliance. Often content with a dull life.

(Continued)

TABLE 2.5
(Continued)

Scale and T-Score Level	Associated Characteristics	Possible Counseling Issues
41–58	Shows a balance of emotionality and level-headedness.	Will likely have reasonable insight.
59–65	Pleasant, optimistic, conforming, denies problems, has high social needs but is insecure and superficial.	May minimize problems and resist psychological explanations but accept advice.
>65	Naive, poor insight, denies problems, demanding, flirtatious, infantile, suggestible, uninhibited.	Often worries about performance and relationships. May have had a rejecting father. May respond to support and reassurance. May end therapy if own views are challenged.
4–Pd	The Psychopathic Deviate scale measures conflict, struggle, respect for society's rules, anger, social poise, and exploitation.	When interpreting this scale, consider frustrating events in the person's situation. Scores usually decrease with age, and are a bit higher for African Americans and males.
<40	Conventional, avoids unpleasantness, enjoys routine, passive, rigid, self-critical, noncompetitive, low sex drive.	Can become dependent and accept advice but may avoid taking charge of self-change. Often needs reassurance about own abilities.
41–58	Has good relationships, balances meeting own needs with understanding others' needs.	At the higher end of this range may have a personal sense of fairness and be alert to the counselor's approach.
59–65	Assertive, energetic, likable, self-confident, diverse interests, poised, easily bored, intellectualizes, cynical, impatient, resentful, hedonistic.	This level is common for people concerned with social problems and with adolescents. May be willing to bend rules for personal advantage. Attending to other people's feelings will help in relationships.
>65	Lacks empathy, insensitive, angry, breaks the rules, self-centered, quick to anger, doesn't learn from experience, manipulative. Above T75: irresponsible, potential for violence.	May experience emotional numbing. Problems with work, family, substance abuse, or the legal system are common. Often have an underlying fear of abandonment, and deny the need to change. May respond to encouragement and empathy.
5–Mf, Male	The Masculinity/Femininity scale indicates interest in activities and behaviors that are stereotypically masculine or feminine.	Scores increase with education and social class. T-score levels would be 10 points higher on 1930 MMPI norms.
<40	Tough, independent, self-confident, adventurous, macho, crude, reckless, inflexible, unsympathetic.	Men with scores in this range often avoid therapy. Those that do come in may be action oriented. Many have underlying doubts about masculinity and seek to protect macho self-image.

(Continued)

TABLE 2.5
(Continued)

Scale and T-Score Level	Associated Characteristics	Possible Counseling Issues
41–55	Conventional, practical, balanced, easy-going, contented.	Will have a range of interests and some flexibility concerning definitions of masculine tasks.
56–68	Interest in the arts, expressive, sensitive, peace-loving, intelligent, common sense, curious, social, some passivity.	Typical elevation for college-educated males, especially in the arts. May be well read and have greater fund of psychological knowledge.
>68	Ambitious, warm, tolerant, socially passive, dependent, insecure, sex-role conflicts, effeminate.	May have gender identity conflicts, discomfort with sex-role demands, or have homoerotic concerns.
5–Mf, Female	The Masculinity/Femininity scale indicates interest in activities and behaviors that are stereotypically masculine or feminine.	Low scores are interpreted more positively when the person is more highly educated.
<40	High feminine interest, capable, conscientious, idealistic, coy, seductive, petulant, helpless, passive, insecure, dependent.	May have underlying doubts about their femininity. Often defer decisions to the therapist. May manipulate with charm.
41–55	Easy-going, competent, empathic.	Will probably be comfortable with feminine traits without being passive.
>55	Confident, logical, practical, competitive, vigorous, spontaneous, tough, coarse, unemotional, unfriendly, dominating.	May be unaware of the impact of aggressive tendencies. May anger other people, including therapist. Often does not see herself as typically feminine.
6–Pa	The Paranoia scale indicates level of trust, sensitivity, and suspiciousness.	Often indicates a person's fear of assault on character or ability. African Americans and adolescents score somewhat higher.
<40	Cheerful, conventional, orderly, trusting, loyal, bland, gullible, touchy, stubborn, evasive, guarded.	Well-adjusted clients will have the more positive traits, poorly adjusted will have the negative.
41–60	Clear thinking, reasonable, adaptable, cautious, sensitive.	Well-balanced people usually score in this range. Toward the higher range, will be more guarded and sensitive to interpersonal slights.
>60	Angry, resentful, mistrustful, suspicious, hostile, rigid, blames others, guarded, assumes others are against them.	Especially above T65, person will have difficulty trusting therapist and scan for insults, testing therapist's patience. Difficult to engage in therapy. Craves validation of own experience.
7–Pt	The Psychasthenia scale detects worry, anxiety, doubts, tension, discomfort, and obsessiveness.	Anxiety is uncomfortable and often motivates people in therapy. Because the scale tends to measure trait anxiety, it is important to assess the person's long term coping methods.

(Continued)

30

TABLE 2.5
(Continued)

Scale and T-Score Level	Associated Characteristics	Possible Counseling Issues
<40	Self-confident, many interests, values success, persistent, responsible, adaptable, relaxed, may appear lazy.	Probably had an emotionally secure place in family of origin.
41–58	Reliable, adaptable, trusting.	Stress symptoms are likely to be related to situational demands.
59–65	Organized, reliable, punctual, conservative, introspective, high-strung, impractical, tense, self-doubting, self-critical.	Likely to be hard workers and not see selves as anxious. May overwork and not feel successful.
>65	Meticulous, perfectionistic, compulsive, ruminative, fearful, tense, obsessive, dependent, insecure, socially awkward, agitated, guilty, has stress-related physical complaints, difficulty concentrating.	May be inefficient or suffer interruptions at work because of ruminations, rituals, or panic symptoms. Cognitive and behavioral stress management techniques may help. May have an underlying fear of failure. May resist therapeutic interpretations but make slow steady progress.
8–Sc	The Schizophrenia scale measures odd thinking and social alienation.	Adolescents, college students, and African Americans often score a bit higher on this scale.
<40	Friendly, cheerful, trusting, conventional, controlled, restrained, superficial, unimaginative.	Structure and routine may be important. Often are unable to generate solutions to problems and will defer to the therapist.
41–58	Well-balanced, dependable.	Will be able to engage in logical thinking and participate in the therapeutic process.
59–65	Creative, spontaneous, avant-garde, impractical, idiosyncratic, high-strung, different, moody, eccentric, aloof, impersonal.	May have a low interest in people, but be highly creative. May be highly sensitive to personal slights by the therapist.
>65	Adventuresome, generous, imaginative, bizarre, confused, disoriented, anxious, irritable, hostile, rejected, inferior, alienated, withdrawn, unresponsive.	May benefit from social skills instruction. May be sexually preoccupied or be conflicted about sex role. At elevations above T75, thinking process is disrupted and communication is often difficult. May benefit from a caring relationship, which was often missing in childhood.
9–O	The Hypomania scale indicates the level of excitability and psychic energy.	Scores tend to decline with age but African Americans score slightly higher. Moderate elevations in college populations are common.
<40	Quiet, modest, humble, sincere, practical, conscientious, unpopular, listless, lethargic, depressed, controlled.	May have grown tired during the testing. May have generally low energy. Interest in the family is not uncommon. Exercise is a possible intervention.

(Continued)

TABLE 2.5

(Continued)

Scale and T-Score Level	Associated Characteristics	Possible Counseling Issues
41–58	Energetic, sociable, responsible, reliable, pleasant, realistic.	At the upper level, will have vitality.
59–65	Gregarious, talkative, eager, outgoing, hard-working, competitive, action-oriented, bores easily, tense, excitable, anxious, aggressive, superficial.	May have doubts about self-worth, worry about failure, and overextend selves to compensate. Helping them accept personal limitations may provide some relief.
>65	Confident, talkative, euphoric, expansive, flighty, restless, agitated, irritable, confused, manipulative, grandiose, impulsive, labile, hostile.	May have difficulty focusing and take on too much. Inconsistent attendance or drop out of therapy. Drug use is not uncommon. May have had demanding and domineering parents.
0–Si	The Social Introversion scale indicates people orientation.	Introversion tends to be trait-like and stable over time. Couples who score very differently may experience difficulties agreeing on social activities.
<40	Extroverted, gregarious, sociable, poised, mixes well, verbal, vigorous, confident, persuasive, assertive, status-seeking, self-indulgent, impulsive, exhibitionist, manipulative.	Will value the counseling relationship and expect warm interaction. May have difficulty working or studying alone. Sometimes anger others with their flamboyance.
41–58	Active, energetic, friendly, warm.	Usually show a balance of wanting contact with people and needing time alone.
59–65	Reserved, cool, retiring, aloof, compliant, conventional, dependable, serious.	May prefer being with a close friend instead of a large group. Group therapy may be stressful. May need help managing social contact.
>65	Introverted, reliable, compliant, conventional, reserved, shy, isolating, socially uncomfortable, sensitive, submissive, cautious, controlled, insecure, indecisive, rigid, irritable.	May be actively withdrawing from others due to stress and need stress management techniques. If they do not know the social rules, may benefit from social skills training.

measured by that scale, and the third column contains important counseling issues to consider when interpreting the scale. The sections next to the scale abbreviation have general comments and issues that may apply to all scale elevation levels. Subsequent rows for each scale are arranged so that the first column defines a range of scores and the second contains descriptive adjectives for that range. The third column has behavioral descriptions, issues that may surface during therapy, and possible interventions. The descriptive adjectives are loosely arranged in order from the positive to the negative. One can expect the positive adjectives to be a better fit for well-adjusted people, and the negative adjectives to be more descriptive of poorly adjusted people. Keiller and Graham (1993) produced some evidence that low scores indicate generally less of the negative traits associated with a scale.

The counseling and interpretation issues are also loosely arranged in a progressive hierarchy so that later issues are more associated with higher scores. The counselor may scan the adjective lists and counseling issues in adjacent T-score levels before settling on an interpretation for the current level. Issues present at lower levels of interpretation are often present at higher levels. Higher scale elevations usually indicate a greater number of problems, more disruption in functioning, and greater intensity. The data for interpreting the MMPI-2 clinical scales presented in Table 2.5 were compiled from a number of sources (Butcher et al., 1989; Butcher & Williams, 1992; Duckworth & Anderson, 1995; Graham, 1993; Greene, 1991; Lewak et al., 1990; Meyer & Deitsch, 1996.

Harris and Lingoes (1955, cited in Graham, 1993) developed MMPI scale subdivisions because heterogeneous content in the clinical scales is difficult to interpret. Subscales for content-specific groups of items within scales 2, 3, 4, 6, 8, and 9 have been retained on the MMPI-2. After interpreting the main scale elevation, the counselor can consult the subscales interpretation in the manual to see which content areas are elevated. Subscales have also been developed for scale 0 by Hostetler, Ben-Porath, Butcher, and Graham (1989, cited in Butcher et al., 1989). Interpretation for these scales is presented in the administration manual.

Supplemental and Research Scales

Not all supplementary scales that were developed for the MMPI have been retained on the MMPI-2 because of item changes and deletions. The supplementary scales that follow have proven their worth in counseling and will be useful to consider when interpreting the profile. Interpretive data that follow were compiled from Butcher et al. (1989), Butcher and Williams (1992), Duckworth and Anderson (1995), Graham (1993), and Greene (1991).

The Ego Strength (Es) scale indicates the person's level of general psychological health or vulnerability. Scale Es (Barron, 1953) was developed by contrasting the answers of those who succeeded in treatment with answers from those who did not. Because 12 items on this scale were deleted on the MMPI-2, it is considered experimental. Below T45, people think poorly of themselves and may feel helpless to change. They often do not succeed in therapy despite good intentions. The counselor should determine if they lack the ability to solve their problems or if they only believe they lack them. Between T45 and T60, people will probably feel they have enough emotional resources to deal with life's problems. If a college student scores toward the lower end, the student may have low confidence in his or her abilities. Above T60, people believe that they have the resiliency necessary to rebound from most difficulties. They often do well in therapy unless they do not recognize that they have problems. College students often score in this range.

The Over-Controlled Hostility (OH) scale was developed by Megargee, Cook, and Mendelsohn (1967) by contrasting the answers of prisoners with no assault to extreme assaultiveness records. Above T65 suggests the person keeps tight control on negative emotions. This is sometimes a positive social adaptation. If people have poor emotional coping ability they may have outbursts and benefit from anger management techniques.

The Marital Distress (MDS) scale is new to the MMPI–2 and was developed by identifying items that address family relations (Hjembo, Almagor, & Butcher, as cited in Butcher et al., 1989). Items were selected if they identified people reporting poor marital adjustment. People with scores above T60 are likely to report that problems in their relationship are a current stressor.

Substance Abuse Scales

We have placed the three major MMPI–2 substance abuse scales in a separate area because substance abuse issues may exist alone or coexist with other problems. The MacAndrew Alcoholism Scale–Revised (MAC–R) is a criterion scale that was originally designed by comparing the MMPI answers of people with alcohol abuse problems to those of psychiatric patients without alcohol problems. Some items ask directly about alcohol use, but most are more subtle items that are statistically related to addictive problems. It is usually scored in raw score points and interpreted if the raw score is above 23 points. The scale does not definitively identify current substance abuse problems. It works better as an indication of the person's tendency to become addicted to alcohol, drugs, gambling, and possibly sex. In the 24 to 27 point range, the person may not exhibit addictive behavior problems. Over a raw score of 27 the person is more likely to have a problem with addiction, but currently sober people with past problems may also score high. If a person has a high score and does not have an addiction, the counselor should assess the person's stress level and coping abilities, because stress puts the person at risk for further substance abuse. Also, people who score high are often willing to take risks that can have legal or health consequences.

The Addiction Potential Scale (APS) is new criterion scale designed similarly to the MAC–R. It can be interpreted the same way if the score is above T65. People with scores in the T60–T65 range may also have life-styles characteristic of people who abuse drugs or alcohol. The Addiction Acknowledgment Scale (AAS) is a content scale that asks directly about alcohol and substance abuse problems. Because the item content is obvious, people who want to deny their problems can easily skew their answers to indicate they do not have a problem. Using APS and AAS together will give the counselor an indication of the person's awareness of a tendency to abuse alcohol and drugs. Interpretive information for the substance abuse scales presented in Table 2.6 was compiled from several sources (Butcher et al., 1989; Butcher & Williams, 1992; Duckworth & Anderson, 1995; Graham, 1993; Greene, 1991).

Content Scales

The content-specific scales (Butcher, Graham, Williams, & Ben-Porath, 1990) for the MMPI-2 are completely new. They were authored to replace the previous Wiggins (1969) content scales and to supplement interpretation of the main MMPI-2 profile. In contrast to the clinical scales, these scales were constructed by grouping items with similar meaning. The scales are completely independent from each other because items appear in only one scale. In contrast to the main scales, each scale score is free to vary relative to the other scales.

The consistent item content and scale independence make the scales easier to interpret than the criterion scales. Answer patterns directly represent the person's self-description or conscious presentation of problems. For example, in the Depression scale the person may have agreed to items that inquire about symptoms of depression such as "I feel sad all the time"

TABLE 2.6
Substance Abuse Issues Scales

Scale and T-Score Level	Associated Characteristics and Counseling Issues
MAC–R 24–27 Raw	The MacAndrew Alcoholism Scale–Revised was developed to identify alcoholics, but works better as a measure of susceptibility to addictive behaviors of any type. Raw scores in this range are suggestive of addictive behaviors, but will misidentify many people.
>27 Raw	Is often extroverted and a risk taker, and is likely to have addictive behavior patterns. Some people control the behaviors, but are more susceptible to them under stress.
APS >65	The Addictions Potential scale is new to MMPI-2, and has a similar aim to the MAC–R. The higher the score, the more likely it is the person has or will develop problems with substance abuse.
AAS >65	The Addictions Acknowledgment scale inquires about admitted participation in substance use and addictive behavior. High scorers may be thinking about past problems, and low scorers may be denying problems. Used in conjunction with APS, it can provide an avenue to exploring the person's attitudes about alcohol and drug use.

(sad affect), "I can't seem to get going" (lack of energy), and "I feel my problems cannot be solved" (hopelessness). If the person is aware of the problems the person can respond directly to the content. Contrast this type of item with an item that might be found on the criterion scale for depression (D), such as "My thinking is slow" and "I have trouble remembering things."

Duckworth and Anderson (1995) suggested that the counselor begin feedback by talking about the problems suggested by content scales. The person may be more resistant to discussing behavior related to the other scales, especially if the defensiveness indicators are high. Brief summaries of the interpretive data for the content scales presented in Table 2.7 were compiled from several sources (Butcher et al., 1989; Butcher & Williams, 1992; Duckworth & Anderson, 1995; Greene, 1991). The counselor should interpret the scale if the score is near or above T65.

Case Example

The case, the same as used in Chapter 4, is presented according to the interpretive strategy presented earlier.

1. The Context of the Assessment. Martha is a 42-year-old secretary, assistant to the personnel manager in a large hospital. She is a college graduate with a major in elementary education. During her student teaching she had several unpleasant experiences, including difficulty keeping order, and she felt inept much of the time. Rather than enter the educational field, she tried several jobs for brief periods and settled on secretarial work, in which she has felt fairly comfortable. Recently, however, with a change in bosses, she is having trouble adjusting and is consulting a counselor. A significant but not exclusive issue in the counseling is career suitability, so a fairly thorough battery of measures is in order, including an interest inventory, an ability measure, a measure of normal personality (16PF), and a measure of psychopathology (MMPI–2). For a more complete discussion of details of this case the reader is referred to Chapter 4, where, in the context of a 16PF interpretation, Martha's ability and interest results are also presented.

2. The Answer Sheet. The answer sheet is carefully filled in with no special pattern of marks discernable by inspection, and with very neat, well-marked answer spaces. All the demographic information is included.

3. The Validity Scales. Martha did not omit any items, so her Cannot Say score is zero, and does not constitute a hindrance to interpretation. Her scores on the L, F, and K validity scales are 61, 55, and 54 respectively, none so high as to prevent use of the ordinary rules of interpretation. The score

TABLE 2.7
MMPI–2 Content Scales

Scale	Scale Name, Interpretive Information, and Issues
Internal Symptoms and Problems	
ANX	The Anxiety scale identifies individuals who report nervousness, sleep disturbance, and worries, including losing their mind.
FRS	The Fears scale detects specific fears such as the sight of blood, high places, fire, and animals.
OBS	The Obsessiveness scale reports trouble making decisions because of excessive rumination. Change is stressful.
DEP	The Depression scale inquires about symptoms of depression such as guilt, hopelessness, emptiness, and thoughts of death.
HEA	The Health Concerns scale will be high when the person agreed to items about minor physical ailments and poor health.
BIZ	The Bizarre Mentation scale inquires about unusual beliefs, hallucinations, and distorted thinking.
External Aggressive Tendencies	
ANG	The Anger scale identifies people who admit to problems with anger expression such as irritability, swearing, or smashing things.
CYN	The Cynicism scale identifies people who have a negative view of other's motives and believe people are not to be trusted.
ASP	The Antisocial Practices scale inquires about legal troubles, admiration of criminal activity, and respect for the law.
TPA	The Type A scale will be elevated when a person admits to being hard-driving, impatient, aggressive, and work-oriented.
Negative Self-View	
LSE	The Low Self-Esteem scale identifies individuals who have a low opinion of their own appearance, confidence, coordination, and ability.
General Problem Areas	
SOD	The Social Discomfort scale will be elevated when respondents agree that they feel uncomfortable, shy, or uneasy around people.
FAM	The Family Problems scale detects the person's view of difficulties within the family, including poor support, bickering, and unhappiness.
WRK	The Work Interference scale identifies problems that disrupt work performance, such as stress, difficulty making decisions, and negative views of coworkers.
TRT	The Negative Treatment Indicators scale identifies people who are likely to be pessimistic about therapy. High scorers doubt the efficacy of mental health workers, physicians, and therapy. May feel unable to discuss problems and prefer to give up rather than change.

of 61 on the L scale may be considered in the low moderate range, from Table 2.3, suggesting the possibility of an overvirtuous presentation. Also with reference to the table, the F score of 55 suggests candidness in responding, and perhaps the existence of problems in a single symptom complex. The K score of 54 suggests a generally functional person—adaptive, self-controlled—but it is at the higher end of the mid-range for defensiveness. We can certainly use the ordinary rules of interpretation, but we are left with a certain ambiguity as to how much Martha was candid or defensive on her responses.

4. Overall Level of Distress. The average of her eight pathological scales (1, 2, 3, 4, 6, 7, 8, 9) is about 62, quite high but not really florid. She has two of the eight pathology scales well above 65, scales 2 and 7. She may be considered distressed, but not extremely so.

5. Probable Behavior and Attitudes. In conceptual order according to Table 2, her MMPI–2 scores are as shown in Table 2.8.

Before getting into the interpretation of individual scores and two-point code, a glance at the conceptual outline given earlier prompts a few comments. Her highest scores, on the average, are in the discomfort section, as opposed to the social nonconformity or the alienation section. Within that section, the higher are the neurotic, so that she is likely to be feeling her stress—anxious and somewhat depressed—rather than playing it out in her muscles and bones. Of the two somatizing scales, Hy is higher, so she is likely to have some defensiveness, lack of insight into the psychological nature of her problems. In the social nonconformity area her low Ma (low energy) is consistent with the high depression already noted, as is the high introversion denoted by the relatively high score on Si.

Moving to the two-point code, the Pt score is quite high, 11 points higher than the next lowest (D = 83). After the D score, two others are also in the high range: Hy and Sc are 65. These patterns suggest that, although we may have a fair confidence in the 2–7 code, in a few months the scores may change enough so that the two highest would be 7–3 or 7–8. A glance at Table 2.2 reveals that the first of these, the 7–8 code, signals a more serious behavior pattern, not so much characterized by worry as by bizarre thought and behavior. The 3–7 code, not in the table because of its relative infrequency, is noted by one author to be associated with low academic drive, anxiety, and insomnia, not so very different from the current 2–7 code. This code, in which we have fair confidence, signals the prominence of worry, the likelihood of anxiety problems, and the achievement drive. Not in the

TABLE 2.8
Martha's MMPI–2 Scores

Discomfort				Social Nonconformity		Alienation		Nonpathology	
Neuroticism		Somatization							
2	7	1	3	4	5	6	8	5	0
D	Pt	Hs	Hy	Pd	Ma	Pa	Sc	Mf	Si
72	83	63	65	55	39	56	65	45	59

table but noted by many practitioners is the likelihood of dependency among persons with a 2–7 pattern. This interpretation is consistent with the 16PF interpretation in Chapter 4.

Turning to the highest clinical scores, we begin with Pt (= 83), which, from Table 2.4, suggests perfectionism, anxiety and guilt, and stress problems. Under Counseling Issues we note the possibility of steady progress despite some resistance, plus the suggestion to try behavioral or cognitive therapy. Comments on the D score of 72 include the likelihood of low self-regard and guilt, and again a suggestion of cognitive therapy along with exercise and social networking. The Sc score of 65 signals the possibility of feelings of alienation and confusion, which need to be checked by interview. Again suggestions for therapy include social networking, but here focused on skills training. The high score on Hy (65) suggests naivete and poor insight, and a tendency to minimize problems. Support and reassurance are suggested for this client, and a caution for the counselor not to be too challenging or confrontive.

In summary so far, it seems quite likely that Martha is very worrisome (consistent with her high Anxiety on the 16PF) and depressed, perhaps feeling alienated and confused, and prone to low self-insight and minimization of her problems. It is suggested that the counselor proceed gently and supportively, and try cognitive and/or behavioral methods. A further suggestion is to encourage and help Martha to develop her social support network and her social skills.

Finally, Martha's scores on the two nonpathological scales (5 and 0) can be considered. Her score on Mf (scale 5) of 45 suggests, from Table 2.4, that she is about average between high feminine interest and its opposite, leaning toward femininity—competent and empathic, comfortable with her femininity and not passive. The score of 59 on Si is in the introverted direction, again consistent with the 16PF but not so extreme. From the table we see her as probably reserved, aloof, serious.

6. Specific Questions for This Assessment. Consistent with the discussion of this case in Chapter 4, we posit four issues specific to this assessment:

1. What Leary calls *functional diagnosis*, focusing on the probable interaction between client and counselor.
2. Probable occupational fit, or degree of resemblance between Martha and persons in various occupations.
3. Martha's strengths in terms of coping with her life and her occupational situation, as revealed in the MMPI.
4. Aspects of Martha's personality that may make adjustment difficult and that she may wish to work on.

One way to conceptualize functional diagnosis is to think what it will be like for the counselor to work with a person like Martha, who is anxious, introverted, and perhaps naive and has poor insight. The anxiety, being a significant source of discomfort, is likely to be a motive for Martha to work at the counseling. The introversion is likely to be a hindrance to smooth communication, because it will be difficult at best for Martha to reveal personal matters. The introversion can be difficult for beginning counselors particularly, because as counselors we rely on verbal feedback to see how we are doing. The possible dependency signaled by the 2–7 code may present a difficulty if through its attendant submissiveness Martha is kept from talking about important issues or disagreeing with the counselor when appropriate. Finally, as a counselor I evaluate my similarity to Martha in as many ways as I can, personality among them. Martha, with her two-point code, tends to anxiety and perhaps dependency—if I share or have shared any of those characteristics I have an advantage in understanding Martha.

The second specific issue, resemblance of Martha to various occupational groups, is handled more appropriately by measures of ability, interest, and normal personality and is deferred to the discussion in Chapter 4, where it is concluded that poor job fit is probably no more than a component in her discomfort, not a major factor. Martha's current job situation may be magnifying her distress, but it is probably not the only thing. More specifically, the symptoms Martha shows on the MMPI–2 may well be partly situational, but the possible underlying personality characteristics—dependency, naivete, worrisomeness—are most likely of earlier origins, and need separate consideration.

To begin the third specific issue, Martha's strengths, we note first the likelihood of high expectations taken from the 2–7 code description in Table 2.4. No matter what she does, Martha will probably expect herself to do a good job. In addition, Martha is likely to stay with therapy once she begins it. From a description of Martha's score range on the Mf scale (Table 2.4), we note the likelihood of a range of interests and practicality.

The fourth specific issue, areas for Martha to consider working on, has been suggested in some of the preceding comments. Martha shows high anxiety, social introversion, and the possibility of dependency and of naivete and lack of self-insight. The last of these, the naivete and lack of self-insight, we discuss first because of their treatment implications. If these are verified in the interview, they suggest a gentle, nonintrusive manner in therapy, one that does not require a great insight on the part of the client. Generally the therapist should not expect much growth in this area with a client who shows a fairly high score on Hy, except over a very long period.

Persons with anxiety as high as Martha's are often found to express discomfort about work as well as other areas of activity. To address the high anxiety, one might suggest relaxation procedures and behavioral/cognitive therapy techniques. The relaxation procedures show promise with Martha because, being so introverted, she is likely to respond quickly to conditioning techniques. Introversion may also be a problem at work if the job requires social interaction at more than a minimal level. Martha may be helped by encouragement and instruction about creating and accessing a social support network, and perhaps even by role-play activities to practice social skills. For the same set of problems Martha may profit from systematic assertiveness training groups such as were common 10 or 20 years ago. Finally, for the possible dependency, Martha might be encouraged and instructed in self-care habits—clothing, food, living quarters, friends, and so forth.

RESEARCH

There are thousands of published research articles applicable to the MMPI and MMPI-2. There are some disagreements about the usefulness of individual scales, but overall the research shows that the test is psychometrically sound and clinically valid for a variety of settings and populations. Research that addresses use of the test with different cultural populations has generally shown that there are few test performance differences due to culture (Graham, 1993). Apart from these few comments, we cannot provide here adequate coverage of the research. Fortunately, there are many good sources that provide summaries of the clinical research data.

The reader should review Graham's (1993) book on the MMPI-2. It is clearly written, precise, and thorough. Research findings are presented in sections pertaining to test features and interpretation issues. Graham reviewed the pertinent reliability and validity research, research on clinical use of each scale, sources for behavioral correlates, use with special groups including multicultural issues, use in vocational settings, and the validity of computer assisted interpretation. He also presented examples of interpretive process, case information, profiles, professional reports, and computer generated interpretation.

We also suggest reading Duckworth and Anderson's (1995) book. It was written for the person using the MMPI-2 in a university counseling center, outpatient private practice, or mental health clinic. The book was organized around the test structure and contains numbered lists of research findings pertinent to the interpretation of each scale and profile type. The authors included chapters on multicultural issues, use of the test in medical settings, and case examples interpreted by each author. They had a unique approach to interpretation that included important supplementary scales. Interpretive information in the book contains comments on client behaviors, interpersonal issues, suggestions for interventions, and reactions to treatment.

Lewak et al. (1990) took a different approach to using the MMPI/MMPI–2. This book was less research oriented than most and focused on using the first 13 scales to assess treatment issues and provide client feedback. Descriptive adjectives for individual scales and high-point codes were organized by client concerns, thoughts, emotions, and behaviors. The authors then provided clear hypotheses about the client's early learning experiences, interpersonal style, behavior in therapy, and medication possibilities. They provided extensive lists of well-defined feedback statements along with self-help suggestions for the client. Case examples included dialogue between client and counselor.

Meyers and Deitsch's (1996) book was unique because it integrated test data from several psychological tests. The authors concentrated on interpretive information from the MMPI–2 and the Sixteen Personality Factor Inventory. Detailed interpretation sections were organized around *DSM–IV* diagnoses and behavioral features. The appendices contained a structure for interview data, a list of self-help books, and examples of relaxation techniques. The authors provided multimodal treatment suggestions for each diagnosis, making this book a valuable reference source in treatment planning.

Greene's (1991) book balanced detail with usefulness. He provided the standard interpretive data and research findings along with case examples. He presented a great amount of case data including his own approach to profile interpretation and various computer-generated reports. The information headings were similar to those found in Greene and Nichols' (1995) interpretive strategy described earlier. Multicultural issues for test interpretation were also reviewed.

Butcher and Williams (1992) also provided a general resource for interpretation and research information on the MMPI–2 and the MMPI–A. The book contained data on the clinical, content, and supplemental scales, as well as the code types. Interpretive data were presented in easy-to-use tables and text for both tests. Research evidence for test validity with various clinical samples was included with the interpretive data.

EVALUATION AND FUTURE DIRECTIONS

The MMPI–2 is so popular that it is the standard by which most other personality inventories are judged. It is well accepted in numerous settings as a valid personality and pathology assessment tool. It is relatively easy to use and inexpensive, and provides an abundance of information for a reasonable investment of time. More applied research is needed to match profile characteristics with effective interventions, and to determine variables that predict outcomes in counseling. For example, researchers could match counselor, client, and treatment characteristics to determine efficient treatment delivery. Research is needed to validate test use in vocational and medical settings. Validity methods need to be adjusted for content scale interpretation. We see continuing development in interpretation strategies based on the content scales. Items will be developed from clearly defined psychological constructs and then refined through psychometrics.

REFERENCES

Barron, F. (1953). An ego-strength scale which predicts response to psychotherapy. *Journal of Consulting Psychology, 17,* 327–333.

Butcher, J. N., Dahlstrom, W. G., Graham, J. R., Tellegen, A., & Kaemmer, B. (1989). *MMPI-2: Manual for administration and scoring.* Minneapolis: University of Minnesota Press.

Butcher, J. N., Graham, J. R., Williams, C. L., & Ben-Porath, Y. S. (1990). *Development and use of the MMPI-2 content scales.* Minneapolis: University of Minnesota Press.

Butcher, J. N., & Williams, C. L. (1992). *Essentials of MMPI-2 and MMPI-A interpretation.* Minneapolis: University of Minnesota Press.

Butcher, J. N., Williams, C. L., Graham, J. R., Archer, R. P., Tellegen, A., Ben-Porath, Y., & Kaemmer, B. (1992). *MMPI-A: Manual for administration and scoring.* Minneapolis: University of Minnesota Press.

Caldwell, A. (1996). *Caldwell report.* Los Angeles, CA: Author.

Cohen, R. J., Swerdlik, M. E., & Phillips, S. M. (1996). *Psychological testing and assessment: An introduction to tests and measurement* (3rd ed.). Mountain View, CA: Mayfield.

Duckworth, H. C., & Anderson, W. P. (1995). *MMPI interpretation manual for counselors and clinicians* (4th ed.). Bristol, PA: Accelerated Development.

Edwards, D. W., Morrison, T. L., & Weissman, H. N. (1993). The MMPI and MMPI-2 in an outpatient sample: Comparisons of code types, validity scales, and clinical scales. *Journal of Personality Assessment, 1,* 1–18.

Gilberstadt, H., & Duker, J. (1965). *A handbook for clinical and actuarial MMPI interpretation.* Philadelphia, PA: W. B. Saunders.

Graham, J. R. (1993). *MMPI-2: Assessing personality and psychopathology.* New York: Oxford University Press.

Greene, R. L. (1991). *The MMPI-2/MMPI: An interpretive manual.* Boston: Allyn & Bacon.

Greene, R. L., Brown, R. C., & Kovan, R. E. (1998). *MMPI-2 Adult Interpretive System, Ver. 2.* Odessa, FL: Psychological Assessment Resources.

Greene, R. L., & Nichols, D. S. (1995). *MMPI-2 Structural Summary.* Odessa, FL: Psychological Assessment Resources.

Hathaway, S. R., & McKinley, J. C. (1943). *The MMPI manual.* New York: Psychological Corporation.

Keiller, S. W., & Graham, J. R. (1993). The meaning of low scores on MMPI-2 clinical scales of normal subjects. *Journal of Personality Assessment, 2,* 211–223.

Lanyon, R. I. (1978). *Psychological Screening Inventory test manual.* Port Huron, MI: Sigma Assessment Systems.

Lewak, R. W., Marks, P. A., & Nelson, G. E. (1990). *Therapist guide to the MMPI & MMPI-2: Providing feedback and treatment.* Bristol, PA: Accelerated Development.

Marks, P. A., Lewak, R. W., & Nelson, G. E. (1996). *Marks Adult Interpretive Report for the MMPI-2 and MMPI.* Los Angeles: Western Psychological Services.

Marks, P. A., & Seeman, W. (1963). *The actuarial description of abnormal personality: An atlas for use with the MMPI.* Baltimore, MD: Williams & Wilkins.

Megargee, E. I., Cook, P. E., & Mendelsohn, G. A. (1967). The development and validation of an MMPI scale of assaultiveness in overcontrolled individuals. *Journal of Abnormal Psychology, 72,* 519–528.

Meyer, R. G., & Deitsch, S. E. (1996). *The clinician's handbook* (4th ed.). Boston: Allyn and Bacon.

Pope, H. S., Butcher, J. N., & Seelen, J. (1993). *The MMPI, MMPI–2, & MMPI–A in court.* Washington, DC: American Psychological Association

Rainwater, G. D. (1995). *MMPI–2 report 3.0.* Melbourne, FL: Psychometric Software.

Schuerger, J. M., Watterson, D. G., & Croom, W. C. (1994). *Psychological variables and their applications* (7th ed). Unpublished manuscript, Cleveland State University.

Strong, E. K., Jr. (1927). *Vocational Interest Blank.* Stanford, CA: Stanford University Press.

Welsh, G. S., & Dahlstrom, W. G. (Eds.). (1956). *Basic readings on the MMPI in psychology and medicine.* Minneapolis: University of Minnesota Press.

Wiggins, J. S. (1969). Content dimensions in the MMPI. In J. N. Butcher (Ed.), *MMPI: Research developments and clinical applications* (pp. 127–180). New York: McGraw-Hill.

3

The California Psychological Inventory

Harrison G. Gough
Institute of Personality and Social Research,
University of California, Berkeley

The goal of the California Psychological Inventory (CPI; Gough & Bradley, 1996) is to put information into the hands of a qualified interpreter that may be used to construct a true-to-life picture of the person who was tested. This purpose involves several important considerations. One is that the focus is always on the individual, not on nomothetic or aggregated data. A second is that the interpreter of the inventory should have proper training and background, and should possess the intuitional and empathic skills that accurate psychodiagnosis demands. A third is that the scales of the inventory should be relevant to, and predictive of, consequential criteria in the daily life of the individual. A fourth consideration is that the information conveyed by each scale, and by configurations of scales, should be in a form that builds on and takes advantage of the interpreter's lifelong experiences and natural observational talents.

To achieve these objectives, five basic principles or axioms have guided the choice of variables for inclusion in the inventory, and the methods employed to construct and validate these scales. *Axiom 1* pertains to the choice of measures, and to the decision to assess "folk concepts," that is to say, constructs about personality that all people, everywhere, use in their daily lives to comprehend their own behavior and the behavior of others. Insofar as possible, these constructs should be cultural universals, operative everywhere that people live together under societal terms. CPI scales for dominance (Do), responsibility (Re), tolerance (To), and flexibility (Fx) may be cited as examples. Part of the research agenda for the CPI is to

45

demonstrate the transcultural utility of measures such as these for understanding and predicting the behavior of individuals.

Axiom 2 may be called the "open system" axiom. It pertains to the question, "How many scales will the system include?" The import of Axiom 2 is that a sufficient number of scales shall be included so as to allow the prediction of any consequential, recurring form of interpersonal behavior, either from a single scale (the rare case) or from a combination of two, three, or even four scales (the usual case). If an important criterion turns out to be unpredictable from the set of scales as then constituted, a new measure may and probably should be added to the system. On the other hand, if a scale in the system seldom or never demonstrates predictive relevance, it may and probably should be dropped. The idea that scales may be added, or dropped, according to their links to nontest criteria is what is meant by the *open system*. In the history of the CPI from its inception almost 50 years ago, down to the present, scales have in fact been added, and scales have in fact been dropped.

Axiom 3 may be described as the "instrumental" axiom. It pertains to the question, "What are the specific intentions of each scale?" In personality assessment there are two major answers to this query. One of these may be termed the *definitional* approach, based on concepts of trait definition and measurement, with desiderata of maximal internal consistency, minimal interscale correlations, and unambiguous location in a factor-analytic matrix. Ordinarily, in the development of scales by means of these methods, no attention is paid to nontest criteria or to the ability of the measure to predict behaviors within the realm of applicability envisaged for the full inventory. In contrast, the instrumental approach places primary emphasis on the pragmatic relevance and utility of the scale, from its initial development down to its validation and elaboration of meanings. For the scales of the CPI, two and only two basic requirements are posited: (1) to forecast with reasonable accuracy what people will say and do in defined situations, and (2) to identify people who will be described in meaningful and differentiated ways by those who know them well. If these objectives can be attained without attention to the punctilios of orthodox psychometrics, well and good.

Axiom 4 refers to the psychometric topography of the profile of scales, answering the question, "How shall the scales be related to each other?" The axiom states that interscale correlations for the CPI should resemble as closely as possible the intercorrelations among the designated concepts as used by ordinary people in their everyday lives. The goal, in other words, is not orthogonality, or psychometric independence within the set of scales, but rather, the attainment of a pattern of relations that accurately maps the topography of folk usage of the inventory's concepts.

Axiom 5 provides an answer to the question, "Should measurement be restricted to single, key dimensions or should facets within those dimensions be separately scaled?" For the CPI, major themes such as introversion/extroversion are assessed by a family of intercorrelated scales, indicative of subtleties and nuances in the manner in which the general disposition is manifested. For example, the first sector on the CPI profile contains seven scales depicting different but related ways in which self-confidence, poise, and participative propensities are expressed. The second sector also contains seven scales, each indicative of a facet within the realm of self-regulative interpersonal values. By attending to configurations among these seven scales, or facets, an interpreter will know the degree of dependability and rule-observing behavior to be expected, but also the style or manner in which these proclivities will be expressed.

FORM 434

The current form of the CPI contains 434 items, 28 fewer than the prior 462-item version published in 1986 (Gough, 1987). The first published form of the CPI (Gough, 1957) contained 480 items. In agreement with the open-system axiom, in addition to dropping items from earlier versions, items were modified, where necessary, so as to eliminate awkward constructions, sexist language, inquiries contraindicated by legislation such as the 1991 Americans with Disabilities Act, and items referring to outmoded or time-dated content.

Scoring of the inventory is reported for 20 folk, 3 vector, and 7 special-purpose scales. The standard profile report form presents the folk measures on a profile sheet, and gives raw and standard scores for the 7 special-purpose scales. The 3 vector scales are used to classify the respondent within the three-dimensional model of personality structure theorized to underly the totality of the inventory. Later in this chapter a brief account will be given of this model and its historical background.

These 30 scales may be scored in full on Forms 480 and 462 of the CPI, as well as (of course) on Form 434. Also, scales as scored on Form 434 are of the same length as scales scored on Form 462, permitting approximate comparability of descriptive statistics for data based on Form 462 testing with findings for scales scored on Form 434. Analytic equivalence is also maintained, as verified by very high correlations between scales in their Form 462 and Form 434 keying. As reported in the 1996 manual, these coefficients ranged from a low of .96 to a high of 1.00.

The inventory can be administered in from 40 to 50 min, in most instances. For slow readers, or in circumstances where testing is very anxiety arousing, more time will be required. If testing is done in groups, the examiner can read the instructions aloud while the respondents read silently, after which they proceed at their own pace. Most college students can simply be asked to read the instructions on the booklet and answer sheet, and then to go ahead until finished. Occasionally, clients are asked to take booklet and answer sheet home, to bring back for the next appointment. The existence of empirically developed algorithms for identifying invalid protocols (Lanning, 1989) allows the counselor to detect any answer sheet of questionable reliability.

INTERPRETIVE MEANINGS OF SCALES

Table 3.1 lists the 30 scales, along with a short statement of their intended function and a summary of their major interpretive implications. Much more complete information about these scales may be found in the 1996 manual, including the specifics of their development, illustrative research fundings, and a systematic account of their behavioral and descriptive significants. Information about how to interpret patterns and configurations among the scales may be found in McAllister's *Practical Guide to CPI Interpretation* (McAllister, 1996).

TABLE 3.1
Intentions and Implications of Form 434 CPI Scales

Measures of interpersonal style and orientation

Do   (Dominance). *Length*: 36 items. *Purpose*: To assess prosocial interpersonal dominance. *Implications*: High scorers tend to be confident, assertive, dominant, and task oriented. Low scorers tend to be cautious, quiet, unassuming, and hesitant to take the initiative. Persons with very high scores are often domineering and overbearing.

Cs   (Capacity for Status). *Length*: 28 items. *Purpose*: To measure personal qualities that are associated with and that lead to high social status. *Implications*: High scorers tend to be ambitious, to have many and varied interests, and to value success. Low scorers tend to be unsure of themselves, to dislike direct competition, and to be uncomfortable with uncertainty or complexity.

Sy   (Sociability). *Length*: 32 items. *Purpose*: To identify people who are outgoing, socially affiliative, and who enjoy social participation. *Implications*: High scorers tend to be sociable, gregarious, and at ease in most situations. Low scorers tend to be shy, inhibited, and attention avoiding.

Sp   (Social Presence). *Length*: 38 items. *Purpose*: To identify people characterized by feelings of self-assurance, confidence in dealing with others, and versatility. *Implications*: High scorers tend to be socially poised, spontaneous, clever, verbally fluent, and pleasure seeking. Low scorers tend to be self-denying, reserved, hesitant to express personal opinions, and subdued.

Sa   (Self-acceptance). *Length*: 28 items. *Purpose*: To identify persons with high self-esteem and a strong sense of personal worth. *Implications*: High scorers tend to be talkative, self-confident, and sure of themselves. Low scorers tend to be self-doubting, taciturn, self-blaming, and conciliatory.

In   (Independence). *Length*: 30 items. *Purpose*: To assess the twin elements of psychological strength and interpersonal detachment. *Implications*: High scorers tend to be self-sufficient, resourceful, detached, and persistent in seeking goals whether others agree or not. Low scorers tend to lack self-confidence, to seek support from others, to avoid conflict, and to have difficulty in making decisions.

(Continued)

TABLE 3.1
(Continued)

Em (Empathy). *Length*: 38 items. *Purpose*: To identify persons with affective insight, with a talent for understanding how others feel and think. *Implications*: High scorers tend to be liked and accepted by others, are aware of and sensitive to social nuances, and are optimistic in outlook. Low scorers are unempathic, skeptical about the intentions of others, limited in their range of interests, and defensive about their own feelings and desires.

Measures of normative orientation and values

Re (Responsibility). *Length*: 36 items. *Purpose*: To identify persons who are aware of societal rules and who can and do comply with them when appropriate. *Implications*: High scorers are responsible, reliable, ethically perceptive, and serious about duties and obligations. Low scorers are self-indulgent, undisciplined, careless, and indifferent to personal responsibilities.

So (Socialization). *Length*: 46 items. *Purpose*: To assess the degree to which societal norms have been internalized and become autonomously operational within the individual. *Implications*: High scorers are conscientious, well-organized, productive, and rule respecting. Those with very high scores can be overly conforming and rule dominated. Low scorers are rule-resistant, nonconforming, often rebellious, trouble-prone, and unconventional in views and attitudes.

Sc (Self-control). *Length*: 38 items. *Purpose*: To identify persons with a strong, affective cathexis of societal constraints, and whose ego control mechanisms are suppressive. *Implications*: High scorers try to control their emotions and to deny anger, suppress hostile and erotic impulses, and take pride in being self-disciplined. Low scorers have strong feelings and emotions, make little effort to hide or deny what they feel, have problems of undercontrol and impulsivity, and seek new experience and adventure.

Gi (Good Impression). *Length*: 40 items. *Purpose*: This scale has two goals, first, for very high scores (approximately raw score 30 and above), to identify protocols too strongly characterized by social desirability criteria and overly favorable self-presentation, and second, to identify persons whose self-presentational style emphasizes ingratiation and compliance. *Implications*: High scorers want to make a good impression, try to do what will please important others (sometimes to the point of being obsequious and sycophantic), and behave in conventional, formal ways. Low scorers insist on being themselves, even if this causes friction, or annoyance to others, are dissatisfied with many things, often complain, and are easily irritated.

Cm (Communality). *Length*: 38 items. *Purpose*: This scale also has two purposes. The first is to identify protocols with too many deviant or unusual responses to permit ordinary interpretation. The second is to define a continuum of latent beliefs and attitudes along which low scores are indicative of unconventionality and/or deviance, and high scores are indicative of realistic and friction-free ego functioning. *Implications*: High scorers fit in easily, see themselves as quite average, and make little effort to change things in their social context. Low scorers see themselves as different from others, as unconventional or nonconforming, are often changeable and moody, and would like many things to be different in the social milieu. Raw scores of approximately 25 and below are suggestive of careless or random answering.

Wb (Well-being). *Length*: 38 items. *Purpose*: To assess feelings of physical and psychological well-being. Very low scores (raw scores of 20 and below) are suggestive of exaggerated or unwarranted emphasis on personal problems, and even of deliberate attempts to fake bad. Above this point, scores may be psychologically interpreted. *Implications*: High scorers see themselves as in reasonably good physical and mental health, are optimistic about their future, and are cheerful. Low scorers are concerned about health, or personal problems, are given to complaining, see themselves as being treated unfairly, and are pessimistic.

TABLE 3.1

(Continued)

To   (Tolerance). *Length*: 32 items. *Purpose*: To assess attitudes of tolerance, forbearance, and respect for others. *Implications*: High scorers tend to be tolerant of others' beliefs, even when different from or counter to their own, and try to behave in fair-minded, reasonable, and tactful ways. Low scorers tend to be distrustful, fault-finding, and extrapunitive, and often harbor vengeful and vindictive feelings.

Measures of cognitive and intellectual functioning

As   (Achievement via Conformance). *Length*: 38 items. *Purpose*: To assess achievement potential in well-defined and clearly structured situations. *Implications*: High scorers have a strong drive to do well, like to work in settings where tasks and expectations are clearly defined, are efficient and well organized. Low scorers have difficulty in doing their best work in settings having strict rules and regulations, are easily distracted, and tend to withdraw from or abandon tasks when things do not go well.

Ai   (Achievement via Independence). *Length*: 36 items. *Purpose*: To assess achievement potential in open, minimally defined situations. *Implications*: High scorers have a strong drive to do well, like to work in settings that encourage freedom and individual initiative, are clear-thinking and good at taking the initiative. Low scorers have difficulty in doing their best work in settings that are vague, poorly defined, and lacking in precise specifications, and have limited interest in intellectual or cognitive endeavors.

Ie   (Intellectual Efficiency). *Length*: 42 items. *Purpose*: To assess the degree to which intellectual resources are efficiently utilized. *Implications*: High scorers are efficient in the use of intellectual resources, can keep on at a task where others might give up or become discouraged, are insightful and good at logical analysis. Low scorers find it difficult to get started on cognitive tasks, and to see them through to completion, feel unsure of themselves, express ideas awkwardly, and behave in self-defeating ways.

Measures of role and personal style

Py   (Psychological-mindedness). *Length*: 28 items. *Purpose*: To identify people who think psychologically, that is, who are interested in motives and the determinants underlying human behavior. *Implications*: High scorers tend to be insightful and perceptive, are good at appraising others but are not necessarily nurturant or supportive. Low scorers are more interested in the practical and concrete than the abstract, look more at what people do than at how they feel or think, and are often apathetic and unresponsive to intellectual challenges.

Fx   (Flexibility). *Length*: 28 items. *Purpose*: To assess a continuum going from resistance to change and novelty at one pole, to fluidity and delight in change at the other. *Implications*: High scorers are flexible, seek out change and variety, are easily bored by routine, everyday experience, and become impatient with the commonplace; they are also clever and imaginative, but careless and loosely organized. Low scorers like a steady pace and well-organized and predictable situations, tend to be conservative in their social and political views, and do not cope well with complex or rapidly changing interpersonal environments.

F/M   (Femininity/Masculinity). *Length*: 32 items. *Purpose*: To assess a continuum going from agentic masculinity at one pole to communal or nurturant femininity at the other. *Implications*: Among males, high scorers tend to be sensitive, esthetically reactive, and high-strung, whereas low scorers tend to be action oriented, tough-minded, un-sentimental, and aggressive. Among females, high scorers tend to be sympathetic, warm, sentimental, and modest, but also dependent and vulnerable to threat. Both females and males with low scores tend to be independent, tough-minded, decisive, and self-sufficient.

(Continued)

TABLE 3.1

(Continued)

The vector scales

v.1   (vector 1). *Length*: 34 items. *Purpose*: To define a continuum going from involvement, participative inclinations, and extraversion at one pole, to detachment, a need for privacy, and introversion at the other. *Implications*: High scorers tend to be quiet, reserved, reluctant to commit self to any definite or irreversible course of action, and inhibited in the expression of emotions or personal feelings. Low scorers tend to be assertive, talkative, power oriented, and self-confident.

v.2   (vector 2). *Length*: 36 items. *Purpose*: To define a continuum going from a rule-questioning perspective at one pole to a rule-favoring perspective at the other. *Implications*: High scorers tend to have strong ethical beliefs, to have efficient, industrious, and thorough work habits, and to be self-disciplined and reliable. Low scorers tend more toward unconventionality, adventurousness, impulsivity, and mischievousness, and toward skepticism concerning moral posture and alleged selflessness in others. At very low scores on v.2 there are potentialities for reckless and rule-violating behavior.

v.3   (vector 3). *Length*: 58 items. *Purpose*: To define a continuum going from general dissatisfaction, psychological inadequacy, and poor ego integration at one pole, to self-realization, psychological competence, and good ego integration at the other. *Implications*: High scorers tend to be capable, insightful, foresighted, fair-minded in their dealings with others, and relatively free of neurotic trends and disabling self-doubt. Low scorers tend to have many problems, feel victimized by life, have narrow interests, and deal poorly with stress and interpersonal conflicts.

The special-purpose scales

Mp   (Managerial Potential). *Length*: 34 items. *Purpose*: To identify people with an interest in management, and with effective interpersonal skills. *Implications*: High scorers are productive and efficient, impress others as trustworthy, have long-range time perspectives, like to be with people, and have high aspirations for self. Low scorers are easily offended, withdraw or give up when things go badly, avoid making decisions, and tend to keep people at a distance.

Wo   (Work Orientation). *Length*: 40 items. *Purpose*: To identify people with a dutiful work ethic, and a strong sense of commitment to their jobs. *Implications*: High scorers are seen as dependable and responsible, as asking for little in the way of praise or commendation, and as self-disciplined. Low scorers often push against and test limits, are careless, tend to distrust others, and to behave in self-centered and temperamental ways.

CT   (Creative Temperament). *Length*: 42 items. *Purpose*: To identify people of an imaginative, creative temperament, with the potential for coming up with original ideas and solutions to problems. *Implications*: High scorers have a wide range of interests, use their imaginations freely, think in unconventional ways, tend to be rebellious and nonconforming, and react strongly to esthetic stimuli. Low scorers tend to be plodders, conventional in thinking and behavior, overcontrolling of emotional feelings, narrow in interests, and reserved.

Lp   (Leadership). *Length*: 70 items. *Purpose*: To identify people who have good leadership skills, who like to be in positions of leadership, and who will be accepted as leaders by others. *Implications*: High scorers are self-confident, socially at ease, enterprising, energetic, ambitious, and resourceful; others turn to them for advice and reassurance and they are willing to give advice. Low scorers are distractible, pessimistic, fluctuating in mood, concerned about their own adequacy, and ill at ease in many situations.

(Continued)

TABLE 3.1
(Continued)

Ami (Amicability). *Length*: 36 items. *Purpose*: To identify people who are amicable, amiable, friendly, and considerate of others. *Implications*: High scorers behave in an ethically consistent manner, are protective of those close to them, do not seek control or power, and are appreciative, modest, patient, and pleasant. Low scorers are often self-dramatizing, opportunistic, nonconforming, headstrong, quarrelsome, and self-centered.

Leo (Law Enforcement Orientation). *Length*: 42 items. *Purpose*: To identify people who view law enforcement and societal rules favorably, and whose temperament and demeanor are suitable for work in the law enforcement area. *Implications*: High scorers favor conservative values, judge self and others in conventional terms, have a stable, optimistic view of the future, and are self-confident, practical, and hard working. Low scorers tend to be nonconforming, given to daydreaming, introspective, changeable, complicated, and worrying.

Tm (Tough-mindedness). *Length*: 36 items. *Purpose*: To assess a continuum going from tender-mindedness (reflective, soft-hearted, trusting) at one pole to tough-mindedness (frank, hard-headed, unemotional) at the other. *Implications*: High scorers are realistic in their thinking, not given to far-fetched fantasies, able to comprehend and logically analyze complex problems, and impress others as capable, determined, self-confident, and thorough. Low scorers are often anxious, poor at dealing with stress or trauma, self-defeating, easily distracted, sensitive, and submissive.

Skilled use of the CPI rests in part on thorough understanding of the personological implications of each scale, and an ability to think inductively. That is, from observing those scales with high and low standing on the respondent's profile, the interpreter must evolve a more total picture of the individual, one that entails the specific indicators but that goes beyond them in the elaboration of expectations for likely behavior and for how others will react to the person under scrutiny.

McAllister's interpretational manual (McAllister, 1996) can be of great help to a student of the CPI, in showing how to understand the meaning of scale configurations and patterns. Consider the configuration of high Do (above 65 standard score) and low F/M (below 40 standard score). McAllister stated that these persons are often domineering, pushy, and blunt, and that they will be impatient with subordinates. What if a low (below 40) score on Em is added to the configuration? McAllister remarked that these persons will be even more likely to exhibit domineering behavior, and that as managers they will create morale problems because of their tendency to mistreat their employees.

THE THREE-VECTOR THEORETICAL MODEL

After the first 480-item version of the CPI appeared, there were many factor analyses of its 18 scales published, all of which agreed that there were two primary themes referring to interpersonal and normative orientations

(Megargee, 1972). Nichols and Schnell (1963) developed scales for these themes, naming them Person Orientation and Value Orientation. Later, using Guttman's technique of smallest space analysis (Guttman, 1968, 1982), Karni and Levin (Karni & Levin, 1972; Levin & Karni, 1970) detected a possible third theme in which the overall covariation among the scales was concentrated into a single focus. From these studies, and what has followed, it can now be seen that the CPI and its scales encompass three fundamental orientations: toward people, toward societal values and rules, and toward self.

In the 1940s and 1950s, psychologists interested in factorial issues published extensively on the number and nature of the basic variables in personality. Eysenck (1947) identified two major themes, one pertaining to general neuroticism and the other to a bipolar dimension of hysteria–dysthymia or extraversion–introversion. Psychoticism, as a third key dimension in Eysenck's formulation, came later (see Eysenck & Eysenck, 1976). Welsh (1956), in an early analysis of the Minnesota Multiphasic Personality Inventory (MMPI), found two primary factors that he called *anxiety* and *repression*. Leary (1957) proposed dominance–submission and love–hate as the two axes for his interpersonal circumplex. However, the work closest to what is now called the three-vector model is that of Philip Vernon (1953).

From his survey of factor analyses of personality variables, Vernon concluded that the "most pervasive or far-reaching dimension might be termed dependability—a blend of persistence, purposiveness, stability, and good character" (Vernon, 1953, p. 12). Vernon identified extraversion–introversion as the other basic theme in personality structure. A graphic display of Vernon's model is given in Fig. 3.1.

Vernon's extraversion–introversion axis is obviously similar to the interpersonal orientation theme in the CPI, even though Vernon drew more on psychopathological than on normal terminology to specify its meaning. This axis, dealing with one's orientation toward people, is now assessed by the first vector or v.1 scale of the CPI.

Vernon's undependability–dependability axis corresponds to the dimension defined by the second vector or v.2 scale, with one important provision: Vernon's axis is heavily loaded with evaluative and even pejorative terms, whereas v.2 is relatively free of any negative or invidious implications at either pole. On the v.2 scale, persons with low scores are characterized by norm-questioning dispositions, which may be expressed in creative and socially useful ways, as well as in negative or wayward behavior. Implications are likewise for persons scoring high on v.2: their behavior may vary from admirable compliance with social values to undue conventionality, overconformity, and rigid ego control. It might be noted that in Vernon's circumplex, Eysenck's major axis of hysteria–dysthymia appears as a subordinate theme, as does Leary's major axis of dominance–submission.

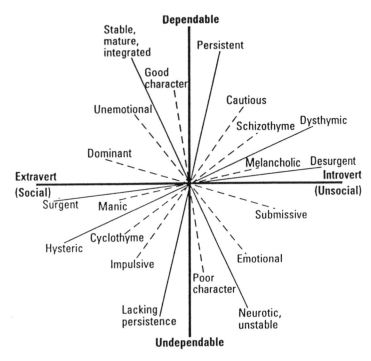

FIG. 3.1. The two basic dimensions of personality as proposed by Philip E.
Vernon. From Vernon (1953). Reprinted by permission of Methuen & Company,
publisher, London.

To develop the three vector scales, target clusters among the folk measures were posited, based on the locations of these scales in the smallest
space analyses of Karni and Levin. Items were chosen for each of the three
scales that had maximum correlations with each target cluster, and minimal
correlations with the other two. The goal of these analyses was to produce
three scales, free of overlap, as orthogonal (uncorrelated) as possible, and
consonant with the personological implications of the three fundamental
orientations. This task is easy to describe, but carrying it out was a long
and arduous labor. Finally, in the early 1980s, the three scales were completed and ready for presentation (Gough, 1987).

Conceptualization of the three scales as a model of personality structure
is illustrated in Fig. 3.2. Conjoint consideration of the v.1 (externality to
internality) and v.2 (norm-questioning to norm-favoring) scales defines four
ways of living or lifestyles, termed the *Alpha, Beta, Gamma,* and *Delta.*
Approximately 25% of the norm population for the CPI manifest each of
these ways of living. Alphas are involved and participative persons, who
believe societal norms to be in general good and proper. Betas are detached, seek and need privacy, and also tend to approve of social conven-

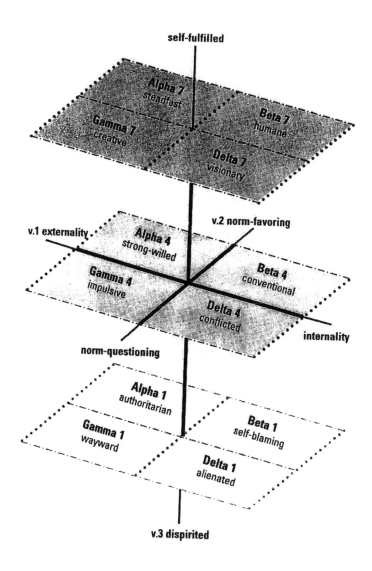

FIG. 3.2. Schematic representation of the three-vector or cuboid model of personality structure, showing cross sections at levels 1, 4, and 7 of ego integration. Modified and reproduced by special permission of the Publisher, Consulting Psychologists Press, Inc., Palo Alto, CA 94303 from CPI Manual, Third Edition by Harrison G. Gough and Pamela Bradley. Copyright © 1996 by Consulting Psychologists Press, Inc.

tions. Gammas like and respond to interpersonal activity, but are dubious about the constrictive and limiting effects of many folkways. Deltas have an internal orientation, resist self-revelation, and also see many of society's rules as unduly restraining and inhibiting.

Each of these lifestyles has its own potentiality for self-realization, and its own risks for malfunctioning and psychopathology, and none is intrinsically superior to the other three. The degree to which the positive possibilities for any lifestyle have been achieved is indexed by the score on the v.3 scale. Seven categories are specified for v.3, with 8% of the norm population classified at the lowest level (Level 1), 12% at Level 2, 19% at Level 3, 22% at Level 4, 19% at Level 5, 12% at Level 6, and 8% at Level 7 (the highest level). Classification of any person within this model is easily expressed by type and level, as, for example, an Alpha-4, a Beta-7, a Gamma-2, or a Delta-5. In short, the v.3 scale assesses a sort of g-factor in personality, to the respondent seen as self-realization, to the ordinary observer seen as psychological competence, and to the professional seen as ego-integration.

Alphas at their best (ranking high on v.3) can be charismatic leaders, directing effort toward worthy and consensual objectives. At their worst, they are authoritarian, rule-dominated, and punitive. At their best (ranking high on v.3), Betas are humane, admirable models of goodness and virtue. At their worst, they are inhibited, repressed, and conformist. Gammas at their best are creative and innovative; at their worst they are wayward and impulse-ridden. Deltas at their best are visionary, often finding a voice in art, music, or literature; at their worst, they experience deep inner conflicts that may lead to fragmentation of the ego.

Although the CPI is intended primarily for use with normal persons, and is scaled for variables relevant to everyday occupational and interpersonal life, the three-vector model does have implications for understanding psychopathology. Betas at low ranks on v.3 are prone to repressive disorders, depression, and somatic conversions. Gammas at low levels on v.3 are at risk for narcissistic, exhibitionistic, and histrionic personality disorders, and for criminality. Deltas at low levels on v.3 may fragment to the point of psychosis, and have severe problems in the control of aggression, whether directed at self or at others. At low levels on v.3, Alphas also manifest typical problems, such as ethnocentrism, and often affiliate with paramilitary or other extremist groups. Unpublished studies of police officers (who tend to be Alphas) reveal that employing excessive force in making arrests, or in dealing with prisoners, is a problem to be guarded against in low-level Alphas. It should be noted, in this little excursion into psychopathology, that clinical psychiatry has well-developed diagnostic and therapeutic concepts for the Beta, Gamma, and Delta pathologies, but tends to view Alpha pathology as reprehensible, and better treated by the courts than by mental health professionals.

In addition to its implications for individual behavior, the three-vector model can be predictive of the functioning of groups. What if the normal balance of approximately 25% of each type is not approximated, and one type or two types predominate? A study of the Rajneeshi colony in Antelope, OR (Sundberg, Latkin, Littman, & Hagan, 1990), found only one Alpha and only one Beta among 67 residents, along with 38 (56.7%) Gammas and 27 (40.3%) Deltas. The prosocial leadership roles played by Alphas and the interpersonal bonding functions of Betas were dangerously underrepresented in this group, and not long after the survey was taken the colony fell apart in acrimonious internal conflict and intrigue.

In their book on use of the CPI in industrial and organizational psychology, Meyer and Davis (1992) discussed a number of managerial teams composed of different mixes of the four lifestyles, and showed how imbalances and asymmetries among the four lifestyles can lead to difficulties. One of the companies they studied had a top management team of five people, four men and one woman. All of the men were Alphas, whereas the woman was a Gamma. During the consultations, the group came to recognize that the Gamma-5 female was viewed as different from the others. The Alphas felt that she took action without keeping them informed, and did not talk to them about her ideas. These are common Alpha criticisms of the change-oriented and innovation-seeking behavior of Gammas. For her part, the Gamma-5 woman felt that the others did not confront her directly, or tell her explicitly when they wanted information. Nonconfrontive, conflict-suppressing behavior is common among Alphas in managerial roles.

The CPI manual (Gough & Bradley, 1996) gives type frequencies for a variety of educational and occupational samples. Some examples of samples with 45% or more members in the Alpha category are sales managers, military officers, male and female applicants for work as a police officer, parole and probation officers, high-school students nominated as leaders, and male applicants for medical school. Examples of groups with a preponderance of Betas are correctional officers, registered nurses, and high-school students in general. Some examples of groups with a preponderance of Gammas are psychology graduate students, social work graduate students, art institute students, and juvenile delinquents. Deltas are most numerous in groups such as male and female prison inmates, and high-school disciplinary problems.

College going among high-school graduates is strongly related to the CPI lifestyles. A survey of 3,487 graduates from 16 cities (Gough & Bradley, 1996) found college-going rates of 61% for Alphas, 40% for Gammas, 39% for Betas, and 27% for Deltas. In some academic settings, Deltas are even less frequent. For example, among 1,413 cadets at West Point only 4% were in the Delta category. Deltas are also very seldom found in managerial or executive positions. In college, Alphas tend to major in fields such as engineering and business administration. Betas move toward nursing, primary school teaching, and religious studies. Gammas like the social sciences, in particular political science, psychology, and sociology. Deltas, insofar as they are present, seek out the humanities and music. A recent paper (Gough, 1995) reviews CPI data of this kind in reference to career planning.

To conclude this section, findings from a survey of graduate students of counseling should be considered. These data were very kindly made available by Professor Morag B. Colvin Harris of East Texas State University. In her sample of 67 male students, 40.3% were Alphas, 16.4% Betas, 35.8% Gammas, and 7.6% Deltas. For 275 female graduate students in counseling the percentages were 38.9% Alphas, 10.5% Betas, 35.3% Gammas, and 15.3% Deltas. Alphas are the most numerous, followed closely by Gammas. Betas and Deltas are much less frequently found in these programs. From what is known about managerial styles (Meyer & Davis, 1992), it seems likely that Alpha counselors and Gamma counselors will have different preferred techniques of counseling, and different ways of dealing with clients.

Using the profile norm samples of 3,000 men and 3,000 women, standard scores with a baseline mean of 50 and standard deviation of 10 were computed for these students of counseling. Scales with means of 59 or more for either the 67 males or 275 females were Do (means of 61 and 59), Sa (60 and 58), Em (62 and 59), To (59 and 59), Ai (62 and 63), Py (58 and 59), v.3 (60 and 60), Mp (60 and 60), and CT (60 and 60). Moderate elevations for both subsamples were found for Cs, Sy, Sp, and In in the first sector, plus Ac, Ie, Fx, and Lp. The other scales were at or near the midpoint of 50, except for v.1 (internality), on which both groups scored in the 40s. Aspirants in the field of counseling, it appears, are characterized by prosocial leadership skills (Do, Mp, and Lp), interpersonal insight (Em and Py), tolerance (To), independent achievement motivation (Ai), maturity (v.3), and a capacity for creative thinking (CT). Lest this sound like too much self-approval and too much concern with making a good impression, the means of close to 50 on the Gi scale for both subsamples should be noted.

The current research bibliography of publications in the English language numbers more than 2,000 entries, far more than can be discussed in a brief overview. Instead of an attempt to cover all of this work, representative major examinations of issues relevant to counseling are cited. Leadership is one example. A study (Gough, 1990) was carried out of 7,331 persons (4,253 men, 3,078 women), using six different criteria of leadership, such as ratings of performance in leaderless group discussion experiments, Q-sorts descriptions specifying effective leadership, and peer ratings for leadership. Correlations of CPI scales with these criteria in each of 11 subsamples were computed, and then median values derived. The highest correlation was for the Do (Dominance) scale with a coefficient of .33, the second was for Independence ($r = .28$), the third was for Self-acceptance (r

= .26), and the fourth was for Empathy (r = .25). The largest negative correlation (−.26) was for the v.1 scale. A study of award-winning school psychologists (Davis & Sandoval, 1992) reported standard score means for these 64 persons of 63 on Do, 61 on In, 58 on Sa, and 57 on Em, a pattern consonant with the findings for leadership in the larger inquiry.

Creativity is another topic that has been extensively investigated by means of the CPI. A recent general survey (Gough, 1992) found 11 CPI scales to be significantly ($p \le .05$) related to ratings of creativity for both 623 men and 405 women seeking doctoral degrees in psychology. The largest correlations (.25 for men, .33 for women) were reported for the CT (Creative Temperament) scale, a measure developed on these samples. Among other CPI scales, largest coefficients were noted for Intellectual Efficiency (.21 for men, .30 for women), Achievement via Independence (.20 and .34), and Tolerance (.20 and .24). In a type/level analysis, based on the theoretical three-vector model, Gammas were rated as more creative than the other three types at all rankings on level, Alphas and Deltas were intermediate, and Betas were rated lowest. In other samples, the CT scale had correlations of .47 with rated creativity of 57 male PhDs in mathematics, of .46 with similar ratings of 41 female PhDs in mathematics, of .33 with rated creativity of 45 research scientists, and of .44 with rated creativity of 124 male architects.

Prejudice was studied in a sample of 450 men and 428 women (Gough & Bradley, 1993), wherein the criterion was based on evaluations by spouses, or by same-sex peers. Tolerance (To) was the CPI scale with largest correlations (−.30 for men, −.28 for women). Socialization had correlations of −.25 for men and −.18 for women, and Responsibility had correlations of −.19 and −.23. Well-socialized, responsible individuals with a disposition toward tolerance do impress those who know them well as relatively free of prejudice. In a type/level analysis of these same persons, Gammas manifested the most prejudice at all rankings on level (score on v.3), and Betas were rated as least prejudiced. Level itself was negatively related to prejudice, with correlations of −.21 for men and −.22 for women.

A rather specialized criterion, esthetic interests and artistic good taste as assessed by the Barron-Welsh Art Scale, was studied in relation to the CPI in samples of 1,020 men and 531 women (Gough, Hall, & Bradley, 1996). Among the 20 folk scales, Fx (Flexibility) had the largest correlations, .33 for men and .20 for women. An interesting contrast occurred for the two scales for achievement potential. Achievement via Independence (Ai) had positive correlations of .24 and .12, whereas Ac (Achievement via Conformance) had negative correlations of −.17 and −.13. Strongest relations, however, were noted in the type/level analysis. Gammas and Deltas scored distinctly higher than Alphas and Betas, at all ranks on level, and level itself was positively related to the esthetic measure.

Among the other domains that have been extensively studied in regard to the CPI may be mentioned delinquency and criminality (Gough &

Bradley, 1992), alcoholism and its treatment (Cooney, Kadden, & Litt, 1990; Kadden, Litt, Donovan, & Cooney, 1996; Kosson, Steurwald, Newman, & Widom, 1994; Kurtines, Ball, & Wood, 1978), ego development and personality change in adulthood (Cartwright & Wink, 1994; Helson & Roberts, 1994; Wink & Helson, 1993), and personal adjustment (Bayer, Whissell-Buechy, & Honzik, 1980; Cartwright, Wink, & Kmetz, 1995; Cook, Young, Taylor, & Bedford, 1996; Montgomery, Haemmerlie, & Edwards, 1991; Peskin, Jones, & Livson, 1997; Picano, 1989). In-depth reviews of individual scales of the CPI have also appeared in the 1990s, including one of the Re (Responsibility) scale (Weekes, 1993) and another of the So (Socialization) scale (Gough, 1994).

The work just cited all pertains to behavioral and other criteria external to the CPI. There is also an extensive literature pertaining to internal psychometric issues. One characteristic of the CPI that is often remarked in reviews and textbook accounts is item overlap. That is, items of the inventory often appear on two or more scales. The CPI is not alone, of course, in this respect. The MMPI, as one example, has about the same degree of item overlap as the CPI, and tests such as the Myers–Briggs Type Indicator (Myers, McCaulley, Quenk, & Hammer, 1998) and the Millon Clinical Multiaxial Inventory (Millon, 1983) have even more. Psychometric formalists assert that the existence of overlapping items will obscure or unduly influence the true factorial structure of a multivariate instrument. However, studies of the factor structure of the CPI in which overlap has been removed either by restricting items to one scale only or by statistical adjustments of interscale correlations so as to remove the effect of overlap, have shown that overlap has almost no influence on the number and definitions of the factors (Rogers & Shure, 1965). In a series of three papers that began with the hypothesis of overlap as a distorting influence on CPI factor structure, Farley and Cohen (Cohen & Farley, 1977; Farley & Cohen, 1974, 1980) ended with the conclusion that "no negative contribution of item overlap was found." On the contrary, these authors observed, the use of common items is an economical technique for increasing the total number of items in scales, thus improving scale internal reliability without adding to the overall number of items in the inventory.

Many but not all of the references cited so far contain information pertinent to the use of the CPI in counseling. There are many studies in addition to these that deal specifically with topics in counseling such as CPI profiles for people in different majors and different professional programs, relation of the CPI to scholastic aptitude tests used by colleges, differences between more and less successful student assistants, counselor characteristics as related to counseling effectiveness, and personality changes associated with college attendance. At the end of this chapter a list of 30 references is given, citing studies that are directly relevant to the theory and practice of counseling but that have not been specifically cited in the text.

INTERPRETATION

Interpretation of a CPI protocol follows a pathway from the general to the specific. Step 1 is to examine the record for any sign of invalidity, or distortion of responses. For impressionistic readings, this can be done by looking at the scores on Gi, Cm, and Wb, to note whether the first is too high, or either of the other two is too low. In the computer narrative, these examinations make use of precise statistical algorithms, applied in a decision-tree sequence. This review can answer the question, "Has this person responded to the inventory in a manner sufficiently similar to the responses of people in general, so that a valid, individualized interpretation may be attempted?"

The second step is to compare the protocol with broad groupings of people, specifically to groupings known to be relevant to the inventory, and known to be useful for the attainment of psychological understanding. For the CPI, this means classifying the protocol in regard to type (lifestyle) on the v.1 and v.2 scales, and in regard to level on v.3. The CPI manual furnishes generalized formulations for each of the four ways of living, and also descriptive statements for the seven levels of self-realization or ego integration.

The third step takes up the 20 folk scales and their interactions, looking for individuating implications that hold for the particular person who was tested. In general, attention is directed to scales with standard scores of approximately 60 and over, or of approximately 40 or below. Consider a profile with highest scores of 63 on Sa and 60 on Ie, and lowest scores of 39 on Re and 36 on Sc. In this context, we could say that our client is likely to be seen by others as self-centered, intelligent, irresponsible, and impulsive. If the type/level classification had been Gamma-6, we now have enough information to begin a psychological portrait that should be a helpful starting point for counseling, for predicting many behaviors, and for understanding some of the intrapersonal and interpersonal problems he or she will encounter.

This push toward individuation in interpretation can be carried into the special-purpose scales, if desired. Suppose that our client also had scores of 65 on CT (Creative Temperament), 32 on Leo (Low Enforcement Orientation), and 61 on Tm (Tough-mindedness). These additional findings can be introduced into the portrait, or psychological model, that we are trying to create.

This is about as far as one can go in an impressionistic interpretation of the record. In the computer narrative, however, one more step is taken, a test-based formulation of the personality by means of Block's (1961) 100-item California Q-set. Embedded in the logic of the computer program are 200 algorithms, one for each Q-sort item for men, and the same for women. The goal of this analysis is to produce a CPI-based Q-sort formulation that will approximate what an insightful, informed, and benevolent observer would say. The algorithms were developed empirically on 547 men and 393 women. Each algorithm yields a score along the 1 to 9 scale established for the 100 items, after which these scores are classified into the five most salient, the eight next most salient, and so on down to the five least salient or "true" statements about the respondent. This CPI-based Q-sort may be validated against a Q-sort from an actual observer, or panel of observers.

A validational study of this kind was carried out on 82 men and 65 women, none of whom had been used in the development of the algorithms. The Q-sort criterion for each person was based on the consensual Q-sort by five psychologists who had observed the person in intensive assessment settings, but who had had no access to the CPI or other test data. The range of correlations in the full sample of 147 persons was from .09 to .89, with medians of .65 for both the 82 men and the 65 women. One of the factors related to the magnitude of these validity coefficients was the interjudge agreement for each panel. The alpha index of interjudge agreement correlated at .39 with the correspondence between the CPI and the panel's Q-sorts.

CASE ILLUSTRATION

To illustrate application of the CPI to individuals, the case of Dan M. is presented. Dan is a 19-year-old second-year college student majoring in psychology. Looking ahead, he hopes for a career in counseling, working with adults. Next year he hopes to be allowed to take a graduate seminar in counseling psychology, and he plans to volunteer as a student assistant for a campus service offering help on contraception and related issues. He also has a strong interest in humanistic psychology and in subjects such as music, film, and philosophy.

He grew up in poor economic circumstances. His father died when he was still a child, but several years later, when his mother remarried, family income was higher, in the "middle class" range in his own judgment. His mother has worked throughout his life, in secretarial and supervisory posts. There was extended family support from aunts and uncles, and grandparents. In high school Dan did well academically, and took part in groups formed to preserve the environment and to foster the humanities. He dated occasionally, and enjoyed social gatherings. In college, so far, he has had a smaller circle of friends, and has been more serious about his academic work. His grade average is a bit above 3.00. Both his mother and his stepfather are strongly supportive of his educational aspirations, without being pushy or demanding. However, he is expected to take care of himself and to function independently. Dan sees himself now as intelligent and self-confident, perhaps a little aggressive but at the same time lacking in assertiveness.

Figure 3.3 shows Dan's classification in the CPI type/level schema. On the v.1 scale he scores in the participative-extraverted portion of the continuum, and on the v.2 scale he is on the norm-questioning side of the dimension, leading to a classification in the Gamma quadrant. Gammas, as described earlier, tend to be involved, participative, and rule-questioning. At their best, they are adept in spotting the flaws and incongruities in conventions, including those of the workplace, and nearly always are eager for

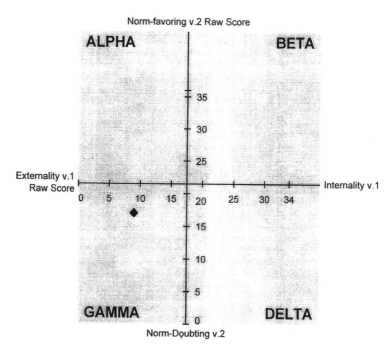

Classification for type:	**Gamma**		
Classification for level:	**7**		
Type and Level Scores:	Raw	Standard	
	9	35	v.1 (internality)
	17	41	v.2 (norm-favoring)
	52	72	v.3 (ego integration)

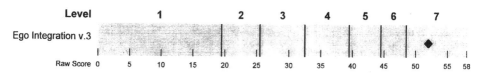

FIG. 3.3. Classification of Dan M. in the CPI three-vector model of personality structure.

change and innovation. They are also creative in their own thinking, and persuasive in convincing others that change is needed. At their worst, they resist control or advice from others, and are apt to behave in impulsive and self-serving ways. Because Dan ranks at the highest classification on the v.3 scale, one can expect that he will be an effective, well-integrated Gamma. For Gammas at level 7 one can anticipate superior intellectual ability, verve, spontaneity, and a zest for new experience.

Figure 3.4 gives Dan's CPI profile on the 20 folk measures. Three scales have standard scores above 70 (Cs, Sp, and Em). From these elevations we can infer that Dan is ambitious, alert to opportunity, and enterprising, that he is verbally fluent and articulate, at ease in nearly any situation, and that he is insightful concerning how others feel and think. Scores of 60 or greater may be noted on Sy, Sa, In, Gi, Wb, To, Ac, Ai, and Ie. The first three (Sy, Sa, and In) are in sector 1 of the profile where they add emphasis to the inferences based on the three highest points on Cs, Sp, and Em. Within this first sector, the only score below 60 is on the Do scale, consonant with Dan's remark to his interviewer that although aggressive he is somewhat lacking in assertiveness.

In the second sector of measures of intrapersonal values and self-regulation, four scales were close to the central baseline of 50 (Re, So, Sc, and Cm). To and Wb, at 60 and 62, betoken optimism and self-confidence, along with a worldview valuing relationality and tolerance. The elevation of 61 on Gi (Good Impression), however, is less favorable in its implications, suggesting a certain lack of self-insight concerning his own egoistic and self-evaluative motives. One of McAllister's (1996) configurations postulates high scores on Cs, Sy, and Gi, for which McAllister suggested a manipulative tendency to get ahead and to take advantage of others in one's drive for success.

The third profile sector dealing with measures of achievement motivation and intellectual functioning shows scores of 64 for Ac, 67 for Ai, and 65 for Ie. This is one of the 152 configural signs discussed by McAllister. When it is present, as it is for Dan, McAllister (1996) suggested the following interpretation:

> They easily learn new things and want to be seen as knowledgeable. They can work within a structure and a game plan, but prefer a measure of individual freedom. They do not like close supervision. They are likely to be seen as quick, adept, and resourceful, and generally are efficient and well-organized. (p. 81)

The last three scales (Py, Fx, and F/M) are between 50 and 57 in elevation, and hence not candidates for interpretive comments, were it not for the fact that Dan has already announced his desire to pursue advanced study in

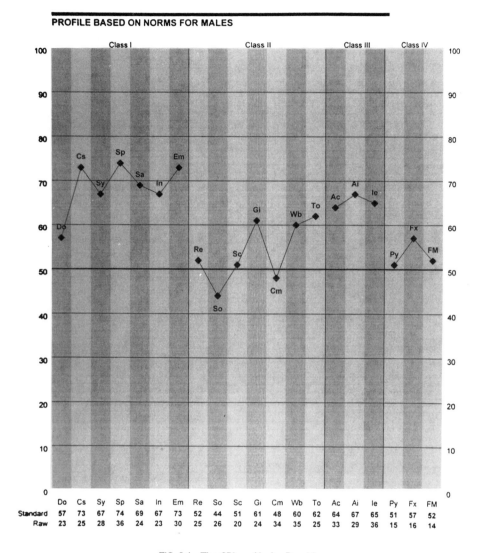

PROFILE BASED ON NORMS FOR MALES

	Do	Cs	Sy	Sp	Sa	In	Em	Re	So	Sc	Gi	Cm	Wb	To	Ac	Ai	Ie	Py	Fx	FM
Standard	57	73	67	74	69	67	73	52	44	51	61	48	60	62	64	67	65	51	57	52
Raw	23	25	28	36	24	23	30	25	26	20	24	34	35	25	33	29	36	15	16	14

FIG. 3.4. The CPI profile for Dan M.

psychology and a career in counseling. Given these goals, the relatively average score on Py may presage future difficulties as he moves along these pathways.

Among the seven special-purpose scales, Dan had four above 60: Managerial Potential (Mp), Creative Temperament (CT), Leadership Potential (Lp), and Tough-mindedness (Tm). Taken together, Mp, Lp, and Tm indicate confidence and competence in leadership roles, and an ability to think independently and to take decisive action when necessary. CT is indicative of superior creative potential.

In the final section of the interpretive narrative, the 100 items in the California Q-set (Block, 1961) are arrayed in order of salience, using the algorithms derived by means of empirical analyses. To list all 100 of these items with their estimated Q-sort placements would take far too much space, and could even result in information overload. Instead, only the five items placed in the topmost category for salience plus the eight items in the next highest category will be cited, matched at the bottom by the eight and five items in the least salient categories.

Q-sort items placed in Category 9 (extremely characteristic or salient):
 Is subjectively unaware of self-concern; feels satisfied with self (7.55)
 Interested in members of the opposite sex (7.30)
 Has social poise and presence; appears socially at ease (7.28)
 Is verbally fluent, can express ideas well (7.16)
 Values own independence and autonomy (7.09)

Items placed in Category 8 (quite characteristic or salient):
 Behaves in an assertive fashion (6.91)
 Initiates humor (6.84)
 Emphasizes being with others; gregarious (6.83)
 Responds to humor (6.63)
 Is cheerful (6.62)
 Is personally charming (6.52)
 Has a wide range of interests (6.45)
 Is calm, relaxed in manner (6.43)

Items placed in Category 2 (quite uncharacteristic, or negatively salient):
 Is moralistic (3.25)
 Has a readiness to feel guilty (3.17)
 Is subtly negativistic; tends to undermine and obstruct or sabotage (3.13)
 Is unpredictable and changeable in behavior and attitudes (3.12)
 Overreactive to minor frustrations; irritable (3.07)
 Has a brittle ego-defense system; has a small reserve of integration; would be disorganized and maladaptive when under stress or trauma (2.91)

Give up and withdraws where possible in the face of frustration and adversity (2.70)

Is vulnerable to real or fancied threat (2.69)

Items placed in Category 1 (extremely uncharacteristic or negatively salient):

Reluctant to commit self to any definite course of action; tends to delay or avoid action (2.65)

Genuinely submissive; accepts domination comfortably (2.58)

Feels a lack of personal meaning in life (2.36)

Is self-defeating (2.20)

Feels cheated and victimized by life; self-pitying (2.06)

To conclude this section on Dan and his CPI protocol, the final comments by his life history interviewer may be quoted:

Dan is an extraverted and socially active person. He appears to be genuinely concerned about others and their welfare, and expresses mature and tolerant values. His professional goal is to do counseling with "normal" persons, in particular the resolution of family problems. He seems to be little interested in the research side of psychology, nor in psychodynamic or in-depth methods of psychotherapy. In his own life, he seems not as yet to have worked out the ambivalences in his relation to his step-father, and also has unresolved reservations about his mother's dual commitment to career and family. Nonetheless, he is highly motivated, seeking experiences that will extend his knowledge and increase his depth of self-understanding, and barring unforeseen trauma should be able successfully to pursue his stated objectives.

IMPLICATIONS FOR COUNSELING

Had Dan sought counseling, it is quite likely that his ambivalence toward his stepfather could have been discussed. His feelings about his mother's distance or even aloofness from the children might also merit analysis. One would also hope that through counseling Dan would become aware of the underside of some of his strengths, in particular his tendency to manipulate people so as to gain his own ends, and his lack of insight about his own need for approval. At a deeper level, his egoistic, narcissistic feelings might be examined. Although Dan did not seek counseling for himself, he did continue along the path he set forth at the time of testing, and approximately 12 years later earned a PhD degree in psychology. As of our most recent follow-up he was engaged in family counseling in a clinic specializing in family conflicts and problems.

REFERENCES

Bayer, L. M., Whissell-Buechy, D., & Honzik, M. P. (1980). Adolescent health and personality. *Journal of Adolescent Health Care, 1*, 101–107.

Block, J. (1961). *The Q-sort method in personality assessment and psychiatric research*. Springfield, IL: C. C. Thomas. (Reprinted 1978, Consulting Psychologists Press, Palo Alto, CA)

Cartwright, L. K., & Wink, P. (1994). Personality change in women physicians from medical student years to mid-40s. *Psychology of Women Quarterly, 18*, 291–308.

Cartwright, L. K., Wink, P., & Kmetz, C. (1995). What leads to good health in midlife women physicians? Some clues from a longitudinal study. *Psychosomatic Medicine, 57*, 284–292.

Cohen, A., & Farley, F. H. (1977). The common-item problem in measurement: Effects on cross-cultural invariance of personality structure. *Educational and Psychological Measurement, 37*, 757–760.

Cook, M., Young, A., Taylor, D., & Bedford, A. P. (1996). Personality correlates of psychological distress. *Personality and Individual Differences, 20*, 313–319.

Cooney, N. L., Kadden, R. M., & Litt, M. D. (1990). A comparison of methods for assessing sociopathy in male and female alcoholics. *Journal of Studies on Alcohol, 51*, 42–48.

Davis, J. M., & Sandoval, J. (1992). School psychologists' personalities: Award winners contrasted with a random sample. *Professional Psychology: Research and Practice, 23*, 418–420.

Eysenck, H. J. (1947). *Dimensions of temperament*. London: Routledge & Kegan Paul.

Eysenck, H. J., & Eysenck, S. B. G. (1976). *Psychoticism as a dimension of personality*. London: University of London Press.

Farley, F. H., & Cohen, A. (1974). Common-item effects and the smallest space analysis of structure. *Psychological Bulletin, 81*, 766–772.

Farley, F. H., & Cohen, A. (1980). Common items and reliability in personality measurement. *Journal of Research in Personality, 14*, 207–211.

Gough, H. G. (1957). *Manual for the California Psychological Inventory*. Palo Alto, CA: Consulting Psychologists Press.

Gough, H. G. (1987). *The California Psychological Inventory administrator's guide*. Palo Alto, CA: Consulting Psychologists Press.

Gough, H. G. (1990). Testing for leadership with the California Psychological Inventory. In K. E. Clark & M. B. Clark (Eds.), *Measures of leadership* (pp. 355–379). West Orange, NJ: Leadership Library of America.

Gough, H. G. (1992). Assessment of creative potential in psychology and the development of a creative potential scale for the CPI. In J. C. Rosen & P. McReynolds (Eds.), *Advances in psychological assessment* (Vol. 8, pp. 227–259). New York: Plenum.

Gough, H. G. (1994). Theory, development, and interpretation of the CPI socialization scale. *Psychological Reports, 75*, 651–700.

Gough, H. G. (1995). Career assessment and the California Psychological Inventory. *Journal of Career Assessment, 3*, 101–122.

Gough, H. G., & Bradley, P. (1992). Delinquent and criminal behavior as assessed by the revised California Psychological Inventory. *Journal of Clinical Psychology, 48*, 298–308.

Gough, H. G., & Bradley, P. (1993). Personal attributes of people described by others as intolerant. In P. M. Sniderman, P. E. Tetlock, & E. G. Carmines (Eds.), *Prejudice, politics, and the American dilemma* (pp. 60–85). Stanford, CA: Stanford University Press.

Gough, H. G., & Bradley, P. (1996). *California Psychological Inventory manual* (3rd ed.). Palo Alto, CA: Consulting Psychologists Press.

Gough, H. G., Hall, W. B., & Bradley, P. (1996). Forty years of experience with the Barron-Welsh Art Scale. In A. Montuori (Ed.), *Unusual associates: A festschrift for Frank Barron* (pp. 252–301). Cresskill, NJ: Hampton Press.

Guttman, L. (1968). A general nonmetric technique for finding the coordinate space for a configuration of points. *Psychometrika, 33,* 469–506.

Guttman, L. (1982). Facet theory, smallest space analysis, and factor analysis. *Perceptual and Motor Skills, 54,* 491–493.

Helson, R., & Roberts, B. (1994). Ego development and personality change in adulthood. *Journal of Personality and Social Psychology, 66,* 911–920.

Kadden, R. M., Litt, M. D., Donovan, D., & Cooney, N. L. (1996). Psychometric properties of the California Psychological Inventory socialization scale in treatment-seeking alcoholics. *Psychology of Addictive Behaviors, 10,* 131–146.

Karni, E., & Levin, J. (1972). The use of smallest space analysis in studying scale structure: An application to the California Psychological Inventory. *Journal of Applied Psychology, 56,* 341–346.

Kosson, D. S., Steurwald, B. L., Newman, J. P., & Widom, C. S. (1994). The relation between socialization and antisocial behavior, substance use, and family conflict in college students. *Journal of Personality Assessment, 63,* 473–488.

Kurtines, W. M., Ball, L. R., & Wood, G. H. (1978). Personality characteristics of long-term recovered alcoholics: A comparative analysis. *Journal of Consulting and Clinical Psychology, 46,* 971–977.

Lanning, K. (1989). Detection of invalid response patterns on the California Psychological Inventory. *Applied Psychological Measurement, 13,* 45–56.

Leary, T. (1957). *Interpersonal diagnosis of personality.* New York: Ronald Press.

Levin, J., & Karni, E. (1970). Demonstration of cross-cultural invariance of the California Psychological Inventory in America and Israel by the Guttman-Lingoes smallest space analysis. *Journal of Cross-Cultural Psychology, 1,* 253–260.

McAllister, L. W. (1996). *A practical guide to CPI interpretation* (3rd ed.). Palo Alto, CA: Consulting Psychologists Press.

Megargee, E. I. (1972). *The California Psychological Inventory handbook.* San Francisco, CA: Jossey-Bass.

Meyer, P., & Davis, S. (1992). *The CPI applications guide.* Palo Alto, CA: Consulting Psychologists Press.

Millon, T. (1983). *Millon Clinical Multiaxial Inventory manual* (3rd ed.). Minneapolis, MN: National Computer Systems.

Montgomery, R. L., Haemmerlie, F. M., & Edwards, M. (1991). Social, personal, and interpersonal deficits in socially anxious people. *Journal of Social Behavior and Personality, 6,* 859–872.

Myers, I. B., McCaulley, M. H., Quenk, N. L., & Hammer, A. L. (1998). *MBIT manual* (3rd ed.). Palo Alto, CA: Consulting Psychologists Press.

Nichols, R. C., & Schnell, R. R. (1963). Factor scales for the California Psychological Inventory. *Journal of Consulting Psychology, 27,* 228–235.

Peskin, H., Jones, C. J., & Livson, N. (1997). Personal warmth and psychological health at midlife. *Journal of Adult Development, 4,* 71–83.

Picano, J. J. (1989). Development and validation of a life history index of adult adjustment for women. *Journal of Personality Assessment, 53,* 308–318.

Rogers, M. S., & Shure, G. H. (1965). An empirical evaluation of the effect of item overlap on factorial stability. *Journal of Psychology, 60,* 221–233.

Sundberg, N. D., Latkin, C. A., Littman, R. A., & Hagan, R. A. (1990). Personality in a religious commune: CPIs in Rajneeshpuram. *Journal of Personality Assessment, 55,* 7–17.

Vernon, P. E. (1953). *Personality tests and assessments.* London: Methuen.

Weekes, B. S. (1993). Criterion-related validity of the responsibility scale of the California Psychological Inventory. *Psychological Reports, 73,* 315–320.

Welsh, G. S. (1956). Factor dimensions A and R. In G. S. Welsh & W. G. Dahlstrom (Eds.), *Basic readings on the MMPI in psychology and medicine* (pp. 264–281). Minneapolis, MN: University of Minnesota Press.

Wink, P., & Helson, R. (1993). Personality change in women and their partners. *Journal of Personality and Social Psychology, 65,* 597–605.

30 ADDITIONAL CPI REFERENCES RELEVANT TO COUNSELING

Adams, S. H. (1994). Role of hostility in women's health during midlife: A longitudinal study. *Health Psychology, 13,* 488–495.

Blake, R. J., Potter, E. H., Jr., & Slimak, R. E. (1993). Validation of the structural scales of the CPI for predicting the performance of junior officers in the U.S. Coast Guard. *Journal of Business and Psychology, 7,* 743–448.

Bohn, M. H. (1973). Personality variables in successful work-study performance. *Journal of College Student Personnel, 14,* 135–140.

Boyle, B. P., & Coombs, R. H. (1971). Personality profiles related to emotional stress in the initial year of medical training. *Journal of Medical Education, 46,* 882–888.

Campagna, W. D., & O'Toole, J. J. (1981). A comparison of the personality profiles of Roman Catholic and male Protestant seminarians. *Counseling and Values, 26,* 62–67.

Domino, G. (1968). Differential prediction of academic achievement in conforming and independent settings. *Journal of Educational Psychology, 59,* 256–260.

Domino, G. (1971). Interactive effects of achievement orientation and teaching style on academic achievement. *Journal of Educational Psychology, 62,* 427–431.

Donohue, M. V. (1995). A study of the development of traits of entry-level occupational therapy students. *American Journal of Occupational Therapy, 49,* 703–709.

Downs, E., Stephens, J. C., & Jenkins, S. J. (1996). Scores on the California Psychological Inventory for men and women majoring in counseling. *Psychological Reports, 78,* 562.

Dyer, E. D., & Winward, E. J. (1995). Persistence of SCII and CPI scores of students entering a baccalaureate nursing program during a seven-year period. *Psychological Reports, 76,* 1362.

German, S. C., & Cottle, W. C. (1981). The use of the CPI to ascertain differences between more and less effective student paraprofessional helpers. *Journal of the National Association of Women Deans, Administrators, and Counselors, 44,* 11–16.

Gough, H. G., & Kirk, B. A. (1970). Achievement in dental school as related to personality and aptitude variables. *Measurement and Evaluation in Guidance, 2,* 225–233.

Gough, H. G., & Lanning, K. (1986). Predicting grades in college from the California Psychological Inventory. *Educational and Psychological Measurement, 46,* 205–213.

Helson, R., & Moane, G. (1987). Personality change in women from college to midlife. *Journal of Personality and Social Psychology, 53,* 176–186.

Helson, R., Roberts, B., & Agronick, G. (1995). Enduringness and change in creative personality and the prediction of occupational creativity. *Journal of Personality and Social Psychology, 69,* 1173–1183.

Hogan, R., Mankin, D., Conway, J., & Fox, S. (1970). Personality correlates of undergraduate marijuana use. *Journal of Consulting and Clinical Psychology, 35,* 58–63.

Johnson, D., Shertzer, B., Linden, J., & Stone, S. C. (1967). The relation of counselor candidate characteristics and counseling effectiveness. *Counselor Education and Supervision, 6,* 297–303.

Kegel-Flom, P. (1992). What kinds of leaders are entering optometry school? *Optometry and Vision Sciences, 69,* 991–996.

King, G. D., McGowen, R., Doonan, R., & Schweibert, D. (1980). The selection of paraprofessional telephone counselors using the California Psychological Inventory. *American Journal of Community Psychology, 8*, 495–501.

Kurtines, W., & Hogan, R. (1972). Sources of conformity among unsocialized college students. *Journal of Abnormal Psychology, 80*, 49–51.

Lindholm, B. W., & Touliatos, J. (1995). Personality traits and curricular choices of undergraduate women in home economics. *Psychological Reports, 76*, 579–586.

McGinley, H., & Van Vranken, R. A. (1992). Common structure dimensions of the American College Testing Program academic test and the California Psychological Inventory. *Psychological Reports, 71*, 491–498.

Mordock, J., & Patterson, C. (1965). Personality characteristics of counseling students at various levels of training. *Vocational Guidance Quarterly, 13*, 265–269.

Palladino, J. J., & Domino, G. (1978). Differences between counseling center clients and nonclients on three measures. *Journal of College Student Personnel, 19*, 497–501.

Pfeifer, C. M., Jr., & Sedlacek, W. E. (1974). Predicting black student grades with non-intellectual measures. *Journal of Negro Education, 43*, 67–76.

Plant, W. T. (1965). Personality changes associated with college attendance. *Human Development, 8*, 142–151.

Rapaport, K., & Burkhart, B. R. (1984). Personality and attitudinal characteristics of sexually coercive college males. *Journal of Abnormal Psychology, 93*, 216–221.

Reich, S. (1976). California Psychological Inventory: Profile of a sample of first-year law students. *Psychological Reports, 39*, 871–874.

Sprafkin, R. P. (1972). Personal problems versus vocational problems: Personality differences between clients. *Journal of Clinical Psychology, 28*, 114–116.

Ying, Y., & Liese, L. H. (1990). Initial adaptation of Taiwan foreign students to the United States: The impact of prearrival variables. *American Journal of Community Psychology, 18*, 825–845.

4

The Sixteen Personality Factor Questionnaire (16PF)

James M. Schuerger
Cleveland State University

BACKGROUND, CONCEPTUAL AND HISTORICAL

Raymond B. Cattell, the author of the Sixteen Personality Factor Questionnaire (16PF), distinguished three domains (Cattell & Warburton, 1967) within which human characteristics may be assessed: the ability domain, what one can do; the motive domain, what one wants to do; and the personality domain, one's style, how one typically acts. The 16PF and other similar measures are in the personality domain. In addition to the three assessment domains, Cattell distinguished three data sources or levels (Leary, 1957) from which one may get information about a person's characteristics: life data (L-data), which consist of observations from real, everyday events, or reports of what a person does; question data (Q-data), what a person says about self—what Leary (1957) called the level of conscious communication; and test data (T-data), in which a person reacts to a set of contrived circumstances, as contrasted to the naturally occurring situations of L-data. Q-data, the form of information in which personality questionnaires are found, is the only one in which the person consciously reports about self. In the other two (L-data and T-data) the person *does* something that can be the basis for inference about personality.

When the three domains are crossed with the three data sources, one gets the grid shown in Fig. 4.1, which may serve as an extensive if not exhaustive map of possible assessments. The 16PF and other personality questionnaires are in cell 4, personality by questionnaire. The grid allows

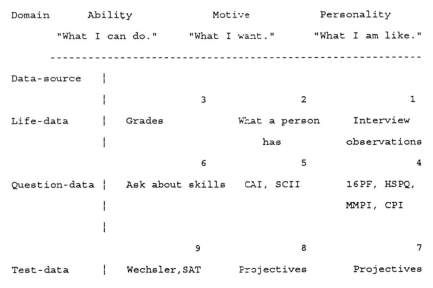

Domain	Ability	Motive	Personality
	"What I can do."	"What I want."	"What I am like."

Data-source			
	3	**2**	**1**
Life-data	Grades	What a person has	Interview observations
	6	**5**	**4**
Question-data	Ask about skills	CAI, SCII	16PF, HSPQ, MMPI, CPI
	9	**8**	**7**
Test-data	Wechsler, SAT	Projectives	Projectives

FIG. 4.1. Assessment procedures by domain and data source.

opportunity to point out that T-data do not include questionnaires, which are sometimes loosely called tests. Tests include the usual ability measures such as IQ tests or precollege tests and, under the motive and personality domains, projective tests such as the various inkblot, drawing, and picture-story measures. In a test the client does something, in contrast with questionnaires, in which the client reports on self. Leary (1957) referred to the T-data level as the level of private perception. This is considered to be the deepest level, the level of fantasy and dreams, the level that is tapped by projective tests and word association, as contrasted with the conscious self-presentation that occurs in Q-data.

Parenthetically, one can see from the grid that in any assessment that includes measures from more than one domain and/or more than one data source there is the possibility of inconsistency—within cells or across cells, within domain or across domains, within data source or across data sources. For example, many counselors are familiar with situations in which a client has an Artistic pattern on some measure of Holland's typology and on the 16PF or another personality measure looks more like a business executive, which is in Holland's Enterprising type. How many counselors have seen an excellent student, a model citizen as reported by teachers and peers (L-data), who shows pathology in the interview or on a questionnaire (Q-data) measure of pathology? I recall a young woman who presented herself as outgoing and dominant on the 16PF (Q-data) and who in the interview looked pathetic and forlorn (L-data). In an interview, the client's self-descriptions are Q-data, whereas the observables are L-data.

From one point of view, inconsistencies are a nuisance and weaken one's ability to make convincing inferences. In fact, if the purpose of assessment is to predict from Q-data to L-data (to predict behavior), inconsistencies are a source of invalidity. From another point of view, however, inconsistencies are merely part of the information about a client. Inconsistencies as well as consistencies address the basic assessment question, "What does it mean for this person to present self in this way in this circumstance?" Concretely, one might ask, "What does it mean for this person to present self as outgoing and dominant on the 16PF and seem timid and forlorn in the counseling sessions?" Leary (1957) suggested that inconsistencies be understood as part of the effort to reduce survival anxiety. The reader is referred to his stimulating book for further treatment of this topic. The validity of the 16PF in predicting behavior (L-data) from self-report (Q-data) is addressed later, in the Interpretation and the Research sections.

Returning to cell 4, personality by questionnaire, one can see that assessing personality in this way is like a self-administered interview. A person answers questions about his or her preferences, attitudes, life history, behavior, personal traits, and perhaps other aspects of personal life. The responses are put together in a particular way, into "scales" or collections of items, and are compared with the responses of other persons. The personality questionnaire is a way for a person to present him- or herself in a particular context.

Researchers who create personality questionnaires have various aims and differing ideas about how to form the item clusters, or scales. For this reason, there are many commercial questionnaires. There are two distinctions among them that are relevant here: (a) the distinction between measures of normal personality, like the 16PF, and measures of psychopathology, like the Minnesota Multiphasic Personality Inventory (MMPI; Hathaway & McKinley, 1989), and (b) the distinction according to how items are assigned to the various scales—by contrasting various groups, by writing items for a particular construct, or by a method called domain sampling. As to the first, the 16PF is a measure of normal personality, which means that it does not have items that represent severe pathology. As to the second, the 16PF was constructed to be an adequate sample of the entire domain of normal personality by questionnaire.

To create such an instrument, Cattell and his colleagues began by studying the trait adjectives collected by Allport and Odbert (1936). This collection was taken as a de facto definition of the domain of personality by questionnaire, and consists of trait adjectives like *worrying, dependable*, or *submissive*. The researchers reduced the original 4,500 trait terms to a representative set of 171 bipolar terms, and then again down to 35. This final sample became a rating scale (L-data), which was tried out on a sample of 208 adults. Later the researchers wrote Q-data items to sample the same domain, and these became the original 16PF. By a statistical procedure known as factor analysis the researchers identified 16 clusters of items, and, by inspecting the meaning of the items, gave the clusters their original names. This entire procedure—identifying a domain, writing items to sample the domain, trying out items, and using factor analysis to identify clusters of items—is an example of domain sampling.

There are two implications for practice that hold for instruments created by the domain-sampling method: (a) the instrument will have adequate coverage of normal personality by questionnaire, and (b) the scales will represent unitary, construct-ordered scales. The first implication differentiates the 16PF from instruments that concentrated on some limited domain, like psychopathology, or self-concept, or depression. The second differentiates it from an instrument that does not attempt to measure constructs, like the MMPI.

ADMINISTRATION AND SCORING

The 16PF, unlike many other personality questionnaires, is available in a number of forms, so the counselor needs to make a decision about form based on the population being worked with. For most purposes this will be the most recent form, the 16PF Fifth Edition, suitable for general adult use for ages ranging from 15 or 16 years to late adulthood (the norm group includes persons from 15 to 92!). A low-literate form, Form E, is recommended for adults with limited intellectual ability. For adolescents aged 11 to 18 the High School Personality Questionnaire (HSPQ), a downward revision of the 16PF, may be used, and for children aged 8 to 12 the Children's Personality Questionnaire (CPQ) is appropriate. One form of the 16PF, the Clinical Analysis Questionnaire (CAQ), includes a pathology supplement in addition to the 16 normal factors. Earlier forms for adults are still in use— Forms A, B, C, and D—but are being superseded by the 16PF Fifth Edition. All forms are available in soft cover booklets with separate answer sheets.

For all forms administration is simple and straightforward, following ordinary canons of courtesy and common sense. Administration maybe to a single individual or to a group of reasonable size. Clients need to be comfortable, to know why they are completing the 16PF, and to know what use will be made of the information. Administration generally takes less than an hour for any form, and sometimes as little as half an hour. The instrument is untimed and may be answered in pen as well as pencil, unless the sheets are to be scanned by optical mark reader.

Scoring may be done by hand in a few minutes with the use of scoring grids and norm tables; it may be also accomplished by mail-in service, by FAX, or on one's own PC with software from the test publisher (IPAT;

telephone 1-800-252-IPAT). For all scoring options except hand scoring a number of computerized options are available. If the presenting problem is career suitability, counselors may want to consider the Personal Career Development Profile (PCDP), an interpretive report for the 16PF that provides, in addition to the primary and global factors, several pages of text that address problem solving, coping, interpersonal interaction, occupational role, career activity interests, and life-style effectiveness. The wording is generally user-friendly, and many counselors report client satisfaction with the report. For more clinical applications, one can use the Karson Clinical Report (KCR), couched in more clinically relevant terms. To use the Couple's Counseling Report (CCR), which gives not only a separate profile for each partner but also a comparison of profiles and four to six pages of text, the counselor administers, to each partner, a special form of the 16PF that includes supplementary items on relationship history and satisfaction. If none of these specialties is needed, the counselor can request the Basic Interpretive Report (BIR), which most find cost-effective and well done. It provides, beyond the standard score profile, a section of descriptive text organized according to the global factors, a second section listing and describing several criterion scores, and a final section relating the person's scores to Holland types. If the counselor chooses the hand-scoring option, the counselor can obtain the 16 primary scores in Fig. 4.2 in less than 5 min, and,with about 5 to 10 min additional work can calculate the five global scores from combinations of the 16 primaries. For many counselors, especially more seasoned ones, these will be adequate. For others, or for those with special testing goals, the added cost of the computerized reports may well be offset by the substantial value added over and above the basics—additional scores, relevant interpretive test, specific focus.

RESEARCH

Psychometric Properties

Under this heading one usually finds the topics of test reliability and test validity. Here I only present test reliability, saving validity for a heading of its own. Test reliability may be presented briefly under two headings, *homogeneity*, which has to do with the degree to which items on a single scale or factor are interrelated, and *temporal stability*, which has to do with how much the ranking of persons on any scale changes over time. On both these counts the 16PF Fifth Edition is well within industry standards. The *Administrator's Manual* (Russell & Karol, 1994) put the average 2-month stability at .70, and the average homogeneity, based on a sample of 2500, at .74. In a large meta-analysis of studies in this area, Schuerger, Zarella, and Hotz

Primary Factors	Low Score Description	High Score Description
A: Warmth	Reserved, Impersonal	Warm, Outgoing, Attentive
B: Reasoning	Concrete	Abstract
C: Emotional Stability	Reactive, Changeable	Emotionally Stable, Mature
E: Dominance	Deferential, Cooperative	Dominant, Assertive
F: Liveliness	Serious, Restrained	Lively, Animated
G: Rule-Consciousness	Expedient, Nonconforming	Rule-Conscious, Dutiful
H: Social Boldness	Shy, Threat-Sensitive	Socially Bold, Thick-Skinned
I: Sensitivity	Utilitarian, Unsentimental	Sensitive, Aesthetic
L: Vigilance	Trusting, Unsuspecting	Vigilant, Suspicious, Wary
M: Abstractedness	Grounded, Practical	Abstracted, Imaginative
N: Privateness	Forthright, Genuine	Private, Discreet, Non-Disclosing
O: Apprehension	Self-Assured, Complacent	Apprehensive, Self-Doubting
Q1:Openness to Change	Traditional	Open to Change, Experimenting
Q2:Self-Reliance	Group-Oriented, Affiliative	Self-Reliant, Individualistic
Q3:Perfectionism	Flexible, Tolerates Disorder	Perfectionistic, Organized
Q4:Tension	Relaxed, Placid	Tense, High Energy, Impatient

Global Factors	Low Score Description	High Score Description
EX:Extraversion	Introverted, Inhibited	Extraverted, participating
(A, F, H, N-, Q2-)		
AX:Anxiety	Low Anxiety, Unperturbed	High Anxiety, Perturbable
(C-, L, O, Q4)		
TM:Tough-Mindedness	Receptive, Open-Minded	Tough-Minded, Resolute
(A-, I- M-, Q1-)		
IN:Independence	Accommodating, Agreeable	Independent, Persuasive, Willful
(E, , L, Q1)		
SC:Self-Control	Unrestrained, Follows Urges	Self-Controlled, Inhibits Urges
(F-, G, M-, Q3)		

FIG. 4.2.   16PF factors. From Russell and Karol (1994). Adapted by permission.

(1989) found very similar values. Other forms of the 16PF tend to have similar temporal stabilities, but slightly lower for the HSPQ as would be expected of the younger subjects, and generally lower homogeneities (Schuerger et al., 1989).

Criterion Validity of the 16PF

A large number of studies report the validity of the 16PF in various contexts, placing it among the most researched of personality questionnaires (see, e.g., Graham & Lilly, 1984, p. 234). Research studies before 1970 are reported in the early handbook (Cattell, Eber, & Tatsuoka, 1970), and subsequent bibliographies are to be found in the *16PF Research Bibliography* (Hussong et al., 1977), the early *Administrator's Manual* (IPAT Staff, 1986), and the more recent 16PF Fifth Edition *Administrator's Manual* (Russell & Karol, 1994) and *Technical Manual* (Conn & Rieke, 1994). For the academically inclined reader, the early handbook is recommended for its information density and for a chance to peek into the mind of a great thinker; it can be heavy going, however. More recently, Schuerger did two summaries, one general (Schuerger, 1992) and one specific to occupational concerns (1995). Schuerger and Watterson (1996) wrote a monograph that listed a great many occupational studies along with three interpretational paradigms, based on over 700 references having to do with the 16PF and occupation. Spotts and Schontz (1991) recently did a limited meta-analysis of 16PF data in clinical and substance-abuse populations, and Krug's 1977 summary, *Psychological Assessment in Medicine*, still has currency. Two practicing clinicians have used their clinical databases as sources for books, one by Karson and O'Dell (*A Guide to the Clinical Use of the 16PF*, 1976) and one by Cattell (*The 16PF: Personality in Depth*, 1989). Both are recommended for their solid basis and clinical acuity.

A Word of Caution

Because the 16PF is available in many forms, cross-form comparison is an issue with this instrument, unlike other instruments that exist in only one form. Schuerger (1992) summarized cross-form correlations for versions of the instrument that predate the 16PF Fifth Edition. For the global factors the correlations average between .59 and .73, in the range in which one usually finds short-term temporal stability for personality instruments (Schuerger et al., 1989). For the primary factors the correlations are lower, averages running from .38 to .49, somewhat less than short-term stability. Correlations between the 16PF Fifth Edition and the earlier Form A are mostly above .50 for the primary factors, with the notable exception of factors M and N. Correlations of the 16PF Fifth Edition global factors and Form A globals average .66, ranging from .38 for TM to .81 for EX. The caution is that the practitioner who gets used to interpreting one form needs to exercise caution in applying the generalizations to another form. For the modern user this would ordinarily mean settling in with the 16PF Fifth Edition. As for utilizing research results from earlier forms with the 16PF Fifth Edition, the correlations are high enough that for most factors it is not a problem, factors M and N being the exception. As more data become available for the 16PF Fifth Edition the current generalizations can be checked, and to date most of the research is confirmatory.

INTERPRETATION

For a client, the 16PF is a self-administered interview. For the counselor interpreting the 16PF, the issue is to understand the person's responses. The basic question is, "What does it mean to be this person answering these questions this way in these circumstances?" One can posit three levels of interpretation, three levels of answer to the question. The first and most direct level is the Q-data level. At this level, the counselor takes the scores at face value—they are, after all, the person's self-description, and they represent clear concepts derived directly from the person's self-descriptive statements. Interpretation at this level is descriptive, not inferential. For example, one may always say of a person with a high score on Factor A (see Fig. 4.2), "The client presented self as having a high level of interpersonal warmth." For a client with a low score on Factor A, one could say, "The client described himself on the personality questionnaire as objective and preferring some privacy rather than outgoing."

A second level of interpretation, and one that requires inference, is the L-data level. That is, one often wants to predict the client's behavior from 16PF scores. For example, the counselor might say about a person high on Factor A that such a person would probably feel more comfortable in a job with person contact than in a laboratory job. This is a data-based inferential statement.

At a third level, it is also possible to make inferences from 16PF scores about deep-seated feelings and early learnings, the kind of psychological entities one could categorize under Leary's third level, the level of private perception. This level, usually tapped by projective tests, can be approached to some degree from Q-data as well. For example, it would be fair to say that a person with a high score on Factor A (Warmth) may very well have dependency needs. Inferences at this level are rarely data-based, usually originating in clinical observations. They should be made with caution.

The rest of this section is divided into five headings: (a) Constructs: The Meaning of the 16PF Factors; (b) Configurations: Combinations of 16PF Scores; (c) Motivational Distortion; (d) Cross-Cultural and Gender Findings; and (e) An Interpretive Strategy. The first heading presents the meat of the chapter, a description of the constructs measured by the 16PF and some L-data findings for each factor. The second section presents combinations of scores that have been found important in understanding a client's self-presentation. The next two headings present material that is necessary for a thorough interpretation of the 16PF, how a person's scores can be influenced by the context of the assessment, including temporary states and more permanent ones like the person's ethnic/cultural background or gender. The final heading presents a traditional method of interpreting the 16PF along with some practitioner's hints.

Scores on the 16PF are stens, standard scores with mean = 5.5 and standard deviation = 2.0. By convention, when interpreting an individual profile, scores below 4 are considered low, and scores above 7 are considered high. Thus, about 10% of persons will have low scores, 10% will have high scores, and 80% will be in the average range, with scores of 4 to 7. The 16PF factors are bipolar: both ends have meaning.

Constructs: The Meaning of the 16PF Factors[1]

Figure 4.2 presents the variables measured by the 16PF, created by systematic sampling from the domain of personality-by-questionnaire. The 16 primary factors were developed by factor analysis of a large set of questions written to typify the domain, as described earlier. When these 16 variables were themselves factor analyzed, several global factors emerged, now called Extraversion (EX), Anxiety (AN), Tough-Mindedness (TM), Independence (IN), and Self-Control (SC), as presented in Fig. 4.2. The letters in parentheses under each global factor denote the primary factors that are most directly related to the global factor. For example, under Self-Control, F– signifies that primary factor F is negatively related to global Self-Control. Persons high on Self-Control tend to have low scores on F, that is, to be Serious and Restrained.

The following section presents descriptions of the factors, arranged according to their contributions to the global factors. Each description begins with the factor name and acronym, and with some typical item contents. This is followed by comments about the occupational relevance of the factor. References are given as relevant, with this exception: A sample that is proprietary and cannot be identified specifically is simply referenced "prop." Clinical findings are mostly taken from summaries by Cattell (1989), Karson and O'Dell (1976), Krug (1981), and Meyer (1989). The factor names and descriptions are those of the 16PF Fifth Edition (Russell & Karol, 1994).

Extraversion (EX). The Extraversion global factor includes primary factors A, F, and H, and factors N and Q2 reversed, as noted in Table 4.2. That is to say, consistent with a high Extraversion score are high scores on A, F, and H, and low scores on N and Q2. Persons scoring high have presented themselves as warm, lively, and socially competent. High scores are found particularly among the Holland Social and Enterprising types, and low scores among the Investigative types (Schuerger & Sfiligoj, 1998; see also Russell & Karol, 1994). Clinically, this factor tends to be high for persons with narcissistic or histrionic characteristics, and low for persons with schizoid, schizotypal, or avoidant characteristics (Terpylak & Schuerger, 1994).

Factor A, Warmth; low score is reserved, high score is warm. Items on Factor A have to do with spending time with others, with the warmth of friendships, with expressing emotions, with working in person-centered jobs. *Occupational findings* include average sten scores below four (<4) for engineers (DiFiore, 1981; Franklin, 1983), scientists (Bachtold, 1976; Cattell et al., 1970), and artists (Anonsen, 1985; Cattell et al., 1970). High scores (>7) are found in some samples of nurses (Adams & Klein, 1970), school coun-

---

[1]Much of this material is taken, with permission, from Schuerger and Watterson (1996).

selors (Johns, 1985), social workers (Cattell et al., 1970), and consulting accountants (Cattell et al., 1970; Osman, 1973). The factor is known to be positively correlated with performance for sales workers and negatively correlated for production, mechanical, and creative workers (Schuerger, 1995). *Clinical findings* for persons high on the factor include proneness to hasty decisions, gullibility, and desire for approval (Cattell, 1989). Persons low on the factor sometimes display what Karson and O'Dell called the "burnt child" syndrome, difficulty securing satisfactory relationships because of trauma in childhood (Karson & O'Dell, 1976). In marital relationships, husbands with low A scores will often find it difficult to provide emotional nurturance to their partners (Cattell, 1989).

Counselor comments include the following: High scores on the factor emphasize contact with others. People with such scores are often described as warm, friendly, responsive to others. Their faces evidence emotional contact. They are interested in being with people, can be engaging and participative, and like to work in groups and associations. Sweney (undated note) held that high scores on this factor represent the social needs of the person, as opposed to the skills, which are reflected in scores on H (Social Boldness). Low A scores indicate a higher interest in things rather than people. Such individuals prefer roles where there is more exposure to ideas and practical applications than with people. They appear more reserved, cool, and aloof. There is less emotional expression displayed, and others find them harder to read. In general, contact with others is less of a priority and typically their skills of interpersonal engagement are less developed. Counselors can find themselves frustrated working with such persons because their level of social feedback is so low.

Factor F, Liveliness; low score is serious, high score is lively. Items on Factor F have to do with being stylish, in the middle of social excitement, talking about social events, enjoying racy or spicy humor. *Occupational findings* include low scores (<4) for some samples of scientists and artists (Cattell et al., 1970); Bachtold (1976) presented a sample of scientists that is just a bit above 4.0 on this factor. Some samples of technicians and systems analysts (Schuerger & Watterson, 1996) have scores just above 4.0, as do a few samples of religious persons (Grant, 1975; Schuerger & Watterson, 1996). High scores (>7, or just below 7) are found in some samples of Roman Catholic priests (Scordato, 1975), three samples of nurses (Adams & Klein, 1970; Franklin, 1983; Hobin-Hopkins, 1975), five samples of teachers (DeLamatre, 1995; Foell & Locke, 1984; Henjum, 1966; Taylor & Armstrong, 1975; White & Anderson, 1975), and several samples of sales and managerial personnel (Bartram, 1992; Hartson & Mottram, 1976; Mahan & Mahan, 1982; Schuerger & Watterson, 1996). Rodeo cowboys (McGill, Hall, & Moss, 1986) and school principals (Sternad, 1991) also show high scores on this factor. The factor is known to be positively correlated with performance for sales and managerial workers and negatively correlated for production, mechanical and creative workers (Schuerger, 1995). *Clinical findings* include a tendency for persons high on the factor to externalize inner conflicts (Krug, 1981). High scores sometimes go with hysterical disorders, and are sometimes a sign of low behavior controls (Cattell, 1989). Low scores are seen as a sign of a tendency to internalize conflicts, and of high behavior control (Krug, 1981). Cattell (1989) noted that the behavior control associated with this factor is not superego or ego, but desurgency, avoidance of punishment. She cautioned against use of disinhibiting strategies with such clients unless there are other signs of behavior control as well, such as high scores on C, G, or Q3.

Counselor comments include the following: High scores on the factor are seen in persons who are energetic and enthusiastic. They tend to be optimistic and frequently display high energy and enthusiasm. Stress and surprise can sometimes raise levels to an agitated state. Low F score individuals demonstrate a serious and somber quality that emphasizes few displays of enthusiasm or emotional expression. If upset, displeased, or disappointed, they show limited visible recognition of it other than a matter-of-fact statement. They can do well in repetitive and objective-oriented roles. A low score may, however, raise a question about depressive aspects that can be important to explore.

Factor H, Social Boldness; low score is shy, high score is bold. Items on Factor H have to do with ease in starting conversation with strangers, comfort with new groups, enjoyment of the limelight. *Occupational findings* include scores below 4 for only a few samples known to us, mostly small samples of highly technical groups. If the definition of low is modified somewhat (<5), low scores are seen for some Realistic, Investigative, and Artistic groups: engineers (Hartson & Mottram, 1976), artists (Anonsen, 1985), miners (Cattell et al., 1970), and machine operators (Schuerger & Watterson, 1996). High scores (>7) are found in many samples of managers (Bartram, 1992; Schuerger, 1995; Schuerger & Watterson, 1996), and in one sample each of high-school principals (Sternad, 1991), psychologists (Cattell et al., 1970), and police (Johns, 1985). The factor is known to be positively correlated with performance for managers and sales persons and negatively correlated for production and mechanical workers and systems analysts (Schuerger, 1995). *Clinical findings* for high scorers include possibility of risk and sensation seeking (Cattell, 1989). Low scores on Factor H correlate with risk of physical illness, especially stomach ulcer, and are often found in alcoholics. For persons with low scores on Factor H, the disinhibiting effects of alcohol are much valued, and such persons often show dramatic personality changes after drinking (Cattell, 1989).

Counselor comments include the following: High scores on the factor are usually associated with individuals who are socially bold and adventurous in seeking new contact and relationships. They are frequently fond of travel and variety. They are typically confident in moving into new circumstances, and they find energy and reward in new contacts and associations. Low-scoring individuals are typically shy, socially hesitant and reserved. They are often uneasy and self-conscious when in a group or meeting. New social occasions are trying and energy draining. They have a preference for one-on-one settings with family or close friends. They sometimes enjoy just being alone. Extensive interpersonal contact at work may place higher degrees of stress. They tend to be better at detailed work with low people contact.

Factor N, Privateness; low score is forthright, high score is private. Items on Factor N have to do with difficulty speaking of personal matters, with being hard to get close to. *Occupational findings include* low scores (<4–4.5) for many occupations in Holland's Social type: nurses (Cattell et al., 1970; Franklin, 1983), psychologists (Johns, 1985), counselors (Dawson, 1973; Hubele, 1970; Payne, 1977; Roberts, 1975), teachers (Start, 1966; Widdop & Widdop, 1975), and religious personnel (Grant, 1975; Scordato, 1975). Three Artistic groups also show low scores (Anonsen, 1985; Cattell et al., 1970; Johns, 1985). High scores (>7) are known to be in only one sample of undergraduate students in a religious program (Byrd, 1981), and from two small proprietary samples in Holland's Conventional type. The factor is not known to have correlations with performance (Schuerger, 1995). *Clinical findings* include problems in intimate relationships for persons with high scores (Cattell, 1989), and behavior control problems for persons with low scores (Krug & Laughlin, 1976). Also noted is the propensity for some persons with low N scores to get into trouble because of their simplicity or naivete (Cattell, 1989).

Counselor comments include the following: High scores on the factor are seen in scoring individuals who have a desire to keep their thoughts and feeling to themselves. They tend to be private, not so much from a need to be manipulative as from a desire to keep their own thinking to themselves. Their reasons for the privacy may vary: feeling vulnerable, being different, or concern about being criticized. Persons with high scores on the factor can be difficult for counselors because it is so hard for them to reveal. Low N individuals have a strong preference to be open and forthright about their thoughts and feelings. They are bold in self-expression with a push to express and verbalize inner realities. This can be spontaneous and refreshing or in poor judgment and socially awkward. Such persons may have high quantity of personal revelation rather than high-quality openness.

Factor Q2, Self-Reliance; low score is affiliative, high score is self-reliant. Items on Factor Q2 have to do with spending long periods of time alone, preferring to make one's plans by oneself, preference of solitary work over teamwork. *Occupational findings* include few low scores, and none below 4.0. Some Social groups show scores below 5 (<5): nurse (Cattell, 1970; Hobin-

Hopkins, 1975; Smith, 1965), school counselor (Cattell et al., 1970; Johns, 1985), Roman Catholic priests (Griffin, 1970; Noty, 1974), social worker (Cattell et al., 1970), teacher (White & Anderson, 1975; Widdop & Widdop, 1975). High scores (>7) are found mostly in a few samples of Holland's Realistic, Investigative, and Artistic types: engineer (Hay, 1964), woman scientist (Bachtold, 1976), pharmacist (Johns, 1985), artist (Anonsen, 1985; Bachtold, 1976; Johns, 1985). The factor is known to be positively correlated with creative performance and school achievement (Schuerger, 1995). *Clinical findings* include, for persons with high scores, the possibility of severe withdrawal, particularly if one of the anxiety components (L, O) is also high (Cattell, 1989). Medically, high scores are related to incidence of coronary heart disease, hypertension and peptic ulcers (Sherman & Krug, 1977). Persons with low scores on the factor are endorsing need for the company with others, and may signal dependent tendencies. In combination with high scores on L, low scores may indicate an approach–avoidance conflict; similarly, persons with otherwise low Extraversion scores (low A, F, or H) are often found to be emotionally needy yet cool or socially inept.

Counselor comments include the following: High scores on the factor express a high regard for one's own perspective and conclusions. Persons high on this factor like their own opinions and they tend to be highly self-sufficient in their activities. They believe it best to do it themselves. It is sometimes hard for them to ask for help and they put a premium on their own resources. This tendency may look like aloofness and superiority to others, but the ones with the high scores do not often see themselves that way. Sweney (undated note) held that high scores on this factor are often found among "technically oriented introverts, who have not learned the values of cooperative efforts." Clients with high Q2 scores will often profit from enhancing their already existing coping behaviors. The counselor may ask, "What works best for you now?" Low Q2 scores are from individuals who look to others (the group) for ideas, direction, and support for their thoughts and actions. They have strong group loyalty, and they may seek social approval. They like and are open to suggestion and direction. They prefer to operate in groups and committees where consensus and team action are valued.

Anxiety (AN). The Anxiety global factor includes Primary Factors L, O, and Q4, and Factor C reversed, as noted in Table 4.2. Consistent with a high Anxiety score are high scores on L, O, and Q4, and low scores on C. Persons scoring high on the factor have presented themselves as emotionally reactive, untrusting, apprehensive, and tense. No occupational groups are known to have high scores on this factor, although a few, mostly in the Holland Artistic type, are a bit higher than average (Schuerger, 1995). Many clinically labeled groups show elevated scores on this factor (Meyer, 1989).

Factor C, Emotional Stability; low score is reactive, high score is emotionally stable. Items on Factor C have to do with being able to cope with problems, feeling satisfied with one's life, recovering quickly from upsets, and not being particularly emotionally labile. *Occupational findings* do not include low scores (<4) for any occupational group except for one sample of English secondary school teachers (Start & Laundy, 1973). High scores (>7) are found in many Realistic occupations: Firefighters (Johns, 1985), mechanics (Cattell et al., 1970), airline pilots and police officers (Johns, 1985; Tatar, 1982). It is also high in some manager samples (Mahan & Mahan, 1982; Murray, 1993) and some religious samples (Schuerger & Watterson, 1996). The factor is known to be positively correlated with performance for sales workers and production/mechanical workers (Schuerger, 1995). Although low C alone is not sufficient to infer pathology, *clinical findings* for persons low on the factor frequently have the flavor of poor practical adjustment to life, or, as Skidmore (1977) says, "inability to roll with the punches." Specific deficits for persons with low C may include poor prognosis for therapy (Krug, 1981), implications for poor physical health (Sherman & Krug, 1977), and any of four variants of low ego strength (Cattell, 1989): (a) unawareness of feelings; (b) failure to consider possible courses of action; (c) poor timing; and (d) failure to act.

Counselor comments include the following: High scores on the factor reflect calmness and stability. Persons with high scores like to be seen as even-tempered, unflappable, hard to rattle. With setbacks they bounce back quickly, and they are emotionally resilient. Sweney (undated note) stated that high scores on this factor are seen in persons who are low in their ability to empathize with others, perhaps because their own Olympian sense of well-being separates them from the trials of ordinary persons. Low C score individuals show high susceptibility to being easily emotionally disrupted, frequently from more minor events. Their ability to bounce back from change, disruption, or disappointment is low. They may show volatility and inappropriate bursts of anger, self-assertion, and distress. They can appear inconsistent, reactive, and lacking in persistence and stability.

Factor L, Vigilance; low score is trusting, high score is wary. Items on Factor L have to do with cynicism about the motives of others, distrust of being frank and open with others. *Occupational findings include* low scores (<4) on average, for just a few mixed samples: accountants (Anonsen, 1985), pilots (Cattell et al., 1970), and police and firefighters (Johns, 1985). High scores (>7) are rare, and are found, paradoxically, mostly in a few samples in the Social type: counselors (Roberts, 1975), teachers (Foell & Locke, 1984; Ruffer, 1976; White & Anderson, 1975; Zimmerman & Williams, 1971), nurses (Hobin-Hopkins, 1975; Smith, 1965). Seminarians who did not persist toward the Roman Catholic priesthood score very high (8.1; Scordato, 1975) on this factor, as do rodeo cowboys (7.3; McGill et al., 1986). The factor is not known to be positively or negatively correlated with job performance (Schuerger, 1995), although as a component of the global factor Anxiety it would seem likely that it has a generally detrimental effect on employee behavior, especially at high levels. *Clinical findings* include, according to Karson and O'Dell (1976), the fact that of all 16PF scales, this one is the most suggestive of clinical relevance just from item content. It is not a measure of paranoia, because there are no delusions, no restricted affect (Cattell, 1989), but it does identify persons who are "fault-finders" and "injustice-collectors." They envy others' possessions (Cattell, 1989). It is the third most important factor medically (Krug, 1981), and is implicated, at the high end, in heart problems. High scores on the factor may serve as a defense against feelings of inadequacy for persons who are also high on Apprehensiveness (O+). Low scores are not known to be clinically relevant.

Counselor comments include the following: High scores on the factor are seen in individuals who are wary of others and their agendas. They like to investigate and question situations. They are generally slow to trust others and they tend to blame events and people for their misfortune. Ownership of life tends to be more outside of themselves; thus, they need to remain more vigilant. They do not typically operate well in a team or participative situation. They often report that they feel resentful of life's dealings with them, and expect a "dirty deal." Clients with such scores can present a difficulty for counselors in that the clients' difficulty with trust gets in the way of the therapeutic relationship. Low L scores characterize individuals who tend to trust others and accept themselves at face value. They also accept responsibility for their own life and their own behavior, and they are less likely to blame or criticize others. They may not be as investigative or curious. They may tend to be hard on themselves and willing to accommodate others. They work well with groups with a cooperative and participative attitude. They can be taken advantage of and may be somewhat naive or gullible.

Factor O, Apprehension; low score is self-assured, high score is apprehensive. Items on Factor O have to do with worry, with feeling sensitive to the actions of others, with being self-critical. *Occupational findings* include low scores (<4) on average, for several Realistic or Investigative occupations: firefighters (Johns, 1985), mechanics (Cattell et al., 1970), scientists (Cattell et al., 1970), and dentists (Boyd, 1985; Schuerger, 1995) and several proprietary samples of managers. High scores (>7) are rare, found in only three samples I know of: nuns (Campbell, 1985), teachers (Start, 1966), and accountants (Osman, 1971). The factor is known to be negatively correlated with performance for sales workers, managers, and for production and mechanical workers (Schuerger, 1995). *Clinical findings*, as evident in this factor's manifest content and major contribution to global anxiety, include high scores in most disorders characterized by anxious or depressive symptoms. The scores do not diagnose—high scores on this factor do not automatically mean disorder, nor do they always occur in the presence of disorder. However, one often sees it in borderline, schizotypal, antisocial, avoidant, and dependent personality disorders, and in schizophrenic, substance abuse, anxiety, and obsessive-compulsive symptom disorders (Meyer, 1989). Cattell (1989) noted the importance of other factors in interpreting high scores on O: Along with G+, one sees negative self-censure; Along with G–, one sees identity problems; along with Q3+, one sees inadequacy and shame; along with E–, one sees submissiveness; along with F–, one sees the possibility of depression. Along with descriptions of these subtypes, she offered suggestions for intervention. She also suggested, for persons with low scores (1, 2, or 3) on Factor O, the strong possibility of repression of negative aspects of the personality. Alternatively, very low scores may indicate behavior control problems (Karson & O'Dell, 1976).

Counselor comments include the following: High scores on the factor describe individuals with a high degree of worry and apprehension as a key facet to their life. They tend to doubt and second-guess themselves on plans, decisions, and actions. They may frequently exercise concern over issues outside their control. They can easily become stressed or discouraged. Low O-scoring individuals emphasize a strong comfort with themselves, and these individuals can appear confident and high on self-esteem. They tend not to doubt themselves much or question their choices, abilities, or motives. There may be blind and negative aspects of the actions or statements that they make, and they may lack a strong drive to change or grow personally. They can endure stress and pressure, and they are likely to be seen in responsible roles or ones under some pressure.

Factor Q4, Tension; low score is relaxed, high score is tense. Items on Factor Q4 have to do with getting annoyed by changes in plans, becoming easily frustrated, showing restlessness when kept waiting. *Occupational findings* include low scores (<4–4.5) for engineers (Hay, 1964; Nowak, 1980), firefighters and police (Johns, 1985; Snibbe, Fabricatore, & Azen, 1975), some religious groups (Noty, 1974; Schuerger & Watterson, 1996), and just a few business samples (Anonsen, 1985; Bartram, 1992; Schuerger, 1995). High scores (>7) are found in only one sample, a group of 53 accountants (Osman, 1973). In fact, in the entire database there are only ten samples with scores over 6.5 (>6.5) on this factor. The factor is known to be positively correlated with performance only in a few particularly tense environments (Schuerger, 1995), although some (Schuerger & Watterson, 1996) have noted its contribution to achievement motive. *Clinical findings* are preceded by noting that items on this factor are the clearest "cry for help" in the inventory (Karson & O'Dell, 1976). The factor is a major contributor to global anxiety, and elevated scores on the factor are common in many conditions: borderline personality disorder, schizotypal personality disorder, avoidant personality disorder, obsessive-compulsive disorder, somato-form disorder, various anxiety disorders (Meyer, 1989). Apart from often signaling low general motivation (Cattell, 1989), low scores do not generally carry any negative implications. When accompanied by high scores on O they can suggest the possibility of depression (Cattell, 1989).

Counselor comments include the following: High scores on the factor demonstrate an experienced high level of tension. Persons high on this factor usually show physical components that are related to experienced nervousness and discomfort. There may be associated sleeplessness and a lack of satisfaction. Sweney (undated note) cited the motivational aspect of high scores on this factor, and the items themselves bespeak the "Type A" quality of persons with high scores. Some consultants prefer to think of this factor as the tension associated with high energy. Low Q4-scoring individuals express a low tension level and fewer agitated feelings. They appear calm, relaxed, and tranquil. They do not show much upset or emotional disruption. They may also reflect low drive and a low sense of urgency, possibly even complacency. They probably sleep well and have fewer physical ailments. They can tend to be highly satisfied and comfortable with their current surroundings.

Tough-Mindedness (TM). The Tough-Mindedness global factor includes primary factors A, I, M, and Q1, all in the negative or reversed direction, as noted in Fig. 4.2. That is to say, consistent with a high Tough-Mindedness score are low scores on A, I, M, and Q1—persons scoring high have presented themselves as reserved, unsentimental, practical, and traditional. Factor A has been discussed earlier, under Extraversion, and is not discussed here; Factor Q1 is discussed later under the global factor Independence. High scores on Tough-Mindedness are found particularly in the Holland Realistic type, and low scores in the Artistic type (Schuerger & Sfiligoj, 1998).

Factor I, Sensitivity; low score is unsentimental, high score is sensitive. Items on Factor I have to do with appreciation of beauty, reading rather than action, imagination rather than doing. This factor resembles Jung's feeling–thinking dimension. *Occupational findings* include low scores (<4) on average, for technical personnel, engineers (DiFiore, 1981; Franklin, 1983), pilots (Cattell et al., 1970), and equipment salespersons (Mahan & Mahan, 1982). Low scores are also seen in sales managers (Cattell et al., 1970; prop.). High scores (>7) are found in many samples in Holland's Artistic and Social types: nurses (Adams & Klein, 1970), counselors (Cattell et al., 1970; Dawson, 1973; Hubele, 1970; prop.), social workers (Cattell et al., 1970), teachers (Johns, 1985; Start, 1966; Taylor & Armstrong, 1975), religious (Campbell, 1985; Grant, 1975; Griffin, 1970), and artists (Cattell et al., 1970; Schuerger & Watterson, 1996). The factor is known to be positively correlated with creative productivity, and negatively correlated for production, mechanical, and managerial workers (Schuerger, 1995). *Clinical findings* include, for persons with high scores, an inability to distance self from painful feelings (Cattell, 1989). High scores are related to medical problems, particularly heart and hypertension (SK), the latter particularly so if Factor C is low (Birkett-Cattell, 1989). High scores in men are associated with greater marital satisfaction. Low scores suggest repression of feelings (Cattell, 1989) and are associated with asthmatic symptoms (Sherman & Krug, 1977).

Counselor comments include the following: High scores on the factor are typical of individuals of a more sensitive, compassionate, and cultured nature. They usually possess strong feelings of kindness and concern for others, although sometimes this is also for their own feeling. Thus, they can easily be sensitive to criticism. They usually show a dislike of anger and confrontation, and they tend to avoid conflict and disagreement. Coping with life is stressful, particularly when much anger, loss, and emotional pain are present. Low I-scoring individuals show a tough, factual approach, and they like to be seen as objective and realistic. They show little expression of feelings or soft emotion. Low levels of compassion and empathy are likely; however, low scorers also can handle work that involves conflict and critical business decisions in tumultuous times, and they can withstand criticism and dissension more easily than persons high on the factor.

Factor M, Abstractedness; low score is practical, high score is abstracted. Items on Factor M have to do with attending to inner thoughts rather than practical matters, to losing track of time, to daydreaming. It is related to Jung's Sensation–Intuition dichotomy. *Occupational findings* include low scores, if the term low is expanded a bit (<4.5), for occupations mostly in Holland's Realistic or Conventional categories: miners (Cattell et al., 1970), machine operators (Schuerger & Watterson, 1996), equipment installers (Schuerger & Watterson, 1996), and firefighters and police (Johns, 1985; Lawrence, 1980; Tatar, 1982). Low scores are also seen in sales managers (Cattell et al., 1970; prop.). High scores (>7) are found in many samples in Holland's Artistic and Social types: nurses (Adams & Klein, 1970), counselors (Cattell et al., 1970; Dawson, 1973; Hubele, 1970; prop.), social workers (Cattell et al., 1970), teachers (Johns, 1985; Start, 1966; Taylor & Armstrong, 1975), religious (Campbell, 1985; Grant, 1975; Griffin, 1970), and artists (Cattell et al., 1970; Schuerger & Watterson, 1996). The factor is known to be positively correlated with creative productivity, and negatively correlated for production, mechanical, and managerial workers (Schuerger, 1995). *Clinical findings* include frequent job changes (Barton & Cattell, 1972), accident proneness, and patient-management problems (Krug, 1981) for persons with high scores. Higher than average scores were noted by Cattell et al. (1970) for persons with schizophrenia, substance-abuse problems, and major depression. Persons with low scores, even if they are intellectually capable, may lack innovative and integrative capacities. As clients, such persons may find insight difficult (Cattell, 1989).

Counselor comments include the following: High scores on the factor emphasize a highly active mental inner life. Images and ideas are constantly playing of the screen. Associative leapsare common, and persons with high scores tend to do poorly on concentration tasks of here-and-now details. They tend to be more creative and easily distracted. Dreams and fantasies are prevalent. They are good in roles requiring innovation and/or vision. When they become stressed, they may tend to be accident prone. Low M-scoring individuals usually identify themselves as focused on day-to-day issues in a practical and pragmatic manner. They are less absorbed with ideas and imaginative issues, and they like to be seen as logical and realistic. They may be somewhat literal and short-term focused, and vision is sometimes lacking. Thought flexibility may be low, and their thinking skills may not be as well developed as desired. On the other hand, they follow procedures well, tend to routine details, stay in the here-and-now, and exercise higher alertness to repetitive activities.

Independence (IN). The Independence global factor includes primary factors E, L, and Q1, all in the positive direction, as noted in Fig. 4.2. Factor L is also seen under the Anxiety global factor, and is not presented again here. Persons scoring high on the factor have presented themselves as dominant, vigilant or suspicious, and progressive, open to change. High scores are found particularly among the Holland Investigative, Artistic, and Enterprising types (Schuerger & Sfiligoj, 1998). Clinically, persons with histrionic, borderline, and paranoid personality traits tend to show elevated scores, and those with obsessive-compulsive traits tend to show low scores (Terpylak & Schuerger, 1994).

Factor E, Dominance; low score is deferential, high score is dominant. Items on Factor E reflect comfort in directing others, the ability to be tough with others if necessary. At the opposite end are items reflecting cooperativeness and unwillingness to confront. *Occupational findings* include low scores (<4) for two samples of nurses (Adams & Klein, 1970; Hobin-Hopkins, 1975), and one sample of Roman Catholic teaching nuns (Healy, 1966), as well as a proprietary sample of persons from a fundamentalist religious group (Schuerger & Watterson, 1996). High scores (>7) are found among scientists (Cattell et al.,1970), psychologists and counselors (Cattell et al., 1970; Dawson, 1973; Johns, 1985), artists (Johns, 1985; Schuerger & Watterson, 1996), and managers (Bartram, 1992; Bush & Lucas, 1988; Mahan & Mahan, 1982; Schuerger & Watterson, 1996; Smith, Dowling, & Barry, 1985). The factor is known to be positively correlated with performance for sales workers and managers (Schuerger, 1995). *Clinical findings* for persons high on the factor include many potential indicators of interpersonal problems: aggression and stubbornness (Sweney, undated note), ability to externalize hostile feelings (Karson & O'Dell, 1976), the possibility of being controlling, extrapunitive (Cattell, 1989), and, together with low scores on any of C, G, or Q3, possible violence. Cattell also noted that either extreme on the factor can be disruptive of interpersonal relationships. Low scores can be seen in some clients who are neurotic and/or self-defeating, and in alcoholics but not in narcotic addicts (Krug, 1981). For the clinical interpretation of the factor much depends on the levels of other factors, as detailed later.

Counselor comments include the following: High scores on the factor indicate a strong desire for control through the typical tools of dominance, which may take the form of assertiveness or aggressiveness depending on other factors such as Warmth. Frequently, purposefulness and being goal directed are seen in individuals strong on this dimension. For a person in a leadership role and possessing high scores on this factor it is an advantage to have good social skills. Low-E-score individuals reflect high acceptance and adaptability. They accept direction easily from others, and they hesitate to make assertive statements or take decisive actions. They are typically seen as passive and conforming. If in roles of responsibility, they may tend to rely on the rules, structures, and procedures of the organization to control and get results.

Factor Q1, Openness to Change; low score is traditional, high score is open to change, progressive. Items on Factor Q1 have todo with liking new and better ways of doing things, inclination to change the status quo, preference for progressive rather than tradition always of doing things. *Occupational findings* include low scores (<4–4.5) mostly in samples of conservative religious groups (prop.; Byrd, 1981; Grant, 1975), physical education teachers (Widdop & Widdop, 1975; prop.), and janitors and kitchen workers (Cattell et al., 1970). High scores (>7) are found in alternative samples of religious persons—nuns (Campbell, 1985) and Roman-Catholic priests (Noty, 1974)—women scientists and psychologists (Bachtold, 1976), and UK and Australian managers (Bartram, 1992; Smith, 1965). The factor is not generally known to have positive or negative performance correlations (Schuerger, 1995). *Clinical findings* for persons high on the factor include anger at authority, consistent with Karson and O'Dell's (1976) interpretation of this factor as indicative of unresolved Oedipal conflict. In work and social settings they often have a reputation for being "rabble-rousers," not from a motive of personal gain but out of principle (Cattell, 1989). Persons low on the factorare likely to find therapeutic change difficult because of their conservative tendencies. Low scores are reported by Meyer (1989) for persons with anorexia and somatoform disorders.

Counselor comments include the following: High scores on the factor show interest in rapid progress, change, and development. If embedded in a slow-moving or restrictive environment, persons with high scores may become frustrated. If outspoken, they can sound critical or caustic. This dimension is very helpful to have in a role as a change agent or a person responsible for innovation and experimentation. In marriage counseling, merely talking about problems is not enough for persons with high scores on this factor—they need change. Low Q1-scoring individuals are usually conservative people who prefer current conditions and work to maintain rather than change. They resist experiments and risk-taking actions, and they endorse traditional beliefs and attitudes. They put energy into avoiding mistakes, and they exercise caution and analysis with each step.

Self-Control (SC). The Self-Control global factor includes primary factors G and Q3, and Factors F and M reversed, as noted in Fig. 4.2. Factor F was discussed earlier, under Extraversion, and M under Tough-Mindedness; these are not revisited here. Persons high on this factor present themselves as oriented to the rules, well organized, and not distractible. High scores are found in almost all occupations, but particularly among the Holland Realistic, Enterprising, and Conventional types (Schuerger & Sfiligoj, 1998).

Factor G, Rule-Consciousness; low score is nonconforming, high score is rule conscious. Items on Factor G have to do with adherence to moral standards, good manners, attention to the rules, what Cattell (1989) called "mainstream cultural ideas," Kohlberg's 4th and 5th steps. *Occupational findings* include low scores (<4), on average, for some samples of scientists (Cattell et al., 1970), artists (Anonsen, 1985; Cattell et al., 1970), psychologists (Johns, 1985; Cattell et al., 1970; Bachtold, 1976), counselors and social workers (Dawson, 1973; Roberts, 1975; Cattell, 1970), and certain religious persons, notably Roman-Catholic priests (Noty, 1974; Scordato, 1975; Grant, 1975; Cattell, 1970). High scores (>7) are found among dentists (Boyd, 1985; prop.), systems analysts, mechanics and technicians (prop.), many samples of managers (Chakrabarti & Kundu, 1984; Law & Schuerger, 1982; prop.), and in some samples of nurses (Adams & Klein, 1970; Hobin-Hopkins, 1975) and equipment sales personnel (Mahan & Mahan, 1982; Schuerger, 1995). Interesting in the light of the low scores for some religious groups noted earlier is the fact of high scores on the factor for certain other religious groups, notably Roman-Catholic sisters (Healy, 1966) and certain groups closer to fundamentalism (Schuerger & Watterson, 1996). The factor is known to be positively correlated with performance for production, mechanical, sales, management, and computer workers (Schuerger, 1995). *Clinical findings* include, for persons with high scores, the possibility that they may be perceived as parent figures. Such persons may also find their high super-ego function conflicting, by rigid morality, with reasonable ego flexibility (Cattell, 1989). Persons with low scores may display behavior control problems (Karson & O'Dell, 1976) and accident proneness (Krug,1981). While most persons with low scores, not endorsing cultural values, will be either amoral, morally immature, or at least unconventional, some will have very high, postconventional moral standards (Cattell, 1989).

Counselor comments include the following: High scores on the factor reflect a strong orientation to rule awareness. Boundaries and expectations are clearly defined, and energy is spent to remain within these boundaries. Operating within systems, procedures, and structure is comfortable for persons high on this factor. There is a high degree of dutifulness to follow the expectations of others, particularly the authority dimensions. A strong commitment and adherence is emphasized here, and it is important to understand the reference group associated with this commitment. Sweney (undated note) called this factor the "tendency to be efficient in executing prescribed work," and noted that it is often an excellent predictor of grades in college. Low-G individuals show a preference for flexibility and a thirst for boundary-free existence. There is not a strong regard for roles, procedures, or regulations. This may be controlled or focused by dominance and drive to a goal, or adherence to strong values beyond the rules. However, it may also be a low sense of purpose, high defiance, high creativity, or high autonomy. There may be a higher insistence to pursue their own goals than to meet the expectations of the organization or others.

Factor Q3, Perfectionism; low score is flexible, high score is perfectionistic, organized. Items on Factor Q3 have to do with planning ahead, keeping one's belongings in tip-top shape, and belief in doing a job thoroughly. *Occupational findings* show no scores below 4 in English-speaking occupational samples. A few samples, all Holland's Artistic or Social types, show scores below 5: artist (Anonsen, 1985), English teacher (Johns, 1985), nurse (Franklin, 1983), counselor (Dawson, 1973; Roberts, 1975), Roman Catholic religious (Campbell, 1985; Cattell, 1970; Healy, 1966; Scordato, 1975), and teachers (Henjum, 1966; Ruffer, 1976; Widdop & Widdop, 1975). High scores (>7) are found in a good many samples across Holland types, of which I mention only a few: mechanics and pilots (Cattell, 1970), dentists (Boyd, 1985), nurses (Hobin-Hopkins, 1975; Smith, 1965), missionaries (Schuerger & Watterson, 1996), accountants (Osman, 1971), and secretaries (Johns, 1985). The factoris known to be positively correlated with performance for managers and systems analysts, and negatively correlated for creative workers in certain rare circumstances (Schuerger, 1995). Although high scores on this factor generally signal good behavior controls and a strong sense of self, *clinical findings* nonetheless include high Q3 scores in some syndromes: paranoid personality disorder, schizoid personality disorder, compulsive personality disorder, and somatoform symptom disorder (Meyer, 1989). Cattell (1989) perceptively noted that persons who show profiles with high Q3 coupled with high O (low self-esteem) or low C (low ego strength) may well be experiencing difficulties in general adjustment that have deep roots. Low scores on the factor are associated with most manifestations of anxiety, and are rarely adaptive. Exceptions in my experience are usually artistic or religious persons, deeply committed to their callings.

Counselor comments include the following: High scores on the factor show a high attention to detail and precision. Persons high on this factor can be very meticulous and precise in their activities and work well in jobs requiring accuracy and neatness. They may have compulsive dimensions that can be either situationally productive or distracting, or perfectionistic tendencies that can be disruptive. Low-Q3 individuals tend to be less attentive to details and less orderly in their activities. They are not necessarily meticulous and precise, and they prefer broader concepts and ideas. They can be seen as casual and spontaneous, and often show a free-spirit attitude. They may go against social custom, and appear sloppy and careless. They also may lack self-discipline and focus, and they may prefer to follow their own urges and emotions.

Factor B. One additional factor on the 16PF does not measure personality, but ability, and as such it is not organized under one of the global factors. This is Factor B, Reasoning, with Concrete as the low score and Abstract as the high score. Items on Factor B tap three abilities: verbal reasoning, numerical reasoning, and logical reasoning. *Occupational findings* include just a few samples with scores less than 5, mostly low-skill jobs in Holland's Realistic or Conventional types. High scores (>7) are found in over 100 occupational samples; scores above 7.5 are found in over 50 samples, with Holland's Investigative type and high-level professional occupations prominent. The factor is known to be positively correlated with performance in most jobs (Schmidt, Ones, & Hunter, 1992; Schuerger, 1995).

Counselor comments include the following: High scores reflect general reasoning ability, ability to learn and conceptualize. This factor is related to academic success. People with high scores tend to be alert, mindful of intellectual pursuits, and engaged with ideas and theories. Low B scores denote less developed verbal abstract reasoning skills and/or low academic exposure. Such persons may be highly anxious, depressed, or not motivated to do well on problem-solving items. They tend to be more down-to-earth in their thinking, and thus like to have a demonstration rather than an explanation.

Configurations: Combinations of 16PF Scores[2]

Also important for interpretation of the 16PF are the various configurations, or patterns of scores relative to other scores. For example, to describe a person by saying that she had her highest scores on global factors TM and SC would be to use the configural method. Another example of this method is the two-point code system used in MMPI interpretation. For the 16PF there is no standard configural method like that of the MMPI, although

---

[2]Much of this material is taken, with permission, from Schuerger and Watterson (1996).

various authors have made contributions. Chief among these is Krug's systematic *Interpreting 16PF Profile Patterns* (1981), a catalog of profiles organized according to elevation on the first four global factors, EX, AN, TM, and IN. Each of these factor scores is classified 1 if the score is low, 2 if the score is average, and 3 if the score is high. A profile then takes the form 1331—an example of a person with low EX, high AN and TM, and low IN. For each profile coded this way, Krug gave a one-page description including clinical and occupational findings.

The configural patterns presented in this chapter, by contrast, come from many sources: Karson and O'Dell's *A Guide to the Clinical Use of the 16PF* (K; 1976), Meyer's *Clinician's Handbook* (M; 1989), Schuerger, Watterson, and Croom's *Psychological Variables and Their Applications* (SWC; 1996), Schuerger and Watterson's *Occupational Patterns in the 16 Personality Factor Questionnaire* (SW; 1994), Heather Birkett Cattell's *The 16PF: Personality In Depth* (BC; 1989), or the clinical experience of Dr. David Watterson (W) or Dr. James Schuerger (S). What I present here is a sample of what is available in the sources; the interested reader is referred to them for more extensive study.

Category I. The first configurations to be presented are made up of primary factor scores all within a single global factor. The principle is to examine carefully any profile in which the factors that contribute to one global factor score are not consistent. Most of these patterns are noteworthy because they exemplify violations of the principle that if the trend is low among primary factors for a global factor, all of the primaries should be low. For example, if Factor G, Rule-Consciousness, is low, so should be Factor Q3, Perfectionism. When this principle does not hold for a client's profile, it means that the client presented self in an uncommon way. Sometimes these uncommon ways have useful interpretations. A few examples follow:

Under Extraversion, if A, F, and H are low, in the Introverted direction (Reserved, Serious, Shy), and Q2 is in the Extraverted direction (Group-Oriented, affiliative), look for deep dependency in the client (BC). If A islow (Reserved) and F is high (Lively), look for the client to seek change and variety in romantic attachments (BC). If A is low and His high, look for a callous disregard for others (BC). If A (Warmth) is high and Q2 (Group-Oriented) is low (the need component of EX) whereas F and H are both low (Serious, Restrained, Shy), look for high need for social interaction frustrated by lack of skills.

Under Anxiety, if C and Q4 are in the anxious direction (Reactive, Tense) and O is in the low anxious direction (Self-Assured), look for a person who is denying important needs—psychodynamically, defense mechanisms are maintaining self-esteem (low O) by denying guilt, but the low C and high Q4 indicate that the process is incomplete (BC). If C is low (Reactive, low ego strength) and O is high (Apprehensive, self-Doubting) but Q3 is also high (Perfectionistic, Organized), two hypotheses are available, one of "bound anxiety," anxiety but such that the client can function and perhaps even be motivated by the anxiety (K), and the other hypothesis that the client is experiencing inadequacy and shame, indicated by the high perfectionism and high guilt-proneness from Factor O.

Under Tough-Mindedness, if I is low (Utilitarian, Unsentimental) and M is high (Abstract, Imaginative), look for a fruitful combination of innovation and objectivity (BC), particularly if factor B is also high; if the converse is found, high I and low M, look for a kind, sensitive person without much self-insight.

Category 2. A second category has configurations that have high or low scores across, not within, global factors. A good many of these patterns involve Factor E, a component of Independence, with one or more factors from some other global factor. Again, a few examples:

If Factor E is low (Deferential, Cooperative) and Factor C is also low (Reactive, Changeable, low ego strength), look for a person who is uninvolved, one who gives in to the desires of others (BC). If E is low and Factors I (Sensitive) and L (Suspicious) are both high, look for a distrustful person who is highly sensitive to criticism (W).

If Factor E is high (Dominance) and L (Suspicious) and B (Abstract) are also high, look for intellectualized hostility, particularly if Q1 (Experimenting) is also high (K). If E is high and I (Sensitive) is high, look for a polarity or tension between dominance and nurturance needs (SWC). If E is high and any two or three of the control factors are in the low-control direction (low C, G, and Q3, high F—Reactive, nonconforming, Flexible, and Lively), look for the possibility of violence when threatened with loss.

Category 3. A third category consists of patterns based on occupational data from three large databases (Schuerger, 1995). Figure 4.3 has these data in summary form. The figure is straightforward, as illustrated by the first row. If Extraversion is high and Independence is high, then there is a high probability of membership in the Enterprising type, and a low probability of Realistic and Conventional types. Salary is higher than average in the database for persons with these scores. Thirty percent of persons in the occupational database show this pattern of high scores (high >6.5). Lower in the table are four patterns of primary factors that show occupational patterns, read in a similar fashion.

In summary, if EX is high, the probability of membership in an Enterprising occupation is high, Realistic and Conventional low. If EX is low, the probability of membership in a Realistic occupation is high, particularly if TM or SC is high. If IN is high, the probability of membership in a Conventional occupation is high, particularly if TM or SC is also high.

Global Factors		Percent	Descriptive Probabilities		
EX+	IN+	30	E Hi, R Lo, C Lo	Salary Hi
EX+	SC+	24	E Hi	
EX-	SC+	10	E Lo, R Hi, C Hi	
EX-	TM+	10	E Lo, R Hi	
TM+	SC+	24	R Hi	
TM+	IN-	2	E Lo, C Hi	
TM+	IN+	25	E Hi, C Lo	Salary Hi
IN-	SC+	11	E Lo, C Hi	
Primary Factors				
A+ Q2+		2	E Hi, R Lo	Salary Hi
A- Q2-		1	E Lo, R Hi	Salary Lo
I+ L+ M+		2	E Lo, C Hi	
I- M-		15	R Hi	

FIG. 4.3.   Combinations of scores.

Among the primary factors, in the second half of the table, if A and Q2 are high, the probability of membership in an Enterprising occupation is high, Realistic low; the converse is true if both are low. Factors I, L, M, and sometimes N are called the "Realistic valley." If I and M are low, the probability of membership in a Realistic occupation is high. High scores on I, L, and M together denote a person who has portrayed self as sensitive, suspicious and resentful, and imaginative—prone to muse over ills, easily hurt. This pattern is also related to lower probability of membership in an Enterprising occupation, higher in Conventional.

Motivational Distortion

Motivational distortion is a term used by Cattell (1973) to denote inaccuracy in questionnaire responses, a third factor to consider when interpreting the 16PF. Other authors use other terms, including *test-taking attitude* or *questionnaire invalidity*, for example. In general, the idea is that a person's self-presentation on a personality questionnaire is not always an accurate self-portrait, one that reflects the person's deepest sense of self, or one that is similar to what several knowledgeable friends would say. Out-and-out falsification of responses is not the issue here. People do lie, and it is easy to lie on personality questionnaires, but this seems to be uncommon (Goffin, Christiansen, & Johnston, 1994). The larger issue is the subtle changes in presentation that can occur as circumstances change.

It is well established that, although personality by questionnaire is relatively stable (Schuerger et al., 1989), many persons' self-presentations will change with the circumstances. A person presents one way in the therapist's office and another way in a preemployment situation. A person trying for a job may be expected to feature his or her mental health, interpersonal skills, and conscientiousness, whereas a suspected criminal might feature symptoms in the hope of a not-guilty verdict or light sentence. In other words, most persons will have some "test-taking attitudes" that will vary as circumstances vary, and counselors have concerns about whether these attitudes will interfere with accurate interpretation of responses.

When we speak of "interpretation" of scores in the context of test-taking attitude we mean only inferential interpretation. For scales with homogeneous content, descriptive interpretation is always appropriate—"Mr. Smith presented himself on the personality questionnaire as person-oriented." Inferential interpretation involves a leap from the self-presentation data to life data—"Persons with patterns like this are often found in occupations which require attention to detail." It is only for inferential interpretation that the question of the "validity" of the results is important. If we question the validity of questionnaire results, we are, in effect asking, "Is the person's self-presentation so distorted that we are hesitant to use the usual rules for inferential interpretation?"

Form A of the 16PF has two measures that address this question, one that emphasizes presenting self in a favorable light and one that emphasizes presenting self in an unfavorable way. These two scales are called FG (fake good) and FB (fake bad). The names of the scales convey their origins in experiments with various instruction sets for taking the 16PF, as noted earlier. On the 16PF Fifth Edition the major test-taking attitude scale is Impression Management (IM); on the older Form C it is called MD (motivational distortion). The scales have different origins but correlate highly (~.50) with measures of social desirability (Conn & Rieke, 1994).

On the older forms of the 16PF the scores from the FG scales were often used to "correct" or modify the obtained scores. Such corrections are possible because it is known that when a person presents self favorably, the direction of bias is in stereotypical, socially accepted ways. Concretely, under the impetus to present favorably, the Extraversion variables go up, the Anxiety and other pathology variables go down, and the Self-Control variables go up. Correcting for high FG scores involved bringing these scores closer to the population mean. For the 16PF Fifth Edition, however, the test authors no longer recommend using the IM score for correction, in line with current evidence (Goffin et al., 1994). Instead, the counselor may wish to use it for an indication of how well the client's presentation represents traditional, socially acceptable indicators. A score that is very high may indicate some inability to see his or her defects, a fact that would have implications for the client–counselor interaction.

Cross-Cultural and Gender Findings

Just as varying circumstances influence a person's presentation on personality questionnaires, so does group membership have an influence. Average
16PF scores differ by gender or cultural background, but not much. Earlier-
forms of the 16PF (Hinman & Bolton, 1980; Hubbard, 1982; Mulhausen, 1990;
Whitworth & Perry, 1990) show only slight differences in the personality
factors by ethnic group, usually less than half a sten. Gender differences
tend to be small as well. In brief, minorities will show substantial differences
from the general norms only on Vigilance (Factor L); women show substantial differences only on Sensitivity (Factor I). The *Technical Manual* for the
16PF Fifth Edition (Conn & Rieke, 1994) shows similar findings for the most
recent version of the 16PF. The counselor needs to be sensitive to ethnic
and racial background in interpreting 16PF scores, but need not expect large
differences.

An Interpretive Strategy

As a suggested strategy for interpretation of the 16PF I suggest the following
steps:

1. Consider the context of the assessment, including the age, gender,
   ethnicity, and status of the client, the purpose of the assessment, and
   who will use the information—client, counselor, or some institution.
2. Examine the answer sheet for missing items, patterned responses, faint
   marks, crossed-out marks, extremely neat marks, and so on.
3. Go over the validity scales (Motivational Distortion) to see if there is
   any doubt about using the standard rules in interpreting the 16PF.
4. Review the 16PF scores and combinations of scores in the following
   order: global scores and patterns of globals; any inconsistencies of
   primary factor scores within the globals; very high or very low primary
   scores; patterns of primary factor scores.
5. Apply the information to specific questions or issues that are the focus
   of the assessment.

This strategy is illustrated in the case example here.

Case Example

1. The Context of the Assessment. Martha is a 42-year-old secretary,
assistant to the personnel manager in a large hospital. She is a college
graduate with a major in elementary education. During her student teaching
she had several unpleasant experiences, including difficulty keeping order,

and she felt inept much of the time. Rather than enter the educational field, she tried several jobs for brief periods and settled on secretarial work, in which she has felt fairly comfortable. Recently, however, with a change in bosses, she is having trouble adjusting and is consulting a counselor. A significant but not exclusive issue in the counseling is career suitability, so a fairly thorough battery of measures is in order, including an interest inventory, an ability measure, a measure of normal personality (16PF) and a measure of psychopathology (MMPI; Chap. 2). Purposes of the various measures are as follows: For the client's direct use, the interest and ability measures are included to help assess Martha's fit to various occupations and to identify particular strengths she may have. These two measures and the 16PF are directly relevant to her question about career suitability. The 16PF in addition addresses strengths and areas to work on. Less directly relevant to career choice, the MMPI can still be useful to Martha as a source of information about strengths and areas to work on. Aside from usefulness directly for the client, the MMPI and 16PF are useful to the counselor. The MMPI is helpful in identifying serious pathology, and both instruments help is assessing personality disorders. If either kind of disorder is present, it is to the counselor's advantage to know about it. The 16PF can be useful for the counselor in another way, in that it reveals personal style—the counselor can make informed surmises about how to appeal to the client and perhaps what *not* to try. The counselor can also estimate his or her own similarity to the client and the probable areas of mutual understanding and/or misunderstanding.

As a final note on context, it will be helpful for the reader to know that on the ability measure Martha is at the 91st percentile on general population norms, with a difference of about 5 percentage points between her verbal and quantitative abilities, the verbal being higher. On the interest inventory she has a CSA Holland pattern, with the Conventional and Social scores at about 55 T-score each, and the Artistic about 10 points lower. Her high basic interest scores are all in the Social and Conventional areas—scores of about 65 for Teaching, Domestic Activities, and Office Practices. Among occupational scales, her highest were Elementary Teacher, Special Education Teacher, and Food Service Manager (60), with Nurse and Secretary (50) at the next level. The reader is referred to Chapter 2 for an interpretation of the MMPI.

2. The Answer Sheet.
The answer sheet is carefully filled in with no special pattern of marks discernable by inspection, but with very neat, well-marked answer spaces. All the demographic information is included.

3. The Validity Scales.
Martha's score on Impression Management is 54 (percentile), well within the average range, so it is safe to say that she did not lean either toward symptomatology or toward excessive health and

well-being in her self-presentation. This presentation is consistent with her reason for coming for counseling, but one might have expected a bit more presentation symptom, given her presenting problem. In any event, there is no concern as to using the standard rules and suggestions for interpretation.

4. Review of 16PF Scores for Relevant Information. Martha's 16PF scores, in the usual order, are:

A	B	C	E	F	G	H	I	L	M	N	O	Q1	Q2	Q3	Q4		EX	AN	TM	IN	SC
5	10	4	1	2	8	1	7	4	5	9	5	1	8	6	10		2	8	5	1	7

These scores are on the 10-point sten scale described earlier. Descriptively, from the five global scores first, Martha presents herself as introverted (EX = 2) and submissive (IN = 1), high in anxiety (AN = 8) and self-control (SC = 7). The Krug pattern for these scores, to be discussed later, is 1321. As to inconsistencies among primary factor scores that are related to the globals, those related to EX are consistently in the introverted direction except for Factor A, Warmth, which is average (A = 5, F = 2, H = 1, N = 9, Q2 = 8; recall that for N and Q2 the low score is in the extraverted direction). One might say that she presents herself as liking people and yet finds it very hard to socialize and reveal personal matters. Her high AN score shows moderate anomalies among the related primary scores: Tension is very high (Q4 = 10) and she is emotionally very reactive (C = 1), but Apprehension is only about average (O = 5), and on Factor L she is actually a bit on the low anxious side (Trusting; L = 4). One can say that she presents herself as tense and emotional, but without deep-set guilt feelings or anger at others. Both of her related scores on TM are near the middle, with M being a bit in the practical direction (M = 5) and I toward sensitivity (I = 7). On IN both primary scores are very much in the agreeable or passive direction. Dominance is at the accommodating end (E = 1) and Openness to Change is at the traditional end (Q1 = 1). Both of the related primary factors on SC are in the direction of high Self-Control (G = 8; Q3 = 6), particularly Factor G, Rule-Consciousness.

As to high and low primary factor scores and patterns of primary scores, many of the extreme scores are presented in the preceding paragraph and may be summarized here. Included is the very high score on general learning ability or Reasoning (B = 10), not yet mentioned. Martha has presented herself as very bright, an abstract reasoner (B = 10), with high attention to rules (G = 8) and very traditional attitudes (Q1 = 1). She is extremely shy (H = 1) and accommodating (E = 1) and does not find it easy or proper to speak about personal matters (N = 9). She is currently very tense (Q4 = 10) and emotional (C = 1) and shows profound desurgency and restraint (F = 2).

Turning to more inferential interpretation, one notes first that the Krug pattern 1321 is considerably more frequent in clinical populations than among normals (Krug, 1981), and suggests a "strong need for emotional support from others." Krug also noted that persons with this profile are more than usually prone to health problems, and that the profile has the highest neuroticism index of all the classifications. The combination of very low extraversion and independence, along with high anxiety, might prompt the counselor to look for signs of a personality disorder, perhaps avoidant or dependent (Terpylak & Schuerger, 1994; see also earlier discussion of global factor Extraversion).

Patterns of primary factors are also suggestive of hypotheses for the counselor to evaluate, as noted earlier. The combination of low E (Accommodating) and low C (Emotionally Reactive) was noted by Cattell (1989) to be associated with giving in to the desires of others; low C along with high Q4 (Tense) and low O (Self-Assured; O is 5 here, not really low, but not high) denotes a denial of one's own important needs; high I (Sensitive) along with low M (Practical; again, M is 5, not truly low, but tending in that direction) suggests a kind, sensitive person without much self-insight.

An attempt at integrating the various aspects of all this material, both descriptive and inferential, portrays Martha as a very bright person, conservative and highly rule-conscious, with considerable anxiety and a tendency to keep herself in the background. She probably has personal needs that are not well cared for, perhaps not even known to Martha. She has strengths in her very high intellectual ability and capacity for attention to detail and rule orientation. An additional strength may be seen in her sensitivity and care for others, which may also hinder her by including tendencies to dependency.

5. Focus on Issues Specific to the Assessment. Consistent with the discussion of this case in Chapter 2, I posit four issues specific to this assessment:

1. What Leary calls *functional diagnosis*, focusing on the probable interaction between client and counselor.
2. Probable occupational fit, or degree of resemblance between Martha and persons in various occupations.
3. Martha's strengths in terms of coping with her life and her occupational situation, as revealed in the 16PF.
4. Aspects of Martha's personality that may make adjustment difficult and that she may wish to work on.

One way to conceptualize functional diagnosis is to think what it will be like for the counselor to work with a person like Martha, who is anxious, introverted, and submissive or accommodating. The anxiety, being a significant source of discomfort, is likely to be a motive for Martha to work at the counseling. The introversion and submissiveness are likely to be a hindrance to smooth communication, because it will be difficult at best for Martha to reveal personal matters. With such a low dominance score she might be inclined not to speak up if she disagreed with the counselor. The low extraversion and difficulty in speaking of her personal matters can be difficult for beginning counselors particularly, because as counselors we rely on verbal feedback to see how we are doing. Finally, as a counselor I evaluate my similarity to Martha in as many ways as I can, personality among them. Martha is introverted—if I am also introverted we have that in common and are more likely to feel comfortable with each other. Martha is high on self-control—if I am not so high on that factor I may have to be alert so that I understand her point of view and do not project my own expectations onto her. And so on.

The second specific issue, resemblance of Martha to various occupational groups, requires information that is not easy to present here—mean profiles of a number of occupational groups. The reader is referred to other sources that contain a number of such profiles (Cattell et al., 1970; Schuerger, 1995; Schuerger & Watterson, 1996). Here, a few comparisons can be made using only the global factors and comparing Martha's scores with those of secretaries, her current job, and elementary school teachers, her college major. The mini-table here presents all three:

	EX	TM	IN	SC	Ranks
Martha	2	5	1	7	3 2 4 1
El. education	6	5	5	6	2 4 3 1
Secretaries	4	5	3	7	3 2 4 1

The scores of the two occupations are rounded, to remove decimals. Anxiety has not been included because it does not discriminate well among occupational groups. To the right of the profiles, the global scores are ranked so that the highest score gets a rank of 1, the second highest ranks 2, and so on. Thus for Martha, EX has third rank (3), TM is second (2), IN is fourth (4), and SC is first (1). The ranks of Martha's global factors are 3 2 4 1. The ranks are based on the actual scores including decimals, so deciding between tied ranks is not arbitrary. In her personality scores Martha resembles secretary more than elementary school teacher—her 2 on EX is closer to the 4 of secretary than to the 6 of teacher, and her 1 on IN is closer to the 3 of secretary than to the 5 of teacher. Furthermore, the ranking of her global scores is identical to that of secretary. Based on these results, Martha resembles secretaries more than she does teachers, and, by inference, has a higher likelihood of feeling comfortable in that occupation.

Here one can see specifically what the 16PF can add to interest and ability measurement when evaluating occupational fit. Martha seems to be more similar to teachers than to secretaries on the interest measures, and on ability alone Martha resembles persons in jobs with much decision-making responsibility. On the 16PF she has more resemblance to secretaries than to teachers, and the key elements seem to be exactly the introversion and submissiveness that are so notable in her profile. Thus, when considering her reason for entering counseling, one could not rule out poor occupational fit as a component in her discomfort (because of the ability and interest measures), but one might understand why she chose secretarial work in terms of her low scores on extraversion and independence—she was more comfortable without the responsibility and need for truly interpersonal contact. In a secretarial job her concern for others would compensate for the need for privacy and introversion.

To carry these inferences further, one might consider her current situation. What had been a stable, if not perfect, adjustment has been upset by a change of bosses, and perhaps by the pressures of mid-life crisis. Martha is very bright and recognizes her lack of fit to the job in this respect, and is reevaluating. A tension has surfaced—a tension between her high intellectual ability on the one hand and on the other her need for privacy, shyness, unwillingness to confront, and extreme conservatism. From the discussion of patterns of primary scores it seems that Martha may not have much self-insight, despite her high score on Factor B, so the emergence of this discomfort only under these multiple stresses is not surprising. Questions of how much general pathology Martha shows and the interaction between pathology and occupational fit have been discussed in Chapter 2 on the MMPI. What remains here is to consider Martha's strengths as revealed in the 16PF and areas that she may want to work on.

The third specific issue, Martha's strengths, has been touched upon already, and is summarized here. She is very bright on two separate measures, a general ability test and Factor B of the 16PF. She presents herself as very conscientious, high on Factor G and Q3. These two together, high intelligence and conscientiousness, are generally held to be the best psychometric predictors of job performance. No matter what she does, Martha has a high probability of doing a good job of it. In addition, Martha is a caring person, one who finds it rewarding to attend to the needs of others.

The fourth specific issue, areas for Martha to consider working on, has also been touched on and is summarized here with suggestions for counseling intervention. It was noted earlier that she is introverted, submissive, conscientious, and conservative, all to a high degree. Although any or all of these characteristics might fit her for many jobs, they all tend to be constrictive, to bind Martha in to herself. As one area to work on, one might suggest assertiveness training to help her get more ways to express her own wants and ideas. Another potential problem area is her high anxiety, particularly shown in Factor Q4, Tension. This area was also noted in the discussion of the MMPI (Chap. 2). To address this possible problem, one might suggest relaxation procedures and/or cognitive therapy techniques. I do not suggest insight therapy because of Martha's probable lack of self-insight. The relaxation procedures show promise with Martha because, being so introverted, she is likely to respond quickly to conditioning techniques. Finally, for the sensitivity and possible dependency, Martha might be encouraged and instructed in self-care habits—clothing, food, living quarters, friends, and so on.

USE OF THE 16PF: PURPOSE AND PRACTICE

Given the conceptual background, description of variables, and sample case, it now may seem that a counselor could use the 16PF whenever he or she wants a systematic sample of normal personality by the client's own self-description. More specifically, experience suggests that it is appropriate in areas of use such as career counseling, clinical counseling, marriage and family work, addiction counseling, medical counseling, personnel selection, placement and development, and team building. Empirical studies are available in all these areas. Further, they are all areas in which personality is a significant contributor to understanding and prediction, and the 16PF is actively employed in all these areas and functions. Finally, when practitioners are asked for a list of measures that they believe trainees should learn, or asked what measures they themselves use on a regular basis, the 16PF is among the highest ranked (often the highest) among measures of normal personality (Pietrowski & Keller, 1989).

EVALUATION AND FUTURE DIRECTIONS

Comparative Advantages of the 16PF

In evaluating a normal personality questionnaire one may consider three aspects: (a) does it cover the needed area or domain, (b) are the concepts satisfying to practitioner and/or client, and (c) is there adequate empirical evidence to demonstrate correlations with real-life criteria? As to the first, the reader is no doubt aware that there are at least half a dozen commercially available instruments in the normal personality sphere, many or most of which cover the domain fairly well (Croom, Wallace, & Schuerger, 1989; Schuerger & Allen, 1986). Many make no claim to be systematic samples of the imperfectly defined domain of personality by questionnaire, and, without saying that the 16PF is the best or the only such instrument, I do claim that Cattell and his colleagues have made such an effort, and that their procedures were systematic and well documented. As to the second of the criteria, to a certain extent this must be a matter of personal "psychological" taste. Do the concepts and their theoretical framework appeal to me? One can and should look at the items as well, and at the level of homogeneity to see that these are appropriate, but after such an exploration, it is the concepts and their explanation that becomes convincing to each counselor's taste. Regarding the third criterion, the 16PF is well endowed, as noted in the validity section.

Future Directions

The recent 16PF Fifth Edition seems to be well launched, and well supported by its administrator's and technical manuals and by workshops across the country. Research studies using this edition are appearing in the journals, and I expect the trend to continue. The high-school version (HSPQ) is currently being revised as well and will include a pathology supplement in addition to the normal factors. Other versions of the 16PF are also showing their age and need review and revision—the CPQ for children and the CAQ for adults when a pathology supplement is needed. It would also be useful for practitioners to have an L-data version of the 16PF, so that one could compare an individual's self-reported scores (Q-data) with ratings by peers—fellow employees, or one spouse, for example. Counselors can readily see the possibilities of having such an instrument as supplement to the 16PF.

REFERENCES

Adams, J., & Klein, L. R. (1970). Students in nursing school: Considerations in assessing personality characteristics. *Nursing Research, 19,* 4, 362–366.

Allport, G. W., & Odbert, H. S. (1936). Trait-names, a psycholexical study. *Psychological Monographs, 47*(1, whole No. 211).

Anonsen, M. K. (1985). *Personality and interests of artists and accountants.* Unpublished master's thesis, Cleveland State University.

Bachtold, L. M. (1976). Personality characteristics of women of distinction. *Psychology of Women Quarterly, 1*(1), 70–78.

Barton, K., & Cattell, R. B. (1972). Personality factors related to job promotion and turnover. *Journal of Counseling Psychology, 19*(5), 430–435.

Bartram, D. (1992). The personality of UK managers: 16PF norms for short-listed applicants. *Journal of Occupational and Organizational Psychology, 65,* 159–172.

Boyd, M. A. (1985). Comparing personality profiles: Preadmission and pregraduation. In *Proceedings of the 2nd Annual Conference on the 16 PF Test* (pp.). Champaign, IL: IPAT.

Bush, A. J., & Lucas, G. H. (1988). Personality profiles of marketing vs. R.&D. managers. *Psychology and Marketing, 5*(1), 17–32.

Byrd, J. E. (1981). A comparison of measurement of change in maturation of undergraduate religious education students in an in-service intern program and non-church vocation students at Louisiana College. *Dissertation Abstracts International, 42*(4-A), 1571.

Campbell, V. M. (1985). *Responses on three personality inventoriesby women religious and former religious as a function of different situational contexts.* Doctoral dissertation, Hofstra University.

Cattell, H. B. (1989).*The 16PF: Personality in depth.* Champaign, IL: Institute for Personality and Ability Testing.

Cattell, R. B. (1973). *Personality and Mood by Questionnaire.* San Francisco: Jossey-Bass.

Cattell, R. B., Eber, H. W., & Tatsuoka, M. M. (1970). *Handbook for the Sixteen Personality Factor Questionnaire.* Champaign, IL: IPAT.

Cattell, R. B., & Warburton, F. W. (1967).*Objective personality & motivation tests: A theoretical introduction and practical compendium.* Chicago: University of Illinois Press, Urbana.

Chakrabarti, P. K., & Kundu, R. (1984). Personality profiles of management personnel. *Psychological Studies, 29*(2), 143–146.

Conn, S. R., & Rieke, M. L. (1994). *The 16PF Fifth Edition technical manual.* Champaign, IL: IPAT.

Croom, W. C., Wallace, J., & Schuerger, J. M. (1989). Jungian types from Cattellian variables. *Multivariate Experimental Clinical Research, 9,* 1, 35–40.

Dawson, R. W. (1973). Personality and peer counsellors: An Australian study. *Personnel and Guidance Journal, 52*(1), 46–48.

DeLamatre, J. E. (1995). *Personality dimensions of education majors: Holland Type and the 16PF.* Unpublished doctoral dissertation, University of Akron.

DiFiore, E. W. (1981). *Personality, occupational intersts, and job preferences of R. and D. engineers.* Master's thesis, Cleveland State University.

Foell, N. A., & Locke, D. C. (1984). A profile of students preparing to become industrial cooperative training coordinates. *College Student Journal, 18*(1), 52–55.

Franklin, E. C. (1983). *A comparison among the sex-role orientation, self-esteem/general adjustment, and personality profiles of men and women in male-dominated and female-dominated professions.* Unpublished doctoral dissertation, Kent State University.

Goffin, R. D., Christiansen, N. D., & Johnston, N. G. (1994, April). *Correcting for faking: Effects on the predictive validity of the 16PF.* Paper presented at the annual conference of the Society for Industrial and Organizational Psychology, Nashville, TN.

Graham, J. R., & Lilly, R. S. (1984). *Psychological Testing.* Englewood Cliffs, NJ: Prentice-Hall.

Grant, G. (1975). An objective evaluation of an eleven-week supervised pastoral education program. *Journal of Pastoral Care, 29,* 254–261.

Griffin, J. J., Jr. (1970). *An investigation of the work satisfaction of priests of the archdiocese of Boston.* Unpublished doctoral dissertation, Boston College.

Hartson, W. R., & Mottram, R. D. (1976). *Personality profiles of managers: A study of occupational differences.* ITRU (Industrial Training Research Unit) Publication SL9, University College London, Cambridge, England.

Hathaway, S. R., & McKinley, J. C. (1989). *Manual for Administering and Scoring MMPI-2.* Minneapolis: University of Minnesota.

Hay, J. E. (1964). *The relationship of certain personality variables to managerial level and job performance among engineering managers.* Unpublished doctoral dissertation, Temple University.

Healy, M. M. I. (1966). *Assessment of academic aptitude, personality characteristics, and religious orientation of Catholic sister-teacher trainees.* Unpublished doctoral dissertation, University of Minnesota, Minneapolis.

Henjum, A. E. (1966). *The relationships between certain personality characteristics of student teachers and success in student teaching.* Unpublished doctoral dissertation, University of Minnesota, Minneapolis.

Hinman, S., & Bolton, B. (1980). Motivational dynamics of disadvantaged women. *Psychology of Women Quarterly, 5*(2), 255–275.

Hobin-Hopkins, F. T. (1975). *A study of the relationships between freshman student nurses' academic performance, SAT scores, and specified personality variables.* Unpublished doctoral dissertation, University of Toledo, OH.

Hubbard, D. L. (1982). Differentiation of Black and White college females on the second-order factor Tough Poise as measured by the 16 PF. In *Proceedings of the 2nd Annual Conference on the 16 PF Test* (pp. 56–59). Champaign, IL: IPAT.

Hubele, G. E. (1970). *An investigation of personality characteristics of counselors, administrator, teachers and "non-helping" professionals.* Unpublished doctoral dissertation, University of Illinois.

Hussong, M. A., Sherman, J. L., & Ferris, G. R. (1977). *16PF Research Bibliography: 1971–1976.* Champaign, IL: IPAT.

IPAT Staff (1986; 1991). *Administrator's Manual for the 16 Personality Factor Questionnaire.* Champaign, IL: IPAT.

Johns, E. F. (1985). *Holland's occupational taxonomy in terms of personality traits and discriminant functions.* Unpublished master's thesis, Cleveland State University.

Karson, S., & O'Dell, J. W. (1976). *A guide to the clinical use of the 16PF.* Champaign, IL: IPAT.

Krug, S. E. (1977). *Psychological Assessment in Medicine.* Champaign, IL: IPAT.

Krug, S. E. (1981). *Interpreting 16PF profile patterns.* Champaign, IL: IPAT.

Krug, S. E., & Laughlin, J. (1976). *Handbook for the IPAT Depression Scale.* Champaign, IL: IPAT.

Law, G. D., & Schuerger, J. M. (1982). Personality and the hospitality industry: A comparative study of practicing managers and chefs. *Journal of Hospital Education, 7,* 1, 57–63.

Lawrence, R. A. (1980). *Relationship of officers' scores on the Police Stress Inventory and the 16PF Test.* Unpublished doctoral dissertation, Sam Houston State University.

Leary, T. (1957). *Interpersonal diagnosis of personality.* New York: Ronald.

Mahan, T. W., & Mahan, A. M. (1982). *The 16PF and organizational development: Helping managers grow. Second International Conference on the 16PF Test: 1982 Proceedings.* Champaign, IL: IPAT.

McGill, J. C., Hall, J. R., & Moss, R. F. (1986). Personality characteristics of professional rodeo cowboys: An initial descriptive review. *Journal of Sports Behavior, 9*(4), 143–151.

Meyer, R. G. (1989). *Clinician's handbook.* Boston: Allyn & Bacon.

Mulhausen, W. P. (1990). *Racial/ethnic differences for male offenders on three personality inventories.* Unpublished doctoral dissertation, Kent State University.

Noty, C. (1974). *Personality, interest and motivational correlates of persistence in religious vocations.* Unpublished doctoral dissertation, Loyola University, Chicago.

Nowak, M. (1980). *The Sixteen Personality Factor Inventory and job success in engineers.* Unpublished master's thesis, Cleveland State University.

Osman, A. C. (1973). Personality comparison of men and women students. *Accountant, 169*(5162), 696–697.

Payne, L. L. (1977). *A comparison of personality variables and predicted counseling effectiveness of guidance associates and counselor trainees.* Unpublished doctoral disertation, Texas Tech University.

Roberts, C. D. (1975). *Values and personality characteristics of rehabilitation counselors in agency and educational settings.* Unpublished doctoral dissertation, University of Arizona.

Ruffer, W. A. (1976). Two studies of personality: Female graduate students in physical education. *Perceptual and Motor Skills, 42*(3 Pt. 2), 1268–1270.

Russell, M., & Karol, D. (1994).*The 16 PF Fifth Edition: Administrator's manual.* Champaign, IL: Institute for Personality and Ability Testing.

Schmidt, F. L., Ones, D. S., & Hunter, J. E. (1992). Personnel selection. *Annual Review of Psychology, 43,* 627–70.

Schuerger, J. M. (1992). The Sixteen Personality Factor Questionnaire and its junior versions. *Journal of Counseling and Development, 71,* 231–244.

Schuerger, J. M. (1995). Career assessment and the Sixteen Personality Factor Questionnaire. *Journal of Career Assessment, 3,* 2, 157–175.

Schuerger, J. M., & Allen, L. C. (1986). Second-order factor structure common to five personality questionnaires. *Psychological Reports, 58*, 119–126.

Schuerger, J. M., & Sfiligoj, T. (1998). Holland codes and 16PF global factors: Sixty-nine samples. *Psychological Reports, 82*, 1299–1306.

Schuerger, J. M., & Watterson, D. G. (1996). *Occupational patterns in the 16 Personality Factor Questionnaire*. Chagrin Falls, OH: WAI.

Schuerger, J. M., Watterson, D. G., & Croom, W. C. (1994). *Psychological variables in counseling*. Cleveland: Authors.

Schuerger, J. M., Zarrella, K., & Hotz, A. (1989). Factors which influence the stability of personality by questionnaire. *Journal of Personality & Social Psychology, 56*, 5, 777–783.

Scordato, A. J. (1975). *A comparison of interest, personality and biographical characteristics of seminary persisters and non-persisters from St. Pius X Preparatory Seminary*. Unpublished doctoral dissertation, University of Wyoming.

Sherman, J. L., & Krug, S. E. (1977). Personality-somatic interactions: The research evidence. In S. E. Krug (Ed.), *Psychological assessment in medicine* (pp. 63–114). Champaign, IL: IPAT.

Smith, G. A., Dowling, P. J., & Barry, B. (1985). Australian managers' norms on the 16PF. *Australian Psychologist, 20*(3), 293–301.

Smith, G. M. (1965). The role of personality in nursing education: A comparison of successful and unsuccessful nursing students. *Nursing Research, 14*, 54–58.

Snibbe, H. M., Fabricatore, J., & Azen, S. P. (1975). Personality patterns of white, black, and Mexican-American patrolmen as measured by the Sixteen Personality Factor Questionnaire. *American Journal of Community Psychology, 3*(3), 221–227.

Spotts, J. V., & Shontz, F. C. (1991). Drugs and personality: comparison of drug users, nonusers, and other clinical groups on the 16PF. *International Journal of the Addictions, 26*(10).

Start, K. B. (1966). The relation of teaching ability to measures of personality. *British Journal of Educational Psychology, 36*, 158–165.

Start, K. B., & Laundy, S. (1973). Successful teachers in the secondary school. *Research in Education, 9*(May), 1–15.

Sternad, J. A. (1991). *Use of the Sixteen Personality Factor Questionnaire to predict pre-service principals' assessment center scores*. Unpublished doctoral dissertation, Cleveland State University.

Sweney, A. (undated). *Interpreting 16PF Profiles*.

Tatar, M. (1982). *The police personality and desirable qualities of hostage negotiators: An investigation of psychological dimensions and approaches to the assessment of state policeman who volunteer for training as hostage negotiators*. Unpublished doctoral dissertation, Syracuse University.

Taylor, L. E., & Armstrong, T. R. (1975). Personality factors associated with the predicted role of activity-centered versus textbook-centered preservice elementary science teachers. *Journal of Research in Science Teaching, 12*(3), 229–234.

Terpylak, O., & Schuerger, J. M. (1994). Broad factor scales of the 16PF fifth edition and Millon Personality disorder scales: A replication. *Psychological Reports, 74*, 124–126.

White, W. F., & Anderson, J. (1975). Personality differences among female student teachers of relatively high and low mental ability. *Perceptual and Motor Skills, 41*(1), 29–30.

Whitworth, R. H., & Perry, S. M. (1990). Comparison of Anglo- and Mexican-Americans on the 16 PF administered in Spanish or English. *Journal of Clinical Psychology, 46*, 6, 857–863.

Widdop, J. H., & Widdop, V. A. (1975). Comparison of the personality traits of female teacher education and physical education students. *Research Quarterly, 46*(3), 274–281.

Zimmerman, R. E., & Williams, J. D. (1971). Personality characteristics of innovative and non-innovative teachers. *Psychological Reports, 29*, 2, 343–346.

5

The Myers–Briggs Type Indicator[1] in Counseling

Mary H. McCaulley

Center for Applications of Psychological Type, Inc., Gainesville, Florida

BACKGROUND

The Myers–Briggs Type Indicator (MBTI) falls into the family of personality assessment instruments designed to make it possible to test and use a specific psychological theory. The theory behind the MBTI is C. G. Jung's theory of psychological types (Jung, 1921/1971), that part of Jung's overall theory that is specifically concerned with the way people consciously use their minds. MBTI users apply Jung's powerful framework for looking at individual differences in their relationships with others, their work, and their inner lives.

The MBTI was developed by Isabel Briggs Myers and her mother Katharine Cook Briggs. Katharine Briggs became interested in personality differences when her daughter, Isabel, brought home her future husband, Clarence Myers, to meet the family. She described him later as "an admirable young man, unlike anyone in our family before." As a way of understanding her son-in-law, Mrs. Briggs went to the Library of Congress and read biographies. From her analyses she created her own typology. After Jung's *Psychological Types* was published in English in 1923, she recognized the match between Jung's observations and her own independently developed types. As her daughter Isabel described it in her book *Gifts Differing*

---

[1]Myers–Briggs Type Indicator and MBTI are registered trademarks of Consulting Psychologists Press.

(Myers with Myers, 1980, p. 23), Briggs's *meditative type* was consistent with Jung's *introverts*; her *spontaneous type* corresponded with Jung's *perceptive extraverts*; her *executive type* corresponded with Jung's *extraverted thinking types*; and her *sociable type* corresponded with Jung's *extraverted feeling* types. Katharine Briggs studied Jung's *Psychological Types* intensively, and introduced the concepts to Isabel Myers. Together, mother and daughter became type watchers for two decades, testing Jung's observations against their experiences of their family and friends. This incubation period was an important first step to creating the MBTI. An insight into Isabel Myers's character comes from her own words about the impetus for her long journey in developing and researching the MBTI.

> In the darkest days of World War II when the Germans were rolling irresistibly along and my shoulders ached with trying to hold them back and a horrible sinking feeling lived in the pit of my stomach, the thought came to me one day (I was making my bed at the time) that by letting them spoil my life that way I was helping them win, bringing destruction to pass by my own doing. So I stopped, just like that. I made up my mind that there was no logical justification for turning possible future unhappiness into certain present unhappiness by being afraid of it. Do what you can to make a better world, but don't throw away one day or one minute of the world you've got. What I did, as it turned out, was the Type Indicator. (I. B. Myers, personal communication, 21 December 1970)

The long process of creating the MBTI by solving a series of technical difficulties, to be faithful to the theory, is described in the MBTI *Manual* (Myers & McCaulley, 1985, referred to as the *Manual* from here on[2]). Isabel Myers began by creating forced-choice questions that were intended to let people indicate the effects of Jungian preferences in everyday life. Almost at once she discovered type differences in the way people interpreted the question choices; as a result, each choice is presented in the frame of reference of the types for whom it is intended. In this way, questions became a "stimulus to evoke a type response." Myers understood that type theory was complex and sophisticated; the questions were not intended to tap the theory directly, but to be "straws in the wind," showing which way the wind blows.

Working alone at home, with only family financial support, Isabel Myers painstakingly constructed a series of versions of the MBTI. She collected data on over 9,000 high-school students, over 5,000 medical students, and over 10,000 nursing students, hand scoring the answer sheets. She obtained

---

[2]There have been three published manuals for the MBTI—Myers, 1962, Myers and McCaulley, 1985, and Myers, McCaulley, Quenk, and Hammer, 1998. References to the *Manual* from here on refer to the 1985 edition.

and analyzed data on aptitude and achievement for all three samples, and specialty choice for the medical students. Information about this early research can be found in the *Manual*, and in McCaulley (1977, 1978).

In 1962 Educational Testing Service (ETS) published the MBTI as an instrument to be used only for research (Myers, 1962). In preparation, ETS psychologists added the MBTI to other measures in the College Student Characteristics Study, and these data were included in the 1962 *Manual*. Purchasers were required to specify their research plans, and to return answer sheets to the author on request. During the ETS period, Dr. Sukeyori Shuba, a Japanese psychologist, discovered the MBTI and carried information about it back to the Nippon Recruit Center in Tokyo. Under a contract with Isabel Briggs Myers, Takeshi Ohsawa at the Nippon Recruit Center in Tokyo oversaw the translation of the MBTI. The Japanese translation began to be used in 1968. During this period, Donald MacKinnon at the University of California at Berkeley began including early versions of the MBTI in the test battery of the creativity studies of the Institute for Personality Assessment (IPAR).

By 1975 MBTI research had confirmed Isabel Myers's work, and counselors and others were applying it. Consulting Psychologists Press (CPP) became the publisher and added the MBTI to its catalog of instruments for professional applications. In that same year, Isabel Myers and Mary McCaulley established the nonprofit Center for Applications of Psychological Type (CAPT) for research, scoring, training, and other professional services related to the MBTI. Four years later, in 1979, a membership organization, the Association for Psychological Type (APT), was formed for persons interested in psychological type.

In 1975, the MBTI was relatively unknown. Since then, in a little over a two decades, use of the MBTI has grown exponentially to the point where it will soon be the most widely used psychological tool for "normal people." Counselors use the MBTI with individuals, groups, couples, and families; with children, young people, and adults. They use type to help clients understand themselves, to improve relationships with others, and to choose careers. Other counselors use Jung's type dynamics as part of a Jungian analytical approach that includes consideration of archetypes, the collective unconscious, animus, anima, the persona, and the road to individuation. Counseling uses for individuals are the focus of this chapter, but the principles apply also to families, groups, and organizations.

Educators use the MBTI with teachers and students to work with type differences in teaching styles, learning styles, academic aptitude, achievement and motivation, dropout, and college roommate matching. Organizations in business, industry, and government use the MBTI to deal with type differences in communication, teamwork, management styles, leadership development, and lifelong career planning. In the religious community, the

MBTI is used to value type differences in spiritual development and ministry. The MBTI has been translated into languages of every continent, and is used worldwide.

In 1980, the year of her death, Isabel Myers's book for the public and for the professional was published. *Gifts Differing* described Jung's theory and the 16 types, and distilled a lifetime of reflection on type and early learning, learning styles, occupations, marriage, and type development.

CONCEPTUAL FOUNDATIONS OF THE MBTI

What is there about type theory and the MBTI that led to such rapid growth in so many fields where psychological tests are seldom used? In Isabel Myers's words (Myers & McCaulley, 1985, p. 1):

> The essence of the theory is that much seemingly random variation in behavior is actually quite orderly and consistent, being due to basic differences in the way individuals prefer to use their perception and judgment. Perception involves all the ways of becoming aware of things, people, happenings, or ideas. Judgment involves all the ways of coming to conclusions about what has been perceived. If people differ systematically in what they perceive and in how they reach conclusions, then it is only reasonable for them to differ correspondingly in their reactions, interests, values, motivations, skills, and interests.

Because almost every waking act involves perceiving or decision making, type differences touch all aspects of life.

Overview of Jung's Theory of Psychological Types

The MBTI cannot be understood without also understanding Jung's type theory.

The MBTI Was Designed to Reflect Jung's Theory. The MBTI is not a "test" in the meaning of a measure of better or worse, right or wrong. It simply lets a person "indicate" preferences between equally valuable opposites described in Jung's theory. The MBTI scales indicate four bipolar, theoretically dichotomous, preferences.

> Extraversion (E) or Introversion (I): Attitude toward the outer or inner worlds. Sensing Perception (S) or Intuitive Perception (N): The balance between perceiving the present realities (S) or envisioning future possibilities ((N). Thinking Judgment (T) or Feeling Judgment (F): The balance between reaching judgments through impersonal logic (T) or personal values (F). Perceiving (P) or

Judging (J): The balance between taking in information (P) or drawing conclusions (J).

Each Indicator question forces choices between the poles of one of the four preferences. The 16 types are denoted by the letters for the preferred pole (e.g., ISTJ, ENFP, ESFJ, etc.). To describe a group, the types are arranged in a conventional order, known as the *type table*, such that every type shares three preferences in common with each neighboring type. Characteristics of type groupings are described in the *Manual* (pp. 31–38).

Type Is Concerned With the Balance of Opposites. As in other aspects of Jung's theory, the tensions and striving for balance between opposites create the dynamic interplay that leads to growth.

Everyone Uses All Preferences, but Not Equally. Both poles of the four preferences are valuable and necessary. Everyone uses E, I, S, N, T, F, J, and P daily. Types sharing letters share the characteristic behaviors and traits denoted by the shared letters. However, in each of the 16 types, the pattern of interests and skills associated with one preference is modified by the other three preferences. For example, the extraverted attitude appears differently in ESTJ (a tough-minded executive type) and in ESFJ (a helpful, sociable type.)

The Four Functions: Building Blocks of Type. The functions, or mental processes, described by Jung and the MBTI, are sensing (S), intuition (N), thinking (T), and feeling (F). In Jung's type theory, conscious mental activity falls into one of these four categories. Sensing and intuition refer to two different kinds of *perceiving*; thinking and feeling refer to two different kinds of *judging*.

Sensing perceiving (S) refers to perceptions of the senses, and brings to awareness what is occurring in the present moment. Development of differentiated skills of sensing is expected to lead to characteristics such as realism, acute powers of observation, memory for details, practical common sense, and the ability to enjoy the present moment. Correlations of sensing scores with constructs from other personality instruments include practical outlook, economic interests, conventional, natural, favors conservative values, uncomfortable with complexity, contented. In careers, sensing scores correlate with scores for banker, management, skilled and unskilled trades, clerks, accounting, and any other fields requiring close attention to detail (*Manual*, pp. 207, 212). The CAPT *Atlas of Type Tables* (Macdaid, McCaulley, & Kainz, 1986) provides data on type distributions in normative samples and careers.

Intuitive perceiving (N) refers to perceiving the intangible by way of insight—future possibilities, associations, meanings, abstractions, symbols. Jung described intuition as "perception by way of the unconscious." For example, when a person uses sensing to describe a peanut, the words are likely to be *crisp, rough, shiny on the inside, two symmetrical nuts*. When a person uses intuition to describe the same peanut, you may hear *peanut butter, take me out to the ball game, elephants,* or *George Washington Carver*. Significant correlations between the N scale and other instruments reported in the *Manual* (pp. 207 and 212) include complexity, academic interests, individualistic, artistic, creative, theoretical, foresighted, resourceful. Occupations significantly correlated with intuition are counselor, artist, physicist, chemist, reporter, foreign language teacher—all fields requiring skills in dealing with abstractions and patterns of symbols. Because it is intuition that sees new possibilities and patterns, it is not surprising that creative samples show a large majority of intuitive types. (*Manual*, pp. 74 and 75)

Thinking judging (T) is the rational process that reaches conclusions through an impersonal process of logic or cause and effect. Differentiation of thinking is, in theory, expected to be associated with objectivity, analytical ability, skepticism, critical judgment, and concern with justice and fairness. Significant correlations between T and other instruments include mechanical, skeptical, masculine orientation, theoretical, distrust, dominance. Thinking types significantly choose occupations requiring skills with the inanimate, logic, or mathematics, including engineering, business, sciences, computer technologies, and other technical fields.

Feeling judging (F) is the rational process that reaches conclusions by weighing values and the merits of people, things, and ideas. Feeling judges subjectively; thinking judges objectively. Differentiation of feeling is, in theory, expected to be associated with appreciation, empathy, desire for harmony, and an understanding of and concern for other people. The distinction in psychology between "tough-minded" and "tender-minded" relates to TF differences. Significant correlations between F and other instruments include nurturance, affiliation, altruism, tender-minded, social and religious values. Examples of occupations of interest to feeling types include social service, counseling, religious activities, teaching, health care, and any other occupations where one can work with people.

The Attitudes: Orientations to the World. Jung described the attitudes of *extraversion* (outward-turning) and *introversion* (inward-turning) as directions of energy flow. Extraversion and introversion describe universal aspects of personality. Most other researchers who have tried to describe human personality comprehensively have measured—or discovered—extraversion and introversion. The MBTI includes a scale for indicating extraversion–introversion (EI).

Extraversion (E) describes the attitude in which energy flows out or is drawn out to the environment. The world around us provides stimulation, and we wish to interact with the people and things around us. The characteristics expected to result from preferring the extraverted attitude include sociability, action orientation, impulsivity, and ease of communication. The largest significant correlations between the MBTI EI scale and other instruments are the extraversion–introversion scales of those instruments, generally in the range of .69 to .79. MBTI extraversion also correlates significantly with scales of sociability, dominance, leadership, expressed inclusion, expressed affection, exhibitionism, and being venturesome. Extraverts tend to be attracted to occupations that have action, outdoors or travel, and contact with people.

Introversion (I), in Jung's theory, is an important normal variant of human personality. When a person introverts, energy is drawn from the environment and is directed inward to the world of concepts and ideas. People who habitually take the introverted attitude develop the characteristics associated with introversion: interest in the clarity of concepts and ideas, reliance more on enduring concepts than on transitory external events, a thoughtful, contemplative detachment, and enjoyment of privacy. Correlations significantly associated with MBTI introversion include self-sufficient, reserved, and introspective. Occupations that attract introverts tend to require working alone, one-to-one contacts, longer attention span, and work with ideas. Introverts are in the majority among computer programmers, engineers, statisticians, librarians, accountants, or anesthesiologists.

Extraversion–introversion is an important dimension in the therapeutic relationship. Extraverts appear to be the valued majority, so that introverts often report feeling different. In many correlations with personality measures, extraversion is associated with positive qualities—ego strength and emotional stability, personal integration, and self-esteem. Introversion is more likely to be associated on other scales with negative qualities—anxiety, guilt, and neuroticism. Some of this difference comes from the extravert's greater comfort with the environment, but some of the negative descriptions of introverts can stem from society's lack of appreciation of the strengths of introversion.

The outward-turning of extraverts can lead them to look more to others and less to themselves as the cause of their problems. Counselors often see extraverts who are astonished to find they are themselves important actors in their own drama, not simply responding to external forces. The inward-turning introverts are likely to blame themselves for their difficulties. Counselors often see introverts who are amazed at the counselor's suggestion that perhaps others might also be at fault in their problems. For extraverts, the counselor will try to distinguish the deserved confidence of well-developed extraverts from the overconfidence of the less mature extraverts. For introverts, counselors must distinguish the introspection, anxieties, and need for solitude of healthy introverts from the chronic anxiety and despair of introverts in psychological pain. In any case, it is useful to keep in mind that many personality tests, as well as the larger society, describe extraversion as if it were a more positive attribute than introversion.

Extraversion–introversion is one of the most widely used personality constructs. Most instruments treat the construct as one continuous trait. Introversion can be seen as a lack of extraversion, or vice versa. Jung saw extraversion and introversion as different constellations of actions, each with its consequent behaviors and traits. He believed there were no "pure extraverts" or "pure introverts." Extraversion is always associated with one of the four functions. There are extraverted sensing types, extraverted intuitive types, extraverted thinking types, extraverted feeling types, but there are no "extraverts"—and similarly with introverts. This point is clarified in the section on dynamics, but it is important because it is alien to most of the work in personality theory.

Judging (J) and perceiving (P) refer to the orientation to the outer (extraverted) world. The JP scale indicates whether extraverted behaviors are more likely to reflect the perceptive functions (S or N) or the judging functions (T or F). JP is used in two ways in the MBTI. First, it identifies observable behaviors important in their own right. Second, JP helps identify the dynamic pattern for each type by pointing to the dominant and auxiliary functions.

In any new situation it is important to take the perceiving attitude—seeing everything, and being curious and interested. At some point, one has seen enough (P) and is ready to reach a judgment (J). Characteristics in scales of other instruments associated with perceiving are complexity, flexibility, autonomy, change-as-challenge, and happy-go-lucky. Measures associated with judging include self-control, stronger superego, rule-bound, and dependability. Many personality scales describe J characteristics more positively than P characteristics. For example, P scores are positively correlated with scales named impulsivity, rebellious, procrastinating, changeable, and restless. J-types occur in greater numbers than P-types in the general population, and J-types are clearly in the majority in samples of managers in business, government, and education. The terms *judgment* and *judging* are often associated in clients' minds with *judgmental*. The MBTI use of the word *judgment* is closer to the meaning of when one speaks of exercising good judgment. In MBTI terms, being "judgmental" or "closed-minded" comes from judging without the balance of perceiving.

Nature and Nurture. Both Jung and Myers believed that nature determines the basis of type, and nurture is important in influencing its development. Environment is important, because families and cultures can disconfirm natural preferences and lead to a "falsification" of type. Jung commented that falsification can lead to an adult neurosis, and counseling may be needed in adulthood to help find the lost path.

Preferences Are Dichotomous

The preferences—EI, SN, TF, and JP—are indicated as a way station to identify the types. They are not traits. In the psychology of personality, most psychological tests measure traits. For example, a scale of assertiveness assumes that assertiveness is normally distributed, with high scores meaning high assertiveness, low scores meaning low assertiveness, and middle scores meaning average assertiveness. In type theory and the MBTI, the preferences are seen as dichotomies. Preferring one pole over the other is like taking one fork in a road rather than the other. A person who takes one fork (e.g., sensing) develops qualitatively different interests, motivations, behaviors, and skills from a person who takes the other fork (e.g., intuition). The most misunderstood (and debated) aspect of type theory and the MBTI is that the preferences are not traits. In type theory there is the assumption of bipolarity; preferences are dichotomous.

Dynamic Interaction of the Preferences

Type theory predicts a lifelong developmental pattern for each type. The dynamic pattern for each type predicts the order in which S, N, T, and F develop to produce the characteristics of the 16 types.

The assumptions for these dynamic patterns are stated briefly next. Some are familiar because they are part of other theories; some are specific to type theory. Counselors working with the MBTI use type theory to understand the reasons for the characteristics of each type, and, more importantly, to plan treatment that builds on the strengths of the type.

The Dominant and Auxiliary Functions.

Type theory assumes that everyone uses sensing, intuition, thinking, and feeling, but that one of these will be the leading or first function (called the *dominant*). A second function will assist (called the *auxiliary*). The dominant function provides consistency of general direction in life. In normal development, the dominant is the most conscious, most differentiated function. Interests, motivations, and skills come from its use.

The personality needs balance. The second or auxiliary function develops to provide balance in two ways. The dominant and auxiliary appear in different attitudes—one provides adaptation to the outer world (E) and the other to the inner world (I). The dominant and auxiliary also provide balance between perception and judgment. If the dominant is a perceiving function (S or N), the auxiliary will provide judgment (T or F) (or vice versa). The well-developed type will therefore be able to deal comfortably with outer and inner events, and will have the skills to take in information and make decisions.

The Less-Developed Functions. The third and fourth functions are assumed to be necessary but less developed. The opposite of the dominant function is called the fourth or inferior function; it is assumed to be nearest to the unconscious, a powerful source for growth. Because the inferior is the least developed, it is also the source of vulnerability (von Franz, 1971). Two recent books, *Beside Ourselves: Our Hidden Personality in Everyday Life* (Quenk, 1993) and *In the Grip: Our Hidden Personality* (Quenk, 1996), described the eruption of the inferior function.

Figure 5.1 shows the relationship of the four functions for each of the 16 MBTI types.

Deficiencies Can Result From Focus on Strengths. When members of any type are developing and focusing on the activities of the dominant process, they cannot *at the same moment* focus on and develop its opposite. Students who have focused on immediate details with dominant sensing can have blind spots about the broad implications or future possibilities of those details. Others whose dominant intuition is differentiated in seeing

ISTJ			ISFJ			INFJ			INTJ		
#1 DOMINANT	S	(I)	#1 DOMINANT	S	(I)	#1 DOMINANT	N	(I)	#1 DOMINANT	N	(I)
#2 AUXILIARY	T	(E)	#2 AUXILIARY	F	(E)	#2 AUXILIARY	F	(E)	#2 AUXILIARY	T	(E)
#3 TERTIARY	F	(E)	#3 TERTIARY	T	(E)	#3 TERTIARY	T	(E)	#3 TERTIARY	F	(E)
#4 Inferior	N	(E)	#4 Inferior	N	(E)	#4 Inferior	S	(E)	#4 Inferior	S	(E)
ISTP			ISFP			INFP			INTP		
#1 DOMINANT	T	(I)	#1 DOMINANT	F	(I)	#1 DOMINANT	F	(I)	#1 DOMINANT	T	(I)
#2 AUXILIARY	S	(E)	#2 AUXILIARY	S	(E)	#2 AUXILIARY	N	(E)	#2 AUXILIARY	N	(E)
#3 TERTIARY	N	(E)	#3 TERTIARY	N	(E)	#3 TERTIARY	S	(E)	#3 TERTIARY	S	(E)
#4 Inferior	F	(E)	#4 Inferior	T	(E)	#4 Inferior	T	(E)	#4 Inferior	F	(E)
ESTP			ESFP			ENFP			ENTP		
#1 DOMINANT	S	(E)	#1 DOMINANT	S	(E)	#1 DOMINANT	N	(E)	#1 DOMINANT	N	(E)
#2 AUXILIARY	T	(I)	#2 AUXILIARY	F	(I)	#2 AUXILIARY	F	(I)	#2 AUXILIARY	T	(I)
#3 TERTIARY	F	(I)	#3 TERTIARY	T	(I)	#3 TERTIARY	T	(I)	#3 TERTIARY	F	(I)
#4 Inferior	N	(I)	#4 Inferior	N	(I)	#4 Inferior	S	(I)	#4 Inferior	S	(I)
ESTJ			ESFJ			ENFJ			ENTJ		
#1 DOMINANT	T	(E)	#1 DOMINANT	F	(E)	#1 DOMINANT	F	(E)	#1 DOMINANT	T	(E)
#2 AUXILIARY	S	(I)	#2 AUXILIARY	S	(I)	#2 AUXILIARY	N	(I)	#2 AUXILIARY	N	(I)
#3 TERTIARY	N	(I)	#3 TERTIARY	N	(I)	#3 TERTIARY	S	(I)	#3 TERTIARY	S	(I)
#4 Inferior	F	(I)	#4 Inferior	T	(I)	#4 Inferior	T	(I)	#4 Inferior	F	(I)

FIG. 5.1. Priorities and Directions of Functions in Each Type. From *Manual: A Guide to the Development and Use of the Myers–Briggs Type Indicator* by Isabel Briggs Myers and Mary H. McCaulley (1985). Palo Alto, CA: Consulting Psychologists Press. Reprinted with permission.

broad new possibilities and symbolic interrelationships may miss facts that are obvious to a sensing type. Dominant thinking types may discount even their own feeling values, and dominant feeling types may not see the beauty and clarity of logic. It is easier to accept, and remedy, the deficiencies of the third and fourth functions when these deficiencies are seen as the natural consequence of having spent more energy on the first and second functions.

Type Development as a Lifelong Process

Type development is a lifelong process. Youth is the time of specialization by developing the dominant and auxiliary functions. Midlife gives the opportunity to develop the third and fourth functions. The journey toward wholeness seeks *individuation*—loyalty to one's own type preferences, with an increasing ability to move from one preference to another with ease and skill as the situation demands. The "midlife crisis" with "Is this all there is?" may be seen as a development of the third and fourth functions to seek individuation. (In Jung's larger theory, individuation includes also the assimilation of the contents of the collective unconscious into consciousness, and divesting the self of the false wrappings of the persona.) In essence, life's journey and individuation are directed toward expanding consciousness.

Electing to Use the MBTI in Counseling

The MBTI differs from other tests used by counselors. Most psychological tests are designed for specific purposes. The MBTI is broadly based on Jung's model of how human beings use their minds. Most tests provide information primarily for the counselor. The MBTI provides information primarily for the client. Most tests provide diagnostic high and low scores. Isabel Myers did *not* design the MBTI for diagnosing psychopathology. Her first goal was to give people a tool to indicate their inborn preferences: "Who am I?" Her second was to indicate the pathway toward wholeness and consciousness: "How do I develop my gifts?" Her third was to "enable us to expect certain personality differences in particular people and to cope with the people and the differences in a constructive way" (Myers with Myers, 1980, p. 1).

Isabel Myers originally developed the MBTI as a tool for career counseling. It has many other counseling uses over a wide range of age groups and presenting issues.

The counselor using the MBTI first helps the client identify the type that fits best. The history and presenting problem enter into assessment of the client's ability to perceive clearly (through sensing or intuition); and to make good decisions (through thinking or feeling). The counselor also helps the client discover whether energy is focused on the external world of people and things (extraversion) or on the inner world of ideas (introversion).

Experienced counselors will recognize that this assessment in the terminology of psychological type is consistent with other models of psychotherapy.

Counselors find that type theory and the MBTI give useful lenses for their counseling strategies to:

Establish rapport with clients.

Increase self-understanding and hope.

Provide a framework for interpreting other tests.

Individualize the stages of career counseling.

Improve problem solving and teamwork for individuals and groups.

Help students manage their learning.

Help adults understand the individuation process of midlife and aging.

Teach effective strategies for coping with change, illness, substance abuse, family violence, and other life stresses.

Counselors use the MBTI at many levels. In one case they may simply use the type description to affirm the client's gifts. In other cases the counselor focuses on developing the dominant and auxiliary and recognizing the effects of being in the grip of the inferior function. For other clients, the counselor shows how the client is being affected by the "type environment" (e.g., introverts will have different work experiences in the introverted environment of physics from that of the extraverted environment of sales). Or the focus will be on showing how type differences are interfering with communication, and what to do about it.

When used appropriately and competently, Jung's model and the MBTI can foster an appreciation of one's own individuality and gifts, and a greater understanding of others. Differences are valued, and used constructively rather than destructively. As counselors help clients gain greater command of their dominant and auxiliary functions, and less vulnerability to their inferior function, the type development process leads to more consciousness in all spheres of their lives.

The four cases later in this chapter show how counselors can use type theory, type tables, and type dynamics to develop hypotheses and choose interventions for their clients.

TEST ADMINISTRATION AND SCORING

MBTI Materials

The standard form of the MBTI from 1977 to 1998 was Form G (126 items). In 1998 the standard form became Form M (93 items). Other forms include Form F (166 items), Form K (131 items) and Form J (290 items). Isabel Myers constructed Form F (1962) and Form G (1977) and of course all earlier forms beginning in 1944. Forms J and K, using her items, were developed by David Saunders after her death in 1980. Form M was developed by a research team in 1998. Forms F, G, J, and K include research questions not scored for type but included by Myers to study individual differences within types.

All items in all MBTI forms are in forced-choice format to permit choices between the desirable opposites in each preference. Choices are always in the same preference (E or I; S or N; but never E or N; T or J).

There are two item types: phrase questions and word pairs. Phrase questions present a stem followed by two choices, such as "Are your interests (A) few and lasting, or (B) varied?" Word pairs simply present two words with the instructions, "Which word in each pair appeals to you more?" Phrase questions may reflect influences in everyday life; word pairs may reflect a truer preference.

Except for the research questions, all MBTI questions are scored to determine the preferred pole of the four indices—EI, SN, TF, and JP, and to generate the four letters of the type preferences, i.e. ESTJ, ISFJ, INFP, ENTP.

Isabel Myers was an astute observer of people. She recognized that members of the same type could be quite different in some ways. She assigned items within EI, SN, TF, and JP into 5 behavioral clusters as subscales to show different ways in which a preference might manifest itself in behavior. (In type theory, traits and behaviors develop from exercising the action tendencies of the preferences. For example, extraverted energy may lead to becoming gregarious, or outspoken, or physically active.)

From the beginning, Isabel Myers added a few "nontype" questions for her research on type development. These items are not used to score EI, SN, TF, or JP.

After her death, Form J was published. Saunders included all questions (scored for type and research questions) in any version of the MBTI during Isabel Myers's lifetime, plus a few new research questions from his own research.

Saunders also developed Form K, to add to Form G a few questions not weighted for type, but needed for Form K reports of the subscales of the four preferences—the Expanded Analysis Report (EAR) scored by CPP, and the Expanded Interpretive Report (EIR) scored by CAPT.

Administration

The MBTI is essentially self-administering. Instructions on the question booklets and on the answer sheets are designed to avoid a right–wrong mind set and to show how the respondent will benefit by answering honestly. Omissions are permitted but not encouraged. The goal is to assess type preferences from what the respondent is clear about, not from random guessing. Procedures for individuals and groups follow standard professional and ethical practice. For poor readers or sight-impaired persons, the questions can be read aloud; readers must be careful to be even-handed lest they make the responses favored by their own type sound more attractive.

Scoring

Scoring the MBTI is designed to indicate the direction of preferences, E or I, S or N, T or F, J or P, in order to identify the type, such as ESTJ or ISFP. The MBTI is scored for four indices: EI, SN, TF, and JP. Each answer to each item is weighted 0, 1, or 2; weights take into account the popularity of the item, social desirability, omissions, and differences in the way males and females answer some items on the TF scale. The first step in scoring is to sum the item weights for each pole of each preference. These eight raw score totals are called *points*. Letters are assigned for the pole with the highest number of points. (For example, 15 points for E and 9 points for I would indicate a preference for E.) A linear formula transforms the points to a preference score, which takes into account the difference and direction of the two poles and allows for breaking ties. The four preference scores are the important MBTI scores; each consists of a letter and a number (e.g., E 11, T 29, etc.). The greater the difference in points between one pole and the other, the higher the preference score. The letter indicates the *direction* of the preference, and the number reflects the *consistency* with which the preference is reported. (A high preference score does not imply the level of skill in using the preference.) Hand-scoring templates generate four preference scores (e.g., I 19, S 31, T 17, J 11). The letter portions of the four preference scores indicate the type (e.g., ISTJ).

Continuous Scores. Isabel Myers knew that most researchers in psychology start with a trait perspective. Inevitably, they would correlate MBTI preferences with their trait measures. Therefore she created the formula for continuous scores so that researchers would report their findings in the same way. Continuous scores treat the dichotomies as if there were an underlying continuum. The midpoint is set at 100, and scores are subtracted from 100 for preferences E, S, T, or J; scores are added to 100 for preferences I, N, F, and P. Thus the continuous score for a preference score of E 19 would appear as 81, and a preference score of I 19 would appear as 119. When MBTI continuous scores are correlated with scale scores from other instruments, negative correlations indicate an association between the other measure and E, S, T, or J; positive correlations indicate a correlation between the other measures and MBTI I, N, F, or P. An example from the *Manual* shows correlations of −.75 with the Omnibus Personality Inventory Social Extraversion Scale (p. 181) and +.63 with the MMPI Social Introversion scale (p. 180). Examples of MBTI scores appear in the case studies later in this chapter.

Until recently, most research with the MBTI used continuous scores to compare preferences separately with trait measures. Recent studies (e.g., Pearman & Fleenor, 1996) are taking seriously that "type is the unit of measurement for the MBTI" and are finding predicted differences among the 16 types.

Form F and Form G optical-scanning answer sheets can be scored by computer or by using templates. Form G is also available in a self-scoring version. Hand-scoring is accomplished with five hand-scoring templates— one each for EI, SN, TF male, TF female, and JP. (During construction of the MBTI, all item analyses examined weights for males and females separately; the TF scale is the only one where item weights require separate male and female keys.) Instructions on the templates show how to transform raw scores into preference scores. Computer reports (see case studies) provide a number of subscores and interpretive information. Report forms for recording hand-scored results are available.

Computer scoring by the publisher for Forms J and K also provides expanded information from subscales for MBTI users qualified to purchase Level B tests. An expanded Step II report provides a narrative interpretation of the EAR scales. A Type Differentiation Indicator (TDI) report from Form J is available to MBTI users qualified to purchase Level C tests. The TDI provides scores for seven "comfort scales" from Myers's research items. Other computer-generated reports for couples, managers, careers, learning styles, and other applications are also available or in development by CPP. [Editor's Note: In the fall of 1998, after this book was in production, Consulting Psychologists Press completed a major revision of the MBTI and published Form M, now the standard version of the MBTI, and a revised *Manual* (Myers, McCaulley, Quenk, & Hammer, 1998). Scoring data and research cited in this chapter come from Form G, which will be available for an indefinite period. The new form M followed the same principles Myers used in the earlier forms and does not change any of the theoretical and interpretive sections of this chapter.

In 1977 Isabel Myers completed the Form G revision essentially alone. In 1998 Form M was developed by a team of experts. Myers mainly used student samples. The Form M revision included one sample more representative of the total population and another sample of adults who had verified the accuracy of their Form G type preferences.

Form G has 126 items, 94 scored for type, plus 32 research items. The Form M team began with a set of 290 items tried out by Myers over the years plus 290 more suggested by others. The team, in a series of studies, narrowed down the list of 580 items to 93, using Item Response Theory to validate each item's accuracy in identifying type and to establish new item weights. Of the 94 Myers Form G items, 51 are retained in Form M's 93 items, all of which are scored for type. Scoring is simplified to unit weights and the same TF key can be used for males and females.

Form G and Form M both use items in forced-choice format and include phrase questions and word pairs. The MBTI is based on the assumption that type preferences are not continuous "trait" scores, but reflect different pathways to excellence and are dichotomous "type" scores. Myers attempted in all previous forms to weight items to achieve precision at the midpoint. Form M scoring substantially increases precision.

Reliabilities of Form M are mainly in the .90 range, slightly higher than those of Form G. The 1998 *Manual* includes many of the validity data of the 1985 *Manual*, plus validity of new research using Form M. Most of the validity data in the 1985 *Manual* focused on the preferences for EI, SN, TF, and JP. The 1998 *Manual* also includes validity data separately for the 16 types.

Form M simplifies earlier versions of the MBTI in three ways: all questions have just 2 choices; item weights on the TF scale are the same for males and females; and all weights are 0 or 1. Like Form G, Form M can be hand-scored or computer-scored. Both are also available in a self-scorable version.]

The Final Step in Scoring: Translating the Type Formula Into Type Descriptions

MBTI scoring generates a four-letter code to indicate one of the 16 types. The last step in scoring is the *type description*. Myers's type descriptions describe Jung's type dynamics in everyday language. Each description is a portrait of a well-developed type, ending with the type's problems when perception or judgment is undeveloped. Reading the best-fit description is usually self-confirming. Gifts can be acknowledged. Weaknesses can be recognized as blind spots coming from the emphasis on gifts. The concept of "mutual usefulness of opposites" promotes appreciation for one's own qualities and respect for others. The dynamic aspects of type theory provide a useful map for type development, for recognizing our vulnerabilities when "in the grip" of the inferior function, and for integrating previously unrecognized preferences in the process of lifelong growth. The four cases present the data from scoring and Myers's type descriptions.

In addition to the type description for the individual, a unique feature of the MBTI is the description of groups in *type tables*. Type tables provide a wealth of information for understanding career patterns, family interactions, teamwork in work groups, and even implications for the larger society. For example, what is the likelihood of one-sided social decision making when samples of managers in business, government, education, the military, and the police fall strongly in the four "tough-minded" TJ types whose gifts are in logical analysis and decisiveness? How does society create structures that balance the TJ emphasis of the power structure by giving weight to "the people side" values (F) and openness to new viewpoints with adaptability to change (P)?

MBTI Normative Data

The purpose of the MBTI is to indicate types—that is, the four letters. The most useful "normative data," therefore, concern the question, "How frequent is my type?" If INFJ and ESFJ females each tell the counselor "I feel as if I have no kindred spirits," the counselor will interpret the two comments very differently. INFJ is in fact a relatively rare type, whereas ESFJ is a frequent type among females. The *Manual* (pp. 46–51) provides data on distributions of the types for males and females by age and education level. Means and standard deviations of each preference by age groups were reported in Appendix C (pp. 239–241). The *CAPT Atlas of Type Tables* (Macdaid et al., 1986) provides extensive data on samples grouped by age, education level, and occupation. Because "type is the unit of measurement for the MBTI," the MBTI is concerned with categorical measurement. Norms as used in IQ tests or diagnostic instruments such as the MMPI are not appropriate for the MBTI.

MBTI INTERPRETATION

Initial Explanation

The first important task for the counselor is to help clients discover their best-fit preferences and best-fit type. The *Manual* chapters on Initial Interpretation and Verification (pp. 52–62) and Uses of Type in Counseling (pp. 63–73) describe this process. It is not always possible to identify the best-fit type in one session; sometimes one or more preferences may be in doubt at first. Because a counselor using the MBTI in type development will be helping clients find their unique paths to excellence in their own preferences, it is important to understand what those preferences are. If earlier life has caused true preferences to go underground and be falsified, the counselor would not want to increase falsification. In many cases, the client's reactions to the type description give little doubt about the accuracy of the report. An extreme example was a client who said with astonishment, "I feel as if it X-rayed my soul!" Often there are doubts and questions. These should be taken seriously, especially when the client is being tested during an emotional upheaval or life crisis. As one client described a change in her type report, "My world had fallen in and ISFJ was my hanging-on-by-myfingernails type—I wasn't a very good ISFJ but I was living one day at a time and trying to get my life under control. Now that I'm back on my feet, I come out a spontaneous ENFP where I belong." The *Manual* gave strategies for resolving such issues.

During the initial interpretation, the counselor develops hypotheses. Good type development requires clear perception (through sensing and intuition) and good decision making (through thinking and feeling) It requires a comfortable balance between the inner life (introversion) and the outer world (extraversion). And it leads to understanding oneself and appreciating others. (Experienced counselors will recognize that these goals in the terminology of psychological type are consistent with other models of psychotherapy.)

MBTI reports are very unlike clinical reports written for a professional to integrate with other test data. Myers assumed clients would be told their types and would be taught to use type concepts. Her type descriptions begin with the characteristics of a type with good type development, and end with a brief mention of problems the type may encounter if the dominant and auxiliary are undeveloped. She published privately in 1970 her *Introduction to Type*, written for the persons who answer the Indicator. It described the preferences, the dominant and auxiliary, and the descriptions of each of the 16 types in everyday language. The booklet also briefly described applications in communications, relationships, career choice, in work situations, and in problem solving. As use of the MBTI has grown, other explanatory materials, brief and extended, have appeared and are available from Consulting Psychologists Press, the Center for Applications of Psychological Type, and other sources.

When MBTI results are introduced to individuals or groups, the explainer usually provides a blank profile, describes each preference, and lets the respondent make a self-assessment of how he or she came out on the MBTI. The client writes down the preferred letter, and may plot the estimated strength of preference on the profile. Sometimes, the "Effects of Each Preference in Work Situations" from *Introduction Type* are checked off and discussed. The report from the MBTI is then produced. The counselor is careful to say, "You *came out* an ENFP," never "You *are* an ENFP." The type description is read carefully, "to see if it fits." If the client's earlier self-assessment is another type, the description for that type is read and compared with the MBTI description.

Chapter 5 of the MBTI *Manual* described assumptions about type that are shared with the client, and other specific details of the process of explaining type to individuals or groups. In sessions with clients, counselors use type theory in many ways. For example:

"You said in your MBTI answers that having a constant challenge is important to you" (N).

"When you made that decision, were you following your head (T) or your heart (F)? Can you tell which gave you better advice?"

"We agree that you have been really successful with past jobs where your knowledge of details (S) made you a star. This new assignment is uncomfort-able—it calls on you to use your imagination and look at the 'big picture' (N). You haven't suddenly become incompetent—you are simply moving into an area you haven't developed yet."

"In our culture, women are socialized toward feeling—concern with other peo-ple, tact, sympathy. It sounds as if you have always thrived on logical analysis and being a tough-minded skeptic (T). Your thinking skills serve you well in being a successful engineer. Your mother taught you the social skills, and you can 'turn them on' when you have to. Can you stop feeling guilty that when you use Feeling it seems mechanical to you, and when you use Thinking you 'come alive'? That's your way, and it's legitimate, even if it is not the way of the majority of women."

MBTI Counseling in Different Settings

The MBTI is interpreted at many different levels. Sometimes the main goal is simply to establish the fact that people indeed are different in predictable ways, and that these differences are interesting and valuable. Sometimes the feedback focuses on a specific use—learning styles, teaching styles, communication patterns, or career choices.

A useful strategy to introduce the MBTI is to put people in "type-alike" groups with instructions to discuss their type descriptions. Groups report their consensus of characteristics others need to know to understand their type. Group leaders often give type-related exercises before the members of a group receive their MBTI reports. After group members have received their reports, they see the reasons for their differences in the exercises. Members of type-alike groups describe the experience with words such as "We were all on the same wavelength," "I instantly felt comfortable," "I knew I would be understood," and "We laughed a lot at how alike we were." The group leader shows how type dynamics appear in the similarity and differ-ences of groups. For example, the comment for Extraverted Thinking Types, ESTJ and ENTJ, may point out that "both report high activity and logical decisiveness (ETJ characteristics), but notice that ESTJ talks about practical outcomes and ENTJ talks about leading toward a vision (the difference in the S or N auxiliary)."

Myers's decision-making model is useful with individuals, couples, and groups. Briefly, it involves answering four questions:

What is the situation? (S)

What are the possibilities? (N)

What are the logical consequences of different courses of action? (T) What values must be weighed in the decision? What do you care about? (F)

Myers predicted that the dominant function will carry most weight in this process, but taking all four functions into account will broaden consideration of factors to consider before coming to a final decision.

When the MBTI is used with couples, they may be asked to answer for themselves, and then answer as if they were their partner. The counselor faces a very different situation when the members of a couple are different and know it, from the case when members of a couple are different but each partner sees the other as like oneself. In couples or families, interpretations focus on communications and type differences in behavior, with the goal of creating a climate with respect for and constructive use of differences. Psychotherapists also use the MBTI as an integral framework for reconstructive therapy. Discussions of these issues from practicing therapists can be found in Jones and Sherman (1997), Quenk (1984, 1993), and Provost (1993).

Counselors often find it useful to share their own type preferences with a client. For example, "You prefer to use sensing, and you have learned to be realistic and practical. I prefer to use intuition; my head keeps popping up with new ideas. You are feeling stuck right now. I'm going to let my intuition pop up with new ideas, and then you can let your sensing see if any of them are practical." Here the counselor is teaching "the constructive use of differences" and demonstrating the use of a function that comes less readily to the client.

Experienced counselors often say, "You cannot help others with type until you understand your own type." The MBTI counseling process teaches type development, not only to the client, but to the counselor as well. NF counselors, for example, discover when their intuitive hunches and feeling values are or are not trustworthy. "My intuition with clients is usually on target, but I've learned to trust it less if the issue is my own issue about asking for help." As they grow in knowledge of type, NF counselors gain new respect for their own less preferred sensing and thinking and grasp opportunities to learn more about S and T (often from clients of types different from themselves).

Cautions

The MBTI can be seen as deceptively simple. Type descriptions can seem like those in popular magazine "personality tests." Type theory is powerful, but of course it is not infallible. The counselor needs to be alert for the danger that the client puts too much weight on the type and type description. This danger is greater with the MBTI types than with trait instruments, where a shift of T-scores from 49 to 55 does not have the significance that a shift of letters from S 7 to N 7 will have.

It is easy also for the client, and the counselor, to assume that a clear preference necessarily means high skill. It is logical to assume that if people are clear about preferences, they will be more likely to follow them and develop the skills that go with the exercise of those preferences. This logical sequence often occurs, but there can be many events—lack of opportunity, competing pressures, lack of basic ability—that can cause a discrepancy between preferences and acquisition of the abilities of those preferences.

The MBTI is a self-report instrument. Like any self-report instrument, validity is increased if the respondent is motivated to answer honestly. Because the MBTI is administered in so many nonclinical settings, the counselor must be especially aware of environmental pressures that interfere with true responses. Especially in organizational settings where respondents are not sure what use will be made of the information, there is a strong motivation to answer "as I think 'they' want me to."

As with any other psychological testing, results should be treated with great caution when the MBTI is answered by persons in severe distress. It is useful sometimes to see if the client can answer "as you are feeling today" and "as you used to feel when you were well." We have found it helps in family conferences in an inpatient setting to engage the family in the early stage of guessing types, before the MBTI reports are given. Insights from the discussion about whether the patient is acting as an introvert now, or has always been an introvert, have opened new communications.

CASE EXAMPLES

A major use of the MBTI in counseling is as a tool to conceptualize the problem and the client–counselor interaction. The four cases that follow show how the counselor uses different strategies, and focuses on different aspects of the problem, as a function of the client's type. The cases represent examples of the four combinations of perception and judgment:

Case A: Henry Gray (ESTJ)—Attend to realities (S); decide with objective analysis (T).

Case B: Jean White (ESFJ)—Attend to realities (S); decide with personal warmth (F).

Case C: George Black (ENFP)—Attend to possibilities (N); decide with personal warmth (F).

Case D: Tracy Brown (INTP)—Attend to possibilities (N); decide with objective analysis (T).

A basic strategy when using type in counseling is the familiar "build on strengths to overcome weaknesses." In the context of type, this means:

Assess the development of the dominant and auxiliary functions.

Consider the likelihood that the auxiliary is not providing sufficient balance.

Consider whether the third and fourth functions are available when needed.

Use the motivation of the dominant and auxiliary to develop the third and fourth functions. (Isabel Myers spent years on MBTI statistics [tertiary S and inferior T] to create an instrument that would help people—a goal desired by her dominant feeling and her auxiliary intuition.)

If the problem seems to reside in the inferior or fourth function, do not attack the problem head on; the inferior function is the source of the greatest vulnerability, as well as holding the potential for positive change. Von Franz (1971) and Quenk (1993) discussed these issues in some detail.

Consider issues such as the frequency of the type, the types of others in the environment, whether life history has encouraged falsification of type, and whether there is a match or mismatch between the type and current occupation.

For students, consider the relationship between type and intelligence. Note especially unexpected failures or unexpected successes—for example, the unexpected failure of an "IN academic type" who is not interested in learning, or the unexpected success of the "hands-on, just-do-it" ESTP type who is excelling in academic work.

Be aware of the communication style of the client's type, including pacing, words, use of symbolism and metaphors, and the amount of interaction or quiet for contemplation needed to establish rapport.

Consider the counselor's own type, values and blind spots, and especially communication style, in the therapeutic interaction. An example may make this point clearer. A dominant thinking type and a dominant feeling type were discussing their attitudes toward family therapy. The feeling type counselor said, "It is so rewarding to bring harmony after strife, but even after all these years, when they yell and scream at each other, my stomach knots up." The thinking type counselor replied, "Not for me. I am so interested in analyzing what remark set off what reaction that I don't react to the screaming at all."

In short, type provides a rich tapestry of hypotheses and expectations to be tested in the therapeutic encounter.

Case A. Henry Gray (ESTJ)

Henry Gray was a 47-year-old successful businessman who had taken the MBTI with his wife at a parent group conducted by the school counselor. He had come out an ESTJ (extraverted thinking type with sensing). Figure 5.2 shows the ESTJ type description given to Mr. Gray, and Fig. 5.3 shows the detailed scoring information provided to the counselor. Mr. Gray's preferences were clear and consistent. (Refer back to the section on scoring as a reminder about points, preference scores, and continuous scores.)

Later, Mr. Gray made a separate appointment to discuss with the counselor his frustration with his son Jim, now a high-school sophomore. In the appointment, he described his attitude toward the responsibilities of parenthood. In brief terms, he listed his duties to be a good parent: (1) Make him tough because it's a tough world out there; (2) make him persistent because no one ever gets anywhere if he gives up; and (3) make him an upright citizen because we need morality in our society.

He listed Jim's misbehaviors. The counselor repeatedly asked variations of, "Why do you suppose Jim does that when he knows you don't like it?" The responses were variations of, "He mustn't do it. It is wrong for him."

As he described his interactions with Jim, the counselor saw a picture of a constant stream of commands, complaints, and corrections. Even when father and son did things together, Henry seemed to use the occasions to correct Jim's every effort. Behind what came across as a barrage of nagging, the counselor began to see great love and concern for Jim.

"Mr. Gray, every time I ask you how the situation may look from Jim's point of view, you tell me how wrong Jim is. I am not there when you talk to Jim, but what you describe is a constant stream of criticism from you. I believe you are doing this because you love Jim and are trying to help him be a good and successful man in a difficult world. I am asking you to stop and think what your interactions seem like to *Jim*."

Mr. Gray stopped, sat quietly, and shook his head.

"If Jim were here, and I asked him, 'Jim, what does your father think of you,' what would he say?"

After a pause, Mr. Gray said slowly, "He would probably say, 'Dad thinks I'm no good and I never do anything right.' "

"If a person feels no good and that he never does anything right, how easy is it for him to motivate himself to try harder?"

"Impossible, I would estimate."

"Mr. Gray, you love Jim and want him to be a strong, good man. You are trying to teach him by showing him whenever he is off track. The result isn't

Myers–Briggs Type Indicator Report

This report was prepared for
HENRY GRAY   CASE A

Here is the report of the Myers-Briggs Type Indicator (MBTI) which you answered on February 11th, 1998. The MBTI indicates sixteen types of people. Your answers to the MBTI questions came out the type called **Extraverted Thinking with Sensing**, also known by the letters **ESTJ**.

The author of the MBTI, Isabel Briggs Myers, wrote sixteen descriptions of the types at their best; the end of each report describes problems which persons of that type may have when not at their best. This page of your report describes type ESTJ. Page 2 and 3 give reasons why the sixteen types are different from one another, and tell more about your answers. Some people prefer to read their description first; others prefer to read the reasons first. Whichever way you prefer, be sure to read all three pages to see your full report.

ESTJ
Extraverted Thinking with Sensing

ESTJ people use their thinking to run as much of the world as may be theirs to run. They like to organize things and get them done. Reliance on thinking makes them logical, analytical, impersonal, objectively critical, and not likely to be convinced by anything but reasoning.

They focus their thinking on the people and things in the world around them. They organize facts, situations and operations well in advance, and make a systematic effort to reach their carefully planned objectives on schedule. They have little patience with confusion or inefficiency, and can be tough when the situation calls for toughness.

They think conduct should be governed by logic and they govern their own behavior by logic as much as they can. They live their lives according to a definite set of rules that embody their basic judgments of the world. Any change in their ways requires a conscious change in their rules.

They are more interested in seeing present realities than future possibilities. This makes them matter-of-fact, practical, realistic, fact-minded, concerned with here and now. They use past experience to help them solve problems. ESTJ's are more curious about new facts and new things than about new ideas. They want to be sure that ideas, plans and decisions are based on solid fact. As they do not listen to their own intuition very much, they usually need an intuitive around to sell them on the value of new ideas.

They like jobs where the results of their work are immediate, visible and tangible. They have a natural bent for business and industry, production and construction. They enjoy administration, and like to decide what ought to be done next and give the necessary orders. Getting things done is their strong suit.

Like the other decisive types, ESTJ's run some risk of deciding too quickly before they have fully seen the situation. All the decisive types need to stop and listen to the other person's side of the matter, especially with people under them who can't talk back. This is seldom easy for ESTJ's. But IF they do not take time to understand, they may judge too hastily, without enough facts or enough regard for what other people think or feel.

ESTJ's may rely so much on the logical approach of thinking that they overlook their feeling values--what they care about and what other people care about. They may decide that something they value is not important, just because it isn't logical to care about it. Thinking and feeling can often lead to different decisions. If ESTJ's always let their thinking suppress their feeling, their feeling will not develop and be manageable. If feeling values are ignored too much, they may build up pressure and explode in most inappropriate ways.

ESTJ's need to find positive ways to take feeling values into account. One useful way to use feeling is to appreciate other people's merits. ESTJ's see what is illogical so they are naturally critical; therefore appreciation comes harder for ESTJ's than for the feeling types. But ESTJ's can learn to make it a rule to mention what is well done, not merely what needs correcting. The results will be worthwhile, both in their work and in their private lives.

FIG. 5.2. Myers–Briggs Type Indicator Report (Case A). *Note:* Copyright 1991 by Publisher, Consulting Psychologists Press, Palo Alto, California, 94306. All rights reserved. Printed by Center for Applications of Psychological Type, Inc., 2815 NW 13th Street, Suite 401, Gainesville, Florida, 32609 under license from Publisher. Reprinted with permission.

Myers-Briggs Type Indicator

Detailed Scoring Information

Professional report for
Dr. Mary McCaulley

MBTI results for
HENRY GRAY CASE A

E Extravert	Introvert I
S Sensing	Intuition N
T Thinking	Feeling F
J Judgment	Perception P

59 49 39 29 19 9 9 19 29 39 49 59

ESTJ - Extraverted Thinking with Sensing

FULL SCALE RESULTS (*Parts I,II and III of the MBTI*)

		EI Direction of Energy	SN Perception Function	TF Judgment Function	JP Extraverted Attitude		Total Points	
ESTJ	Preference Scores:	E 15	S 39	T 51	J 27	E	18	I 10
			Auxiliary (Introverted)	Dominant (Extraverted)		S	23	N 3
						T	27	F 1
						J	21	P 7

PHRASE QUESTIONS (*Parts I and III of the MBTI*).
These questions ask for responses to everyday events and may therefore be more influenced by the demands of these events.

						Phrase Points	
					E	13	I 9
					S	10	N 2
ESTJ	Preference Scores: E 7	S 15	T 15	J 17	T	8	F 0
					J	13	P 4

WORD PAIR QUESTIONS (*Part II of the MBTI*).
Word pairs are less affected by everyday events and may be nearer to true preferences.

						Word Pair Points	
					E	5	I 1
					S	13	N 1
ESTJ	Preference Scores: E 7	S 23	T 37	J 9	T	20	F 1
					J	8	P 3

Answer Sheet Information

Sex	Male
Computed Age is	47
Highest grade completed	16
Are you a student?	No
Likes practical skills best	
Are you working?	Yes
Date of birth	01/28/51
Form G answered on	02/11/98
Total items available	126
Last item answered was	126

Continuous Scores

	Full Scale	Phrase	Word Pair	X Half	Y Half
EI	85	93	93	93	93
SN	61	85	77	81	81
TF	49	85	63	67	81
JP	73	83	91	77	97

Group Code	4U	-98
Case Id	#5161-3	
Date Scored	10/26/98	

Item Omissions

EI	scored items omitted	0
SN	scored items omitted	0
TF	scored items omitted	0
JP	scored items omitted	0
Subtotal of omissions		0
Research items omitted		1
Total omissions	.	1

FIG. 5.3. Myers–Briggs Type Indicator Detailed Scoring Information (Case A).
Note: Copyright 1991 by Publisher, Consulting Psychologists Press, Palo Alto, California, 94306. All rights reserved. Printed by Center for Applications of Psychological Type, Inc., 2815 NW 13th Street, Suite 401, Gainesville, Florida, 32609 under license from Publisher. Reprinted with permission.

what you want; he is becoming resentful and losing confidence in himself. There are strategies that work better. Let me give you some well-established facts about children his age, to see if we can find a better strategy."

The counselor briefly outlined research that children model after people they admire, and by whom they feel loved. He described in practical terms the implications of Jim's developmental level. Together, the counselor and Mr. Gray developed a plan whereby Mr. Gray would (a) work to listen and understand, (b) work to suspend judgment, (c) teach Jim in a relaxed way, with Jim's level in mind, (d) watch for Jim's successes—even small ones—and make an appreciative comment, and (e) schedule activities together that they both could enjoy on a man-to-man basis.

The counselor did not see Mr. Gray again, but she noticed that Jim's grades began to improve and he seemed better able to stand up for himself with his classmates.

In terms of type dynamics, Mr. Gray was using his dominant thinking to comment on what was out of line in Jim's behavior, but was not using his thinking to look at the logical outcomes of these constant criticisms. The counselor tried to get him to turn off his dominant thinking and use his auxiliary sensing to observe and understand Jim. She gave him specific behavioral guidelines for making these observations of Jim so that he could develop empathy by experience. (Intuition and feeling are the functions most closely associated with empathy and insight; N and F are less accessible to ESTJs.)

The counselor tried to convey psychological insight in practical, logical, sequential terms suitable to Mr. Gray's ST style of dealing with the world. His original logical formula for being a good parent was made specific and a more appropriate formula was put in its place. He was also encouraged to suspend judgment (T) and stay more of the time in the perceptive attitude (using his S) so that he could understand Jim more. The counselor was brief, to the point, and factual. The door was open if he wished to discuss other problems, but the counselor did not expect Mr. Gray would seek or see much sense in treatments that involve "just sitting around and talking."

Case B. Jean White (ESFJ)

Jean White was a 42-year-old married woman with two children. Her son, Tom Junior, was a freshman in college; her daughter, Susan, was a junior in high school. Mrs. White had been a secretary in an interior design firm when she married her husband Tom, a civil engineer. She gave up her job when Tom Junior was born. During the early child-rearing years, she was active in the Parent Teacher Association and other community groups. She met the counselor when he explained the MBTI to a board on which she served. After the meeting, Mrs. White took the counselor aside and asked for an appointment to discuss "family problems."

Mrs. White appeared for her first appointment, attractive, well-groomed, and confident. She began by saying she was feeling angry at her children and her husband "for no reason at all." She took control of the interview, volubly describing her husband, her perfect marriage, her children, and the many demands of her life. Suddenly she became quiet, and then added slowly, looking away, that she came to counseling because for no good reason she was very unhappy.

As the counselor had listened for themes in the deluge of words, he had heard, "I try so hard but they don't appreciate me." "I can see so clearly what they need, and I tell them and tell them, but they won't listen to me. In fact, they tell me not to be so bossy." "They hurt my feelings but they don't mean to." She had watched the counselor carefully. Twice she asked, "Am I giving you what you need?"

After the session, the counselor reviewed Mrs. White's MBTI reports. Figure 5.4 shows the type description the counselor had given Mrs. White at the board meeting. Figure 5.5 is the counselor's detailed scoring information for Mrs. White's MBTI scores. She had come out an ESFJ (extraverted feeling dominant, with sensing her introverted auxiliary and thinking her introverted inferior function).

Based on the reports and his knowledge of extraverted feeling types, the counselor set his tentative goals and expectations:

Extraverted feeling is very sensitive to disharmony, and anxious to please. He must be alert that she not hide her real feelings in order to be a "good patient." Transference issues may have to be dealt with if her need for affiliation leads to her putting him on a pedestal.

There is probably considerably more friction in the family than she acknowledges to herself. With her dominant feeling, she will probably try to explain away others' behaviors that hurt her.

Extraverted feeling types tend to look outward for validation of self-worth. Is she working too hard to gain the approval of others?

As her youngest child leaves the nest, where will she use her ESFJ gift of nurturing others? One quiet, self-sufficient, engineer husband cannot comfortably absorb all the dynamic, loving energy of an ESFJ.

Is she ready at midlife to take some "Jean time"? Has she been denying herself time to develop talents in herself because of her concerns for the family?

In the early weeks of counseling, Jean controlled the sessions with her voluble descriptions of the week's events. A picture emerged of her increasingly desperate attempts to make the family do what was good for them, and the family's increasing resistance. With quiet questions from the counselor about the specifics of events, Jean began to see that many times she would see something that clearly would be helpful, and rush in and take

Myers-Briggs Type Indicator Report

This report was prepared for
JEAN WHITE CASE B

Here is the report of the Myers-Briggs Type Indicator (MBTI) which you answered on May 11th, 1998. The MBTI indicates sixteen types of people. Your answers to the MBTI questions came out the type called **Extraverted Feeling with Sensing**, also known by the letters **ESFJ**.

The author of the MBTI, Isabel Briggs Myers, wrote sixteen descriptions of the types at their best; the end of each report describes problems which persons of that type may have when not at their best. This page of your report describes type ESFJ. Page 2 and 3 give reasons why the sixteen types are different from one another, and tell more about your answers. Some people prefer to read their description first; others prefer to read the reasons first. Whichever way you prefer, be sure to read all three pages to see your full report.

ESFJ
Extraverted Feeling with Sensing

ESFJ people radiate warmth and fellowship. They are concerned chiefly with people and they place a high value on harmonious human contacts. They are particularly warmed by approval and sensitive to indifference. Much of their pleasure and satisfaction comes from the warmth of feeling of people around them and from their own warm feelings.

ESFJ's enjoy admiring people, and so they tend to concentrate on the admirable qualities of other people. They base their decisions on their personal values and they try to live up to their ideals. They are loyal to respected persons, institutions or causes, often to the point of idealizing whatever they admire.

They are unusually able to see value in other people's opinions. Even when opinions are in conflict, they have faith that harmony can somehow be achieved and they often manage to bring it about. They are friendly, tactful, sympathetic, and can almost always express the right feeling. To bring harmony, they are ready to agree with other people's opinions within reasonable limits; in this process, they need to be careful that they don't concentrate so intensely on other people's viewpoints that they lose sight of the value of their own ideas.

They are mainly interested in the realities perceived by their five senses, so they become practical, realistic, and matter-of-fact. ESFJ's appreciate and enjoy their possessions. They take great interest in the details of their experiences. They like to base their plans and decisions upon known facts. They enjoy variety but usually adapt excellently to routine.

They are at their best in jobs that deal with people and any situations where cooperation can be brought about through good will. ESFJ's are found in jobs such as selling, some kinds of direct supervision, teaching, preaching, face-to-face cooperative work, etc. Their compassion and awareness of physical conditions often attract them to health fields where they can provide patient care. They are less likely to be happy in work demanding mastery of abstract ideas or impersonal analysis.

They think best when talking with people, and enjoy talk. They have to make a special effort if they are to be brief and businesslike and not let sociability slow them down on the job.

They like to have matters decided or settled, but they do not need or want to make all the decisions themselves. They have many definite "shoulds" and "should nots" and may express these freely. They are persevering, conscientious, orderly even in small matters, and are inclined to expect others to be the same.

They run some risk of jumping to conclusions before they understand a situation. IF they have not taken time to gain firsthand knowledge about a person or situation, their actions may not have the helpful results they intended. For example, ESFJ's beginning a new project or a new job may do things as they judge they *should* be done, instead of taking the pains to find out how the organization works or what is *really* wanted.

ESFJ's find it harder than other types to see things they wish were not true. They find it especially hard to admit the truth about problems with people or things they care about. IF they fail to face disagreeable facts, or IF they refuse to look at criticisms that hurt, they will sweep their problems under the rug instead of finding good solutions.

Myers-Briggs Type Indicator
Detailed Scoring Information

Professional report for
Dr. Mary McCaulley

MBTI results for
JEAN WHITE CASE B

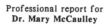

E Extravert		Introvert **I**
S Sensing		Intuition **N**
T Thinking		Feeling **F**
J Judgment		Perception **P**

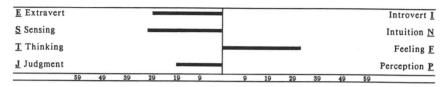

| 59 | 49 | 39 | 29 | 19 | 9 | | 9 | 19 | 29 | 39 | 49 | 59 |

ESFJ – Extraverted Feeling with Sensing

FULL SCALE RESULTS (*Parts I, II and III of the MBTI*)

		E I Direction of Energy	**S N** Perception Function	**T F** Judgment Function	**J P** Extraverted Attitude		**Total Points**		
ESFJ	Preference Scores:	E 29	S 31	F 33	J 19	E	21	I	6
			Auxiliary (Introverted)	Dominant (Extraverted)		S	21	N	5
						T	4	F	20
						J	20	P	10

PHRASE QUESTIONS (*Parts I and III of the MBTI*).
These questions ask for responses to everyday events and may therefore be more influenced by the demands of these events.

Phrase Points

ESFJ	Preference Scores:	E 23	S 15	F 19	J 15	E	16	I	4
						S	11	N	3
						T	0	F	9
						J	13	P	5

WORD PAIR QUESTIONS (*Part II of the MBTI*).
Word pairs are less affected by everyday events and may be nearer to true preferences.

Word Pair Points

ESFJ	Preference Scores:	E 5	S 15	F 15	J 3	E	5	I	2
						S	10	N	2
						T	4	F	11
						J	7	P	5

Answer Sheet Information

Sex	Female
Computed Age is	42
Highest grade completed	14
Are you a student?	No
Likes _ best	
Are you working?	No
Date of birth	01/30/56
Form G answered on	05/11/98
Total items available	126
Last item answered was	126

Continuous Scores

	Full		Word	X	Y
	Scale	Phrase	Pair	Half	Half
EI	71	77	95	83	89
SN	69	85	85	83	87
TF	133	119	115	113	121
JP	81	85	97	89	93

Group Code	4U -98
Case Id	#5161-2
Date Scored	10/26/98

Item Omissions

EI	scored items omitted 0
SN	scored items omitted 0
TF	scored items omitted 0
JP	scored items omitted 0

Subtotal of omissions	0
Research items omitted	2
Total omissions	2

FIG. 5.5. Myers–Briggs Type Indicator Detailed Scoring Information (Case B).
Note: Copyright 1991 by Publisher, Consulting Psychologists Press, Palo Alto, California, 94306. All rights reserved. Printed by Center for Applications of Psychological Type, Inc., 2815 NW 13th Street, Suite 401, Gainesville, Florida, 32609 under license from Publisher. Reprinted with permission.

over, making great effort. She then m! .mized the efforts she had made and shook off thanks. People began to expect her to take over and took her efforts for granted. Worse, especially at home, the family saw her helpful actions as nagging and interference. She began to see how she was losing the appreciation she so wanted, and often deserved, by jumping before she fully understood the problem from others' points of view.

She began to stop and learn what would be appreciated before she offered help. Slowly she began to separate her times of genuine, relaxed helpfulness from the helpfulness forced on others so she could be appreciated. To her surprise, she found that her "go slow and ask" approach was bringing better solutions and more cooperation.

Always voluble in the sessions, she began to feel safe enough to become quiet and share the desperation of her unhappiness. "I am in a boat in a lake. Everyone around the shore is having fun. I am all alone, and calling for help. No one listens to me." Gingerly she began to explore the desperation of her need to please, including pleasing the counselor. Slowly, as they explored the process together, she found it was safe to "say what I really think." She began to explore her secret dreams for her future—tentatively, because taking time for herself seemed selfish.

The counselor was sensitive to the deep hurts beneath the socially poised facade, and helped her appreciate that when she went overboard trying to be helpful, she had "got in wrong trying to do right." They processed her feelings of hurt and rejection when the counselor was late or took a vacation, at which times she became superficial and overly "understanding" of his need for time away from "demanding people like me."

At the conclusion of counseling she was more at peace with her family and friends, and with herself. She was planning to return to college, and to prepare herself to teach middle school where she could help children at a critical developmental stage. Some of the insights she shared with the counselor were:

"I was out of touch with how sensitive I am. I didn't know how things hurt me a lot. I used to pretend it didn't happen. I would say 'I don't need you!' I learned about feeling my feelings."

"It took me six months to hear you say 'Why do you want to be perfect?' It was such an alien thought. Then I had another insight. If I don't have to be perfect, they don't have to be perfect."

"I can make requests now, not demands. Somehow they do more of the things I ask them to. And we feel closer. I don't push as much. I am able just to be alive. And when I don't try to do everything I get more done."

In terms of type dynamics, Jean had been so ruled by need for harmony of her dominant feeling that she had not achieved the balance of her sensing auxiliary. She needed the balance of using her perception before imposing her extraverted feeling on her world. As she learned to slow down and see more around her, she learned to trust her common sense and her feeling judgments became more appropriate. Her litany of "You must do this for your own good" subsided. She could listen more to Tom Junior and Susan, and they began to share more with her. As she developed her introverted side, she became better able to enjoy "alone time" with no outside demands. She could listen to "Jean's needs" without feeling selfish, and she became less vulnerable to the demands or criticisms of others.

Case C. George Black

George Black was a 31-year-old counseling student in the second year of a doctoral program. Before graduate school he taught social studies in an inner-city high school. He was a popular teacher, committed to his students and to helping them become better citizens. George found projects in the community where students could "learn by doing." With his high energy and good humor, he became a community leader. After 7 years in teaching, he became restless for new challenges. He was dismayed to find that some students he tried to help continued to have problems, and had decided he needed more skills. After inquiring from friends and colleagues, he had settled on counseling and gained admission to a rigorous program 100 miles from his home. The first year was a dramatic change of pace from his high-energy, high-involvement former life. He took the MBTI as part of a course in using tests in counseling, and agreed that ENFP described him well. George was gratified to see that ENFP is a frequent type among counselors; he had made a good choice. Figure 5.6 shows the ENFP type description given to George. Figure 5.7 is his advisor's detailed scoring information for George's MBTI scores.

When the class discussed type dynamics, he learned that his dominant function was intuition, used in an extraverted way. Looking back on his life, he could see how galvanized he had always been by possibilities for action. And he agreed that there had been times when, once the challenging part of a project was past, he had dropped it to go on to the next challenge. The challenges that energized him most had always been "possibilities for people" (extraverted dominant N, auxiliary introverted feeling). He began to understand problems he was having at his stage in the program: too many papers (introversion), too much study (introversion), too little "action" (extraversion). He had 6 long months to go before exams. Then practicum would come—he could work with people again and apply his new-found knowledge.

Suddenly, a new possibility for volunteering part time with a boys group was too good to resist. He threw himself into it, getting to know the boys,

Myers–Briggs Type Indicator Report

This report was prepared for
GEORGE BLACK CASE C

Here is the report of the Myers-Briggs Type Indicator (MBTI) which you answered on April 17th, 1998. The MBTI indicates sixteen types of people. Your answers to the MBTI questions came out the type called **Extraverted Intuition with Feeling**, also known by the letters **ENFP**.

The author of the MBTI, Isabel Briggs Myers, wrote sixteen descriptions of the types at their best; the end of each report describes problems which persons of that type may have when not at their best. This page of your report describes type ENFP. Page 2 and 3 give reasons why the sixteen types are different from one another, and tell more about your answers. Some people prefer to read their description first; others prefer to read the reasons first. Whichever way you prefer, be sure to read all three pages to see your full report.

ENFP
Extraverted Intuition with Feeling

ENFP people are the enthusiastic innovators in the field of action. They care warmly about new possibilities--new ways of doing things, or new and fascinating things that might be done. They have a lot of imagination and initiative for starting projects and a lot of impulsive energy for carrying them out. They are sure of the worth of their inspirations and tireless with the problems involved. They are stimulated by difficulties and most ingenious in solving them. They get so interested in their newest project that they have time for little else.

They get other people interested, too. They are extremely perceptive about the attitudes of other people, and they aim to understand people rather than to judge them. Sometimes, by putting their minds to it, they achieve an uncanny knowledge of what different people will respond to and they use this understanding to win support for their projects. They adapt to others' opinions in the way they present an objective, but never to the point of giving it up. Their faith in their intuition makes them too individualistic to conform exactly to any group.

Their energy comes from a succession of new enthusiasms; in their world which is full of possible projects, they must pick those that have the greatest potential, either intrinsically or for the ENFP's own development. When it comes to decision-making, ENFP's like to use feeling values rather than thinking. Their feeling is useful in selecting projects by weighing the values of each. Their feeling also shows in the ENFP's concern for people. They are skillful in handling people and often have remarkable insight into their possibilities and

interest in their development. They are much drawn to counseling, where each new person presents a fresh problem to be solved and a fresh insight to be communicated. They can be inspired and inspiring teachers, particularly where they have freedom to innovate. And they can succeed in almost any field that captures their interest--such as in art, journalism, science, advertising, sales, ministry, writing, and so on.

In their quieter moments, their feeling gives them some balancing introversion, and adds depth to the insights supplied by their intuition. At its best, their insight, tempered by judgment, may amount to wisdom.

A real difficulty for ENFP people is that they hate uninspired routine and find it remarkably hard to apply themselves to humdrum detail unconnected with any major interest. Worse yet, they may get bored with their own projects as soon as they have solved the problems and come to plain sailing. They need to learn to carry through and finish what they begin, but they are happiest and most effective in jobs that permit of one project after another, with somebody else taking over as soon as the situation is well in hand.

Because ENFP's are always being drawn to the exciting challenges of new possibilities for action, it is essential that they develop their judgment. IF their judgment is undeveloped, they may commit themselves to ill-chosen projects, fail to finish anything, and squander their inspirations, abilities and energy on irrelevant, half-done jobs. At their worst, they are unstable, undependable, fickle and easily discouraged.

FIG. 5.6. Myers–Briggs Type Indicator Report (Case C). *Note:* Copyright 1991 by Publisher, Consulting Psychologists Press, Palo Alto, California, 94306. All rights reserved. Printed by Center for Applications of Psychological Type, Inc., 2815 NW 13th Street, Suite 401, Gainesville, Florida, 32609 under license from Publisher. Reprinted with permission.

Myers-Briggs Type Indicator
Detailed Scoring Information

Professional report for
Dr. Mary McCaulley

MBTI results for
GEORGE BLACK CASE C

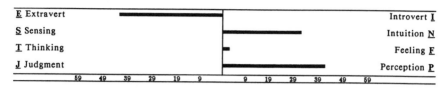

E Extravert	Introvert **I**
S Sensing	Intuition **N**
T Thinking	Feeling **F**
J Judgment	Perception **P**

59 49 39 29 19 9   9 19 29 39 49 59

ENFP - Extraverted Intuition with Feeling

FULL SCALE RESULTS *(Parts I,II and III of the MBTI)*

		EI Direction of Energy	SN Perception Function	TF Judgment Function	JP Extraverted Attitude	Total Points			
ENFP	Preference Scores:	E 43	N 33 Dominant (Extraverted)	F 3 Auxiliary (Introverted)	P 43	E	24	I	2
						S	5	N	21
						T	9	F	10
						J	5	P	26

PHRASE QUESTIONS *(Parts I and III of the MBTI).*
These questions ask for responses to everyday events and may
therefore be more influenced by the demands of these events.

						Phrase Points			
						E	19	I	2
						S	2	N	11
ENFP	Preference Scores:	E 33	N 19	F 1	P 33	T	3	F	3
						J	2	P	18

WORD PAIR QUESTIONS *(Part II of the MBTI).*
Word pairs are less affected by everyday events and may be
nearer to true preferences.

						Word Pair Points			
						E	5	I	0
						S	3	N	10
ENFP	Preference Scores:	E 9	N 15	F 1	P 11	T	7	F	7
						J	3	P	8

Answer Sheet Information

Sex	Male
Computed Age is	31
Highest grade completed	16
Are you a student?	Yes
Likes <u>history</u> best	
Are you working?	No
Date of birth	11/07/66
Form G answered on	04/17/98
Total items available	126
Last item answered was	126

Continuous Scores

	Full Scale	Word Phrase	X Pair	Y Half	Half
EI	57	67	91	73	85
SN	133	119	115	119	115
TF	103	101	101	91	111
JP	143	133	111	121	123

Group Code	4U -98
Case Id	#5161-1
Date Scored	10/26/98

Item Omissions

EI	scored items omitted 1
SN	scored items omitted 0
TF	scored items omitted 0
JP	scored items omitted 0

Subtotal of omissions	1
Research items omitted	1
Total omissions	2

FIG. 5.7. Myers–Briggs Type Indicator Detailed Scoring Information (Case C).
Note: Copyright 1991 by Publisher, Consulting Psychologists Press, Palo Alto, California, 94306. All rights reserved. Printed by Center for Applications of Psychological Type, Inc., 2815 NW 13th Street, Suite 401, Gainesville, Florida, 32609 under license from Publisher. Reprinted with permission.

creating new projects for them, and giving it his all. He became so caught up in it that he no longer *had* the project, the project had *him*. His intuition was totally engaged. Deadlines for the project and deadlines for term papers were upon him. He picked up his pace, juggling academic and volunteer work with frenzied energy. Suddenly he awoke to find himself in the infirmary. A fellow student had found him unconscious. He was totally exhausted and had slept 24 hours before awakening. His adviser visited, found his life was not in danger, and together she and George pieced together what had happened. She learned about the volunteer project, and the insights from his term paper. She was enthusiastic about both, and the contributions George had been making in class discussions. She made it clear that with his capacity for insight and creativity, and his dedication to helping others, he was on the road to becoming a very good counselor.

Then she listened to his account of the days before his collapse, and asked him, "When did you eat?" George didn't remember. "When did you get some sleep?" George didn't remember. "Do you remember being hungry or sleepy?" George pondered. "I think maybe, but I was on such a roll getting everything done that I didn't pay much attention." The advisor told George that in the 1960s the Counseling Center at Auburn University found that students who were hospitalized in the infirmary for exhaustion were significantly more likely to have dominant intuition on the MBTI.

The adviser and George tested how type theory might explain what happened to George. His dominant intuition had clearly been in charge. His inferior function, sensing, was alert to the signs of exhaustion. Sensing sent messages, "You haven't eaten." The intuition drowned them out. Sensing sent messages, "You haven't slept." Intuition drowned them out. Finally, the inner sensations that had been ignored built up such force that George could no longer ignore them and he collapsed. They talked about how George had handled overload in the past, and George remembered that when he was caught up in exciting possibilities, his mother told him he "always made himself sick by not taking care of himself." The adviser described George's dilemma from a type perspective:

Extraverted intuitives will always find themselves taking on exciting challenges for action. These are what make life worth living. Given that intuitives are likely to underestimate the time it will take to work out the challenges that excite them, they are more vulnerable to overload than the other types. If they are to achieve their special gifts of understanding and helping people, they need to develop in two ways. First, before accepting new challenges, or when they are already on overload, they need to stop. Ask their auxiliary introverted feeling to weigh the importance of all the competing claims on their attention, and help them choose what is really important. Second, remember that their least developed function is sensing. They are likely to underestimate the complexity of the details that must be handled to accomplish the vision, and the time it will take. They are also unlikely, as George had discovered, to give enough weight to signals that their bodies are on overload. George agreed that when he was very busy, he needed to go against his natural tendency to work harder, and instead should schedule meals and sleeping time.

In working with George, his adviser used type dynamics, first to help him appreciate the gifts of his dominant intuition, second to see the need to use his auxiliary feeling to weigh the importance of the possibilities that attracted him, so that he would not fritter away his time on things he actually cared less about, and third, to be aware of the blind spots of his inferior sensing, in underestimating the importance of details and of messages from his body.

Case D. Tracy Brown (INTP)

Tracy Brown was a 25-year-old brilliant medical student in the second half of her third year in medical school. She was doing very well in a combined MD–PhD program, and thoroughly enjoying her dissertation research. What brought her to the counselor was a very low rating in clinical care during her rotation on obstetrics. She was criticized for her care of a 16-year-old who was expecting her first child within 2 weeks and was frightened that she would die. Tracy had focused on the need for better contraception to prevent future pregnancies. With another patient, she missed essential facts in the family history because, as the patient later told the nurse, "She seemed so cold I didn't want to talk to her." Worse, she was frustrated by patients who would not follow her orders, when it was clearly logical that they needed to stay on their diets and take prescribed medication.

Tracy had taken the MBTI with others of her class, and knew the counselor from the feedback session. She had come out INTP (an introvert with dominant thinking, intuition as auxiliary and feeling as her inferior function) and agreed that the description fitted her well. Figure 5.8 is the INTP description given to Tracy.

INTP is one of the types most attracted to science, with great intrinsic interest in learning for its own sake. Up to now, Tracy had been succeeding in the world of her strengths—ideas (I), theory and abstractions (N), and logical analysis (T). These matters had consumed her interest since high school. She had always found social life dull except when she could talk science with those who shared her interests. Now she was confronted with a situation calling on her neglected extraversion (comfort with interpersonal interactions), and her inferior feeling (warmth, harmony, and interpersonal understanding). She somewhat reluctantly admitted she liked to help patients for the intellectual challenge of "solving the case" (NT) but that she didn't seem to get as personally involved (F) as her classmates. As

Myers–Briggs Type Indicator Report

This report was prepared for
TRACY BROWN CASE D

Here is the report of the Myers-Briggs Type Indicator (MBTI) which you answered on May 23rd, 1998. The MBTI indicates sixteen types of people. Your answers to the MBTI questions came out the type called **Introverted Thinking with Intuition**, also known by the letters **INTP**.

The author of the MBTI, Isabel Briggs Myers, wrote sixteen descriptions of the types at their best; the end of each report describes problems which persons of that type may have when not at their best. This page of your report describes type INTP. Page 2 and 3 give reasons why the sixteen types are different from one another, and tell more about your answers. Some people prefer to read their description first; others prefer to read the reasons first. Whichever way you prefer, be sure to read all three pages to see your full report.

INTP
Introverted Thinking with Intuition

INTP people look for principles that explain outcomes. They rely on thinking to develop these principles. As a result, they become logical, analytical, impersonal, objectively critical, and are not apt to be convinced except by reasoning.

Being introverts, they use their thinking to find the principles underlying whatever they become aware of. They can become so absorbed with an idea that they persevere with it, without depending on external circumstances. They organize ideas and knowledge; they usually do not organize situations or people, unless they must for the sake of their work. In the field of ideas they are decisive and sure. Socially they may be rather shy except with close friends.

INTP's are quiet, reserved, detachedly curious, and quite adaptable so long as their ruling principles are not violated. Then they stop adapting. Their main interest lies in seeing possibilities beyond what is present or obvious or known. Their intuition heightens their quickness of understanding, insight, ingenuity, intellectual curiosity, and their fertility of ideas about problems.

Depending on their interests, INTP's are good at pure science, research, mathematics, or the more complex kinds of engineering; they may become scholars, teachers, or abstract thinkers in fields such as economics, philosophy or psychology. They are more interested in the challenge of reaching solutions to problems than of seeing the solutions put to practical use.

A special problem for INTP's is to make themselves understandable. They want to state the exact truth, but often make it so complicated that few can follow them. If they will scale their points down until they seem too simple to be worth saying, their ideas will be more widely understood and accepted.

INTP's need to check out even their most attractive intuitive ideas against the facts and the limitations the facts impose. They need to be rigorous in checking *all* the facts; they can easily neglect those facts which don't support their idea. Unless INTP's develop their perception, they are in danger of gaining too little knowledge and experience of the world. Then their thinking is done in a vacuum and nothing will come of their ideas.

INTP's may rely so much on the logical approach of thinking that they overlook what other people care about and what they themselves care about. They may decide that something they value is not important, just because it isn't logical to care about it. IF INTP's always let their thinking suppress their feeling values, their feeling will not develop and be manageable. If feeling values are ignored too much, they may build up pressure and explode in most inappropriate ways. Feeling contributes to good personal relationships by stressing that it *does* matter how the other person feels. Small things make a great difference--a word of appreciation where honestly due, or mention of the extent of agreement before any disagreement is spoken. Thinking types are naturally critical and it is harder for them to express appreciation than it is for other types. But if they try, they can develop appreciation and will find it helpful on the job as well as in personal relationships.

FIG. 5.8. Myers–Briggs Type Indicator Report (Case D). *Note:* Copyright 1991 by Publisher, Consulting Psychologists Press, Palo Alto, California, 94306. All rights reserved. Printed by Center for Applications of Psychological Type, Inc., 2815 NW 13th Street, Suite 401, Gainesville, Florida, 32609 under license from Publisher. Reprinted with permission.

Myers–Briggs Type Indicator

Detailed Scoring Information

Professional report for
Dr. Mary McCaulley

MBTI results for
TRACY BROWN CASE D

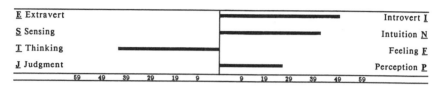

E Extravert	Introvert **I**
S Sensing	Intuition **N**
T Thinking	Feeling **F**
J Judgment	Perception **P**

59 49 39 29 19 9   9 19 29 39 49 59

INTP – Introverted Thinking with Intuition

FULL SCALE RESULTS (*Parts I,II and III of the MBTI*)

		E I Direction of Energy	S N Perception Function	T F Judgment Function	J P Extraverted Attitude		Total Points		
INTP	Preference Scores:	I 51	N 43 Auxiliary (Extraverted)	T 43 Dominant (Introverted)	P 27	E 1 S 2 T 23 J 6		I 26 N 23 F 1 P 19	

PHRASE QUESTIONS (*Parts I and III of the MBTI*).
These questions ask for responses to everyday events and may therefore be more influenced by the demands of these events.

Phrase Points
E 1   I 20
S 0   N 12
T 7   F 0
J 4   P 13

INTP	Preference Scores:	I 39	N 25	T 13	P 19

WORD PAIR QUESTIONS (*Part II of the MBTI*).
Word pairs are less affected by everyday events and may be nearer to true preferences.

Word Pair Points
E 0   I 6
S 2   N 11
T 16   F 1
J 2   P 6

INTP	Preference Scores:	I 13	N 19	T 29	P 9

Answer Sheet Information

Sex	Female
Computed Age is	25
Highest grade completed	16
Are you a student?	Yes
Likes <u>science</u> best	
Are you working?	No
Date of birth	03/11/73
Form G answered on	05/23/98
Total items available	126
Last item answered was	126

Continuous Scores

	Full		Word	X	Y
Scale	Phrase		Pair	Half	Half
EI	151	139	113	125	127
SN	143	125	119	123	121
TF	57	87	71	75	83
JP	127	119	109	123	105

Group Code	4U -98
Case Id	#5161-4
Date Scored	10/26/98

Item Omissions

EI	scored items omitted	0
SN	scored items omitted	2
TF	scored items omitted	3
JP	scored items omitted	3
Subtotal of omissions		8
Research items omitted		2
Total omissions		10

FIG. 5.9. Myers–Briggs Type Indicator Detailed Scoring Information (Case D). *Note:* Copyright 1991 by Publisher, Consulting Psychologists Press, Palo Alto, California, 94306. All rights reserved. Printed by Center for Applications of Psychological Type, Inc., 2815 NW 13th Street, Suite 401, Gainesville, Florida, 32609 under license from Publisher. Reprinted with permission.

she explored her attitudes toward patients, and her concern at her lack of competence in the clinical area, she began to see that she had major blind spots in the interpersonal side of medicine. The counselor commented that this was not infrequently a problem for an INTP, and there was a logical reason for it. Up to now, Tracy had been developing along the lines of her intrinsic strengths—introversion, thinking, and intuition—natural at her time of life. She hadn't been pressed to develop her extraversion and feeling— they were less important for academic success. Clearly, if her attention had been on I and T, it was not surprising that she had overlooked E and F. Tracy now saw a logical (T) reason to develop E and F skills in order to become the competent doctor she had always imagined she would be. And she intended to be a well-rounded doctor.

Tracy and the counselor developed a plan of action. She decided she could not attain and did not need the high levels of empathy that seemed to come so naturally to her classmates with extraversion and feeling—but she *did* need to learn EF skills. Two strategies were set forth. Tracy would observe classmates with these skills to learn formulas of comfort and support until she had found her own empathic style. Second, she would use her intuition to see patterns that would help her understand patients better. As she did these experiments, her thinking would, as always, check them out for cause and effect, so that she could see if she was on target. With a logical reason to do so, Tracy began to spend more time on extraverted activities and on people watching. To her surprise, but not that of the counselor, she began to find that not only was she doing better with patients, but somehow her relationships with her peers and faculty became warmer and more satisfying.

In working with Tracy, the counselor started with the fact that Tracy's MBTI preferences were clear and consistent (see Fig. 5.9, the counselor's detailed scoring information for Tracy's MBTI scores). The principle of type dynamics hypothesized to fit Tracy was that she had neglected her third and fourth functions until confronted with the crisis in patient care. Her dominant logic told her that if she were to succeed, she must be able to manifest more empathy. With the spur from her dominant T, the neglected F activities acquired higher valence. Her auxiliary intuition was challenged to find facts about people's values (F) and behavior (S) that she had hitherto missed. Together her favored N and T made "people watching" intellectually interesting. She forced herself to do more extraverting, because her thinking decided it was the logical way to learn people skills. In short, she developed her less-developed S and F preferences in the service of goals desired by her T and N dominant and auxiliary.

All four of these cases can, of course, be conceptualized differently, and all have other dynamic issues not discussed here. The cases show how type theory provides a framework for looking at counseling issues in a practical and matter-of-fact ST type (Henry Gray), a sympathetic and friendly SF type (Jean White), an enthusiastic and insightful NF type (George Black), and a logical and ingenious NT type (Tracy Brown).

MBTI RESEARCH ISSUES

From the time Isabel Myers and Mary McCaulley founded the Center for Applications of Psychological Type, CAPT has maintained the bibliography for the MBTI. The number of entries in 1975 was 337, in 1985 was 1,022, and in 1991 was 1,736. As of this writing in 1998 references are over 6,300, and growing rapidly in English and other languages. The staff of the Isabel Briggs Myers Memorial Library at CAPT has assisted hundreds of researchers in searching the MBTI Bibliography for references of interest to their research. The 20th Anniversary Special Issue of the *Journal of Psychological Type* (Carskadon & McCarley, 1997) recognized 380 authors of MBTI research from 143 academic institutions. Another indication of the increase in research on the MBTI is that the 1985 *Manual* has 307 pages and the 1998 *Manual* has 420 pages.

The Isabel Briggs Myers Memorial Library is building its collection of overseas MBTI research, with journals and studies from England, Australia, and Japan. In 1997 the library received dissertations from Macedonia and South Africa.

Increase in the use of the Indicator has been accompanied by increase in research and in applications. The 1985 MBTI *Manual* covered reliability and validity from Isabel Myers's early work until 1985. Consulting Psychologists Press has published two updates of MBTI research since 1985. The first is *MBTI Applications: A Decade of Research on the Myers-Briggs Type Indicator*, edited by Allen L. Hammer (1996a). It covers new material on reliability and validity by Robert J. Harvey (1996); career management and counseling by Allen Hammer (1996b); management and leadership by Christa Walck (1996); teams by Allen Hammer and Gregory Huszczo (1996); counseling and psychotherapy by Naomi and Alex Quenk (Quenk & Quenk, 1996); education, learning styles, and cognitive styles by John K. DiTiberio (1996); multicultural applications by Linda Kirby and Nancy Barger (1996); and health, stress, and coping by John Shelton (1996). The second research review is *Developing Leaders: Research and Applications in Psychological Type and Leadership Development*, edited by Catherine Fitzgerald and Linda Kirby (1997). The contributing authors provide a review of the literature on type and leadership, and chapters about type differences in responses to change, decision-making styles, and leadership development. Other contributors relate type differences to measures commonly used in leadership development, includ-

ing the FIRO-B, the 360-Degree Management Feedback Instruments, SYMLOG
Profiles, and management simulations.

Two statements by the authors of these reviews occur repeatedly. First,
Isabel Myers based her work on her understanding of Jung's theory of
psychological types. Her research supported Jung's theory. Research in the
last decade has confirmed and extended Myers's findings. There is solid
support for the construct validity of the MBTI. Second, too much of the
research looks at the four preferences separately, correlating these with
trait measures of other researchers. It is time researchers take seriously
that "type is the unit of measurement for the MBTI." Correlational methods
are popular because most personality research assumes the constructs are
traits. MBTI research needs to move toward analyses of the differences in
the 16 types. The 1998 *Manual* answers these criticisms by citing many
analyses of type differences, not merely correlations with EI, SN, TF, and JP.

The following sections summarize major research findings on the reliability and validity of the MBTI, with a focus primarily on issues important to
counselors and educators. Specifics can be found in the 1985 and 1998
*Manual*s and in *MBTI Applications*.

Reliability

Internal consistency and test–retest reliabilities are presented in Chapter 10
of the 1985 *Manual* and chapter 8 of the 1998 *Manual*. Robert J. Harvey
reviewed recent research on reliability and validity in Chapter 2 of *MBTI
Applications*.

Internal Consistency Reliabilities. Internal consistency reliabilities are
reported for EI, SN, TF, and JP separately, using split-half correlations of
continuous scores and coefficient alpha. Harvey (1996) commented on a
dilemma in split-half reliability for the MBTI. In general, split-half reliabilities
go up when the individual items in a scale correlate highly with each other,
that is, the items are homogeneous. However, when Isabel Myers created
the MBTI, she knew that the action tendencies of each preference led to
many different behaviors. (For example, extraversion might appear in sociability, or being outspoken, or seeking many acquaintances.) She created
behavioral clusters within EI, SN, TF, and JP to reflect the heterogeneity of
behaviors within each. (This fact was not generally known in 1985.) Harvey
pointed out the dilemma for the MBTI because Isabel Myers sought broad
content validity in her items: If the total scale split-half reliability shows
great homogeneity, then Myers's clusters are not showing the heterogeneity
she sought. On the other hand, if the clusters lead to lower reliabilities, the
MBTI will look less reliable than trait instruments with homogeneous characteristics. Myers anticipated this dilemma when she divided the MBTI into

X-half and Y-half for internal consistency reliability research. She selected X and Y items to be sure they gave similar coverage of each cluster.

Reliability estimates for most trait-based personality scales are concerned with scale scores. The MBTI reliability estimates for continuous scores for EI, SN, TF, and JP are comparable to those of trait instruments. Split-half X and Y correlations of continuous scores for 55,971 Form F records and 32,671 Form G records from the MBTI data bank fall between .75 and .86 for EI; .73 and .91 for SN; .76 and .88 for TF; and .80 and .92 for JP. Median split-half correlations for smaller research samples from seventh grade through adults were EI .82, SN .82, TF .77, and JP .92. The lowest correlations occur, as Myers predicted, in small samples of younger, underachieving students; correlations for younger gifted students are in the adult ranges. (Myers was always alert to reliabilities in samples assumed to be at different levels of type development. Her assumption was that good type development implies more consistent judgment, showing itself in more consistency in answering the MBTI.) Harvey (1996) conducted a meta-analysis of the *Manual* internal consistency reliabilities, weighting each correlation by the number of persons in that study. Meta-analysis reliabilities for males were EI .82, SN .85, TF .82, and JP .87, and for females EI .83, SN .85, TF .80, and JP .86. Harvey also reported alpha correlations from his own work on a sample of 2,400. He found a range of alpha estimates of internal consistency reliability of .83 to .86 for females, and .83 to .87 for males. These data are consistent with coefficient alpha reliabilities in the *Manual* (p. 169).

Harvey concluded that the MBTI internal consistency reliabilities may be underestimating the true reliabilities because of the heterogeneity of the scales. The published MBTI split-half reliabilities and the alpha-coefficient reliabilities compare favorably with those of the currently popular trait-based instruments (many of which have longer scales).

Test–Retest Reliabilities.   Three questions are asked when two administrations of the MBTI are compared: First, how high is the correlation between continuous scores for the first and second testing on EI, SN, TF, and JP? Second, how high is the percentage of agreement for E or I, S or N, T or F, and J or P? Third, how often do people come out the same type? Estimates of test–retest reliabilities are expected to be lower than internal consistency reliabilities, because of intervening events and different test conditions. The longer the interval between test and retest, the lower the reliability coefficient is expected to be. The MBTI, however, is designed to indicate types. Therefore reliability estimates also look at consistency of choosing the same preference (E or I, S or N, T or F, and J or P), or of choosing the same four-letter type.

Data reported in the *Manual* for 24 groups with retest intervals from 1 week to 4 years showed median continuous score correlations of EI .84, SN

.81, TF .72, and JP .81. Retest reliabilities showed no consistent patterns of change in two studies with different retest conditions—mood manipulation (Howes, 1977) and career instructions (Parham, Miller, & Carskadon, 1984).

Test–retest agreement of type categories (i.e., letters) for 20 groups including seventh-grade students, college students, medical students, and elementary-school teachers retested after 5 weeks to 6 years yielded a range of agreement from 68% to 89% for E or I, 64% to 92% for S or N, 69% to 88% for T or F, and 66% to 92% for J or P.

To come out the same MBTI type, all four letters must be the same on retest, an event expected to occur by chance only 6.25% of the time. The range for test and retest coming out the same type in 20 samples was from 24% to 61% with a median of 45%. (In the sample with the longest interval, 94 elementary-school teachers retested 6 years later, 61% came out the same type.) In the composite of 13 samples with complete data, the range of samples with either three or four letters the same was 59% to 98% with the median at 77%. In the 12 samples with full data on retest, only 1 person of 1,928 changed all four letters on retest, and only 35 had changed three letters on retest. Additional analysis showed that most changes occurred when the original preference score was low. The median agreements on retest were 68% for low preference scores, 79% for moderate preferences, and 90% for clear preferences.

In summary, for Form G the test–retest reliabilities of the four individual scales are comparable to those of other personality instruments. In the 1998 *Manual*, Form M internal consistency and test–retest reliabilities are higher than those of Form G. On retest, about three-fourths of a sample will come out with three or four letters the same. Most of the changes occur in one preference only, usually a preference with low scores. Counselors, of course, should be alert to a greater possibility of change, because they are seeing people whose type may have been falsified, or who are reporting preferences clouded by distress.

Validity

The MBTI was designed at every step to represent Jung's theory of psychological types. Type theory provides testable hypotheses for construct validity research. Chapter 9 of the 1985 *Manual* and chapter 9 of the 1998 *Manual* covered validity, including correlations of MBTI continuous scores with the scale scores of 30 personality and career interest tests. Thorne and Gough (1991) provided extensive data on construct validity from the creativity studies of the Institute for Personality Assessment and Research at the University of California at Berkeley.

The 1996 *MBTI Applications* and 1997 *Developing Leaders* also reported validity research. The *CAPT Atlas of Type Tables* (Macdaid, McCaulley, & Kainz, 1986) provided construct validity for the hypothesis that people are more likely to select careers that fit their type preferences. Representative findings of interest to counselors appear next.

Career Choice. Myers predicted early in her work that the most important type differences for career selection and satisfaction would be ST, SF, NF, and NT. Sensing and intuition would lead to interests and motivation for work dealing with the specifics and tangible (S) or the symbolic and big picture (N). Thinking and feeling would lead to interests in working with materials and ideas using impersonal analysis (T) or with people and ideas using personal understanding (F). She also predicted that choices of work settings would be associated with EI (E for action and outside work, or I for ideas and inside work), and with JP (J for systems and order, or P or flexibility and change).

Extensive data on type differences in career choice, specialty choice, career satisfaction, turnover, and practical advice for career counseling can be found in the 1985 and 1998 *Manuals*, *MBTI Applications*, and the *Atlas of Type Tables*, as well as in Hammer and Macdaid (1992), Hammer (1993), McCaulley and Martin (1995).

Research shows that all 16 types appear in every career. The pattern of types selecting specific careers is consistent with predictions from type theory. Hammer and Macdaid (1992) listed for each of the 16 MBTI types the top 50 occupations out of the 207 occupations in the *Atlas*. There was almost no overlap between the top 50 occupations of opposite MBTI types. Hammer (1996a) also reported, in the 10-year research review of *MBTI Applications*, that opposite types on the MBTI are associated with opposite themes on Holland's vocational personality types. Turnover is higher when the occupation is a poor fit with type preferences. Research on job satisfaction shows more type-related differences when satisfaction is measured by specific aspects of the job than when global measures of satisfaction are used. MBTI types differ in career values and career decision making. Career counselors find that type enters into each stage of career counseling. Data on college majors and specialties within careers also show type differences congruent with type theory.

Academic Success. Beginning with studies of high-school students and medical students by Isabel Myers, and continuing to the present, extensive research shows type differences in academic aptitude, achievement, learning styles, and teaching styles (*Manual*, Chapter 8; *MBTI Applications*, Hammer, 1996a, Chapter 7). All 16 types can and do succeed academically. To the extent that education requires reading, mathematics, and working with symbols, type theory predicts that student preferring intuition, the function that deals with abstractions and symbols, will have an advantage. Extensive research from the 1950s to the 1990s on academic aptitude in high school, college, graduate school, and professional school confirms that intuitive types average higher academic aptitude scores. Perceiving types, whose curiosity helps them garner a wide range of information, also score higher than the more decisive judging types. When it comes to grades, however, the judging types have a slight edge. These data do not mean that intuitive types are more intelligent than sensing types. Indeed, sensing types do very well (a) when the subject material has more factual, tangible aspects, and (b) when the teacher instructs in the clear, sequential ways that fit a sensing learning style. Data support the hypothesis that the more "academic" IN types (less frequent in the general population) score higher on aptitude and academic achievement tests. They also seek graduate training in proportionately greater numbers. The IN types are concerned with knowledge for its own sake; their opposite ES types are the most likely to see little use in knowledge that cannot be put to practical use. In addition to the *Manual*, considerable research on type differences in learning styles and teaching styles is providing better ways to reach all students.

Correlations With Other Personality and Interest Measures. The *Manual* (pp. 177–206) reported correlations of continuous scores of EI, SN, TF, and JP with scales of personality and interest measures. Some significant relationships were noted early in this chapter in the descriptions of the preferences. Among the largest correlations are those between MBTI EI and the scales of other instruments measuring extraversion or introversion. In general, correlations are in the predicted directions, and MBTI scales do not correlate with measures of unrelated constructs.

Analyses of type differences on scores on other personality tests will enrich test interpretation. Robert McHenry and his colleagues at Oxford Psychologists Press in the United Kingdom have embarked on extensive studies including demographic variables and many psychological tests and other indicators of individual differences.

The type perspective sometimes casts new light on meanings of personality scales that differ from the construct suggested by their names. For example, Thinking Introversion on the Omnibus Personality Inventory is not correlated with Thinking or Introversion. It *is* correlated with Intuition. The manual describes Thinking Introversion as "academic interests," a construct consistent with intuition (*Manual*, Table 11.1, p. 181). The correlation of OPI Intellectual Interests with SJ is less surprising when the manual describes the scale as measuring learning for practical use. On the other hand, the strong correlations of Complexity and Autonomy with NP, the "independent spirits," is consistent with predictions from type theory.

MBTI and Behavioral Ratings

Extensive data from the Institute for Personality Assessment (IPAR) at the University of California at Berkeley (Gough, 1981; Thorne & Gough, 1991) were reported in the *Manual*, and earlier in this chapter. Trained IPAR raters conducted interviews and observed behavior of highly creative people, and a wide range of college students. Researchers at IPAR and elsewhere reported that preferences for intuition (N) and to a lesser extent for perception (P) are significantly associated with measures of creativity (*Manual*, pp. 214–221). Pearman and Fleenor (1996) and Fleenor (1997) reported on behavioral measures for participants in the programs at the Center for Creative Leadership (CCL). These data were reported for the 16 types separately, and were part of a series of studies on the CCL database. The data support predictions from type dynamics.

Individual Agreement with MBTI Reports. An important validation for the MBTI occurs when individuals who answer the MBTI agree with the MBTI results. The first critical task for a counselor is to help the client identify the best-fit type. These issues were described in Chapter 5 of the *Manual*. In some studies, students who read descriptions of types, including their MBTI type and its opposite, significantly more often chose their MBTI type and did not choose its opposite (Carskadon, 1982; Carskadon & Cook, 1982). In other studies, participants went through exercises to identify their work type and their best-fit type, and significantly selected the type in their MBTI reports. When size of scores is taken into account, most of the disagreements occur in cases where the MBTI preference score is low. In summary, both the retest reliability data and the best-fit data show agreement with MBTI type a high percentage of the time, and most disagreements are in preferences that were low (Carskadon, 1982; Carskadon & Cook, 1982; Hammer & Yeakley, 1987; Kummerow, 1988; Walck, 1992; Ware & Yokomoto, 1985). Harvey (1996), in *MBTI Applications*, reviewed the best-fit research and the need for further research, but concluded that "the best-fit type paradigm is perhaps one of the most powerful means of assessing the validity of the instrument's type assignments, and the results of past best-fit studies have been generally quite supportive" (p. 23).

Counselors, of course, should never take the reported type of clients for granted without careful verification.

Research About Counselors and Clients. C. G. Jung, describing reasons for his theory of psychological types in 1936, wrote, "it is an essential means for describing the 'personal equation' of the practicing psychologist, who, armed with an exact knowledge of his differentiated and inferior functions, can avoid many serious blunders in dealing with his patients" (Jung, 1921/1971, p. 555).

What types become counselors? What types seek counseling to help solve their problems? These issues were discussed in the *Manual* (Chapter 6) and *MBTI Applications* (Hammer, 1996a, Chapter 6). Canadian data were reported in Casas and Hamlet (1984). In overview, counselors are more likely to prefer intuition, and, secondarily, feeling. Clients who seek counseling are also more likely to prefer intuition. In theory, intuition is associated with the ability to see patterns and to read between the lines; feeling is associated with motivation to work with and understand people. Figure 5.10 shows a type distribution of counselors from the *CAPT Atlas of Type Tables* (Macdaid et al., 1986). All 16 types are represented. Sixty-three percent are intuitives, and 46% fall in the enthusiastic, insightful NF column.

Almost all samples of mental health professionals show intuitives in the majority. In 13 samples from the *CAPT Atlas of Type Tables*, the median for intuition was 70%. Counselors in the more practical specialties (vocational and rehabilitation counseling) are more evenly divided between S and N types. In contrast to the predominance of intuition among counselors, three-fourths of the general population prefer sensing.

Counselors differ also on the other MBTI preferences. Extraverts outnumber introverts in school, college, and crisis counselors; psychiatrists and psychologists are more closely divided between extraverts and introverts. Feeling types are in the majority among counselors; those counselors who prefer thinking are found in rational-emotive and behavioral specialties.

Quenk and Quenk (1996), in Chapter 6 of *MBTI Applications*, reviewed MBTI research on interest in becoming a counselor, the accuracy of the counselor's interpretations, student–supervisor relationships, preferred methods of counseling, types most likely to seek counseling to solve problems, client–counselor interactions and satisfaction, and outcome. Most studies used EI, SN, TF, and JP preferences, not the 16 types. Specific research questions yielded more significant type differences than broad questions. Intuitive student counselors found it easier to understand non-communicative clients, and to use metaphors and guided imagery. Type enters into counselor preferences for counseling strategies (see reviews in Carskadon, 1979; Carskadon, McCarley, & McCaulley, 1987; Coan, 1979; Levin, 1978; Witzig, 1978). In considering nature versus nurture, extraverted counselors put more weight on the environment. Introverted counselors give greater weight to biological determinism. Sensing counselors tend to emphasize factual and quantitative issues in sessions with clients, and measure their success by behavior change in the client. Intuitive counselors tend to use fantasy, imagery, dreams, and symbolism in their sessions, and measure their success by the client's new insights. Counselors who prefer thinking tend to choose rational, informational, cognitive, and behavioral

		ISTJ	ISFJ	INFJ	INTJ
A	General	6.7	6.2	6.0	3.7
B	Rehab.	5.1	7.3	5.1	3.4
C	Voc. & Ed.	7.4	6.4	5.0	3.1
D	School	5.6	5.9	4.9	1.7
E	Runaways	2.6	6.8	3.4	1.7
F	Crisis	3.4	5.3	9.5	2.7
G	Psychodrama	2.9	2.4	11.8	2.9
H	Social Work	8.6	7.9	8.1	4.4
I	Psychology	3.0	2.5	7.0	10.7

		ISTP	ISFP	INFP	INTP
A	General	1.9	2.9	11.9	3.4
B	Rehab.	3.4	4.5	11.3	4.0
C	Voc. & Ed.	1.5	2.2	11.3	3.6
D	School	1.4	2.4	13.0	1.4
E	Runaways	1.7	7.7	18.8	6.0
F	Crisis	0.4	0.8	15.7	6.5
G	Psychodrama	0.0	1.2	9.4	4.7
H	Social Work	1.0	2.5	11.5	5.0
I	Psychology	1.5	1.2	14.7	8.5

		ESTP	ESFP	ENFP	ENTP
A	General	1.6	3.9	17.7	4.6
B	Rehab.	1.7	6.2	20.3 +	4.5
C	Voc. & Ed.	1.0	3.9	16.8	4.8
D	School	1.4	4.2	18.5	4.9
E	Runaways	3.4	1.7	19.7	4.3
F	Crisis	1.5	2.3	17.2	6.1
G	Psychodrama	0.0	1.8	29.4 +	7.1
H	Social Work	1.5	4.6	15.2	4.6
I	Psychology	0.5	1.2	18.4	6.0

		ESTJ	ESFJ	ENFJ	ENTJ
A	General	7.1	7.0	10.2	5.2
B	Rehab.	7.9	5.7	6.2	3.4
C	Voc. & Ed.	8.6	7.6	10.9	5.9
D	School	8.4	9.4	11.9	5.2
E	Runaways	2.5	3.4	12.0	4.3
F	Crisis	3.0	6.5	12.6	6.5
G	Psychodrama	1.2	3.5	12.9	8.8
H	Social Work	6.3	6.5	7.7	4.6
I	Psychology	2.7	2.2	8.2	11.7

FIG. 5.10. Myers–Briggs Type Indicator Patterns of Counselors in Different Fields. *Note:* Numbers preceding bar graphs represent the percent of the sample falling in that type. If the percentage exceeds 20%, a + follows the bar. The individual tables from which these samples were drawn appear in the chapter on Counseling and Mental Health in the *CAPT Atlas of Type Tables* by Macdaid, McCaulley, and Kainz (1986). Reprinted with permission.

approaches, and are more oriented toward objectivism and impersonal causality. Counselors who prefer feeling are more attracted to experiential and affective approaches with a focus on personal will and the quality of the therapeutic relationship. Counselors who prefer perceiving find it easier to remain open, following the client where the session leads; counselors who prefer judging find it easier to provide structure, goals, and direction. Counselors include more perceiving types than other health professions (McCaulley, 1977). In Levin's (1978) study of counselors, over three-fourths of gestalt and experiential counselors were P types; over 70% of psychoanalytic and rational-emotive counselors were J types.

Counseling training provides a wide range of options to prospective counselors, who can choose those that fit them best. Research with counselors will clarify the treatment methods easiest for counselors of different types. Are there some methods so alien to any given type that counselors of that type are unable to use them therapeutically? What do counselors need to know to "talk the language" of each type? All counselors must be able to go beyond their preferred methods to help clients very different from themselves. Type theory gives a rationale for choices of counseling strategies.

Who Seeks Counseling, and What Do They Expect From It? Research reported in the *Manual* (pp. 73–75) and in *MBTI Applications* (Hammer, 1996a, pp. 110–111) showed that more intuitives than sensing types seek psychological treatment. (As a sensing client said, "I didn't come at first because I didn't see what just talking about it could do." Another said, "I thought I felt so bad because I was physically sick.") Sensing types may be more likely to see psychological problems in physical terms.

Quenk and Quenk (1996) found many MBTI studies from university counseling centers. These found that N and P types are more likely to come in for personal counseling, and S and J types for academic advisement or career counseling. Other research found that extraverted clients expected to talk openly and that benefits would come quickly. Intuitives expected treatment would take longer. Feeling clients placed a high value on the positive regard of the counselor. Perceiving types, perhaps overwhelmed with options, expected the counselor would tell them what to do. Intuitive types valued treatments that involve participation in laboratory learning, fantasy, mental imagery, dreams, and journal keeping. Cann (1979) even found type differences in dream content. Sensing types reported more dreams of everyday life, and intuitives reported more dreams with archetypal content.

The fact that intuitives are in the majority among counselors and their clients raises questions for the entire field of counseling. Will NF counselors develop appropriate treatment strategies for sensing and thinking clients whose approach to life is so different from their own? One ENFP counselor was caught up short by an ISTJ client. "You keep talking about ways for me to be happy. I am not here to be happy. I am here to solve my problems! Happy is irrelevant." Sensing counselors, a minority in their profession, have a special opportunity to interpret the sensing majority in the general population to their colleagues, and to alert intuitive counselors to misperceptions and lost opportunities in reaching the sensing types.

In summary, both counselors and clients differ in predictable ways in their expectations of counseling, and in their preferences for treatment methods. Jung's framework should be increasingly useful as more is known about type differences in diagnosis and effective treatment.

Mind–Body Issues in Counseling. John Shelton (1996) discussed type differences in health, stress, and coping in Chapter 9 of *MBTI Applications.* Type theory gives new insights to mind–body issues. For example, type theory predicts that introverts with sensing dominant (ISTJ and ISFJ) will be the most observant of inner sensations of the body. Also, the inferior intuition of introverted sensing types is more likely to see pessimistic than optimistic possibilities. Jungian analysts noted early that the complete and circumstantial detail in reporting symptoms and the focus on negative possibilities may cause ISTJ and ISFJ to be diagnosed hypochondriacs. Shelton (1996) reviewed a number of studies where ISTJ and ISFJ were actually overrepresented in samples of patients diagnosed with coronary heart disease, allergic reactions, and chronic pain. Type theory alerts counselors to be watchful that the ISTJ and ISFJ style of reporting not be written off as hypochondria when serious illness is present. In contrast, however, in theory, extraverted intuitives (ENFP and ENTP) whose sensing is inferior may have the opposite problem of ignoring physical symptoms (see the case of George Black earlier in this chapter).

Counselors will be interested in Shelton's review of type differences in reactions to stress and strategies for coping with stress. Quenk (1993, 1996) described what stresses precipitate each of the 16 types into the inferior function, how they experience being "in the grip," and how they regain control of the dominant and auxiliary. Counselors using the MBTI will find this application of type dynamics useful to their clients.

Limitations of the MBTI in Counseling

The MBTI is designed to indicate inborn pathways to development and wholeness—"gifts differing." The MBTI is not designed to assess psychopathology. The MBTI indicates preferences for taking in information and making decisions. It does not assess skills. Type theory and the MBTI can, however, be used by counselor in establishing conceptual frameworks of

(a) possible strengths and weaknesses, (b) typical and atypical behaviors, (c) effects of environmental pressures, and (d) developmental pathways. The case studies earlier in this chapter provide examples of using type theory to establish hypotheses and to test them in the course of counseling.

MBTI data can also alert the counselor to type biases that are reflected in the culture and sometimes in assessment instruments. For example, the cultural bias that extraversion is healthier than introversion appears as positive correlations between MBTI extraversion and "mental health" scales for self-confidence, ego strength, and emotional stability. Neuroticism, depression, and psychasthenia scores show low positive correlations with MBTI introversion. (See Table 11.1 of the *Manual*.) Type theory helps the counselor look at scores of tests of psychopathology from two perspectives. Is the behavior true pathology or characteristic of a given type? (Is the patient schizoid, or introverted? Is this behavior manic or merely enthusiastic extraversion?)

Personality assessment is complex and we have no perfect personality instruments. The MBTI has the limitations of all self-report instruments. It is essential to consider the motivation of the client in answering the MBTI and to consider hypotheses from type theory along with other data.

The fact that MBTI reports are in terms of 16 types, not scale profiles, poses several problems for counselors. Some types (especially ENFPs) resist the entire idea of type as being "boxed in." They are slow to see that type describes a developmental pathway, not a restriction. The type descriptions can be seen as pop psychology rather than as an integrated set of hypotheses, exemplifying a complex theory with considerable empirical support. Some types may reify the descriptions, casting them in concrete. An example is an ISFJ for whom type had become extremely important as part of her identity. She was asked to take the MBTI in a course, and became panicky waiting for the results, fearing that she might not be an ISFJ after all.

EVALUATION AND FUTURE DIRECTIONS

Jung believed his type theory described universal human mental processes. Until recently, Jung's rich and comprehensive theory was relatively neglected in this country. His work relating to psychological type was little appreciated, even by Jungians. Isabel Myers's work, carried on apart from academia, was also unknown. Her attempt to provide simple explanations of Jung's insights led many to think of her work itself as simple. In being faithful to Jung's theory, Isabel Myers had to solve many psychometric problems of which we in psychology are seldom aware. These include type differences in interpreting the questions, the assumption of dichotomies, and the consequent need for precision at the midpoint of the scales.

When I first became acquainted with the MBTI, I consistently underestimated it. After intensive work with Isabel Myers, and after using the MBTI for over 25 years as a counseling tool, a research instrument, and a teaching tool, I have come to a deep appreciation of its depth and complexity, both in theoretical assumptions and in psychometrics. As of 1998, the MBTI, created in the early 1940s and published only for research from 1962 to 1976, has been available for professional applications for 22 years. Almost unknown in 1976, it is now used around the world. A large body of research now supports Jung's theory and Myers's instrument. The explosion of interest in psychological type points to many future directions.

Type Is Known to the General Public

Every application of the MBTI leads to requests for more detailed information, and for support materials. Information generated by MBTI users in counseling, careers, education, families, organizations, and spirituality is being integrated into the overall body of knowledge about psychological type. In addition to many new books for those who use the MBTI in their professional work, the MBTI is becoming familiar in settings far from the counselor's office. Popular books cover applications of psychological type—in personal development, in families and childrearing, in teaching and learning, in the world of work, and in spiritual life. Many of these books include type descriptions related to the theme of the book. Some of these follow Myers in describing well-developed types. Others simply describe traits and behaviors characteristic of the types.

In addition to Isabel Myers's *Gifts Differing* (Myers with Myers, 1980), books with general descriptions of psychological type include Brownsword (1988), Corlett and Millner (1993), Hirsh and Kummerow (1990), Kroeger and Thuesen (1988), Martin (1997), Myers (1970, 1987, 1993), Myers and Kirby (1994), Pearman and Albritton (1997), and Quenk (1993, 1996). Other popular books about type in families and childrearing include Farris (1991), Ginn (1995), Jones and Sherman (1997), Murphy (1992), Neff (1995), Penley and Stevens (1994), Provost (1990), and Tieger and Barron-Tieger (1997).

In education, books for teachers include Bargar, Bargar, and Cano (1994), Fairhurst and Fairhurst (1995), Lawrence (1993), Mamchur (1996), Provost and Anchors (1987), Provost (1988), Thompson (1997), and Van Sant and Payne (1995). Books for students include DiTiberio and Hammer (1993), DiTiberio and Jensen (1995), Golden and Lesh (1994), Lawrence (1997), and Provost (1992).

Popular books about careers and the world of work are also increasing. Examples are Barger and Kirby (1995), Barr and Barr (1989), Demarest (1997), Hammer (1993), Hennessy (1995), Hirsh and Kummerow (1990), Hirsh and Kise (1996), Kummerow, Barger, and Kirby (1997), Martin (1995), and Tieger and Barron-Tieger (1995).

Type differences in spiritual life are described in Edwards (1993), Ginn (1994), Grant, Thompson, and Clarke (1983), Harbaugh (1988), Hirsh and Kise (1997), Kise, Stark, and Hirsh (1996), and Richardson (1996).

Popularity and rapid growth have their costs. Enthusiasts can describe type with such vigor that more skeptical types wonder if type is a cult rather than a body of theory and research. The MBTI is used in organizations, religion, and education by some whose training has not alerted them to the caution needed when any psychological instrument is used with complex human beings. Misled by the seeming simplicity of the MBTI, they misinform. For example, people are told that their type cannot succeed in the career of their choice. MBTI data show all 16 types in all careers, but there are more of the types whose interests match the tasks to be accomplished, for example, more ST types in civil engineering, more SF types in hands-on patient care, more NF types in counseling, and more NT types in physics. It goes beyond the data to assume that rare types in any occupation will not perform well. Rare types may report feeling like outsiders, or that they offer a different perspective that is valuable. People have been told their types are incompatible for marriage, although research shows that all type combinations have produced both successful and unsuccessful marriages. Type can be used negatively instead of for "the constructive use of differences." The presenter can make some types sound much better than others, a phenomenon particularly likely in organizations where the "desirable types" are described with TJ characteristics, and where members of an organization may hesitate to answer the MBTI honestly, or to admit to a preference for feeling. (As organizations recently have begun to appreciate the need for better communication and for adaptability to change, there is a trend for feeling and perceiving preferences to be more appreciated.)

Other Type Instruments

Twenty-five years ago, most psychology students learned about Freud. Jung was mentioned only in passing. By the 1990s Jungian Societies had been formed all over the United States, even in smaller cities.

In the 1960s the Jungian Type Survey or Gray–Wheelright Test (Wheelright, Wheelright, & Buehler, 1964) was developed by Jungian analysts in San Francisco. It has scales for extraversion–introversion, sensing–intuition, and thinking–feeling. Most research on the Jungian Type Survey was published in the 1960s. In 1984 an experimental instrument, the the Singer–Loomis Inventory of Personality, was developed by Jungian analysts June Singer and Mary Loomis to identify Jung's basic functions and attitude combinations. It is now published as the Singer–Loomis Type Deployment Inventory (Singer & Loomis, 1997). It does not use Isabel Myers's interpretation of Jung's description of the auxiliary function as "in every respect different from the nature of the primary function" (Jung, 1921/1971, p. 406), which is the basis of type dynamics in the MBTI.

Keirsey and Bates in *Please Understand Me* (1984) described four classical temperaments, and derived 16 types as variants of these four temperaments. They included "portraits" of 16 types, using MBTI type letters. In MBTI terms, the Keirsey–Bates temperaments are SJ, SP, NF, and NT. A "temperament sorter" was included in the book to help readers understand temperament/type differences. The sorter, not developed through research, is sometimes mistaken for the MBTI.

Other books on type also use question lists to give readers of the book a way of applying type concepts to themselves. These lists were not intended by their authors to be used as type indicators (e.g., Lawrence, 1993; Mamchur, 1984, 1996).

Working from an abstract systems science model, Lowen (Lowen with Miike, 1982) generated types that have characteristics in common with Jungian types.

Scales for the concepts indicated by the MBTI—the EI, SN, TF, and JP scales—have been used in tests of personality (e.g., Millon, 1994), of personal styles in business (e.g., Hogan & Champagne, 1993), and in student styles (e.g., Oakland, Glutting, & Horton, 1996). These instruments tend to be trait based, without the MBTI psychometric concerns of precision at the midpoint and type dynamics.

A fascinating scientific discovery has confirmed the basic preferences described by Jung and the MBTI. The NEO-PI (Costa & McCrae, 1989, 1992; McCrae, 1996; McCrae & Costa, 1990) was developed by factor analysis of terms for traits. This atheoretical procedure generated the Five-Factor Model (Goldberg, 1993) of "enduring personality traits." The five factors, like Jung's psychological types, assume stability over time. Factor 1, Neuroticism, is not related to the MBTI scoring, but does correlate negatively with the Type Differentiation Indicator "Comfort Scales" (see earlier section on Scoring). Factor 2, Extraversion, correlates positively with extraversion on MBTI EI; Factor 3, Openness to experience, correlates with intuition on MBTI SN; Factor 4, Agreeableness, correlates with feeling on MBTI TF; and Factor 5, Conscientiousness, correlates with judging on MBTI JP.

The five factors are interpreted as traits. In their early work, Costa and McCrae described high scores for factors 2–5 positively and low scores negatively. Later, low scores were described more neutrally, but the scales are still used in diagnosis of pathology (Costa & Widiger, 1993). Newman (1996) reported on a 1993 symposium comparing the NEO-PI and the MBTI.

When two instruments, the MBTI and the NEO-PI, come from such opposite sources and find the same personality variables, I believe they must be describing fundamental human characteristics.

Type and Children

MBTI users have long asked for an indicator for children. Item analyses for Form G of the MBTI began at fourth grade, but the MBTI is most useful at eighth grade or older. Cohen (1981) described research at Glassboro State College in New Jersey to develop the Cosiol–Jones–Cohen Children's Personality Scale (no longer available). In 1987 Consulting Psychologists Press published the Murphy–Meisgeier Type Indicator for Children (Meisgeier & Murphy, 1987). The MMTIC was designed to reflect Jungian types in children from Grades 2 to 8. The Consortium for Type Development, a longitudinal study by Elizabeth Murphy and Martha Wilson Alcock, is collecting MMTIC and MBTI data, neurological data, and videos of child and adult subjects ages 0–5, 6–18, 19–40, and 41 years and older (personal communication, Elizabeth Murphy).

Future Developments of Interest to Counselors

Growing Focus on the Characteristics of the 16 Types. The trend toward focus on the 16 types rather than the four type preferences will provide more rigorous tests of type dynamics (e.g., Mitchell, 1991) and more precise suggestions for treatment of specific types (e.g., Otis & Louks, 1997). Building on the research a decade ago (Hobby, Miller, Stone, & Carskadon, 1987; McCarley & Carskadon, 1987; Ware & Yokomoto, 1985), ongoing Center for Creative Leadership studies by Pearman and Fleenor (1996) and by Fleenor (1997) reported type differences on scores of personality tests and observer ratings of behaviors. The future will bring more information on type similarities and differences related to cultural group, educational level, work, and intelligence.

Research on the relationship between type and gender, building on the work of Stokes (1987a, 1987b), is underway by Lawrence Demarest at CAPT. The issues are important to counselors, because the culture is more accepting of women who prefer feeling and men who prefer thinking. Preliminary data suggest that gender differences in research can often be explained as well or better by MBTI thinking or feeling preferences.

Research with clients will continue to clarify type differences in presenting problems, risk behaviors, diagnostic categories, most effective treatments, responses to medication, reactions to stress, patient compliance, counselor–client interactions, and communication with health professionals. Neuropsychologists will continue to find support for Jung's type theory in patterns of the brain (e.g., Newman, 1990; Wilson & Languis, 1989, 1990).

Counselors will develop better strategies to foster type development of all types. More attention will be paid to type development in midlife. Increasing knowledge of type differences will lead to more effective treatment strategies for sensing types who are less likely to see counseling as helpful.

Predictive Validity.   Much of past MBTI validity research focused on construct and concurrent validity. Research on predictive validity will be expanded. Does counseling with the MBTI lead to measurable improvement in communication between couples? In decision making? In academic achievement? More research predicting how interventions affect different types is needed, particularly in health and education.

Applications in Education.   In the field of education, type differences in academic aptitude, achievement, interest in reading, learning styles, and teaching styles are well established. At this time of major changes in education, from concerns over dropouts to computers in the classroom, action research is needed at all levels from elementary school to adult education. Teachers will take type into account in their lessons and learning software. Students will discover their own best ways to learn. Teachers can make their presentations more effective for all 16 types by asking their students to serve as consultants to evaluate the quality of the lesson from the perspective of their own type.

Special opportunities will occur in classrooms with multicultural diversity. The MBTI focus on respect for differences allows students in type-alike groups to see that ENFPs and ISTJs can look at situations differently because of the ways they use their minds, not because of the color of their skin.

Applications in the Workplace.   Type differences in choosing careers are well established (see the *CAPT Atlas of Type Tables*, Macdaid et al., 1986). The next *Atlas* will provide career data separately by gender and other groupings. The next decade will provide career counselors with more precise information about type differences in career choices, career satisfaction, burnout, and the characteristics of tasks that continue to motivate, or lead to boredom. Career counselors will take type differences into account at each stage of the counseling process (McCaulley & Martin, 1995). Career counselors who use the MBTI can contribute to the body of MBTI career information if they periodically review their case records to see if type behaviors they observe in their work stand up under analysis and should be shared.

Cultural Diversity.   Since the first edition of this book a decade ago, the expansion of type across cultures has been dramatic. New translations appear each year. Use of the MBTI across cultures is just beginning to teach us about the universal aspects of the 16 types, and about aspects of each culture that foster or falsify type development.

When I attend international MBTI conferences, I have this conversation: "Jung believed type preferences are universal in the human species. He also believed the preferences of any individual are inborn, and that family and cultural influences determine whether inborn preferences develop toward excellence and wholeness, or are falsified. Translation of the MBTI is complex, because the translator needs to take into account the nuances of Jung's theory and how to represent these for each culture. And yet, you tell me that this instrument, developed in the middle of this century by a White middle-class woman in the United States, works in your country. Can this be true?" Despite the effects of very different cultures, despite the fallibility of any translation, I have been assured it is true!

Data so far show all 16 types in every culture. The type tables differ. The behaviors associated with type preferences show the effects of the culture. Extraversion and introversion, for example, are recognized in all cultures, but extraversion may look different in cultures where extraverts are in the majority, and in cultures where they are a minority.

As the MBTI is translated into languages around the globe, we are finding that type brings a common human perspective that promotes understanding. Parents everywhere recognize the challenges for introverted parents with extraverted children, or for practical parents with imaginative children. Developments over the next decade will clarify these early trends.

More Resources for Learning About Type

As the MBTI has become more widely known, many counselors have been sharing their observations about type differences in the *Bulletin of Psychological Type, Journal of Psychological Type*, and at conferences of the Association for Psychological Type, the Center for Applications of Psychological type, and other professional meetings. The next decade will bring many more materials for the professional and the public, to bring Jung's concepts to life.

In summary, MBTI applications in counseling, education, organizations, and spirituality have expanded and become more sophisticated. More is known, and more materials exist for applying type. Knowledge of the MBTI has spread to the general public. International use of the MBTI has grown rapidly in the past decade, with more translations in Europe, Asia, and Africa.

The world is changing rapidly as we near a new millennium. Since the last revision of the MBTI in 1977, changes in society have affected meaning of words and the desirability of behaviors. The team who developed Form M of the MBTI which appeared in 1998 closely examined these influences on 580 possible items before selecting the 93 that met their standards.

Research on psychological type will always be challenging. Type theory predicts how types direct their energy toward extraverted or introverted activities. Type theory predicts how types direct their energy toward present events or future possibilities. Type theory predicts whether types use impersonal analysis or personal values to reach conclusions.

Type theory predicts the direction of energy. It does *not* predict specific behaviors that result from that energy. The underlying functions and attitudes can be manifested in many ways at the behavioral level. Moreover, good type development leads to the ability to show behaviors appropriate to the situation, whether or not they are preferred. Nevertheless, for over 50 years, construct validity for the MBTI has been supported by research. More recently, research with the MBTI subscales, and research when the type is the unit of measurement, support type differences predicted from the theory of type dynamics. *MBTI Applications* (Hammer, 1996a) provides a wealth of testable hypotheses for the next generation of MBTI researchers.

In the end, I believe that Jung's insights about the functions and attitudes and their dynamic interaction will prove to be describing human attributes that truly exist, and that the MBTI will remain a sophisticated instrument for identifying them.

RESOURCES FOR THE MYERS-BRIGGS TYPE INDICATOR

Association for Psychological Type (APT)

A nonprofit membership association for all persons interested in psychological type. APT sponsors biennial international conferences and biennial regional conferences. APT facilitates networking through interest area coordinators for careers and occupations, counseling and psychotherapy, education, management and organization development, multicultural issues, psychological theory and research, and religious and spiritual issues. APT also has local groups in each region of the United States and has affiliated international associations. APT publishes a newsletter, *Bulletin of Psychological Type*, and a research journal, *Journal of Psychological Type*.

Address 9140 Ward Parkway, Kansas City, MO 64114, USA; telephone 816-444-3500; fax 818-444-0330; e-mail staff@aptcentral.org; web site http://www.aptcentral.org.

Center for Applications of Psychological Type (CAPT)

A nonprofit international organization founded in 1975 by Isabel Briggs Myers and Mary H. McCaulley. CAPT provides basic and advanced professional training and consultation for MBTI users, and for users of the Murphy–Meisgeier Indicator for Children (MMTIC). CAPT publishes and distributes books, support materials, and training materials for the MBTI, and maintains the Isabel Briggs Myers Memorial Library and the *Bibliography* for the MBTI. In addition to its own research, CAPT provides MBTI research collaboration and consultation, and computer scoring for the MBTI, and is a general information resource for questions about type.

Address 2815 NW 13th St., Suite 401, Gainesville, FL 32609, USA; telephone 800-777-CAPT; fax 352-378-0503; e-mail capt@capt.org; web site http://www.capt.org.

Consulting Psychologists Press (CPP)

Publisher of the MBTI and many other psychological tests. CPP licenses international distributors and translations, grants permissions to quote or copy, and provides scoring services and/or software. Its subsidiary, Davies-Black Publishing, also publishes professional and popular books about MBTI and MMTIC applications.

Address 3803 East Bayshore Road, P.O. Box 10096, Palo Alto, CA 94303, USA; telephone 800-624-1765; fax 415-969-8608; e-mail cpp-db.com; web site www.cpp-db.com.

REFERENCES

Bargar, J. R., Bargar, R. R., & Cano, J. M. (1994). *Discovering learning preferences and learning differences in the classroom.* Columbus, OH: Ohio Agricultural Education Curriculum Materials Service.

Barger, N. J., & Kirby, L. K. (1995). *The challenge of change in organizations.* Palo Alto, CA: Davies-Black.

Barr, L., & Barr, N. (1989). *Leadership equation: Leadership, management, and the Myers-Briggs.* Austin, TX: Eakin Press.

Brownsword, A. W. (1988). *Psychological type: An introduction.* San Anselmo, CA: Baytree.

Cann, D. R. (1979). *Personality structure and the content of dreams.* Unpublished doctoral dissertation, McGill University, Montreal, Canada.

Carskadon, T. G. (1979). Clinical and counseling aspects of the Myers-Briggs Type Indicator: A research review. *Research in Psychological Type, 2,* 2–31.

Carskadon, T. G. (1982). Myers–Briggs Type Indicator characterizations: A Jungian horoscope? *Research in Psychological Type, 5,* 87–88.

Carskadon, T. G., & Cook, D. D. (1982). Validity of MBTI descriptions as perceived by recipients unfamiliar with type. *Research in Psychological Type, 5,* 89–94.

Carskadon, T. G., & McCarley, N. G. (Eds.). (1997). 20th Anniversary special issue. *Journal of Psychological Type, 42.*

Carskadon, T. G., McCarley, N. G., & McCaulley (1987). *Compendium of research involving the Myers–Briggs Type Indicator.* Gainesville, FL: Center for Applications of Psychological Type.

Casas, E., & Hamlet, J. (1984). *Psychological types of clients, student-counselors and supervisors in a clinical training center: Study of client-counselor compatibility and therapy internship.* Final Report, CRHSC, Subvention No. 410 834 0428, University of Ottawa, Canada. (Original in French)

Center for Applications of Psychological Type. (1997). *Myers–Briggs Type Indicator Bibliography.* Gainesville, FL: Center for Applications of Psychological Type.

Coan, R. W. (1979). *Psychologists: Personal and theoretical pathways.* New York: Irvington.

Cohen, S. R. (1981). Using the MBTI with teachers, supervisors, administrators and students: A program review. *Research in Psychological Type, 3,* 42–47.

Corlett, E. S., & Millner, N. B. (1993). *Navigating midlife: Using typology as a guide.* Palo Alto, CA: Consulting Psychologists Press.

Costa, P. T., & McCrae, R. R. (1989). Reinterpreting the Myers–Briggs Type Indicator from the perspective of the Five-Factor Model of personality. *Journal of Personality, 57*(1), 17–40.

Costa, P. T., Jr., & McCrae, R. R. (1992). *The Revised NEO Personality Inventory (NEO-PI-R) and NEO Five-Factor Inventory (NEO-FFI) professional manual.* Odessa, FL: Psychological Assessment Resources.

Costa, P. T., & Widiger, T. A. (Eds.). (1994). *Personality disorders and the Five-Factor Model of personality.* Washington, DC: American Psychological Association.

Demarest, L. (1997). *Looking at type in the workplace.* Gainesville, FL: Center for Applications of Psychological Type.

DiTiberio, J. K. (1996). Education, learning styles, and cognitive styles. In A. L. Hammer (Ed.), *MBTI Applications: A decade of research on the Myers–Briggs Type Indicator* (pp. 123–166). Palo Alto, CA: Consulting Psychologists Press.

DiTiberio, J. K., & Hammer, A. L. (1993). *Introduction to type in college.* Palo Alto, CA: Consulting Psychologists Press.

DiTiberio, J. K., & Jensen, G. H. (1995). *Writing & personality: Finding your voice, your style, your way.* Palo Alto, CA: Davies-Black.

Edwards, L. (1993). *How we belong, fight and pray: The MBTI as a key to congregational dynamics.* Washington, DC: Alban Institute.

Fairhurst, A. M., & Fairhurst, L. (1995). *Effective teaching, effective learning: Making the personality connection in your classroom.* Palo Alto, CA: Davies-Black.

Farris, D. (1991). *Type tales.* [Children's stories.] Palo Alto, CA: Consulting Psychologists Press.

Fitzgerald, C., & Kirby, L. K. (Eds.). (1997). *Developing leaders: Research and applications in psychological type and leadership development.* Palo Alto, CA: Davies-Black.

Fleenor, J. W. (1997). The relationship between the MBTI and measures of personality and performance in management groups. In C. Fitzgerald & L. K. Kirby (Eds.), *Developing leaders: Research and applications in psychological type and leadership development* (pp. 115–138). Palo Alto, CA: Davies-Black.

Ginn, C. W. (1994). *Voices of loss.* Gainesville, FL: Center for Applications of Psychological Type.

Ginn, C. W. (1995). *Families: Using type to enhance mutual understanding.* Gainesville, FL: Center for Applications of Psychological Type.

Goldberg, L. R. (1993). The structure of phenotypic personality traits. *American Psychologist, 48*(1), 26–34.

Golden, B. J., & Lesh, K. (1994). *Building self-esteem: Strategies for success in school . . . and beyond.* Scottsdale, AZ: Gorsuch Scarisbrick, Publishers.

Gough, H. G. (1981, July). *Studies of the Myers–Briggs Type Indicator in a personality assessment research institute.* Paper presented at the Fourth National Conference on the Myers-Briggs Type Indicator, Stanford University, Stanford, CA.

Grant, W. H., Thompson, M., & Clarke, T. E. (1983). *From image to likeness: A Jungian path in the gospel journey.* Ramsey, NJ: Paulist Press.

Hammer, A. L. (1993). *Introduction to type and careers.* Palo Alto, CA: Consulting Psychologists Press.

Hammer, A. L. (Ed.). (1996a). *MBTI applications: A decade of research on the Myers-Briggs Type Indicator.* Palo Alto, CA: Consulting Psychologists Press.

Hammer, A. L. (1996b). Career management and counseling. In A. L. Hammer (Ed.), *MBTI applications: A decade of research on the Myers–Briggs Type Indicator* (pp. 31–53). Palo Alto, CA: Consulting Psychologists Press.

Hammer, A. L., & Husczco, G. E. (1996). Teams. In A. L. Hammer (Ed.), *MBTI applications: A decade of research on the Myers–Briggs Type Indicator* (pp. 81–103). Palo Alto, CA: Consulting Psychologists Press.

Hammer, A. L., & Macdaid, G. P. (1992). *MBTI Career Report manual*. Palo Alto, CA: Consulting Psychologists Press.

Hammer, A. L., & Yeakley, F. R. (1987). The relationship between "true type" and reported type. *Journal of Psychological Type, 13,* 52–55.

Harbaugh, G. L. (1988). *God's gifted people*. Minneapolis, MN: Augsburg Press.

Harvey, R. J. (1996). Reliability and validity. In A. L. Hammer (Ed.), *MBTI applications: A decade of research on the Myers–Briggs Type Indicator* (pp. 5–29). Palo Alto, CA: Consulting Psychologists Press.

Hennessy, S. M. (1995). *Thinking cop, feeling cop: A study in police personalities* (2nd ed.). Scottsdale, AZ: Leadership, Inc.

Hirsh, S. K., & Kummerow, J. M. (1989). *LIFETypes*. New York: Warner Books.

Hirsh, S. K., & Kummerow, J. M. (1990). *Introduction to type in organizations: Individual interpretive guide* (2nd ed.). Palo Alto, CA: Consulting Psychologists Press.

Hirsh, S. K., & Kise, J. A. G. (1996). *Work it out: Clues for solving people problems at work*. Palo Alto, CA: Davies-Black.

Hirsh, S. K., & Kise, J. A. G. (1997). *Looking at type in spirituality*. Gainesville, FL: Center for Applications of Psychological Type.

Hobby, S. A., Miller, D. I., Stone, J. A., & Carskadon, T. G. (1987). An empirical test of differing theoretical positions of Myers and Keirsey concerning type similarity. *Journal Psychological Type, 13,* 56–60.

Hogan, R. C., & Champagne, D. W. (1993). *Personal Style Inventory*. King of Prussia, PA: HRDQ. (Earlier editions published 1982, 1985)

Howes, R. J. (1977). *Reliability of the Myers–Briggs Type Indicator as a function of mood manipulation*. Unpublished master's thesis, Mississippi State University.

Jones, J. H., & Sherman, R. G. (1997). *Intimacy and type: A practical guide for improving relationships for couples and counselors*. Gainesville, FL: Center for Applications of Psychological Type.

Jung, C. G. (1971). *Psychological types* (H. G. Baynes, Trans., rev. by R. F. C. Hull). Volume 6 of *The collected works of C. G. Jung*. Princeton, NJ: Princeton University Press. (Original work published 1921)

Keirsey, D. W., & Bates, M. (1984). *Please understand me*. Del Mar, CA: Prometheus Nemesis.

Kise, J. A. G., Stark, D., & Hirsh, S. K. (1996). *LifeKeys: Discovering who you are, why you're here, and what you do best*. Minneapolis, MN: Bethany House.

Kroeger, O., & Thuesen, J. (1988). *Type talk*. New York: Delacorte Press.

Kummerow, J. M. (1988). A methodology for verifying type: Research results. *Journal Psychological Type, 15,* 20–25.

Kummerow, J. M., Barger, N. J., & Kirby, L. K. (1997). *WORKTypes*. New York: Warner Books.

Lawrence, G. D. (1993). *People types and tiger stripes* (3rd ed.). Gainesville, FL: Center for Applications of Psychological Type.

Lawrence, G. D. (1997). *Looking at type and learning styles*. Gainesville, FL: Center for Applications of Psychological Type.

Levin, L. S. (1978). Jungian personality variables of psychotherapists of five different theoretical orientations (Doctoral dissertation, Georgia State University, 1978). *Dissertation Abstracts International, 39*(08), 4042B. (University Microfilms No. 79-01, 823)

Lowen, W., with Miike, L. (1982). *Dichotomies of the mind: A systems science model of the mind and personality*. New York: John Wiley and Sons.

Macdaid, G. P., McCaulley, M. H., & Kainz, R. I. (1986). *CAPT atlas of type tables*. Gainesville, FL: Center for Applications of Psychological Type.

Mamchur, C. M. (1984). *Insights: Understanding yourself and others*. Toronto: Ontario Institute for Studies in Education.

Mamchur, C. (1996). *A teacher's guide to cognitive type theory & learning style*. Alexandria, VA: Association for Supervision and Curriculum Development.

Martin, C. R. (1995). *Looking at type and careers*. Gainesville, FL: Center for Applications of Psychological Type.

Martin, C. R. (1997). *Looking at type: The fundamentals*. Gainesville, FL: Center for Applications of Psychological Type.

McCarley, N. G., & Carskadon, T. G. (1987). Findings and strategies leading to empirically-based type descriptions. *Journal of Psychological Type, 13*, 9–14.

McCaulley, M. H. (1977). *The Myers longitudinal medical study* (monogr. II). Gainesville, FL: Center for Applications of Psychological Type.

McCaulley, M. H. (1978). *Applications of the Myers–Briggs Type Indicator to medicine and other health professions* (monogr. I). Gainesville, FL: Center for Applications of Psychological Type.

McCaulley, M. H., & Martin, C. R. (1995). Career assessment and the Myers–Briggs Type Indicator. *Journal of Career Assessment, 3*(2), 219–239.

McCrae, R. R., & Costa, P. T., Jr. (1990). *Personality in adulthood*. New York: Guilford Press.

McCrae, R. R. (1996). Social consequences of experiential openness. *Psychological Bulletin, 120*(3), 323–337.

Meisgeier, C., & Murphy, E. (1987). *Murphy–Meisgeier Type Indicator for Children: Manual*. Palo Alto, CA: Consulting Psychologists Press.

Millon, T. (1994). *Millon Index of Personality Styles (MIPS)*. San Antonio, TX: Psychological Corporation.

Mitchell, W. D. (1991). A test of type theory using the TDI. *Journal of Psychological Type, 22*, 15–26.

Murphy, E. (1992). *The developing child: Using Jungian type to understand children*. Palo Alto, CA: Davies-Black.

Myers, I. B. (1962). *Manual: The Myers–Briggs Type Indicator*. Princeton, NJ: Educational Testing Service. (Out of print)

Myers, I. B. (1970). *Introduction to type*. Swarthmore, PA: Author.

Myers, I. B. (1987). *Introduction to type* (4th ed., rev. by A. L. Hammer). Palo Alto, CA: Consulting Psychologists Press.

Myers, I. B. (1998). *Introduction to type* (6th ed., rev. by L. K. Kirby & K. D. Myers). Palo Alto, CA: Consulting Psychologists Press.

Myers, I. B., & McCaulley, M. H. (1985). *Manual: A guide to the development and use of the Myers–Briggs Type Indicator*. Palo Alto, CA: Consulting Psychologists Press.

Myers, I. B., with Myers, P. B. (1980). *Gifts differing*. Palo Alto, CA: Consulting Psychologists Press.

Myers, K. D., & Kirby, L. K. (1994). *Introduction to type dynamics and development: Exploring the next level*. Palo Alto, CA: Consulting Psychologists Press.

Myers, I. B., McCaulley, M. H., Quenk, N. L., & Hammer, A. H. (1998). *MBTI Manual: A guide to the development and use of the Myers-Briggs Type Indicator* (3rd ed.). Palo Alto, CA: Consulting Psychologists Press.

Neff, L. (1995). *One of a kind: Making the most of your child's uniqueness*. Gainesville, FL: Center for Applications of Psychological Type. (Original work 1988)

Newman, J. B. (1990). *A cognitive perspective on Jungian psychology*. Gainesville, FL: Center for Applications of Psychological Type.

Newman, J. B. (Ed.). (1996). *Measures of the Five Factor Model and psychological type: A major convergence of research and theory*. Proceedings of the Theory and Research Symposium conducted at the Tenth International Conference of the Association for Psychological Type, July 1993, Newport Beach, CA. Gainesville, FL: Center for Applications of Psychological Type.

Oakland, T., Glutting, J. J., & Horton, C. B. (1996). *Student style questionnaire.* San Antonio, TX: Psychological Corporation.

Otis, G. D., & Louks, J. L. (1997). Rebelliousness and psychological distress in a sample of introverted veterans. *Journal of Psychological Type, 40,* 20–30.

Parham, M., Miller, D. I., & Carskadon, T. G. (1984). Do "job types" differ from "life types"?: The effects of standard vs. vocationally specific instructions on the reliability of MBTI scores. *Journal of Psychological Type, 7,* 46–48.

Pearman, R. R., & Albritton, S. C. (1997). *I'm not crazy, I'm just not you.* Palo Alto, CA: Davies-Black.

Pearman, R. R., & Fleenor, J. W. (1996). Differences in observed and self-reported qualities of psychological types. *Journal of Psychological Type, 39,* 3–17.

Penley, J. P., & Stephens, D. W. (1994). *The M.O.M.S. Handbook: Understanding your personality type in mothering.* Wilmette, IL: Penley & Associates.

Provost, J. A. (1988). *Procrastination: Using psychological type to help students.* Gainesville, FL: Center for Applications of Psychological Type.

Provost, J. A. (1990). *Work, play, and type: Achieving balance in your life.* Palo Alto, CA: Consulting Psychologists Press.

Provost, J. A. (1992). *Strategies for success: Using type to do better in high school or college.* Gainesville, FL: Center for Applications of Psychological Type.

Provost, J. A. (1993). *Applications of the Myers–Briggs Type Indicator in counseling: A casebook* (2nd ed.). Gainesville, FL: Center for Applications of Psychological Type.

Provost, J. A., & Anchors, S. (1987). *Applications of the Myers–Briggs Type Indicator in higher education.* Palo Alto, CA: Consulting Psychologists Press

Quenk, A. T. (1984). *Psychological types and psychotherapy.* Gainesville, FL: Center for Applications of Psychological Type.

Quenk, N. L. (1993). *Beside ourselves: Our hidden personality in everyday life.* Palo Alto, CA: Davies-Black.

Quenk, N. L. (1996). *In the grip: Our hidden personality.* Palo Alto, CA: Consulting Psychologists Press.

Quenk, N. L., & Quenk, A. T. (1996). Counseling and psychotherapy. In *MBTI applications: A decade of research on the Myers–Briggs Type Indicator* (pp. 106–122). Palo Alto, CA: Consulting Psychologists Press.

Richardson, P. T. (1996). *Four spiritualities: Expressions of self, expressions of spirit.* Palo Alto, CA: Davies-Black.

Shelton, J. (1996). Health, stress, and coping. In A. L. Hammer (Ed.), *MBTI applications: A decade of research on the Myers–Briggs Type Indicator* (pp. 197–215). Palo Alto, CA: Consulting Psychologists Press.

Singer, J., & Loomis, M. (1997). *Interpretive guide for the Singer–Loomis Type Deployment Inventory.* Gresham, OR: Moving Boundaries.

Stokes, J. (1987a). Exploring the relationship between type and gender, part 1: Anecdotal experiences of MBTI users. *Journal of Psychological Type, 13,* 34–43.

Stokes, J. (1987b). Exploring the relationship between type and gender, part 2: A review and critique of empirical research and other data. *Journal of Psychological Type, 13,* 44–51.

Thompson, T. C. (Ed.). (1997). *Most excellent differences: Essays on using type theory in the composition classroom.* Gainesville, FL: Center for Applications of Psychological Type.

Tieger, P. D., & Barron-Tieger, B. (1995). *Do what you are: Discover the perfect career for you through the secrets of personality.* Boston: Little, Brown.

Tieger, P. D., & Barron-Tieger, B. (1997). *Nature by nurture: Understand your child's personality and become a better parent.* Boston: Little, Brown.

Thorne, A., & Gough, H. (1991). *Portraits of type: An MBTI research compendium.* Palo Alto, CA: Consulting Psychologists Press, Inc.

Van Sant, S., & Payne, D. (1995). *Psychological type in schools: Applications for educators.* Gainesville, FL: Center for Applications of Psychological Type.

von Franz, M.-L. (1971). The inferior function. In M.-L. von Franz and J. Hillman (Eds.), *Jung's typology* (pp. 1–72). Dallas, TX: Spring.

Walck, C. L. (1992). The relationship between indicator type and "true type": Slight preferences and the verification process. *Journal of Psychological Type, 23,* 17–21.

Walck, C. L. (1996). Management and leadership. In A. L. Hammer (Ed.), *MBTI applications: A decade of research on the Myers–Briggs Type Indicator* (pp. 56–79). Palo Alto, CA: Consulting Psychologists Press.

Ware, R., & Yokomoto, C. (1985). Perceived accuracy of Myers–Briggs Type Indicator descriptions using Keirsey profiles. *Journal of Psychological Type, 10,* 27–31.

Wheelwright, J. B., Wheelwright, J. H., & Buehler, H. A. (1964). *Jungian type survey: The Gray–Wheelwright Test.* San Francisco: Society of Jungian Analysts of Northern California.

Wilson, M. A., & Languis, M. L. (1989). Differences between electrical activity patterns between extraverted and introverted adults. *Journal of Psychological Type, 18,* 14–23.

Wilson, M. A., & Languis, M. L. (1990). A topographic study of differences in P300 between introverts and extraverts. *Brain Topography, 2*(4), 269–274.

Witzig, J. S. (1978). Jung's typology and classification of psychotherapies. *Journal of Analytical Psychology, 4,* 315–331.

6

Cognitive and Behavioral Assessment

Carol R. Glass
Catholic University of America

Thomas V. Merluzzi
University of Notre Dame

In contrast to other chapters in this book, we do not discuss a particular test here, nor do we use terminology such as *personality* or *personality assessment*. Our intent is to review two broad areas of assessment with great clinical relevance, the assessment of behavior and cognition.

Behavioral assessment is closely tied to the field of behavior therapy, providing information on specific problem behaviors that can guide the development of individualized treatment plans and assess the effectiveness of interventions. The term *cognitive assessment* does not refer, in this instance, to intelligence testing or neuropsychological assessment. Rather, cognitive assessment deals with the assessment of the cognitive constructs targeted by cognitively oriented approaches to counseling (e.g., self-statements, beliefs, attributions, cognitive schemas).

We hope to accomplish several goals with this chapter. First, we hope to set cognitive and behavioral assessment techniques in context both historically and conceptually, and we contrast cognitive and behavioral assessment with more traditional approaches to assessment. Our intention here is not to present a case for the superiority of cognitive and behavioral assessment, but to highlight the different assumptions that underlie these approaches and to suggest points of integration. Second, we introduce the reader to the primary methods used for cognitive and behavioral assessment. Finally, due to the breadth of this task, we focus on one particular problem area: social anxiety and social skills deficits. This problem is used to illustrate the application of cognitive and behavioral approaches to assessment, and specific case examples are given.

HISTORICAL PERSPECTIVES

For excellent treatments of the history of cognitive and behavioral assessment, the reader is encouraged to read McReynolds (1986) and Sundberg (1981). These authors provide ample evidence that both assessment approaches had precursors that existed prior to the beginnings of modern-day behavior therapy and cognitive therapy.

Behavioral Assessment

The emergence of behaviorism and eventually behavioral assessment can be traced to the work of Watson (1913) and Skinner (1953), as well as a number of others whose work was related to the scientific traditions of behavior theory (e.g., Pavlov). The reader is likely familiar with the work of these authors and their direct connection to the development of behavioral perspectives in operant and classical conditioning research. Glass and Arnkoff (1992) provided an excellent summary of the history of the practice of behavior therapy.

Direct observation is an integral aspect of behavioral assessment, with roots in other fields as well as psychology (McReynolds, 1986). McReynolds (1986) cited the observation methods of Darwin (1859), the direct observation of children (Gesell, 1925; Goodenough, 1949) and groups (Bales, 1951), and the emphasis on role playing in psychodrama (Moreno, 1983) as less than well-recognized influences on the emergence of behavioral assessment. Further, the ecological perspective of Lewin and Barker (Barker, 1968) has direct connections to the conceptual bases of behavioral assessment, in that the emphasis on environmental influences on behavior was an integral part of Lewin's famous equation, $B = f(p,e)$. Behavior is a function of the person *and* the environment. In citing the influence of these authors, McReynolds noted that interest in direct observation and on ecological variables was not relegated solely to the behavioral perspective. Also, they helped contribute to an intellectual and scientific environment that would support the growth of behavioral assessment.

More recently, the work of Lindsley (1956), Skinner (1953), and Ayllon and Azrin (1968) contributed greatly to the focus on behaviorism. In addition, McReynolds noted the work of Bijou and Patterson (1971) as a major contribution to the systematic development of behavior observation systems. Lindsley (1956) used operant technology to assess behavior deficits in schizophrenics. In a classic book on token economies, Ayllon and Azrin

(1968) underscored the need for thorough and controlled observation in the assessment of behaviors in a hospital setting.

All things considered, however, the major thrust in behavioral assessment seems to have been a function of the behavioral technology used in single-subject designs and the abandonment of traditional assessment and diagnosis by early behaviorists. The intention of behavioral assessment was to reduce the inference in assessment and diagnosis and create methods that would be more science than art (Hersen & Bellack, 1976). That thrust was also prompted by the fact that in behavior therapy, assessment and treatment are closely linked.

The first major books on behavioral assessment were published in 1976 and 1977 and later revised (Bellack & Hersen, 1998; Ciminero, Calhoun, & Adams, 1986). Other volumes published in this period are also excellent reference sources on this subject (Barlow, 1981; Mash & Terdal, 1984). The two journals devoted to the topic (*Journal of Behavioral Assessment* and *Behavioral Assessment*) were first published in 1980. Clearly, behavioral assessment, as a well-defined area of study, is quite young. The remarkable growth in the field appears to be related to the scientific traditions inherent in the behavioral perspective, and the fact that behavioral assessment is indispensable to the practice of behavior therapy.

Cognitive Assessment

Cognitive assessment has a more convoluted history. As opposed to behavioral assessment, which emerged primarily from behavior therapy, cognitive assessment is more of a hybrid. Interestingly, some of the methods used in cognitive assessment were derived from treatments or perspectives that have been labeled cognitive-behavioral. The most notable example of this are the inventories that assess self-statements (also called self-talk or internal dialogue), the thoughts clients have that might either inhibit or facilitate their response. This approach to cognitive assessment can be traced to the work of Meichenbaum (1977), whose influence on the field has been enormous. Meichenbaum's treatment studies, published in the early 1970s, were based primarily on the premise that thoughts were the final common pathway for information related to a problem area such as a phobia or a skill deficit. Thus, early cognitive assessment measures were based on the belief that one could assess dysfunctional thoughts as well as document change in thoughts as a function of treatment.

Because the background and methods of cognitive assessment are so diverse, it is difficult to narrow the focus of the historical developments leading to present-day methods. Therefore, we limit our historical analysis to those people and events that had a major impact on cognitive assessment.

Kelly's personal construct theory (1955), with its emphasis on the psychological construction of one's environment and the importance of expectancies and prediction, is very consistent with the present-day approaches to cognitive assessment. Although Kelly would object to being labeled "cognitive," the richness of the theory and its compatibility with cognitive perspectives contribute to its importance. Neimeyer and Neimeyer (1981, 1993) presented an extended discussion of how cognitive assessment is conducted from a personal construct or constructivist perspective.

The influence of social learning theory is apparent when one considers that cognitive assessment has focused on both behavior and outcome expectancies. Rotter (1954) and Bandura (1986) were essential figures in this area. However, milestones for the cognitive perspective are the publication of Mischel's (1968) book *Personality and Assessment* and, to a greater extent, his 1973 *Psychological Review* article entitled "Toward a cognitive social learning reconceptualization of personality." In that paper he presented what he termed *person variables*, and in a subsequent paper (Mischel, 1981) he explicated strategies for the assessment of such variables.

Brock (1967) and Greenwald (1968) deserve recognition for their work on the elicitation and scoring of thought data in attitude change research, which formed the basis for the cognitive assessment methods called thought listing. There is also a broader context for cognitive assessment, namely, information processing (Merluzzi, Rudy, & Glass, 1981). A volume edited by Ingram (1986) illustrated how the clinical and cognitive sciences have been integrated. In that volume, Lachman and Lachman (1986) provided an insightful history of the information processing paradigm, whereas other chapters of the book illustrated the importance of the paradigm for the future of clinical cognitive psychology. Neimeyer and Neimeyer (1993) also contrasted the cognitive approaches we are focusing on in this chapter with constructivist approaches to cognitive assessment. Here the target of assessment is not a thought or belief, but systems of personal constructs and networks of meaning that tap tacit, core cognitive processes and constructions of self and others.

Perhaps because cognitive and cognitive-behavior therapy have a more recent history compared to behavior therapy (see Arnkoff & Glass, 1992), the first major books on cognitive assessment were not published until the early 1980s (Kendall & Hollon, 1981b; Merluzzi, Glass, & Genest, 1981). At that time, it was rare to find even cognitive therapy outcome studies that employed cognitive measures to assess treatment change. Today, the situation is completely reversed, such that almost every major study on the effectiveness of a cognitive treatment utilizes some form of cognitive assessment. The development of new inventories to assess self-statements continues to outpace studies that demonstrate their validity and clinical utility. And although there have never been individual journals devoted solely to cognitive assessment, review articles on cognitive assessment are now routinely published in *Behaviour Research and Therapy*. Just as many behavior therapists now consider themselves cognitive-behavior therapists, it is interesting that some have referred to this assessment field as "cognitive-behavioral assessment."

CONCEPTUAL FOUNDATIONS

The conceptual underpinnings of behavioral and cognitive perspectives can be best illustrated by comparing the paradigmatic assumptions that drive each perspective with those of more traditional projective and trait approaches to assessment (Merluzzi & Carr, 1992). An overview of these major assessment approaches is presented in Table 6.1.

Projective methods, which are based on the assumption that information obtained from the client can be used to infer intrapsychic conflict, are an example of what Mischel (1968) called a *sign* approach. In contrast, the assumption underlying behavioral assessment is that the observed behavior is a *sample* of the client's typical responses. Trait approaches to assessment, such as the Minnesota Multiphasic Personality Inventory (MMPI), make the assumption that there are stable constellations of characteristics that can be obtained by merely asking the person directly. Because trait approaches are based on large numbers of individuals, a person's score on a particular measure can be compared to the normative score of the population. Thus, trait assessment is based on *nomothetic* assumptions, so that an individual can only be understood when compared with the population at large, whereas behavioral assessment is based on *idiographic* assumptions involving the intensive study of individuals.

Cognitive assessment is founded on the assumption that cognitive processes affect a person's behavioral and emotional responses. However, the environment is also considered a critical aspect of the assessment process, because transformations of stimuli from the environment may be a function of cognitive processes. Cognitive assessment may involve either a sample approach or a sign approach. The methods for assessing self-statements—what Ingram and Kendall (1986) called *cognitive products*—that we primarily focus on in this chapter are a sample of a person's thoughts in a particular situation. However, recent attempts to use the Stroop color-naming task or information-processing perspectives to assess cognitive structures and schemas could be considered a sign approach.

Although the level of measurement in cognitive and behavioral assessment compared to traditional assessment is less global, and the inferences made in the assessment process far less deep, the issues generally encountered in traditional personality trait assessment are nonetheless relevant.

TABLE 6.1

Overview of Projective, Trait, Behavioral, and Cognitive Approaches to Assessment

	Projective	Trait	Behavioral	Cognitive
Aims/goals	Identify dynamics of personality by inferring unconscious processes and issues from personal symbols.	Identify a constellation or configuration of personality characteristics.	Identify behaviors and the antecedents and reinforcers of those particular behaviors.	Identify cognitive processes that interact with affect and influence behavior.
Scope of assessment	Assess intrapsychic functioning to provide a broad-based description of personality.	Assess many or few stable traits to provide a broad or narrow description of personality.	Assess particular behaviors and provide specific information about the antecedents and reinforcers that may provoke and maintain the behaviors.	Assess various aspects of information processing and their relationship to affective and behavioral states. May be broad or narrow in scope.
Assumptions about methods	Information (symbols) is derived by methods that bypass defenses and is used to infer intrapsychic processes not readily available for conscious examination. Idiographic, sign approach. Emphasis on person factors.	Personality constructs are accessible by self-report using instruments that are reliable and valid. Nomothetic approach. Emphasis on stable person factors.	Direct observations in situations provide adequate information about behavior and the antecedents and reinforcers. Idiographic, sample approach. Emphasis on situational factors.	Cognitive processes can be inferred from cognitive products, affective responses and motoric responses. Idiographic and nomethetic, sample and sign approach. Emphasis on person and situational factors.

Conceptualization of clinical problems	Intrapsychic unconscious conflict is responsible for maladaptive affect and behaviors.	Extreme scores on certain traits or on unusual configuration of traits may be associated with maladaptive affect and behavior.	Environmental variables such as aspects of the situation and/or specific reinforcement contingencies cause or maintain maladaptive behaviors.	Dysfunctional information-processing or cognitive processes cause maladaptive affect or behavior.
Uses of assessment results	Assessment results provide descriptive information that may be used to diagnose or to devise goals for therapy. Global predictions regarding prognosis. Conflicts may be identified that may be dealt with in therapy. May not be a sensitive process or outcome measure because of reliability problems.	Assessment results are used to classify and diagnose or to imply broad goals that relate to changes in the structure, level, or configuration of traits. Global predictors regarding prognosis. May not be a sensitive process or outcome measure to assess treatment effects.	Assessment results and treatment are closely connected. Assessment used to select treatments and document the effectiveness of treatment. Sensitive outcome measure but not useful as process measure.	Assessment results may be used to devise goals for treatment. Changes in dysfunctional cognitive processes may be part of treatment. May be useful process and outcome measure.

Note. From Merluzzi and Carr (1992). Reprinted by permission.

That is, reliability and validity, particularly ecological validity, are critical issues in cognitive and behavioral assessment as well.

The distinction between cognitive and behavioral assessment and more traditional assessment methods noted earlier should not lead one to assume that both cognitive and behavioral assessment are based on identical underlying assumptions. Although they might share some common assumptions about the scope of the tasks of assessment, strictly speaking, they are not based on the same conceptual presuppositions. On a more practical level, strict adherents of behavior theory might not value self-reported thoughts concomitant with directly observed behavior. For them, overt behavior is considered the most relevant data to guide the development of a treatment plan and measure the effectiveness of the interventions. Conversely, strict adherents of the cognitive perspective might view a behavior as literally meaningless without the context provided by self-reported thoughts. Thus, thoughts might determine the interpretation of behavior. Despite the differences noted in Table 6.1, however, both the cognitive and behavioral perspectives have empiricism as their method of proof, operationism as a way of describing experimental procedures, and adhere to the rational canons of science (Lachman, Lachman, & Butterfield, 1979).

In recent years, the differences between the perspectives have received less and less attention. Current interest in the integration of psychotherapy approaches (e.g., Norcross & Goldfried, 1992; Stricker & Gold, 1993) has promoted the pursuit of discovering what is common and effective in all approaches to psychotherapy and, presumably, assessment as well.

In the following sections we present basic information about behavioral and cognitive approaches to assessment. For each approach we present information about administration and scoring, interpretation, and finally, a short case example.

BEHAVIORAL ASSESSMENT

Administration and Scoring

Behavioral assessment measures have been developed for a wide array of problem areas ranging from marital discord to phobias, from school behaviors to sexual dysfunction. These assessment procedures can play an important role in initial problem identification and specification as well as treatment planning, evaluation, and revision. The following discussion begins with a brief explanation of six frequently used methods of behavioral assessment. Behavior therapists typically use more than one of these methods (a *multimethod* assessment) in the measurement of target behaviors. We then focus our attention on a selective review of the behavioral assessment of social skills and social anxiety, an area generating a great deal of interest in recent years. In large part, this interest has been due to the association of social skills deficits with a broad range of clinical problems including depression, juvenile delinquency, marital distress, social isolation, and illness (McFall, 1982). Assessment methods used in the evaluation of social skills are presented as representative of the issues and methods germane to behavioral assessment in general.

Behavioral Interviews. The behavioral interview is usually the starting point for assessment in behavior therapy (Morganstern, 1988). According to Spiegler and Guevremont (1998), the behavioral interview is also the most frequently used behavioral assessment method, with 90% of behavior therapists indicating that they used the method with six or more clients within the past year.

Kirk (1989) provided a detailed description of the stages and content of the behavioral interview. During the initial stage of the interview, the counselor simply puts clients at ease and listens to their description of the presenting problems. The next stage assesses the development of the problem, including onset, course (the way it has developed since onset), and predisposing factors (anything in the client's background that made it more likely that the problem would develop).

At the core of the behavioral interview, however, is the behavioral analysis stage, with the goal to discover "how the problem is currently maintained, in what way it is interfering with the patient's life, and whether the problem is serving any useful purpose for the patient" (Kirk, 1989, p. 25). Problems can be analyzed in terms of the conditions under which the problem is most likely to occur—that is, the counselor focuses on the antecedents and consequences of the behavior that increase or decrease the likelihood that the behavior will take place or modulate the intensity of the problem. These antecedents and consequences can involve both situational and behavioral cues, thoughts, mood states, and the behavior of others. The counselor will also want to analyze the factors that maintain the problem behavior, such as the immediate and long-term consequences, and the reduction in anxiety produced by avoidance. The behavioral interview is an essential first step in a comprehensive behavioral assessment. In addition to identifying problems and formulating hypotheses about them, the information gained from the interview can be used to guide the choice of additional forms of behavioral assessment.

Finally, the counselor assesses the coping resources and other assets of the client, psychiatric and medical history, psychosocial situation, and beliefs about the nature of the problem (Kirk, 1989). Other good examples of behavioral interviews include Kanfer and Saslow (1965), Wolpe (1992), and Goldfried and Davidson (1994).

Self-Report Inventories. Although self-report inventories or question-naires were once looked on with disfavor by many behavior therapists, they are now the second most common method of behavioral assessment, em-ployed by 63% of behavior therapists on a frequent basis (Spiegler & Guevremont, 1998). Unlike projective tests or empirically derived invento-ries such as the MMPI, behavioral questionnaires place a strong emphasis on specific behaviors and situations, thus giving them strong face validity, and typically show good criterion-related and convergent validity as well. Jensen and Hayes (1986) outlined a number of functions and goals for self-report questionnaires: collection of historic and demographic information, screening and diagnosis, and identification and specification of target be-haviors, controlling variables, and alternative behaviors.

The use of self-report inventories has many advantages. They are inex-pensive and relatively easy and quick to complete, asking clients to answer true/false or to rate how true items are on Likert-type rating scales. They are available in the form of broad inventories that can screen for a wide range of problems. There are also numerous questionnaires that are tai-lored to very specific behaviors and situations, such as depression, social skills, fear and anxiety, eating disorders, and marital problems. In the face of the proliferation of behavioral self-report questionnaires, users must be cautioned that the development of a valid and reliable instrument requires complex and extensive psychometric development, testing, and analysis. Before a questionnaire is used to make clinical judgments, the counselor should carefully evaluate its validity and reliability along with its appropri-ateness for a specific client and situation. Descriptions and psychometric information about a wide variety of behavioral self-report inventories can be found in the *Dictionary of Behavioral Assessment Techniques* (Hersen & Bellack, 1988a) and *Measures for Clinical Practice* (Fischer & Corcoran, 1994).

Self-Monitoring. Self-monitoring or self-recording refers to the system-atic observation and documentation of one's own behavior. Such procedures are a rich source of assessment information and can also serve as an important component of behavioral self-control interventions (Thoresen & Mahoney, 1974). Self-monitoring provides a relatively simple and highly flexible ap-proach to the collection of a variety of behavioral data, and is frequently used by 56% of behavior therapists (Spiegler & Guevremont, 1998). Types of information collected can include various forms of individual or group behavior, the antecedents and consequences of such behaviors, and any number of environmental aspects of the settings in which these events occur.

Clients who self-monitor their own behavior typically make frequency counts (i.e., how often the behavior occurs in a specified time period), but time-related measures (i.e., the duration of target behavior) and qualitative ratings of a variety of internal or external events can also be included. Common formats for self-recording include narrative descriptions, behavioral diaries, rating scales, checklists, and graphs. In addition, a variety of mechanical, timing, and electronic devices have been developed to aid in self-monitoring (Bornstein, Hamilton, & Bornstein, 1986). Ingenious self-monitoring systems, methods, and aids have been developed for almost every conceivable type of behavior (Mahoney, 1977; Thoresen & Mahoney, 1974). Problems associated with self-monitoring include questions of *reliability* (the honest and accuracy of the data obtained) and *reactivity* (the influence of the self-monitoring process on the behavior being measured). These problems have been the subject of considerable research and discussion and were reviewed in detail by Bornstein, Hamilton, and Bornstein (1986).

Direct or Naturalistic Observation. The direct observation and recording of an individual or group was once the "hallmark" of behavioral assessment (Ciminero, 1986), although it is frequently used today by only 30% of behavior therapists (Spiegler & Guevremont, 1998). Direct or naturalistic observation is usually employed to assess motor and/or verbal behaviors, ranging from discrete activities such as arm or eye movements to more complex behaviors such as social interactions. As Kazdin (1981) pointed out, the selection, operationalization, and measurement of target behaviors in an objective, clear, and complete manner may appear deceptively simple, but require careful planning and execution. Careful training of observers is essential for reliable observational assessment. Factors that must be considered include interrater reliability, observer drift, observer bias, and interactions between the observer and the observed (Foster & Cone, 1986).

Behaviors are usually quantified by using frequency measures, discrete categorizations (e.g., yes/no, correct/incorrect), or measures of the duration of the behavior. Recording procedures can be continuous or carried out at specified time units or intervals. Numerous variations and combinations of measurement and sampling procedures have been devised for behavioral observation programs (Foster, Bell-Dolan, & Burge, 1988). Direct observational assessment has been used very successfully with certain populations such as schoolchildren and the institutionalized. For general outpatient populations, effective naturalistic observation is more difficult because of practical limitations and the inability to control or standardize the assessment setting. For these populations, analogue methods have frequently been used as an alternative.

Analogue Observation. Analogue measures require the client to respond to a contrived situation that simulates or closely resembles the relevant conditions in the natural environment. Analogues provide an alternative form of direct behavioral observation when naturalistic observation is too costly or impractical, and allow the counselor to test hypotheses about the antecedents of the client's target behavior by varying the situation and observing the resulting behavior.

One of the most frequently used forms of analogue assessment is the Behavioral Avoidance Test (BAT), originally described by Lang and Lazovik (1963) in the assessment of snake phobia. Since then, the BAT has been used in the assessment of a variety of avoidant behaviors (Bernstein & Nietzel, 1973). In a typical BAT analogue, the client is instructed to proceed as far as possible through a series of progressively more challenging approaches to a specified object or situation. For example, in assessing spider phobia the client may first be instructed to view a picture of a spider and gradually progress to letting the spider crawl on his or her hand. A BAT typically includes from 5 to 15 progressive approach behaviors, with scoring based on the number of behavioral steps successfully completed.

Role plays are another common form of analogue assessment. A typical role play begins by describing a specific stimulus situation. The counselor or an assistant (confederate) then initiates an interaction that approximates a situation that might occur in the client's natural environment. The behavior of the client is rated according to specific response criteria. Variations on this format include using a written, audiotape, or videotape stimulus in place of a live actor, or having the client write out her or his responses rather than state them (Nay, 1977).

Analogue procedures provide a flexible format for the assessment of a wide range of behaviors within the practical restrictions of a clinical setting, yet simulated observations and role plays are used frequently by only 20–23% of behavior therapists (Spiegler & Guevremont, 1998). As assessment procedures move away from in vivo, naturalistic observation toward contrived analogues carried out in clinical or laboratory settings, the external validity of the analogue measure must be carefully addressed (Merluzzi & Biever, 1987). The generalizability of the client's behavior as observed in an analogue assessment to what she or he actually does in real-life settings is a critical concern.

Psychophysiological Assessment.   Experimental psychology, behavioral medicine, and biofeedback research have been responsible for the development of a number of physiological measures that are useful in behavioral assessment. Devices have been developed to measure multiple parameters of all major physiological systems, including cardiovascular, musculoskeletal, respiratory, electrodermal, gastrointestinal, and central nervous system (Kallman & Feuerstein, 1986; Sturgis & Gramling, 1988). Major applications of psychophysiological assessment include problems such as headaches, hypertension, Raynaud's syndrome, sexual dysfunction, convulsive disorders, anxiety and stress, and sleep disorders.

When measures are properly selected and applied, psychophysiological assessment can be valid and reliable. The major disadvantages are that they often require expensive and elaborate equipment that is often intrusive and restrictive. However, pulse rate (as an indicator of anxiety) is a simple measure that can be used by clients in the natural environment. About 19% of behavior therapists report the frequent use of psychophysiological measurement (Spiegler & Guevremont, 1998).

Assessment of Social Skills

Since the development of the Wolpe-Lazarus Assertiveness Inventory (Wolpe & Lazarus, 1966), numerous social skills and social anxiety assessment measures have appeared in the behavioral literature. The number and variety of these assessment procedures have been matched by the many, often divergent, definitions of social skills found in the literature. Assessment has focused on a number of different aspects, including global ratings of behavior (e.g., social skill, observed anxiety, impression made), numerous different molecular behaviors such as talk time and eye contact, self-ratings of subjective anxiety levels, avoidance of or inhibited social behavior, available repertoires of social responses, and the ability to understand and appropriately respond to social cues.

In spite of this extensive work in the area of social skills assessment, Conger and Conger (1986) pointed out that there is "no theoretically derived nor empirically established listing of (social) skills" (p. 527). Hersen and Bellack (1977) provided a broad, clinically useful definition for social skills by describing the construct as the "effectiveness of behavior in social interactions" (p. 512).

The reader is referred to McFall (1982) for an insightful discussion of current theoretical and assessment issues in the conceptualization of social skills. The formats most frequently used in the behavioral assessment of social skills and anxiety are behavioral interviews, self-report questionnaires, and analogue observational measures. An overview of some of the better known social skills and anxiety measures is provided later. Detailed reviews of social skills measures were provided in Bellack and Hersen (1979), and Glass and Arnkoff (1989) provided a review of the behavioral assessment of social anxiety and social phobia.

Behavioral Interviews. Arkowitz (1981) suggested that a behavioral interview for assessing social inadequacy and anxiety should yield descriptions of potential social contacts and a typical day with reference to social interactions, as well as information on the client's sexual knowledge, experiences, and anxieties. He also suggested assessing social functioning across 21 different areas, including same- and other-sex relationships, casual and intimate relationships, public speaking, and initiating and developing social interactions. The client is asked to estimate his or her level of social skill and social anxiety in each of these areas. Some of the same issues are addressed in the Social Anxiety History Questionnaire (Turner, Beidel, Dancu, & Keys, 1986), an interviewer-administered questionnaire covering topics related to the range of fears experienced by social phobics.

It is unfortunate that there is little research on behavioral interviews, and no reliability and validity information is available for the approaches just described. However, there is considerable overlap between behavioral interviews and one of the major interviews currently employed to diagnose anxiety disorders, the revised Anxiety Disorders Interview Schedule (ADIS-R; DiNardo & Barlow, 1988). In assessing social phobia with the ADIS-R, the interviewer asks clients to rate their level of fear and avoidance in social situations such as parties, meetings, using public restrooms, and eating, writing, and speaking in public. Clients are also asked when these fears were first experienced, and whether anxiety and avoidance are dependent on the formality of the situation, the size of the group, or the degree of acquaintance.

Self-Report Inventories. Self-report inventories have a long history in the assessment of social anxiety and inhibition, and are the most frequently used and most diverse form of behavioral assessment of social skills. The relevant questionnaires can be organized into four major areas: social skills, shyness, social anxiety, and general phobic severity.

The first group of measures, inventories that assess social skills, tend to focus either on assertiveness or skill in social interactions. The most widely used assertiveness scales are the Rathus Assertiveness Schedule (RAS; Rathus, 1973), the College Self-Expression Scale (CSES; Galassi, DeLo, Galassi, & Bastien, 1974), and the Assertion Inventory (AI; Gambrill & Richey, 1975). The RAS contains 30 descriptive statements, to which clients respond on a Likert scale ranging from *very uncharacteristic* to *very characteristic*. On the CSES, clients use a 5-point Likert scale (ranging from "never or rarely" to "almost always") to indicate the likelihood of engaging in each of 50 social behaviors concerned with positive assertion, negative assertion, and self-denial. Most items include both a specific type of assertive behavior and the person or situational context involved. As its name implies, the CSES was tailored for college students; a less frequently used "adult" version has also been developed (Gay, Hollandsworth, & Galassi, 1975). The AI also uses a Likert format, but in contrast to the already-mentioned measures, each descriptive situation is rated separately for the likelihood of engaging in the behavior and the amount of discomfort associated with carrying it out. The AI also provides separate scales for different types of social situations such as declining requests, engaging in social contacts, and expressing negative feelings. See Beck and Heimberg (1983) and St. Laurence (1987) for a more detailed review of the assessment of assertion.

The three best-known self-report measures for the assessment of social skill or social behavior are the Survey of Heterosexual Interactions (SHI;

Twentyman & McFall, 1975), the Social Performance Survey Schedule (SPSS; Lowe & Cautela, 1978), and the Social Situations Questionnaire (SSQ; Bryant & Trower, 1974). The SHI presents 20 situations primarily dealing with the early states of dating. Clients rate on 7-point scales the likelihood that they would actually perform the behavior called for. Williams and Ciminero (1978) developed a parallel version for women in heterosocial situations, the SHI-F. The SPSS is a 100-item scale that assesses self-reported frequency of positive and negative social behaviors. It is especially useful in the early stages of treatment planning and in selecting clients who might benefit from social skills training. Finally, although initially used with undergraduates, the SSQ has also been used with diagnosed social phobic clients. This inventory presents 30 social situations that range from casual to more intimate encounters, and clients are asked to rate the difficulty and frequency of occurrence of each situation.

The three measures of shyness we discuss next were developed by social psychologists and may not be well known to counselors. A chapter by Briggs and Smith (1986) provides more in-depth information in these scales. The Stanford Shyness Survey (Zimbardo, 1977) contains 44 questions dealing with many aspects of shyness, including clients' attributions as to the causes of their shyness, situations and individuals eliciting feelings of shyness, consequences of shyness, and physiological, cognitive/affective, and behavioral symptoms. Cheek and Buss's (1981) Shyness Scale was designed to assess discomfort and inhibition in the presence of others. Both the original 9-item scale and the revised 20-item inventory (Cheek & Melchior, 1985) have shown good reliability. Finally, the Social Reticence Scale (SRS; Jones & Russell, 1982) and its revision (SRS-II; Jones, Briggs, & Smith, 1986) are also measures of discomfort and inhibition in the presence of others. Seven components of dispositional shyness are assessed, including anxiety, inhibition, loneliness, distraction, and isolation.

Among the self-report inventories of social anxiety, Watson and Friend's (1969) Social Avoidance and Distress Scale (SAD) and Fear of Negative Evaluation Scale (FNE) have been the most frequently used. The SAD, which contains 28 true–false items, includes items related to behavioral avoidance as well as subjective anxiety, and is thus not a "pure" measure of the construct. The FNE is a 30-item true–false inventory that focuses more on concerns over negative evaluation by others. More recently, the Social Phobia and Anxiety Inventory (SPAI) has received increasing use and interest (Turner, Beidel, Dancu, & Stanley, 1989).

The last group of self-report questionnaires is inventories of general fear. Perhaps the best known such scale is the Fear Survey Schedule (FSS), of which there are several versions. The FSS-III (Wolpe & Lang, 1964) consists of 75 items reflecting the most common fears seen in clinical practice, and clients rate the degree of their fear on 5-point Likert scales. An additional measure of phobic symptoms related to social phobia, agoraphobia, and blood-injury phobia is the Fear Questionnaire (FQ; Marks & Mathews, 1979). In the social phobia subscale, clients indicate on a 9-point scale how much they would avoid each of five situations. A third general measure of anxiety is the more recently developed Beck Anxiety Inventory (Beck, Epstein, Brown, & Steer, 1988), a measure of the somatic and affective symptoms of clinical anxiety. The BAI has nòt been used in research on social anxiety and phobia, but will probably be increasingly important for counselors.

Self-Monitoring. Self-monitoring or self-observation can allow a unique assessment of real-life interactions. From a record of the client's dates and casual interactions, it is possible to derive measures of the frequency of social contacts (both formal and informal), their antecedents and consequences, the range or number of different people with whom a client interacts, duration of interactions, topics of conversation of types of interaction, and self-ratings of anxiety and skill.

Gambrill and Richey (1985) developed a social contact recording form that allows for the self-recording of a number of aspects of social interactions, including the person contacted along with the setting, nature, and duration of the interaction. In addition, the client rates her or his comfort, confidence, and enjoyment concerning the contact.

The daily log or diary used by Dodge, Heimberg, Nyman, and O'Brien (1987) to study the other-sex interactions of high and low socially anxious undergraduates yielded a good deal of useful information. Analyses of these diaries suggested that high-anxious students had fewer interactions, especially with friends or lovers, experienced higher levels of anxiety, were less satisfied with their performance, and rated it more negatively than did low-anxious students.

Direct or Naturalistic Observation. Although naturalistic observation is generally considered the most valid form of behavioral assessment, it has been infrequently used in the area of social skills. As Bellack and Hersen (1979) noted, "the special character of interpersonal behavior frequently makes such observations impractical or impossible. Intimate and private interactions generally are not privy to outside observers, and many public interactions (e.g., assertion situations, meeting with a stranger) occur too infrequently and unpredictably to permit easy access" (p.87). As a result of these difficulties, a great deal of attention has been turned to the development of analogue measures, as described next.

Analogue Measures. After self-report questionnaires and behavioral interviews, behavioral observation using simulated situations or role plays of various types is the most frequently reported form of behavioral assessment used in the literature on social skills and anxiety. In these analogues, a stimulus situation is presented and the client is then instructed to respond as he or she would in a real situation. Kern (1982) suggested that role-play formats can vary in terms of how closely they approximate more naturalistic behavior. The external validity of such role-play assessments can be increased by making role plays as realistic as possible (Bellack, 1983), by having clients replicate their behavior from prior naturalistic interactions, and by sampling a number of personally relevant situations. Conger and Conger's (1986) chapter on social skills assessment contained an excellent review of the literature on simulated role-play interactions.

As with self-report questionnaires, a wide variety of designs has been reported. Variations involve time periods (ranging from single brief responses to extended face-to-face interactions), different levels of realism in the settings used, different stimulus presentations (ranging from audiotapes to live actors serving as confederates), and differing response modes.

Scoring procedures also vary widely across different analogue assessments. Global ratings of skill and anxiety can be derived from one of three sources: from clients themselves, from their partners or confederates in the interaction, or from external judges who observe the interaction or later view it on videotape. Client ratings of anxiety (often on a 1–7 or 0–100 scale) can be requested at any number of points both before, during, and after the interaction. Obtaining ratings from all three sources is valuable, because self-evaluations of anxiety may be more extreme than levels of anxiety noticeable by others. The perspective of the confederate may also be quite different from that of a judge who has never met the client.

A final issue in analogue assessment involves the level of measurement employed in the behavioral observation. Most of the social anxiety and social skills research has used global ratings, in which raters use Likert scales to specify the client's overall level of social skill, anxiety, likability, attractiveness, effectiveness, and so on. In contrast to such global or molar ratings, a client's interactions can also be analyzed according to specific micro or molecular behaviors, such as talk time, gaze, gestures, smiles, leg movements, and number of questions.

The prototype of the single-response role-play test is the Taped Situation Test (TST, Rehm & Marston, 1968), which consists of 10 heterosocial situations presented on audiotape. A narrator describes the background of each situation, a female confederate delivers a prompt line of dialogue, and clients have 10 sec to respond as they believe they would in real life.

One of very few measures developed for inpatients is the Simulated Social Interaction Test (SSIT; Curran, 1982; Farrell, Curran, Zwick, & Monti, 1983). The SSIT consists of eight brief social interactions, each initiated by confederate prompts delivered in face-to-face interactions. The situations were selected based on factor-analytic results from previous research on social anxiety, and represent a range of social encounters. For example:

Narrator: "Let's suppose you respond to an ad in the newspaper and go for a job interview. As the interview goes on, the interviewer says":

Confederate: "What makes you think you're a good person for the job?" (Farrell et al., 1983, p. 5)

The client then responds as she or he would in an actual situation. Eight such interactions are videotaped, with the client responding to examples of disapproval, assertiveness, confrontation, heterosexual contact, interpersonal warmth, rejection by parents, interpersonal loss, and positive feedback. These tapes are rated by trained judges who use 11-point Likert scales to assess overall assertiveness and overall anxiety. The Behavioral Assertiveness Test (BAT) developed by Eisler, Miller, and Hersen (1973) uses a similar format, where judges rate verbal responses such as duration of reply, loudness, compliance, and requests as well as nonverbal behaviors such as eye contact and smiles.

In a format similar to the above, Mullinix and Galassi (1981) presented participants with four audiotaped statements involving work-related conflict. They were asked to take the role of a coworker and to write down exactly what they would say in response to the taped statement. These statements were then rated by trained judges for level of compliance and presence of annoyance/hostility.

Becker and Heimberg (1988) have criticized single-response role plays for a number of reasons. Such single exchanges are uncommon in real-life interactions, they are unable to assess difficulties that would arise later in the interaction, and some studies have not supported their validity. For these reasons, multiple-response role plays have been developed (e.g., Galassi & Galassi, 1977), where the client's first response is followed by another prompt from the partner, and so on, such that over time the role play resembles an actual interaction. One of the best examples of these extended interaction measures is the Social Interaction Test (SIT; Trower, Bryant, & Argyle, 1978), in which clients are asked to interact for 12 min with a male and female confederate. A 29-item rating scale is used by both partners and judges to evaluate the client's actual verbal and nonverbal behavior and physical appearance. Another more naturalistic analogue procedure, with many of the advantages of direct behavioral observation, was developed by Higgins, Frisch, and Smith (1983). In the Behavioral Assessment Situation (BAS) the client is confronted by a confederate student who, in the course of a conversation, makes a series of increasingly demanding requests to borrow some important class notes from them. The client is unaware that the fellow student is a confederate and that the interaction is being videotaped. The videotape is then scored for overall social skill, tenseness/uneasiness, number of speech disturbances, frequency of conversational questions and feedback, latency of responses, and level of compliance. The reader is encouraged to consult Conger and Conger (1986) and Merluzzi and Biever (1987) concerning issues related to the validity of analogue methods of behavioral assessment of social skill.

Psychophysiological Assessment. Due to the intrusive nature and cost of required instrumentation, little use has been made of psychophysiological measurements as a component in the comprehensive behavioral assessment of social skills and anxiety. Several studies (Kaloupek & Levis, 1980; Monti, Wallander, Ahern, & Munroe, 1984) have used a psychophysiological measure of anxiety (i.e., heart rate) as part of a multidimensional assessment of anxiety and social skills. Although anxiety is often present in individuals with poor social functioning, neither its role in overall social functioning nor its relationship to socially skilled behaviors is currently clear (Bellack, 1979).

Summary. Although the sheer number and variety of assessments may appear confusing, this broad variety is also a significant asset. The variety of choices currently available allows the counselor to select from a wide range of assessment options and select measures that best suit a specific client's needs. Choice of an appropriate set of assessment measures should be guided by a careful assessment of intervention targets (Kanfer, 1985) and should focus on the individual problems and circumstances of the client. The initial interview should suggest hypotheses about target behaviors that can be clarified and tested using multiple methods of behavioral assessment.

Interpretation

Interpretation of behavioral assessment measures most often focuses on the degree of change between pretreatment (baseline) measures and those made during and after treatment. Thus, repeatedly administered measures can detect relatively small changes over the course of treatment and also provide important idiographic information.

Another characteristic of behavioral assessment evaluation is an emphasis on single-subject designs and visual or clinical analysis (Turner & Ascher, 1985). These data-based approaches to analysis illustrate the emphasis that behavior therapy places on the empirical evaluation of clinical practice (Barlow, Hayes, & Nelson, 1984). Thus, although group comparisons are often considered the hallmark of psychological research, it should be noted that single-subject designs have played an important role in the advancement of both clinical and basic research in behavior therapy (Barlow et al., 1984). Some behavior therapists hold that significance tests are not sensitive to important aspects of *individual* change. In addition, differences in sample size and variance can obscure substantial therapeutic effectiveness, whereas at other times statistically significant results can be obtained in spite of trivial clinical differences between groups or failure to demonstrate clinically significant change.

Case Example

Susan is a 29-year-old woman, referred by a friend to a local community mental health center. Her presenting complaint was dissatisfaction with her current social and personal life. Behavioral assessment techniques used by the psychologist who worked with Susan included a structured interview, several self-report questionnaires, role plays, and self-monitoring procedures.

The outline developed by Arkowitz (1981) was used to guide the behavioral interview, which was conducted over several sessions and is briefly summarized here. Susan presented as an appropriately dressed young woman who appeared her stated age and was of average physical appearance. She displayed little eye contact and tended to respond to questions with short monotonic answers. Susan showed little affect except for a brief period of tearfulness. A review of her current functioning and past history showed no evidence of major psychopathology.

The client related that she had come to feel increasingly socially isolated over the past several years. Three years ago she had broken up with her boyfriend after a 4-year relationship and had not dated since. Susan worked as a registered nurse in a local hospital and had been working a night shift since shortly after the breakup with her boyfriend. She had a small group of female friends she saw regularly and with whom she felt at ease. In addition, she had a close relationship with her family. Areas of difficulty included conversations with men, speaking in front of a group, and situations that called for assertiveness (e.g., making complaints, disagreeing with others).

Susan was taken through a broad overview of her social functioning as a child and adult. This discussion was followed by a detailed review of a number of specific areas of social functioning such as casual relationships, intimate relationships, interactions with authority figures, and relationships with family members. She was also asked to review the events in a typical day in her current life. This process was used to help identify specific problem areas and skill deficits. Problematic behaviors were carefully examined in terms of their antecedents and consequences.

The client completed the Social Avoidance and Distress Scale and the Assertion Inventory. Susan's score on the SAD was 19, well above the normative mean of 9. On the AI she had a discomfort score of 115 (normative mean = 94, SD = 21) and a response probability score of 110 (normative mean = 104, SD = 16, with lower scores reflecting a greater probability of displaying the behavior). Areas of highest discomfort on the AI were engaging in social contacts, handling criticism, and disagreeing.

At the close of the first session, Susan was instructed in the use of a social contacts recording form, which she was to keep with her and complete throughout the next week. Following any social contact, she was to record the day, time, general nature, and duration of that contact; information on the other person(s) and their responses; who initiated the exchange, and if it was Susan, what she said; and finally, a brief rating of her comfort, satisfaction, and enjoyment of the interaction. At the time of her second interview, this self-monitoring form was used for further assessment of problem areas and their antecedents and consequences. The information was also used to help identify specific behavioral skill deficits and situations that led to increased anxiety.

Two analogue role plays were conducted during the second session. In the first a male counselor and in the second a female counselor from the agency volunteered to serve as confederates. For each analogue, Susan was simply instructed to maintain a conversation for 5 minutes, pretending that she and the confederate were sharing a table during lunch in a cafeteria. Her psychologist served as an observer for both analogues. After each role play, both the psychologist and Susan gave global ratings of both her social skill and anxiety on a scale from 1 (lowest possible skill or anxiety level) to 10 (highest level). The observer's scores for the male role play were social skill = 3, social anxiety = 7; in the female role play, ratings were social skill = 5, social anxiety = 5. Susan's self-ratings for the male role play were social skill = 3, social anxiety = 8, and in the female role play her self-ratings were social skill = 5 and social anxiety = 7.

This behavioral observation, although not a naturalistic situation, allowed the psychologist to view the client's behavior with both a man and a woman. Observing the role plays gave him the opportunity to discuss later with Susan the relation of her self-perceptions of social skill and anxiety with those of an observer. A comparison of observer and self-ratings of anxiety was used to analyze some of her actions that indicated anxiety, and to explore some the fears that contributed to Susan's social anxiety in the role plays and at other times. Most importantly, the analogues allowed the psychologist to observe, and later discuss with the client, a number of specific components of her social interactions. These included motor behaviors (e.g., eye contact, nodding, and body posture), speech characteristics (e.g., latencies and volume), and conversational style and content (e.g., asking open-ended questions, providing reinforcement, balancing talking and listening).

The information provided by the questionnaires, role plays, and self-monitoring was used to help identify specific problem areas and skill deficits, and in the selection of appropriate treatment strategies. Assessment information was also used to help set treatment goals and priorities. For example, excessive anxiety across a number of social situations served to limit Susan's initiation of conversations and interfered with performance in and enjoyment of social interactions. Selecting anxiety reduction in social situations as an early treatment goal led to instruction in relaxation techniques and other coping strategies that she could use during in vivo exposure to a hierarchy of anxiety-provoking situations.

Another goal identified during the initial assessment was Susan's desire to increase her social contacts with men and improve her skills and increase her enjoyment in these situations. The articulation of this goal led to further assessment of this area, skills training to correct specific behavioral deficits, and exploration of the types of situations that would lead to increased contacts with men in nonthreatening settings.

Susan was seen weekly for approximately 4 months. Throughout her treatment, assessment was seen as an ongoing process. Different forms of self-monitoring were used to help redefine goals and indicate when they had been attained. Daily self-monitoring of social contacts initiated with men also allowed for continuous assessment of progress. Occasional role-play exercises were used to help identify and remediate specific skill deficits in different social settings.

At the next to last treatment session, the SAD and AI were readministered, and the initial two role-play analogues were repeated. Susan's SAD score had decreased from 19 to 10. On the AI, her discomfort score decreased from 115 to 95, while her response probability score improved from 110 to 100. The observer's ratings on the same 10-point scale from the male role play were social skill = 6 and social anxiety = 5, and from the female role play, social skill = 7 and social anxiety = 2. Susan's self-ratings for the male role play were social skill = 7 and social anxiety = 5. In the female role play, her self-ratings were social skill = 7 and social anxiety = 3. All of these scores showed relative improvement since the initial assessment.

By the final session Susan felt that she had met all the specific goals set during the course of counseling. The accomplishment of these various progressive behavioral goals had been documented through the use of self-monitoring procedures throughout treatment, and by readministering the self-report questionnaires and role-play analogue test. She felt that the skills she acquired had greatly enhanced her level of social functioning. Of equal importance, Susan felt she now had the skills to shape her own behavior. She planned to continue to use the self-monitoring and behavioral analysis procedures she had learned in treatment to continue to improve her skills and enhance her enjoyment of social situations in the future.

Psychometric Analysis of Behavioral Assessment: Current Trends

A review of the current literature reveals considerable controversy concerning the validity and reliability of behavioral assessment measures of social skills and social anxiety. Areas of criticism include debates about definitions of social skills, the lack of standardized assessment procedures, the proliferation of measures with questionable psychometric properties, and poor correlations among various social skills measures (Conger & Conger, 1986). These issues are representative of current debates throughout the field of behavioral assessment (Strosahl & Linehan, 1986).

A major factor in all of these concerns is the lack of a standardized definition of social skills, and disagreement as to its basic components (Conger & Conger, 1986). Furthermore, although it is generally recognized that social skills involve multiple components, self-report questionnaires usually yield only a single score. Bellack (1979) noted that because anxiety, skills, and behaviors are often not correlated, it makes little sense to sum them into a single global score.

Although analogue measures are more likely to provide multiple component measures in addition to (or instead of) a single global score, they have been subject to criticism on other grounds. The validity of these components is not clear, especially given the variety of components assessed across studies and the different ways they are measured (Conger & Conger, 1986). In addition, although the behavioral literature stresses the importance of situational specificity in behavioral responses, analogue measures are often very limited in the variety of stimulus situations that they present (Arkowitz, 1981). Galassi and Galassi (1976) demonstrated that variations in analogue design (e.g., length of interaction, live model vs. videotape vs. audiotape) result in significantly different results. Finally, the ecological validity of analogue measures has been unclear in light of research that has shown a lack of correlation between role plays and more naturalistic measures in some instances (Frisch & Higgins, 1986), yet finding adequate correlations in others (Merluzzi & Biever, 1987).

COGNITIVE ASSESSMENT

Following the growth of cognitive and cognitive-behavioral therapies, interest in cognitive assessment has increased. Ingram and Kendall (1986) proposed a broad-based taxonomy for cognitive assessment that included four components: (a) cognitive structures, (b) cognitive propositions, (c) cognitive operations (or processes), and (d) cognitive products. Structures refer to the organization of information, that is, how the information is stored and organized by the individual. Examples of cognitive structures are short-term and long-term memory. Cognitive propositions refer to the information that is contained in those structures. Operations are the procedures or mechanisms by which information is encoded, stored, and retrieved. Finally, cognitive products are the output from the system. The first three components of this taxonomy have been the focus of basic research on cognitive aspects of psychopathology, but have seen little clinical application. Cognitive products, such as thoughts, beliefs, and narratives of which people are consciously aware, have been used extensively and have a great deal of clinical utility.

In the sections that follow, we have chosen to focus on the assessment of several cognitive products that will be of greatest interest to the counselor, namely, self-statements, beliefs, attributions, and expectancies. It is important to recognize that dysfunctional cognition can take one of two forms. Cognitive *deficits* or deficiency refers to the absence of certain thoughts or information processing that could be helpful (e.g., in impulsive children), whereas cognitive *distortions* are more active, negative thinking processes more typically associated with anxiety and depression (Kendall & Dobson, 1993).

Self-Statements

The approach to assessing cognitive products that has generated by far the greatest interest is the assessment of self-statements and internal dialogue. Several classification schemes have been proposed to classify the various methods of assessing thoughts (see Glass & Merluzzi, 1981; Kendall & Hollon, 1981b; Martzke, Anderson, & Cacioppo, 1987). Glass (1993) offered a comprehensive strategy in which methods of assessing thoughts can be viewed according to where they fall on each of four dimensions:

- Structure (endorsement vs. production).
- Timing (retrospective, concurrent, or about future events).
- Response mode (written or oral).
- Nature of stimulus (thoughts "in general," imagined situation, situation viewed on videotape, role play, or in vivo situation).

Endorsement Methods. Endorsement methods, which have the highest degree of structure, are typified by self-statement questionnaires or inventories—what Glass and Merluzzi (1981) classified as "recognition methods." The client is typically presented with a list of thoughts and is asked to check off or rate how frequently he or she has had each one in a particular time period or situation. Such ratings scales might range, for example, from 1 (never) to 5 (very often). These inventories often include 20 to 30 items and have a specific focus such as social anxiety, depression, agoraphobia, and so on. The *response mode* of structured-thought questionnaires is usually written, although in measures for children questions can be read aloud and answers given orally. On the *timing* dimension, such measures are usually administered retrospectively, and it is important to complete self-statement questionnaires as soon as possible after the situation of interest. For example, a depressed client might complete the Automatic Thoughts Questionnaire (ATQ), indicating how frequently negative thoughts occurred over the last week. However, self-statement inventories could also be used in anticipation of a particular task, especially for anxious clients where anticipatory anxiety may be greater than that experienced once in the situation itself. Finally, with respect to the *nature of the stimulus*, assessments can occur after imagined scenes, situations presented on audio- or videotape, role-played scenarios, in vivo situations, or with general instructions to rate how often each thought has been experienced.

Examples of frequently used self-statement inventories are:

- Agoraphobic Cognitions Questionnaire (ACQ; Chambless, Caputo, Bright, & Gallagher, 1984).
- Anxious Self-Statements Questionnaire (ASSQ; Kendall & Hollon, 1989).
- Assertiveness Self-Statement Test (ASST; Schwartz & Gottman, 1976).
- Automatic Thoughts Questionnaire (ATQ; Hollon & Kendall, 1980; depression).
- Checklist of Positive and Negative Thoughts (CPNT; Galassi, Frierson, & Sharer, 1981; test anxiety).
- Children's Cognitive Assessment Questionnaire (CCAQ; Zatz & Chassin, 1985; test anxiety).
- Cognition Checklist (CCL; Beck, Brown, Steer, Eidelson, & Riskind, 1987; depression and anxiety).
- Cognitive Interference Questionnaire (CIQ; Sarason & Stoops, 1978; test anxiety).
- Negative Affect Self-Statement Questionnaire (NASSQ; Ronan, Kendall, & Rowe, 1994).
- Panic Attack Cognitions Questionnaire (PACQ; Clum, Broyles, Borden, & Watkins, 1990).
- Revised Obsessional Intrusions Inventory (ROII; Purdon & Clark, 1994).
- Social Interaction Self-Statement Test (SISST; Glass, Merluzzi, Biever, & Larsen, 1982).

The advantage of endorsement approaches to assessing thoughts is that they are easy to administer and score. After the client completes a checklist or rates how frequently she or he had each thought, the counselor can sum the ratings, usually with separate subscales for positive and negative thoughts. Clark (1988) also suggested that structured questionnaires may facilitate accessibility by priming cognitions through reliance on the recognition process.

The obvious disadvantage of structured inventories is that the statements contained in these questionnaires are prototypical statements and may not reflect an individual client's actual thoughts. Thus, the idiosyncratic nature of the individual's thoughts is not captured. Also, self-statement inventories are devised for a very specific problem, and a counselor would need one measure for each problem area and would need to rely on existing measures with demonstrated reliability and validity. Although such questionnaires have also been criticized for not assessing the impact these thoughts have for clients, counselors can review the questionnaire during a session and probe into the idiosyncratic meaning of each thought.

Production Methods. The production or protocol analysis method requires clients to generate or recall their thoughts. With respect to the *response mode*, these thoughts can be communicated orally (and audiorecorded) or they can be written. Also, production methods may vary on the *timing* dimension: retrospective, concurrent, or thoughts about future events can be obtained. Usually, the client is given a brief period of time to write discrete thoughts, which can be categorized by the counselor and client. Examples of production methods are:

- Thought listings (Cacioppo & Petty, 1981; Cacioppo, von Hippel, & Ernst, 1997).
- Daily Record of Dysfunctional Thoughts (Beck & Emery, 1985).
- Videotape-aided thought recall (VTR; Ickes, Robertson, Tooke, & Teng, 1986).
- Think-aloud (Genest & Turk, 1981).
- Articulated thoughts during simulated situations (ATSS; Davison, Robins, & Johnson, 1983; Davison, Vogel, & Coffman, 1997).
- Thought sampling (Hurlburt, 1997; Hurlburt & Melancon, 1987).

The *thought listing* method (Cacioppo & Petty, 1981; Cacioppo et al., 1997) requires the client to write the thoughts he or she had during a specified period of time (e.g., while waiting for a job interview) or, in the case of test anxiety, while taking an exam. Thus the situation may have occurred in the past or may be one that the client is anticipating. For example, socially anxious clients may be asked to imagine or remember a recent interaction with a stranger and then to "list thoughts that went through your head; whether about yourself, the other person, or the situation; whether positive, negative, or neutral." Usually, the client is given a period of time to complete this task (e.g., 2.5 min). Although thought listings are versatile and can be used across a variety of situations and problems, it is sometimes the case that clients produce relatively few thoughts using this format.

Many cognitive therapists are already familiar with the *Daily Record of Dysfunctional Thoughts,* which is an integral part of the homework tasks used to increase clients' awareness of their thinking styles (Beck & Emery, 1985). Clients are asked to review the day's activities and record the nature of the situation in which they experienced some negative affect (e.g., depression, anxiety, anger), rate the intensity of that emotion on a 1–100 scale, and then list the thoughts that accompanied this feeling. Later on in counseling, clients learn the ways in which these automatic thoughts are reflective of underlying cognitive distortions such as catastrophizing or overgeneralization. As they learn to challenge their thoughts by asking "What's the evidence?," "What's another way of looking at it?," and "So what if it happens?" (Spiegler & Guevremont, 1998), an additional column on the form can be used to write down a more adaptive or positive cognition. Thought Record Forms have the advantage of assessing thoughts directly in real-life situations, although the counselor has less control over the assessment situation and must rely on the client to remember to record all relevant information.

Another method of asking clients to recall thoughts after a real-life or role-played situation has been termed *videotape-aided thought recall* (VTR). VTR is an example of what Kendall and Hollon (1981a) classified as recording methods, and Glass and Merluzzi (1981) called prompted recall. Clients are shown a videotape of their performance and are asked to stop the tape when they recall a thought (Ickes et al., 1986), to verbalize thoughts continuously, or are prompted at regular intervals to report what they were thinking. Typically, clients talk into an audiotape recorder while watching the screen, as if they were "dubbing in" their thoughts to the action, although they can also be asked to list their thoughts. In the VTR approach, one can also study the relationship between the action on the screen (e.g., overt behavior or nonverbal behavior) and the thoughts that accompany those behaviors. One advantage of this approach is that it generates a large sample of cognitive data. Some disadvantages are that reports of thoughts in response to videotape cues may be based largely on the client's post-hoc evaluation of his or her performance, and that self-focused attention may be induced by the presence of the camera. Using a camera that is out of sight, or positioning the camera behind clients to record the interaction from their perspective (Schwartz & Garamoni, 1986a), should reduce or eliminate a reactive effect on performance.

The *think-aloud* technique can also be considered a recording method, although Glass and Merluzzi (1981) used the term *expressive* or *concurrent methods*. Clients are asked to talk or think out loud as they are engaged in a situation or imagine themselves in one. The advantage of this method over VTR is that the stream of thoughts is captured as the situation progresses, thus avoiding problems associated with post hoc evaluation of behavior. The reader is referred to Genest and Turk (1981) for a review of this technique. One of the difficulties with this method, however, is that in certain situations (such as those involving social interaction) one cannot interact and simultaneously report thoughts. Thus the think-aloud method is more applicable to situations in which the person does not have to converse. For example, during treatment of a simple phobia such as acrophobia the counselor might have the person think aloud while engaging in desensitization or in vivo exposure therapy. Similarly, a test-anxious client in a private room would be able to "think aloud" while working on an exam.

Davison and his colleagues have developed a method they call *articulated thoughts during simulated situations* (ATSS; Davison et al., 1983; Davison et al., 1997). While imagining that a series of social interactions presented on tape is happening to them, clients are asked to report aloud their thoughts and feelings at predetermined times. Such simulated situations could be tailored to individual clients in order to enhance validity. Although they are similar to think-aloud in that ATSS methods involve concurrent reports of spontaneous thoughts and do not constrain responses, one disadvantage for counselors is that they require preproduced tapes to provide the stimulus situations.

A final production method is illustrated by the concurrent *thought sampling* work of Hurlburt (Hurlburt, 1997; Hurlburt & Melancon, 1987) and Singer (Pope & Singer, 1978). A sound generator is used to randomly cue clients to list or check thoughts. This approach might be an interesting compromise in those situations where one cannot continually express thoughts.

In each of these six production methods, rating of the thoughts is necessary, such that the protocols generated are scored by raters, counselors, and/or clients. In thought listing studies on social anxiety (e.g., Cacioppo, Glass, & Merluzzi, 1979), the statements generated have been scored as either positive (facilitating social interaction) or negative (inhibiting social interaction). In addition, other scoring systems could be used to assess the intensity or salience of the thoughts, their believability, controllability, impact, or the focus of attention (self, other, or situation). Thoughts could also be rated using a coping category, in which the client makes a negative statement followed immediately by a positive one (Merluzzi, Taylor, Boltwood, & Gotestam, 1991). For example, one spider phobic in their study said, "I'm really afraid, but I *am* going to do this no matter what."

Beliefs

The assessment of beliefs usually focuses on irrational beliefs, based on Ellis's rational-emotive theory (Ellis & Harper, 1961). By far the most frequently used measure of irrational beliefs has been the Irrational Beliefs Test (IBT; Jones, 1969), although a few studies have used Shorkey, Reyes, and Whiteman's (1977) Rational Behavior Inventory. The IBT is a 100-item scale that assesses 10 of the irrational beliefs described by Ellis and Harper (1961), such as demand for approval. A total IBT score as well as 10 subscale scores can be obtained. Despite the obvious clinical advantages, Smith (1982) provided evidence that questionnaire measures of irrational beliefs lack discriminant validity. He argued that they may be measuring emotional distress or general negative affect rather than beliefs. Others have proposed that measures addressing irrational beliefs need to be developed that are specific to different disorders. Thus the Dysfunctional Attitudes Scale (DAS; Weissman & Beck, 1978) so frequently used in depression research could in some ways be seen as a measure of beliefs and attitudes associated with depression.

Attributions

The role of causal attributions and attributional style in clinical work has become a topic of increasing interest. Essentially, attributions refer to the inferences or explanations that people make about the causes of events. Attributions are hypothesized to affect behavior through their influence on expectations for future success. A good example of the clinical use of causal attribution assessment is a study by Peterson, Luborsky, and Seligman (1983). Those authors combed through verbatim transcript materials and noted events and the causes ascribed to those events by the client. The causes offered by the client were then rated on three dimensions, internal versus external, global versus specific, and stable versus transient.

The Attributional Style Questionnaire (ASQ; Seligman, Abramson, Semmel, & von Baeyer, 1979) is perhaps the best-known measure of attributional style. The ASQ consists of 12 vignettes describing situations with either positive or negative outcomes, and with either interpersonal or achievement-related themes. A depressive explanatory style for the causes of negative events involves seeing one's self as responsible (i.e., internal attribution), and seeing the cause as pervasive (i.e., global) and permanent (i.e., stable).

Expectancies

Self-efficacy expectations, which refer to behavior expectancies (i.e., the perceived ability to perform a behavior) and not outcome expectancies (i.e., the perceived consequences of performing that behavior), have also received much recent attention. Self-efficacy theory (Bandura, 1977, 1986) has as one of its central tenets that efficacy expectations may be more predictive of behavior than outcome expectancies or previous behavior in the same situation. Because they are tied to one's sense of efficacy to perform a specific behavior, self-efficacy questionnaires must be developed individually for each behavior and situation. For example, in a study of cognitive processes, anxiety, and performance on doctoral dissertation oral examinations, self-efficacy for test-taking skills was assessed with items such as, "During orals, I can answer questions directly and succinctly," and self-efficacy for the control of thoughts and anxiety with items like, "Before my orals, I can stop myself from thinking about failing" (Arnkoff, Glass, & Robinson, 1992).

Outcome expectancies (Rotter, 1954) assess the perception of the outcome of a particular situation or generalized expectancy about outcomes that may be pervasive across all situations. Thus, an individual may be anxious about cocktail parties and expect that he will have trouble making smalltalk, and therefore become anxious and have a miserable time. If that pattern were to occur across all situations one would have a generalized expectancy. However, if it occurs in one specific situation it is a more situationally discrete expectancy.

Cognitive Assessment of Social Anxiety

The cognitive assessment of social anxiety, and to a greater extent depression, has developed as a function of recent theories as to the role of cognitive factors in those disorders and the increase in research utilizing cognitive and cognitive-behavioral treatments.

An overview of some of the more frequently used measures for the cognitive assessment of social anxiety and social phobia is presented below. The reader is encouraged to consult Arnkoff and Glass (1989) and Glass and Arnkoff (1994) for more information.

Endorsement Methods of Self-Statement Assessment. The most frequently used cognitive assessment methods are endorsement techniques, namely, structured inventories of self-statements. Among these questionnaires, the Assertiveness Self-Statement Test (ASST; Schwartz & Gottman, 1976) and the Social Interaction Self-Statement Test (SISST; Glass et al., 1982) are the best known. The ASST was designed to assess self-statements that may facilitate (i.e., positive thoughts) or inhibit (i.e., negative thoughts) one's ability to refuse unreasonable requests. The client rates 17 positive and 17 negative statements on a 5-point scale (from *hardly ever* to *very often*) indicating how often she or he had a particular thought before, during, or after a situation involving an unreasonable request. A revision of the ASST, consisting of 12 positive and 12 negative self-statements, has also been developed that is relevant to a wider range of assertive behavior situations (Heimberg, Chiauzzi, Becker, & Madraso-Pederson, 1983). These authors have employed the ASST-R with both college student and clinical populations.

The SISST is a 30-item measure, containing 15 positive and 15 negative thoughts that relate to interactions with the other sex (heterosocial encounters). The format is similar to the ASST in that clients rate the frequency of occurrence of each thought on the same 5-point scales. We recommend, however, changing the bottom anchor to *never* so that the measure can better discriminate the absence of negative and positive thinking from the infrequent experience of thoughts. Pronouns on the SISST can be changed so that the scale can be used with reference to interactions with either men or women, and following same-sex as well as other-sex conversations. Although the SISST has been used with minor wording changes in public speaking situations, Glass recently revised the measure in order to increase its validity in these contexts. In the original study, Glass et al. (1982) had participants complete the SISST immediately after interactions with other-sex confederates. Instructions have been modified by other researchers to follow imagined scenes involving social interaction (Zweig & Brown, 1985) and as a general measure of how frequently clients may have experienced each thought without reference to a specific situation (Heimberg, Hope, Dodge, & Becker, 1990).

The SISST has been used with a variety of populations, including prisoners (Segal & Marshall, 1985), general outpatient clients (Merluzzi, Burgio, & Glass, 1984), social phobics (Dodge, Hope, Heimberg, & Becker, 1988; Turner, Beidel, & Jacob, 1994), shy adults (Glass & Furlong, 1990), and socially anxious undergraduates (Myszka, Galassi, & Ware, 1986).

In general, results with self-statement questionnaires such as these indicate that negative, more than positive, thoughts are more highly related to measures of symptomatology, affect, and behavior, and are more sensitive to change as a function of treatment. For the counselor, this suggests that helping clients to become aware of and change negative patterns of thinking may be more important than merely increasing the number of positive thoughts.

Production Methods of Self-Statement Assessment. The thought listing method has been used in a number of studies. For example, Cacioppo et al. (1979) had male undergraduates list thoughts prior to an interaction with a woman with whom they were unacquainted. Negative (but not positive) self-statements discriminated high and low socially anxious groups. Thought listings have also been used in outcome studies for cognitive-behavioral group therapy for social phobia (Heimberg, Dodge, Hope, Kennedy,

Zollo, & Becker, 1990). Immediately after participating in a behavioral simulation of an anxiety-provoking social situation that was personally relevant, clients were asked to list the thoughts they experienced. Both positive and negative thoughts showed significant change as a function of treatment.

In addition to rating positive and negative thoughts, other scoring strategies have been suggested for the production methods. For example, Fichten, Amsel, Robillard, and Tagalakis (1991) scored thought listings on focus of attention; that is, self, other, or situation focused. Johnson and Glass (1989) found that the number of self-evaluative thoughts of shy high-school boys was associated with their self-perceptions of lower social skill as well as with judge's ratings of their anxiety. The clinical utility of focus of attention is particularly evident when working with persons who have anxiety disorders, where the allocation of attention toward the self may affect their ability to encode important external cues.

Daily Reports of Automatic Thoughts, as discussed previously, can provide a flexible assessment tool for the counselor to use with clients. The VTR method has not been used frequently in studies of social anxiety, but has seen some interesting applications in social psychology. Garcia, Stinson, Ickes, Bissonnette, and Briggs (1991), for example, videotaped male–female dyads and asked them to recall their thoughts while watching a videotape of the interaction. After playing back audiotapes of interactions between shy high-school boys and female confederates, Johnson and Glass (1989) found a large number of significant relations between thoughts recalled and self-ratings of social skill and anxiety, as well as with ratings made by partners and judges.

Think-aloud methods, having great appeal from the perspective of obtaining a large amount of cognitive data without relying on retrospective recall, have seen limited use in social skills assessment. As noted earlier, it is impossible to interact naturally in a social situation and simultaneously think aloud. Also, Kendall and Hollon (1981a) noted that there may be a reactive effect that influences the actual flow of self-talk. That is, clients who are asked to think aloud may spend more time on individual thoughts than those who do not think aloud. The technique could be adapted, however, in order to apply it to social anxiety. For example, Goldfried and Sobocinski (1975) and Craighead, Kimball, and Rehak (1979) asked participants to *imagine* themselves in a social situation such as social rejection and to report what was going on in their mind during the interaction. In both studies negative thoughts were significantly correlated with anxiety.

The ATSS methodology has been used to study speech anxiety. Davison, Haaga, Rosenbaum, Dolezal, and Weinstein (1991) found that self-efficacy thoughts verbalized while participants listened to an audio recording of a simulated speech situation were related to their level of speech anxiety. Finally, the thought sampling method has not been directly applied to social anxiety, but could be adapted for research on social interaction. If clients were to carry a sound generator that beeped at random intervals, they could respond by filling out a brief questionnaire and list their thoughts, also indicating the setting (i.e., alone or with someone, etc.).

Beliefs. The Irrational Beliefs Test has shown mixed utility in social anxiety research, perhaps because it measures a more general tendency toward irrationality rather than beliefs specifically about social interactions. Some have suggested that the IBT represents some overarching construct common to many problem areas, namely, anxiety or neuroticism. Thus, it would be useful to develop a well-validated measure addressing irrational beliefs specific to social anxiety. Nevertheless, certain subscales of the IBT may be helpful to counselors working with socially anxious clients. Glass and Furlong (1990), for example, found that IBT scales measuring demand for approval, high self-expectations, and anxious overconcern were associated with having a greater number of negative thoughts and fewer positive thoughts on the SISST. These beliefs were also significantly related to several self-report measures of social anxiety and public self-consciousness.

Attributions. The bulk of the work on causal attributions, utilizing the ASQ, has focused on depression. However, the application of attribution theory to social anxiety may provide a fruitful analysis of the cognitions of socially anxious persons concerning the causes of certain outcomes in social situations. Several studies have found attributional differences between individuals high and low in social anxiety (e.g., Alden, 1987), and social phobics given cognitive-behavior therapy showed significant changes on the attributional dimensions of internality and stability of their causal explanations.

Expectancies. The distinction between behavioral expectancy (e.g., self-efficacy expectations) and outcome expectancies is relevant for the examination of expectations in social anxiety. For example, Moe and Zeiss (1982) developed a Self-Efficacy Questionnaire for Social Skills, which asks clients to rate their expectations as to whether they can behave in a number of positively valued ways (e.g., friendly, warm) in each of 12 social situations. Theoretically, one's perceived self-efficacy should be related to real-life social behaviors. Similarly, Fichten, Bourdon, Amsel, and Fox (1987) developed and presented validation data for a self-efficacy measure called the College Interaction Self-Efficacy Measure. An interesting aspect of their work is that they compare efficacy judgments when the stimulus person is either able-bodied or disabled.

Outcome expectancy has been assessed by measures of the subjective expected utility of certain outcomes. Fiedler and Beach (1978) found that the estimated probabilities that specific consequences would result from either compliance or assertive refusal was related to the intent to behave assertively. Bruch, Haase, and Purcell (1984) named this scale the Subjective Probability of Consequences Inventory, and found that scores on the SPCI accounted for a significant percent of the variance in predicting knowledge of assertive responses.

Interpretation

The discussion of the interpretation of cognitive assessment data will focus primarily on self-statements. The process of interpreting clients' self-statement data can take many forms. For example, a counselor may attempt to determine the idiosyncratic meaning of a client's self-statements. In Beck's approach to cognitive therapy (Beck, Rush, Shaw, & Emery, 1979), he first elicited what he termed *automatic thoughts*, and then explored the meaning of each thought, and how the thought served to maintain depression by representing a distorted thinking style. A counselor might be able to classify thoughts as depressogenic or nondepressogenic, or anxiety-provoking or anxiety-inhibiting thoughts. Thus, the depression- or anxiety-producing function of the thoughts could be emphasized, with the client's subjective meaning used to enhance or refine the analysis of those thoughts.

Although there have been several scoring schemes proposed for self-statement or thought data, the most prevalent dimension assessed has been valence. For example, both the ASST and SISST yield two subscales: positive (facilitating assertion or social interaction) and negative (inhibiting assertion or social interaction). Thus, interpretation of the scores from these instruments involves evaluating the frequency of both positive and negative self-statements. Although norms are not available, one could use previously published data comparing socially anxious or phobic groups with individuals who are not anxious.

In an intriguing approach to the problem of interpreting cognitive assessment data, Schwartz and Garamoni (1986b, 1989) concluded that the evaluative dimension (positive versus negative) appears to be a dominant dimension in the construction of information. Although we are capable of using many other dimensions to construe events, the evaluative dimension appears to be at a higher level of abstraction than many others and applicable to a wide variety of information. They thus propose a *states of mind* (SOM) model that includes five states of mind, each based on a different relative balance between positive and negative cognitions. This SOM ratio is calculated by dividing the number of positive thoughts by the number of positive plus negative cognitions.

Schwartz and Garamoni suggested that the optimal state of mind, *positive dialogue*, is characterized by a ratio of .62 (±.06) and characterizes the well-adjusted individual. This asymmetry would promote a positive, facilitating approach to life while having a sufficient amount of negative thoughts to remain sensitive to problems and to threatening information. For example, a person who exhibits a positive dialogue on the SISST has a greater number of positive cognitions that should facilitate social interaction, but also has sufficient negative cognitions to remain interpersonally sensitive.

In contrast to positive dialogue, the *negative dialogue* pattern is characterized by an SOM ratio of .38 (±.06) and is indicative of a moderate degree of psychopathology. The dominance of negative cognitions generally would promote inhibition and a tendency to discount positive events, even though they may stand out against a backdrop of negative thoughts. An *internal dialogue of conflict*, with a SOM ratio of .50 (±.05), represents individuals with mild levels of anxiety, depression, or obsessionality. Finally, the *positive monologue* and *negative monologue* states of mind have predominantly positive (SOM equal to or above .69) or negative (SOM equal to or below .31) thoughts. Schwartz and Garamoni proposed that these states of mind are typical of forms of hypomania or excessively assertive individuals, on the one hand, or by profound states of depression and other forms of severe psychopathology on the other.

Recent studies (e.g., Amsel & Fichten, 1998; McDermut and Haaga, 1994) have found that extremely positive states of mind were not dysfunctional. Consequently, Schwartz, Reynolds, Thase, Frank, and Fasiczka (1995) suggested a revision to the SOM model, such that low to moderate levels of positive monologue (perhaps up to an SOM ratio of .90) are also considered adaptive and perhaps optimal. Amsel and Fichten (1998) also made two recommendations pertaining to SOM ratios: that those derived from structured inventories be calculated based on rating scales that are converted to start at 0 instead of 1 (in order not to constrain potential ratios mathematically), and that a correction of +1 should be made whenever a client reports either 0 positive or 0 negative thoughts (a problem more common for production measures). Otherwise, no distinction can be made between a client with 0 positive thoughts and 1 negative thought or 10 negative thoughts: her or his SOM ratio would be 0 regardless.

In their review of the cognitive assessment literature covering a variety of assessment methods and problem areas, Schwartz and Garamoni (1986b, 1989) presented convincing evidence supporting the states of mind model. Diverse methods of cognitive assessment (inventories, thought listings, etc.) across a variety of problem areas yield results that functional individuals have a thought balance that typifies a positive dialogue, whereas mildly anxious or depressed individuals engage in an internal dialogue of conflict, and more moderately disturbed clients fall into the negative dialogue range. The advantage of the states of mind model is that it provides an interpretive framework for the assessment of self-statements. The goal of therapy, according to Schwartz (1991), is to restore or achieve a more functional balance of positive to negative thoughts through the course of treatment. Thus, the process of therapy might include frequent monitoring of thoughts and charting the SOM ratio over time and across situations. Schwartz (1991) showed that progress in therapy is associated with frequent shifts in the states of mind. Although a positive dialogue SOM would be the desired endpoint for counseling, a shift from negative dialogue to an internal dialogue of conflict could also be seen as desirable. The reader is encouraged to read Schwartz and Garamoni (1989) for an extended treatment of the states of mind analysis of self-statements.

Case Example

Ralph H. is a 28-year-old software developer for a small computer firm. He has managed a successful career by working long hours and thoroughly devoting himself to his job. He has been shy all his life, particularly in unstructured situations such as informal social gatherings (e.g., a party at the boss's house), and has managed to avoid them as much as possible. He has sought therapy for his shyness as he would like to date and be able to attend social functions with the office staff.

In order to get a precounseling assessment of Ralph's states of mind, the counselor asked him to think of a recent encounter with a woman. He reported that a woman was working temporarily in an adjoining office and that they had a brief conversation one day. He also indicated that she was someone he would like to date. The counselor then asked Ralph to fill out the SISST while thinking about this brief interaction. His Positive subscale score was 46, and Negative thoughts were 50 (SOM = .48). This indicated to the counselor that Ralph was exhibiting an internal dialogue of conflict, indicative of a mild degree of psychopathology. This conflict was very apparent in Ralph's description of his brief interaction with the woman. He vacillated for a very long time before saying hello to her. However, overall it seemed that inhibition prevailed. The conflict was fueled by a fear that rejection was evidence of unattractiveness and unlikability.

The counselor also asked Ralph to imagine himself talking to the same woman in line at the company cafeteria. He was asked to imagine the situation as vividly as possible and then to write down any thoughts he had during the imagined encounter. This approach was used to assess spontaneous idiosyncratic thoughts that he might have in the actual situation.

For this task Ralph was given a standard thought-listing form, a sheet of paper with lines drawn across the page about an inch apart. Ralph was told that he would have about 2 minutes to list his thoughts, writing one thought in each of the sections on the page.

The following is a verbatim transcription of the thoughts Ralph listed on the thought listing form. As an exercise, you may want to try to score these as either negative (e.g., inhibiting social interaction) or positive (e.g., facilitating social interaction).

1. I was thinking that she's merely patronizing me by talking to me. (2)
2. Maybe she is really interested in me. (1)
3. Nah! She thinks I'm a social nerd—a typical software programmer! (3)
4. I'm a nervous wreck. (3)
5. I hope I don't say something stupid. (2)
6. I'll probably spill my tray and really make a fool of myself. (2)
7. I've got to hang in there. (1)
8. I can't be giving up every time I want to engage a woman in conversation. (2)
9. But it is so hard to be calm and talk. (3)
10. Just relax and take it one step at a time. (3)

The counselor had Ralph put a "+" or a "−" sign by each statement to indicate whether it was facilitating or inhibiting. The counselor then had him rate the intensity of each statement, thereby assessing the subjective importance of each thought for Ralph and how salient each thought was during his imagining of the encounter with the woman. These scores are in the parentheses after each statement. Alternatively, Ralph could have been asked to go back and rate the extent to which he believed each thought.

This type of counselor–client interaction and the participation of the client in the assessment process can produce considerable incidental information that may be useful in treatment. It is interesting to note that at times there could be a discrepancy between the counselor's categorizing of the statements and the client's. In this case, the counselor and Ralph agreed on the classification of all but one of the thoughts listed. They agreed that thoughts numbered 1, 3, 4, 5, 6, and 9 were negative or inhibiting, and that 2, 7, and 10 were positive. The disputed item was number 8. The counselor categorized it as positive and Ralph categorized it as negative. The counselor assumed that this was a coping statement that might help foster interaction. Ralph, on the other hand, saw it as a negative statement that expressed frustration and futility in the imagined situation.

When you take into account the client's subjective ratings of intensity, the relative nature of the thoughts begins to emerge. Ralph's idiosyncratic negativity emerges more clearly than if his subjective ratings were absent. If we use the client's categorizing, then the intensity ratings change the SOM ratio from .40 to .30, indicating a slightly more negative pattern characteristic of what Schwartz and Garamoni call a negative monologue rather than negative dialogue.

In the next session, Ralph and his counselor reviewed the individual items on the SISST-Negative scale that he had endorsed at scale values of 4 or 5. He was encouraged to choose those statements most typical of his thinking during interactions with this woman or other women that he was attracted to in the past. These thoughts, as well as those derived from the thought listing, were used as the basis for interventions in subsequent sessions.

In the initial sessions, the counselor assisted Ralph in identifying the thoughts (self-talk or automatic thoughts) and feelings that accompanied social situations. He was also encouraged to examine the fears associated with rejection. In particular, the counselor introduced the rational emotive principle of separating one's intrinsic worth from one's performances or behaviors. Finally, Ralph was encouraged to anticipate social interactions, actually imagine the situation as it might occur, and to "think out loud" as he imagined the situation. The counselor noted any negative dialogue or inhibiting thoughts. After discussing the situation, Ralph imagined the situation again; however, this time he was encouraged to eliminate the negative or inhibiting thoughts and replace them with facilitating or coping thoughts. This process was repeated several times over the next few sessions.

Ralph was given homework assignments that were ordered from relatively easy to difficult. Easy assignments included behaviors such as smiling and making eye contact, tasks of intermediate difficulty included initiating and maintaining a conversation with a woman for a few minutes, and difficult tasks included asking someone for a date. As noted earlier, the counselor had Ralph imagine the task and describe his thoughts in detail, and practice challenging his negative thoughts and substituting positive self-talk. This was followed by later assignments in which Ralph continued this cognitive restructuring while actually engaging in these behaviors.

Counseling continued in this manner for 10 sessions, with Ralph showing marked improvement in his ability to approach women and maintain brief conversations. He continued to report some subjective anxiety in those situations, but had improved his ability to cope with the anxiety by reducing his anticipatory negative self-talk and coping with his fears of rejection by focusing on what he could do differently rather than on global self-incrimination.

A postcounseling administration of the SISST indicated that the SISST-Negative score was 38 and the SISST-Positive was 55, representing an SOM ratio of .59. This represented a shift from an internal dialogue of conflict to the low end of the positive dialogue state of mind.

Psychometric Issues in Assessing Thoughts

In previous sections, we have mentioned the importance of reliability. For endorsement methods of self-statements and questionnaires of beliefs and attributional style, internal consistency is the most appropriate form of reliability to examine, whereas for the production methods of self-statements interrater reliability would be a more appropriate focus. Because we would expect thoughts to change somewhat as a function of the situation, test–retest reliability may not be as important to consider.

In general, cognitive assessment techniques have been used with little attention paid to methodological and psychometric issues (Clark, 1988; Glass & Arnkoff, 1994, 1997). As noted earlier, content validity is important for structured self-statement inventories, in that the sample of thoughts included in the questionnaire should be representative of thoughts that many individuals might think. Therefore, these instruments should be constructed carefully by using production methods first to generate a large number of statements that can be evaluated for inclusion in the final endorsement instrument. We also recommend measures with items that have been shown to differentiate between functional and dysfunctional groups— for example, where socially phobic and nonanxious adults endorse each thought item to a significantly different extent. Finally, most endorsement instruments are designed with a specific population in mind and therefore may not be content valid for use with a different population.

With respect to other types of validity, Glass and Arnkoff (1994, 1997) suggested that the criterion validity of a self-statement measure can be assessed by looking at its relationship to concurrent measures of behavior, affect, or arousal, as well as its ability to predict future behavior. Cognitive assessment methods should also be able to distinguish groups known to differ on some clinically relevant dimension (e.g., depressed vs. nondepressed), and be sensitive to change as a function of counseling. Construct validity is a more difficult problem for measures of thoughts. First, although one might expect that thought data collected by different methods (e.g., endorsement vs. production) would be highly related and thus establish convergent validity, endorsement and production methods do not always correlate significantly. Different methods, therefore, may contribute to different conclusions in research and practice. To establish discriminant validity, thought data should not correlate with other constructs such as self-esteem, intelligence, social desirability, and so on. It is also important to show that cognitive measures correlate more highly with corresponding than with noncorresponding mood states (Clark, 1988).

CONCLUSIONS

It may be evident to the reader that behavioral assessment and cognitive assessment differ from other forms of personality assessment that are based on assumptions about traits or based on the projective hypothesis, and in fact were devised as systems that were in opposition to the traditional assessment methods. The controversy raised as a function of the development of these alternatives to traditional assessment is parallel to the controversy in personality that pits the trait approach against the situationist position. As that controversy brewed, the interactionist perspective (Endler & Magnussen, 1976) emerged and appeared to be a reasonable approach to account for the relative stability of certain behaviors as well as the impact of situations. Even Walter Mischel, an ardent proponent of the situational perspective, can be characterized as an interactionist. His recent work seems to indicate that certain dispositional factors do distinguish people and that certain situations (high demand situations) may exacerbate those initial differences.

Essentially the same process is occurring in assessment, in that some behavioral assessors are now advocating an integration of traditional assessment (such as the DSM diagnostic categories) and behavioral assessment (Hersen & Bellack, 1988b). Several years ago, in fact, 70% of the members of the Association for Advancement of Behavior Therapy who responded to a survey regarded the MMPI as a test with which professionals should have competence (Piotrowski & Keller, 1984). The integration of traditional and behavioral and cognitive assessment will encourage behavioral and cognitive assessors to attend to larger and more abstract patterns of psychopathology. That will, in turn, expand the scope of behavioral and cognitive assessment, and hopefully foster the inclusion of more specific behavioral and cognitive phenomena in the description and diagnosis of psychopathology.

Future Directions

As noted in the previous section, some advocates of behavioral assessment envision that traditional assessment and behavioral assessment will be complementary systems. Recent developments appear to support this trend. Perhaps as a sign of a declining interest in behavioral assessment as a separate field, the journal *Behavioral Assessment* is no longer published as a separate volume, and is included as a subsection at the end of *Behaviour Research and Therapy*. The *Journal of Behavioral Assessment* also recently changed its name to the *Journal of Psychopathology and Behavioral Assessment* to reflect a larger domain of issues that may be included in behavioral assessment. In one chapter, Kendall (1990) reported that half of the assessment-focused articles in this latter journal addressed more traditional objective inventories such as the MMPI, Millon Clinical Multiaxial Inventory, or State-Trait Anxiety Inventory. Thus this integration has already become a reality. In sum, the future of behavioral assessment appears to be as a part of the mainstream of an integrated psychological assessment. The scientific rigor that is evident in behavioral assessment will likely stimulate further improvements in the diagnostic classification system of the DSM.

In addition, the behavioral assessment field has already seen a dramatic downward trend in the assessment of the *frequencies* of target behaviors, and a marked increase in the development of behavioral self-report inventories (Kendall, 1990). Kendall suggested that the time, cost, and other difficulties associated with counting behavioral frequencies have led to this reduction. In addition, results from this more microscopic level of assessment have also not always differentiated between known groups or shown sensitivity to change following treatment. The molecular behavioral assessment in the social skills area, for example, has not captured the incredible complexities of human communication and the reciprocal nature of social interaction, and has difficulty assessing the more process-oriented skills such as sense of timing and social cue discrimination. Thus microbehavioral analyses have sometimes demonstrated poorer external validity compared to judges' and confederates' molar or global ratings, although it should be noted that the literature on marital interaction has seen the development of several excellent behavioral coding systems to assess couples' behavior (see Margolin, Michelli, & Jacobson, 1988).

In contrast, the pragmatic and economic advantages of self-report measures can also be used to assess thoughts and beliefs (Kendall, 1987), and have a better track record in demonstrating group differences and treatment change. We expect this trend to continue in the future, and suggest that it is no coincidence that the decline in interest in coding the frequency of micro or molecular behavior occurred at the same time as the growth of interest in cognitive and cognitive-behavioral interventions.

In addition to the tremendous increase in measure development among structured self-statement inventories, the future of cognitive assessment also appears to be aligned with recent research in cognitive psychology and information processing (Ingram, 1986; Kendall & Ingram, 1987; Merluzzi & Carr, 1992). The rich tradition of methods and research has already made an impact on the assessment of cognitive processes in psychopathology (Nasby & Kihlstrom, 1986). The most well-studied of the disorders from an information processing perspective is depression, although information-processing perspectives on social skill and anxiety also exist (Merluzzi, Rudy, & Krejci, 1986). However, the practical utility of this research for clinical assessment needs to be pursued.

Finally, cognitive assessment has begun to develop into a discipline with the maturity of behavioral assessment. In the past 10 years, work has moved from studying college students to developing measures of cognitive products with clinical populations, and we expect this trend to continue. In addition, there needs to be more attention paid to the subjective world of the client in cognitive assessment methods. Counselors can supplement

cognitive self-statement inventories with methods from cognitive constructivist assessment (Neimeyer & Neimeyer, 1993), in order to assess core
cognitive processes and constructions as well as cognitive products.

REFERENCES

Alden, L. (1987). Attributional responses of anxious individuals to different patterns of social
   feedback: Nothing succeeds like improvement. *Journal of Personality and Social Psychology,*
   52, 100–106.
Amsel, R., & Fichten, C. S. (1998). Recommendations for self-statement inventories: Use of valence, endpoints, frequency and relative frequency. *Cognitive Therapy and Research, 22*,
   255–277.
Arkowitz, H. (1981). Assessment of social skills. In M. Hersen & A. S. Bellack (Eds.), *Behavioral*
   assessment: A practical handbook (2nd ed., pp. 296–327). New York: Pergamon.
Arnkoff, D. B., & Glass, C. R. (1989). Cognitive assessment in social anxiety and social phobia.
   Clinical Psychology Review, 9, 61–74.
Arnkoff, D. B., & Glass, C. R. (1992). Cognitive therapy and psychotherapy integration. In D. K.
   Freedheim (Ed.), *History of psychotherapy: A century of change* (pp. 657–694). Washington, DC:
   American Psychological Association.
Arnkoff, D. B., Glass, C. R., & Robinson, A. S. (1992). Cognitive processes, anxiety, and perform-
   ance on doctoral dissertation oral examinations. *Journal of Counseling Psychology, 39*, 382–388.
Ayllon, T., & Azrin, N. H. (1968). *The token economy: A motivational system for therapy and reha-
   bilitation.* New York: Appleton-Century-Crofts.
Bales, R. F. (1951). *Interaction process analysis.* Cambridge, MA: Addison-Wesley.
Bandura, A. (1977). Self-efficacy: Towards a unifying theory of behavior change. *Psychological*
   Review, 84, 191–215.
Bandura, A. (1986). *Social foundations of thought and action: A social cognitive theory.* Englewood
   Cliffs, NJ: Prentice Hall.
Barker, R. F. (1968). *Ecological psychology: Concepts and methods of studying the environment of*
   human behavior. Stanford, CA: Stanford University Press.
Barlow, D. H. (Ed.). (1981). *Behavioral assessment of adult disorders.* New York: Guilford.
Barlow, D. H., Hayes, S. C., & Nelson, R. O. (1984). *The scientist practitioner: Research and account-
   ability in clinical and educational settings.* New York: Pergamon.
Beck, A. T., Brown, G., Steer, R. A., Eidelson, J. I., & Riskind, J. H. (1987). Differentiating anxiety
   and depression utilizing the Cognition Checklist. *Journal of Abnormal Psychology, 96*, 179–183.
Beck, A. T., & Emery, G. (1985). *Anxiety disorders and phobias: A cognitive perspective.* New York:
   Basic Books.
Beck, A. T., Epstein, N., Brown, G., & Steer, R. A. (1988). An inventory for measuring clinical
   anxiety: Psychometric properties. *Journal of Consulting and Clinical Psychology, 56*, 893–897.
Beck, A. T., Rush, A. J., Shaw, B. F., & Emery, G. (1979). *Cognitive therapy of depression.* New York:
   Guilford Press.
Beck, J. G., & Heimberg, R. G. (1983). Self-report assessment of assertive behavior: A critical
   analysis. *Behavior Modification, 7*, 451–487.
Becker, R. E., & Heimberg, R. G. (1988). Assessment of social skills. In M. Hersen & A. S. Bellack
   (Eds.), *Behavioral assessment: A practical handbook* (3rd ed., pp. 365–395). New York: Per-
   gamon.
Bellack, A. S. (1979). A critical appraisal of strategies for assessing social skill. *Behavioral As-
   sessment, 1*, 157–176.

Bellack, A. S. (1983). Recurrent problems in the behavioral assessment of social skill. *Behaviour Research and Therapy, 21*, 29–41.

Bellack, A. S., & Hersen, M. (Eds.). (1979). *Research and practice in social skills training.* New York: Plenum Press.

Bellack, A. S., & Hersen, M. (Eds.). (1998). *Behavioral assessment: A practical handbook* (4th ed.). Boston: Allyn and Bacon.

Bernstein, D. A., & Nietzel, M. T. (1973). Procedural variation in behavioral avoidance tests. *Journal of Consulting and Clinical Psychology, 41*, 165–174.

Bijou, S., & Patterson, R. F. (1971). Functional analysis in the assessment of children. In P. McReynolds (Ed.), *Advances in psychological assessment* (Vol. 2, pp. 63–78). Palo Alto, CA: Science and Behavior Books.

Bornstein, P. H., Hamilton, S. B., & Bornstein, M. T. (1986). Self-monitoring procedures. In A. R. Ciminero, K. S. Calhoun, & H. E. Adams (Eds.), *Handbook of behavioral assessment* (2nd ed., pp. 176–222). New York: Wiley.

Briggs, S. R., & Smith, T. G. (1986). The measurement of shyness. In W. H. Jones, J. M. Cheek, & S. R. Briggs (Eds.), *Shyness: Perspectives on research and treatment* (pp. 47–60). New York: Plenum Press.

Brock, T. C. (1967). Communication discrepancy and intent to persuade as determinants of counterargument production. *Journal of Experimental Social Psychology, 3*, 269–309.

Bruch, M. A., Haase, R. F., & Purcell, M. I. (1984). Content dimensions of self-statements in assertive situations: A factor analysis of two measures. *Cognitive Therapy and Research, 8*, 173–186.

Bryant, B., & Trower, P. E. (1974). Social difficulty in a student sample. *British Journal of Educational Psychology, 44*, 13–21.

Cacioppo, J. T., Glass, C. R, & Merluzzi, T. V. (1979). Self-statements and self-evaluations: A cognitive response analysis of heterosocial anxiety. *Cognitive Therapy and Research, 3*, 249–262.

Cacioppo, J. T., & Petty, R. E. (1981). Social psychological procedures for cognitive response analysis: The thought-listing technique. In T. V. Merluzzi, C. R. Glass, & M. Genest (Eds.), *Cognitive assessment* (pp. 309–342). New York: Guilford Press.

Cacioppo, J. T., von Hippel, W., & Ernst, J. M. (1997). Mapping cognitive structure and processes through verbal content: The thought-listing technique. *Journal of Consulting and Clinical Psychology, 65*, 928–940.

Chambless, D. L., Caputo, G. C., Bright, P., & Gallagher, R. (1984). Assessment of fear of fear in agoraphobics: The Body Sensations Questionnaire and the Agoraphobic Cognitions Questionnaire. *Journal of Consulting and Clinical Psychology, 52*, 1090–1097.

Cheek, J. M., & Buss, A. H. (1981). Shyness and sociability. *Journal of Personality and Social Psychology, 41*, 330–339.

Cheek, J. M., and Melchior, L. A. (1985, August). *Measuring the three components of shyness.* Paper presented at the annual meeting of the American Psychological Association, Los Angeles.

Ciminero, A. R. (1986). Behavioral assessment: An overview. In A. R. Ciminero, K. S. Calhoun, & H. E. Adams (Eds.), *Handbook of behavioral assessment* (2nd ed., pp. 3–11). New York: Wiley.

Ciminero, A. R., Calhoun, K. S., & Adams, H. E. (Eds.). (1986). *Handbook of behavioral assessment* (2nd ed.). New York: Wiley.

Clark, D. A. (1988). The validity of measures of cognition: A review of the literature. *Cognitive Therapy and Research, 12*, 1–20.

Clum, G. A., Broyles, S., Borden, J., & Watkins, P. L. (1990). validity and reliability of the Panic Attack Symptoms and Cognition Questionnaire. *Journal of Psychopathology and Behavioral Assessment, 12*, 233–245.

Conger, J. C., & Conger, A. J. (1986). Assessment of social skills. In A. R. Ciminero, K. S. Calhoun, & H. E. Adams (Eds.), *Handbook of behavioral assessment* (2nd ed., pp. 526–560). New York: Wiley.

Craighead, W. E., Kimball, W. H., & Rehak, P. J. (1979). Mood changes, physiological responses, and self-statements during social rejection imagery. *Journal of Consulting and Clinical Psychology, 47*, 385–396.

Curran, J. P. (1982). A procedure for the assessment of social skills: The Simulated Social Interaction Test. In J. P. Curran & P. M. Monti (Eds.), *Social skills training: A practical handbook for assessment and treatment* (pp. 348–373). New York: Guilford Press.

Darwin, C. (1859). *The origin of the species*. London: John Murray.

Davison, G. C., Haaga, D. A. F., Rosenbaum, J., Dolezal, S. L., & Weinstein, K. A. (1991). Assessment of self-efficacy in articulated thoughts: "States of mind" analysis and association with speech-anxious behavior. *Journal of Cognitive Psychotherapy: An International Quarterly, 5*, 83–92.

Davison, G. C., Robins, C., & Johnson, M. K. (1983). Articulated thoughts during simulated situations: A paradigm for studying cognition in emotion and behavior. *Cognitive Therapy and Research, 7*, 17–40.

Davison, G. C., Vogel, R. S., & Coffman, S. G. (1997). Think-aloud approaches to cognitive assessment and the articulated thoughts in simulated situations paradigm. *Journal of Consulting and Clinical Psychology, 65*, 950–958.

DiNardo, P. A., & Barlow, D. H. (1988). *Anxiety Disorders Interview Schedule—Revised* (ADIS-R). Albany, NY: Phobia and Anxiety Disorders Clinic, State University of New York.

Dodge, C. S., Hope, D. A., Heimberg, R. G., & Becker, R. E. (1988). Evaluation of the Social Interaction Self-Statement Test with a social phobic population. *Cognitive Therapy and Research, 12*, 211–222.

Dodge, C. S., Heimberg, R. G., Nyman, D., & O'Brien, G. T. (1987). Daily heterosocial interactions of high and low socially anxious college students: A diary study. *Behavior Therapy, 18*, 90–96.

Eisler, R. M., Miller, P. M., & Hersen, M. (1973). Components of assertive behavior. *Journal of Clinical Psychology, 29*, 295–299.

Ellis, A., & Harper, R. A. (1961). *A guide to rational living*. Englewood Cliffs, NJ: Prentice Hall.

Endler, N. S., & Magnussen, D. (1976). *Interactional psychology and personality*. Washington, DC: Hemisphere.

Farrell, A. D., Curran, J. P., Zwick, W. R., & Monti, P. M. (1983). Generalizability and discriminant validity of anxiety and social skills ratings in two populations. *Behavioral Assessment, 6*, 1–14.

Fichten, C. S., Amsel, R., Robillard, K., & Tagalakis, V. (1991). Thoughts about encounters between nondisabled and disabled peers: Situational constraints, states-of-mind, valenced thought categories. *Cognitive Therapy and Research, 15*, 345–369.

Fichten, C. S., Bourdon, C. V., Amsel, R., & Fox L. (1987). Validation of the College Interaction Self-efficacy Questionnaire: Students with and without disabilities. *Journal of College Student Personnel, 28*, 449–458.

Fiedler, D., & Beach, L. R. (1978). On the decision to be assertive. *Journal of Consulting and Clinical Psychology, 46*, 537–546.

Fischer, J., & Corcoran, K. (1994). *Measures for clinical practice* (2nd ed.). New York: Simon & Schuster.

Foster, S. L., Bell-Dolan, D. J., & Burge, D. (1988). Behavioral observation. In A. S. Bellack & M. Hersen (Eds.), *Behavioral assessment: A practical handbook* (3rd ed., pp. 119–160). New York: Pergamon.

Foster, S. L., & Cone, J. D. (1986). Design and use of direct observation. In A. R. Ciminero, K. S. Calhoun, & H. E. Adams (Eds.), *Handbook of behavioral assessment* (2nd ed., pp. 253–324). New York: Wiley.

Frisch, M. B., & Higgins, R. L. (1986). Instructional demand effects and the correspondence among role-play, self report, and naturalistic measures of social skill. *Behavioral Assessment, 8*, 221–236.

Galassi, J. P., DeLo, J. S., Galassi, M. D., & Bastien, S. (1974). The College Self-Expression Scale: A measure of assertiveness. *Behavior Therapy, 5*, 165–171.

Galassi, J. P., Frierson, H. T., Jr., & Sharer, R. (1981). Behavior of high, moderate, and low test-anxious students during an actual test situation. *Journal of Consulting and Clinical Psychology, 49,* 51–62.

Galassi, J. P., & Galassi, M. D. (1976). The effects of role-playing variations on the assessment of assertive behavior. *Behavior Therapy, 7,* 343–347.

Galassi, M. D., & Galassi, J. P. (1977). *Assert yourself! How to be your own person.* New York: Human Sciences Press.

Gambrill, E. D., & Richey, C. A. (1975). An assertion inventory for use in assessment and research. *Behavior Therapy, 6,* 550–561.

Gambrill, E. D., & Richey, C. A. (1985). *Taking charge of your social life.* Belmont, CA: Wadsworth.

Garcia, S., Stinson, L., Ickes, W., Bissonnette, V., & Briggs, S. R. (1991). Shyness and physical attractiveness in mixed-sex dyads. *Journal of Personality and Social Psychology, 61,* 35–49.

Gay, M. L., Hollandsworth, J. G., Jr., & Galassi, J. P. (1975). An assertive inventory for adults. *Journal of Counseling Psychology, 22,* 340–344.

Genest, M., & Turk, D. C. (1981). Think aloud approaches to cognitive assessment. In T. V. Merluzzi, C. R. Glass, & M. Genest (Eds.), *Cognitive assessment* (pp. 233–269). New York: Guilford Press.

Gesell, A. (1925). *The mental growth of the pre-school child.* New York: Macmillan.

Glass, C. R. (1993). A little more about cognitive assessment. *Journal of Counseling and Development, 71,* 546–548.

Glass, C. R., & Arnkoff, D. B. (1989). Behavioral assessment of social anxiety and social phobia. *Clinical Psychology Review, 9,* 75–90.

Glass, C. R., & Arnkoff, D. B. (1992). Behavior therapy. In D. K. Freedheim (Ed.), *History of psychotherapy: A century of change* (pp. 587–628). Washington, DC: American Psychological Association.

Glass, C. R., & Arnkoff, D. B. (1994). Validity issues in self-statement measures of social phobia and social anxiety. *Behaviour Research and Therapy, 32,* 255–267.

Glass, C. R., & Arnkoff, D. B. (1997). Questionnaire methods of cognitive self-statement assessment. *Journal of Consulting and Clinical Psychology, 65,* 911–927.

Glass, C. R., & Furlong, M. (1990). Cognitive assessment of social anxiety: Affective and behavioral correlates. *Cognitive Therapy and Research, 14,* 365–384.

Glass, C. R., & Merluzzi, T. V. (1981). Cognitive assessment of social-evaluative anxiety. In T. V. Merluzzi, C. R. Glass, & M. Genest (Eds.), *Cognitive assessment* (pp. 388–438). New York: Guilford Press.

Glass, C. R., Merluzzi, T. V., Biever, J. L., & Larsen, K. H. (1982). Cognitive assessment of social anxiety: Development and validation of a self-statement questionnaire. *Cognitive Therapy and Research, 6,* 37–55.

Goldfried, M. R., & Davidson, G. C. (1994). *Clinical behavior therapy* (expanded ed). New York: John Wiley & Sons.

Goldfried, M. R., & Sobocinski, D. (1975). Effects of irrational beliefs on emotional arousal. *Journal of Consulting and Clinical Psychology, 43,* 504–510.

Goodenough, F. L. (1949). *Mental testing: Its history, principles, and applications.* New York: Holt, Rinehart, & Winston.

Greenwald, A. G. (1968). Cognitive learning, cognitive response to persuasion, and attitude change. In A. G. Greenwald, T. C. Brock, & T. M. Ostrom (Eds.), *Psychological foundations of attitudes* (pp. 147–170). New York: Academic Press.

Heimberg, R. G., Chiauzzi, E. J., Becker, R. E., & Madraso-Pederson, R. (1983). Cognitive mediation of assertive behavior: An analysis of the self-statement patterns of college students, psychiatric patients, and normal adults. *Cognitive Therapy and Research, 7,* 455–464.

Heimberg, R. G., Dodge, C. S., Hope, D. A., Kennedy, C. R., Zollo, L. J., & Becker, R. E. (1990). Cognitive behavioral group treatment for social phobia: comparison with a credible placebo control. *Cognitive Therapy and Research, 14,* 1–23.

Heimberg, R. G., Hope, D. A., Dodge, C. S., & Becker, R. E. (1990). DSM-III-R subtypes of social phobia: Comparison of generalized social phobics and public speaking phobics. *The Journal of Nervous and Mental Disease, 178,* 172–179.

Hersen, M., & Bellack, A. S. (Eds.). (1976). *Behavioral assessment: A practical handbook.* New York: Pergamon.

Hersen, M., & Bellack, A. S. (1977). Assessment of social skills. In A. R. Ciminero, K. S. Calhoun, & H. E. Adams (Eds.), *Handbook of behavioral assessment* (pp. 509–554). New York: Wiley.

Hersen, M., & Bellack, A. S. (1988a). *Dictionary of behavioral assessment techniques.* New York: Pergamon.

Hersen, M., & Bellack, A. S. (1988b). DSM-III and behavioral assessment. In A. S. Bellack & M. Hersen (Eds.), *Behavioral assessment: A practical handbook* (3rd ed., pp. 67–84). New York: Pergamon.

Higgins, R. L., Frisch, M. B., & Smith, D. (1983). A comparison of role-played and natural responses to identical circumstances. *Behavior Therapy, 14,* 158–169.

Hollon, S. D., & Kendall, P. C. (1980). Cognitive self-statements in depression: Development of an automatic thoughts questionnaire. *Cognitive Therapy and Research, 4,* 383–395.

Hurlburt, R. T. (1997). Randomly sampling thinking in the natural environment. *Journal of Consulting and Clinical Psychology, 65,* 941–949.

Hurlburt, R. T., & Melancon, S. M. (1987). How are questionnaire data similar to, and different from, thought sampling data? Five studies manipulating retrospectiveness, single-moment focus, and indeterminacy. *Cognitive Therapy and Research, 11,* 681–704.

Ickes, W., Robertson, E., Tooke, W., & Teng, G. (1986). Naturalistic social cognition: Methodology, assessment, and validation. *Journal of Personality and Social Psychology, 51,* 66–82.

Ingram, R. (Ed.). (1986). *Information processing approaches to clinical psychology.* New York: Academic Press.

Ingram, R. E., & Kendall, P. C. (1986). Cognitive clinical psychology: Implications of an information processing perspective. In R. E. Ingram (Ed.), *Information processing approaches to clinical psychology* (pp. 3–21). New York: Academic Press.

Jensen, B. J., & Hayes, S. N. (1986). Self-report questionnaires and inventories. In A. R. Ciminero, K. S. Calhoun, & H. E. Adams (Eds.), *Handbook of behavioral assessment* (2nd ed., pp. 150–175). New York: Wiley.

Johnson, R. L., & Glass, C. R. (1989). Heterosocial anxiety and direction of attention in high school boys. *Cognitive Therapy and Research, 13,* 509–526.

Jones, R. G. (1969). A factored measure of Ellis' irrational belief system, with personality and adjustment correlates (Doctoral dissertation, Texas Technological College, 1968). *Dissertation Abstracts International, 29,* 4379B–4380B. (University Microfilms No. 69-6443)

Jones, W. H., Briggs, S. R., & Smith, T. G. (1986). Shyness: Conceptualization and measurement. *Journal of Personality and Social Psychology, 51,* 629–639.

Jones, W. H., & Russell, D. (1982). The Social Reticence Scale: An objective measure of shyness. *Journal of Personality Assessment, 46,* 629–631.

Kallman, W. M., & Feuerstein, M. J. (1986). Psychophysiological procedures. In A. R. Ciminero, K. S. Calhoun, & H. E. Adams (Eds.), *Handbook of behavioral assessment* (2nd ed., pp. 325–350). New York: Wiley.

Kaloupek, D. G., & Levis, D. J. (1980). The relationship between stimulus specificity and self-report indices in assessing fear of heterosexual social interaction: A test of the unitary response hypothesis. *Behavioral Assessment, 2,* 267–281.

Kanfer, F. H. (1985). Target selection for clinical change programs. *Behavioral Assessment, 7,* 7–20.

Kanfer, F. H., & Saslow, G. (1965). Behavioral diagnosis. *Archives of General Psychiatry, 12,* 529–538.

Kazdin, A. E. (1981). Behavioral observation. In M. Hersen & A. S. Bellack (Eds.), *Behavioral assessment: A practical handbook* (2nd ed., pp. 101–124). New York: Pergamon.

Kelly, G. A. (1955). *The psychology of personal constructs.* New York: Norton Press.

Kendall, P. C. (1987). Behavioral assessment and methodology. In G. T. Wilson, C. M. Franks, P. C. Kendall, & J. P. Foreyt, *Review of behavior therapy: Theory and practice* (Vol. 11, pp. 40–83). New York: Guilford Press.

Kendall, P. C. (1990). Behavioral assessment and methodology. In C. M. Franks, G. T. Wilson, P. C. Kendall, & J. P. Foreyt, *Review of behavior therapy: Theory and practice* (Vol. 12, pp. 44–71). New York: Guilford Press.

Kendall, P. C., & Dobson, K. S. (1993). On the nature of cognition and its role in psychopathology. In K. S. Dobson & P. C. Kendall (Eds.), *Psychopathology and cognition* (pp. 3–16). San Diego: Academic Press.

Kendall, P. C., & Hollon, S. D. (1981a). Assessing self-referent speech: Methods in the measurement of self-statements. In P. C. Kendall & S. D. Hollon (Eds.), *Assessment strategies for cognitive-behavioral interventions* (pp. 85–118). New York: Academic Press.

Kendall, P. C., & Hollon, S. D. (Eds.). (1981b). *Assessment strategies for cognitive-behavioral interventions.* New York: Academic Press.

Kendall, P. C., & Hollon, S. D. (1989). Anxious self-talk: Development of the Anxious Self-Statements Questionnaire (ASSQ). *Cognitive Therapy and Research, 13,* 81–93.

Kendall, P. C., & Ingram, R. (1987). The future for cognitive assessment of anxiety. In L. Michelson & L. M. Ascher (Eds.), *Anxiety and stress disorders* (pp. 89–104). New York: Guilford Press.

Kern, J. M. (1982). The comparative external and concurrent validity of three role-plays for assessing heterosocial performance. *Behavior Therapy, 13,* 666–680.

Kirk, J. (1989). Cognitive-behavioural assessment. In K. Hawton, P. M. Salkovskis, J. Kirk, & D. M. Clark (Eds.), *Cognitive behaviour therapy for psychiatric problems: A practical guide* (pp. 13–51). Oxford: Oxford University Press.

Lachman, R., & Lachman, J. T. (1986). Information processing psychology: Origins and extensions. In R. Ingram (Ed.), *Information processing approaches to clinical psychology* (pp. 23–50). New York: Academic Press.

Lachman, R., Lachman, J. T., & Butterfield, E. C. (1979). *Cognitive psychology and information processing: An introduction.* Hillsdale, NJ: Lawrence Erlbaum Associates.

Lang, P. J., & Lazovik, A. D. (1963). Experimental desensitization of a phobia. *Journal of Abnormal and Social Psychology, 66,* 519–525.

Lindsley, O. R. (1956). Operant conditioning methods applied to research in chronic schizophrenia. *Psychiatric Research Reports, 5,* 118–139.

Lowe, M. R., & Cautela, J. R. (1978). A self-report measure of social skill. *Behavior Therapy, 9,* 535–544.

Mahoney, M. J. (1977). Some applied issues in self-monitoring. In J. D. Cone & R. P. Hawkins (Eds.), *Behavioral assessment: New directions in clinical psychology* (pp. 241–254). New York: Brunner/Mazel.

Margolin, G., Michelli, J., & Jacobson, N. (1988). Assessment of marital dysfunction. In A. S. Bellack & M. Hersen (Eds.), *Behavioral assessment: A practical handbook* (3rd ed., pp. 441–489). New York: Pergamon.

Marks, I. M., & Mathews, A. M. (1979). Brief standard self-rating for phobic patients. *Behaviour Research and Therapy, 17,* 263–267.

Martzke, J. S., Andersen, B. L., & Cacioppo, J. T. (1987). Cognitive assessment of anxiety disorders. In L. Michelson & L. M. Ascher (Eds.), *Anxiety and stress disorders* (pp. 62–88). New York: Guilford Press.

Mash, E. J., & Terdal, L. G. (Eds.). (1984). *Behavioral assessment of childhood disorders.* New York: Guilford Press.

McDermut, W., & Haaga, D. A. F. (1994). Cognitive balance and specificity in anxiety and depression. *Cognitive Therapy and Research, 18,* 333–352.

McFall, R. M. (1982). A review and reformulation of the concept of social skills. *Behavioral Assessment, 4,* 1–33.

McReynolds, P. (1986). History of assessment in clinical and educational settings. In R. O. Nelson & S. C. Hayes (Eds.), *Conceptual foundations of behavioral assessment* (pp. 42–80). New York: Guilford Press.

Meichenbaum, D. H. (1977). *Cognitive-behavior modification.* New York: Plenum Press.

Merluzzi, T. V., & Biever, J. (1987). Role-playing procedures for the behavioral assessment of social skills: A validity study. *Behavioral Assessment, 9,* 361–377.

Merluzzi, T. V., Burgio, K. L., & Glass, C. R. (1984). Cognitions and psychopathology: An analysis of social introversion and self-statements. *Journal of Consulting and Clinical Psychology, 52,* 1102–1103.

Merluzzi, T. V., & Carr, P. A. (1992). Cognitive science and assessment: Paradigmatic and methodological perspectives. In D. J. Stein & J. E. Young (Eds.), *Cognitive science and clinical disorders* (pp. 79–97). New York: Academic Press.

Merluzzi, T. V., Glass, C. R., & Genest, M. (Eds.). (1981). *Cognitive assessment.* New York: Guilford Press.

Merluzzi, T. V., Rudy, T. E., & Glass, C. R. (1981). The information processing paradigm: Implications for clinical science. In T. V. Merluzzi, C. R. Glass, & M. Genest (Eds.), *Cognitive assessment* (pp. 77–126). New York: Guilford Press.

Merluzzi, T. V., Rudy, T. E., & Krejci, M. (1986). Social skill and anxiety: Information processing perspectives. In R. Ingram (Ed.), *Information processing approaches to clinical psychology* (pp. 109–129). New York: Academic Press.

Merluzzi, T. V., Taylor, C. B., Boltwood, M., & Gotestam, K. G. (1991). Opioid antagonist impedes exposure. *Journal of Consulting and Clinical Psychology, 59,* 425–430.

Mischel, W. (1968). *Personality and assessment.* New York: Wiley.

Mischel, W. (1973). Toward a cognitive-social learning reconceptualization of personality. *Psychological Review, 80,* 252–283.

Mischel, W. (1981). A cognitive-social learning approach to assessment. In T. V. Merluzzi, C. R. Glass, & M. Genest (Eds.), *Cognitive assessment* (pp. 479–502). New York: Guilford Press.

Moe, K. O., & Zeiss, A. M. (1982). Measuring self-efficacy expectations for social skills: A methodological inquiry. *Cognitive Therapy and Research, 6,* 191–205.

Monti, P. M., Wallander, J. L., Ahern, D. K., & Munroe, S. M. (1984). Multi-modal measurement of anxiety and social skills in a behavioral role-play test: Generalizability and discriminant validity. *Behavioral Assessment, 6,* 15–25.

Moreno, Z. T. (1983). Psychodrama. In H. I. Kaplan & B. J. Sadock (Eds.), *Comprehensive group psychotherapy* (2nd ed., pp. 158–166). Baltimore, MD: Williams & Wilkins.

Morganstern, K. P. (1988). Behavioral interviewing. In A. S. Bellack & M. Hersen (Eds.), *Behavioral assessment: A practical handbook* (3rd ed., pp. 86–118). New York: Pergamon.

Mullinix, S. D., & Galassi, J. P. (1981). Deriving the content of social skills training with a verbal response components approach. *Behavioral Assessment, 3,* 55–61.

Myszka, M. T., Galassi, J. P., & Ware, W. B. (1986). Comparison of cognitive assessment methods with heterosocially anxious college women. *Journal of Counseling Psychology, 33,* 401–407.

Nasby, W., & Kihlstrom, J. F. (1986). Cognitive assessment of personality and psychopathology. In R. Ingram (Ed.), *Information processing approaches to clinical psychology* (pp. 217–239). New York: Academic Press.

Nay, W. R. (1977). Analogue measures. In A. R. Ciminero, K. S. Calhoun, & H. E. Adams (Eds.), *Handbook of behavioral assessment* (pp. 279–328). New York: Wiley.

Neimeyer, G. J., & Neimeyer, R. A. (1981). Personal construct perspectives on cognitive assessment. In T. V. Merluzzi, C. R. Glass, & M. Genest (Eds.), *Cognitive assessment* (pp. 188–232). New York: Guilford Press.

Neimeyer, G. J., & Neimeyer, R. A. (1993). Defining the boundaries of constructivist assessment. In G. J. Neimeyer (Ed.), *Constructivist assessment: A casebook* (pp. 1–30). Thousand Oaks, CA: Sage.

Norcross, J. C., & Goldfried, M. R. (Eds.). (1992). *Handbook of psychotherapy integration*. New York: Basic Books.

Peterson, C., Luborsky, L., & Seligman, M. E. P. (1983). Attributions and depressive mood shifts: A case study using the symptom-context method. *Journal of Abnormal Psychology, 92*, 96–103.

Piotrowski, C., & Keller, J. W. (1984, March). *Attitudes towards clinical assessment by the members of the AABT*. Paper presented at the convention of Southeastern Psychological Association, New Orleans.

Pope, K. H., & Singer, J. L. (Eds.). (1978). *The stream of consciousness: Scientific investigation onto the flow of human experience*. New York: Plenum Press.

Purdon, C., & Clark, D. A. (1994). Perceived control and appraisal of obsessional intrusive thoughts: A replication and extension. *Behavioural and Cognitive Psychotherapy, 22*, 269–285.

Rathus, S. S. (1973). A 30-item schedule for assessing assertive behavior. *Behavior Therapy, 4*, 398–406.

Rehm, L. P., & Marston, A. R. (1968). Reduction of social anxiety through modification of self-reinforcement: An instigation therapy technique. *Journal of Consulting and Clinical Psychology, 32*, 565–574.

Ronan, K. R., Kendall, P. C., & Rowe, M. (1994). Negative affectivity in children: Development and validation of a self-statement questionnaire. *Cognitive Therapy and Research, 18*, 509–528.

Rotter, J. B. (1954). *Social learning and clinical psychology*. Englewood Cliffs, NJ: Prentice Hall.

Sarason, I. G., & Stoops, R. (1978). Test anxiety and the passage of time. *Journal of Consulting and Clinical Psychology, 46*, 102–109.

Schwartz, R. M. (1991, November). *The idea of balance in psychotherapy*. Paper presented to the Association for Advancement of Behavior Therapy, New York.

Schwartz, R. M., & Garamoni, G. L. (1986a). Cognitive assessment: A multibehavior-multimethod-multiperspective approach. *Journal of Psychopathology and Behavioral Assessment, 8*, 185–197.

Schwartz, R. M., & Garamoni, G. L. (1986b). A structural model of positive and negative states of mind: Asymmetry in the internal dialogue. In P. C. Kendall (Ed.), *Advances in cognitive behavioral research and therapy* (Vol. 5, pp. 1–62). New York: Academic Press.

Schwartz, R. M., & Garamoni, G. L. (1989). Cognitive balance and psychopathology: Evaluation of an information processing model of positive and negative states of mind. *Clinical Psychology Review, 9*, 271–294.

Schwartz, R. M., & Gottman, J. M. (1976): Toward a task analysis of assertive behavior. *Journal of Consulting and Clinical Psychology, 44*, 910–920.

Schwartz, R. M., Reynolds, C. F., Thase, M. E., Frank, E., & Fasiczka, A. L. (1995, November). *Optimal and normal affect balance in cognitive therapy and pharmacotherapy of major depression: Evaluation of the balanced states of mind model*. Presented to the Association for the Advancement of Behavior Therapy, Washington, DC.

Segal, Z. V., & Marshall, W. L. (1985). Heterosocial skill in a population of rapists and child molesters. *Journal of Consulting and Clinical Psychology, 53*, 55–63.

Seligman, M. E. P., Abramson, L. Y., Semmel, A., & von Baeyer, C. (1979). Depressive attributional style. *Journal of Abnormal Psychology, 88*, 242–247.

Shorkey, C. T., Reyes, E., & Whiteman, V. L. (1977). Development of the Rational Behavior Inventory: Initial validity and reliability. *Educational and Psychological Measurement, 37*, 527–534.

Skinner, B. F. (1953). *Science and human behavior*. New York: Macmillan.

Smith, T. W. (1982). Irrational beliefs in the cause and treatment of emotional distress: A critical review of the rational-emotive model. *Clinical Psychology Review, 2*, 505–522.

Spiegler, M. D., & Guevremont, D. C. (1998). *Contemporary behavior therapy* (3rd ed.). Pacific Grove, CA: Brooks/Cole.

St. Laurence, J. S. (1987). Assessment of assertion. In M. Hersen, R. M. Eisler, & P. M. Miller (Eds.), *Progress in behavior modification* (Vol. 21, pp. 152–190). Newbury Park, CA: Sage.

Stricker, G., & Gold, J. R. (Eds.). (1993). *Comprehensive handbook of psychotherapy integration.* New York: Plenum Press.

Strosahl, K. D., & Linehan, M. M. (1986). Basic issues in behavioral assessment. In A. R. Ciminero, K. S. Calhoun, & H. E. Adams (Eds.), *Handbook of behavioral assessment* (2nd ed., pp. 12–46). New York: Wiley.

Sturgis, E. T., & Gramling, S. (1988). Psychophysiological assessment. In A. S. Bellack & M. Hersen (Eds.), *Behavioral assessment: A practical handbook* (3rd ed., pp. 213–251). New York: Pergamon.

Sundberg, N. D. (1981). Historical and traditional approaches to cognitive assessment. In T. V. Merluzzi, C. R. Glass, & M. Genest (Eds.), *Cognitive assessment* (pp. 52–76). New York: Guilford Press.

Thoresen, C. E., & Mahoney, M. J. (1974). *Behavioral self-control.* New York: Holt, Rinehart, & Winston.

Trower, P., Bryant, B., & Argyle, M. (1978). *Social skills and mental health.* Pittsburgh: University of Pittsburgh Press.

Turner, R. M., & Ascher, L. M. (1985). *Evaluating behavior therapy.* New York: Springer.

Turner, S. M., Beidel, D. C., Dancu, C. V., & Keys, D. J. (1986). Psychopathology of social phobia and comparison to avoidant personality disorder. *Journal of Abnormal Psychology, 95,* 389–394.

Turner, S. M., Beidel, D. C., Dancu, C. V., & Stanley, M. A. (1989). An empirically derived inventory to measure social fears and anxiety: The Social Phobia and Anxiety Inventory. *Psychological Assessment: A Journal of Consulting and Clinical Psychology, 1,* 35–40.

Turner, S. M., Beidel, D. C., & Jacob, R. G. (1994). Social phobia: A comparison of behavior therapy and atenolol. *Journal of Consulting and Clinical Psychology, 62,* 350–358.

Twentyman, C. T., & McFall, R. M. (1975). Behavioral training of social skills in shy males. *Journal of Consulting and Clinical Psychology, 43,* 384–395.

Watson, D., & Friend, R. (1969). Measurement of social-evaluation anxiety. *Journal of Consulting and Clinical Psychology, 33,* 448–457.

Watson, J. B. (1913). Psychology as the behaviorist views it. *Psychological Review, 20,* 158–177.

Weissman, A. N., & Beck, A. T. (1978, March). *Development and validation of the Dysfunctional Attitude Scale: A preliminary investigation.* Paper presented at the annual meeting of the American Educational Research Association, Toronto, Canada.

Williams, C. L., & Ciminero, A. R. (1978). Development and validation of a heterosocial skills inventory: the Survey of Heterosocial Interactions for Females. *Journal of Consulting and Clinical Psychology, 46,* 1547–1548.

Wolpe, J. (1992). *The practice of behavior therapy* (4th ed.). New York: Pergamon.

Wolpe, J., & Lang, P. (1964). A fear schedule for use in behavior therapy. *Behaviour Research and Therapy, 2,* 27–30.

Wolpe, J., & Lazarus, A. A. (1966). *Behavior therapy techniques: A guide to the treatment of neurosis.* New York: Pergamon.

Zatz, S., & Chassin, L. (1985). Cognitions of test-anxious children under naturalistic test-taking conditions. *Journal of Consulting and Clinical Psychology, 53,* 393–401.

Zimbardo, P. G. (1977). *Shyness: What it is and what to do about it.* Reading, MA: Addison-Wesley.

Zweig, D. R., & Brown, S. D. (1985). Psychometric evaluation of a written stimulus presentation format for the Social Interaction Self-Statement test. *Cognitive Therapy and Research, 9,* 285–295.

VOCATIONAL ASSESSMENT

7

Interpretation of the Strong Interest Inventory[1]

Jo-Ida C. Hansen
Center for Interest Measurement Research,
Department of Psychology,
University of Minnesota

The Strong Interest Inventory is the oldest, continuously used interest inventory available today. As was the case with most interest inventories developed in the 1920s and 1930s, the Strong Interest Inventory had its beginnings in an item pool created just after World War I. The work was done as part of a seminar, conducted by Clarence S. Yoakum at Carnegie Institute of Technology, which explored the problem of using a paper-and-pencil questionnaire to differentiate people in various occupations. The result of the seminar's effort was a pool of 1,000 items that eventually found their way into several instruments (e.g., Occupational Interest Inventory, Freyd, 1923; General Interest Survey, Kornhauser, 1927; and Purdue Interest Report, Remmers, 1929), only one of which, the Strong Interest Inventory, survived the changes of time and society to continue in use today. The longevity of the Strong is due primarily to the revisions that have been done periodically throughout its history.

HISTORY OF THE STRONG INTEREST INVENTORY

The earliest predecessor of the Strong Interest Inventory was the Interest Report Blank, developed by Karl Cowdery in 1926 under the supervision of

---

[1]Strong Interest Inventory is a trademark of the Stanford University Press.

E. K. Strong, Jr., who had been an interested observer of the Yoakum seminar at Carnegie prior to joining the Stanford University faculty (Cowdery, 1926). Cowdery used a sample of items from the original Carnegie item pool for developing his inventory. For reasons that history has not preserved, Cowdery did not pursue his work in interest measurement research. E. K. Strong, however, did continue Cowdery's efforts and improved the Interest Report Blank by adding and deleting items, publishing the first Vocational Interest Blank® in 1927 (Strong, 1927). The instrument later became known as the Strong Vocational Interest Blanks[2]; in 1974 it was renamed the Strong-Campbell Interest Inventory, Form T325 of the Strong Vocational Interest Blank (SVIB-SCII; Campbell, 1974), and in 1985, the Strong Interest Inventory (SII; Hansen & Campbell, 1985). The most recent version of the Strong Interest Inventory is Form T317 of the Strong Vocational Interest Blanks (Harmon, Hansen, Borgen, & Hammer, 1994).

Each revision of the Strong Interest Inventory resulted in an expansion of the profile, and the instrument now provides information about the similarity of a person's interests to 109 occupations. The Strong also measures interests related to Holland's six global types and 25 basic interests, which represent areas commonly recognized as important for understanding the organization and structure of interests as well as the world of work.

The development of the Strong Interest Inventory to its current breadth of interest measurement was a gradual process beginning with a rather modest profile of only 10 Occupational Scales representing the interests of men. The first women's form was developed in 1933 (Strong, 1933), and revisions of the men's and women's forms took place in 1938 (Strong, 1938) and 1946 (Strong, 1946), respectively. These revisions provided the opportunity to expand the occupations represented on the profile as well as to improve the item pools.

The next major innovation in the scale construction technology of the Strong Interest Inventory was the development of the Basic Interest Scales in the 1960s (Campbell, Borgen, Eastes, Johansson, & Peterson, 1968). These scales added tremendously to the instrument, supplementing the profile information provided by the empirically derived and atheoretically developed Occupational Scales.

The next series of changes in the Strong Interest Inventory began with the 1974 revision, which featured two major developments: the merger of the men's and women's forms into one item booklet and profile, and the integration of Holland's theory of vocational types with the empiricism of Strong's Occupational Scales. Subsequent revisions of the instrument

---

[2]Strong Vocational Interest Blanks® is a registered trademark of the Stanford University Press.

(Campbell & Hansen, 1981; Hansen & Campbell, 1985) were designed to address questions of sex equity of the instrument, to expand the Occupational Scales to a wider range of professional and nonprofessional occupations, and to develop better interpretive materials and interpretive aids to accompany the burgeoning profile.

Current Version of the Strong

Development of the 1994 version of the Strong Interest Inventory involved sampling over 55,000 people from across the country and combining them with 12,000 participants used for scale development with the 1985 Strong Interest Inventory. The General Occupational Themes (GOT) and Basic Interest Scales (BIS) were revised; the item pool for the test was modified; new Personal Style Scales were developed, and new Occupational Scales were constructed (Harmon et al., 1994).

Item Pool. The Strong Interest Inventory includes a test booklet composed of 317 items that measure interest in or "liking" for occupations, school subjects, work activities, leisure activities, and various types of people; a short section devoted to estimating self-characteristics; and a set of paired-choice items that reflect work dimensions. Over the years, the psychometric properties of the items included in the Strong booklet have been studied carefully to ensure that the items elicit a wide range of responses among occupations and that their inclusion in the item pool is supported by evidence of predictive, as well as concurrent, validity. In addition, the items are revised periodically to ensure that they are (a) free of sex-role bias, (b) up to date, (c) in good taste, and (d) free of cultural bias. The items also are designed to be unambiguous; in other words, most people reading the items should interpret them in the same way. The reading level has been maintained at the eighth to ninth grade level to accommodate the use of the instrument with a wide range of people.

Profile Report. The Strong Interest Inventory is scored by a computer that calculates the scores for the various scales. Then, the results are printed on a six-page profile report form that begins with a Snapshot page that summarizes the individual's highest scores for the GOT, the BIS, and the Occupational Scales (see Fig. 7.1). The second page reports the GOT and BIS scores (see Fig. 7.2); pages 3, 4, and 5 report the Occupational Scale results (see Figs. 7.3, 7.4, and 7.5), and the final page reports scores on the Personal Style Scales and the Administrative Indexes (see Fig. 7.6).

Appropriate Client Populations. Although the Strong Interest Inventory frequently is used with college-aged young adults, the instrument is appropriate for use with a wide range of ages, for example, high-school students,

Profile report for **A CLIENT**   4692
ID:
Age: 0   Date tested:
Gender: Female   Date scored: 11/4/96

Page 1 of 6

SNAPSHOT: A SUMMARY OF RESULTS FOR
A CLIENT

GENERAL OCCUPATIONAL THEMES

The General Occupational Themes describe interests in six very broad areas, including interest in work and leisure activities, kinds of people, and work settings. Your interests in each area are shown at the right in rank order. Note that each Theme has a code, represented by the first letter of the Theme name.

You can use your Theme code, printed below your results, to identify school subjects, part-time jobs, college majors, leisure activities, or careers that you might find interesting. See the back of this Profile for suggestions on how to use your Theme code.

THEME CODE	THEME	VERY LITTLE INTEREST	LITTLE INTEREST	AVERAGE INTEREST	HIGH INTEREST	VERY HIGH INTEREST	TYPICAL INTERESTS
I	INVESTIGATIVE	☐	☐	☐	☑	☐	Researching, analyzing
A	ARTISTIC	☐	☐	☑	☐	☐	Creating or enjoying art
R	REALISTIC	☐	☐	☑	☐	☐	Building, repairing
C	CONVENTIONAL	☐	☐	☑	☐	☐	Accounting, processing data
E	ENTERPRISING	☑	☐	☐	☐	☐	Selling, managing
S	SOCIAL	☑	☐	☐	☐	☐	Helping, instructing

Your Theme code is IAR—(see explanation at left).
You might explore occupations with codes that contain any combination of these letters.

BASIC INTEREST SCALES

The Basic Interest Scales measure your interests in 25 specific areas or activities. Only those 5 areas in which you show the *most* interest are listed at the right in rank order. Your results on all 25 Basic Interest Scales are found on page 2.

To the left of each scale is a letter that shows which of the six General Occupational Themes this activity is most closely related to. These codes can help you to identify other activities that you may enjoy.

THEME CODE	BASIC INTEREST	VERY LITTLE INTEREST	LITTLE INTEREST	AVERAGE INTEREST	HIGH INTEREST	VERY HIGH INTEREST	TYPICAL ACTIVITIES
R	ATHLETICS	☐	☐	☐	☑	☐	Playing or watching sports
R	MECHANICAL ACTIVITIES	☐	☐	☐	☑	☐	Working with tools and equipment
A	CULINARY ARTS	☐	☐	☑	☐	☐	Cooking or entertaining
I	MEDICAL SCIENCE	☐	☐	☑	☐	☐	Working in medicine or biology
R	NATURE	☐	☐	☑	☐	☐	Appreciating nature

OCCUPATIONAL SCALES

The Occupational Scales measure how similar your interests are to the interests of people who are satisfied working in those occupations. Only the 10 scales on which your interests are *most* similar to those of these people are listed at the right in rank order. Your results on all 211 of the Occupational Scales are found on pages 3, 4, and 5.

The letters to the left of each scale identify the Theme or Themes that most closely describe the interests of people working in that occupation. You can use these letters to find additional, related occupations that you might find interesting. After reviewing your results on all six pages of this Profile, see the back of page 5 for tips on finding other occupations in the Theme or Themes that interest you the most.

THEME CODE	OCCUPATION	VERY DISSIMILAR	DISSIMILAR	MID-RANGE	SIMILAR	VERY SIMILAR
IR	CHEMIST	☐	☐	☐	☐	☑
IRA	BIOLOGIST	☐	☐	☐	☐	☑
RI	FORESTER	☐	☐	☐	☐	☑
IR	COMPUTER PROGR./ SYSTEMS ANALYST	☐	☐	☐	☐	☑
RC	GARDENER/ GROUNDSKEEPER	☐	☐	☐	☐	☑
RI	ENGINEER	☐	☐	☐	☑	☐
IRA	GEOLOGIST	☐	☐	☐	☑	☐
IRA	VETERINARIAN	☐	☐	☐	☑	☐
IRA	DENTIST	☐	☐	☐	☑	☐
AIR	TECHNICAL WRITER	☐	☐	☐	☑	☐

PERSONAL STYLE SCALES measure your levels of comfort regarding Work Style, Learning Environment, Leadership Style, and Risk Taking/Adventure. This information may help you make decisions about particular work environments, educational settings, and types of activities you would find satisfying. Your results on these four scales are on page 6.

FIG. 7.1. Snapshot page of the Strong Interest Inventory for A Client. Reprinted with permission of Consulting Psychologists Press, Inc. "Modified and reproduced by special permission of the Publisher, Consulting Psychologists Press, Inc., Palo Alto, CA 94303 from the *Strong Interest Inventory*™ of the *Strong Vocational Interest Blanks*® Form T317. Copyright 1933, 1938, 1945, 1946, 1966, 1968, 1974, 1981, 1985, 1994 by The Board of Trustees of the Leland Stanford Junior University. All rights reserved. Printed under license from Stanford University Press, Stanford, CA 94305. Further reproduction is prohibited without the Publisher's written consent." *Strong Interest Inventory* is a trademark of and *Strong Vocational Interest Blanks* is a registered trademark of the Stanford University Press.

GENERAL OCCUPATIONAL THEMES

BASIC INTEREST SCALES

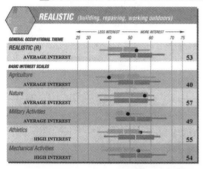

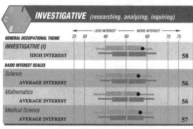

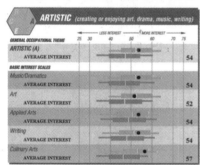

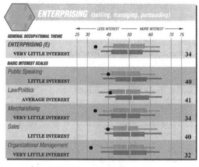

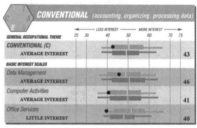

FIG. 7.2. General Occupational Theme and Basic Interest Scale profile for A Client. Reprinted with permission of Consulting Psychologists Press, Inc. "Modified and reproduced by special permission of the Publisher, Consulting Psychologists Press, Inc., Palo Alto, CA 94303 from the *Strong Interest Inventory*™ of the *Strong Vocational Interest Blanks*® Form T317. Copyright 1933, 1938, 1945, 1946, 1966, 1968, 1974, 1981, 1985, 1994 by The Board of Trustees of the Leland Stanford Junior University. All rights reserved. Printed under license from Stanford University Press, Stanford, CA 94305. Further reproduction is prohibited without the Publisher's written consent." *Strong Interest Inventory* is a trademark of and *Strong Vocational Interest Blanks* is a registered trademark of the Stanford University Press.

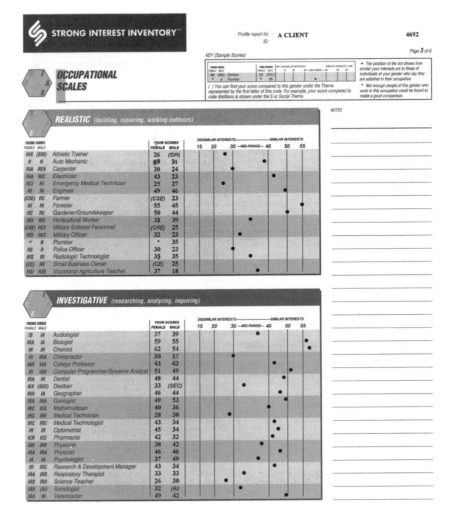

FIG. 7.3. Realistic and Investigative Occupational Scales on the Strong Interest Inventory. Reprinted with permission of Consulting Psychologists Press, Inc. "Modified and reproduced by special permission of the Publisher, Consulting Psychologists Press, Inc., Palo Alto, CA 94303 from the *Strong Interest Inventory*™ of the *Strong Vocational Interest Blanks*® Form T317. Copyright 1933, 1938, 1945, 1946, 1966, 1968, 1974, 1981, 1985, 1994 by The Board of Trustees of the Leland Stanford Junior University. All rights reserved. Printed under license from Stanford University Press, Stanford, CA 94305. Further reproduction is prohibited without the Publisher's written consent." *Strong Interest Inventory* is a trademark of and *Strong Vocational Interest Blanks* is a registered trademark of the Stanford University Press.

232

FIG. 7.4. Artistic and Social Occupational Scales on the Strong Interest Inventory. Reprinted with permission of Consulting Psychologists Press, Inc. "Modified and reproduced by special permission of the Publisher, Consulting Psychologists Press, Inc., Palo Alto, CA 94303 from the *Strong Interest Inventory*™ of the *Strong Vocational Interest Blanks*® Form T317. Copyright 1933, 1938, 1945, 1946, 1966, 1968, 1974, 1981, 1985, 1994 by The Board of Trustees of the Leland Stanford Junior University. All rights reserved. Printed under license from Stanford University Press, Stanford, CA 94305. Further reproduction is prohibited without the Publisher's written consent." *Strong Interest Inventory* is a trademark of and *Strong Vocational Interest Blanks* is a registered trademark of the Stanford University Press.

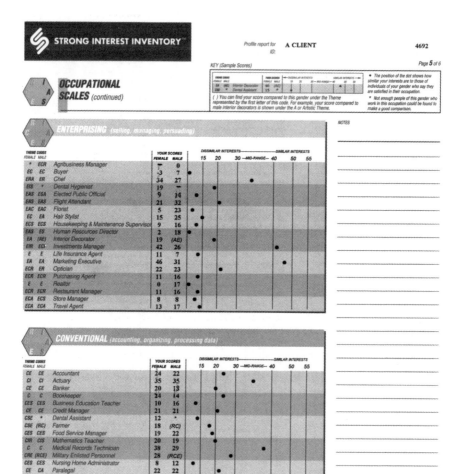

STRONG INTEREST INVENTORY™

Profile report for **A CLIENT**
ID:

4692

KEY (Sample Scores)

Page **5** of 6

FIG. 7.5. Enterprising and Conventional Occupational Scales on the Strong Interest Inventory, reprinted with permission of Consulting Psychologists Press, Inc. "Modified and reproduced by special permission of the Publisher, Consulting Psychologists Press, Inc., Palo Alto, CA 94303 from the *Strong Interest Inventory*™ of the *Strong Vocational Interest Blanks*® Form T317. Copyright 1933, 1938, 1945, 1946, 1966, 1968, 1974, 1981, 1985, 1994 by The Board of Trustees of the Leland Stanford Junior University. All rights reserved. Printed under license from Stanford University Press, Stanford, CA 94305. Further reproduction is prohibited without the Publisher's written consent." Strong Interest Inventory is a trademark of and *Strong Vocational Interest Blanks* is a registered trademark of the Stanford University Press.

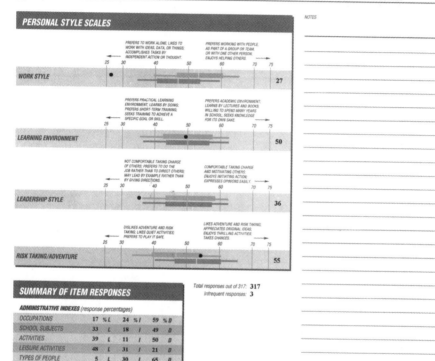

FIG. 7.6. Personal Style Scales and Administrative Indexes of the Strong Interest Inventory, reprinted with permission of Consulting Psychologists Press, Inc. "Modified and reproduced by special permission of the Publisher, Consulting Psychologists Press, Inc., Palo Alto, CA 94303 from the *Strong Interest Inventory*™ of the *Strong Vocational Interest Blanks*® Form T317. Copyright 1933, 1938, 1945, 1946, 1966, 1968, 1974, 1981, 1985, 1994 by The Board of Trustees of the Leland Stanford Junior University. All rights reserved. Printed under license from Stanford University Press, Stanford, CA 94305. Further reproduction is prohibited without the Publisher's written consent." *Strong Interest Inventory* is a trademark of and *Strong Vocational Interest Blanks* is a registered trademark of the Stanford University Press.

individuals who are reentering the labor force or returning to school, persons who are making mid-career changes, clients in rehabilitation settings, or people who are preparing for retirement. The Strong Interest Inventory also is used as one of several assessment instruments in placement and training situations; in research, as the instrument that measures or operationalizes interests; or with a variety of special populations, such as cross-ethnic or international populations, disabled clients, culturally disadvantaged clients, and people seeking career opportunities or training in vocational-technical areas. Thus, the Strong is used by a broad cross section of organizations including secondary and vocational-technical schools, universities, government agencies, mental health centers, hospitals, industry, consulting firms, private institutions, and the military.

Purpose of the Strong. People vary in their motivation for engaging in career exploration, and the Strong is helpful in reaching a variety of goals. For example, some individuals simply wish to confirm a career choice they already have made; others are trying to narrow their range of possible choices; and still others are hoping to identify new options that they may not have considered in the past.

Psychologists and counselors find the Strong useful in understanding the unique qualities of each client, and the individual clients find that the Strong helps them to gain insight about their interests and how they relate to the working world. Ultimately, the information can be used by the counselor and client to provide the client with better self-understanding and with the knowledge and information necessary to make better decisions.

The Strong Interest Inventory usually is not administered before the 10th grade. However, the Strong can be used as an introduction to the world of work and to career exploration with younger students—eighth and ninth graders. The General Occupational Themes and Basic Interest Scales, in particular, will help 13-, 14-, and 15-year-olds identify interests that are beginning to develop and give them new directions to explore. Most people's interests begin to solidify by age 17 or 18, and the Strong then can be used to begin long-range educational and career planning. For younger individuals, or those who may not have the attention span necessary for completing the inventory in one sitting, it is permissible to administer the instrument in two or more shorter sessions.

PSYCHOMETRIC BRIEFING

Three assumptions are basic to the development of any interest inventory. First, interest measurement assumes that a person can give an informed response such as *like, indifferent,* or *dislike* to items that describe activities that are familiar to the person. The second assumption is that the structure of interests underlying these familiar activities is the same structure of interests underlying unfamiliar activities. Third, the responses to the familiar items then can be used to generalize to interests in the unfamiliar areas.

Based on these assumptions, E. K. Strong, Jr., developed the empirical method of contrast groups for identifying items that differentiated the interests of various occupations from people-in-general. Strong's first effort resulted in 10 Occupational Scales; the current form of the Strong has 211 Occupational Scales for women and men that represent the interests of 109 occupations.

Occupational Scale Construction Technique

The method used to construct the Occupational Scales of the Strong Interest Inventory is the empirical method of contrast groups. Essentially, the technique involves the comparison of item responses for two samples, and the identification of the items that differentiate the two groups. This technique has been used in test development with interest inventories and also with personality measures such as the Minnesota Multiphasic Personality Inventory (MMPI; McKinley & Hathaway, 1940) and the California Psychological Inventory (CPI; Gough, 1957).

In the interest measurement field, the two contrast groups typically are a criterion sample representing a specific occupation, such as athletic trainers, and a separate and unique sample of either women- or men-in-general selected from a wide range of occupations. However, the traditional empirical method of contrast groups has been modified somewhat in developing the women- and men-in-general samples (called female and male General Reference Samples) used in the 1994 revision of the Strong. Rather than developing in-general contrast samples composed of participants not included in the criterion samples, 200 respondents were selected from each occupational criterion sample used in the 1994 revision. For those occupational criterion samples with fewer than 200 participants (e.g., 99 female medical illustrators or 96 male plumbers), all members of the criterion sample became part of the in-general sample. As a result, a large proportion of the participants used in the occupational criterion samples also are used in the female General Reference Sample ($N = 9,467$) and in the male General Reference Sample ($N = 9,484$).

The respondents to each criterion sample collection effort are screened on several criteria before inclusion in the sample, with the goal of selecting subjects who are typical representatives of the occupation. The final sample consists of a national sample of people who usually have been in their occupation for a minimum of 3 years, who are satisfied with their occupation, and who pursue their job in a typical fashion for that occupation. The occupational criterion sample generally is composed of about 200 subjects, although a smaller number of subjects will provide a reliable sample if stringent item selection standards are maintained.

Separate-Sex Scales. Although some interest inventories are available that use one set of scales for females and males (e.g., the Self-Directed Search, Holland, 1985b; the Career Assessment Inventory, Johansson, 1986; the Campbell Interest and Skill Survey, Campbell, Hyne, & Nilsen, 1992), several studies conducted with the Strong Interest Inventory to examine the feasibility of combined-sex scale construction indicate that for the Strong Interest Inventory combined-sex scales are less valid for most occupations and often are less reliable than are single-sex scales (Hansen, 1976, 1984; Hansen & Campbell, 1985; Webber & Harmon, 1978). Therefore, the current Strong profile continues to present Occupational Scale scores that are based on separate female and male samples. By using patterns of scores, meaningful interpretations can be provided for both own- and opposite-sex scales.

Weighting the Items. Items with large response percentage differences between the criterion sample and the appropriate-sex General Reference Sample are selected to represent the interests of the occupation on the Occupational Scale. The selected items represent both the "likes," or interests, and "dislikes," or aversions, of the occupation; typically, between 40 and 50 items emerge as those that best differentiate the contrast samples (i.e., occupational criterion sample and General Reference Sample).

The items that the occupational criterion sample prefers are assigned a unit weight of +1; the aversions of the criterion sample also are weighted +1. The net effect of this weighting system is to provide a scale on which an individual will score high if she or he has the same likes and dislikes as the occupational sample. Because the item weights for the various Occupational Scales are trade secrets, a fictitious example is used here to illustrate how the item weights contribute to a person's score on an Occupational Scale. If, for example, a woman responds *like* to an item such as *trigonometry*, and that item is among the preferences of female statisticians, her score on the female Statistician scale will increase. Her score also will increase if she responds *dislike* to the item *disco dancing* because, in this fictitious example, disco dancing is an activity that female statisticians dislike. A *like* response to the item *disco dancing*, on the other hand, would have the opposite effect and would lower the score on the female Statistician scale.

Standardizing the Occupational Scales. The Occupational Scales are standardized to allow the scores on various scales to be compared easily and meaningfully. The original criterion sample is used as the standardization sample for its own scale. First, the criterion sample is scored on the Occupational Scale to obtain a raw score; then, the raw scores are used in a raw-score-to-standard-score conversion formula that yields a mean of 50 and a standard deviation of 10 for the criterion sample. Thus, each criterion sample has a mean standard score of 50 on its own scale.

An individual who scores 50 on an Occupational Scale has responded to the items on the scale at a level similar to that of the average member of the criterion sample and therefore looks similar to the occupation in terms of her or his interests. The interpretive categories for scores on the Occupational Scales are:

Score	Interpretive Comment
19 or below	Very dissimilar
20–29	Dissimilar
30–39	Mid-range
40–49	Similar
50 or higher	Very similar

Basic Interest Scale Construction Technique

The Basic Interest Scales (BIS; Campbell et al., 1968) first were developed to supplement the Occupational Scales, and to provide a heuristic model for understanding the structure of interests and for identifying the clusters of interests that are relevant to the overall interests of occupations. Currently, there are 25 Basic Interest Scales on the profile. The items on each scale originally were grouped together using a cluster analysis procedure. The item selection for the current BIS was guided by factor analyses of the item pool. The item content within each scale, therefore, is highly correlated; the coefficient alphas range from .74 to .94 with a median of .86 (Harmon et al., 1994).

Weighting the Items. The items on the Basic Interest Scales are weighted so that a *like* response is a +1 and a *dislike* response is a −1. Thus, a high score on a particular Basic Interest Scale indicates that the person said *like* to a large number of items included on that scale and representing that cluster of interests.

Standardizing the BIS. A combination of the female and male General Reference Samples was used to standardize the Basic Interest Scales. A raw-score-to-standard-score conversion formula was employed that sets the mean for the GRS equal to 50 with a standard deviation of 10. Thus, a score of 50 on any BIS is a score indicating an average interest as compared to people-in-general.

General Occupational Theme Construction Technique

The General Occupational Themes (GOT) were constructed to provide a more parsimonious organization for the Strong Interest Inventory profile (Campbell & Holland, 1972; Hansen & Johansson, 1972). The original GOT were based on Holland's theory of vocational types (Holland, 1973) and were developed using a rational-theoretical method to select items that represented each of the six types proposed by Holland: Realistic, Investigative, Artistic, Social, Enterprising, and Conventional (Campbell, 1974). The current GOT are slightly modified versions of the original scales that have a high correlation with the original GOT and that continue to represent Holland's six vocational personality types. Like the items on the Basic Interest Scales, the GOT items are highly intercorrelated and the coefficient alphas range from .90 to .94 with a median of .91. (Harmon et al., 1994). The items are weighted with the same scheme as that used with the BIS—+1 for a *like* response and −1 for a *dislike* response. The GOT were standardized using a combination of the female and male General Reference Samples with the standard score mean set equal to 50 and the standard deviation at 10.

Personal Style Scale Construction Techniques

The Personal Style Scales include the Work Style Scale, the Learning Environment Scale, the Leadership Style Scale, and the Risk Taking/Adventure Scale. The empirical method of contrast groups was used to construct the Work Style Scale and the Learning Environment Scale. The Risk Taking/Adventure Scale was among the original BIS identified by cluster analysis in the 1960s, and the Leadership Style Scale emerged from factor analyses of the Strong item pool.

Work Style Scale. The Work Style Scale was developed using contrast samples of participants drawn from the General Reference Samples who consistently preferred the people pole of the World of Work items on the Strong and from those participants who consistently preferred data, things, or ideas. Once the items differentiating these two samples were identified, then the Work Style Scale was standardized on a combined sample of the female and male General Reference Samples using a raw-score-to standard-score conversion formula with the mean set equal to 50 and standard deviation at 10. The higher is an individual's score on the Work Style Scale, the more the person prefers to work with people (Harmon et al., 1994).

Learning Environment Scale. The contrast samples for constructing the Learning Environment Scale were individuals drawn from the General Reference Samples (GRS) who had earned master's and doctoral degrees and individuals from the GRS with degrees from technical or trade schools. The item responses for a sample of MA and PhD degree holders were compared to the item responses of the sample of vocational technical degree holders; the items differentiating the two samples were chosen for the Learning Environment Scale.

The Learning Environment Scale was standardized on a combination of the female and male General Reference Samples with mean set equal to 50 and standard deviation equal to 10. Scores of 55 or higher suggest interests of people who enter academic learning settings, whereas scores of 45 or lower suggest interests similar to those who prefer applied learning situations (Harmon et al., 1994).

Risk Taking/Adventure Scale. The scale called Risk Taking/Adventure on the 1994 Strong was originally developed through cluster analysis as a Basic Interest Scale (Campbell et al., 1968) and appeared on the profile with Realistic type BIS through the 1985 revision of the Strong. The current scale, which has a slightly modified item content, has been moved to the Personal Style section of the 1994 profile.

Like the other Personal Style Scales, the Risk Taking/Adventure Scale is normed on the combined female and male General Reference Samples with a mean set equal to 50 and a standard deviation of 10. As the scale name suggests, high scores reflect a willingness to take risks (Harmon et al., 1994).

Leadership Style Scale. The Leadership Style Scale was identified as one of the scales that emerged in the factor analysis of the Strong item pool that also identified the 25 Basic Interest Scales. Similar to the Work Style Scale, the Leadership Style Scale correlates with the extroversion/introversion construct.

The scale is normed on the combined female and male General Reference Samples, with the mean for that sample set equal to 50 and the standard deviation set equal to 10. People who like to direct others score above the mean of the combined GRS, and those who prefer to work alone score below the mean (Harmon et al., 1994).

ADMINISTRATION

The Strong Interest Inventory may be administered in either a paper-and-pencil or computer-adapted format. The paper-and-pencil version takes about 25 to 35 min for the average individual to complete; the computer-administered version takes about half the time or roughly 15 min. The Strong can be given individually or in groups and is sufficiently robust to be administered in unsupervised settings (e.g., as a take-home assignment or through the mail) or during several sittings if an individual cannot complete the entire inventory at one time. Although the reading level has been maintained at the eighth to ninth grade level to ensure that the majority of clients can understand the item content, it is permissible to provide definitions or explanations for items that may be difficult to understand.

Basic instructions for taking the Strong should include a standard introduction such as the following:

> The Strong Interest Inventory is designed to help you understand your interests in a general way and to identify some types of activities and work in which you may be interested. The booklet lists a variety of jobs, activities, school subjects, types of people, and work dimensions. You are asked to indicate how you feel about each item—whether you feel you "like" the item, are "indifferent" to it, or "dislike" it. Your answers to the items will be compared to people already employed in a wide variety of occupations to see how similar your interests are to theirs. As you respond to the items in the booklet, remember that the Strong is designed to assess only your interests and it does not measure your abilities. As you think about possible jobs and occupations, you will need to consider both your abilities and interests to make the best decisions.

Additional information and instructions, given to the client prior to taking the Strong, will vary according to the situation. Counselors, however, frequently find it helpful to remind the client that most people respond *like* to about one-third of the items, *indifferent* to about one-third, and *dislike* to about one-third of the items. Also, the inventory cannot tell the client what she or he "should do." Rather, the instrument is designed to give some general information that will help the individual to do a thorough self-evaluation of her or his patterns of interests, and the profile is organized to aid the individual in identifying these patterns of interests. Finally, the client should be reminded that career planning is a lifelong activity, and results on the profile can be used for long-range planning as well as for making immediate educational or career planning decisions.

Scores on the Strong Interest Inventory are used, of course, to explore work-related interests, but they also can provide clients with an opportunity to explore other types of interests such as leisure interests, preferences for various types of work, living and recreational environments, and affinity for people with various interests. Although compatibility between interests and work environment is important, compatibility between interests and other life roles also is important. The high and low scores of the General Occupational Themes and the Basic Interest Scales are especially helpful in determining how well a client's lifestyle matches her or his interests. Ultimately, the counseling outcome goal is an integration of the person's various interests into a composite that allows satisfaction through the various roles in her or his life.

INTERPRETATION

The Strong Interest Inventory is used primarily to stimulate respondents to think about activities and occupations that match their interests. The instrument helps them to objectively identify their interests in an efficient manner. The results are organized to provide a framework for relating the interests to career possibilities and for encouraging the individual to consider options that may have been ignored previously. Longitudinal outcome research with the Strong has shown that college students who receive interpretations of their Strong scores tend to participate in more career exploration activities than do students who have not taken the Strong (Randahl, Hansen, & Haverkamp, 1993). However, these same students remember very little about the specific results report on their profiles 1 year before the follow-up study (Hansen, Kozberg, & Goranson, 1994). The results from these studies suggest that the most effective use of the Strong will occur within the context of a career development intervention that goes beyond isolated interpretation of scores.

The GOT, BIS, and Occupational Scales

The three main sets of scales on the Strong profile are the six General Occupational Themes, the 25 Basic Interest Scales, and the 107 female-normed and 104 male-normed Occupational Scales. The Occupational Scales differ from the General Occupational Themes (GOT) and Basic Interest Scales (BIS) in several ways. The GOT and BIS were constructed to measure single interest factors and are composed of items that, within each scale, are highly related to each other. The Occupational Scales, on the other hand, are composed of items that represent several interest factors. As a consequence, the GOT and BIS are somewhat easier to understand and interpret. They provide the best general information about a person's interests and also are useful for exploring nonoccupational interests such as avocational interests or preferences for various work and living environments.

The Occupational Scales also are more complicated to interpret than are the other scales because of the system of assigning positive weights to both the likes and the aversions of an occupation. However, because of their greater length and item complexity, the Occupational Scales are less susceptible to faking than are the GOT and BIS. They also are less susceptible to distortion from extreme response rates and to transient changes in interests. Thus, the Occupational Scales—as they were when E. K. Strong,

Jr., first constructed them—are the preferred scales for predicting future occupational choices.

General Occupational Themes. The six General Occupational Themes— Realistic, Investigative, Artistic, Social, Enterprising, and Conventional— were added to the profile to provide a global view of a person's interests; they also provide a useful starting point for the exploration of an individual's occupational interests. And the GOT contribute to the Strong Interest Inventory in another important way: They are used as part of the procedure for assigning Holland types to the Occupational Scales and the Basic Interest Scales.

Thus, each Occupational Scale is assigned a one- to three-letter Holland code that is useful in identifying the main clusters of interests of the occupation represented by the scale. For example, the Accountant scale is coded C and E, indicating interests that fall in the Conventional and Enterprising areas. Each Basic Interest Scale also has been assigned a primary Holland code based on the BIS scale's highest correlation with the GOT. The Mechanical Activities BIS, for example, has its highest correlation with the Realistic Theme and, therefore, is clustered with other R-Theme BIS on the profile. In turn, the codes assigned to the BIS and Occupational Scales are used to assist in organizing the entire profile; the BIS are clustered together by their Holland type and placed on the profile in Holland's R-I-A-S-E-C order, as are the Occupational Scales.

The General Occupational Themes also can be used in interpretation to better understand the type of counseling intervention that may be most effective with the client. Such matching strategies have been shown to improve counseling outcomes and to increase client satisfaction with the counseling process (Kivlighan, Hageseth, Tipton, & McGovern, 1981).

Most people's interests are represented by some combination of the themes rather than by one pure type, and they find that only some of the descriptors for each type or theme fit their interests. Brief definitions for each of the types are presented on the back of the Strong Inventory profile, and often it is a useful exercise during interpretation of the inventory to ask the client to underline the descriptors that seem to fit her or his interests best.

Holland's theory of vocational types goes beyond the model of matching people and jobs to also suggest that individuals will increase their satisfaction if they match their interests to learning environments, family environments, leisure activities, and living environments (Holland, 1985a). Scores on the GOT will provide clients with a global view of their interests; once they understand the meaning of the six themes, it is useful for them to consider where in their lives these interests fit. For some people, their work and leisure activities, as well as the types of people with whom they wish to associate, are quite similar across settings. For others, their interests are very diverse and they choose to satisfy their many areas of interests by selecting different types of activities for their various roles in life (e.g., family roles, work roles, relaxation roles).

As clients examine their profile scores, it is helpful for them to integrate what they already know about their preferences with their measured interests. They can do this by examining past activities in which they have chosen to engage, past jobs and accomplishments, who their friends have been, where they spend most of their time, and so on. This information, combined with their interest inventory scores, can help them to identify their unique pattern of interests.

Basic Interest Scales.   The Basic Interest Scales (BIS) serve as subdivisions for the more global General Occupational Themes. For example, the Music/Dramatics, Art, Applied Arts, Writing, and Culinary Arts Basic Interest Scales all are related statistically to the Artistic Theme and measure specific areas of interest within the global A-Theme.

The scale names for the BIS provide an idea of the item content and the appropriate interpretation for each scale. Thus, scores on the BIS lend themselves to straightforward interpretations about activities that the client likes or dislikes. These scales can be used in the same way as the GOT to help the client identify jobs, environments, activities, and types of people that appeal to them.

GOT and BIS Profile Information.   The Strong profile presents three types of interpretive information for the GOT and BIS: standard scores, interpretive comments, and interpretive bars. The standard scores are based on a raw-score to standard-score conversion, using the combined female and male General Reference Samples described earlier. The standard score mean for this sample is set equal to 50 with a standard deviation of 10. Therefore, the average score for people-in-general on each scale is 50. The interpretive comments are based on either the female General Reference Sample or the male General Reference sample, and the interpretive bars, shown in Fig. 7.2, represent the distribution of women's and men's scores on each scale.

As the interpretive bars in Fig. 7.2 illustrate, the distribution of scores on many scales does differ for women and men. Consequently, interpretation based on the client's own sex typically provides the most valid and reliable information and the most options for exploration of interests in areas considered nontraditional for one sex or the other. If women and men had the same distribution of scores on the scales, the interpretive comments and the interpretive bars would be unnecessary and the standard scores, based on the female and male General Reference Sample, would be sufficient.

The interpretive comments are assigned to scores based on percentile categories for the client's own sex:

Comment Printed	General Reference Sample Percentile
Very high	91st and above
High	76th to 90th
Average	26th to 75th
Little	11th to 25th
Very little	10th and below

The more similar the distributions of scores for the female and male General Reference Samples are on each of the scales, the more similar the interpretive categories are for each sex. For example, in Fig. 7.2 the distribution of scores for the female and male General Reference Samples on the Realistic Theme differs; the women have a mean score of 47 and the men a mean score of 53. Consequently, a score of 57 would fall in the "high interest range" of scores compared to the female General Reference Sample but in the "average interest range" compared to the male General Reference Sample. Conversely, women and men have similar distributions of scores on the Computer Activities BIS, which is located on the profile under the Conventional category, and a score of 37, for example, would be in the "little interest" range for females and males.

The interpretive bars provide a visual representation of the score distributions, which can be helpful in explaining the profile to the client. The upper bar, shown in Fig. 7.2, represents the distribution of scores for the female GRS and the lower bar represents the scores of the male GRS. The vertical line in the middle of each distribution represents the mean or average score for the female or male GRS. The middle 50% of each distribution (25th to 75th percentile) is represented by the thick portion of the bar, and the area between one end of the thin line and the other is the 10th to 90th percentile.

High and low scores on the GOT and BIS can be used to help clients judge how well their lifestyles match their interests. For example, incompatibility between interests and pursued activities can lead to dissatisfaction with work life if the mismatch is between occupational interests and the chosen job. Conceivably mismatches also can lead to dissatisfaction with personal relationships (Bruch & Skovholt, 1985; Johnson, 1987; Schneider, 1987; Wiggins & Weslander, 1983), living and working environments (Meir, Keinan, & Segal, 1986; Spokane, 1987), or with leisure time (Cairo, 1979), if the incongruence between interests and activities occurs in these domains.

The psychologist's or counselor's role in interpreting the GOT and BIS is to provide plausible hypotheses for high and low scores on the scales, as well as to assist in identifying patterns of interests as they emerge, and to clarify how these interests may relate to a person's educational, work, and personal life. The client must examine her or his own life history to identify what type of interest the scores represent and to determine how best and most fully to satisfy these interests in the future.

Occupational Scales. The most useful scales on the Strong Interest Inventory profile for predicting future occupational choice are the Occupational Scales. They measure the similarity of a person's interests to the interests of people employed in specific occupations. Validity research with the Occupational Scales also has shown that the Strong Inventory can be used to assist clients in their choice of college majors (Hansen & Swanson, 1983; Hansen & Tan, 1992).

The Occupational Scales are standardized so that the mean standard score for each occupation on its own scale is 50. Therefore, an individual who scores 50 on a particular scale has responded similarly to the way an average member of that occupation does and looks similar to the occupation in terms of interests. The profile reports scores for both female- and male-normed scales for 102 occupations. Seven additional Occupational Scales are on the profile that are normed on only female or male samples; they include five scales normed on female samples only—Child Care Provider, Dental Assistant, Dental Hygienist, Home Economics Teacher, and Secretary—and two scales normed on male samples only—Agribusiness Manager and Plumber. These seven occupations are dominated by one sex or the other, and therefore, it has been impossible to locate criterion samples sufficiently large to construct scales for both sexes.

As Figs. 7.3, 7.4, and 7.5 illustrate, regardless of the individual's sex, all Occupational Scales are scored on every profile. The standard scores are printed in the column next to the scale name, and an asterisk for the person's same-sex score is printed at a corresponding point along a pre-printed grid to provide a graphic representation of the similarity between the individual's interests and those of the occupation.

Interpretive categories range from similar interests (scores of 40 and higher) to mid-range (scores from 31 to 39) and dissimilar interests (scores of 30 and below). Scores in the similar category are the most predictive of future choices and should be used in interpretation with clients. The range of scores possible to obtain on the Occupational Scales extends from a low of −47 on female Art Teacher to a high of +90 on female Audiologist (Harmon et al., 1994). A negative score on an Occupational Scale indicates that the person's interests are very dissimilar to those of the occupation.

Although the General Occupational Themes and Basic Interest Scales help an individual to identify global areas of interests that may be satisfied through a variety of activities, the Occupational Scales tie the individual's interests more directly to the world of work. The main objective in interpreting the Occupational Scales is to assist the individual in identifying patterns of interests, and then, from those patterns, to identify occupations that fit the person's area of interests. Although a person usually is quite aware of her or his dislikes, pointing out the lowest scores also may be useful to an individual as she or he examines the profile.

The client and counselor may work together to identify common interests among the occupations represented by the client's highest scores. Eventually, the client will want to focus on a few specific occupations to explore in detail. Initially, however, the exploration may be designed to identify interests highlighted on the profile, as well as to generalize to occupations with related interests that are not represented on the profile by an Occupational Scale.

The codes representing Holland's six types that are assigned to each Occupational Scale are useful both for identifying the areas of interest of the particular occupation and for generalizing to related occupations. Clients should be encouraged to consider all relevant occupations even though they may not have considered them before because of unfamiliarity with the occupation or because of a perception that an occupation may be closed to them on the grounds of such factors as gender, social class, or ethnic background.

For example, the client whose Occupational Scale profile is presented in Fig. 7.3 scored in the similar range on the Biologist scale (located in the Investigative category on the profile). Related occupations for this Occupational Scale include anatomists, bacteriologists, biomedical researchers, ecologists, geneticists, oceanographers, and zoologists. These are occupations that incorporate her interests and are worthy of consideration as career possibilities.

In addition to helping clients identify related occupations, the Holland codes assigned to each Occupational Scale reflect the likes and the aversions of people in the occupation. For example, the Buyer scale (located in the Enterprising category on the profile in Fig. 7.5) is assigned the code EC, suggesting that items in the Enterprising and Conventional areas are weighted as "likes" and that Investigative and Artistic items, which according to Holland's theory of vocational types are least related to interests in the E-Theme and C-Theme areas, are weighted as "dislikes."

Just as the codes can be used to draw attention to the similarities among occupations to aid in generalizing to related occupations, the codes also can be used to help understand how occupations differ from one another. For example (see Fig. 7.3), although engineers (RI) and research and development managers (IR) both have realistic and investigative interests, the order of the codes assigned to their respective Occupational Scales suggest that realistic activities are the primary interests for engineers (RI), whereas investigative activities are the primary interests for research and development managers (IR).

Work Style Scale

The Work Style Scale of the Strong Interest Inventory is a measure that differentiates between people who like to work with data, ideas, or things and those who prefer to work with people. The higher an individual's score on the Work Style Scale, the more interests she or he has in activities that involve working with people. For example, samples of people in occupations such as child-care provision, high-school counseling, and life insurance sales score high on the Work Style Scale (Harmon et al., 1994). On the other hand, low scores represent an interest in working with data, ideas, or things. Samples of people in occupations such as mathematics, physics, or computer programming score low on the Work Style Scale.

The Work Style Scale also is related to Holland's six vocational personality types. High scores that represent an interest in working with people are related to Holland's Enterprising and Social types, and low scores that reflect an interest in data, ideas, and things are related to Holland's Realistic and Investigative types. The client's results shown in Fig. 7.6 reflect the interests of a person who prefers to work with ideas, data, and things rather than people.

Learning Environment Scale

The Learning Environment Scale is not a measure of ability. Rather, the scale was designed to measure the setting in which a person may prefer to learn. For example, a low score on the Learning Environment Scale—say, a score of 35—does not indicate that the person lacks the ability to perform college-level work. The score does indicate, however, that the person may prefer to learn in practical, hands-on learning environments. People with low scores on the Learning Environment Scale who do choose to go to college or even on to graduate school often see a degree as a necessary hurdle for entry into the occupation they are seeking or as a means to an end.

On the other hand, people such as the client in Fig. 7.6 who score 45 or higher on the Learning Environment Scale usually are oriented toward learning in a college or university environment. Those who score at this level, or in the 50s or 60s, should be encouraged to develop a plan for satisfying their academic interests in the future through participation in activities that require acquiring knowledge, developing theories, and understanding underlying principles. College and graduate education provide one mechanism for satisfying academic interests, but other possibilities include continuing or community education courses, entering occupations that require the continual acquisition of knowledge, periodically leaving a well-known job or position to enter a new one that presents a new challenge, or engaging in hobbies and leisure activities that require learning new knowledge and information.

Frequently, individuals who score low on the Learning Environment Scale are oriented toward learning and acquiring knowledge for the purpose of the practical application of the knowledge, rather than for the purpose of understanding the underlying principle. People who do score low on the scale should not be discouraged from entering an educational system, but they may wish to participate in internship experiences or to hold part-time jobs to complement their course work and to provide practical experience in their occupational area.

Risk Taking/Adventure Scale

The Risk Taking/Adventure Scale measures the willingness, or lack thereof, of a person to take risks. High scorers generally are people who need a bit of excitement in their lives because of their adventuresome nature. This willingness to take risks may be realized in several different ways. Some high scorers may engage in physically risky activities such as rock climbing and motorcycle racing. Others may enjoy the excitement of financial risks or of social risks. The woman whose profile is shown in Fig. 7.6 has adventuresome interests relative to other women.

People who score low on the Risk Taking/Adventure Scale generally are more cautious than are high scorers, and they prefer to play it safe in most situations especially new or unfamiliar activities. Generally, men score higher than do women on the Risk Taking/Adventure Scale (on average as much as 6 points higher). Also, young people tend to score higher on the scale than do adults (Hansen, 1992; Hansen & Campbell, 1985; Harmon et al., 1994).

Leadership Style Scale

The Leadership Style Scale is intended to differentiate between people who prefer to do a task themselves—in other words, to work alone—and those who enjoy being in charge of other people. To some extent, the scale reflects the preferences of introverts and extroverts (Harmon et al., 1994). The client in Fig. 7.6 has scored in the introverted direction, which suggests that she may prefer to work alone rather than to be in charge of others. (The case study presented at the end of this chapter illustrates that only part of this hypothesis holds true for this client.)

People who score high on the Leadership Style Scale (say, 55 or higher) are those who like to direct others. They frequently gravitate toward business, corporate, or social service environments that involve persuading others. People who score low (45 or lower), on the other hand, are more likely to avoid being in charge and may even seem to lack initiative to organize group activities, especially in settings that are dominated by extroverts.

Administrative Indexes

The profile for the Strong Interest Inventory reports several administrative indexes that are useful for ascertaining the validity of the profile. These indexes include the Total Responses Index, the Infrequent Responses Index, and the indexes that summarize the *like, indifferent,* and *dislike* response percentages for various sections of the item booklet (LP%, IP%, and DP%).

Total Responses Index. The Total Responses Index simply indicates the number of items on the inventory to which the individual has responded. Most people respond to all 325 items, but occasionally a few items will be missed. Although a large number of items can be deleted without appreciably affecting the profile scores, the computer scoring program is set to print an alert to the counselor on the Snapshot page (Fig. 7.1) of the profile if more than 17 items are missing.

Infrequent Responses Index. The Infrequent Responses Index was developed as a very general indicator of profile validity using those items on the Strong Interest Inventory that generally are answered in the same way by most people. If less than 6% of the female or male GRS said *like* to an item (in other words, most people "dislike" the item), then that item was included on the Infrequent Responses Index. A *like* response to these items would be unusual and would be weighted as an infrequent response on the Index.

Each person is allowed to make several infrequent responses before the computer flags the profile as an unusual one. The range of scores for women is +5 to −7, and for men the range is +7 to −8. Once a large number of infrequent responses has been given, the score becomes a negative number, and this negative number serves as a signal that the profile may be invalid (Harmon et al., 1994).

When a negative Infrequent Responses Index does occur, the best way to determine whether the person has responded honestly to the items is to check with the individual. If the person has understood the instructions, feels positively about taking the Strong Interest Inventory and the career counseling process in general, and indicates honesty in responding to the items, then the interpretation should proceed. In these instances, the person probably does have a valid profile in spite of an unusual pattern of interests, and the profile may be interpreted in the same manner as any other would be.

LP, IP, and DP Indexes. The response percentage indexes are included to provide a mechanism for determining quickly how the person has responded to various sections of the item booklet. For example, the profile illustrated in Fig. 7.6 shows that the client indicated *like* to 17% of the items in the occupations section of the item pool and *dislike* to 59% of those items.

People-in-general have an average response rate across these three indexes of about 32% with a standard deviation of about 12%. Most people respond *like* to somewhere between 14% and 50% of the item pool. The client in Fig. 7.6 has responded *like* to 28% of the items, *indifferent* to 22% of the items, and *dislike* to 50% of the items. If a person has an extremely high (say 65% or higher) or an extremely low (10% or lower) response rate, the result is likely to be an elevated or depressed profile, respectively. Although the profile is an accurate reflection of the individual's interests, the interpretation may need to be modified to accommodate the extreme response rate. Interpretation of elevated, flat, and depressed profiles is discussed in the next section.

People with high *indifferent* response rates may be indecisive or genuinely confused about their interests and the choices available to them. They may need to accumulate additional experience and to learn more about the world of work before proceeding with the decision-making process.

Flat and Depressed Profiles

Occasionally an individual's profile configuration will appear *flat*—the scores will be primarily in the average interpretive ranges—or *depressed*, with scores below average on the General Occupational Themes and Basic Interest Scales and below the mid-range on the Occupational Scales. A flat or depressed profile usually is the result of a low *like* response rate, say, less than 10%.

Flat or depressed profiles may be diagnostic of several different career decision-making situations. For example, people with narrow or well-defined interests may score high on only the one or two scales that correspond to their interests, and as a result, their profiles will appear to be flat or depressed. For others, the flat or depressed profile is symptomatic of limited knowledge about the world of work, indecisiveness or unreadiness to make a career commitment, or simply apathy toward the concept of working (Hansen, 1984). A recent longitudinal study indicated that students with undifferentiated profiles as college freshmen may have more difficulty in selecting college majors and may feel more career uncertainty while in college than do college students with differentiated Strong profiles. However, 12 years after entering college their levels of career accomplishment, certainty of career choice, and job satisfaction were similar to those of the students with differentiated profiles (Sackett & Hansen, 1995).

One method for interpreting flat or depressed profiles is to treat the results as ipsative data. Rather than comparing the individual's responses to the normative samples (e.g., "Your interests look average compared to the male General Reference Sample"), the individual's scores are rank-ordered from high to low and the exploration concentrates on the highest of the person's scores even if none of the scores are higher than average (e.g., "Instead of comparing your interests to those of other people, let's identify the areas of greatest interest to you").

The most useful scores will be the GOT and BIS scores closest to the mean for that person's own-sex standardization sample, and the highest of the mid-range Occupational Scale scores—those that are between about 31 and 39. The key to remember during the interpretation of flat or depressed profiles is to continuously assess how much "sense" the emerging pattern of interests makes. If the profile appears integrated and if the same pattern of interests emerges across the GOT, BIS, and Occupational Scales, then proceeding with the profile interpretation is legitimate. If the results appear random and the interests from one section of the profile to another are unrelated, then caution is advised.

Elevated Profiles

A profile with many scores above average usually is the result of a high *like* response rate. The GOT and BIS are affected more by an elevated response rate than are the Occupational Scales because only the *like* responses determine high scores on those scales, whereas both *like* and *dislike* responses contribute to high scores on the Occupational Scales. Usually an elevated profile reflects diversity in a person's interests or a wide range of interests.

Elevated profiles are less difficult to interpret than are flat or depressed profiles. The general procedure is to focus on the highest of the high scores, for example, the 3 highest GOT, the 8 to 10 highest BIS, and the highest of the "similar" Occupational Scales. People with elevated profiles may find it difficult to make career decisions because of their many interests, and they may be reluctant to choose one area over another. They can be encouraged, however, to explore several alternatives such as (a) pursuing a job that provides contact with a diversity of people or a position that incorporates a variety of tasks and responsibilities, (b) engaging in a range of leisure activities and hobbies that may be quite different from their vocational activities, or (c) planning a career path that will allow changes in jobs periodically (Hansen, 1992).

Opposite-Sex Occupational Scale Interpretation

The same-sex normed Occupational Scales on the Strong Interest Inventory are the most valid for all clients. However, the opposite-sex scores can be used as part of the analysis of patterns of interests that emerge on the profile. In the analysis of these patterns, the absolute values of scores become less important and the combination of scores becomes the primary focus. If, for example, an individual scores high on a same-sex Occupational Scale but scores even higher on the opposite-sex scale for the same occupation, the consistency in level of scores on the two scales is more important than the difference between the scores. (See scores on the female and male Geologist scales, located in the Investigative category on the profile, which illustrate this point in Fig. 7.3.)

If a person scores low on a corresponding-sex scale but high on an opposite-sex scale, the high scores can be used as valid indicators if they contribute to the pattern of interests that is emerging from the GOT, BIS, and other same-sex Occupational Scales. A consistent pattern of interests across the three sets of scales provides support for consideration of an occupation even if the individual has not scored high on the own-sex Occupational Scale. The client in Figs. 7.1–7.6, for example, has a pattern of science interests appearing on the GOT (above average score on the I-Theme), and Occupational Scales (high scores on the female Biologist, Chemist, Dentist, Medical Technologist, Optometrist, Pharmacist and Physicist scales). These scores all support the *similar* score she received on the male Physician scale, and medicine would be a legitimate occupation for her to consider even though she scored in the mid-range on the female Physician scale.

EVIDENCE OF VALIDITY FOR THE STRONG

The most important evidence of validity for the Strong Interest Inventory is predictive validity, because the instrument is used to help make decisions that ultimately will affect an individual's future.

Evidence of Validity for the Occupational Scales

Evidence for the predictive validity of the Occupational Scales has been studied using various criteria (e.g., declared major, job entered, stated occupational goal) for prediction. The classic predictive validity design is to collect a sample of subjects who have completed the Strong Interest Inventory, and store the data for a number of years. After time has passed, the study is reactivated; the original subjects are located, and the criterion questions are asked (usually something like "what is your declared major?" if studying the validity of the Strong for predicting college major, or "what is your occupation?" if the criterion is job entered).

After the follow-up data are collected, the college major or job title is matched to an Occupational Scale as directly as possible. Indirect matches also are made to the Occupational Scales that appear to most closely represent the major or occupation. For example, a major in elementary education would be considered a direct match to the Elementary School Teacher scale; a major in criminology is indirectly matched to the Sociologist scale. The hit rate of prediction for the sample is computed by determining the percentage of the subjects who scored high on the Occupational Scale that represents their college major or career choice.

Predictive validity studies for the merged-sex Strong compare favorably with data collected in the 1930s (Strong, 1935), in the 1950s (McArthur, 1954), and in the 1960s (Brandt & Hood, 1968). For example, over an 18-year interval between initial testing and criterion data collection, Strong found that 66% of a sample of males had scores of 40 or higher on Occupational Scales that were direct matches to their jobs. Spokane (1979) found that 71% of a sample of women and 59% of a sample of men had scores of 40 or higher on Occupational Scales, on the first merged-sex version of the Strong (Campbell, 1974), that were direct matches to their planned occupation. Two revisions later, Hansen (1986) found that 79% of the women and 68% of the men had scores of 40 or higher on Occupational Scales that represented the occupations they were in 12 years after testing with the Strong as freshmen in college. To date, no evidence of predictive validity has been collected for the 1994 Strong. However, the similarity in scale construction techniques between earlier versions of the Strong and the 1994 form should result in similar hit rates for the two versions.

Evidence of Validity for the GOT and BIS

Consistent with the interpretive guidelines that stress the importance of using the Strong Interest Inventory to identify patterns of interests rather than to focus only on the two or three highest scores on the profile, a study by Johnson and Johansson (1972) has shown that the level of consistency between scores on the Occupational Scales and Basic Interest Scales is important. They analyzed data for students who, 10 years earlier, had scored high on either the Physicist or Life Insurance Agent scale. Seventy-five percent of these subjects were in occupations related to the scores on their earlier profiles. They also found that the Basic Interest Scales were useful in determining if the subjects would enter occupations represented by their highest scores or if they would enter related occupations. For example, a subject with consistently high scores on both the Sales BIS and Life Insurance Agent Occupational Scale would be more likely to enter that occupation than would be a subject who scored low on Sales and high on Life Insurance Agent. The latter subject was more likely to enter a related occupation such as advertising.

Similarly, consistency between the GOT and Occupational Scale scores suggests greater predictive validity of the profile. A study conducted by Varca and Shaffer (1982) showed that the GOT also are useful for predicting the avocational and leisure activities in which an individual will participate.

SPECIAL SETTINGS AND SPECIAL POPULATIONS

To use the Strong Interest Inventory with various populations and in various settings, the administration and interpretation of the instrument do not need to be altered extensively from the usual procedure. Components of the career counseling sequence, however, may need to be adapted to special circumstances. For example, an outplacement program for high-level executives will be designed differently from a career exploration course for ninth- or tenth-grade high-school students. In each situation, however, an interest inventory may be given to assist the individuals in structuring their career exploration activities, in efficiently and objectively identifying their interests, and in planning activities that match their interests.

Adult Clients

Adult career development intervention has become a major task of human resource professionals in industry and business. One thing to keep in mind for adults who are considering career changes, however, is the distinction between *career* dissatisfaction and *job* dissatisfaction. In some instances, an individual's interests may be matched appropriately with her or his chosen career but the specifics of the particular job held at that time (e.g., coworkers, salary, level of responsibility, degree of autonomy) may be leading to dissatisfaction (Hansen, 1992). People who are dissatisfied with their particular job often find that the Strong Interest Inventory simply confirms their current occupational choice and offers suggestions for job-situation changes that will produce a better match and greater satisfaction. People who are unhappy with their careers—as opposed to jobs—may find that the Strong profile offers suggestions for new career possibilities.

Cross-Cultural Use

In a series of studies conducted during the last few years, the Strong Interest Inventory has been shown to be a useful career guidance tool for minority racial groups and international populations. Validation studies using the 1985 Strong Interest Inventory with Native Americans (Hansen & Haverkamp, 1988; Haviland & Hansen, 1987), African Americans, Asian Americans and Chicana(o)/Latina(o) college students (Hansen & Haverkamp, 1988) and with Mexicans (Fouad & Hansen, 1987) have shown the instrument to have validity hit rates similar to those found for White college student samples.

On the average, about 65% of the subjects scored 40 (moderately high) or higher on the scale representing their chosen college major. Studies conducted with predominantly White college student populations have shown concurrent validity hit rates for college major of about 68% at the moderately high or higher level (Hansen & Swanson, 1983). Among the racial minority groups, the Chicana(o)/Latina(o) sample had the highest hit rate (73%) and the Native American samples had the lowest hit rate: an average of 56% for females and males in the Haviland and Hansen (1987) and Hansen and Haverkamp (1988) studies. These data, even for the Native American samples, are sufficiently strong to support the use of the Strong Interest Inventory with racial minority college students.

The *Applications and Technical Guide* (Harmon et al., 1994) for the current version of the Strong includes a chapter on the cross-cultural use of the Strong (Fouad, Harmon, & Hansen, 1994). Item response data for ethnic and racial minorities collected during the 1994 revision were analyzed in a variety of ways including mean item responses, GOT and BIS mean scores, and Occupational Scale mean scores. These data were compared to that for Whites who also had participated in the 1994 revision. The authors concluded that, on average, the differences among the various groups (e.g., Whites, Asian Americans, African Americans, Latina(o)s/Chicana(o)s, and Native Americans) were few and that "racial and ethnic minority members of an occupation are very similar to other members of their occupational group" (p. 275).

Vocational-Technical Career Exploration

The addition of nonprofessional Occupational Scales to the profile of the Strong Interest Inventory, beginning with the 1985 Strong, has helped to ensure its usefulness with non-college-bound populations regardless of race or ethnic origin. On the current version of the instrument, about 28% of the scales represent the interests of vocational-technical and nonprofessional occupations, such as carpenters, electricians, florists, food service managers, respiratory therapists, and emergency medical technicians. The addition of the nonprofessional Occupational Scales to the profile, combined with the professional Occupational Scales, makes the Strong Interest Inventory appropriate for a wide range of occupational and educational goals.

Rehabilitation Clients

The Strong has a history of use with clients in rehabilitation or educational settings that serve clients with special physical challenges such as hearing impairment (S. Pressman, personal communication, 1987), spinal-cord injury (Rohe & Athelstan, 1982), or epilepsy (Fraser, Trejo, Temkin & Clemmons,

1982). The work of Rohe and Athelstan (1982), for example, has shown that the mean profile of interests for spinal-cord-injured clients can provide useful considerations for treatment. Spinal-cord-injured clients have a tendency toward introversion that, in a medical setting, frequently is misdiagnosed as depression. They prefer practical activities and probably will respond more positively to rehabilitation programs that focus on concrete goal setting rather than on abstract planning and sharing of feelings.

Other studies have looked at sex differences and vocational interest dimensions for adults with disabilities (Brookings & Bolton, 1986). Holvey, Partridge, and Wagner (1986) showed, for example, that the differences in interests found for women and men in the population-in-general hold true for women and men from rehabilitation populations: Women scored higher on measures of artistic and social interests, and men scored higher on measures of mechanical interests.

Use With the Culturally Disadvantaged

Although many of the concurrent and predictive validity studies with the Strong Interest Inventory have used subjects who are college students or college graduates, several studies have shown that the Strong also is appropriate for use with culturally disadvantaged individuals who may not have had extensive educational opportunities. These studies have shown, for example, that the culturally disadvantaged have identifiable interests, show diversity in their interests, and make vocational decisions that are predicted by the Strong (Anderson & Lawlis, 1972; Harmon, 1970).

CASE STUDY FOR A CLIENT

Figures 7.1–7.6 are the report profile for a client, a 20-year-old Caucasian female who is in her junior year of college at a large research university. She anticipates being elected to Phi Beta Kappa at the end of her junior year and is on track to graduate summa cum laude with a major in biochemistry. She has volunteered to work with faculty on several research projects and is listed as coauthor on two publications. In addition to her academic work, she is active in several campus organizations; she generally serves in a leadership capacity in these organizations. For example, she is president-elect of her sorority, president of the student governing board for the sciences college, and serves as a student representative to the university's board of regents. Her leisure interests include camping, canoeing, sailing, water skiing and downhill skiing, racquetball, golf, travel, theater, music, reading, photography, and dancing. She intends to pursue a PhD after completing her undergraduate education.

The Strong GOT and BIS profile for this woman (see Fig. 7.2) has a relatively large number of average or lower scores—28 of the 31 scales in these two sections are in the average or lower range. Her three scores above average occur in areas related to her academic and leisure interests. She scores high on the Investigative Theme, reflecting her interest in science and research, and high on the Athletics Scale, reflecting her sports leisure activities. The connection of the high score on Mechanical Activities to her activities is less obvious, although laboratory work in biochemistry certainly requires the use of equipment and machinery.

She appears to have some interest or tolerance for all of the basic interest areas representing realistic, investigative, and artistic activities (note the average scores on these scales). She also has a tolerance for activities typical of the conventional type with the exception of Office Services.

In contrast to her organizational activities and her leadership roles in them, her scores on the Social Theme and social BIS and the Enterprising Theme and enterprising BIS all fall in the little interest or very little interest category with the exception of a low average score on Law/Politics. Her Leadership Style score of 36 (see Fig. 7.6) also does not accurately reflect her involvement in organizational leadership. The Work Style score of 27 seems in line with her research and laboratory science interests. However, her Learning Environment score of 50 is lower than one might predict for someone who has done well scholastically in an Investigative field and intends to pursue an advanced degree. For this particular individual the addition of a work values measure, such as the Minnesota Importance Questionnaire (Rounds, Henley, Dawis, Lofquist, & Weiss, 1981), to the use of the Strong might help to generate hypotheses to explain the contradictions between her measured interests and her chosen activities and her educational goals.

Her highest scores on the Occupational Scales—Chemist and Biologist—certainly seem to confirm her choice of college major (see Fig. 7.3). Her other high Occupational Scale scores tend to cluster in the realistic and investigative areas; those in the realistic area—Electrician, Engineer, Forester—reflect her mechanical activities interest as well as her investigative interest. Many of her other high Occupational Scale scores also reflect a combination of interests in mechanical activities and science (e.g., Dentist, Geologist, Medical Technologist, Optometrist, and Physicist). Her few high scores on the artistic Occupational Scales (see Fig. 7.4) occur for those occupations that combine an artistic interest with investigative and/or realistic interests (e.g., Architect, Photographer, and Technical Writer). Consistent with her low scores on the social and enterprising GOT and BIS and her average scores on the Conventional GOT and BIS, she has almost no Occupational Scale scores above the mid-range in these areas (see Figs. 7.4 and 7.5). The two exceptions are Investment Manager and Marketing Executive, which fall in the enterprising area. Individuals with investigative interests often score high on these two Occupational Scales probably reflecting an interest in analyzing and studying data.

This student's interests are quite consistent across the GOT, BIS, and Occupational Scales. The profile taken in total suggests someone with well-defined interests that match her current choice of college major. However, the inconsistencies between her leadership activities and her score on the Leadership Style Scale and between her academic expectations and her Learning Environment score illustrate the usefulness of incorporating measures of several constructs, in this instance interests and values, in career exploration counseling. In addition, the use of values and personality measures might provide additional information to guide interpretation of this client's relatively high score on the Risk Taking/Adventure Scale. These additional measures, combined with the interest profile of the Strong and her academic record, which suggests high ability, would provide a more complete picture and therefore better prediction for purposes of career decision making than can the use of an interest inventory by itself.

REFERENCES

Anderson, R. P., & Lawlis, F. G. (1972). Strong Vocational Interest Blank and culturally handicapped women. *Journal of Counseling Psychology, 19,* 83–84.

Brandt, J. E., & Hood, A. B. (1968). Effect of personality adjustment on the predictive validity of the Strong Vocational Interest Blank. *Journal of Counseling Psychology, 15,* 547–551.

Brookings, J. R., & Bolton, B. (1986). Vocational interest dimensions of adult handicapped persons. *Measurement and Evaluation in Counseling and Development, 18,* 168–175.

Bruch, M. A., & Skovholt, T. (1985). Congruence of Holland personality type and marital satisfaction. *Measurement and Evaluation in Counseling and Development, 18,* 100–107.

Cairo, P. C. (1979). The validity of the Holland and Basic Interest Scales of the Strong Vocational Interest Blank: Leisure activities versus occupational membership as criteria. *Journal of Vocational Behavior, 15,* 68–77.

Campbell, D. P. (1974). *Manual for the SVIB-SCII* (1st ed.). Stanford, CA: Stanford University Press.

Campbell, D. P., Borgen, F. H., Eastes, S., Johansson, C. B., & Peterson, R. A. (1968). A set of Basic Interest Scales for the Strong Vocational Interest Blank for Men. *Journal of Applied Psychology Monographs, 52*(6), Part 2.

Campbell, D. P., & Hansen, J. C. (1981). *Manual for the SVIB-SCII* (3rd ed.). Stanford, CA: Stanford University Press.

Campbell, D. P., & Holland, J. L. (1972). Applying Holland's theory to Strong's data. *Journal of Vocational Behavior, 2,* 353–376.

Campbell, D. P., Hyne, S. A., & Nilsen, D. L. (1992). *Manual for the Campbell Interest and Skill Survey.* Minneapolis, MN: National Computer Systems.

Cowdery, K. M. (1926). Measurement of professional attitudes: Differences between lawyers, physicians, and engineers. *Journal of Personnel Research, 5,* 131–141.

Fouad, N. A., & Hansen, J. C. (1987). Cross-cultural predictive accuracy of the Strong-Campbell Interest Inventory. *Measurement and Evaluation in Counseling and Development, 20,* 3–10.

Fouad, N. A., Harmon, L. W., & Hansen, J. C. (1994). Cross-cultural use of the Strong. In L. W. Harmon, J. C. Hansen, F. H. Borgen, & A. L. Hammer (Eds.), *Strong Interest Inventory applications and technical guide* (pp. 255–280). Palo Alto CA: Consulting Psychologists Press.

Fraser, R. T., Trejo, W. R., Temkin, N. R., & Clemmons, D. (1982, November). *Assessing the vocational interests of those with epilepsy.* Paper presented at the meetings of the American Epilepsy Society, Phoenix, AZ.

Freyd, M. (1923). *Occupational interests.* Chicago: C. H. Stoelting.

Goodyear, R. K., & Frank, A. C. (1977). Introversion-extroversion: Some comparisons of the SVIB and OPI Scales. *Measurement and Evaluation in Guidance, 9,* 206–211.

Gough, H. G. (1957). *Manual for the California Psychological Inventory.* Palo Alto, CA: Consulting Psychologists Press.

Hansen, J. C. (1976). Exploring new directions for Strong-Campbell Interest Inventory occupational scale construction. *Journal of Vocational Behavior, 9,* 147–160.

Hansen, J. C. (1984). *User's guide for the SVIB–SCII.* Stanford, CA: Stanford University Press.

Hansen, J. C. (1986, August). *12-Year longitudinal study of the predictive validity of the SVIB–SCII.* Paper presented at the meetings of the American Psychological Association, Washington, DC.

Hansen, J. C. (1992). *User's guide for the SII* (rev. ed.). Stanford, CA: Stanford University Press.

Hansen, J. C., & Campbell, D. P. (1985). *Manual for the SVIB–SCII* (4th ed.). Stanford, CA: Stanford University Press.

Hansen, J. C., & Haverkamp, B. E. (1988). *Concurrent validity of the SCII for American Indian, Asian, Black and Hispanic college students.* Minneapolis, MN: Center for Interest Measurement Research, University of Minnesota.

Hansen, J. C., & Johansson, C. B. (1972). The application of Holland's vocational model to the Strong Vocational Interest Blank. *Journal of Vocational Behavior, 2,* 479–493.

Hansen, J. C., Kozberg, J. G., & Goranson, D. (1994). Accuracy of student recall of Strong Interest Inventory results 1 year after interpretation. *Measurement and Evaluation in Counseling and Development, 26,* 235–242.

Hansen, J. C., & Swanson, J. L. (1983). Stability of interests and the predictive and concurrent validity of the 1981 SCII for college majors. *Journal of Counseling Psychology, 30,* 194–201.

Hansen, J. C., & Tan, R. N. (1992). Concurrent validity of the 1985 Strong Interest Inventory for college major selection. *Measurement and Evaluation in Counseling and Development, 25,* 53–57.

Harmon, L. W. (1970). Strong Vocational Interest Blank profiles for disadvantaged women. *Journal of Counseling Psychology, 17,* 519–520.

Harmon, L. W., Hansen, J. C., Borgen, F. H., & Hammer, A. L. (1994). *Strong Interest Inventory applications and technical guide.* Palo Alto, CA: Consulting Psychologists Press.

Haviland, M. L., & Hansen, J. C. (1987). Criterion validity of the Strong-Campbell Interest Inventory for American Indian college students. *Measurement and Evaluation in Counseling and Development, 19,* 196–201.

Holland, J. L. (1973). *Making vocational choices: A theory of careers.* Englewood Cliffs, NJ: Prentice Hall.

Holland, J. L. (1985a). *Making vocational choices: A theory of vocational personalities and work environments.* Englewood Cliffs, NJ: Prentice Hall.

Holland, J. L. (1985b). *Professional manual for the Self-Directed Search.* Odessa, FL: Psychological Assessment Resources.

Holvey, J. M., Partridge, E. D., & Wagner, E. E. (1986). Sex differences in vocational interests among rehabilitation clients. *Journal of Applied Rehabilitation Counseling, 17,* 51–53.

Johansson, C. B. (1986). *Career Assessment Inventory: Enhanced version.* Minneapolis, MN: National Computer Systems.

Johnson, J. A. (1987). Influence of adolescent social crowds in the development of vocational identity. *Journal of Vocational Behavior, 31,* 182–199.

Johnson, R. W., & Johansson, C. B. (1972). Moderating effect of basic interests on predictive validity of SVIB occupational scales. *Proceedings, 80th Annual Convention, American Psychological Association*, pp. 589–590.

Kivlighan, D. M., Jr., Hageseth, J. A., Tipton, R. M., & McGovern, T. V. (1981). Effects of matching treatment approaches and personality types in group vocational counseling. *Journal of Counseling Psychology, 28*, 315–320.

Kornhauser, A. W. (1927). Results from a quantitative questionnaire of likes and dislikes used with a group of college freshmen. *Journal of Applied Psychology, 11*, 85–94.

McArthur, C. (1954). Long-term validity of the Strong Vocational Interest Blank in two subcultures. *Journal of Applied Psychology, 38*, 346–354.

McKinley, J. C., & Hathaway, S. R. (1940). A Multiphasic Personality Schedule (Minnesota): I, Construction of the schedule. *Journal of Psychology, 10*, 249–254.

Meir, E. I., Keinan, G., & Segal, Z. (1986). Group importance as mediator between personality-environment congruence and satisfaction. *Journal of Vocational Behavior, 28*, 60–69.

Randahl, G. J., Hansen, J. C., & Haverkamp, B. E. (1993). Instrumental behaviors following test administration and interpretation: Exploration validity of the Strong Interest Inventory. *Journal of Counseling and Development, 71*, 435–439.

Remmers, H. H. (1929). The measurement of interest differences between students of engineering and agriculture. *Journal of Applied Psychology, 13*, 105–119.

Rohe, D. E., & Athelstan, G. T. (1982). Vocational interests of persons with spinal cord injury. *Journal of Counseling Psychology, 29*, 283–291.

Rounds, J. B., Jr., Henley, G. A., Dawis, R. V., Lofquist, L. H., & Weiss, D. J. (1981). *Manual for the Minnesota Importance Questionnaire: A measure of vocational needs and values*. Minneapolis, MN: Department of Psychology, University of Minnesota-Twin Cities.

Sackett, S. A., & Hansen, J. C. (1995). Vocational outcomes of college freshmen with flat profiles on the Strong Interest Inventory. *Measurement and Evaluation in Counseling and Development, 28*, 9–24.

Schneider, B. (1987). The people make the place. *Personnel Psychology, 40*, 437–453.

Spokane, A. R. (1979). Occupational preferences and the validity of the Strong-Campbell Interest Inventory for college women and men. *Journal of Counseling Psychology, 26*, 312–318.

Spokane, A. R. (Ed.). (1987). Conceptual and methodological issues in person-environment fit research. *Journal of Vocational Behavior, 31*, 217–361.

Strong, E. K., Jr. (1927). *Vocational Interest Blank*. Stanford, CA: Stanford University Press.

Strong, E. K., Jr. (1933). *Vocational Interest Blank for women*. Stanford, CA: Stanford University Press.

Strong E. K., Jr. (1935). Predictive value of the Vocational Interest Test. *Journal of Educational Psychology, 26*, 332.

Strong, E. K., Jr. (1938). *Vocational Interest Blank for men* (rev.). Stanford, CA: Stanford University Press.

Strong, E. K., Jr. (1946). *Vocational Interest Blank for women* (rev.). Palo Alto, CA: Stanford University Press.

Varca, P. E., & Shaffer, G. S. (1982). Holland's theory: Stability of avocational interests. *Journal of Vocational Behavior, 21*, 288–298.

Webber, P. L., & Harmon, L. W. (1978). The reliability and concurrent validity of three types of occupational scales for two occupational groups. In C. K. Tittle & D. G. Zytowski (Eds.), *Sex-fair interest measurement: Research and implications* (pp. 77–82). Washington, DC: National Institute of Education.

Wiggins, J. D., & Weslander, D. L. (1982). Tested compatibility in first and second marriages. *American Mental Health Counselors Association Journal, 4*, 25–29.

8

The Kuder Occupational Interest Survey

Esther E. Diamond
Educational and Psychological Consultant

Donald G. Zytowski
Counseling Psychologist

BACKGROUND

The history of the Kuder Occupational Interest Survey, Form DD (KOIS), dates back to the Depression days of the early 1930s, when, as a graduate student at The Ohio State University, Frederic Kuder undertook some very modest research on the relation between interests and vocations. His research and development work continued, still on his own time and with his own funds (e.g., he borrowed on his life insurance), after he joined the University of Chicago. In 1939, after 6 years of research, the first Preference Record–Vocational was distributed by the University of Chicago bookstore. Science Research Associates published it in 1941. Responses yielded scores on seven relatively independent scales: Literary, Scientific, Artistic, Persuasive, Social Service, Musical, and Computational.

Experience with this form suggested the need for more adequate representation of clerical and mechanical interests, and appropriate items for measurement of these interests were compiled and included in the experimental edition of the second Preference Record–Vocational, Form B. The problem of including additional items without increasing administration time as well as reading time was solved by using a triad form in which respondents indicated which of three activities in each item they preferred most and which they preferred least. Form B was published in 1943 by Science Research Associates and was subsequently used in the armed forces during World War II.

Form C, published in 1948, was developed in response to a need for a measure of outdoor interests as well as a Verification scale to identify subjects who responded to the Preference Record carelessly, insincerely, or without understanding. Form C was superseded in 1956 by the Kuder General Interest Survey, Form E, designed to accommodate younger people by lowering the reading level, adding items to increase the reliability, and adding no activities that might be unfamiliar to them. Still another Preference Record—Personal, Form A (also published in the 1940s but no longer in print), measured personal interests that were closely related to preferences for a variety of social and environmental variables in work.

The article "Three Generations: The Continuing Evolution of Frederic Kuder's Interest Inventories" (Zytowski, 1992) provides a succinct review of Kuder's work in interest measurement and its guiding philosophy over approximately 60 years. It briefly discusses the technological and social changes that modified his work and led to the third generation—the person-match approach, developed by one of his long-time associates, Dr. John Hornaday.

Development of the KOIS

The KOIS had its origin in the Kuder Preference Record—Occupational, Form D, in which occupational keys were developed by comparing responses of individuals in an occupational criterion group who had demonstrated satisfaction with their choice of occupation with those of individuals in a general norm or reference group roughly representative of the distribution of occupations in the world of work. This method of scale development was similar to that used for the empirically built scales of the Strong Vocational Interest Blank (SVIB) (Strong, 1943). Items were chosen from Forms C and A so as to be well distributed throughout the factorial space pertinent to occupational choice. Criteria for satisfaction were: ages 25 to 65; having been in the same occupation for at least 3 years; and, given a choice, would choose the same kind of work again.

But as Kuder (1966) pointed out, use of a men-in-general or women-in-general base for developing occupational scales implies that the choice is between a single occupation and the composite of all other occupations, thus losing a great deal of sharpness in differentiation. Responses for which there are large differences between the general reference group and the criterion group, he maintained, are not necessarily the same as those that are best for differentiating among the specific occupations in the general reference group. Using actual differences in proportions of two occupational groups marking each response to an occupational interest inventory would result in greater differentiation, an approach suggested by Findley (1956) and adopted by Kuder.

Clemans's Lambda

Differences in homogeneity of the preferences of occupational groups, however, created a problem with use of proportion sums as scores. The more homogeneous a group, the larger the proportion marking the same choice in the *most* and the *least* columns, and the larger the sum of squared proportions. For a group of the lowest possible homogeneity, on the other hand, with one-third marking each of the three *most* and each of the three *least* response positions, the sum of the squared proportions would be considerably lower. Scores, consequently, would not have the same possible range from occupation to occupation and therefore would not be comparable. If the best cutting point between score distributions for two different occupations—that is, the point at which the two distributions intersect—is other than zero, as it would be in scales of different degrees of homogeneity, then different cutting points have to be computed for the many comparisons that would need to be made.

A solution was to convert proportion scores to Clemans's lambda coefficients (Clemans, 1958). The proportion values for the 600 responses marked by a criterion group represent the continuous variable, and the 200 responses marked by the individual and the 400 not marked represent the dichotomous variable. The lambda coefficient—the ratio of the obtained r point biserial to the maximum r point biserial—represents the correlation between the individual's responses and the modal responses of the given criterion group. The upper limit of the lambda is 1.00 for all groups, regardless of homogeneity.

Differentiation between occupational groups—an essential characteristic of an occupational interest inventory and the hallmark of its construct validity—improved dramatically over the earlier system in comparison studies. The incidence of members of an occupational group obtaining a higher score on a scale other than their own was 32% less when lambda scores were used, and there was a 36% reduction in errors of classification (Kuder & Diamond, 1979).

The KOIS, which Watkins, Campbell, and Nieberding (1994) found to be the third most frequently used vocational assessment by counseling psychologists, currently contains 109 occupational scales representing 76 different occupations. Thirty-three are derived from separate male and female criterion groups, 32 from male groups, and 11 from female groups. In addition, the report includes 40 college-major scales, 14 of which are derived from separate male and female criterion groups, 8 from males only, and 4 from females only.

Eight experimental scores are provided for research purposes, and a Verification (V) score gives an estimate of the sincerity and care with which the responses were marked. Vocational Interest Estimates (VIEs) are also provided for the 10 vocational areas corresponding to those in the Kuder General Interest Survey, Form E: Outdoor, Mechanical, Scientific, Computational, Persuasive, Artistic, Literary, Musical, Social Service, and Clerical.

Scores on all scales, regardless of survey taker's gender, are reported. All scales are arranged in descending rank order of scores, regardless of norm group gender, and are reported to survey takers. Ranks of the scales on the survey taker's opposite gender groups provide important information about possibilities that should be taken into consideration in educational and career planning.

Two versions of the report form are returned to the survey administrator. The first shows Vocation Interest Estimates (VIEs) corresponding to the 10 vocational interest areas in the Kuder General Interest Survey, Form E: Outdoor, Mechanical, Scientific, Computational, Persuasive, Artistic, Literary, Musical, Social Service, and Clerical. The VIE scores are easily converted to Holland's RIASEC personality types: Realistic, Investigative, Artistic, Social, Enterprising, and Conventional (Holland, 1997). Occupational and college major scores are arranged in rank order without numerical scores, and with an explanation designed for the survey taker. The second version contains the same information, but also includes the numerical scores and scores on the experimental scales, as well as an explanation for the survey administrator.

The size and complexity of the scoring protocol necessitated the eventual computerization of the OIS, which is currently available only in a machine-scored version, described later in this chapter.

CONCEPTUAL FOUNDATIONS

Guiding Principles of Interest Measurement

The major premise in the development of the KOIS was that the purpose of an occupational interest inventory is to help young people discover the occupations they will find most satisfying. Kuder stipulated two fundamental requirements that must be met by such an inventory: (a) It must be valid with respect to the criterion of job satisfaction, and (b) it must be suitable for use with young people who may have quite limited backgrounds of training and experience (Kuder, 1977). He cited 12 principles of interest measurement that have guided all of his work in the field:

1. The ability to differentiate well between occupational groups is one of the essential characteristics of an occupational interest inventory.
2. The questions in an occupational interest inventory should be well distributed throughout the domain of interests relevant to vocational choice.

3. The activities described in the questions must be clear and easily understood by the subjects, both by those who answer the inventory for their own guidance and by those who, as members of criterion groups, answer the inventory for the purpose of establishing occupational scoring systems.

4. The use of an interest inventory in occupational counseling rests on the assumption that the domain of interests in generally well understood activities is essentially the same as the domain of interests in activities that are not generally well understood.

5. A form of item should be used that is known to be affected relatively little by changes in context.

6. The form of question should be as free as possible from the effects of response bias.

7. Occupational titles should not be used in the items in an interest inventory intended for use in occupational counseling.

8. The questions should not be unpleasant or threatening.

9. A means should be available for checking on the confidence that can be placed in the answers to the inventory.

10. The same inventory should be use for both sexes.

11. The set of scores from an occupational interest inventory must have high reliability and stability, and these characteristics should be measured in terms of reliability and stability within the person.

12. The most useful form in which to report scores from an interest inventory is in order of magnitude.

Applications of these principles to the KOIS is seen in the studies of differentiation and errors of classification referenced earlier; in the scales available, which represent professional, skilled, white-collar, and service occupations, among others; in the simple descriptions of common activities; in the item format, which minimizes response bias (Cronbach, 1950); in the absence of occupational titles, which might introduce stereotypes into the thinking of respondents; in the existence of the Verification scale; and in the reliability and stability of individual profiles, and differences between pairs of scores (Kuder & Diamond, 1979).

Why Measure Interests?

Holland, Magoon, and Spokane (1981) described interest measurement as possibly the most popular form of vocational assistance. Tyler (1978) saw interest patterns, like value patterns, as structures for processing possibilities: "What may govern one person's choices, occupational or otherwise, is a value structure in which comfort and security rank very high" (p. 147).

These structures enable the individual to select and develop a unique assortment of possibilities from among those available. Anastasi (1988), discussing recent changes in the goals of interest measurement, pointed to the increasing attention accorded to career decision making and, as part of that process, self-exploration. Another change she described was the increasing emphasis on expanding the career options open to the individual.

But why measure interests? Why not simply ask a person what his or her interests are and what kind of work he or she would most like to do? These are frequently asked questions. The answer is that people's occupational and educational choices are too often based on irrelevant influences and information rather than on critical information about themselves and about the fields they are considering. A famous poet, for example, had in his youth thought he would like to be a naturalist. A course in botany, however, caused him to change his mind; he simply had had a very unrealistic idea of what day-to-day activities the career involved and the kind of educational preparation that it required. As Nunnally (1959) noted, young people are often quite unaware of the specific activities performed in different occupations. Nor do expressed, as opposed to measured, interests provide adequate information; Cronbach (1970) pointed out that a single direct question such as "Would you like to be a teacher?" may prompt a response based on lack of information or on a superficial understanding of the vocation. Darley and Hagenah (1955), who worked with E. K. Strong, found that "claimed interests emerge from different causal factors—factors more associated with prestige, family pressures, aspirational levels, transient considerations, and misconceptions of the world of work—than do measured interests" (p. 75).

Using the KOIS in Counseling

The KOIS, which uses work-related activities rather than occupational titles in its items, minimizes chances for stereotyping. Its forced-choice format, which in effect asks the respondent to rank the three activities in each item, greatly reduces response bias or the tendency of respondents to avoid commitment to the extremes of a Likert scale and to choose a safe middle response instead. Jackson (1977) found response bias to account for as much as one-third of the total variance in responding.

The KOIS offers basis for comprehensive educational and vocational planning and decision making. It is appropriate for use with individuals in 10th grade and beyond, college students, and adults. It can be administered to individuals or in group settings, but as Zytowski (1981) suggested, it is best administered when the individual is asking for assistance rather than when there is a scheduled wholesale administration. It is also best used "to enhance self-understanding, to reduce too many choices to a manageable few, or to suggest new possibilities to consider" (p. 1). The inventory can be self-administered, but availability of a counselor is helpful in interpreting the profile of scores, helping the inventory taker discern options he or she might otherwise overlook, and in answering related questions or discussing next steps.

As is true of any assessment instrument, the KOIS should be used with pertinent information about an individual's achievements, past work experience if any, scores on measures of ability and other traits, personal goals and values, and other relevant factors. Moreover, as Tittle (1978) found in her review of the research, studies on the effects of interest inventories suggest that by themselves, without supplementary material, they are not as effective in stimulating exploration as they might be.

Hoffman, Spokane, and Magoon (1981) questioned various studies of the effects of interest inventories and other interventions because of their failure to use multiple short-term outcome measures that had demonstrated validity. In addition, the outcome measures used relied principally on simple recall or on satisfaction with treatment; the treatments lacked equivalence of content or of counselor contact. Hoffman et al. used multiple and multimodal measures to study the impact of three—interest profiles only, audiotape in addition to profiles, and counselor contact in addition to profiles. Significantly more subjects in the counselor contact plus profiles group sought occupational information than subjects in the other two groups, and counselor contact was also found to be significantly related to goal attainment.

Whether administered on an individual or a group basis, interest inventories can be most useful as part of a series of counseling interventions rather than isolated events. Only then can they do more than merely confirm existing self-concepts or thinking about occupations. Interest inventory results can suggest exploratory experiences into hitherto unexplored areas. They also can prompt a client to examine his or her value system and its relationship to occupational goals more intensively.

Paving the Way for Interventions

The KOIS facilitates such exploratory experiences and, through its basic and supplementary materials, paves the way for various interventions following administration of the inventory and discussion of the results. For example:

- Items represent all 15 areas of Forms A and C. Areas from A are preference for being active in groups, for familiar and stable situations, for working with ideas, and for avoiding conflict. From C they are outdoor, mechanical, computational, scientific, persuasive, artistic, literary, musical, social service, and clerical. In addition, two new areas are represented: preference for working independently, and preference for acting spontaneously, in a carefree manner.

- The two-part report of scores, the counselor's copy and the inventory taker's copy, provide interpretive information for each, enabling the inventory taker to understand much of the report and freeing the counselor to pick up the interpretation at the point where questions arise and assistance is needed.

- In addition to the occupational and college major scores, the Verification, or V, score and the scores on the eight experimental scales are reported (on the counselor's copy only). The experimental scores provide a very tentative index of the inventory taker's maturity and of the sincerity of his or her responses.

- The Vocational Interest Estimates, or VIEs, described earlier, provide information for those counselees who are still uncertain about the general area or areas within which their interests lie. Holland codes—Realistic, Investigative, Artistic, Social, Enterprising, and Conventional—may also be estimated from the percentile ranks of the VIE scales. Descriptions of the occupational and college major criterion groups also give the top-ranking VIEs for each.

- Occupational and college major scores provide counselees with information about how closely their KOIS responses resemble those of men and of women in the various criterion groups. The occupational scales cover a broad spectrum of professional and nonprofessional occupations.

- The *General Manual*, 3rd ed. (Kuder & Zytowski, 1991), combined the 1979 *General Manual* and the 1985 *Manual Supplement* with additional material on interpretation and extension of results.

- An earlier *General Manual* (2nd ed., Kuder & Diamond, 1979) presented the history of the development of the KOIS and results of the research studies conducted over the years—including studies of accuracy of classification, reliability and homogeneity, and the factor structure. It also contained descriptions of each of the occupational and college major criterion groups.

- A *Manual Supplement* (Zytowski, 1985) provided updated information pertaining to the 1985 revision of the report form. (The report form was revised on the basis of the recommendations of a panel of experienced counselors representing the major settings in which the KOIS is used.)

- The Kuder DD/PC provided for administration and scoring of the OIS on the personal computer with MS-DOS, a hard disk, and a minimum of 640 K memory. Administration takes 22–30 min, yielding rapid results and enabling interactive online examination of career and college-major data.

- The Kuder *DD/PC User's Guide* (Kuder & Zytowski, 1993) covered installation and use of the computer-based KOIS, with special attention to certain features made possible by computer administration. These "Computer-Kuder" features include a "purpose-setting" question that asks survey takers for which of several reasons they are taking the survey; V-score tracking, which warns the survey taker that her or his responses may be inconsistent and suggests the possibility of going back over previous answers; and when the survey taker's highest occupational scale score is below a critical level, a "bridge" is suggested that gives occupations for consideration derived from the highest VIE scores.

ADMINISTRATION AND SCORING

Introducing the Inventory

The manner of introducing the KOIS will differ with different settings and with different client needs. In college freshman orientation programs, for example, students will be interested in using the inventory for selection (or confirmation) of a choice of course of study. Some may be looking ahead to possible future occupations. In individual personal or college counseling or in industry, the introduction should be tailored to the individual's needs and level of sophistication. As part of a general testing program in a high school, the KOIS lends itself to several modes of presentation—for example, in the homeroom; in an appropriate club, such as a science, mathematics, or journalism club, or Future Farmers of America; or in an English or social studies classroom.

Many inventory takers most likely have already been exposed to some discussion of the nature of interests and how they differ from abilities; how they are related to different fields of study and different hobbies and activities; and how they relate to one's self-concept, values, and past experiences. Nevertheless, a brief recapitulation of such discussion before administering and interpreting the KOIS can often be very helpful in understanding and using the results. It is important, too, to discuss how men and women have been socialized differently in our society and how their interest scores might be affected as a result.

A Word About Ipsativity

The question of ipsativity invariably is raised with regard to forced-choice items. As Anastasi (1988, p. 545) observed, ipsative scoring applies when the individual expresses preference for one activity over another rather than in absolute terms, and the frame of reference for the scores is the individual rather than a normative sample. But as Kuder (1975) pointed out, in the case of the Kuder inventories the intensity of the individual's activity preferences are compared with those of a norm group. That is, the comparison is with the responses of others faced with the same stimulus situation. Illustrating his point, Kuder (1975) stated that "it is not enough to know that an individual strongly likes both 'attending baseball game' and 'attending an opera.' What is important is which he or she prefers to the other when faced with a choice" (p. 6). Furthermore, decisions in our society are rarely limited to such simple choices but are "complicated by the interaction of various motivations determined by all of our previous experiences" (p. 6).

The 100 forced-choice triads, written at sixth-grade level, are contained in a combination survey booklet and optically scanned answer sheet. Because the scoring system requires an enormous amount of computer storage capacity for the table of lambda values for each of 600 possible response patterns for each scale, as shown in Appendix A, the KOIS cannot be scored by hand; they must be scored by computer (results are mailed from the publisher within 48 hr of receipt of answer sheets) or by the DD/PC program described earlier.

The Score Report Form

Two copies of the revised 1985 individualized report form—one for the counselor and one for the inventory taker—contain interpretive information on the back. One important change from the previous form is that the numerical lambda values are reported only on the counselor's copy, although the inventory taker should have access to them if desired.

Four different types of scales, accompanied by explanatory comments, are identified on the report form in separate sections. The first section contains a statement of the dependability or the degree of confidence that can be placed in the results, based on the Verification (V) score, the number of missing or invalidly marked triads, the lambda level, and other indices of usability. The second section contains the percentile scores for the VIEs in the same 10 general interest areas as those offered by the Kuder General Interest Survey, Form E, and based on a general population of men and women KOIS users. VIEs are ranked and grouped into high, average, and low interest areas compared with the responses of criterion groups of men and of women.

In the third and fourth sections, respectively, the 140 occupational and college major scores are reported separately in rank order. They are compared with men and with women in each of the criterion groups, in accordance with Title IX guidelines for nondiscrimination on the basis of sex (U.S. Department of Health, Education, and Welfare, 1975). Scores are grouped as indicating interest patterns "most similar to" those of the criterion group—that is, within .06 lambda points of the inventory taker's highest score, and therefore not significantly different; "next most similar," or between .07 and .12 lambda points of the highest core; and the rest, listed in order of similarity. (Some KOIS scales have been normed only on one sex, but efforts are underway to develop criterion groups for the other sex as subjects become available. There are now 94 "twin" scales—47 pairs of scales—representing 33 occupations and 14 college majors normed on both female and male criterion groups.)

Users of the KOIS sometimes ask why the scales are not grouped by level, industry, job family, broad interest area, or some other classification scheme. Such a system had been considered, but the conclusion was that classification of occupations is seldom clear-cut and usually influences interpretation, implying similarity of occupations in the same classification that may in fact be quite dissimilar in underlying interests and other characteristics. Ranked scores carry no such implications and were deemed best for interpretation (Kuder & Diamond, 1979).

The V score and the scores on the eight experimental scales are shown only on the counselor's copy. The eight experimental scales are just that—experimental; the suggested interpretations should be highly tentative until additional research has been carried out. The M (men) and W (women) scores are lambdas derived from comparisons with general norm groups of men and women. The MBI (men best impression) and WBI (women best impression) scores are derived from comparison with responses of the same individuals asked to respond to the KOIS a second time with instructions to make the best impression possible. Differences between the M and MBI scores and the W and WBI scores for the relevant sex provide an additional rough indication of the degree of confidence that may be placed in the individual's scores.

Zytowski and England (1995) obtained partial validation of these hypothesis in a study that found that higher lambda scores on the occupational scales accompanied by a low M or W score (i.e., when subjects greatly resembled men or women in occupations and more weakly resembled men or women in general) were related to greater stability of interest profiles and greater consistency of results with actual occupation.

The S (sons) and D (daughters) scales are based on the responses of high-school boys and girls, respectively, and the F (fathers) and MO (mothers) scales are based on the responses of the sons' fathers and the daughters' mothers, respectively. Differences between the two scores of the appropriate sex may serve as a rough index of the maturity of the inventory taker's interests.

The DD/PC report form, consisting of eight pages of explanatory text and rank-ordered scores, may be read on screen or printed out locally. An alternative report, for the counselor's use, yields numerical scores but not the text.

Interpreting the Scores

The extent of the counselor's involvement with the KOIS report of scores depends, again, on the setting and the level of maturity and sophistication of the inventory takers. In most cases, the explanations of the various scores on the report form are sufficiently explicit for the initial overview without necessitating the counselor's intercession. For younger respondents, however, or those who seem less sure of themselves (or really uncertain about vocational decisions) or those whose profiles contain unexpected high ranks or a confusing array of high ranks, the counselor may be needed to ensure that the information represented by the scores is as meaningful and useful as possible.

If an interpretive session is held, it should be an interactive one, in which the counselor provides a flexible structure and, through comments and questions, encourages the inventory taker to take the lead in commenting on the scores, finding relationships among them, noting the extent to which they meet expectation or are surprises, asking appropriate questions, and suggesting next steps.

Dependability. For most adults, dependable results will be indicated in the first section of the score report. Younger respondents are likely to receive more than one of the cautionary messages regarding dependability: more than 15 unreadable responses (in which case the answer sheet is returned to the sender); highest lambda between .31 and .39, indicating that interest patterns may not yet have stabilized; V score between 42 and 44, indicating unusual interests; V score below 42, indicating that results may not be accurate; highest lambda lower than .31, indicating that interest patterns may not be sufficiently developed to score for occupations or college majors (only Section 2 results are printed).

The V score has 60 answer positions for 41 items, based on the number of responses marked significantly more frequently by persons instructed to try to make the best possible impression. When the V score is between 42 and 44, and all other indicators are positive, the interest pattern may truly be unique or nontraditional or representative of values unique to a particular culture. This question can be explored with the respondent and, if the high-ranking occupational and college major scores are in keeping with his or her expectations, the report form should be accepted as reliable. When a caution message appears with a V score below 42, poor reading or inattention is a likely cause, and even though a report of scores is issued, it might be advisable to ask if the inventory-taker understood the content of the survey, and to have him or her retake it if carelessness or inattention appears to have been the problem.

Vocational Interest Estimates. Because the KOIS items were derived from the Kuder Preference Record—Vocational, Form C, and the Kuder Preference Record—Personal, Form A, short scales from Form C are the basis for the VIEs. VIE percentile norms were obtained by selecting answer sheets submitted for a wide geographic distribution of high-school, college, and private agency users (mental health, vocational rehabilitation, military, and private vocational counseling agencies). VIEs are reported in rank order within high, average, and low groupings. The boundaries for high and low percentiles are the 75th and the 25th percentiles, respectively. Scale descriptions are given on the back of the report form. To relate the inventory taker's KOIS scores to his or her VIEs, the counselor might refer to Appendix B of the *Manual Supplement*, which gives the highest three VIEs for each scale, for the appropriate sex. Page 6 of the *Manual Supplement* also provides a table for converting VIE percentiles to Holland codes, based on data Holland (1979) used to indicate equivalence of Kuder's scales to his six personality types: Realistic, Investigative, Artistic, Scientific, Enterprising, and Conventional.

- Occupational and college major scores provide counselors with information about how closely their KOIS responses resemble those of men and of women in the various criterion groups. The occupational scales cover a broad spectrum of professional and nonprofessional occupations; they relate to all 12 of the work groups in the U.S. Department of Labor *Guide for Occupational Exploration* (1979).

- Inventory takers should examine the ranks for their own gender first, then look at ranks on the other-gender list for occupations and college majors not on their own-gender list. They may have questions about why the scales are separated by norm-group gender, and the counselor may wish to discuss with them how differences in sex-role socialization and different expectations of males and females traditionally have led to differences in responses to the activities represented by the items. As Kuder (1977) found, on the average, men obtain higher scores compared with men, and women obtain higher scores compared with women for any occupation for which scales have been developed separately by sex.

- An earlier version of the *General Manual* (Kuder & Diamond, 1979) presented the history of the development of the KOIS and the results of the research studies conducted over the years—including studies of accuracy of classification frequency of differences, predictive validity, interests and job satisfaction, reliability and homogeneity, and the factor structure. It also contained descriptions of each of the occupational and college major criterion groups.

- The counselor—whose copy of the score report contains the actual lambda values—can also advise the inventory taker about the magnitude of differences between scores on male-normed and female-normed scales. Because everyone will have *some* highest ranks compared with members of the other sex, those that have considerably lower lambdas than on own-sex norms should be interpreted with caution, especially if there are large differences in scores on "twin" scales—scales for the same occupation or college major that have been developed on both sexes.

Counselors can also help inventory takers—especially those who are less experienced in occupational and educational exploration—to look for patterns in their top-ranking occupations and college majors and those that are "next most similar." For example, do the ranks show a pattern of interest in health-related occupations, or in mechanical work? Inventory takers may even find patterns in ranks that are least similar, indicating fields of work and study that they might find dissatisfying.

Relating occupational and college major scores to VIEs provides an even broader basis for discovering patterns. More than 10 or 12 "most similar" scales, however, may represent undifferentiated interests and may be confusing for the inventory taker to interpret. The counselor may want to sound out the inventory taker as to possible underlying reasons; for example, do the ranks represent leisure-time interests or hobbies, or some deeply hidden aspirations? As Zytowski (1981) pointed out, homemakers returning to work often have profiles with a high proportion of high-ranking social service and literary occupations. These usually reflect many of the activities in which women at home engage.

The Experimental Scales. Although inferences based on scores on the experimental scales must remain highly tentative until further research has been carried out, the counselor may want to consider the scores in conjunction with other information. For example, if the V score and/or the lambda level is questionable, the counselor may want to look at differences between the M and MBI or the W and WBI scores. If the BI scores are more than 10 points greater, the inventory taker may have responded insincerely. On the other hand, he or she may be truly social-service oriented or have other interests that are not traditional in our society.

As stated earlier, the difference between the S and F scores and the D and MO scores may provide some indication of maturity, but there are insufficient data at present to justify such an inference. The difference between M and W scores should never be considered as an indication of masculinity or femininity; at most, it represents differences between general interests of men and general interests of women. For a number of criterion groups (e.g., female physicians and female computer programmers, male clinical psychologists) the difference is very small; for others (e.g., female librarians, male computer programmers, male police officers) the difference is considerably larger (Diamond, 1981).

Further Cautions Regarding Interpretation

Some counselors may be tempted to overinterpret a profile, making clinical or other inappropriate inferences from the scores or the session in which the scores are interpreted. The KOIS is not a clinical or diagnostic instrument, and the counselor should not infer attitudes, personality characteristics, or other attributes not specifically measured by the inventory. The occupational exploration implications of the scores should constitute the principal framework for the interpretive session. Even when an inventory taker brings up feelings, self-doubts, and the like, the discussion should remain within the context of how they affect the occupational exploration and decision-making process.

The KOIS is not recommended for selection for either employment or a program, except in combination with other appropriate measures and validated for that purpose. The counselor should also make it clear to the inventory taker that the KOIS is not a test of ability, nor does it tell the person what he or she "should" do.

SANDRA HARRIS: A CASE EXAMPLE

Sandra Harris is a 30-year-old "re-entry" woman—returning to work after several years of raising a family at home. She is a high-school graduate and held several office and salesclerk jobs until marriage. She now has two young children in primary school and wants to go back to work, but is not sure what she wants to do. She has a chance to take an office job again or to take a job in a small neighborhood boutique, but neither option appeals to her very much; she would like to "try something new." She took the KOIS at a community college counseling center and has looked at her score report, but she is now seeking help interpreting it in depth and in getting answers to a number of questions.

Presented here are numerical scores for Vocational Interest Estimates, Occupations, and College Majors, compared with men and compared with women, from the counselor's copy of Sandra Harris's KOIS report form (Fig. 8.1). (Numerical scores are not given on Sandra's copy.) Scores are listed as those most similar and those next most similar. The remaining scores are simply listed in the order of similarity.

Kuder Occupational Interest Survey Report Form

Name HARRIS SANDRA

Sex FEMALE **Date** 08/14/86

Numeric Grid No. **SRA No.** 00379

1 **Dependability:** How much confidence can you place in your results? In scoring your responses several checks were made on your answer patterns to be sure that you understood the directions and that your results were complete and dependable. According to these:

YOUR RESULTS APPEAR TO BE DEPENDABLE.

2 **Vocational Interest Estimates:** Vocational interests can be divided into different types and the level of your attraction to each type can be measured. You may feel that you know what interests you have already — what you may not know is how strong they are compared with other people's interests. This section shows the relative rank of your preferences for ten different kinds of vocational activities. Each is explained on the back of this report form. Your preferences in these activities, as compared with other people's interests, are as follows:

Compared with men		Compared with women	
HIGH		HIGH	
OUTDOOR	81	MECHANICAL	98
CLERICAL	77	OUTDOOR	87
AVERAGE		AVERAGE	
MECHANICAL	75	MUSICAL	68
MUSICAL	61	CLERICAL	65
SOCIAL SERVICE	45	COMPUTATIONAL	39
LITERARY	31	PERSUASIVE	27
COMPUTATIONAL	29	LITERARY	26
LOW		LOW	
PERSUASIVE	19	SOCIAL SERVICE	17
SCIENTIFIC	04	SCIENTIFIC	06
ARTISTIC	04	ARTISTIC	02

3 **Occupations:** The KOIS has been given to groups of persons who are experienced and satisfied in many different occupations. Their patterns of interests have been compared with yours and placed in order of their similarity with you. The following occupational groups have interest patterns *most* similar to yours:

Compared with men		Compared with women	
AUTO MECHANIC	.43	OFFICE CLERK	.50
CARPENTER	.43	FLORIST	.47
ELEM SCH TEACHER	.42	BOOKKEEPER	.47
INTERIOR DECOR	.42	BANK CLERK	.46
POSTAL CLERK	.42	DEPT STORE SALES	.45
WELDER	.42	ELEM SCH TEACHER	.45
BRICKLAYER	.41	SECRETARY	.45
MACHINIST	.41	VETERINARIAN	.45
ELECTRICIAN	.40	BANKER	.44
PLUMBER	.40	BEAUTICIAN	.44
PAINTER, HOUSE	.39	EXTENSION AGENT	.44
FLORIST	.39		

Compared with men

MOST SIMILAR, CONT.

FORESTER	.38
TRUCK DRIVER	.37
BOOKSTORE MGR	.37

THESE ARE NEXT
MOST SIMILAR:

BANKER	.36
BOOKKEEPER	.36
PLUMBING CONTRAC	.36
BLDG CONTRACTOR	.36
SUPERVSR, INDUST	.36
FARMER	.36
NURSE	.36
BUYER	.35
PLANT NURSRY WKR	.35
X-RAY TECHNICIAN	.35
TRAVEL AGENT	.34
INSURANCE AGENT	.34
TV REPAIRER	.34
PRINTER	.34
EXTENSION AGENT	.34
LIBRARIAN	.33
CLOTHIER, RETAIL	.33
METEOROLOGIST	.33
FILM/TV PROD/DIR	.33
DENTIST	.32
POLICE OFFICER	.32
ENGINEER	.32
MATHEMATICIAN	.32
AUTO SALESPERSON	.32
PHOTOGRAPHER	.31
VETERINARIAN	.31

THE REST ARE
LISTED IN ORDER
OF SIMILARITY:

PHYS THERAPIST	.30
MATH TCHR, HS	.30
REAL ESTATE AGT	.29
COMPUTER PRGRMR	.29
ARCHITECT	.29
OPTOMETRIST	.29
SCIENCE TCHR, HS	.28
AUDIOL/SP PATHOL	.28
PHARMACIST	.27
PHYSICIAN	.27
RADIO STATON MGR	.27
LAWYER	.27
CHEMIST	.26
JOURNALIST	.25
MINISTER	.23
ACCT, CERT PUB	.23
PERSONNEL MGR	.23
SCHOOL SUPT	.23
STATISTICIAN	.22

FIG. 8.1. Sandra Harris' KOIS Report Form.

278

Compared with women		Compared with men		Compared with women	
THESE ARE NEXT MOST SIMILAR:		REST, CONT.			
NURSE	.42	COUNSELOR, HS	.22		
MATH TEACHER, HS	.41	PODIATRIST	.22		
ACCT, CERT PUB	.41	PHARMACEUT SALES	.22		
OCCUPA THERAPIST	.41	SOCIAL WORKER	.20		
DENTIST	.40	PSYCHOLOGIST	.17		
PHYS THERAPIST	.40				
X-RAY TECHNICIAN	.40				
LIBRARIAN	.39				
COMPUTR PRGRMR	.38				
DENTAL ASSISTANT	.38				

4 College Majors: Just as for occupations, the KOIS has been given to many persons in different college majors. The following college major groups have interest patterns *most* similar to yours:

THE REST ARE LISTED IN ORDER OF SIMILARITY:		Compared with men		Compared with women	
ARCHITECT	.37	AGRICULTURE	.40	PHYSICAL EDUC	.46
BOOKSTORE MGR	.36	ANIMAL SCIENCE	.40	HOME ECON EDUC	.44
FILM/TV PROD/DIR	.36	FORESTRY	.35	MATHEMATICS	.43
PHYSICIAN	.36			BUSINESS EDUC	.42
ENGINEER	.35	THESE ARE NEXT		MUSIC & MUSIC ED	.40
INSURANCE AGENT	.35	MOST SIMILAR:			
AUDIOL/SP PATHOL	.33			THESE ARE NEXT	
DIETITIAN	.33	MUSIC & MUSIC ED	.32	MOST SIMILAR:	
SCIENCE TCHR, HS	.32	PHYSICAL EDUC	.32		
INTERIOR DECOR	.32	ELEMENTARY EDUC	.31	ELEMENTARY EDUC	.39
JOURNALIST	.31	ENGINEERING	.31	HEALTH PROFESS	.39
COL STU PERS WKR	.30	FOREIGN LANGUAGE	.31	NURSING	.38
NUTRITIONIST	.30	ART & ART EDUC	.30	DRAMA	.37
COUNSELOR, HS	.29			FOREIGN LANGUAGE	.37
RELIGIOUS ED DIR	.28	THE REST ARE		BIOLOGICAL SCI	.36
SOCIAL WORKER	.28	LISTED IN ORDER		ART & ART EDUC	.35
LAWYER	.24	OF SIMILARITY:			
PSYCHOLOGIST	.24			THE REST ARE	
		ARCHITECTURE	.26	LISTED IN ORDER	
		SERV ACAD CADET	.26	OF SIMILARITY:	
		MATHEMATICS	.25		
		BUSINESS ADMIN	.25	HISTORY	.33
		PHYSICAL SCIENCE	.24	SOCIOLOGY	.30
		BIOLOGICAL SCI	.22	PSYCHOLOGY	.29
		SOCIOLOGY	.21	ENGLISH	.28
		ECONOMICS	.20	POLITICAL SCI	.25
		ENGLISH	.20		
		HISTORY	.20		
		PREMED/PHAR/DENT	.19		
		PSYCHOLOGY	.17		
		POLITICAL SCI	.14		

Experimental Scales.		V-SCORE 53		
M .39	MBI -.12		M .46	WBI -.13
S .38	F .34		D .42	MO .42

FIG. 8.1. (Continued)

The counselor tells her:

In scoring your responses, several checks were made on your answer pattern to be sure you understood the directions and that your results were complete and dependable. Your results do appear to be dependable.

The next part of your report shows how your interests compare with those of females and those of males—that is, the relative rank of your interests—in the following 10 broad vocational areas:

Computational—Working with numbers.

Scientific—Solving problems and discovering facts.

Persuasive—Meeting and dealing with people, promoting projects, selling things and ideas.

Outdoor—Being outside, working with plants or animals.

Clerical—Working with precision and accuracy.

Musical—Making or listening to music.

Literary—Reading and writing.

Social Service—Helping people.

Artistic—Involving visually creative work with design, color, form, and materials.

Mechanical—Using machines and tools.

Compared with females, your scores are high in Mechanical and Outdoor interests; compared with males, they are high in Outdoor and Clerical interests. Compared with females, they are average in Musical, Clerical, Computational, Persuasive, and Literary interests, and low in Social Service, Scientific, and Artistic interests. Compared with females, they are lowest in Social Service, Scientific, and Artistic interests, and compared with males, they are lowest in Persuasive, Scientific, and Artistic interests.

Sandra is especially concerned about her ranks "compared with men" and "compared with women." Why is she getting both kinds of scores, she asks, and why are they different? For example, on her VIEs she is high on Outdoor and Clerical compared with men and only average in Mechanical, but compared with women she is high in both Mechanical and Outdoor. The counselor explains the rationale for the different norms and points out that Sandra's mechanical and outdoor interests are high compared with women because, unlike herself, women in general don't express much interest in work-related mechanical and outdoor activities. In general, however, men are much more interested in mechanical activities than women are, and they mark many such activities in the KOIS more frequently than she did. If Mechanical was only average compared with men, Sandra inquired, why was her rank on Auto Mechanic her highest occupational rank compared with men? Also, her ranks on Office Clerk, Bookkeeper, Secretary and such occupations were her highest ranking compared with women, but her VIE

Clerical rank was her highest compared with men and only average compared with women. Here the counselor has a more difficult explanation to make. She tells Sandra that the VIEs are based on the activities marked most frequently by men in general or women in general, and women in general mark clerical activities much more frequently than men do. The VIE ranks for each scale are based on the percentage of inventory takers who obtained lower ranks than she did. The occupational ranks, however, represent a direct comparison with the typical responses of a specific group of people, regardless of the percentage of inventory takers who obtained lower ranks. The two types of ranks or scores, then, are not directly comparable. Sandra seems to have some difficulty understanding this, and she abandons the effort when the counselor tells her that the important thing to concentrate on is the general idea of how her interests compare with those of men and of women, her ranks in each group, and the patterns they suggest.

Why is it, Sandra asks, that compared with men she seems to be interested in jobs she's never even considered, "mostly things you do with your hands . . . mechanical kinds of things," whereas compared with women she seems to be interested mostly in the kind of work she's always done or could have done—"women's kind of work." The counselor asks Sandra what she thinks of the fact that professional and social-service-oriented occupations are among her lowest ranking, compared with both men and women. This seems to make sense to Sandra; she's never really been interested in that kind of work.

Perhaps, the counselor suggests, Sandra isn't aware of all the choices open to her. They discuss her college-major ranks and the outdoor occupations suggested by the top-ranking scales compared with men, as well as the "next most similar" engineering rank. The highest ranking scales compared with women do not appeal to her—especially home economics education and business education; they represent what she has been trying to get away from.

Then, taking a different tack, the counselor asks Sandra if she's ever had a course in home mechanics or industrial arts. Well, she did have a course where she learned to fix mechanical things around the house . . . "you know, repair burned-out wire, change washers, learn how the different parts of a sewing machine work, things like that." And yes, she was pretty good at fixing the children's toys and "kind of liked doing that." But auto mechanic, carpenter, welder . . . she gives a little shrug of uncertainty, perhaps tinged with distaste. She has seen a few women construction workers, but she always thought they had to be kind of rough, not very feminine. She has always prided herself on her femininity; it is very important to her and she thinks it is very important to set an example for her daughter. "And I'll bet the men in these jobs give women a hard time." Still maybe the work is more exciting than being an office clerk or a salesperson. And it probably pays better ... "It sure is hard to decide."

She seems to be pleading silently with the counselor to tell her what to do. The counselor says Sandra must make the decision herself, but that if there is no pressure to decide immediately, there are a number of things she can do that might help her. To begin with, she might want to find out more about her top rankers compared with women and compared with men in the *Guide for Occupational Exploration*. She might also want to visit some job sites and talk with some people working in those jobs; the counselor can help set up such visits. Sandra can also investigate appropriate training at the technician level at the community college, the counselor suggests. Sandra responds with unexpected eagerness. Yes, it might even be fun to go back to school for a while, and she could get a part-time job to fill in until she really knows what she wants to do. "I guess I really have to do some homework on this," she admits. She realizes that she needs to determine a sequence of next steps and that she needs to obtain more occupational information. A time was set to come back to discuss her progress and to obtain any help she might want with further planning.

Note that the counselor has been very careful not to sanction or disapprove any of the judgments Sandra has expressed. She has acted as a facilitator, enabling Sandra to examine her own values, her experiences, and her feelings about work and about herself, to consider the possibilities open to her, and to outline important next steps. And she has let Sandra know of her support and availability as a resource person.

KOIS RESEARCH

Some of the research on the KOIS was mentioned earlier in this chapter in the context of a particular question or problem. In this section the major relevant research studies are described more systematically, albeit briefly. (For a complete description of the research see Kuder, 1977, and Kuder & Diamond, 1979.)

Early research on the KOIS was limited to intensive study of the scores of 3,000 subjects in 30 core groups selected as being most representative of the spread of occupations and college major fields for which scales had been developed. Where possible, subjects were selected from cross-validation groups whose responses were not used to develop scales; the remainder were chosen at random from the criterion groups. (For the original 148 occupational and college-major scales, the paired comparisons that were basic to much of the research would have amounted to 1,087,000.)

In generalizing from the research on the 30 core groups, one must take into account the fact that all KOIS scales were developed in the same way, with the same standards for membership in a criterion group, and with an acceptable level of homogeneity in criterion group responses. Given these conditions, and on the assumption that the core group scales are representative of the complete set of KOIS scales, differentiation should generally be as good for the other scales. Later studies reported here (e.g., follow-up studies and factor analyses) go far beyond the original core research and lend further credence to the inferences drawn on the basis of KOIS results.

Validity

Validity studies included (a) an errors of classification study, an examination of the frequency with which members of an occupational group achieved a higher score on a scale other than their own, (b) the rank of scores of the 30 core group members on their own scale, (c) the frequency of differences of varying magnitudes between a person's score on his or her own scale and his or her highest score, (d) predictive validity studies, and (e) factor analysis, which provides evidence of the construct validity of the KOIS.

Errors of Classification: New Scoring System vs. General Reference Group. How did the KOIS scoring system compare with a system that uses a general reference group? Responses for six KOIS cross-validation groups consisting of 90 subjects each were scored on all six scales, including their own—first on Form D scales, developed with the use of a general reference group, and then on KOIS scales. That is, there were two sets of five comparisons each for the 540 subjects. Form D scores were converted to standard scores, based on the means and standard deviations of the original criterion groups. For each pair of occupations, the number of persons from one group who obtained a higher score on the scale for the other group than on their own was tallied. A similar tally was made based on the KOIS scoring system.

On the scales developed with a general reference group, subjects scored higher on an occupation other than their own 209 times. When lambdas were used, the number of errors of classifications was reduced to 142—a reduction of 32%, and 31% when ties were counted.

In a second errors-of-classification study, the 30 core groups were scored on all 30 scales. The number of errors ranged from 0% to 29% with a mean of 6.2%. Many of the so-called errors occurred in very closely related fields— for example, a number of electrical engineers scored highest on other engineering scales, and 16 social workers obtained their highest score on the clinical Psychologist scale.

Frequency of Differences. The frequency of differences between a score on the person's own scale and that person's highest score was obtained for the 3,000 core group members. In 64% of the cases, the score on the subject's own scale was either the highest score or within .009 of the highest. For 71% it was within .019, or one standard error of measurement, of the highest score; for 90%, it was within .069 of the highest score. Only 10% had a score for their own occupation .070 or more removed from their highest score, indicating a significant difference between the two scores.

Predictive Validity. Zytowski (1976) located more than 1,000 men and women 12 to 19 years after they had taken the Kuder Preference Record Occupational, Form D, which contained the same items as the KOIS, in high school or college. Answer sheets were rescored for the KOIS. Data for 882 subjects were available. Of these, 51% were employed in an occupation that would have been suggested to them by scores on the KOIS scales. These results were close to the maximum obtainable concurrent validity in the light of the population, which was extremely variable in socioeconomic status and in consistency of career progression. The college major scales were slightly more predictive than the occupational scales.

Zytowski and Laing (1978) followed up 206 persons from the same population that was used in Zytowski's 1976 study and who were in occupations predictable by one of the 28 KOIS "twin" scales—scales for the same occupation or college major developed on male and female criterion groups. They investigated the predictive validity of own- and other-gender-normed scales, as well as the rank-order correlations between male- and female-normed scales. The predictive validity of scores on the two sets of norms was about equivalent, regardless of the gender of the person taking the inventory. Slightly more than 43% of the sample were in occupations corresponding to their five highest-ranked scales on own-gender norms, and more than 50% were in occupations corresponding to their five highest-ranked scales on other-gender norms.

Interests and Job Satisfaction. Herzberg and his associates (Herzberg, Mausner, Petersen, & Capwell, 1957) long ago asserted that of all types of tests used in counseling, interest tests had the strongest factual justification: "the pattern of interests as measured by objective tests has a demonstrable positive relationship to the satisfaction the individual derives from his job" (p. 215).

In his follow-up study, Zytowski (1976) attempted to learn whether persons in jobs congruent with their measured interests were more satisfied than persons in jobs not congruent with their measured interests. Direct responses to a question about degree of satisfaction showed no relationship, but a question as to whether the respondent would consider changing jobs or occupations if given the chance did show a relationship with congruence, for men only.

Dawis (1994) pointed out that empirically keyed interest inventories like the KOIS are designed to predict occupational membership, which he asserted has a low correlation with job satisfaction. Thus, the KOIS and similar instruments should not necessarily be expected to correlate with job satisfaction.

Although there have been no other studies relating the KOIS to job satisfaction, data from at least nine studies involving other forms of the Kuder interest inventories testify to this relationship and appear to be generalizable to the KOIS, particularly because many of the items from those forms are included in the KOIS, the same broad general areas are tapped, and the same principles of interest measurement governed its construction.

The most definitive job-satisfaction study is one by McRae (1959) involving the Kuder Preference Record—Vocational, Form C. McRae studied the scores of 1,164 young people from 61 secondary schools in 31 states. They had taken the inventory in high school and responded to a questionnaire 7 to 10 years later on how well they liked their work. Analysis of the results showed that 728 persons were in work consistent with their interests as measured in high school, and 436 were in work not consistent with their earlier interests. Of the "consistent" group, 62% were satisfied with their work, as opposed to only 34% in the "inconsistent" group. Also, the proportion of dissatisfied workers in the inconsistent group was about three times as great as in the "consistent" group. These results are in close agreement with a study by Lipsett and Wilson (1954).

Kuder (1977) noted that there are problems with the use of job satisfaction as a criterion, especially because there are great variations in the degree to which people find occupations attractive. Similar observations have been made by Clark (1961) and Strong (1955), among others. For additional studies on job satisfaction and discussion of job satisfaction as a criterion, see Kuder (1977).

Factor Analyses. Seven factor analyses of KOIS response proportions were conducted between 1963 and 1976 by different researchers. In the first involving 124 variables, 15 principal factors were extracted: best impression, femininity/masculinity, skilled trades, behavioral sciences, artistic, scientific-mathematical, sales, youth, literary, medical, religious, outdoor, and three unidentifiable factors.

In the next three analyses, 13 factors were identified: skilled trades, business-accounting, artistic, social welfare, sales, food, clerical, journalism, physical sciences, medical, nutrition, library science, and young women.

In the fifth analysis 20 factors were extracted: drive, aggressiveness; femininity/masculinity; mechanical; medical; literary; social welfare; artistic; dietetics; persuasive; outdoor; religious; engineering; political science, power; science-mathematics; accounting-clerical; musical; physical education; library science; and two unidentifiable factors.

In the sixth analysis, 23 factors were identified, 15 of which were similar to those identified in the fifth analysis. The other 8 were identified as adult women; adult men; young women; occupational dissatisfaction; sales; typical responses; behavioral sciences; and journalism.

The last factor analysis was conducted separately for male- and female-normed scales, using lambda scores converted to z scores. For male-normed scales, 11 factors emerged: skilled trades; helping; political science vs. language; medical service; mathematic-numeric; art; psychology; physical science vs. language; physical science vs. business; active, military, persuasive vs. sedentary; and agriculture. For female-normed scales, 9 factors emerged—7 of them the same as or similar to those for male-normed scales: lower level, easy access; helping; sociopolitical science; medical service; language; mathematic-numeric; art; psychology; and homemaking.

For more complete information on the factor analyses and the methodologies employed, see Kuder (1977) and Kuder & Diamond (1979).

Validity of Using Other-Gender Norms. In counseling women or men, questions arise as to how to interpret scores based on data from the other sex. The important consideration is whether scores for occupations based on data from men fall in the same relative order for a woman as would scores based on data from women.

Early in the development of the KOIS, Kuder studied the scores of 99 females on scales for 13 occupations for which both male and female norms had been developed. Subjects were high-school girls, college women, and women in a variety of occupations. Median correlation between the two sets of scores was .74 for high school girls, .77 for college women, and .81 for employed women. Scales that yielded the highest scores on one set of norms generally yielded high scores on the other set.

Diamond and Raju (1977) obtained scores on 28 pairs of KOIS scales, male-normed and female-normed, for occupations and college majors with the same or similar names. The sample consisted of 639 males and 353 females who took the KOIS in 1973. Correlations between ranks on the two sets of sales were obtained for each individual. The median correlation was .87 for male and .86 for females, and ranged up to .97. Only 5 of the 982 individual correlations fell below .60, indicating that scales generally ran in the same order for a person on male and female norms.

Zytowski and Laing (1978), in a study mentioned earlier in this chapter, found scores on two sets of twin scales to be highly correlated and approximately equal predictive validity.

Diamond (1981) investigated the degree of overlap between scores on male-normed and female-normed KOIS scales for KOIS occupational criterion group profiles as an index of sex-typical and sex-atypical interests. The scores of female-normed professional occupational groups had far more overlap with male-normed scores than did the scores of criterion groups for less-skilled occupations, both female-normed and male-normed. In fact, most female-normed professional criterion groups exhibited greater score overlap than did their male counterparts.

Reliability

Several types of KOIS reliability have been investigated and are reported in Kuder and Diamond (1979). The first refers to the reliability of individual profiles, or the consistency of an individual's scores on two administrations (test–retest reliability). The second refers to the stability of individual profiles over time. A third type refers to the consistency of the differences between scores on each pair of scales. Reliability of the VIE scales has also been studied.

Reliability of Individual Profiles. One hundred independent determinations of profile reliability were made for equal proportions of male and female high-school seniors and college students, each involving from 25 to 28 pairs of scores. All had satisfactory V scores. The two administrations were approximately 2 weeks apart. Median reliability for all cases as .90. Fifteen of the 100 reliabilities were below .80, and only 7 were below .75.

In another study, individual test–retest reliabilities were computed for 92 high-school senior boys and 50 college senior women on 142 scales. Median correlation for the former was .93 and for the latter .96. Standard errors of measurement ranged from .011 to .052, with a median of .01.

Stability Over Time. Gehman and Gehman (1968) studied the stability of KOIS scores of engineering students over 3 to 4 years. All had taken the KOIS as freshmen and again as seniors. Median reliability was .89.

A case study of the stability of four KOIS profiles from a single individual over a 30-year period has been offered by Zytowski (1996), who identified several consistent and emergent career themes over the span of years and compared them with actual job duties and expressed job satisfaction. The results were interpreted as supporting a broader, thematic interpretation of interest inventory data rather than an approach that begins, "You ought to be a . . . ." Jepsen (1996), in a commentary, added that interest inventories may be as well suited to predict intrinsically rewarding activity (that is, selected aspects of a job common to diverse occupations) rather than occupational roles alone.

Consistency of Score Difference. Differences between scores in each possible pair of scores on four scales were obtained in two administrations to 92 high-school senior boys. Correlations ranged from .84 to .92, demonstrating a high degree of consistency for the scales involved.

Reliability of VIE Scales. VIE scales have KR-20s ranging from .63 to .85, except for the Persuasive scale, which has a KR-20 for only 47. (For more reliable estimates of broad vocational interests, administration of the two earlier instruments is suggested.) All of the scale intercorrelations but one are either negative or below .30, indicating the relative independence of the scales. The highest correlation is .46, between Outdoor and Mechanical.

Homogeneity

The extent to which criterion group members express the same preference for KOIS activities is a measure of their homogeneity (Kuder & Diamond, 1979). The more homogeneous a group, the larger the proportion marking the same *most* and *least* choices, and the larger the sum of the squared proportions of the 100 combined *most* and *least* responses. For a group with perfect homogeneity, where 100% mark the same choices throughout the inventory (theoretically possible, but highly unlikely), the sum of the squared combined proportions over the 100 triads would be 400. For a group of the lowest possible homogeneity, with one-third of its members marking each of the *most* and each of the *least* response positions, the sum of squared proportions over the 100 triads would be 267.

For each of the KOIS criterion groups, the sum of the squared proportions for the 600 *most–least* patterns of response was found. Values ranged from a low of 329.33 to a high of 363.48. Values were generally higher for social-service-oriented groups and lower for manual workers, who closely resembled the heterogeneous men-in-general group. In general, as Kuder (1977) observed, the greater the degree of specialization in an occupation, the more homogeneous the group is likely to be.

EVALUATION AND FUTURE DIRECTIONS

As Kuder (1977) commented:

> Interest inventories are fallible and do not furnish all the answers needed for every counseling situation. . . . We now know a great deal more about the role of interests in occupational choice than we knew fifty years ago. It is notable that reviewers do not advocate abandoning the use of interest inventories even in their present imperfect form. The justification for their use in guidance

must be essentially the same as that for any psychological instrument: namely, that they contribute to being a better job of counseling. (p. xi)

KOIS Strengths and Weaknesses

The most notable strength of the KOIS—one that has clearly enhanced the use of interest measurement in counseling—is its innovative method of scale development and scoring. The ability to make direct comparisons between an individual's responses to an interest inventory and the typical responses of various occupational and college major groups is a clear advantage over reliance on items that differentiate between the responses of a general reference group and those of a criterion group. Strong himself (1943) discovered that scales based on a reference group consisting of a sample of the general population did not produce good differentiation between professional groups. He found that no single reference group was satisfactory for the whole range of occupations. The errors of classification and the frequency of differences studies cited earlier (Kuder & Diamond, 1979) affirm the very significant improvement in classification obtained by the use of the KOIS rationale, and consequently in the validity of the inferences drawn from the scores.

Moreover, as both Laime and Zytowski (1964) and Johnson (1978) found, the fact that most women's responses on the Strong Vocational Interest Blank (and, in Johnson's study, the Strong-Campbell Interest Inventory) are unlike those of the men-in-general group apparently contributes to inflated scores on male-normed scales. Scores on other-gender scales on the KOIS, on the other hand, permit a more straightforward interpretation in counseling.

Another strength of the KOIS is its item content and item type. The KOIS avoidance of occupational titles and use of easily understood work-related activities discourages the favoring of occupational stereotypes. The forced-choice item format minimizes response bias, or the tendency of some inventory takers to avoid extreme responses (*like very much, dislike very much*), or to answer from different reference points, so that the reliability of the responses over respondents is very low.

The availability of materials to help with the counseling uses of the KOIS is still another strength. These include the VIEs; the two-part report of scores with their comprehensive interpretive sections; a simulation of a typical counseling session on audiocassette; and the *General Manual* and *Manual Supplement*, which contain the technical information for the KOIS.

The KOIS's main weakness is the relatively limited number of occupational scales and the fact that a number of them are in need of updated norms; most of the scales were developed between 1955 and 1965, and the remainder between 1967 and 1981. Although the scales cover a broad range of professional and nonprofessional occupations, the technology has changed for some of them, some occupations have become outdated, and new occupations have entered the world of work. Also, where possible, more scales normed on women are needed to match scales normed on men. Use of the KOIS cross-culturally has not been systematically investigated. Because of cultural differences, the V score and the lambda score levels may be lowered, rendering the results potentially questionable. For use outside the Western countries and generally with non-English-speaking populations, problems of appropriate translation and of scale development (new criterion group responses would be needed for all scales) are considerable obstacles. Nevertheless, this area is an important one in which to encourage research. Finally, the pencil-and-paper KOIS can only be centrally scored; turnaround time, in most cases, is 48 hours plus mailing time. What is being done to rectify these shortcomings is discussed later in this chapter.

Comparison with Other Interest Inventories

Zytowski (1981) discussed the problem of administering more than one inventory and finding inconsistencies in the profiles for a given individual. He pointed out correctly that some people are not always consistent even when they take the same inventory twice and when the inventory has been shown to be reliable across persons. In addition, inventories that have similar kinds of scales may have very different items and different modes of responding, or the composition of norm groups may differ in such characteristics as age range or specialties within the occupation (e.g., research vs. application). If a client takes two inventories and the results show differences, Zytowski suggested that the counselor present both sets of results, discuss the possible reasons for the inconsistency with the client, and let him or her base next steps on the one that seems to more accurately reflect the client's interests. Or, the information from the two inventories can be used to complement each other, especially if one has scales not represented in the other.

The inventory with which the KOIS can be compared most directly is the Strong Interest Inventory (SII; Harmon, Hansen, Borgen, & Hammer, 1994), because both deal principally with occupational interests, as opposed to broad general interest areas, and scales for both are empirically developed rather than internally developed. There are, nevertheless, a number of major differences. The principal difference is the method of scale construction and scoring. The SII uses the significant differences between general-reference-group and criterion-group responses to items in the inventory to build a scale. SII standard scores and are based on these differences; the disadvantages of using a general reference group for scale building and scoring have already been dealt with in detail earlier in this chapter. The

KOIS, on the other hand, develops scales directly from the response proportions of the criterion group. Scores are lambdas—correlations between the modal responses of the criterion group and the responses of the individual. Although lambdas are not reported on the student copy of the score report, the scales are ranked on the basis of their lambda values.

In addition, item content and type of response also differ greatly. The KOIS contains 100 groups of three activities each, for which the inventory taker selects one most preferred and one least preferred, in effect rank-ordering them. No occupational titles are used. The SII, on the other hand, includes 135 occupations, 39 school subjects, 46 work-related activities, 29 leisure activities, and 20 types of people, all rated *like, indifferent*, or *dislike*; plus 30 items assessing preference between pairs of activities, 12 ratings of personal characteristics, and 6 paired comparisons of data, people, things, and ideas.

The third difference is in number and types of scales. Both inventories have indexes with which to check the dependability of an administration. Both have homogeneous scales reported in percentiles: the KOIS 10 VIEs; the SII 6 General Occupational Themes and 25 Basic Interest Scales. The KOIS is scored for 109 occupational scales representing 76 different careers, including 33 scored for both men and women, 32 based exclusively on men, and 11 based on women. They are presented in rank order based on the unique lambda coefficient. The SII is scored for 211 occupational scales representing 109 careers, only a few of which are not represented by both genders. They are grouped by Holland type and reported as T-scores. The KOIS includes college major scales; the SI does not. The KOIS presents scores on eight experimental scales, which are not recommended for interpretation; the SCII yields four "personal style" scores.

As mentioned earlier, the KOIS scales were developed mainly between 1955 and 1965, with a number of new scales added and two scales updated between 1967 and 1981. Almost half of the SII scales were updated in the 1994 edition. General Reference Groups were also updated. Both inventories offer comprehensive manuals, and both also offer ancillary materials.

Plans in Progress or Under Consideration

The KOIS lends itself to continuous updating rather than periodic new editions. New scales, chiefly of women in occupations already represented by male scales, have been added, and additional scales are planned. In the Kuder DD/PC, the "Bridge" to occupations can be used to access the *Occupational Outlook Handbook*, either in print or on the Internet, where it has been published by America Online. An alternative is for users to access the computer database Fast Facts, which incorporates Occupational Outlook-style sketches of every occupation and college major for which the KOIS is scored.

Career Matching: A New Concept in Interest Measurement

The traditional task in occupational counseling—matching people to occupations—"really involves person-to-people matching . . . trying to match a specific individual to a group of people in an occupation," Kuder (1977, p. 163) observed. However, he went on to point out, in real life, perfect matching does not occur. "Even the members of an occupational group do not match their group perfectly;" considerable variation exists among them, although the greater the degree of specialization the more homogeneous the group will be. The original objective, then, of matching people to jobs might be better achieved by matching people to individuals they resemble and who are enthusiastic about their work, Kuder concluded. No longer would the composition of occupational groups be a problem. The task, instead, would be to build a pool of people from as many occupations as possible and from all strata in life with whom to compare the individual. Detailed personal histories of the closest matches would be presented to the survey taker. New occupations could be represented in the system as soon as data from a few people in the occupation could be obtained.

Zytowski (1992) described the evolved methodology of such a system, now named the Kuder Career Search Schedule. The personal job histories, or career sketches, of nearly 1,500 people have been collected and published in *The Kuder Book of People Who Like Their Work* (Hornaday & Gibson, 1995). The KOIS can now be scored to identify the people who like their work, whose interests are most similar to those of the survey taker. Of course, as Kuder pointed out, additional research must be undertaken to determine the reliability and stability of such a novel approach. Eventually, additional exploratory research needs to be directed to determining the reliability and stability of individual results for a number of persons who have taken the KOIS twice. The system could well extend beyond the field of interests and encompass "the whole range of information that can be collected about human beings" (Kuder, 1977, p. 167). Indeed, the future of the KOIS is filled with promise for vastly expanded ways of measuring human characteristics.

REFERENCES

Anastasi, A. (1988). *Psychological testing* (6th ed.). New York: Macmillan.
Clark, K. E. (1961). *Vocational interests of nonprofessional men.* Minneapolis: University of Minneapolis Press.

Clemans, W. V. (1958). An index of item-criterion relationship. *Educational and Psychological Measurement, 18*, 167–172.

Cronbach, J. (1950). Further evidence on response sets and test design. *Educational and Psychological Measurement, 10*, 3–31.

Cronbach, L. J. (1970). *Essentials of psychological testing* (3rd ed.). New York: Harper & Row.

Darley, J. G., & Hagenah, T. (1955). *Vocational interest measurement*. Minneapolis: University of Minnesota Press.

Dawis, R. V. (1994). Vocational interests, values, and preferences. In M. D. Dunnette & L. M. Hough (Eds.), *Handbook of industrial and organizational psychology* (2nd ed., Vol. 2, pp. 834–871). Palo Alto, CA: Consulting Psychologist Press.

Diamond, E. E. (1981). Sex-typical and sex-atypical interest of Kuder Occupational Interest Survey criterion groups: Implications for counseling. *Journal of Counseling Psychology, 28*, 229–242.

Diamond, E. E., & Raju, N. S. (1977). *Technical supplement, Career development inventory* (rev. ed.). Chicago: Science Research Associates.

Findley, W. G. (1956). A rationale for evaluation of intem discrimination statistics. *Educational and Psychological Measurement, 16*, 175–180.

Gehman, W. S., & Gehman, L. H. (1968). Stability of engineering interests over a period of four years. *Educational and Psychological Measurement, 28*, 367–376.

Harmon, L. W., Hansen, J. C., Borgen, F. H., & Hammer, A. L. (1994). *Strong interest inventory: Applications and technical guide*. Palo Alto, CA: Consulting Psychologists Press.

Herzberg, F., Mausner, B., Petersen, R. O., & Capwell, D. F. (1957). *Job attitudes: A review of research and opinion*. Pittsburgh: Psychological Service of Pittsburgh.

Hoffman, M. A., Spokane, A. R., & Magoon, T. M. (1981). Effects of feedback mode on counseling outcomes using the Strong Campbell Interest Inventory: Does the counselor really matter? *Journal of Counseling Psychology, 28*, 119–135.

Holland, J. L. (1979). *Vocational preference inventory manual*. Palo Alto, CA: Consulting Psychologists Press.

Holland, J. L. (1997). *Making vocational choices: A theory of vocational personalities and work environments*. Odessa, FL: Psychological Assessment Resources.

Holland, J. L., Magoon, T. M., & Spokane, A. R. (1981). Counseling psychology: Career interventions, research and theory. *Annual Review of Psychology, 32*, 279–305.

Hornaday, J. A., & Gibson, L. A. (Eds.). (1995). *The Kuder book of people who like their work*. Amherst, NH: Motivation Press.

Jackson, D. N. (1977). *Jackson Vocational Interest Survey Manual*. London, Ontario: Research Psychologists Press.

Jepsen, D. A. (1996). Commentary: Inventory scores and work experiences. *Career Development Quarterly, 46*, 104.

Johnson, R. W. (1978). Relationships between male and female interest scales for the same occupations. In C. K. Tittle & D. G. Zytowski (Eds.), *Sex-fair interest measurement: Research and implications* (pp. 95–101). Washington, DC: National Institute of Education.

Kuder, F. (1966). *General manual: Kuder DD occupational interest survey* (1st ed.). Chicago: Science Research Associates.

Kuder, F. (1975). *Manual: Kuder E General Interest Survey*. Chicago: Science Research Associates.

Kuder, F. (1977). *Activity interests and occupational choice*. Chicago: Science Research Associates.

Kuder, F., & Diamond, E. E. (1979). *General manual: Kuder DD occupational interest survey* (2nd ed.). Chicago: Science Research Associates.

Kuder, F., & Zytowski, D. G. (1991). *Kuder Occupational Interest Survey, general manual* (3rd ed.). Monterey, CA: CTB/McGraw-Hill.

Kuder, F., & Zytowski, D. G. (1993). *Kuder DD/PC user's guide*. Monterey, CA: CTB/McGraw-Hill.

Laime, B. F., & Zytowski, D. G. (1964). Women's scores on the M and F forms of the SVIB. *Vocational Guidance Quarterly, 12*, 116–118.

Lipsett, L., & Wilson, J. W. (1954). Do suitable interests and mental ability lead to job satisfaction? *Educational and Psychological Measurement, 14,* 373–380.

McRae, G. G. (1959). *The relationships of job satisfaction and earlier measured interests.* Unpublished doctoral dissertation, University of Florida.

Nunnally, J. C., Jr. (1959). *Tests and measurements.* New York: McGraw-Hill.

Strong, E. K. (1943). *Vocational interests of men and women.* Stanford, CA: Stanford University Press.

Strong, E. K. (1955). *Vocational interests 18 years after college.* Minneapolis: University of Minnesota Press.

Tittle, C. K. (1978). *Sex bias in testing: A review with policy recommendations.* Princeton, NJ: Educational Testing Service.

Tyler, L. E. (1978). *Individuality.* San Francisco: Jossey-Bass.

U.S. Department of Health, Education, and Welfare. (1975). Nondiscrimination on the basis of sex. *Federal Register, 40,* 24128–24145.

U.S. Department of Labor. (1979). *Guide for occupational exploration.* Washington, DC: U.S. Government Printing Office.

Watkins, C. E. Jr., Campbell, V. L., & Nieberding, R. (1994). The practice of vocational assessment by counseling psychologists. *The Counseling Psychologist, 22,* 115–128.

Zytowski, D. G. (1976). Predictive validity of the Kuder Occupational Interest Survey. *Journal of Counseling Psychology, 23,* 221–233.

Zytowski, D. G. (1981). *Counseling with the Kuder occupational interest survey.* Chicago: Science Research Associates.

Zytowski, D. G. (1985). *Manual supplement: Kuder DD occupational interest survey.* Chicago: Science Research Associates.

Zytowski, D. G. (1992). Three generations: The continuing evolution of Frederic Kuder's interest inventories. *Journal of Counseling and Development, 71,* 245–248.

Zytowski, D. G. (1996). Three decades of interest inventory results: A case study. *Career Development Quarterly, 45,* 432–459.

Zytowski, D. G., & England, R. J. L. (1995). Indices of career maturity in the Kuder Occupational Interest Survey. *Measurement and Evaluation in Counseling and Development, 28,* 148–151.

Zytowski, D. G., & Laing, J. (1977). Validity of other-gender normed scales on the Kuder Occupational Interest Survey. *Journal of Counseling Psychology, 25,* 205–209.

9

A Complete Career Guidance Program: The COPSystem

Lisa Knapp-Lee

EDITS, San Diego, California

BACKGROUND OF THE COPSystem

The Career Occupational Preference System Interest Inventory (COPS) (R. R. Knapp & Knapp, 1974, 1982; Knapp-Lee, Knapp, & Knapp, 1995) is designed to assist individuals in the career decision-making process. The COPS is a carefully and systematically developed instrument yielding job activity interest scores based on occupational clusters, and may be used as a first step in career exploration. Using the extensive interpretive material presented with the COPS leads the way to utilization of most occupational information systems and consideration of educational choices, resulting in actual career decision making. The COPS Interest Inventory provides for time-effective administration, scoring, and interpretive procedures based on Career Occupational Preference System (COPSystem) occupational clusters, which have been established and refined through an extensive series of theoretical and factor-analytic studies begun over three decades ago (R. R. Knapp, 1967). The measurement of interests provided by the COPS combined with measurement of abilities, Career Ability Placement Survey (CAPS) (L. Knapp & Knapp, 1976), and measurement of values, Career Orientation Placement and Evaluation Survey (COPES) (R. R. Knapp & Knapp, 1978; Knapp-Lee, Knapp & Knapp, 1995), provides a coordinated system for career exploration and decision making. For purposes of career exploration, a classification system is clearly needed. There are over 20,000 occupations listed in the *Dictionary of Occupational Titles* (DOT; U.S. Department of Labor,

1991) that are available for consideration as possible careers. The structural form arrived at for the classification of occupations has great practical implications for career guidance. Clients should be directed to focus their consideration primarily on those occupations consistent with their interests, abilities, and values. Furthermore, this field of focus should broaden their perspective by including all, or virtually all, occupations within such a categorization. With these prescribed goals in mind, appropriate techniques can be chosen to arrive at the most meaningful classificatory structure.

The structure of interests may be presented from empirically sampling specific occupations or theoretically based on hypothetical groupings demonstrated through a statistical technique known as factor analysis. Among all possible choices, factor analysis is the most efficient tool used to clarify structure and has been used in the development of the COPSystem occupational clusters. In test development, factor analysis is a mathematical technique used to examine the clustering of test items. This grouping or clustering of highly related items defines a factor.

The development of the COPSystem occupational clusters followed closely the pioneering work of previous researchers. The early work of Thurstone (1931), who first applied factor-analytic techniques to the interest domain, and the following work of Guilford, Christensen, Bond, and Sutton (1954) led to a clearer understanding of the structure of interests in terms of groups of occupations based on focus of activities performed in the occupations. Kuder (1948) also reported scales including the eight basic group interest factors. During the researching of the structure of occupations, it became apparent that occupational interest could also be clustered by levels based on concepts, such as levels of responsibility, aspiration, and manipulative versus intellectual or planning activities. This distinction was first operationally defined in an inventory developed by Guilford, Shneidman, and Zimmerman (1948) and formally summarized by Roe (1956).

The technique of factor analysis yielded occupational classificatory systems that laid the groundwork for the development of the COPSystem structure of occupations. The available factor analytic studies presented structures similar enough in content to form a classification system by groups, based on focus of activity, and levels and degrees of responsibility and achievement. This approach, following the work of Guilford et al. (1948), has been empirically demonstrated and refined by R. R. Knapp (1967), R. R. Knapp and Knapp (1974, 1982) and L. Knapp-Lee, Knapp, and Knapp (1995). Virtually all available factor analyses have been based on items written to reflect the major focus of activity performed in a wide range of occupations. This categorization by primary focus of activity, which is reflected in the COPSystem (R. R. Knapp, Knapp, & Knapp-Lee, 1990), follows from a long history of research into the structure of occupations guided by theory and empirically confirmed through factor analysis. The milepost stepping stones in the evolution of the structure of occupations can be summarized (Table 9.1).

TABLE 9.1
Classification of Job Interests by Primary Focus
of Activity Summary of Factor-Analytic Studies

COPS group factors, Knapp & Knapp	Roe	Guilford	Kuder	Thurstone
Science	Science	Scientific	Scientific	Science
Technology	Technology	Mechanical	Mechanical	Science
			Computational	
Outdoor	Outdoor	Natural	Outdoor	
Business	Business Contact	Mercantile	Persuasive	People
		Leadership		
Clerical	Organization	Clerical	Clerical	Business
Communication	General Cultural	Literary	Literary	Language
Art	Arts and	Aesthetic	Artistic Musical	Language
	Entertainment	Expression		
Service	Service	Service	Social Service	People

Factor Analysis and the Group Structure of Interests

In the statistical foundation for a cluster structure of occupations dating back to the pioneering work of Thurstone (1931), four primary factors were identified among professional-level occupations, and the direction was set for the scientific study of occupational classification. Application of the factor-analytic model to the clarification of the interest domain has paralleled developments in the application of this technique in the ability area, both of which were accelerated by advances in computer technology. The technique may be used to demonstrate multiple, lower order factors at the secondary factor level or at the primary factor level, as Thurstone (1938) did in establishing the concept of primary mental abilities. As noted, the necessity of such a classification with multiple broad factors to explain the world of work becomes evident when confronted with a comprehensive list of occupational titles such as that in the *Dictionary of Occupational Titles* (U.S. Department of Labor, 1991). Although that document is an exemplary compendium of information about specific occupations, its use in occupational exploration is severely limited. Such information is highly useful when keyed to a structure that is based on a primary focus of activity.

Some ad hoc classification systems, which have not been based on either empirical or theoretical research, have been presented. An example of such a classification is one in which occupations are clustered by industry, such as transportation. Such a cluster groups together occupations involving activities as diverse as a truck driver, ticket agent, accountant, bookkeeper, and dispatcher. Similarly, other work-group arrangements have categorized together a wide diversity of occupations. One cluster identified as leading–influencing, for example, includes programmer, statistician, teacher, psychologist, lawyer, purchasing agent, radio station manager, business manager, securities trader, newspaper editor, police lieutenant, mine inspector, hotel manager, travel agent, literary agent, and railroad dining car steward. Nonetheless, categorization by the concept of leading–influencing is perhaps better than no categorization at all.

Other systems of classification, while based on a measurement foundation, provide no information concerning relationship between jobs. Empirically developed scales are illustrative of this approach to interest measurement. Responses of students or other examinees are compared with responses of seasoned persons on the job on the assumption that similarity between responses of, for example, a 15-year-old high school sophomore and a 30-year-old PhD psychologist will indicate a positive prognostication for satisfaction as a psychologist. As Lunneborg and Lunneborg (1978, p. 165) stated, an outstanding example of an interest measure without a theoretical base lies in the empirically constructed Strong-Campbell Interest Inventory (SCII) occupational scales (Campbell, 1974). Instruments such as the SCII attempt to provide a comprehensive coverage of major occupations by adding occupational scales. Although not directly derived from factor-analytic techniques, Kuder (1948) developed and refined his series of scales to the point where the General Interest Survey Form C, introduced in 1948, represented all eight of the group interest factors represented in Roe's model. (Actually the General Interest Survey Form C presented 10 scales, 8 of which parallel those classified by Roe, 1956, and are listed in Table 9.1, with the addition of two others, Computational and Musical.)

In that same year, Guilford et al. (1948) published an inventory based on Guilford's factor-analytic research that reflected eight interest dimensions but also yielded two social service dimensions, Social Activity and Personal Assistance. The publication of this inventory was the first to present scales representing levels and defined the primary interest structure later elaborated upon by Roe (1956). The first application of a groups-by-levels classification in the measurement of interests thus appeared.

One of the most consequential factor resolutions of this theoretically based classificatory system was a seven-factor resolution published by Guilford et al. in 1954, based on a sample of male Air Force personnel. Factors obtained in that study were mechanical, scientific, social welfare, aesthetic expression, clerical, business, and outdoor. The first six of these were among those also hypothesized by Guilford et al. (1954, p. 28). Although clearly emerging in the analysis, outdoor was not among those hypothesized in that study and thus was not listed among the verified factors in that study. It was this study that Holland (1973, p. 5) felt represented the most explicit forerunner of his typology of personality. Of course, selecting a six-category typology omits not only the outdoor work interest factor but also the well-established linguistic or verbal-interest factor, which was apparent in Guilford's other research as well as in most factor-analytic studies of occupational interests (Roe, 1956).

Lunneborg and Lunneborg (1975, 1978) presented data in support of this eight-dimensional structure. The pattern of item correlations against the eight scales and intercorrelations of the scales was interpreted by the authors as supporting this structure. Meir and Barak (1974) presented a simple inventory using occupational titles to measure the eight group factors. Their data from occupational samples of working adults and intercorrelations among the scales were interpreted as supporting the validity of that inventory.

The model depicting these eight factors can be conceptualized in a number of ways. Roe and Klos (1969) suggested a circular model, and there is some evidence from the use of the COPS Interest Inventory that supports this (R. R. Knapp, Knapp, & Buttafuoco, 1978). However, there has been some suggestion that the order may be better explained with several slight changes (Tracey & Rounds, 1994). It seems apparent that more research needs to be conducted to confirm the order of the structure, but support for the number of clusters to be included is apparent (Gati, 1979, 1991; Guilford et al., 1954; R. R. Knapp et al., 1990; Lunneborg & Lunneborg 1975, 1978; Meir, 1970, 1973).

COPSystem Structure of Occupations

In the development of the COPSystem structure of occupations, factor analysis has been the mathematical procedure chosen as the most appropriate technique for establishing, as well as confirming and monitoring, the theoretical classification of occupations. The resulting structure represents the most parsimonious system for the cluster grouping of occupations.

Early Item Factor Analysis. In the early research (R. R. Knapp, 1967) to establish the COPSystem occupational structure, Roe's (1956) classification of occupations (following the work of Guilford et al., 1948) into major groups and then into levels within each group served as the hypothesis. In the model originally presented, the eight groups were based on the primary focus of activity and were identified as: I, Service; II, Business Contact; III, Organization; IV, Technology; V, Outdoor; VI, Science; VII, General Culture; and VIII, Arts and Entertainment. These groups were each further classified by Roe into hierarchical levels reflecting degree of responsibility, training, capacity and skill. In the study by R. R. Knapp (1967), items were written to reflect occupations in each of five of these levels within each of the eight major groups, yielding 40 cells in the model. An experimental set of items was developed and administered to a sample of unselected students from the freshmen classes of two colleges and from the junior and senior classes of one high school. The individual item responses were submitted to factor analysis. The factor analyses (R. R. Knapp, 1967; R. R. Knapp & Knapp, 1974) yielded the eight broad, interpretable factors on which the occupational clusters in the COPSystem are based. They are defined subsequently in the section entitled The 14 COPSystem Occupational Clusters. Inspection of the intercorrelational matrix within each of the eight factors suggested high- and low-level clusters within the areas of Science, Technology, Business, Communication, Arts, and Service.

From this initial development, it was hypothesized that clusters of variables representing professional level occupational interests and skilled level interests would appear. Based on the original logical groupings of items into levels, 14 hypothesized factors were submitted for verification to patterned equamax rotation. All 14 factors emerged in the rotated matrix.

Reexamination of Item Factor Structure. The 1982 revision of the COPSystem Interest Inventory was undertaken to update and simplify wording of some items in the inventory, to reflect changes in certain job categories, and to achieve a better sex balance in response to items on certain scales. The COPSystem Interest Inventory was revised again in 1995. This revision included updated items to reflect contemporary job trends. To determine what effect these changes might have on the structure of the occupational classification, it was necessary to submit the data from the revised instrument to another series of factor analyses.

Professional and Skilled level clusters were confirmed for five groups: Science, Technology, Business, Arts, and Service. The Professional and Skilled levels emerged separately, indicating clusters that were differentiated based on level of responsibility. Separate level clusters did not seem appropriate for the Outdoor, Clerical, or Communication groups. In this and subsequent studies, only five of the eight levels were clearly differentiated at the Professional and Skilled levels. Inspection of item content in the two Technology Skilled clusters suggested two logical groupings, which are represented in the COPSystem as Technology Skilled and Consumer Economics. Although the activities reflect occupations generally confirmed as being in the Technology group, two Skilled level clusters provide better representation for this, the largest occupational group. Confirmatory factor-analytic results support these clusters. In terms of focus of activity represented by occupations in the two clusters, the Technology Skilled cluster, as contrasted with the Consumer Economics cluster, might be thought of as a dirty hands versus clean hands categorization within the Technology group. The Consumer Economics factor has appeared in all recent factor-analytic studies and is most clearly defined in the COPS-R analysis (L. J. Knapp-Lee, Knapp, & Knapp, 1989).

Structure of the 1982 COPS items was established through a series of factor analyses based on the new pool of single items. A technique employed to reconfirm the structure at the item level was Bentler's (1971) monotonicity analysis. A second technique using subscores based on highly homogeneous items also confirmed the factors. Although some changes occurred, these analyses generally replicated the results from earlier analyses. Structure of the 1995 COPS clusters was confirmed through a series of factor analyses.

Using the factor analytic techniques to periodically reexamine the structure existing within a given set of job activity items is advantageous because it provides flexibility in revising and updating item content. Items can be rewritten to reflect changing job activities, as, for example, the ever-increasing application of computer input in the Clerical area. Other examples are application of the technique to a set of sex-balanced items to construct a single sex-normed instrument, the COPS Interest Inventory, Form-R (COPS–R) (R. R. Knapp & Knapp, 1980a, 1980b); application to sets of items at the Professional level only to broaden and refine measurement for the college-oriented client, the COPS Interest Inventory, Form-P (COPS–P) (L. J. Knapp-Lee et al., 1982); and confirmation of the appropriateness of the instrument for specialized samples, such as the adult handicapped population (Brookings & Bolton, 1986).

CONCEPTUAL FOUNDATIONS OF THE COPSystem

An assumption underlying development of the COPSystem is that the career guidance process begins by assisting individuals in defining areas for occupational investigation that are specific and appropriate to their personal interests. Investigation of a great many related occupations within a specific area broadens the scope of career exploration, yet supplies an avenue to systematically narrow the choices to consider. Through this process, individuals are more quickly and systematically introduced to those occupations in which they are likely to be employed. Interests, what an individual likes to do, along with abilities and temperament play a major role in career selection and also influence the educational preparation that students will consider and select for their career preparation.

Systematic consideration of occupations appropriate to a given individual's personal aspirations and unique characteristics has grown increasingly complex as the number of occupations has multiplied. Test results can help the individual by presenting a wide scope of occupational choices and isolating a smaller segment for consideration in terms of personal interests, abilities, and values. This function of assessment through a testing program is described in the present system as clustered occupational exploration.

Occupational clusters in the COPSystem are keyed to training and school curriculum. Determination of those clusters representing an examinee's individual interest and ability patterns will help the individual in the choice of curriculum and the selection of particular courses and training available to him or her.

In summary, current trends in career guidance emphasize the broadening of occupational knowledge prior to making a specific vocational choice. Guidance may be most effective if first directed at the identification of occupational clusters or families related to the examinees' interests, abilities, and values rather than focusing on the selection of a particular job or occupation. Identification of the appropriate cluster of similar, interrelated occupations and the obtaining of information on a wide range of occupations within the cluster are prime objectives of the career guidance unit. Thus, the need exists for instruments providing systematic measurement of examinees' interests, abilities, and values related to clusters of meaningfully related occupations.

Sample occupations for each of the 14 clusters are presented in the *Self-Interpretation Profile and Guide*, the interpretive booklet accompanying the measurement instruments. These occupations are keyed to occupational information systems. By following this up, examinees are referred to current, detailed information about these and other related occupations in their area of interest. Additional activities are suggested for examinees in evaluating their interests, skills, choice of curriculum, college majors, and job information. The worksheets presented in the *Self-Interpretation Profile and Guide* define the career decision-making guidelines and provide the exercises to put the career decision-making process into action. Examinees are told to identify the areas (e.g., Business, Science), the level (either Professional or Skilled) in which they have relatively high or low interests, and to list their three highest interest areas. Examinees then relate their highest interest areas to sample occupations listed under each cluster in the *Self-Interpretation Profile and Guide* by choosing sample occupations to look up in independent sources of information. Selected occupations are chosen and information is provided on the interpretive material or sources consulted, from which the examinee lists skills required and tasks performed in these jobs, as well as the courses available and training appropriate to the occupations selected. This research by the examinee, based on measurement scores, results in a clear-cut step-by-step decision-making process.

The COPSystem thus provides a career awareness unit based on interest, ability, and value scores keyed to occupational clusters, job information, and curriculum or training programs. Scores used in interpretation are based on instruments providing measurement in three areas: interest, abilities, and values. There are five forms of the interest inventory: the COPS Intermediate Inventory (COPS II) (R. R. Knapp & Knapp, 1976), the COPS-R (R. R. Knapp & Knapp, 1980a), the COPS (L. Knapp-Lee et al., 1995), the COPS-P (L. J. Knapp-Lee et al., 1982), and the COPS-PIC (Knapp-Lee, 1993).

These five interest inventories may be used with the CAPS (L. Knapp & Knapp, 1976) ability battery and the COPES (L. Knapp-Lee & Knapp, 1995) work values survey. All of these instruments are keyed to the eight major occupational clusters measured in the COPSystem. All of the instruments are available in self-scoring format and all but the COPS II may be machine scored.

Description of the Interest Inventories in the COPSystem

COPS II (Career Occupational Preference System Intermediate Inventory). The COPS II is a self-scoring booklet at the fourth-grade reading level designed to complement the widely used COPS. The COPS II extends measurement to younger, elementary-grade students and to those students at higher grade levels for whom reading or language present difficulties or where other motivational considerations interfere with administration of the COPS Interest Inventory. The COPS II incorporates graphics and requires less intensive reading than most inventories. With COPS II, measurement is based on a knowledge of familiar school courses and activities, rather than exclusively on knowledge of job-related activities, which may not be familiar to some students. Examinees receive scores in eight areas, five of which are divided into Professional levels and at least one Skilled level. These same 14 occupational clusters are measured in the other forms of the COPSystem. The interpretive material is included in the booklet. The interpretation consists of descriptions of the occupational clusters, sample job titles, lists of skills and abilities, and suggested activities to get experience. The job activity worksheets facilitate career exploration and program planning.

COPS–PIC (COPS Picture Inventory of Careers). The COPS–PIC was developed to meet the need for a brief inventory of interests providing systematic measurement of job activity preferences in terms of clusters of meaningfully related occupations in a simplified format with virtually no reading required. Most interest inventories are based on the ability to read in order to make decisions about the desirability of a job activity or occupations and have been used with those who are illiterate, or have limited English skills. The COPS–PIC was developed to help in determining a more accurate measure of interest for these individuals.

COPS–R (Career Occupational Preference System Interest Inventory, Revised Edition). The COPS–R is designed to assist individuals in the career decision-making process. Like the earlier COPS Interest Inventory, the COPS–R is a carefully and systematically developed instrument yielding job activity interest scores based on occupational clusters. The COPS–R provides a simplified format with sex-balanced items presenting interpretation based on single sex norms.

COPS–R administration, scoring, and interpretation are accomplished through a single, self-contained booklet. Items are written at a sixth-grade level, with the whole unit presented in an easy-to-follow programmed booklet. All words in the COPS–R are at a sixth-grade reading level as determined by the vocabulary of Harris and Jacobson (1972).

COPS (Career Occupational Preference System Interest Inventory). The COPS Interest Inventory measures job activity interests in the eight major occupational clusters. Four of these clusters are divided into Professional and Skilled clusters, three are undifferentiated by these levels, and one, Technology, is divided into one Professional level and two Skilled level clusters. The COPS was revised in 1995 with the major goal of revising item content to reflect contemporary job activities such as the increased use of computers. A second objective was to examine the gender differences on the scales. Renorming was completed to reflect current attitudes toward the occupational activities in the COPS clusters, which would include changes reflecting diminished occupational stereotypes.

The objective to reduce the sex differences between certain of the scales was achieved, as evidenced by the fact that male–female mean differences for the two editions were reduced in 11 of the 14 scales. Although differences on these scales were reduced, they still were statistically significant and were of such a magnitude as to require separate male and female profile norms. These remaining differences are, of course, due to cultural differences between the sexes in terms of expressed occupational activity preferences on the items that were not revised. For those users who require a single sex-normed profile, a sex-balanced inventory is available in the form of the COPS–R.

Both the COPS and the COPS–R inventories consist of 168 job activity descriptions reflecting work performed in a wide variety of occupations. Examinees respond to these items according to their degree of like or dislike for each activity. Items reflect actual tasks performed in specific occupations rather than being phrased in terms of often unfamiliar occupational titles. Response alternatives allow the examinee to indicate *(L) Like very much*, *(l) like moderately*, *(d) dislike moderately*, or *(D) Dislike very much*. This free-choice response format allows examinees to state their degree of like or dislike for each activity without forcing a choice between activities that may be equally appealing or distasteful.

COPS–P (Career Occupational Preference System, Form P). The COPS–P measures interest within the eight major career clusters and follows the structure of occupations developed by the research with the COPS.

The COPS–P inventory was developed to refine measurement of the eight broad group factors at the Professional level into subclusters for use by college and professionally oriented individuals in the career decision-making process. The further division of the eight clusters into demonstrated subclusters can be used to help in pinpointing an individual's specific areas of interest and choice of college majors and training programs. Persons seeking career changes would be expected to benefit from the specificity of subclusters.

A list of the subclusters measured by the COPS–P is as follows:

Science: medical life, physical

Technology: electrical, mechanical, civil

Outdoor: agribusiness, nature

Business: finance, management promotion

Computation

Communication: written, oral

Arts: entertaining–performing, fine arts–design

Service: instructional, social–health

ABILITY: CAPS (CAREER ABILITY PLACEMENT SURVEY)

The CAPS consists of a battery of eight 5-minute ability tests providing a comparatively brief and time- and cost-effective measure of ability for career development. The battery was developed as a system for ability measurement, and may be used in conjunction with measures of interests and values in terms of the resultant occupational clusters provided in the COPSystem. A complete description of the rationale and development of the battery is presented in the CAPS Technical Manual (L. Knapp, Knapp, & Knapp-Lee, 1992).

The CAPS measures abilities in terms of the following eight tests:

Mechanical Reasoning

Spatial Relations

Verbal Reasoning

Numerical Ability

Language Usage

Word Knowledge

Perceptual Speed and Accuracy

Manual Speed and Dexterity

Current career development theory indicates that there are many important factors to be considered in career exploration. Perhaps the most important among these are the individual's interests and abilities. There is currently a host of tests available designed to evaluate these areas separately, most of which require several hours of testing time. However, little has been done to integrate the interpretation of measurement in these areas to provide individuals with an overall picture of their interests and abilities, as related to a career choice, in a reasonable length of time. This would seem to be a necessary adjunct to a holistic approach to career counseling. The CAPS is designed as a step in this direction. When interpreted in conjunction with the COPSystem occupational clusters, it provides an individual with a profile or picture of his or her abilities in terms of these occupational clusters. Thus, the CAPS is presented as an instrument providing examinees, instructors, and counselors with a powerful tool to aid them in the planning, organization, and evaluation of career development.

The recognition that there are many aspects to mental ability is the basis for defining individual differences in abilities appropriate to jobs in the various clusters. Thus, an individual high in verbal ability and language usage but low in numerical ability and/or manual dexterity may find occupations in the Communication cluster the most satisfying. Another individual who is high in spatial ability, numerical ability, and manual dexterity and low in verbal ability may be most satisfied in jobs in the Technology cluster.

Features of the CAPS include optimal use of testing time, ease of administration, and ease and flexibility of scoring alternatives. The complete battery can be administered in less than 1 hr, and both machine-scoring and self-scoring forms are available.

VALUES: COPES (CAREER ORIENTATION PLACEMENT AND EVALUATION SURVEY)

Contemporary trends in occupational decision-making theory have placed an increasingly greater emphasis on personality characteristics as they relate to occupational selection. As individuals have become more free to choose how they occupy their time, these characteristics have come to play a greater role in job choice and satisfaction. These characteristics are variously described under such general personality or motivational terms as work values, work needs, or work satisfactions, and all fall within the noncognitive, personality domain.

The perceived importance of the work one chooses has been reiterated by counselors, teachers, therapists, and those actually involved in jobs reflecting all the levels and varied activities represented in the world of work. Dimensions reflected in the COPES have been observed as being related to the type of work a person chooses and the satisfaction derived from the work one does.

Each of the eight COPES dimensions is measured by 16 two-choice, paired-comparison items. A complete description of the development of the COPES may be found in the COPES Manual (L. Knapp & Knapp, 1986) and the COPES Examiner's Manual (Knapp & Knapp-Lee, 1996). The eight dimensions measured by the COPES are:

Investigative versus accepting
Practical versus carefree
Independence versus conformity
Leadership versus supportive
Orderliness versus flexibility
Recognition versus privacy
Artistic versus realistic
Social versus reserved

The COPES was developed as a measure of work values and may be used in conjunction with measures of interests and abilities and interpreted in terms of the career clusters provided in the COPSystem. The COPES was revised in 1995 with new items, and data were gathered to support interpretation of both ends of the values scales.

COPSystem ADMINISTRATION AND SCORING

The COPSystem allows the administrator to choose the method of scoring (machine or self-scoring) and to choose the method of interpreting all three or any one or two of the career units, COPS (Interests), CAPS (Abilities), and COPES (Values). The COPSystem also allows for either group or individual administration.

Scoring of the Instruments

The COPS, COPS–PIC, COPS–R, and COPS–P Interest Inventories can be scored either by hand or by machine. Scoring is accomplished by summing the response weights for the items in each occupational cluster. For hand scoring, especially where immediate self-scoring by the examinees themselves is desired, the self-scoring form is used and responses are made directly on the self-scoring booklet. The first step in scoring is done on the booklet, and scoring is completed on the Self-Interpretation Profile and Guide. Self-scoring by students is usually accomplished in 10 to 20 minutes. Research presented in the COPSystem Technical Manual (L. J. Knapp-Lee, Knapp, & Knapp, 1990) regarding the accuracy of self-scoring indicates a very small percentage of error regarding the clusters considered for career exploration.

For machine-scoring, the COPS machine-scoring booklet may be used and can be electronically scored by computer through the use of local optical readers with licensing agreement from EdITS/Educational and Industrial Testing Service. Scoring services are also provided for these forms when returned to EdITS and results are reported in terms of individually plotted profiles for maximum counseling usefulness. See Fig. 9.1, later in this chapter, for a sample of a computer-generated profile.

The COPS II is available in the self-scoring form only. Responses are reported in terms of raw scores in each of the COPSystem clusters. The COPS II may be used with the CAPS and the COPES and summarized on the COPS II Summary Guide.

Description of the Norm Groups

Scores for the COPS, COPS–R, and COPS–P are reported in terms of the COPSystem occupational clusters both as raw scores and percentile scores. The COPS reports scores in two separate interpretive booklets, one for a high-school norm group and another for a college norm group. Norms for the 1995 edition were based on a national sampling of 19,702 intermediate and high-school students in Grades 7 through 12 collected during the 1996–1997 school year. Norms for the college level were based on a national sampling of 5,043 students. Periodic updating of normative data will be continued.

CAPS scores reflect examinees' relative ability in eight major ability dimensions as compared with others at their age and educational level. Scores are interpreted in terms of national norms, which have been established for the tests and are presented in two ways. First, profiles may be plotted on the CAPS Ability Profile based on norms determined separately for each of the eight tests. A second method of scoring and interpreting the scores involves various combinations of the eight stanine scores for each of the COPSystem occupational clusters.

Norms for the CAPS are based on a national sampling of intermediate (Grades 8–9), high school (Grades 10–12), and community college/college students and are presented in separate norm supplements. Norming data were collected in 1997 for a total sample of 19,651 students. A stratified sample was composed of rural and urban samples from five geographical areas, including minority samples in the proportions reported in the 1990 census data. Norming data will be reestablished in the coming years.

Scores on the COPES reflect an individual's work values in terms of the COPSystem clusters. These are interpreted through the COPES profile in such a way as to help examinees identify those work-related values that are most important to them as compared to others in their peer group.

For interpretive purposes, opposite end poles for each major dimension are described on the profile sheet. Because neither pole of the dimension would be interpreted as good or bad, descriptive words and phrases have been chosen to describe both ends of the dimension in a positive way. Examinees should thus be made aware that low scores are not negative attributes, but rather a way of clarifying the dimensions being measured.

The COPES scores are interpreted in terms of a profile that compares the individual's scores with those from the normative sample. Norms for the COPES are based on a national sample of 19,702 intermediate and high-school students in Grades 7 through 12 and 2,163 college and community college students. Means based on the samples for Grades 7 through 12 and the separate college sample were not meaningfully different for interpretive purposes and consequently were combined to form a single norms sample.

COPSystem INTERPRETATION

Occupational Areas

Statistical results based on factor analysis yielded eight broad interpretable area factors on which the COPSystem is based. These areas are Science, Technology, Outdoor, Business, Clerical, Communication, Arts, and Service. Occupational activities performed in the jobs represented within each area are seen as being more similar to other jobs in that area than to jobs in the other areas.

The COPSystem occupational clusters group together those occupations that are most similar in terms of activity preference. Interest scores based on such clusters provide a more meaningful basis for career decision making than scores based on any other set of items because they maximize the use of the psychological relationship among activities performed in the jobs in each of the clusters. For example, when an individual's activity interests (or occupation) change, it is more likely to be to another activity within the same cluster than to an activity or occupation in any other cluster (R. R. Knapp, Knapp, & Buttafuoco, 1978). Such a cluster system is more useful in career exploration than other systems, such as the U.S. Office of Education (USOE) industry-based job families. In the COPSystem, a truck driver would be grouped with a heavy equipment operator, machine tool operator, welder, and so on, rather than with an air traffic controller or travel agent. In the COPSystem, a surgeon would be grouped with occupations such as a chemist, microbiologist, and physicist, rather than with a medical records librarian. For user convenience, the COPSystem occupational clusters are also cross-referenced to the USOE job groups. Cross-references from the COPSystem occupational clusters to other job groupings are indicated on the COPSystem career guides. In addition to the keying of clusters to the USOE, DOT, and *Occupational Outlook Handbook* (OOH, 1998), cross-references are also available between the COPSystem occupational clusters and many statewide occupational systems (for example, VIEW and OIS).

Professional and Skilled Clusters

Among major considerations in career exploration are questions involving levels of training and of responsibility required by various occupations under consideration. Based on the structure of occupations into groups and levels suggested by Guilford et al. (1948) and Roe (1956) and demonstrated by R. R. Knapp (1967), the COPSystem organizes occupations into Professional and Skilled level clusters. Such division, of course, has great implications for the interpretive usefulness of the instrument. Measurement of occupational interests provided by the COPS Interest Inventory at the Skilled as well as the Professional level will be of assistance equally to the vocationally oriented individual as well as to the college or professionally oriented individual.

Interest scores for five of the eight occupational areas are represented for both Professional level and Skilled level occupational clusters; these include the Science, Technology, Business, Arts, and Service areas. An examination of the occupations in the two levels suggests certain characteristics that, for interpretive purposes, have been labeled Professional or Skilled. The Technology Skilled cluster is further subdivided into two Skilled level clusters; Technology Skilled, encompassing the so-called dirty hands occupations, and Consumer Economics, representing the clean hands technology occupations. The clusters of Outdoor, Clerical, and Communication are undifferentiated in terms of Professional and Skilled levels.

In general, occupations in the Professional level typically require college training and often advanced degrees, especially in the areas of Science, Technology, and Service. Occupations at this level are characterized by a high degree of autonomy and responsibility. In addition to interest in these areas, personal qualifications of ability and personality typically will have to be met.

Occupations in the Skilled level usually require specialized training that would be obtained in trade or vocational school and on-the-job training. These occupations may also require little or no specialized training, such as waiter or usher in the Service area; however, some Skilled level occupations may require a college degree.

The 14 COPSystem Occupational Clusters

The 14 COPSystem clusters are:

Science, Professional occupations involve responsibility for the planning and conducting of research and the accumulation and application of systematized knowledge in related branches of mathematical, medical, life and physical sciences.

Science, Skilled occupations involve observation and classification of facts in assisting in laboratory research and its application in the fields of medicine and life and physical sciences.

Technology, Professional occupations involve responsibility for engineering and structural design in the manufacture, construction, or transportation of products or utilities.

Technology, Skilled occupations involve working with one's hands in a skilled trade concerned with construction, manufacture, installation, or repair of products in related fields of construction, electronics, and mechanics.

Consumer Economics occupations are concerned with the preparation and packaging of foods and the production and care and repair of clothing and textile products.

Outdoor occupations are concerned with activities performed primarily outdoors involving the growing and tending of plants and animals and the cultivation and accumulation of crops and natural resources in the areas of agriculture and nature, as in forestry, park service, fishing, and mining.

Business, Professional occupations involve positions of high responsibility in the organization, administration, and efficient functioning of business and governmental bureaus in regard to finance and accounting, management, and business promotion.

Business, Skilled occupations are concerned with sales and promotion and the correlated financial and organizational activities of businesses.

Clerical occupations involve recording, posting, and filing of business records requiring great attention to detail, accuracy, neatness, orderliness, and speed in office work and in resultant contact with customers in regard to compilation of records.

Communication occupations involve skill in the use of language in the creation or interpretation of literature or in the written and oral communication of knowledge and ideas.

Arts, Professional occupations involve individualized expression of creative or musical talent and ability in fields of design, fine arts and performing arts.

Arts, Skilled occupations involve application of artistic skill in the fields of graphic arts and design.

Service, Professional occupations include positions of high responsibility involving interpersonal relations in caring for the personal needs and welfare of others in fields of social service, health, and education.

Service, Skilled occupations involve providing services to persons and catering to the tastes, desires and welfare of others in fields of personal service, social and health-related service, and protection and transportation.

CAPS Ability Areas

The eight CAPS tests are:

MR: Mechanical Reasoning measures how well a person can understand mechanical principles and devices and the laws of physics. This ability is important especially in courses in industrial arts and occupations in technology as well as skilled level jobs in science.

SR: Spatial Relations measures how well a person can visualize or think in three dimensions and can mentally picture position of objects from a diagram or drawings. This ability is important in courses in arts and industrial arts and jobs in science, technology, and arts.

VR: Verbal Reasoning measures how well a person can reason with words and the facility for understanding and using concepts expressed in words. This ability is important in general academic success and in jobs requiring written or oral communication, especially those Professional level occupations in communication, science, and service involving high levels of responsibility and decision making.

NA: Numerical Ability measures how well a person can reason with and use numbers and work with quantitative material and ideas. This ability is important in school courses and jobs in fields of science and technology involving mathematics, chemistry, physics, or engineering and in business and clerical fields.

LU: Language Usage measures how well a person can recognize and use correct grammar, punctuation, and capitalization. This ability is especially important in jobs requiring written or oral communication and in clerical jobs as well as professional level occupations in science, and in all levels of business and service.

WK: Word Knowledge measures how well a person can understand the meaning and precise use of words. This is important in communication and all professional level occupations involving high levels of responsibility and decision making.

PSA: Perceptual Speed and Accuracy measures how well a person can perceive small detail rapidly and accurately within a mass of letters, numbers, and symbols. This ability is important in office work and other jobs requiring fine visual discrimination.

MSD: Manual Speed and Dexterity measures how well a person can make rapid and accurate movements with the hands. This ability is important in arts–skilled and technology–skilled occupations and other jobs requiring use of the hands.

COPES Work Values Dimensions

Eight work values are measured by the COPES:

Investigative versus Accepting: Intellectual curiosity and the challenge of solving a complex task are major values of persons scoring high on this scale. The need for information is very important to such people. Low scorers value clear-cut activities in which they see the concrete results of their work and do not need to solve many complex problems.

Practical versus Carefree: Showing proper appreciation for one's personal belongings and appreciation of practical and efficient ways of doing things are major values of persons scoring high on this scale. Such persons value activities in which they take good care of their property and work with things to make them more practical and efficient. Low scorers value activities where others take care of equipment and keep things in good working order.

Independence versus Conformity: Independence from rules, regulations, and social conventions and the freedom to work on their own are major values of persons scoring high on this scale. Such persons value activities in which they are relatively free of rules and regulations and are not restricted by social obligations. Low scorers value working under careful supervision where clear directions and regulations can be followed.

Leadership versus Supportive: Making decisions, directing others, and speaking for the group are major values of persons scoring high on this scale. Such persons have a need to be seen as important and usually take positions of leadership. Low scorers value activities in which they can be a good follower and do not need to direct others or tell others what to do.

Orderliness versus Flexibility: Orderliness and keeping things neat and in their proper place are major values of persons scoring high. Such persons value activities in which they keep things tidy and do what they are expected to do. Low scorers value activities in which they can take things as they come and do not need to keep things orderly.

Recognition versus Privacy: To become well-known and famous and to know important people are major values of persons scoring high on this scale. Such persons seek the admiration of others as well as the rewards of honorary degrees. Low scorers value keeping their activities private and are not concerned with being considered a famous person.

Aesthetic versus Realistic: Artistic appreciation and the enjoyment of music and the arts are major values of persons scoring high on this scale. Such persons value activities in which they appreciate beauty, show artistic and emotional sensitivity and appreciate music and the arts. Low scorers are not involved with appreciation of artistic qualities.

Social versus Reserved: Helping others and appreciating the work of charitable service groups are major values of persons scoring high on this scale. Working with people in a friendly situation is important to such persons. Low scorers value activities in which they spend time on their own projects and tend to their own affairs rather than helping others.

Initial Interpretation of COPS, CAPS, and COPES Scores

COPS scores reflect the examinees' degree of interest in 14 occupational clusters. These scores are presented in such a way as to help examinees identify those occupational families in which their interests are greatest compared to others in their peer group. Because items reflect the nature of the activities performed in each occupational family, it is felt the scores more accurately reflect interest independent of considerations of status, salary, and advancement. Instructions are also written to maximize consideration of interest independent of other factors. The Inventory scores, thus, may be thought of as reflecting professed interest to be considered in career selection, along with separate indexes of abilities, values, and personality characteristics.

A basic concept guiding development of the CAPS was that test results should provide for maximum interpretive usefulness. Use of the test data should initiate activities resulting in greater self-awareness in relation to career development. The CAPS may be interpreted separately as well as in terms of occupational clusters. It may also be used in the COPSystem in conjunction with the COPS and the COPES. Thus, the CAPS scores are presented with interpretive material so that the results of the CAPS can have immediate application for career planning, such as in the selection of school courses and training programs as well as through participation in specific programs and community activities. Every effort has been made in development of the CAPS to maximize the interpretive usefulness of the test results.

Each CAPS occupational cluster score on the career profile is based on a combination of individual ability test stanine scores. This combined score represents the contribution variance for tests measuring those dimensions that historically have been shown to yield the greatest predictive validity for success in the jobs in each cluster.

Some examinees will have satisfactory ability scores in clusters not representing their highest interest. If, however, they have some interest in jobs in those clusters (e.g., scores above the 50th percentile) these may represent fields that the examinees may wish to consider further because of ability.

Furthermore, the abilities measured are, of course, not the only factors to be considered in career exploration. Ability may be high in areas for which the examinee does not wish to pursue the vigorous training required to obtain necessary skills for jobs in the cluster. On the other hand, if interest and motivation are high and ability scores are low or fall in the shaded portion of the profile, the examinee may wish to take related courses of study required to improve these skills. Also, it must be remembered that skills other than those measured by the CAPS may be involved in any specific occupation.

When analyzing ability scores in a particular area in which high interest is indicated, the examinee may wish to examine separate ability test scores that comprise the total CAPS Career Profile cluster score. For example, in the Science Skilled area, a stanine score of 5 or above (average or above) may be obtained for Spatial Ability and the remaining tests. However, the Mechanical Reasoning stanine score may be only 1 or 2 (below average). This might indicate that the examinee could benefit from courses or special training in principles of mechanics. The examinee might want to consider occupations within the cluster that do not require a great deal of mechanical skill.

The COPES scores are interpreted by a profile comparing the individual's scores with those from the normative sample. The taxonomy of work values presented in the COPES accounts for eight dimensions that are held to be pervasive work value constructs and are related to the COPSystem occupational clusters.

The concept of work values is sometimes more elusive for examinees to grasp than the concepts of interests and abilities. Once one understands it, however, the importance of values in career planning will become apparent. Reviewing some of the questions from the COPES might help to see what values are being measured. The COPES asks that a choice be made between such pairs of statements as:

work with ideas
work with my hands
team up with others
work on my own

Answers to questions such as these help to identify things considered to be important in work: what rewards an individual needs to get from work in order to be satisfied. Such satisfiers are called *values*, and they are very strong influences in our lives. Most career researchers feel that people act according to what they feel is important to them. For instance, if status or recognition is important to you, you are likely to seek out jobs and friends that contribute to meeting that need. If you do not, you will most probably feel unsatisfied and restless.

Full descriptions of the COPES work values appear on the *Self-Interpretation Profile and Guide*. A table relating the COPES work values to the COP-System occupational clusters is also presented.

Summarization of the COPS, CAPS, and COPES on a Single Profile

The COPS, CAPS and COPES may be summarized separately on their respective *Self-Interpretation Profile and Guides*. If using all three instruments together or in any combination of two of the instruments, results should be summarized on the *Comprehensive Career Guide*. The *Comprehensive Career Guide* contains individual profiles for each inventory and a means of summarizing the scores from the CAPS and COPES on the COPS Interest Inventory profile.

The COPS profile is plotted in the normal manner as described on the *Comprehensive Career Guide*. Below the profile are three rows of boxes, labeled Interests 1, Abilities 2, and Values 3 (see Fig. 9.2 for an example). It is suggested for interpreting the COPS that examinees explore their three highest areas of interest, according to percentile score, or peaks on the profile, as opposed to raw score. Three pluses should be put in the row labeled Interests 1, or perhaps four pluses if there is a tie between the third and fourth highest areas of interest. These are the clusters that the examinee should begin to explore in terms of interest.

The CAPS results are plotted on the *Comprehensive Career Guide* in the same manner that they are on the CAPS *Self-Interpretation Profile and Guide*. Any score on the CAPS Career Profile that is in the white portion, or the very upper part of the lightest shaded portion, will receive a plus in terms of ability. These pluses are transferred to row 2 below the interest profile to indicate the COPSystem cluster that should be explored in terms of interest and ability combined. Any cluster that contains a plus for interest and ability would be the direction to explore in the first stages of career guidance.

The COPES results are plotted on the *Comprehensive Career Guide*, once again, in the same manner that scores are plotted on the COPES *Self-Interpretation Profile and Guide*. Examinees are advised to choose their three highest scores on the COPES and record them on their profile. A sample of this summary profile is found later in this chapter in the case study in Fig. 9.2. Once the pluses are put in the appropriate boxes on each row of the

COPS profile, examinees are ready to explore the clusters in which, first of all, their interests, abilities, and values match.

The next step in the career exploration process is to examine the career clusters and the information contained on the profile sheet. On each profile sheet there is information on the definition of the career cluster and related courses of study. Below this information is a list of occupational titles. Each of these occupational titles is keyed to the DOT (U.S. Department of Labor, 1991). The titles are also keyed to the current OOH, the COPSystem Career Briefs Kit, and the COPSystem Career Cluster Booklet Kit. Cross-references between various statewide systems are available, such as VIEW and OIS. Below the selected occupations for each cluster are listed some skills and abilities needed on the jobs in that particular cluster, suggested activities to get experience, and college majors.

Once the examinee has studied the individual profile for each instrument, studied the summarized profile for all three instruments combined, and briefly examined the clusters that are to be explored, there are additional work sheets to complete that are contained in both the *Comprehensive Career Guide* and the *Self-Interpretation Profile and Guide*. Not only do examinees get a measure of themselves, but they are encouraged to actively use results obtained about themselves. The work sheet entitled Using Your Scores in Career Planning allows examinees to thoroughly explore the career clusters and the information provided on the profile sheet. Along with this work sheet is one for educational planning, which may be used by the high-school student for establishing a four-year program plan for school. For the college student or adult, this form may be used to outline pertinent classes completed and future schooling and/or training that would be helpful in reaching a desired career goal. A local interview form is the final work sheet and may be used as a structured guide for an informational interview or as a planning guide to conduct an interview.

The COPSystem has major interpretive values that make it extremely useful in the counseling situation. In this system, examinees are guided not to a single specific job title but rather an organized system of exploring the world of work. A cluster of occupations to explore is more useful than a single occupational title. In addition, the COPSystem is a time-effective battery. The entire battery may be administered in 2 hr and self scored in another 2 hr. Also, any one or two of the three instruments may be used to yield results that relate these measured dimensions to clustered career exploration.

Although the COPSystem instruments are administered and interpreted in a group setting, they do not eliminate the need for individual counseling. They are helpful tools for the counselor to guide the examinee in the most productive avenue for the client.

SAMPLE CASE STUDIES

Following are two case studies that are illustrative of the interpretive usefulness of the COPSystem instruments. The COPSystem is effective as a base for communication between the counselor and client. The results are indicators of areas and occupations that the client should explore.

Sample Case: Roger Wu

Roger is a 15-year-old high-school sophomore who is enrolled in a career exploration unit as part of his high-school curriculum. He has completed the machine scoring version of the COPS, CAPS, and COPES as part of the career unit in his English class, and his results are presented in Fig. 9.1. His career counselor has brought him in for an individual counseling session to explain the results of the COPSystem. At the meeting, Roger told the career counselor that he wants to be a disc jockey.

In examining his COPSystem results, it can be seen that his three highest interest scores are Communication, Business Professional, and Science Professional, with percentile scores of 94, 89 and 88, respectively. His interest scores are consistent with his desire to be a radio announcer.

However, his ability profile does not match the COPS profile. On the CAPS Career Profile, Roger's probability of success in terms of ability is highest in the clusters of Consumer Economics, Outdoor, Technology Skilled, Service Skilled, Arts Skilled, Science Skilled, Clerical, and Business Skilled. Although his percentile scores on the CAPS Career Profile are somewhat low, his scores are still above the printed shaded area on the profile. For example, Roger's ability score in the Business Skilled cluster is at the 22nd percentile (percentiles are printed to the left of the cluster title), but his score is above the printed shaded area. The shaded areas are indicators that an individual has a high enough ability level at this time for probable success, if the score obtained is at the top or above this shaded area. If Roger wants to explore the remaining clusters, where his scores fall in the shaded area of the profile, he will probably need to consider ways to improve his ability.

Examination of the CAPS Ability Profile indicates his specific areas of weakness. He has moderate to high scores on all but three of the ability tests. He is in the bottom third of the distribution on Verbal Reasoning (stanine 2), Language Usage (stanine 1), and Word Knowledge (stanine 2). He would thus seem to have some difficulty in the language areas, which might cause problems if he pursues the career of a radio announcer.

His COPES values indicate that he has high values in Investigative, Recognition, Flexibility, and Aesthetic. That he values Recognition and Aesthetics seems to indicate that radio announcing would meet some of his values needs. He also has high value scores on Investigative, which corresponds with his interest in Business and Science. He wants to become well known and appreciates music and the arts, both of which are consistent with his occupational interest.

The Summary section of the printout summarizes Roger's interests, abilities, and values. As can be seen, there is an inconsistency in the profile. In two of the areas, his interests and values match (Business Professional and

---

CAREER OCCUPATIONAL PREFERENCE SYSTEM
(COPSYSTEM) SUMMARY

ROGER WU   423144387   GR: 9
DATE: 12/34   AGE: 12

You are interested in an occupational training course and would like help in: reading, language, study skills, interpersonal skills, career planning, educational planning, finding college information, applying to a college, finding job information.

SECTION I INTERESTS (COPS)

YOU HAVE RECENTLY COMPLETED THE COPSYSTEM INVENTORIES. YOUR HIGHEST INTEREST CAREER GROUPS ARE:

Communication
Business Professional
Science Professional

Your interest profile is plotted below. A percentile number is printed at the end of the row of x's. Each number shows your approximate position on each scale as compared to other people at your educational level who have taken the COPS. If your score is near 50, about half (50%) of others fall below you. The higher your score the greater your interest is compared to others.

COPS INTEREST INVENTORY PROFILE

RAW SCORE		PERCENTILE SCORES
		LOW AVERAGE HIGH
		10 20 30 40 50 60 70 80 90
23	Science Professional	XXXXXXXXXXXXXXXXXXXXXXXXXXXXXXXXXXXXXXXXXXXXXXXXXXXXXXXXXXXXXXXXXXXXX88
13	Science Skilled	XXXXXXXXXXXXXXXXXXXXXXXXXXXXXXXXXXXXXXXXXXXXXXXXX64
22	Technology Professional	XXXXXXXXXXXXXXXXXXXXXXXXXXXXXXXXXXXXXXXXXXXXXXXXXXXXXXX75
14	Technology Skilled	XXXXXXXXXXXXXXXXXXXXXXXXXXXXXXX32
10	Consumer Economics	XXXXXXXXXXXXXXXXXXXXXXXXXXXXXXXXXXXXXXXX52
19	Outdoor	XXXXXXXXXXXXXXXXXXXXXXXXXXXXXXXXXXXXXXXXXXXXXX60
24	Business Professional	XXXXXXXXXXXXXXXXXXXXXXXXXXXXXXXXXXXXXXXXXXXXXXXXXXXXXXXXXXXXXXXXXXXXXX89
14	Business Skilled	XXXXXXXXXXXXXXXXXXXXXXXXXXXXXXXXXXXXXXXXXXXXXXXXXXXX68
15	Clerical	XXXXXXXXXXXXXXXXXXXXXXXXXXXXXXXXXXXXXXXXXXXXXXXXXXXXXXX75
25	Communication	XXXXXXXXXXXXXXXXXXXXXXXXXXXXXXXXXXXXXXXXXXXXXXXXXXXXXXXXXXXXXXXXXXXXXXXXXXXXXXXXX94
18	Arts Professional	XXXXXXXXXXXXXXXXXXXXXXXXXXXXXXXXXXXXXXXXXXXXXXXXXXXX68
13	Arts Skilled	XXXXXXXXXXXXXXXXXXXXXXXXXXXXXXXXXXXXXXXXXX52
16	Service Professional	XXXXXXXXXXXXXXXXXXXXXXXXXXXXXXXXXXXXXXXXXXXXX56
10	Service Skilled	XXXXXXXXXXXXXXXXXXXXXXXXXXXXXXXXXXXXXX40

SECTION II ABILITIES (CAPS)

Your score is marked with a plus if it is in the white portion or at the upper edge of the lightest shaded portion of each career group. These are groups in which you have measured abilities indicating a high enough level at this point in your career for probable success. Remember, for success it is neccessary that you continue to get the training and skills needed in these groups.

In interpreting your profile, concentrate on the distance of your scores from the dark shaded area. Peaks in the profile may not be significant because the shaded areas are different heights. Consider whether other things you know about yourself are consistent with your profile.

In groups where your ability scores are in the dark portion of the career profile, but your interest and motivation are high, you may wish to take related courses of study needed to improve your skills. Your COPSystem Comprehensive Career Guide will help you in these choices.

CAPS CAREER PROFILE

Percentile Scores		
22	Science Professional	
+59	Science Skilled	
18	Technology Professional	
+61	Technology Skilled	
+82	Consumer Economics	
+67	Outdoor	
18	Business Professional	
+22	Business Skilled	
+38	Clerical	
18	Communication	
32	Arts Professional	
+86	Arts Skilled	
2	Service Professional	
+59	Service Skilled	

FIG. 9.1. Roger Wu. Career Occupational Preference System (COPSystem) Summary. Reproduced from the COPSystem Comprehensive Career Guide. Copyright © 1998, EdITS, San Diego, CA. Reproduced with permission.

YOUR SEPARATE ABILITY SCORES ARE PLOTTED BELOW.
CAPS ABILITY PROFILE

STANINE SCORES

	LOW		AVERAGE		HIGH		
1	2	3	4	5	6	7	8	9

Mechanical Reasoning	. . XXXXXXXXXXXX-XXXXXXXXXXX . . .	Mechanical Reasoning measures how well a person can understand mechanical principles.
Spatial Relations	. . . . XXXXXXXXXXXX-XXXXXXXXXXX .	Spatial Relations measures how well a person can visualize or think in three dimensions.
Verbal Reasoning	XXXXXXXXXXXX-XXXXXXXXXXXX	Verbal Reasoning measures how well a person can reason with words.
Numeric Ability	. . XXXXXXXXXXXX-XXXXXXXXXXXX . . .	Numerical Ability measures how well a person can reason with and use numbers.
Language Usage	-XXXXXXXXXXXX	Language Usage measures how well a person can recognize and use standard English grammar and punctuation.
Word Knowledge	XXXXXXXXXXXX-XXXXXXXXXXXX	Word Knowledge measures how well a person can understand the meaning and precise use of words.
Perceptual Speed and Accuracy	. . . . . XXXXXXXXXXXX-XXXXXXXXXXX	Perceptual Speed and Accuracy measures how well a person perceives small detail rapidly and accurately.
Manual Speed and Dexterity	. . . . . XXXXXXXXXXXX-XXXXXXXXXXX	Manual Speed and Dexterity measures how well a person can make rapid and accurate hand movements.

10	20	30	40	50	60	70	80	90

PERCENTILE SCORES

Those scores marked as a line of x's show your abilites compared to others at your educational level. Scores extend from the *middle* of the score and do not represent a single point. If your score is near the 50th percentile score, about half (50%) of others fall below you. The higher your score, the greater your ability. See your Comprehensive Career Guide for a further description of your results.

SECTION III WORK VALUES (COPES)
COPES WORK VALUES PROFILE

```
                        - - - - 50  - - - -
Accepting .................................................    .........................................XXXXXXX-X Investigative
Carefree  .................................................    .XXXXXXXX-XXXXXXXX......................... Practical
Conformity .................................................    ..................XXXXXXX-XXXXXXXX........ Independence
Supportive .....................XXXXXXXX-XXXXXXXX......     .................................................. Leadership
Flexibility .XXXXXXXX-XXXXXXXX.......................     .................................................. Orderliness
Privacy   .................................................    .................................XXXXXXX-XX Recognition
Realistic .................................................    .......................XXXXXXX-XXXXXXXX... Aesthetic
Reserved  .................................................    .........XXXXXXXX-XXXXXXXX................. Social
                        - - - - 50  - - - -
```

Those scores marked as a line of x's show your work values as compared to others who have taken the COPES. Scores falling to the left of center show strength in values described on the left, scores to the right of center show strength in those values given on the right. See your COPSystem Comprehensive Career Guide for a description of these values.

SUMMARY

Those career groups below where your (1) interest, (2) abilities, and (3) values have +'s show you the groups you may wish to explore. First consider those groups where your interests, abilities, and values are high and all three marked with a plus. Next, consider those groups where your interests and abilities are both marked with a plus. Your COPSystem Comprehensive Career Guide will help you in your career exploration.

```
  I  II III
INT AB VAL
 +    +SCIENCE PROFESSIONAL - Planning and conducting research in math, medical, life and physical sciences.
      +  SCIENCE SKILLED - Observing and classifying facts in assisting with laboratory research.
      +  +TECHNOLOGY PROFESSIONAL - Engineering and structural design in the manufacture, construction or transportation of products.
      +  TECHNOLOGY SKILLED - Working with one's hands in the skilled trades of construction, installation, repair and manufacturing.
      +  CONSUMER ECONOMICS - Preparation and packaging of foods, making and care of clothing and textile products.
 +       OUTDOOR - Activities performed primarily out of doors such as growing and tending plants and animals.
      +  +BUSINESS PROFESSIONAL - Positions of high responsibility in organization and administration of business.
      +  BUSINESS SKILLED - Sales promotion, marketing and finance in regard to promotion of business.
      +  CLERICAL - Recording, posting and filing business records with attention to detail, accuracy and speed.
 +    +COMMUNICATIONS - Language skill in the written and oral communication of knowledge and ideas.
      +ARTS PROFESSIONAL - Individualized expression of creative or musical talent.
 +    +ARTS SKILLED - Application of artistic skill in photography, graphic arts and design.
         SERVICE PROFESSIONAL - Positions of high responsibility in caring for the personal needs and welfare of others, such as teacher or social worker.
         SERVICE SKILLED - Providing services to persons and catering to the tastes, desires and welfare of others; examples are flight attendant or taxi driver.
```

FIG. 9.1. *(Continued).*

Communication). However, none of his interests and values correspond to his abilities. The discrepancy is made evident by returning to the CAPS profile. His language skills indicate weakness; language is important to both of these clusters. The career counselor, while interviewing Roger, asks why Roger thinks the CAPS language scores are low and is informed that English is a second language in Roger's home.

There are several options that Roger has, although it is immediately apparent that he should improve his English skills. Private tutoring and additional high-school classes should be of help. It is also possible that

Roger may become a DJ in his native language, because in large cities there are often many different language stations. He might also consider work in the technical area of radio broadcasting, perhaps becoming a technician as he has a fairly high degree of interest in both Science and Technology. He might do well as a copywriter if his writing skills improve.

After discussing the summary with his counselor, Roger has made some decisions as to immediate steps to be taken to help him reach his future goals. Because Roger is still in high school and has very little work experience, he plans to do further occupational research. He plans to explore careers in the Communication, Business Professional, and Science areas by examining the cluster descriptions and occupational titles on the profile sheet. Roger and his career counselor are planning to outline a high-school program with an emphasis on improving language skills. He has been encouraged by the career counselor to get tutoring and to enroll in the journalism class offered at school. Roger has time in his coming high-school years to explore a course of study related to occupations that interest him. He now has a better conceptualization of his interests and values as well as areas of strengths and weaknesses.

Sample Case: Kyla Jones

Kyla is a college sophomore who has come to the career counseling center and has indicated that she is uncertain about choosing a college major. She has been encouraged by her parents to pursue a science major, but she feels very uncertain about a particular vocational goal. The COPS–P is usually used for college students when selecting college majors, but Kyla is so uncertain about her professional goals that the career counselor decided to give her the COPS, which will allow her to consider both Professional and Skilled level occupations. At this point in her education, she has completed much of the basic required course work but now wants to know if she should stay in college and continue to seriously consider a science major. Examination of her COPS profile (Fig. 9.2) shows that her three highest interest areas are Service Professional, Business Professional, and Communication, with percentile scores of 92, 91, and 87, respectively. Kyla is guided to explore these three areas.

She has also completed the CAPS ability battery. Scores on the eight tests indicate that she would probably succeed in terms of ability in the following areas where her scores fall into the white or at the top of the lightest shaded portion of the profile: Science Skilled, Technology Professional, Technology Skilled, Consumer Economics, Outdoor, Business Professional, Business Skilled, Clerical, Communication, Service Professional, and Service Skilled. In examining the CAPS Career Profile, it is important to focus not only on the scores in the white portion of the profile, but also on the distance from the dark shaded portions to the obtained score. For example, the results

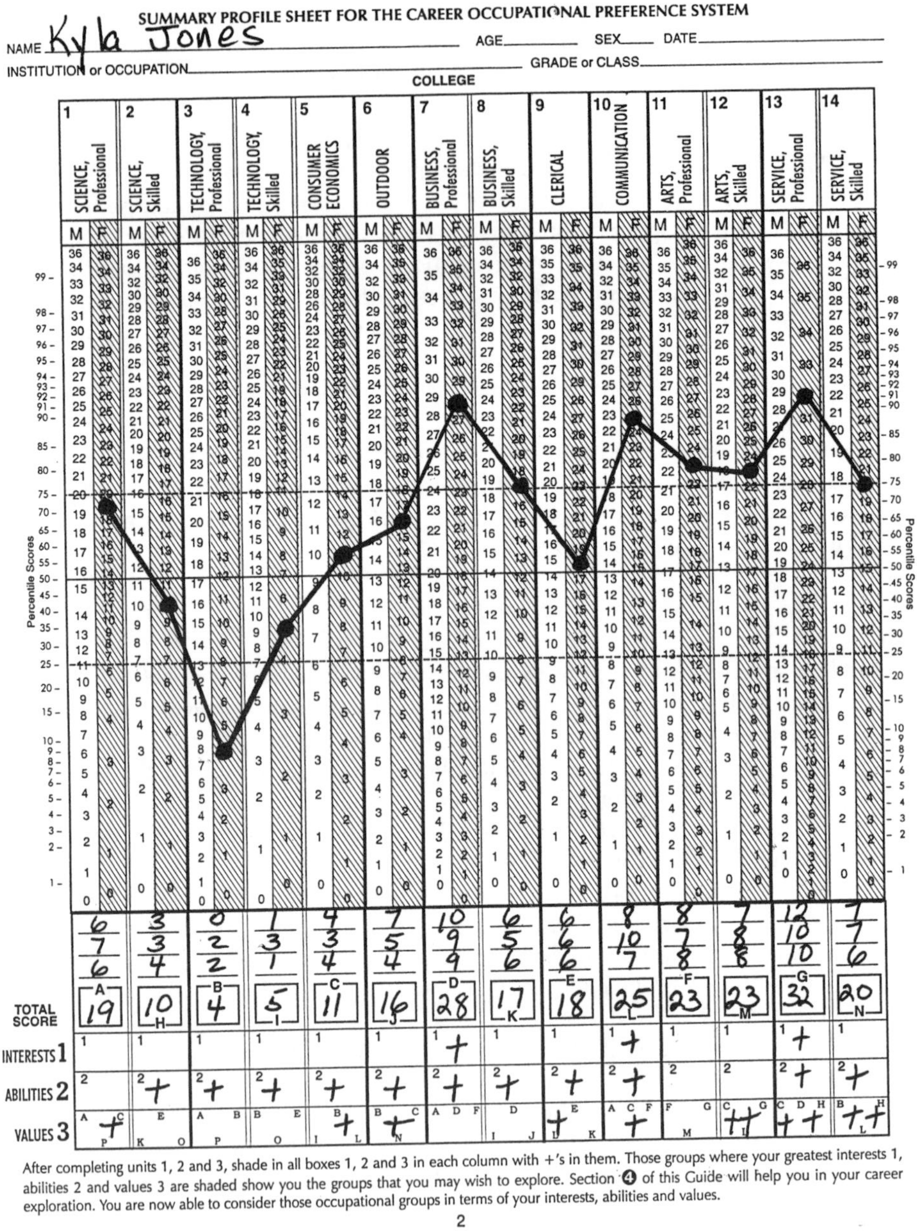

FIG. 9.2. Kyla Jones. Summary Profile Sheet for the Career Occupational Preference System. Reproduced from the COPSystem Comprehensive Career Guide. Copyright · 1998, EdITS, San Diego, CA. Reproduced with permission.

FIG. 9.2. (Continued)

CAPS CAREER PROFILE

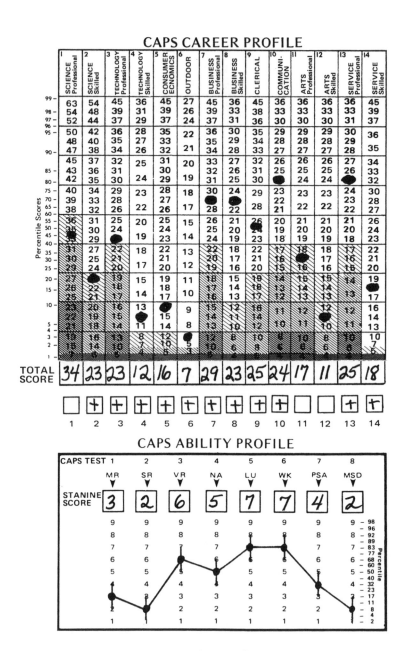

	1 SCIENCE Professional	2 SCIENCE Skilled	3 TECHNOLOGY Professional	4 TECHNOLOGY Skilled	5 CONSUMER ECONOMICS	6 OUTDOOR	7 BUSINESS Professional	8 BUSINESS Skilled	9 CLERICAL	10 COMMUNI-CATION	11 ARTS Professional	12 ARTS Skilled	13 SERVICE Professional	14 SERVICE Skilled
99 -	63	54	45	36	45	27	45	36	45	36	36	36	36	45
98 -	54	48	39	31	39	26	39	33	38	33	33	33	33	39
97 -	52	44	37	29	37	24	37	31	36	30	30	30	31	37
96 -														
95 -	50	42	36	28	35	22	36	30	35	29	29	29	30	36
	48	40	35	27	33		35	29	34	28	28	28	29	
90 -	47	38	34	26	32	21	34	28	33	27	27	27	28	35
85 -	45	37	32	25	31	20	33	27	32	26	26	26	27	34
	43	36	31		30		32	26	31	25	25	25	26	33
80 -	42	35	30	24	29	19	31	25	30	●	24	24	●	32
75 -	40	34	29	23	28	18	30	24	29	23	23	23	24	30
70 -	39	33	28		27		●	●		22			23	28
65 -	38	32	26	22	26	17	28	22	28	21	22	22	22	27
60 -														
55 -	36	31	25	20	25	15	26	21	26	20	21	21	21	26
50 -	35	30	24		24		25	20	●	19	20	20	20	24
45 -		29		19	23	14	24	19	23	18	19	19	18	23
40 -	●		●											
35 -	31	27	23	18	22	13	22	18	22	17	18	18	17	22
30 -	30	25	21		21		20	17	21	16		17	16	21
25 -	29	24	20	17	20	12	19	16	20	15	16	16	16	20
20 -	27	●	19	15	19	11	18	15	19	14	15	15	14	19
15 -	26	22	18	14	18		17	14	18	13	14	14	13	●
	25	21	17		17	10	16	13	17	12	13	13		17
10 -	23	20	16	13	●	9	15	12	16	11	12	12	12	16
	22	19	15	●	15		14	11	14	10	11	●		14
5 -	21	18	14	11	14	8	13	10	12	9	11	10	11	13
4 -														
3 -	19	16	13	8	12		11	8	10	8	10	8	8	10
2 -	16	14	10	7	10	5	10	6	8	6	8	6	6	7 5
1 -														

Percentile Scores

TOTAL SCORE	34	23	23	12	16	7	29	23	25	24	17	11	25	18

☐	✝	✝	✝	✝	✝	✝	✝	✝	✝	☐	☐	✝	✝
1	2	3	4	5	6	7	8	9	10	11	12	13	14

CAPS ABILITY PROFILE

CAPS TEST	1	2	3	4	5	6	7	8
	MR ▼	SR ▼	VR ▼	NA ▼	LU ▼	WK ▼	PSA ▼	MSD ▼
STANINE SCORE	3	2	6	5	7	7	4	2

									Percentile
9	9	9	9	9	9	9	9	9	– 98
8	8	8	8	8	8	8	8	8	– 96 / – 92
7	7	7	7	7	7	7	7	7	– 89 / – 83 / – 77
6	6	6	6	6	6	6	6	6	– 68 / – 60
5	5	5	5	5	5	5	5	5	– 50 / – 40
4		4	4	4	4	4	4	4	– 32 / – 23
3			3	3	3	3	3	3	– 17 / – 11
2			2	2	2	2	2	2	– 8
1			1	1	1	1	1	1	– 4 / – 2

FIG. 9.2. *(Continued)*

indicate a prediction of success, in terms of the measured abilities at a higher probability level for a Service Skilled career than in a career in the Science Skilled cluster, even though the percentile scores are similar in these two career areas. This is because her abilities relating to most Service Skilled professions are considerably greater than the level generally demanded in that cluster (the latter level being defined by the shaded area on the profile).

The next step in interpreting the CAPS battery is to examine the individual scores from each test. Based on the examination of her stanine scores, her CAPS Ability Profile shows that she is average to strong in Verbal Reasoning, Language Usage, Word Knowledge, and Numerical Ability. Her Mechanical Reasoning and Perceptual Speed and Accuracy are in the mid to low range, with Spatial Relations and Manual Speed and Dexterity low. However, considering that her three highest interest areas were Service Professional, Business Professional, and Communication, it is predicted that she will do satisfactorily in terms of ability in those three occupational clusters. Her strong abilities are thus most consistent with her three highest interest areas. However, should she still wish to consider a science career, in which her ability scores fell into the shaded areas, she may need to consider remedial course work or select science careers that require little mechanical reasoning or spatial ability.

Kyla's COPES scores indicate that her three highest value areas are Social, Independence, and Supportive. These three value areas were determined to be her most important areas, those that are the farthest from the midpoint on either side as evidenced by her coded scores. She values helping others and working with people. She is able to work on her own and still work with people, which will help in selecting a specific career.

In the examination of the complete summary profile, Kyla has best agreement in interest, ability and value scores for the clusters of Business Professional and Service Professional. In the Service Professional cluster, she might want to consider occupations such as psychologist or counselor, perhaps in private practice, to use her interest, ability, and value in the business area. Her high value score of Independence will encourage her to set up a private practice where she can work on her own. She also might consider teaching, maybe at a high school or even the university level, as this will match her desire to help and guide individuals and might additionally give her an arena in which to do scientific work that will satisfy her Independence value and moderate interest in Science. Her ability, however, is not clearly confirmed in this latter area. Teaching is consistent with her interest in Communication and Service and also will be consistent with her high verbal language abilities. In either of these occupations she should do well, if she continues to get the necessary educational training.

The counselor should be able to suggest a course of study in line with her high interest areas that will help her set her goals. This profile should be a confirmation to Kyla to strongly question a science major or a heavy course load of science classes. Kyla might go back to the COPS booklet and circle some of the items that she marked as *(L) Like very much* as they should indicate the specific job activities that most appeal to her. She might then begin to explore these occupations, map out a plan for college, and then declare a college major. It might be of help to Kyla to return to the career counselor at the end of her junior year for follow-up and to take the COPS–P to help pinpoint her educational and occupational goals.

RESEARCH ON THE COPSystem

Reliability and validity of the COPS, CAPS, and COPES are summarized here. More in-depth information may be found in the technical manuals for each of these instruments.

Reliability: COPS

Reliability may be defined as the consistency with which a test measures what it purports to measure. Reliability is an important characteristic, especially for tests designed for use in individual guidance.

Alpha and Test–Retest Reliability

Indices of reliability of the COPS Interest Inventory, 1995 edition, have been determined in terms of alpha coefficients and test–retest data. Alpha reliability coefficients range in magnitude from .86 to .93 and demonstrate the high degree of internal consistency of the scales. These reliability coefficients compare favorably with those of other instruments and are not statistically different from reliabilities reported for other basic interest scales.

Long-Term Reliability

Further evidence concerning the reliability of the COPS structure is reflected in the analysis of changes in interest. To examine the nature of changes in major clusters of interests measured in one school year as compared with those obtained in the succeeding school year, R. R. Knapp, Knapp, and Buttafuoco (1978) analyzed profiles for 1,243 students tested in Grades 7 through 12 for whom test–retest scores were available from successive school years.

Profiles for each student were plotted against the national norms for both administrations of the Interest Inventory and frequencies were plotted for first- and second-year peaks (cluster of greatest interest). In comparing first-year administration with second-year administration, 565 (45%) of the students had the same highest interest cluster for the 2 successive years. When the first and second areas of greatest interest are considered, over three-fourths (nearly 80%) of the students had one of their two highest interest areas in common over the period of a year. When the top three areas are suggested for consideration, as is recommended for use in the COPSystem for career exploration, virtually all students (93%) will be considering occupations in those clusters that will still be of greatest interest to them over long periods of time. These data illustrate the effectiveness for most individuals in the clustered career exploration approach for delineating a specific spectrum of the world of work for more detailed exploration.

Reliability: CAPS

To maximize the time-effectiveness of a battery, it is far more efficient to provide several unique, short measures than to have a few very long measures. Thus, the trend in modern testing theory is reflected in the CAPS battery, which is composed of many short tests. As Ruch and Ruch (1963) suggested, it is more efficient to add unique new tests to a battery than to increase the length of the most valid one.

Theoretical and empirical evidence has demonstrated that individual tests in a battery may be considerably shortened without resulting in a serious decrease in the composite validity of the battery. Brokaw (1951) compared the validity of a battery of six predictor tests of different lengths against grades in Aircraft and Engine Mechanics School. Each test was split in half so that validities could be obtained based on full-length and half-length tests. Reliabilities of the full-length tests ranged from .80 to .90, and dropped to .69 to .79 for the half-length tests. The composite validity for the full-length test battery was .57, whereas validities for the half-length tests were .55 for the first half battery and .56 for the second half battery, leading the author to conclude that previous belief in the necessity for using quite long tests is unfounded when the tests are to be used in a battery. Thus, although increasing time effectiveness by shortening the lengths of a number of tests in a battery results in a moderate loss of reliability, it is possible to effect considerable saving of testing time without significant loss of validity.

As Guilford and Fruchter (1973, p. 42) pointed out, knowing the reliability of a short test makes it possible to determine how long a test would have to be to attain any desired level of reliability simply by using the Spearman–Brown formula in reverse. Thus, based on a 5-min test with a reliability of .70, doubling testing time to 10 min increases reliability only .12, to .82. It should be noted that increases in reliability are also negatively accelerated as a function of test length.

A number of methods are available for estimating test reliability. Because of the highly speeded nature of some CAPS tests, wherein many examinees do not complete each test, the split-half method of estimating test reliability is inappropriate. However, it is of interest to note the split-half reliability for the first six tests where the speeded nature of the tests is secondary. The coefficients ranged from .76 to .95.

Test–retest reliability coefficients were based on a sample of high-school students tested 2 weeks apart. Coefficients ranged from .70 to .95, which may be considered to be further evidence for the high reliability of the CAPS tests. However, test–retest reliability for certain tests may not be the most appropriate index.

In the process of test development, parallel forms of the CAPS tests were utilized. Correlations ranged from .70 to .89 between alternate forms, which were considered promising and well within acceptable ranges based on reported coefficients for available aptitude tests (most of which are of considerably greater length).

Reliability: COPES

To examine the internal consistency of COPES scale scores, alpha reliability estimates were obtained for two different samples. Coefficients ranged from .70 to .87, which are considered to represent an acceptable level of reliability commensurate with other values inventories.

Validity: COPS

Evidence of validity, the extent to which an instrument measures what it purports to measure, is available for the COPS, CAPS, and COPES in a number of forms. Internal validation techniques concerned with the item content, stability, and factorial structure of the inventories define what the instrument measures. External validation techniques, including correlations with other instruments and relationships to criteria, such as college major choice and occupational choice, provide further evidence of construct validity.

Factorial Validity/Construct Validity. A major source of validity information for the COPS is represented in the extensive factorial data on which development of the COPS is based. The evidence for factorial validity, a form of construct validity for the structure of the COPSystem clusters and COPS item data, has been previously presented. However, to examine individual item loadings on the 14 scales, a series of clustran item factor analyses was undertaken. Using this technique, the items written to reflect job activities of the occupations in each of the 14 COPSystem clusters were submitted as variables in the factor analysis. For the analysis, each item was hypothesized as belonging to its respective cluster. The factor loadings showed that each item was more highly related to the cluster hypothesized than to any other cluster. Thus, the item "Perform chemical and microscopic tests to determine the causes of disease" has its highest loading (.56) on Factor 1, Science Professional, whereas "Test urine and make blood counts" is most heavily loaded (.51) on the Science Skilled factor.

The data from the clustran factor analyses confirmed the hypothesized content of each activity item and supported the 14 cluster scales presented in the COPSystem Interest Inventory.

The circularity of the clusters may be used to demonstrate the structure of the interest clusters. In order to statistically test the hypothesis of order (presented on the profile) of the major COPSystem groupings derived from Roe's major groupings, it was necessary to combine the levels within each major area. When combined in this manner and following the procedure used by Roe, Hubbard, Hutchinson, and Bateman (1966), a change from any area to one adjacent to it on either side, such as from 2 to 1 or from 2 to 3, is a one-step change. A four-step change is the largest possible for eight areas, such as from area 1 to area 5, or vice versa. The frequency for each step fell in descending order. A test for goodness of fit yielded a chi-square of 25.0, significant beyond the .01 level, indicating that the observed frequencies were not random.

Another requirement for circularity is that shifting should be as likely in one direction as another. Moves from 3 to 2, for example, should be as likely as from 3 to 4. A test of goodness of fit for these data yielded a chi-square value of 5.23, which is not significant. Thus, frequency of change in major areas of interest in one direction is not significantly different from changes in the other direction.

Analysis of data demonstrated that classification and changes with these classifications based on the COPSystem are not random, but are consistent with the model of occupational structure on which the system is based.

Concurrent Validity: Relationship of the COPS to Similar Instruments. Correlations of inventories, such as the COPSystem Interest Inventory, with other similar inventories provide information concerning the construct validity of the instruments. In particular, in the case of the COPS, correlations with the other interest inventories in the COPSystem series are useful in evaluating validity of the constructs measured by these instruments. The correlations between scales of the COPS and the corresponding scales of the COPS–R, based on a sample of 284 high-school students, ranged from .61 to .78 and were held to be of sufficiently high magnitude to support the construct validity of the dimensions measured. To determine the relationship of the COPS to the COPS–P scales, correlations were computed between the inventories based on the responses of 205 entering college freshmen. Correlations between the conceptually similar scales of the COPS–P and the COPS Professional level scales ranged from .70 to .93 with a median correlation of .84. As might be expected, in every instance, the COPS–P scale was more highly correlated to the corresponding COPS Professional level scale than the Skilled level scale.

Relationship of the COPS to the Kuder General Interest Survey (GIS; Kuder, 1975) has been reported based on adult and grade-school student samples. F. Savage (personal communication, 1976) reported correlations based on a sample of 57 adult females. As would be expected, correlations were highest between the correspondingly named scales of these instruments. These correlations generally ranged between .5 and .7.

In another study comparing the Kuder GIS with the COPS, Best and Knapp-Lee (1982) reported results based on a sample of 177 unselected eighth-grade students. Similar scales on the two instruments were compared in terms of correlations between the scales. The pattern of correlation wherein the magnitude of positive correlation was higher between conceptually similar scales than between any other scales in the array again provides construct validity for these scales.

As Kuder (1969) suggested, comparison of the agreement of two interest inventories should be based on the extent to which they lead to similar results in counseling. To examine this, profiles were plotted for each inventory and the three highest areas of interest identified for each subject on both instruments. Results of this analysis indicate that among a sample of eighth-grade students, 25% would be directed to the same top three interest areas for further exploration and 89% would find at least one of their top three interest areas congruent, based on measurement of the two instruments.

Concurrent Validity: Relationship to the Choice of College Major. To examine the validity of the COPS in regard to the choice of college majors made by students, a study was undertaken to determine the relationship between the declared major of entering college freshmen and their measured interests (R. R. Knapp, Knapp, & Michael, 1979). The sample consisted of 366 entering college freshmen who took the COPS and who had declared their major. The cluster representing declared major and the peak measured interest clusters were determined for each student. A test of goodness of fit for these clusters gave chi-squares that were significant at the .01 level in all cases. When the three highest interest groups were examined, 71% of the students would have had a correct prediction of the cluster containing their declared major. Analyses of data demonstrate that measured occupational interest clusters are meaningfully related to, and thus predictive of, declared college major upon entry to college.

Predictive Validity, Longitudinal Research. An issue of concern to counselors involves the degree to which a measurement instrument directs individuals to examine occupations in clusters for which they seek training and from which they eventually choose jobs. To determine the extent to which interpretation of the COPS results directs individuals to explore occupations for which further training or job entry is selected, a follow-up study was initiated based on inventory results obtained between 1974 and 1980.

A follow-up questionnaire was sent to each student from the participating schools for whom COPS scores were available. The follow-up questionnaire included questions about current educational and occupational status. Questions covered present employment and past employment (including job description and title), job satisfaction, colleges attended, major courses of study, and future occupational goals.

Of the 1,091 individuals included in the analysis for whom data were available, 660 (61%) were in educational programs or jobs representing occupational clusters consistent with their prior measured interests. When analyzed by sex, 319 of 479 (67%) of the males had jobs or college majors consistent with their prior measured interests and were categorized as hits, and 341 of 612 (56%) of the females were classified as hits. When analyzed by grade in which the students were administered the inventory, 354 of 623 (57%) of the 10th graders had jobs or college majors consistent with their prior measured interests and were classified as hits, 223 of 330 (68%) 11th graders were hits, and 83 of 138 (60%) 12th graders were hits. Analyses of the data demonstrate that when the COPS was administered during the high-school years, the majority of students were correctly directed in their job search to those clusters representing their job or educational goal 2 to 6 years later (R. R. Knapp, Knapp, & Knapp-Lee, 1985).

Validity: CAPS

Internal validation techniques concerned with item content, stability, and intercorrelations of the tests define the structure of the CAPS battery. External validation techniques including correlations with other instruments and relationships to criteria such as course grades, vocational course choice, and predictive validity in terms of occupational choice provide further evidence of the construct validity of the CAPS.

Concurrent Validity: Relationship of the CAPS to Similar Instruments. Correlations of the CAPS tests with the Differential Aptitude Tests (Bennett, Seashore, & Wesman, 1974) have been obtained for a number of samples (R. R. Knapp, Knapp, & Michael, 1977). Illustrative of this are the correlations based on a sample of 160 10th-grade students, in which conceptually similar tests correlations ranged from .47 to .77 and provided evidence of the validity of the CAPS tests.

Correlations of CAPS tests with conceptually similar tests in the General Aptitude Test Battery (GATB) (U.S. Employment Service, 1973) provide further evidence of construct validity for these tests (L. Knapp, Knapp, Strnad, & Michael, 1978). The CAPS Word Knowledge test, which is conceptually the most similar to measures provided by the GATB Verbal Aptitude (vocabulary) subtest, correlated at .80 with the GATB. The CAPS Numerical Ability test correlated at .67 with the GATB. Correlations between the CAPS Spatial Relations and Perceptual Speed and Accuracy tests and the corresponding tests in the GATB were .63 and .70, respectively.

Correlations between the CAPS tests and the conceptually similar tests of the Iowa Tests of Educational Development are in the .70 range, which further supports the contention that the CAPS measures abilities important to achievement in various areas.

The CAPS tests were correlated with the Metropolitan Achievement Tests (MAT) (Durost, Bixler, Wrightstone, Hildreth, & Lund, 1970) in an eighth-grade sample of 105 students. The correlations of conceptually similar tests ranged from .51 between CAPS Numerical Ability and MAT Total Math to .74 between CAPS Word Knowledge and MAT Total Reading.

Predictive Validity: Relationship to School Marks. Correlations with marks are presented in the CAPS Technical Manual. Generally, the patterns of correlations within particular curriculum areas are consistent with theoretical expectations. In general, industrial arts classes are significantly related to Mechanical Reasoning with significant correlations ranging from .35 to .63. Also, as would be predicted, Spatial Relations and Manual Speed and Dexterity are, in most instances, significantly related to these courses.

The highest correlations with English marks are for Language Usage and Word Knowledge, as would be expected. Marks in virtually every class are significantly correlated to these two tests in differing degrees. Similarly, marks in math classes are significantly related to Numerical Ability with the exception of the geometry course, which places emphasis on logical proof of theorems. Verbal Reasoning was most highly correlated with geometry classes. Marks in typing classes in most of the schools are significantly correlated with either Perceptual Speed and Accuracy or Manual Speed and Dexterity.

School marks in classes that provide training for many jobs in a given CAPS Career Cluster may be used to provide validity criteria for the combined CAPS Career Cluster scores. To examine validity of these scores, correlations were computed against school marks. The resulting relationship of course marks to CAPS career scores supported the predictive validity of the instrument, because high correlations were found between school subjects related to their associated career cluster.

To further examine the predictive validity of the CAPS ability profile, a follow-up study is being conducted on a sample of 2,093 9th through 12th graders who have graduated from high school, have taken the CAPS in 1979, 1980, and 1981, and for whom home addresses are available. In summarizing the results, a hit was defined as correspondence of a college goal (or the present job, if no college attendance was indicated) with a CAPS career area designated by the subjects' CAPS scores. By chance, a 71% hit rate would be expected. However, the hit rate in this sample was 97%. Although this follow-up study is not complete, it does, at this point, provide evidence for the predictive validity of the CAPS scores.

Validity: COPES

The concept of the effectiveness of using separate measures for the interests and the values domains has received empirical support. For example, Pryor and Taylor (1986) found that when separate measures of values and interests are combined, they provide more information relevant to course choice than each one does separately.

To provide evidence concerning the relationship between measures of the domains of interests and values, a study was conducted by R. R. Knapp and Knapp (1979) in which scores obtained from the COPES work values instrument were correlated with occupational activity interests as measured by the COPS. Coefficients ranged in magnitude from .0 to .47. Although correlations between the theoretically similar scales of the COPS and the COPES work values scale are sufficiently low as to justify use of both instruments, the pattern of greatest magnitude generally is theoretically consistent. These correlations are consistent with the majority of previous studies, which show a generally low order of relationship between measures of the values and of the interest domains. The present results are thus consistent with the concept that it is feasible and desirable to utilize independent measures of the concepts in these two domains.

Evidence of construct validity for dimensions measured by the COPES has been presented in terms of the factor structure of the COPES items. Other evidence of construct validity is available based on correlations with other instruments. Correlations of the COPES with values dimensions presented by Guilford et al. (1956) and by Allport and Vernon (1970) between like-named, conceptually similar scales are significant and of moderate to high magnitude, thus providing evidence for construct validity of the scales.

Two studies were undertaken to further consider the relationship of the 16 dimensions of the COPES to the 14 COPSystem Career Clusters. Students were selected who had a single high COPS Interest Inventory peak of a 75th percentile or greater with any second interest area being at least 15 percentile points lower and all other interest areas at least 30 percentile points lower than the highest interest area. The two sets of groups were selected from two separate large populations. Both samples were made up of 8th-

through 12th-grade students. Sample 1 ($N = 15,298$) came from data gathered between 1992 and 1994. Sample 2 ($N = 4,970$) was made up of data gathered between 1989 and 1993. To consider the COPES values for these two sets of groups, the rank of the percentile conversion for the average COPES scores for each group was determined. This rank was based on the absolute value of the distance from the norm mean for each sample in terms of the percentile point conversion. Although it should be emphasized that this research is based on only high-school students, in most cases it confirms the research referred to previously for weighting the values commonly measured. This COPES study is very useful in incorporating in terms of careers, the values defined at the opposite end of the eight pervasive values found in most studies of the values domain.

Support is found for weighting at least a third lower bound value to be considered with the two previously closely associated values to each Career Cluster. This relationship is shown in the *Comprehensive Career Guide*. In a few instances it was found that a previously determined pertinent value was perhaps best replaced by a more appropriate value when it was found that the previously positively weighted value was in fact highly negatively weighted in the studies of students with one clear-cut interest.

The results of this study were thus persuasive in changing some values heretofore hypothesized as being most closely associated with a particular Career Cluster. However, perhaps the most pervasive findings are the confirmation of the previously determined values to be weighted and also the indication of at least a third value from the opposite end of the eight scales that were previously exclusively weighted.

In the school situation, it is interesting to examine the relationship between work values and school achievement, as classes in school can be considered miniature work situations. Subject-matter classes correspond to jobs representing occupational clusters. For example, performance in an English class might be considered comparable to performance on a job in the Communication area. It is assumed that individuals who do well in scientific laboratory courses will be successful in jobs in the Science area. A study (L. J. Knapp & Michael, 1980) was conducted to examine the relationship between work values and academic success in the following courses, which had been shown to be related to performance in actual work situations: science, English, social studies, arts, industrial arts, and typing. These data presented for representative samples of students and vocational groups provide evidence of the validity of the COPES values used in interpreting inventory results in career guidance.

To examine the predictive validity of the COPES work values profile, a follow-up study is being conducted on a sample of 9th through 12th graders who have graduated from high school and had taken the COPES in 1979, 1980, and 1981. The results of a questionnaire requesting the job now held or the course of study now being pursued was analyzed for the 267 students who replied to an initial mailing. Based on this preliminary sample who replied to the questionnaire, 238 (89%) were categorized as hits. By chance, a 64% hit rate would be expected. This preliminary analysis does provide evidence for the predictive validity of the COPES scores in terms of the COPSystem occupational clusters.

EVALUATION AND FUTURE DIRECTIONS FOR THE COPSystem

A primary principle guiding the development of the battery of instruments represented in the COPSystem is to provide the maximum degree of validity per unit of testing time. The COPSystem instruments have been established through extensive theoretical and factor-analytic research. The sound theoretical basis with statistical support lends confidence to the counseling usefulness of the instruments.

There is a continual need for the updating and validation of the instruments, as is the case for all measurement instruments. Longitudinal validity studies of the instruments are continuing, and results will be presented as more data become available. In addition to following up examinees to determine if their occupations correspond to their scores on the COPS, CAPS, and COPES instruments, research needs to be conducted in terms of concurrent validity. That the COPSystem compares favorably to similar instruments provides substantial concurrent validity support. The COPS Interest Inventory has been correlated to numerous instruments measuring similar concepts, and results support the validity of the COPS scales.

Research into values or the type and level of ability required within specific occupational clusters could be further enhanced by additional studies. CAPS ability tests have been firmly established by past research, but perhaps future studies will yield more specifics on the level of ability required within an occupation. Evidence for the structure of work values is of extreme importance because it is clear that values are crucial in the career decision-making process. It is impossible to pinpoint all the value aspects that go into making career decisions, yet the COPES contributes to this understanding. Following up more individuals that have completed the COPES, and possibly expanding the range of values measured in order to establish the congruence of values and career choice, will be useful.

The COPSystem is valuable in the career counseling process because it is a complete battery of coordinated instruments well established through research, all related to a proven structure of occupations and of very practical relevance to the client and counselor. That the COPS interests, CAPS abilities, and COPES values are time-effective and interpreted in terms of clusters of occupations further enhances the counseling usefulness. Both the self-scoring and machine-scoring options add flexibility for the counselor while yielding the same interpretive information for the examinee. The instruments may also be used individually if some aspects have been previously measured, or if particular measurement aspects are not necessary. Self-scoring for immediate feedback is a major advantage.

The comprehensive measuring of the individual facilitates the counseling process. The measurement of interests, abilities, and values allows both counselor and examinee to interact in a knowledgeable manner about occupational options. Results are presented in such a way as to clarify structure and initially expand options, rather than immediately presenting the choice of only one or two occupational options. The client may use the inventory results to move forward in a positive direction toward the best suited career goals. The interpretation material accompanying any one or all three of the measurement dimensions is an exceptional strength of the COPSystem. The career decision-making process is thus enhanced by extensive meaningful decision-making exercises that accompany the measurement instruments.

In years hence, the goal is to continue the development and counseling usefulness of the COPSystem. Data will be submitted to factor analysis to reconfirm the cluster of occupations. Just as career exploration is an ongoing changing process, so is the process of test validation and refinement. It may be that the changing world of work will affect the structuring of occupations in terms of interests, abilities, and values. Perhaps the decline in interest in some outdoor occupations will increase, and the now glamorous computer field will continue to sway more interest into computer technology. Factor analyses of items in the development of the COPS–P tend to support this later trend. It may be the case that the gender gap may close; however, preliminary new data indicate that this is not happening in all career areas. The 1995 norms revision for the COPS indicates an increase in interest for both males and females in the Business clusters. The gender gap seems to have narrowed in the Technology Skilled and Arts Skilled areas. The continued use of factor-analytic technique to examine the structure of interests, abilities, and values will make the instruments both more valid and more useful.

REFERENCES

Allport, G. W., & Vernon, E. (1970). *A study of values*. Boston: Houghton Mifflin.

Bennett, G. K., Seashore, H. G., & Wesman, A. G. (1974). *Differential aptitude tests, manual* (5th ed.). New York: Psychological Corporation.

Bentler, P. M. (1971). Clustran, a program for oblique transformation. *Behavioral Science, 6*, 183–185.

Best, S., & Knapp-Lee, L. (1982). Relationship of interest measurement derived from the COPSystem Interest Inventory and the Kuder General Interest Survey: Construct validation of two measures of occupational activity preferences. *Educational and Psychological Measurement, 42,* 1289–1293.

Brokaw, L. D. (1951). Comparative validity of short vs. long tests. *Journal of Applied Psychology, 35,* 325–330.

Brookings, J. B., & Bolton, B. (1986). Vocational interest dimensions of adult handicapped persons. *Measurement and Evaluation in Counseling and Development, 18,* 168–175.

Campbell, D. P. (1974). *Manual for the Strong-Campbell interest inventory.* Stanford, CA: Stanford University Press.

Durost, W. N., Bixler, H. H., Wrightstone, J. W., Hildreth, G. H., & Lund, K. W. (1970). *Metropolitan Achievement Tests, 1970 edition.* New York: Harcourt, Brace & World.

Gati, I. (1979). A hierarchical model for the structure of vocational interests. *Journal of Vocational Behavior, 15,* 90–106.

Gati, I. (1991). The structure of vocational interests. *Psychological Bulletin, 109,* 309–324.

Guilford, J. P., Christensen, P. R., & Bond, N. A., Jr. (1956). *The DF Opinion Survey.* Los Angeles, CA: Sheridan Psychological Services.

Guilford, J. P., Christensen, P. R., Bond, N. A., Jr., & Sutton, M. A. (1954). A factor analysis study of human interests. *Psychological Monographs, 68*(4).

Guilford, J. P., & Fruchter, B. (1973). *Fundamental statistics in psychology and education* (5th ed.). New York: McGraw-Hill.

Guilford, J. P., Shneidman, E., & Zimmerman, W. S. (1948). *The Guilford-Shneidman-Zimmerman interest study.* Beverly Hills, CA: Sheridan.

Harris, A. J., & Jacobson, M. D. (1972). *Basic elementary reading vocabularies.* London: Macmillan.

Holland, J. L. (1973). *Making vocational choices: A theory of careers.* Englewood Cliffs, NJ: Prentice Hall.

Knapp, L., & Knapp, R. R. (1976). *Career Ability Placement Survey (CAPS).* San Diego, CA: EdITS.

Knapp, L., & Knapp, R. R. (1982). *Career Occupational Preference System, 1998 edition.* San Diego, CA: EdITS.

Knapp, L., & Knapp, R. R. (1986). *COPES manual.* San Diego, CA: EdITS.

Knapp, L., Knapp, R. R., Strnad, L., & Michael, W. B. (1978). Comparative validity of the Career Ability Placement Survey (CAPS) and the General Aptitude Test Battery (GATB) for predicting high school marks. *Educational and Psychological Measurement, 38,* 1053–1056.

Knapp, L., Knapp, R. R., & Knapp-Lee, L. (1992). *CAPS technical manual.* San Diego, CA: EdITS.

Knapp, L., & Knapp-Lee, L. (1996). *COPES Examiner's Manual.* San Diego, CA: EdITS.

Knapp, L. J., & Michael, W. B. (1980). Relationship of work values to corresponding academic success. *Educational and Psychological Measurement, 40,* 487–494.

Knapp, R. R. (1967, November). *Classification of occupational interests into groups and levels.* Paper presented at the Society of Multivariate Experimental Psychology meeting, Berkeley, CA.

Knapp, R. R., & Knapp, L. (1974). *COPS Technical Manual, 1974 edition.* San Diego, CA: EdITS.

Knapp, R. R., & Knapp, L. (1976). *Career Occupational Preference System Intermediate Inventory (COPS II).* San Diego, CA: EdITS.

Knapp, R. R., & Knapp, L. (1978). *Career Orientation Placement and Evaluation Survey (COPES).* San Diego, CA: EdITS.

Knapp, R. R., & Knapp, L. (1979). Relationship of work values to occupational activity interests. *Measurement and Evaluation in Guidance, 12,* 71–78.

Knapp, R. R., & Knapp, L. (1980a). *Career Occupational Preference System Interest Inventory, revised edition (COPS-R).* San Diego, CA: EdITS.

Knapp, R. R., & Knapp, L. (1980b). Second-order group interest factors based on sex-balanced items: Factorial validity of the COPSystem occupational structure. *Educational and Psychological Measurement, 40,* 1091–1098.

Knapp, R. R., Knapp, L., & Buttafuoco, P. M. (1978). Interest changes and the classification of occupations. *Measurement and Evaluation in Guidance, 11,* 14–19.

Knapp, R. R., Knapp, L., & Knapp-Lee, L. (1985). Occupational interest measurement and subsequent career decisions: A predictive follow-up of the COPSystem Interest Inventory. *Journal of Counseling Psychology, 32*, 348–354.

Knapp, R. R., Knapp, L., & Knapp-Lee, L. (1990). *COPSystem technical manual.* San Diego, CA: EdITS.

Knapp, R. R., Knapp, L., & Michael, W. B. (1977). Stability and concurrent validity of the Career Ability Placement Survey (CAPS) against the DAT and the GATB. *Educational and Psychological Measurement, 37*, 1081–1085.

Knapp, R. R., Knapp, L., & Michael, W. B. (1979). The relationship of clustered interest measures and declared college major. Concurrent validity of the COPSystem Interest Inventory. *Educational and Psychological Measurement, 39*, 939–945.

Knapp-Lee, L. (1993). *COPS Picture Inventory of Careers (COPS-PIC).* San Diego, CA: ERAS.

Knapp-Lee, L., Knapp, L., & Knapp, R. R. (1995). *Career Occupational Preference System, 1995 edition.* San Diego, CA: ERAS.

Knapp-Lee, L. J., Knapp, L., & Knapp, R. R. (1982). *Career Occupational Preference System Interest Inventory, Professional Level, Form P.* San Diego, CA: EdITS.

Knapp-Lee, L. J., Knapp, L., & Knapp, R. R. (1990). *COPS-R technical manual.* San Diego, CA: EdITS.

Knapp-Lee, L., & Knapp, L. (1995). *Career Orientation Placement and Evaluation Survey (COPES).* San Diego, CA: ERAS.

Kuder, G. F. (1948). *General Interest Survey, Form C.* Chicago: Science Research Associates.

Kuder, G. F. (1969). A note on the comparability of occupational scores from different interest inventories. *Measurement and Evaluation in Guidance, 2*, 94–100.

Kuder, G. F. (1975). *General Interest Survey, Revised.* Chicago: Science Research Associates.

Lunneborg, C. E., & Lunneborg, P. W. (1975). Factor structure of the vocational models of Roe and Holland. *Journal of Vocational Behavior, 7*, 313–326.

Lunneborg, C. E., & Lunneborg, P. W. (1978). Construct validity of four basic vocational interest factors. *Journal of Vocational Behavior, 12*, 165–171.

Meir, E. I. (1970). Empirical test of Roe's structure of occupations and an alternative interest factors. *Journal of Counseling Psychology, 17*, 41–48.

Meir, E. I. (1973). The structure of occupations by interests—A small space analysis. *Journal of Vocational Behavior, 3*, 21–31.

Meir, E. I., & Barak, A. (1974). A simple instrument for measuring vocational interests based on Roe's classification of occupations. *Journal of Vocational Behavior, 4*, 33–42.

Pryor, R. G. L., & Taylor, N. B. (1986). On combining scores from interest and value measures for counseling. *Vocational Guidance Quarterly, 34*, 178–187.

Roe, A. (1956). *The psychology of occupations.* New York: Wiley.

Roe, A., Hubbard, W. D., Hutchinson, T., & Bateman, T. (1966). Studies of occupational history. Part 1: Job changes and the classification of occupations. *Journal of Counseling Psychology, 13*, 387–393.

Roe, A., & Klos, D. (1969). Occupational classification. *Counseling Psychologist, 3*, 84–89.

Ruch, F. L., & Ruch, W. W. (1963). *Employee aptitude survey, technical report.* Los Angeles: Psychological Services.

Thurstone, L. L. (1931). A multiple factor study of vocational interests. *Personnel Journal, 10*, 198–205.

Thurstone, L. L. (1938). *Primary mental abilities.* Psychometric Monographs, No. 1. Chicago: University of Chicago Press.

Tracey, T., & Rounds, J. (1994). An examination of the structure of Roe's eight interest fields. *Journal of Vocational Behavior, 44*, 279–296.

U.S. Employment Service. (1973). *General Aptitude Test Battery.* Washington, DC: Author.

U.S. Department of Labor. (1998). *Occupational outlook handbook.* Washington, DC: U.S. Government Printing Office.

U.S. Department of Labor, Employment, and Training Administration. (1991). *Dictionary of occupational titles* (4th ed., rev.). Washington, DC: Author.

10

The Self-Directed Search: A Theory-Driven Array of Self-Guiding Career Interventions[1]

Arnold R. Spokane
Michelle Catalano
Lehigh University

The Self-Directed Search (SDS; Holland, 1994a) is a pair of booklets for independent use by clients, accompanied by a growing set of derivative career tools. Because the SDS booklets derive directly from Holland's (1997) theory of the behavior of persons in vocational environments, the array of career interventions that can be conducted using the SDS is also theory driven. The SDS is unique among interest inventories and has established a special niche based on four essential qualities: (a) the organizing system provided by the theory, (b) the self-guiding nature of the inventory booklets—the SDS scoring system requires no electronics, and the scoring process is open to inspection by the respondent, thus becoming an informational intervention in itself, (c) the growing base of studies examining its "functional utility" or therapeutic effects, and (d) its modest cost (Reardon, 1996).

Since its development in 1970, the SDS has been revised and broadened three times (1977, 1985, 1994) to include a coordinated set of forms and closely related products and tools for use in career counseling, organizational development and intervention, workshops, classes, groups and with families. Table 10.1, from Loughead and Linehan (1996), lists the inventories

---

[1]This chapter is an update of a combination of Spokane (1990), with permission of Lawrence Erlbaum Associates, Inc., and Spokane and Holland (1995), with permission of Psychological Assessment Resources. Portions of the text, tables, and figures have been excerpted from the originals.

TABLE 10.1
Self-Directed Search and Supplemental Materials

Title	Purpose
Self-Directed Search Form R	
Self-Directed Search Form R: Software System	Assesses career interests; appropriate for high school, college, and adults.
Self-Directed Search Form R: Computer Version	Computer administration, scoring, and interpretive report.
Self-Directed Search Form R: Interpretive Report	Mail-in service; interpretive report mailed within 24 hr.
Self-Directed Search Form R: Professional Report Service	
Self-Directed Search Form R: Spanish Edition	
Self-Directed Search Form R: Braille Edition	
Self-Directed Search Form R: Vietnamese Edition	
Self-Directed Search Form R: English Canadian	
Self-Directed Search Form R: French Canadian	
Self-Directed Search Form E	Assesses career interests for individuals with limited reading skills; fourth-grade reading level.
Self-Directed Search Form E: English Canadian	
Self-Directed Search Form E: Spanish	
Self-Directed Search Form CP: Career Planning	Assesses long-term career planning; appropriate for those at upper levels of career responsibility.
Self-Directed Search Form CP: Computer Version	Computer administration, scoring, and interpretive report.
Self-Directed Search Form CP: Interpretive Report	Computer interpretive report.
Self-Directed Search Form CP: Professional Report Service	Mail-in interpretive report service.
Self-Directed Search-Career Explorer	Assesses and explores interests for future education and career planning; appropriate for middle- or junior-high-school students.
Self-Directed Search Career Explorer: Interpretive Report	Computer interpretive report.
Self-Directed Search Career Explorer: Professional Report Service	Mail-in interpretive report service.

Position Classification Inventory	Classify jobs or positions in the work environment.
Position Classification Inventory: Professional Report Service	Mail-in interpretive report service.
Vocational Preference Inventory	Assesses career interests using a brief personality inventory; appropriate for adults and older adolescents.
Vocational Preference Inventory: Computer Version	Computer administration, scoring, and interpretive report.
Vocational Exploration and Insight Kit (VEIK)	Career guidance beyond the SDS; appropriate for highly motivated students and adults.
SDS Career Counselor's Kit	Comprehensive kit with samples of four SDS forms: R, E, CP, Career Explorer; EOF, DHOC, and DEO.
1994 SDS Professional User's Guide 1994 SDS Technical Manual	Two manuals detail development, administration, scoring, and interpretation of the SDS.
You and Your Career	Eight-page booklet to enrich the experience of taking the SDS.
Dictionary of Holland Occupational Codes (DHOC)	Provides SDS Summary Codes for 12,860 occupations.
Dictionary of Holland Occupational Codes Computer Search	Computer program provides SDS Summary Codes for 7,500 occupations and 900 programs of study.
The Educational Opportunities Finder (EOF)	Provides educational and vocational areas that match SDS Summary Codes.
Dictionary of Educational Opportunities (DEO)	Description of educational programs that match SDS Summary Codes.
Educational Opportunities: Interpretive Report	Matches Summary Codes to postsecondary school programs and provides program descriptions.
Leisure Activities Finder	Locates leisure activities that match SDS Summary Codes.
Leisure Report: Interpretive Program	Computer interpretive report.
Leisure Report: Professional Report Service	Mail-in interpretive report service.
Making Vocational Choices	Book that presents a comprehensive theory of careers.
Discovering Career Options: Introduction to the Self-Directed Search	Video that introduces the SDS system of career exploration.

Note. Reproduced by special permission of the publisher from *SDS Professional Users Guide* by J. L. Holland, A. B. Powell, and B. A. Fritzche, 1994, Odessa, FL: Psychological Assessment Resources Inc. Copyright © 1985, 1987, 1994 by Psychological Assessment Resources, Inc. Further reproduction is prohibited without permission of PAR Inc.

and applications, which include the six SDS scales (Realistic, Investigative, Artistic, Social, Enterprising, Conventional—hereafter RIASEC) in a clear and concise manner.

This complete set of assessment materials offers a wide range of low-cost career assistance options for the client. These brief, cost-effective, counselor-free interventions are an increasingly popular component of the career counselor's professional array.

PERSON–ENVIRONMENT INTERACTION THEORY: THE ORGANIZING FRAMEWORK FOR THE SDS

The theory that undergirds the SDS has been revised periodically (Holland, 1997) as evidence accumulates testing the theory and its propositions. An understanding of the Holland theory is a prerequisite to competent interpretation of the SDS profile. The theory contains seven principal elements, the first four of which describe how people and jobs are organized:

Principle 1. "Most people can be categorized as one of six personality types labeled Realistic, Investigative, Artistic, Social, Enterprising, or Conventional" (Holland, 1992, pp. 3–5).

Principle 2. "There are six kinds of environments: Realistic, Investigative, Artistic, Social, Enterprising, or Conventional" (Holland, 1992, pp. 3–5).

Principle 3. "People search for environments that will let them exercise their skills and abilities, express their attitudes and values, and take on agreeable problems and roles" (Holland, 1992, pp. 3–5).

Principle 4. "A person's behavior is determined by an interaction between his or her personality and the characteristics of the environment" (Holland, 1992, pp. 3–5).

Table 10.2 contains complete descriptions of the six Holland types derived from empirical studies of their characteristics.

In 1958, Holland described the core of the theory—the projection of one's personality onto the world of work:

> The choice of an occupation is an expressive act which reflects the person's motivation, knowledge, personality, and ability. Occupations represent a way of life, an environment rather than a set of isolated work functions or skills. To work as a carpenter means not only to have a certain status, community role, and a special pattern of living. . . . In this sense, the choice of an occupational title represents several kinds of information: the S's motivation, his knowledge of the occupation in question, his insight and understanding of himself, and his abilities. In short, item responses *may be thought of as limited*

TABLE 10.2
The Six Holland Personality Types and Their Salient Characteristics

	Realistic	Investigative	Artistic	Social	Enterprising	Conventional
Traits (self-ratings)	Hardheaded	Analytical	Aloof	Capable	Aggressive	Content
	Mechanical	Intellectual	Artistic	Enthusiastic	Dominant	Not artistic
	Scientific	Curious	Broad interests	Friendly	Enterprising	Not idealistic
	Quiet	Mechanical	Careless	King	Good Leader	Normal
	Reserved	Scholarly	Disorderly	Kind	Good Leader	Practical-minded
	Unassuming	Scientific	Dreamy	Persuasive	Not Quiet	Shrewd
	Highly trained	Broad interests	Idealistic	Not scientific	Not Scientific	Speculative
	Low self-understanding	Precise	Imaginative	Sincere	Persuasive	Conforming
		Thorough	Intellectual	Trusting	Pleasure-seeking	Conventional
			Introspective	Understanding	Popular	Not original
			Intuitive	Generous	Power-seeking	Conscientious
			Not conforming	Receptive	Practical-minded	Rebellious
			Original	Social	Shrewd	Neat
			Radical	Warm	Sociable	
			Rebellious		Speculative	
			Sensitive		Striving	
			Sophisticated		Versatile	
			Unconventional		Confident	
			Unusual		Energetic	
			Verbal			
			Witty			
			Complicated			
			Power-seeking			
Stereotypes of types	Skilled	Scientific	Creative	Important	Ambitious	Precise
	Mechanically inclined	Intelligent	Imaginative	Influential	Aggressive	Mathematical
	Trained	Studious	Talented	Helpful	Leaders	Methodical
	Builders	Scholarly	Expressive	Devoted	Shrewd	Meticulous
	Practical	Brilliant	Sensitive	Patient	Busy	Unimaginative

(Continued)

343

TABLE 10.2
(Continued)

	Realistic	Investigative	Artistic	Social	Enterprising	Conventional
	Well paid	Inventive Introverted Respected	Interesting Unconventional Temperamental	Understanding Friendly	Responsible Status seeking Dynamic	Invaluable Dull
Inventory and scales	Mechanical Dogmatic	Open Academic type Analytical Curious Mechanical Scholarly Scientific Broad interests	Open Nonconforming Feminine Introverted Original Expressive Nonconformist type	Extroverted Sociable Enthusiastic Liking to help others Feminine Dependent Understanding of others Cooperative Interest in religion Collegiate type	Extroverted Sociable Dominant Enthusiastic Adventurous Dependent (group) Leadership Sociability Self-confidence (social) Popularity Collegiate type	Conservative Dogmatic Vocational type
Values	Institutional restraint Christian conservative Docility Freedom True friendship (–) Ambitious Self-controlled (–) Forgiving (–)	Self-determination Theoretical Adolescent revolt Wisdom Family security (–) True friendship (–) Intellectual Logical Ambitious Cheerful (–)	Self-expression World of beauty Equality Imaginative Courageous Obedient (–) Capable (–) Responsible (–) Clean (–) Logical	Service to others Social Friendly interest Equality Mature love (–) Exciting life (–) Helpful Forgiving Capable (–) Logical (–) Intellectual (–)	Control of others Economic/political Dominant/striving Freedom World of beauty (–) Ambitious Forgiving (–) Helpful (–)	Institutional restraint Christian conservative Economic/political Docility Comfortable life Self-respect (–) World of beauty (–) True friendship (–) Ambitious Polite Obedient Imaginative (–) Forgiving (–)

TABLE 10.2
(Continued)

	Realistic	Investigative	Artistic	Social	Enterprising	Conventional
Life goals	Inventing apparatus or equipment Becoming outstanding athlete	Inventing valuable product Theoretical contribution to science Technical contribution to science	Becoming famous in performing arts Publishing stories Original painting Instrumental musician or singer Musical composition played or published	Helping others in difficulty Making sacrifices for others Competent teacher or therapist Being religious person Being good parent Leader in church Contributing to human welfare	Being well dressed Being community leader Influential in public affairs Expert in finance and commerce	Expert in finance and commerce Producing a lot of work
Aptitudes and competencies	Technical competencies Mechanical ability	Intelligence Mechanical comprehension Arithmetic ability Scientific competencies Math ability Research ability Scientific ability	Musical talent (Seashore) Art judgment (Meier) Spatial Visual (MPFB) Art competencies Foreign language competencies Artistic ability	Interpersonal problem-solving assessment Social and educational competencies Leadership and sales competencies Interpersonal competency	Leaderless group discussion Leadership and competencies Social and educational competencies Business and clerical competencies Interpersonal competency	Clerical aptitudes (Minn. clerical) Business and clerical competencies Clerical ability
Greatest ability lies in area of	Mechanics	Science	Arts	Human relations	Leadership	Business
Identifications	Thomas Edison Admiral Byrd	Madame Curie Charles Darwin	T. S. Eliot Pablo Picasso	Jane Addams Albert Schweitzer	Henry Ford Andrew Carnegie	Bernard Baruch John D. Rockefeller

Note. Reproduced by special permission of the publisher from *SDS Professional Users Guide* by J. L. Holland, A. B. Powell, and B. A. Fritzche, 1994, Odessa, FL.: Psychological Assessment Resources Inc. Copyright © 1985, 1987, 1994 by Psychological Assessment Resources, Inc. Further reproduction is prohibited without permission of PAR Inc.

but useful expressive or projective protocols. (Holland, 1958, p. 336, italics added).

This notion of interests as a reflection of personality provides a more comprehensive basis for clinical interventions, and for extracting more personal meaning from interest inventory scores (Savickas, 1995). Interests, are, in this view, complex indicators of values, needs, self-confidences, and motivations expressed as work preferences.

The remaining theoretic principles describe three diagnostic indicators (congruence, consistency, differentiation), which, when used in combination, constitute one of the few comprehensive, theoretically driven, and empirically validated vocational diagnostic systems.

Principle 5. "The degree of congruence between a person and an occupation (environment) can be estimated by a hexagonal model" (Holland, 1992, p. 4).

Principle 6. "The degree of consistency within a person or an environment is also defined by using the hexagonal model" (Holland, 1992, p. 4).

Principle 7. "The degree of differentiation of a person or an environment modifies predictions made from the SDS profile, from an occupational code, or from their interaction" (Holland, 1992, p. 4).

Congruence. Congruence is a measure of the degree of fit between an individual's personality and the type of work or educational environment that individual inhabits (e.g., an IRC individual in an IRC environment). Congruence can be calculated using first-letter codes in a simple matching formula, using three-letter codes, and using six-letter codes in complex combinations. Congruence is also estimated using one of several mathematical indices (Brown & Gore, 1994; Camp & Chartrand, 1992) in such a way that the properties of the resulting distributions of congruence scores can be examined for skewness, normality, and so on. Unlike most of the indices, the most recent index, "C" (Brown & Gore, 1994), results in an underlying normal distribution, an advantage when conducting multivariate analyses in congruence research studies.

Consistency. Consistency is a measure of the internal harmony within an individual's summary code. Consistency is determined using the first two letters of the three-letter code on the hexagon. Types that are adjacent to each other on the perimeter of the hexagon (e.g., Realistic and Investigative) are more common and therefore harmonious than types that are opposite each other on the perimeter of the hexagon (e. g., Enterprising and Investigative). An individual with an I-E type would be inconsistent. Enterprising and Investigative interests are not often found together and require very different repertoires of behavior.

Differentiation. Differentiation is a measure of the crystallization of interests and provides information about the relative definition of types in an individual's profile. Differentiation can be defined as the highest minus the lowest score among the six types, or it can be calculated using a mathematical index. As Holland indicated, "My purpose was to create a concept that would capture what clinicians mean by a well-defined profile" (Holland, 1992, p. 26).

Finally, the concept of *identity* describes how clear an individual's personality subtype or code is, or, in describing a vocational environment, how clear that environment is. Table 10.3 is a summary of the the diagnostic constructs and interpretive ideas that can be calculated using the code subtypes, and notations in the manual where formulas for these ideas can be found. Empirical evidence for the theory and its propositions, which provide the understructure for the construction, use, and interpretation of the SDS, can be drawn from hundreds of research investigations far too numerous to discuss here. In a recent article, however, Holland (1996) concluded:

Studies show that people flourish in their work environment when there is a good fit between their personality type and the characteristics of the environment. Lack of congruence between personality and environment leads to dissatisfaction, unstable career paths, and lowered performance. (Holland, 1996, p. 397)

CAREER INTERVENTIONS: AN ARRAY OF EFFORTS VARYING IN COUNSELOR AND CLIENT INTENSITY

Figure 10.1 depicts the possible range of strategies available in a comprehensive counseling center, and is based on work to strengthen the career offerings several years ago at the University of Maryland Counseling Center. The treatment array depicted in Fig. 10.1 was first suggested by Magoon (1980), and later described in detail by Westbrook, Gelso, and Spokane, 1989). As the figure implies, interventions can be ordered according to level of counselor involvement on one axis, and level of client investment in time and effort on the other. The complete range of interventions from a brief, counselor-free pamphlet in the upper left quadrant to an extensive individual counseling intervention in the lower right quadrant is ordinarily offered in most counseling centers. The array is ordered on the basis of treatment intensity, which appears to be the only significant treatment characteristic found to produce differential effects in career intervention outcome research studies (Lipsey & Wilson, 1993; Oliver & Spokane, 1988; Spokane & Oliver, 1983).

TABLE 10.3
Summary of Interpretive Ideas and Indexes

Question	Diagnostic construct	Indexes or information	Source
	Basic interpretive ideas		
Degree of fit between:	Congruency	Hexagonal model (no calculation necessary)	Chapter 4; see Appendix B for norms
Current aspiration or occupation and SDS Code?		Zener–Schnuelle Index (7 steps; no calculation necessary)	Table 5; see Appendix B for norms
Current occupation and alternative occupation? Any pair of occupations, aspirations, people?		Iachan Agreement Index (simple arithmetic calculation)	Table 6; see Appendix B for norms
Interest/personality (Interests, traits, life goals, values)	Personality type and SDS profile	Descriptions of the types	Table 12; Holland (1992)
	Supplementary interpretive ideas		
Persistence, tenure, or stability of vocational aspirations, choice, or career	Coherence of vocational aspirations	Summary Code of aspirations (weighted or unweighted)	Chapter 4
		Summary Code of work history	Chapter 5
	Consistency of two-letter code or entire profile	Hexagonal model (adjacent types = very consistent; alternate types = moderately consistent; opposite types = inconsistent)	Chapter 4, Holland (1992); see Appendix B for norms
	Differentiation of entire profile	Highest summary score minus lowest summary score	Chapter 4; see Appendix B for norms
		Iachan Differentiation Index	Table 7; see Appendix B for norms
		Visual inspection: Does the profile of summary scales have high peaks and low valleys or is it relatively flat?	
	Common or rare one-, two-, or three-letter code	Common codes associated with stability; rare codes with change	Chapter 5; see Appendix A for norms

Note. Reproduced by special permission of the publisher from *SDS Professional Users Guide* (p. 42), by J. L. Holland, A. B. Powell, and B. A. Fritzche, 1994, Odessa, FL: Psychological Assessment Resources Inc. Copyright © 1985, 1987, 1994 by Psychological Assessment Resources, Inc. Further reproduction is prohibited without permission of PAR Inc.

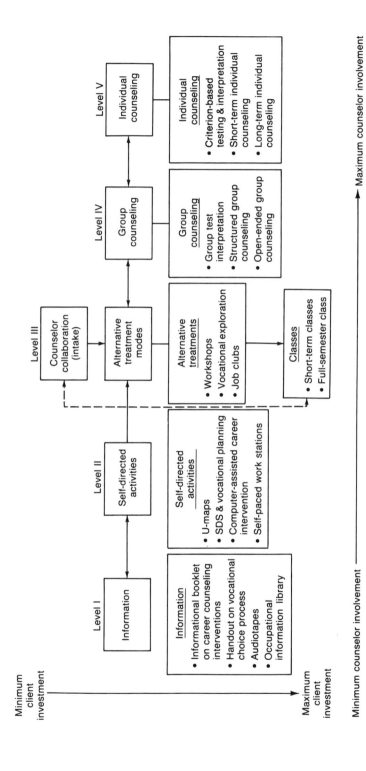

FIG. 10.1. Career intervention at a comprehensive counseling center. From *Testing in Counseling Practice* edited by E. Watkins and V. Campbell, 1990, Hillsdale, NJ: Lawrence Erlbaum Associates.

349

Figure 10.1 presumes a common set of underlying assumptions and processes across diverse intervention strategies. Some writers, with good reason, define career counseling as those counselor-intensive, individual and group strategies (Rounds & Tinsley, 1990) (lower right quadrant of Fig. 10.1). Career counseling in this more limited frame is considered to be a subset of psychotherapy, which can be explained by similar models and theories. Others (Spokane, 1991) include alternative and self-paced interventions (upper left quadrant of Fig. 10.1) in a continuum, arguing that similar client processes underlie the full array of interventions (Holland, Magoon, & Spokane, 1981), and might differ from psychotherapy in important ways. As we learn more about the process of career intervention and counseling (Hill & Spokane, 1995; Spokane et al., 1993), new light may be shed on the nature of client changes involved in the process of career assistance.

THE SDS IS THE BENCHMARK FOR SELF-GUIDED PSYCHOLOGICAL TREATMENTS

The main assumption underlying self-guiding career interventions is that with a minimum of assistance, clients can engage in a systematic exploration of career possibilities and better understand those activities and career options that are appropriate choices considering a client's characteristics. The introduction of self-guiding interest inventories mirrors the emergence of self-help strategies in psychotherapy (Ellis, 1993; Ogles, Lambert, & Craig, 1991; Rosen, 1988, 1993; Scogin, Bynum, Stephens, & Calhoun, 1990), and offers the potential for providing career assistance to a much wider client population than otherwise might receive assistance through traditional diadic interventions. As earlier works have noted (Spokane, 1990), the SDS is the epitome of a self-help psychological intervention. Although caution must be exercised in ensuring that such interventions are employed in a reasonable professional manner (Rosen, 1988, 1993), there is considerable empirical evidence of consistent effects, there are no studies of significant detrimental effects, and clear and unambiguous instructions as well as appropriate cautions are embedded in the materials. In most respects, then, the SDS is the benchmark for self-help psychological devices.

The SDS falls at the upper left quadrant of Fig. 10.1—indicating that it is both low-intensive from the standpoint of the client's investment of energy and time, and low-involving with respect to professional time.

The SDS can serve as a free-standing intervention with modest but consistent outcomes, or as a springboard to more intensive interventions. Reardon (1996) described a comprehensive self-directing career intervention program (including computer-based systems such as the SDS, choices, discover, SIGI plus, card sorts, resources directories, books, audiovisual materials, modules, worksheets, and consumable paper materials). Reardon then compared the costs associated with this self-guiding intervention to those associated with individual career counseling. This comprehensive cost analysis of more than 8,000 self-directing clients and 5,000 individual career counseling clients calculated a variety of fixed and variable costs (e.g., staff coverage, and capacity) associated with each intervention strategy. This remarkable analysis calculated costs for every semester from summer 1989 through spring 1993 at a university career center. The findings revealed that the cost per hour for the self-directed approach was "2.4 times lower" or only 39% of the cost per hour associated with the individual counseling. Although anecdotal evidence is provided for the effectiveness of and client satisfaction with the self-directed intervention (Reardon, 1996) and other evidence supports the consistent effectiveness of self-directing interventions, it is still the case that individual approaches result in more gain (clearly at a much greater cost) than do brief counselor-free alternatives (Oliver & Spokane, 1988; Spokane & Oliver, 1983). Self-guided interventions, however, may reach a different audience that would otherwise have been unable to receive services. Without this complete treatment array (see Fig. 10.1) it is unlikely that most career centers could meet the demand for services placed on them.

The SDS and its theoretical model provide career assistance to individuals, groups, workshops, and classes, and the typology can also be used to organize and interpret client and occupational information in career centers, libraries, and industry settings. This information can also be used in evaluation studies, research, labor-force projections, and strategic and succession planning. In a recent book on applications of the SDS in business and industry, Rose (1996) outlined selection and employee development uses for the RIASEC types.

THE PRIMARY SDS COMPONENTS: THE ASSESSMENT BOOKLET AND THE OCCUPATIONS FINDER

The SDS assessment booklet gauges a person's resemblance to six interest or personality types, and the occupational classification booklet organizes occupations into the same six categories employed in the assessment booklet. Consequently, the respondent can complete the assessment booklet and search the Occupations Finder for compatible occupations. All forms of the SDS employ the same two booklet system. In addition, a third booklet—*You and Your Career* (Holland, 1994b)—provides supplemental information for the respondent on the theory and the interpretation of Holland codes. The SDS contains a daydreams section in which the individual lists occupations under consideration. Called expressed choices, these lists are surprisingly robust estimates of the occupations that respondents eventually enter (see Holland, Fritzsche, & Powell, 1994, p. 4, for a list of these studies on the validity of expressed choice). There are four parts in the SDS that contribute to the calculation of the summary code. These sections are:

- Activities (six scales of 11 items are endorsed like or dislike), which measure personal involvement and potential (e.g., sketch, draw, paint).
- Competencies (six scales of 11 items endorsed yes or no), which estimate proficiencies and skills (e.g., I can play a musical instrument).
- Occupations (six scales of 14 occupational titles endorsed yes or no).
- Self-estimates (two ratings per type of abilities and skills) (e.g., clerical ability, office skills).

After completing the assessment scales, the totals for the subsections of the SDS are transferred to a summary page and added to obtain a total score for each of the six Holland types (Realistic, Investigative, Artistic, Social, Enterprising, Conventional). The highest three total scores indicate the three-letter summary code for use with the Finders. The SDS takes about 35–50 min to complete, and the hand scoring by client or counselor generally takes about 5 min.

Presently there are separate forms for middle-school and high-school students (SDS Career Explorer; Holland & Powell, 1994), both of which can be completed in one class period. There are several forms for adults. There is a form (Form CP) for business and industrial clients who require a version tailored to their unique needs and concerns. There are also forms in Braille and a form for those who read below the sixth grade level (Form Easy). There have been numerous translations of the SDS, and the Spanish, Vietnamese, and French Canadian editions are published in the United States. The SDS inventories are also available in computer versions that administer, score, interpret, and/or embed a person's responses in the context of other client information, although less is known regarding the psychometric properties of these computer-assisted versions of the SDS (McKee & Levinson, 1990).

DERIVATIVE SDS MATERIALS AND TOOLS

User experience with the SDS led to the development of multiple supplementary materials, based on the Holland theory, that are designed to perform specific ancillary functions.

For example, an alphabetized Occupations Finder was developed first to assist test takers in locating occupational codes in the Occupations Finder as the number of occupations included in the Finder increased. Demands for a more comprehensive Occupations Finder led Gary Gottfredson to develop a conversion formula to derive three-letter Holland codes for all occupations in the U.S. labor force—resulting in the *Dictionary of Holland Occupational Codes* (Gottfredson & Holland, 1989; Gottfredson, Holland, & Ogawa, 1982).

Because the dictionary did not allow for unique or eccentric work environments, and because the dictionary was occasionally incomplete regarding a very specific work environment, the Position Classification Inventory (PCI; Gottfredson & Holland, 1991) was developed to permit a small number of employees or supervisors (eight or nine) to rate their work environment using Holland's system. The PCI is an 84-item inventory containing six 13-item scales corresponding to each of the six Holland work environment types. Correlations between supervisor and employee ratings of the same jobs using the PCI were substantial, ranging from .59 to .79. Alpha coefficients ranged from .70 to .94 for a mixed sample of employees and supervisors across scales (Gottfredson & Holland, 1991). There are, as a result of the PCI, two empirical–theoretical tools for classifying any occupational environment.

Three additional exploration devices include the Educational Opportunities Finder (Rosen, Holmberg, & Holland, 1994), a classification of 750 education and training opportunities, and its more elaborate counterpart, the *Dictionary of Educational Opportunities* (Rosen et al., 1994), and the Leisure Activities Finder (Holmberg, Rosen, & Holland, 1990)—a classification of 760 avocations, hobbies, and sports. Because these devices share the same coding system and theoretical underpinning, clients and counselors should find these tools easy to understand and integrate with other information.

The Holland types can also be assessed using the Vocational Preference Inventory (VPI; Holland, 1985), the new Strong Interest Inventory (SII; Harmon, Hansen, Borgen, & Hammer, 1994), the Career Assessment Inventory (CAI; Johansson, 1976), the new ASVAB workbook, a clever and colorful intervention for students (U.S. Department of Defense, 1993), the Vocational Insight and Exploration Kit (VEIK) (Takai & Holland, 1979), and other vocational card sorts. The interchangeability of type scores derived from these various instruments is largely unexplored.

THE SDS MANUALS AND DOCUMENTATION: RELIABILITY, VALIDITY, AND FUNCTIONAL UTILITY

The SDS technical manual (Holland, Fritzsche, & Powell, 1994) summarized the information and history of all SDS forms, including the 1994 edition. Detailed information on the 1994 revision is contained in the 1994 *Technical*

Manual. Although this chapter focuses on the use and effects of the inventory with clients, the substantial database testing the Holland model, the characteristics of the types, and the nature of person–environment interactions is unprecedented as background support for a model underlying an interest inventory (Brown & Brooks, 1996; Holland, 1997; Osipow & Fitzgerald, 1996; Spokane, 1996).

Reliability of the SDS

Internal consistency coefficients (KR-20) for the 1994 edition of the SDS are reported for high-school students, college students, and adults. Coefficients for the summary scales range from .90 to .93 (Holland, Fritzsche, & Powell, 1994). Four- to 12-week test–retest reliabilities for 73 respondents ranged from .76 to .89. Scale differences less than 8 or 9 points are within limits of standard error and are therefore judged to be nonsignificant.

Validity of the SDS

Validity evidence comes from concurrent and predictive studies of the SDS scales when used to predict eventual occupation and or vocational aspirations using the McArthur method. Average hit rate for the 1994 revision was 54.7% (Holland, Fritzsche, & Powell, 1994). The manual summarizes these concurrent and predictive validity findings: "Concurrent validities have ranged from 46.7% to 76.0% hit rates, and predictive validities for 1 to 7 years have ranged from 39.6% to 79.3%" (Holland, Fritzsche, & Powell, 1994, p. 27).

A very large number of studies provide evidence of the convergent and discriminant validity of the SDS types. This information is summarized in Holland, Fritzsche, and Powell (1994) and in Holland (in press). Independent reviews of this body of work support the existence of the types, if not their quasi-circular or hexagonal structure (Herr & Cramer, 1996; Osipow & Fitzgerald, 1996; Spokane, 1991; Walsh & Betz, 1990).

Functional Utility of the SDS

Functional utility is the extent to which the experience of completing an inventory and receiving an interpretation of the results provides useful outcomes for the client. Messick (1995) argued that validity is no longer simply a function of the psychometric properties of the instrument. Validity is also a function of the consequence of any actions that result from an instrument's public use. In his paper on "unified validity," Messick concluded that validity is an integrative combination of traditional psychometric properties, as well as the consequences of utilizing an inventory for various assessment purposes. The outcomes of applying an inventory, then, may be as important to its overall evaluation as its traditional psychometric properties. The SDS is unique among interest inventories in providing substantial evidence for the functional utility of the SDS experience. More than two dozen studies have examined the outcomes of exposure to the SDS, and the moderators that influence those outcomes (Holland, Fritsche, & Powell, 1994; Power, Holland, Daiger, & Takai, 1979).

A brief summary of these outcomes is provided here:

- The SDS provides modest but consistent outcomes (mean effect size about .10) for a variety of individuals at about one third to one half the cost of individual counseling (Reardon, 1996).
- The SDS is most effective with high identity, low indecision clients. Fretz and Leong (1982), for example, concluded that highly indecisive students were less satisfied with the SDS experience than were decisive students. Low-identity students were also less satisfied.
- The SDS will generally increase options under consideration by one serious option that would not otherwise have been considered.
- Task-oriented individuals (I and C types) will derive more benefit than socially oriented individuals (S and E types) (Kivlighan, Hageseth, Tipton, & McGovern, 1981; Kivlighan & Shapiro, 1987).
- No negative or deterioration effects have been associated with the SDS experience.
- Regular sex differences of 5 or 6 points (within error limits) are found on C, E, and I types. Women score higher (8 points) on the Artistic type (within error) and Social type (16 points) and lower on the Realistic type (24 points) than men (Holland, Fritzsche, & Powell, 1994). Although these sex differences can be substantial, an excellent case can be made for considering these differences to be real estimates (Eagly, 1995; Gottfredson, 1983) of existing differences between men and women. The SDS, a raw-score instrument, is one of the only established interest measures that can be used without automatic norm corrections. As Gottfredson argued, the SDS is a reflection of what is, not of what ought to be, in interest measurement. Because of these regular sex differences, however, men and women will differ in the profiles they receive. Women will more likely be Social types, and men more likely Realistic types.

Practitioners will find a comprehensive account of the potential application and interpretation of all SDS forms in the *Professional User's Guide* (Holland, Powell, & Fritzsche, 1994). The information about the use of all SDS forms, reported earlier in manuals and guides, is now integrated in a single guide. Although the essential findings from the technical manual are summarized in the *User's Guide*, its main purpose is application. Figure 10.2,

Step 1

Using the Self-Assessment Booklet, a person:

- lists occupational aspirations
- indicates preferred activities in the six areas
- reports competencies in the six areas
- indicates occupational preferences in the six areas
- rates abilities in the six areas
- scores the responses he/she has given and calculates six summary scores
- obtains a three-letter code from the three highest summary scores

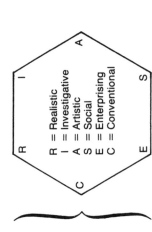

R = Realistic
I = Investigative
A = Artistic
S = Social
E = Enterprising
C = Conventional

Step 2

Using the Occupations Finder, a person:

- locates among the 1,156 occupations those with codes that resemble his/her summary code

Step 3

The person compares the code for his/her current vocational aspiration with the summary code to determine the degree of agreement.

Step 4

The person is encouraged to take some "Next Steps" to enhance the quality of his/her vocational decision-making.

FIG. 10.2. Steps in the SDS exploration process. Reproduced by special permission of the publisher from *SDS Professional Users Guide* by J. L. Holland, A. B. Powell, and B. A. Fritzche, 1994, Odessa, FL: Psychological Assessment Resources Inc. Copyright © 1985, 1987, 1994 by Psychological Assessment Resources, Inc. Further reproduction is prohibited without permission of PAR Inc.

for example, taken from the *User's Guide*, is a diagram of the exploration process that occurs when a respondent completes the SDS.

Even though the SDS and its associated interventions are designed to be self-interpreting, and to require minimal assistance from a counselor, there are ways to strengthen counselor-mediated interpretations of the SDS when they occur in the context of more comprehensive career counseling interventions in individual, group, workshop or class settings. The use of these methods can help to maximize the amount of information from the inventory that is absorbed and retained by the client. One excellent guide to test interpretation prepared by Tinsley and Bradley (1986) was the source of several of these suggestions. Tinsley and Bradley's (1986) general guidelines for test interpretation are easily adapted for self-guiding interest inventories if references to the counselor are exchanged for references to the interpretive materials accompanying the self-guided inventory. For example, Tinsley and Bradley cautioned that the counselor should understand fully what the test scores mean. Certainly, a self-guided interpretation should have as its primary goal the client's complete understanding of the test scores. Tinsley and Bradley offered several additional suggestions for test interpretation that also apply to interest inventories, including: (a) Integrate test results with other available information, (b) keep the client's goals in mind, (c) consider the precision of the test, (d) accentuate positive information but don't avoid the negative, (e) encourage client reaction and feedback, and (f) show the client the test profile.

Similarly, Pope (1992) outlined 10 critical responsibilities professionals have during the process of providing psychological test feedback to clients. These responsibilities include: (a) viewing the testing situation as a feedback process, (b) clarifying roles and tasks of both the professional and the client, (c) responding effectively in a crisis, (d) placing the feedback within a cognitive framework, maintaining records, documentation, and follow-up, (e) considering future uses of the test feedback, (f) acknowledging the fallibility of the test, (g) minimizing the possibility of misuse, distortion, or bias resulting from the feedback, and (h) gauging the client's reactions to the process. It seems reasonable to apply these standards to self-guiding interpretations, and to bear in mind the necessity for clear and unambiguous instructions in a self-guiding assessment procedure.

In addition to these general suggestions, a self-guiding interpretation should accomplish three additional outcomes, as follows.

Provide a Cognitive Framework for Understanding Test Scores. Holland et al. (1981) argued that advanced cognitive organizers could improve the amount of information the client absorbed and retained following interpretation of an interest inventory. Indeed, Fogg (1983) showed that providing a cognitive framework such as UMAPs (see Fig. 10.3 and Jacoby, Rue, &

Find Yourself

AT MARYLAND

Which of these descriptions sound most like you?

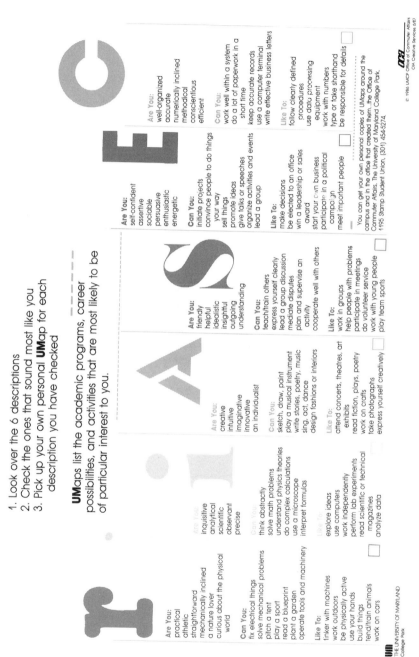

FIG. 10.3. U-MAP. Copyright © 1986 by University of Maryland College Park, Office of Commuter Affairs. Reprinted with permission.

Allen, 1984) prior to the SDS improved the client's ability to remember the information presented in the inventory. The UMAPs teach the Holland system as a way of understanding college majors and academic and nonacademic opportunities available at the University of Maryland. Subjects who received the UMAP intervention showed significantly higher posttest absorption rates $(F = 5.35, df = 1, 26, p .< 05)$ than subjects who received no such framework. Those subjects who received the organizer reported needing significantly less posttest information than those who did not receive the organizer.

Provide a Direct Link to a Valid Job Classification System and to Educational Options. Revised APA–AERA test standards require that when job possibilities are suggested to a client, the system used to attach these jobs to the inventory results must be provided in the interpretive materials. The SDS provides not only a theory-driven set of links in the form of the Finders and the Holland dictionary (Gottfredson & Holland, 1989), but also, an empirical link to the *Dictionary of Occupational Titles* (DOT; U.S. Department of Labor, 1977) and its embedded classification system. In some cases, computer-assisted interventions employing the SDS can be customized to use a corporation's job base as its linking mechanism.

Provide Referral and Resource Information. Referral information can be in the form of books, materials for further reading, or suggestions for locating further professional assistance. The SDS provides referral resources at the national level. Individual centers that employ the inventory usually provide supplemental resources as well (Reardon, 1996).

WHY THE SDS?

Rayman (1982) offered six reasons for selecting an interest inventory, three of which are relevant to self-guiding inventories such as the SDS. Interest inventories provide a systematic way of thinking about one's interests, and about the world of work. According to Rayman, this orderly understanding is the first step toward an informed career choice. Second, Rayman argued, interest inventories simulate broad, systematic exploration of options—an outcome that the SDS has repeatedly been shown to accomplish (Fretz & Leong, 1982). Finally, Rayman noted, interest inventories reassure clients of the validity of their choices, thereby releasing energy previously tied up in indecision, or ambivalence. The release of energy that accompanies confirmation of one's choices can then be directed toward self-enhancing action (mobilization) on the part of the client.

A self-guiding inventory can be given to the client to complete as a homework assignment that provides imediate feedback and a sense of accomplishment. Rayman concluded that the SDS is the treatment of choice at several career development centers because it is cost-effective and convenient, and because the open nature of its scoring adds to the educational value of the intervention.

For Ruth, the case that follows, the SDS was a growth and confirmation experience, taken not because a decision was imminent, but simply to confirm a satisfactory choice. In normal practice, however, the SDS is taken home with the client, and then discussed during one or more counseling sessions in the context of other information and inventory information. Although in Ruth's case no other intervention was necessay or desireable, had this been a more comprehensive counseling case, or had substantial barriers or impediments existed, it may well have been adviseable to use the SDS in the context of other criterion-based inventories such as the SII, the Kuder, or the CISS.

RUTH—A NATURAL COUNSELOR: A SAMPLE CASE USING THE SDS

A professional colleague, Ruth, a 43-year-old school guidance counselor with a master's degree, completed the SDS, and used the Leisure Activities Finder in addition to the regular Finder. Ruth reports being very satisfied in her job, which she has held for 3 years. "I think it's perfect. I feel competent in it, and I think I am paid fairly. I still have a lot of things to learn, but I look forward to learning them." She agreed to complete the SDS in order to learn more about the instrument and its potential for use with high-school populations. Ruth had never taken an SDS herself, but was familiar with the theory and with the SDS as an instrument.

Figure 10.4 contains the Summary Page from Ruth's SDS. Ruth's summary code was SIE, and she reports being surprised at how high her "I" score was. "I think I have more I competencies than I do I interest." Ruth made one minor scoring error, resulting in a one-point discrepancy in her Social high point code. In order to better interpret the meaning of these scores, we used the norm tables in the *Technical Manual* to calculate the percentile levels for the summary code scores, differentiation, consistency, and congruence. Table 10.4 contains Ruth's summary codes and their percentile ranks. The SIE code is a fairly common one, occurring in 2.22% of the 1994 validation sample. Her Social score (82nd percentile) is clearly a high one, although her Investigative score (78th percentile) is also high. Ruth's differentiation score when calculated by the traditional method [highest score (42) minus lowest score (10) = 32] is at the 74th percentile. Using the Iachan

How To Organize Your Answers _____

Start on page 4. Count how many times you said **L** for "Like." Record the number of **Ls** or **Ys** for each group of Activities, Competencies, or Occupations on the lines below.

Activities (pp. 4-5)	3	3	5	10	6	0
	R	I	A	S	E	C

Competencies (pp. 6-7)	4	7	0	7	5	5
	R	I	A	S	E	C

Occupations (p. 8)	0	4	2	12	4	0
	R	I	A	S	E	C

Self-Estimates (p. 9) (What number did you circle?)	4	6	3	6	4	2
	R	I	A	S	E	C

	2	5	1	7	5	3
	R	I	A	S	E	C

Total Scores (Add the five R scores, the five I scores, the five A scores, etc.)	13	25	11	42	24	10
	R	I	A	S	E	C

The letters with the three highest numbers indicate your Summary Code. Write your Summary Code below. (If two scores are the same or tied, put both letters in the same box.)

Summary Code

S	I	E
Highest	2nd	3rd

FIG. 10.4. SDS summary page for Ruth, a 43-year-old guidance counselor. Reproduced by special permission of the publisher from *Self-Directed Search Form R: 1994 Edition (Assessment booklet, p. 10),* by J. L. Holland, 1994, Odessa, FL: Psychological Assessment Resources Inc. Copyright © by Psychological Assessment Resources, Inc. Further reproduction is prohibited without permission of PAR Inc.

TABLE 10.4
Ruth's Summary Code Scores and Percentile Ranks

Type	R	I	A	S	E	C
Raw score	13	25	11	42	24	10
Percentile	44	78	19	82	52	9

Note. Reproduced by special permission of the publisher from *SDS Professional Users Guide* by J. L. Holland, A. B. Powell, and B. A. Fritzche, 1994, Odessa, FL: Psychological Assessment Resources Inc. Copyright © 1985, 1987, 1994 by Psychological Assessment Resources, Inc. Further reproduction is prohibited without permission of PAR Inc.

Differentiation Index (see SDS *Technical Manual*), which utilizes the relative differentiation of the first three scores in the code from the fourth, however, the differentiation score is at the 97th percentile, a better reflection of the high level of differentiation we see in Ruth's code. The formula for the Iachan Differentiation Index is a straightforward one:

$$L_1 = \frac{1}{2}\left[X_1 - \frac{X_2 + X_4}{2}\right]$$

where

X_1 = highest score in a profile

X_2 = second highest score

X_4 = fourth highest score

Consistency for Ruth's code is moderate, with the first two letters of her code SI being one removed (one apart, but not opposite or adjacent) from each other around the hexagon (see Fig. 10.5), a consistency score in the 38th percentile using the consistency norms in the SDS *Technical Manual*. This consistency score reflects the fact that an SI code may not comfortably fit together, and may indicate some internal friction or conflict between aspects of Ruth's personality (SA or SE would have been more consistent). The hexagon, then, is a two-dimensional representation of the statistical distances among the six Holland types in naturally occurring three-letter codes.

Finally, if we presume the work environment of a counselor to be S, or SER using the Holland dictionary (Gottfredson & Holland, 1989), we can calculate congruence using the Zener and Schnuelle (1976) conversion, which would yield a congruence level at the 73rd percentile, or we can use the Iachan congruence formula, which is calculated using Table 10.5.

The Iachan procedure yields a congruence score at the 90th percentile—again a better estimate of the degree of congruence in the profile and more consistent with the client's self-expressions regarding her satisfaction with her job. A somewhat different work environment profile for a counselor was generated by a sample of 11 counselors in the PCI manual, and is reprinted

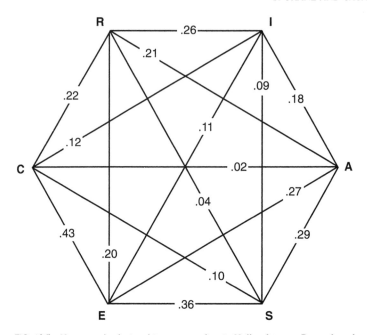

FIG. 10.5. Hexagonal relationships among the six Holland types. Reproduced by special permission of the publisher from *SDS Professional Users Guide* by J. L. Holland, A. B. Powell, and B. A. Fritzche, 1994, Odessa, FL: Psychological Assessment Resources Inc. Copyright © 1985, 1987, 1994 by Psychological Assessment Resources, Inc. Further reproduction is prohibited without permission of PAR Inc.

TABLE 10.5
Calculation of the Iachan Agreement Index Using SDS Summary Code

Occupation Code	First-Letter Match	Second-Letter Match	Third-Letter Match	No Match
First letter	22	10	4	0
Second letter	10	5	2	0
Third letter	4	2	1	0

Note. Reproduced by special permission of the publisher from *SDS Professional Users Guide* by J. L. Holland, A. B. Powell, and B. A. Fritzche, 1994, Odessa, FL: Psychological Assessment Resources Inc. Copyright © 1985, 1987, 1994 by Psychological Assessment Resources, Inc. Further reproduction is prohibited without permission of PAR Inc.

in Fig. 10.6. Use of the profile from the PCI manual would result in even higher congruence estimates for Ruth.

Ruth used the Leisure Finder to explore avocational activities, and discovered that three seemed interesting to her—Social Activism, Self-Help Groups, and Adult Education. Indeed, Ruth reports having engaged in each

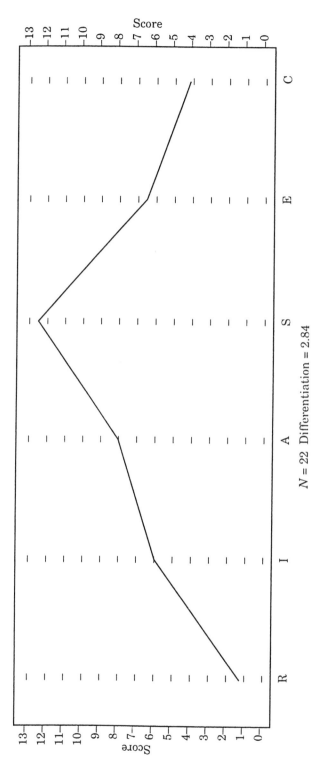

FIG. 10.6 Sample PCI profile for the occupation of Counselor ($n = 11$). From *Position Classification Inventory* (p. 14), by G. D. Gottfredson and J. L. Holland, 1991, Odessa, FL: Psychological Assessment Resources. Copyright © 1991 by Psychological Assessment Resources. Reprinted with permission.

$N = 22$ Differentiation = 2.84

of these activities at one time in her life and had worked in adult education for several years. Ruth did note that many of the activities she was interested in were SR in nature—a reflection of her outdoor interests, and, interestingly, consistent with the counselor type.

In short, Ruth has a highly differentiated three-letter code with a strong Social component. She demonstrates many of the skills associated with the Social Holland type, including strong interactive skills with a wide range of individuals, and very good counseling skills. She is congruent, although moderately inconsistent in theoretical terms, and her profile is quite consistent with her self-reports regarding her feelings about her job.

A 3-year follow up of Ruth finds her having changed schools within her district to obtain a permanent job and certificate. Ruth is still happy with her job, reports very heavy work loads, but enjoys the work immensely. She has developed strong collegial relationships, and has excellent rapport with students. Ruth now has tenure, and reports every intention of staying with her present job and school on a permanent basis

THE FUTURE OF THE SDS AS A SELF-GUIDING INTEREST INVENTORY

Estimates by the publisher indicate that the SDS is the most popular interest inventory in use today. Its popularity is based on its desireable psychometric properties, its theoretical undepinning, its functional utility, its modest cost, and constant efforts by its author and publisher to expand and enhance the set of SDS materials. Work on the theory continues and is reflected in Holland's 1996 APA Award paper and in his new book (1997), which should stimulate another wave of theory-related research. Several topics are the focus of more recent and forthcoming research efforts. These topics include expanded examination of the overlap between interests and personality as measured by the NEO-PIR (Costa, McCrae, & Holland, 1984), especially when neuroticism is removed from the comparisons (Borgen, 1986). Additionally, there seems to be renewed interest in well-controlled laboratory studies of the interaction of people in environments (Helms, 1996), stimulated in part by decreasing returns from descriptive and correlational field studies and in part by the more complex hypotheses and questions being raised as person–environment interaction theory matures.

Although the move to "over-the-counter" interest inventories predicted in an earlier edition of this book has not materialized (Spokane, 1990), users are increasingly employing computer-assisted versions of psychological tests (Gati & Blumberg, 1991). We are probably not far from online career interventions on the Internet, similar to those online interventions such as CAREER-POINT offered to employees at major corporations. Emerging work at Stanford University and elsewhere suggests several possible such interventions.

CONCLUDING COMMENT

The SDS and its derivative materials have dramatically altered the shape of career interventions and our thinking about the process, goals, and outcomes of career intervention. These theory-driven inventories have a firm place in the array of career interventions. When self-guiding interpretation materials are properly designed and evaluated they result in modest but reliable gains for more healthy users. The future of self-guided interventions such as the SDS lies in improved understanding of the underlying mechanisms inducing gain in these interventions, and in strategies to increase their potency and relevancy for all users.

REFERENCES

Borgen, F. H. (1986). New approaches to the assessment of interests. In W. B. Walsh and S. H. Osipow (Eds.), *Advances in Vocational Psychology, Vol. 7. The Assessment of Interests* (pp. 83–125). Hillsdale, NJ: Lawrence Erlbaum Associates.

Brown, D., & Brooks, L. (1996). *Career choice and development* (4th ed). San Francisco: Jossey-Bass.

Brown, S. D., & Gore, P. A. (1994). An evaluation of interest congruence indices: Distribution characteristics and measurement properties. *Journal of Vocational Behavior, 45*, 310–327.

Camp, C. C., & Chartrand, J. M. (1992). A comparison and evaluation of interest congruence indices. *Journal of Vocational Behavior, 41*, 162–182.

Costa, P. T., Jr., McRae, R. R., & Holland, J. L. (1984). Personality and vocational interests in adulthood. *Journal of Applied Psychology, 69*, 390–400.

Eagly, A. H. (1995). The science and politics of comparing women and men. *American Psychologist, 50*, 145–158.

Ellis, A. (1993). The advantages and disadvantages of self-help therapy materials. *Professional Psychology: Research and Practice, 24*, 335–339.

Fogg, N. J. (1983). *Use of advanced cognitive organizers in the interpretation of interests inventories.* Unpublished master's thesis, University of Maryland, College Park.

Fretz, B. R., & Leong, F. T. L. (1982). Career development status as a predictor of career intevention outcomes. *Journal of Counseling Psychology, 29*, 388–393.

Gati, I., & Blumberg, D. (1991). Computer versus counselor interpretation of interest inventories: The case of the Self-Directed Search. *Journal of Counseling Psychology, 38*, 350–366.

Gottfredson, G. D., & Holland, J. L. (1989). *Dictionary of Holland occupational codes* (2nd ed.). Odessa, FL: Psychological Assessment Resources.

Gottfredson, G. D., & Holland, J. L. (1991). *Position Classification Inventory manual* Odessa, FL: Psychological Assessment Resources.

Gottfredson, G. D., Holland, J. L., & Ogawa, D. K. (1982). *Dictionary of Holland occupational codes.* Palo Alto, CA: Consulting Psychologists Press.

Gottfredson, L. S. (1983). The sex fairness of unnormed interest inventories. *Vocational Guidance Quarterly, 31*, 128–132.

Harmon, L. W., Hansen, J. C., Borgen, F. H., & Hammer, A. L. (1994). *Strong Interest Inventory: Applications and technical guide.* Palo Alto, CA: Consulting Psychologists Press.

Helms, S. T. (1996). Some experimental tests of Holland's cogency hypothesis: The reactions of high school students to occupational stimulations. *Journal of Career Assessment, 4*, 253–268.

Herr, E. L., & Cramer, S. H. (1996). *Career guidance and counseling through the lifespan* (5th ed.). New York: Harper Collins.

Hill, A., & Spokane, A. R. (1995). Career counseling and possible selves: A case study analysis. *Career Development Quarterly*

Holland, J. L. (1958). A personality inventory employing occupational titles. *Journal of Applied Psychology, 42*, 336–342.

Holland, J. L. (1985). *Manual for the Vocational Preference Inventory.* Odessa, FL: Psychological Assessment Resources.

Holland, J. L. (1992). *Making vocational choices: A theory of vocational personalities and work environments.* Odessa, FL: Psychological Assessment Resources.

Holland, J. L. (1994a). *The Self-Directed Search (1994 edition).* Odessa, FL: Psychological Assessment Resources.

Holland, J. L. (1994b). *You and your career.* Odessa, FL: Psychological Assessment Resources.

Holland, J. L. (1996). Exploring careers with a typology: What we have learned and some new directions. *American Psychologist, 51*, 397–406.

Holland, J. L. (1997). *Making vocational choices: A theory of vocational personalities and work environments* (3rd ed.) Odessa, FL: Psychological Assessment Resources.

Holland, J. L., Fritzche, B. A., & Powell, A. B. (1994). *Technical manual for the Self-Directed Search.* Odessa, FL: Psychological Assessment Resources.

Holland, J. L., Magoon, T. M., & Spokane, A. R. (1981). Counseling psychology: Career interventions, research, and theory. *Annual Review of Psychology, 32*, 279–305.

Holland, J. L., & Powell, A. B. (1994). *SDS career explorer.* Odessa, FL: Psychological Assessment Resources.

Holland, J. L., Powell, A. B., & Fritzsche, B. A. (1994). *Professional users guide of the Self-Directed Search .* Odessa, FL: Psychological Assessment Resources.

Holmberg, K., Rosen, D., & Holland, J. L. (1990). *The Leisure Activities Finder.* Odessa, FL: Psychological Assessment Resources.

Jacoby, B., Rue, P., & Allen, K. (1984). UMAPS: A person–environment approach to helping students make critical choices. *Personnel and Guidance Journal, 62*, 426–428.

Johansson, C. B. (1976). *Manual for the career assessment inventory.* Minneapolis, MN: National Computer Systems.

Kivlighan, D. M. Jr., & Shapiro, R. M. (1987). Holland type as a predictor o benefit from self-help counseling. *Journal of Counseling Psychology, 34*, 326–329.

Kivlighan, D. M., Jr., Hageseth, J. A., Tipton, R. M., & McGovern, T. V. (1981). Effects of matching treatment approaches and personality types in group vocational counseling. *Journal of Counseling Psychology, 28*, 315–320.

Lipsey, M. W., & Wilson, D. B. (1993). The efficacy of psychological, educational, and behavioral treatment: Confirmation from meta-analysis. *American Psychologist, 48*, 1181–1209.

Loughead, T. A., & Linehan, P. (1996). The basics of using the Self-Directed Search in business and industry. In M. Shahanasarian (Ed.). *The Self-Directed Search (SDS) in business and industry: A resource guide* (pp. 1–26). Odessa, FL: Psychological Assessment Resources.

Magoon, T. M. (1980). The eye of a beholder. *Counseling Psychologist, 8*, 26–28.

McKee, L. M., & Levinson, E. M. (1990). A review of the computerized version of the Self-Directed Search. *Career Development Quarterly, 38*, 325–333.

Messick, S. (1995). Validity of psychological assessment: Validation of inferences from person's responses and performances as scientific Inquiry into score meaning. *American Psychologist, 50*, 741–749.

Ogles, B. M., Lambert, M. J., & Craig, D. E. (1991). Comparison of self-help books for coping with loss: Expectations and attributions. *Journal of Counseling Psychology, 38*, 387–393.

Oliver, L. W., & Spokane, A. R. (1988). Career counseling outcome: What contributes to client gain? *Journal of Counseling Psychology, 35*, 447–462.

Osipow, S. H., & Fitzgerald, L. (1996). *Theories of career development* (4th ed.). Boston: Allyn & Bacon.

Pope, K. S. (1992). Responsibilities in providing psychological test feedback to clients. *Psychological Assessment, 4,* 268–271.

Power, P. G., Holland, J. L., Daiger, D. C., & Takai, R. T. (1979). The relation of student characteristics to the influence of the Self-Directed Search. *Measurement and Evaluation in Guidance, 12,* 98–107.

Rayman, J. R., (1982). *Selecting an interest inventory: A case for the SDS.* Unpublished manuscript, Iowa State University, Ames, IA.

Reardon, R. (1996). A program and cost analysis of a self-directed career decision-making program in a university career center. *Journal of Counseling and Development, 74,* 280–285.

Rose, R. (1996). Using the RIASEC scales in selection and development in business. In M. Shahanasarian (Ed.), *The Self-Directed Search in business and industry: A resource guide* (pp.). Odessa, FL: Psychological Assessment Resources.

Rosen, D., Holmberg, K., & Holland, J. L. (1994). *The Educational Opportunities Finder.* Odessa, FL: Psychological Assessment Resources.

Rosen, G. M. (1988). Self-help treatment books and the commercialization of psychotherapy. *American Psychologist, 42,* 46–51.

Rosen, G. M. (1993). Self-help or self-hype? Comments on psychology's failure to advance self care. *Professional Psychology: Research and Practice, 24,* 340–345.

Rounds, J. B., & Tinsley, H. E. A. (1994). Diagnosis and treatment of vocational problems. In S. D. Brown & R. W. Lent (Eds.), *Handbook of Counseling Psychology* (pp. 137–177). New York: Wiley.

Rounds, J. B., & Tracey, T. J. (1990). From trait-factor to person-environment fit counseling: Theory and Process. In W. B. Walsh & S. H. Osipow (Eds.), *Career counseling: Contemporary topics in vocational psychology* (pp. 1–44). Hillsdale, NJ: Lawrence Erlbaum Associates.

Savickas, M. L. (1995). Examining the personal meaning of inventoried interests during career counseling. *Journal of Career Assessment, 3,* 188–201.

Scogin, F., Bynum, J., Stephens, G., & Calhoun, S. (1990). Efficacy of self-administered treatment programs: Meta-analytic review. *Professional Psychology: Research and Practice, 21,* 42–47.

Spokane, A. R. (1990). Self-guided interest inventories as career interventions: The Self-Directed Search. In C. E. Watkins & V. L. Campbell (Eds.), *Testing in counseling practice* (pp. 285–316). Hillsdale, NJ: Lawrence Erlbaum Associates.

Spokane, A. R. (1991). *Career intervention.* Englewood Cliffs, NJ: Prentice Hall.

Spokane, A. R. (1996). Holland's theory of personalities in work environments. In D. Brown & L. Brooks (Eds.), *Career choice and development* (4th ed., pp.). San Francisco: Jossey-Bass.

Spokane, A. R., Fretz, B. R., Hoffman, M. A., Nagel, D. P., Davison-Aviles, R. M., & Jaschik-Herman, M. L. (1993). Forty cases: A framework for studying the effects of career counseling on career and personal adjustment. *Journal of Career Assessment, 1,* 118–129.

Spokane, A. R., & Oliver, L. W. (1983). Outcomes of vocational intervention. In S. H. Osipow & W. B. Walsh (Eds.), *Handbook of vocational psychology* (Vol. 2, pp. 99–136). Hillsdale, NJ: Lawrence Erlbaum Associates.

Takai, R., & Holland, J. L. (1979). Comparative influence of the Vocational Card Sort, the Self-Directed Search, and the Vocational Exploration and Insight Kit. *Vocational Guidance Quarterly, 27,* 312–318.

Tinsley, H. E. A., & Bradley, R. W. (1986). Test interpretation. *Journal of Counseling and Development, 64,* 462–466.

U.S. Department of Defense. (1993). *Exploring careers: The ASVAB workbook.* Chicago: Author, HQUSMEPCOM/MEPCO.

U.S. Department of Labor (1977). *Dictionary of occupational tables* (4th ed.). Washington, DC.: U.S. Government Printing Office.

Walsh, W. B., & Betz, N. E. (1990). *Tests and Assessment* (2nd ed.). Englewood Cliffs, NJ: Prentice Hall.

Westbrook, F. W., Gelso, C. J., & Spokane, A. R. (1989). Unpublished document, Counseling Center, University of Maryland, College Park, MD.

Zener, T. B., & Schnuelle, L. (1976). Effects of the Self-Directed Search on high school students. *Journal of Counseling Psychology, 23*, 353–359.

11

Using Vocational Card Sorts in Career Counseling

Robert B. Slaney
Pennsylvania State University

Fiona MacKinnon-Slaney
Bowling Green State University

This chapter explores the use of vocational card sorts in career counseling and career exploration. The chapter begins by examining briefly the status of career counseling in counseling psychology. The exploration of this issue presents an important backdrop for the chapter, and it emphasizes how the card sort technique may provide at least a partial response to some of the current concerns that seem relevant and somewhat troubling to career counseling. After the introductory exploration of these concerns, the background and development of the vocational card sorts are explored. Available card sorts are briefly reviewed. Then the use of the card sort technique with clients is examined, a description of its administration is provided, and a discussion of some of its effects on clients is presented. A case example is included. Finally the available research is reviewed, the card sort technique is evaluated, and future directions for development and research are explored.

CURRENT STATUS OF CAREER COUNSELING

There is a skit done by "Monty Python and the Flying Circus" that has a reporter approaching a man on the street to get his opinion on an issue. The man declines to give his opinion because, as he says, "I am an accountant and therefore too boring to be of interest to anyone." It appears that career counselors may be perceived as being in a somewhat similar situation within applied psychology. The results of a number of studies seem consistent with this possibility. More specifically, the studies seem to suggest that counseling psychologists (especially younger counseling psychologists) who have been trained in and associated with career counseling are considerably less interested in this endeavor than they are in individual counseling/therapy (Birk & Brooks, 1986; Fitzgerald & Osipow, 1986; Gelso et al., 1985; Pinkney & Jacobs, 1985; Watkins, Lopez, Campbell, & Himmell, 1986).

Fitzgerald and Osipow (1986), for example, concluded that "vocational psychology and its applied arm, vocational/career counseling, long the single most identifiable characteristic of counseling psychologists, appear to be eroding as the foundation of the discipline" (p. 537). Similarly, Watkins et al. (1986) noted that if vocational work "continues to be engaged in minimally and is increasingly unattractive to counseling psychologists, a reevaluation of its place in counseling psychology may be needed" (p. 307). Although these recent studies suggest that concerns about the status of career counseling are particularly widespread at present, it can be legitimately argued that they have been in clear evidence for at least the last 15–20 years. There may be some change in the degree to which the importance of career counseling is being questioned, there may be increased openness in discussing this issue, and there may be some additional reasons for this questioning, but the issue itself does not seem to be new.

Whether the issue is new or not, the effect seems evident. Career counseling is perceived, at least by some, as less important than the provision of "personal" counseling or psychotherapy. If this is the case, then a central question that deserves attention is, why has this perception developed? This question is only touched on in this chapter. The intent is not to provide an exhaustive discussion of this topic but simply to mention a number of possible issues that seem important. These issues are also seen as forming a backdrop for the presentation of the vocational card sort technique and for why the technique seems particularly relevant at present.

There are at least five possible issues related to the perception of career counseling as less important than counseling/psychotherapy: (a) the position of counseling psychology relative to clinical and the other helping professions; (b) the status and isolation of courses on career theories and career development in graduate training; (c) the status of career counseling in practicum training and counseling services; (d) the position of career theories in counseling psychology in particular and in psychology in general; and (e) the techniques and approaches that are used in career counseling. These are discussed briefly here.

The first hypothesized reason for the current status of career counseling concerns the status of counseling psychology relative to the other helping professions. Although it perhaps oversimplifies issues, there appears to be some truth to the statement that counseling psychologists generally do not wish to be mistaken for the much maligned and stereotyped high-school guidance counselor. On the other hand, some counseling psychologists may object very little, if at all, to being mistaken for clinical psychologists. This attitude may suggest syllogistically that: (A) clinical psychologists are better than counseling psychologists, (B) clinical psychologists do therapy and they *do not do* career counseling, and (C) therefore, doing therapy is better. These attitudes, if accurate, seem connected to the pecking order that many perceive in the helping professions in general and in professional psychology specifically. This order places counseling psychologists somewhere between counselors and clinical psychologists. It may be that career counseling, in the minds of many, is more closely related to the tasks appropriate for the counselor than to the tasks appropriate for a psychologist. The acknowledgment of this attitude is often impeded by a closely related second attitude that suggests that it is not in good taste to openly express the first attitude.

A second reason for the secondary status of career counseling relates to the place of courses in career theories or career development in the graduate curriculum. As graduate students we took a course in vocational behavior. We have also taught such courses for several years, and have observed similar courses being taught for even more years. It seems clear, from our admittedly limited sample, that typically, graduate students in counseling psychology enter graduate study with little or no background in this topic. In addition, courses on career development, vocational behavior, career guidance, or whatever they are named, are often perceived as isolated or different from the rest of the courses and curriculum in counseling psychology. In many curricula, this perceived isolation has an element of reality. This isolation does not work in favor of career counseling because career counseling does not command a central role in most graduate programs. Beyond this, graduate students, despite a lack of background in career courses, frequently expect the course or courses on career topics to be uninteresting.

The status of career counseling in practica and counseling services also has an important effect on its perception. Some programs do not require practicum experience in career counseling, and those that do often find students have less interest and give less attention to their career clients. This is illustrated in the recent study by Gelso et al. (1985). Perhaps this attitude toward career counseling also relates to the pecking order that may determine who actually provides career counseling in particular counseling services. In many centers there is a clear, if often unstated, difference in the status in those who do career counseling and those who do "personal" counseling or psychotherapy. At times, there may appear to be a realistic basis for some of these attitudes. It is sometimes suggested that this basis is the repetitive and frustrating nature of a number of the issues that are raised by some of the clients who seek career services. For example, consider the client who, when first seen on Monday, begins by stating, "I have to choose a major by Friday." However, although these clients do exist, a relevant question is whether or not similarly frustrating clients are not seen for "personal" concerns. It appears that the attitudes that are held by the present and future members of the profession and conveyed to students are more central in the determination of the status of career counseling than is the nature of the client concerns that are presented to counselors.

A fourth factor that is suggested is the current lack of activity in the development and expansion of work on theories of career choice and development. This factor also relates to the apparent isolation of theories of career choice and development from other major theories of counseling and psychotherapy. At this point the theories of Super and Holland are the most dominant in the field. Holland's (1985a) recent revision of his theory may or may not breathe new life into a theory that has generated a truly remarkable amount of research but currently seems to be receiving less attention in the professional literature. Only Linda Gottfredson (1981) has added a relatively recent theoretical statement. Her statement has not, thus far, received the attention that it seems to deserve. Overall, the current lack of activity in theorizing about career development may be both a cause and a result of the apparent decline of interest in career counseling.

The final reason for the status of career counseling may also be the most important in considering the provision of career counseling. This reason suggests that the lack of interest in career counseling may be related to the manner in which counselors often approach career counseling. Increasingly the tendency appears to be to focus on the use of inventories, computers, career libraries, career information, Holland types, exercises, workshops, and other interventions. The effect often appears to be that a service is provided that seems time limited, technique oriented, and fragmented. In ways that are perhaps related to the isolation of career courses and theorizing, career counseling often seems to encourage the isolation of career considerations from other aspects of clients' lives.

In looking over the reasons just listed, the striking commonality is that they are all professional issues. That is, the lack of interest in career counseling services does not come from clients. There is and has been a steady and persistent demand for career services over the years, especially on college campuses. The issue, it seems clear, is most centrally a professional one. The effect is that counselors often have a lack of enthusiasm and interest in career counseling relative to "personal" counseling.

The perception by counselors that career counseling is less interesting than "personal" counseling is of great importance. This perception undoubtedly gets conveyed to clients, colleagues, and graduate students, and creates a negative attitude toward career counseling. It also suggests that when counselors do career counseling they may be less than vitally involved and interested in their duties. For counselors, the importance of maintaining interest in the process of counseling, though given very little attention in the literature, seems central. We have both observed occurrences when counselors seemed to discover that their career clients, although not at all certain of their career choices, were also suffering from a lack of self-esteem or some other more "personal" issue. Given the choice between attending to the lack of clarity about career choices and the lack of self-esteem, the tendency we have seen all too frequently is for the counselor to wish to address the lack of self-esteem and put the career issues on hold until the self-esteem issues are "fixed." Such priorities raise the suspicion that the counselor may simply be more interested in self-esteem concerns. Such priorities seem highly arguable to us in terms of the probabilities of positive gains, especially if there are time constraints on counseling, as there often are. However, despite our suspicions, we have never heard a counselor state that the reason that the personal issues were attended to was that the counselor simply found them to be more interesting than career issues.

It is intriguing to speculate about why "personal" concerns are seen as more interesting than career concerns. One reasonable-sounding scenario suggests that this is so because the primary reason most counseling psychology students choose this career is because they wish to be intimately engaged with whole persons who are dealing with issues that are of primary concern to them. "Personal" concerns are simply seen as being more intimate and involving than career concerns. This attitude is probably accentuated by the fragmentary approaches that are often passed on to graduate students as appropriate approaches to career counseling. It is also consistent with the striking and almost total lack of research or even speculation about the importance of the counseling relationship in career counseling. These two factors probably have an additive effect. For example, when primary attention is placed on an inventory or a printout, less energy may be devoted to listening carefully and understanding the client. Counselors frequently need time (sometimes months) to build rapport in "personal" counseling. Seldom is such a need heard in career counseling. The sense that career counseling does not call for a full and vital relationship with a client may be extremely influential with persons who choose counseling because they wish to develop those types of relationships. The perception that career counseling does not require a counseling relationship may also explain, partially, how counselors may acknowledge intellectually that career concerns are of vital importance yet respond behaviorally as if these concerns were mundane and uninteresting.

If the preceding case seems reasonable, then it follows that the lack of interest in career counseling is a problem that the profession needs to address. It also follows that increasing the involvement of counselors in career counseling might be addressed by approaching treatment for career concerns by relating to clients as whole persons who need to be understood and involved in a counseling relationship as an integral part of career counseling. Although this is not a new or a particularly creative idea, it does seem different from what frequently occurs. We also assume that this approach to treatment will deal directly with the career concerns of the clients who are counseled in a way that is relevant and involves the clients in the process.

VOCATIONAL CARD SORTS AS ONE RESPONSE TO THESE CONCERNS

This chapter develops the theme that the approach to career counseling fostered by the vocational card sort technique is one approach to career exploration that is relevant and involving for both counselors and clients. The card sorts are not suggested as a panacea for all of the concerns about career counseling that have been raised, but they do seem to get counselors more involved and interested in the process. When counselors are involved, clients have no difficulty getting involved. Having been associated with the vocational card sort for over 10 years, as counselors, researchers, and supervisors, we have both come to believe that it is an extremely effective and involving approach to career counseling. When we have introduced students to the approach, they seem to become more interested in their career clients and more interested in career counseling. The process is often described as much more "clinical" and interesting than, for example, the use of inventories. It also appears that the counselors who use the vocational card sort know more about their clients, like them better, and actually get excited about the approach. In essence they feel more involved in a relationship with the client. Given the introduction, these effects seem particularly important for career counseling.

Although one should be aware of the limitations of testimonials, we are not alone in our belief that card sorts are an effective, involving, and innovative approach to career counseling. For example, Williams (1978) wrote an article about the potential uses of the card sort approach. He noted that the card sort provided immediate feedback, and he examined a variety of means of looking at the sorting procedure, some quite creative, to extract meaningful information from the clients' responses as well as their styles of responding. Reviews by both Cochran (1985) and Crites (1985) of a particular version of the card sort, although not enthusiastic about the development of the version reviewed, both seemed to suggest that they saw the card sort approach as potentially useful. Dolliver (personal communication, 1988), the person most identified with the card sort approach, believed that it makes clients more thoughtful about the reasons behind their preferences, including their values. But one of the most thoughtful statements and perhaps the strongest endorsement was provided in a paper by Leo Goldman (1983). Goldman saw the card sort as a technique for counseling as much as an assessment instrument, and he seemed to agree with Dolliver that it was essentially "a structured interview technique." Goldman noted that:

> The technique's distinctive and valuable contribution is that it permits—actually requires—each client to project onto a number of occupational titles ... that individual's idiosyncratic classification of occupations in terms of values, goals, interests, abilities, or whatever the person wants to focus on in answering the question.... What results is usually a much richer depiction of the person's self-concept regarding occupations than one obtains from standardized inventories that have already defined the categories or scales into which responses must be placed during the scoring process.... Similar to a work sample or a projective test, the card sort thus permits observation of the person's approach to the task—fast or slow, decisive or hesitant, specific or vague, clear or cloudy, simple or complex, informed or uninformed about the world of work. These are many of the components of the concept of career maturity as that concept has been developed in recent years. Leading a client through the card sort in that manner requires time and active, skillful counseling. (p. 108)

In closing, Goldman stated:

> To understand this kind of use of the card sort technique [i.e., to understand concepts], a counselor should find it helpful to read the Tyler (1961), Dolliver (1967), Dewey (1974) and Williams (1978) articles. I hope that counselors will do that, because this is perhaps the most valuable single method I have ever found for helping people of almost all ages to examine what they want from their work. (p. 109)

We agree. It is our hope that this chapter will encourage others to examine the potential of the card sort technique in career counseling and in carefully developed research.

BACKGROUND AND DEVELOPMENT OF VOCATIONAL CARD SORTS

Tyler's Research on Choices

The origin of the currently available vocational card sorts can be traced to a paper by Leona Tyler. This paper was, in fact, her 1960 presidential address to the APA Division of Counseling Psychology. Interestingly enough, her focus in the paper was not on career exploration or issues that were particularly related to career choice or career development. Rather, she was pursuing her central concern with the study of individual differences. Tyler had arrived at the idea that "the core of individuality consists of a person's choices and the way he [sic] organizes them," and her address was a description of her research and thoughts in exploring that general hypothesis. Her research combined methods taken from interest measurement, as well as research on concept formation, and used items that were related to four topics: occupations, leisure activities, first names, and community organizations. Of primary interest here, Tyler's approach to research consisted of three steps that are the basis for procedures that are still a fundamental part of most card sort techniques. For this reason, they are presented in some detail as Tyler described them.

First, the subject was seated in front of a board on which 100 cards were arranged in a standard order. Each card had the name of an occupation (leisure activity, first name, or community organization) printed on it, After a short statement about the purpose of the study, these directions were given:

> I would like you to place over here in the "Would Not Choose" column all of the occupations you see as out of the question for a person like you and to place in the "Would Choose" column those you see as possibilities for a person like you. If you can't make a decision, place the card under "No Opinion." (Tyler, 1961, p. 195)

After this preliminary sorting was completed by the subject, the second step was introduced. For this step the "No Opinion" items were removed from the board and the following instructions were given:

> Now I would like you to break up these bigger groups into smaller groups of occupations that for some reason go together in your mind. Place those you reject for one reason into one group, those you reject for another reason into a second group, and so on. On the positive side, place those you would choose for one reason in one group, those you would choose for another reason in a second group, and so on. There are no rules for the number of groups you should come out with or about the number of cards in each group. (Tyler, 1961, p. 196)

The third step involved interviewing the subject on the topics that were used and the reasoning behind the choices that were made. Tyler described this step by writing that:

> I ask him [sic] to tell me what it is that each of his groups represents. I record on the data sheet the label or explanation he gives for each and the numbers of the items he classifies together under this heading. At this stage it is pos-

sible to carry on enough inquiry to make sure that I understand what he means by the distinctions he makes. Finally I ask him which of the negative groups and which of the positive groups he sees as most important for him. We then go through the same procedure with the set of leisure time activities. (p. 196).

It is clear that Tyler thought that this approach to data gathering captured some of the uniqueness of individuals as they were involved in the choice process. At the same time, she was also painfully aware of the difficulty of determining whether this method could be a useful scientific approach to gathering data on the choice process. Tyler's paper is particularly interesting because, in a very real sense, she thought in print about these difficulties. Her attempts at using traditional approaches to measuring reliability and validity are of some interest. But, as she noted, "Dealing with the content or meaning of the responses posed a much more difficult problem" (p. 198). Her approach to this latter issue is interesting in itself but is seen later to still have potential relevance.

Tyler began her research by interviewing about 150 subjects using the occupations and the leisure activities items. (It appears from the article that she did all of the interviews and analyses herself.) Three months later she did a second interview of the subjects who were available. Half repeated the sorting of the occupations and the other half sorted the leisure activities a second time. To make sense of these data, Tyler concealed names and other identifying information and combined and randomized the two sets of interviews. Then for each protocol she wrote down as many statements about the person who had been interviewed as she could generate. When this laborious task was completed, she identified and paired the protocols and compared the two sets of statements she had made to identify "how many of the statements I had made were identical or very nearly so in meaning" (p. 198). For occupations, the percentage of overlapping statements was 61%. For leisure activities, the percentage was 54%. For Tyler these results were encouraging. She then randomly paired some of the protocols and found a noticeably lower percentage of overlap of 24%. It is of relevance that Tyler, although pleased by the data, was more impressed by her sense that protocols for the same person contained "few, if any, real contradictions," whereas contradictions for the randomly paired protocols were "fairly frequent."

Overall, these results were seen as supportive of the card sort approach as a reliable method for capturing some of the uniqueness of individual subjects that could be an important addition to more traditional approaches to measurement. Tyler was also aware that the issue of validity was even more important, and she was less optimistic about locating a solution to this problem. The difficulty, according to Tyler, was caused by the fact that "individual differences of many kinds are so large and striking that they outweigh any sort of group differences" (p. 200). Of course, this statement supports the fact that the approach devised by Tyler to get at the uniqueness of individuals in making choices was effective. As Tyler noted, "it is just this 'individual' component that I was after when I set up this procedure. The Strong Blank gets at the common components far better than this" (p. 200).

Finally, toward the end of her address, Tyler made statements that are of particular interest to the development of the card sorts as interventions for career exploration. Tyler wrote:

> One finding that I had not anticipated when I set up the original study was that the process of carrying out this assigned task apparently constituted an important experience for some subjects. Enough of them mentioned spontaneously, "This kind of thing is good for you. It makes you think," and related it to their own plans and goals so that I began to see it as possibly a *part* of the counseling process itself rather than just a way of assessing personality. (p. 200)

Although Tyler mentioned a number of studies on the counseling process that were in progress that were designed to tell whether the method had something to offer to the counseling process, it does not appear that those studies were published. Indeed, the next apparent attention that was given to the vocational card sort as an intervention for career exploration came from Dolliver, who used the card sort in his dissertation (1966). Dolliver published an article in 1967 that described the vocational card sort that he had used. It is clear in this article that Dolliver's card sort, although referred to as an "adaptation of the Tyler vocational card sort," was an important expansion, clarification, and improvement over the basic outline provided by Tyler.

Dolliver's Contributions to the Card Sort Technique

Dolliver (1967) noted that although the card sort had some characteristics of a test or inventory, he thought it was best described as a structured interview technique. In administering the card sort, Dolliver used three 4 × 6 cards with the categories "Would Not Choose," "Might Choose," and "In Question" printed on them. He used the 51 occupations from the then current men's form of the Strong Vocational Interest Blank, which were printed on 3 × 5 cards.

Dolliver divided the task into four steps. The first step involved sorting the cards into the three piles. In the second task, the subjects grouped the "Would Not Choose" cards and gave their reasons for not choosing these occupations. Then the "Would Choose" cards were grouped and the basis for choosing these occupations was specified. Step three was Dolliver's addition to the task. Subjects were asked to select and rank order the 10 occupations that were most preferred. Dolliver assumed that the subjects were also choosing and ranking the importance of the values associated with these occupations. Step four also involved an addition to the task by Dolliver. He used the Requirements for an Ideal Job Checklist (Rosenberg et al., 1957) to help clients clarify their motives in selecting an occupation. These requirements or motives were also rank ordered. The client then was asked to add any occupations to the hierarchy that were under consideration but that had not been included in the original cards. The remainder of the task involved a summary and evaluation of the entire procedure. Dolliver estimated that the task took between 15 and 45 min, depending on how verbal the client was.

Dolliver's article provided an example of the use of the Tyler Vocational Card Sort (TVCS) and illustrated how the counselor could raise questions and help integrate the information gathered in the process of completing the TVCS. A particular point of emphasis for Dolliver's approach to the card sort involved his use of Kelly's theorizing about personal constructs as a theoretical rationale for making sense of the results. Dolliver concluded by addressing the issues of reliability and validity that had interested Tyler. He noted that:

> The method [i.e., of sorting occupational titles] is a structured interview technique that deals mainly with a client's reasons for making the choices. The concepts of validity and reliability have quite a different meaning in relation to an interview than they have in relation to a test. There is often a low "validity" and a low "reliability" between an early counseling interview and a later one, since from early topics of discussion there evolve new, more pertinent topics. To see whether this modified TVCS procedure has validity, one would ask whether its use led more quickly than would a test or a straight interview to the identification of important vocational counseling topics for discussion. (p. 920)

Dolliver continued by noting that reliability would be negatively valued in counseling because clients' reasons and choices change. Dolliver's statements about establishing reliability and validity for the TVCS as a structured interview represent one perspective for considering reliability and validity for the card sorts. This perspective may, however, be most useful in helping us to recall that the TVCS is basically a career intervention and should be studied in terms of its process and outcome effects on clients. This perspective, although important, does not, of course, deny that the TVCS also contains elements of an instrument that could also be explored in terms of more standard approaches to reliability and validity issues.

With Dolliver's statements about the reliability and validity of the card sort in mind, it may seem ironic that it was Dolliver's work on the predictive validity of expressed vocational choices that provided very important support for the use of expressed vocational interests in counseling. The term *expressed interests* referred to occupations that persons would mention if asked what career choices they were considering or other similar questions. In 1969 Dolliver published an article in the *Psychological Bulletin* that compared the predictive validity of expressed and inventoried vocational interests. The review was done against a backdrop of common wisdom that stated that the expressed interests of clients were clearly inferior to inventoried vocational interests, that is, those derived from measures like the Strong Vocational Interest Blank. In contrast to the expectation of the superiority of inventoried interests, Dolliver concluded that expressed interests had predictive validity—in terms of college majors or career choices—that equaled or exceeded that of inventoried interests. This conclusion was based on his review of the research comparing expressed vocational interests and interests taken from the Strong Vocational Interest Blank. Dolliver's conclusion was also supported by a related review by Whitney (1969) and a study by Holland and Lutz (1968). Both papers reached conclusions similar to Dolliver's. In addition, a substantial number of studies conducted since that time, using a variety of subject groups, time intervals, instruments, and methodologies, consistently support the superiority of expressed vocational interests (Bartling & Hood, 1981; Borgen & Seling, 1978; Cairo, 1982; Dolliver & Will, 1977; Gade & Soliah, 1975; Gottfredson & Holland, 1975; Holland & Gottfredson, 1975; O'Neil & Magoon, 1977; Touchton & Magoon, 1977). Clearly this support for the predictive validity of expressed vocational interests also seems to support the usefulness of the sorting of occupations that is central to the vocational card sorts. This relationship between card sorts and expressed interests was noted by Dolliver when he referred to the TVCS as an "expressed-interest method" (Dolliver & Will, 1977, p. 53).

The 1967 paper by Dolliver was quite important in taking the basic outline suggested by Tyler and using it as a basis for developing an intervention for career exploration. The 1969 paper was also extremely important in adding a strong note of legitimacy to the incorporation of expressed vocational interests, via the card sorts, into career counseling. It can be noted that although his contributions have been quite important in the development of the vocational card sort approach to career exploration, Dolliver has been quite gracious in attributing credit for the technique to Tyler, while being less attentive to the importance of his own contributions.

A SELECTIVE REVIEW OF CURRENTLY AVAILABLE CARD SORTS

Based primarily on the original work of Tyler and the expansions, clarifications, and improvements of Dolliver, a number of additional card sorts were developed. Five of those that are commercially available are reviewed here, as is a sixth version that has been used mainly in a series of studies on the approach. The five are the Non-Sexist Vocational Card Sort, (NSVCS); the Missouri Occupational Card Sort, College Form (MOCS); the Occ-U-Sort (O-U-S); the Vocational Card Sort that is incorporated into the Vocational Exploration and Insight Kit (VEIK); and the Missouri Occupational Preference Inventory (MOPI). These card sorts were reviewed as a group by Dolliver (1981), and reviews of the O-U-S and the VEIK were also located in the *Ninth Mental Measurements Yearbook* (Mitchell, 1985). Interested readers are referred to those reviews and to the more recent review of available card sorts by Slaney, Moran, and Wade (1994). Only some of the more important characteristics and differences in these sorts are noted here.

Dewey's Non-Sexist Vocational Card Sort

Dewey's paper entitled "Exploring Interests: A Non-Sexist Method" introduced the Non-Sexist Vocational Card Sort (NSVCS) and was published in 1974. Basically, she followed the steps articulated by Dolliver in administering the card sort although she omitted the use of the Rosenberg checklist and made no mention of Kelly's theory of personal constructs as a rationale. Dewey did include the Holland high point codes of the 76 individual occupations that were presented on the cards. In her article she presented the distribution of the occupations across the Holland types, and she stated that the "occupations included in the card sort were chosen as being representative of a wide range of vocational values." However, exactly how they were selected was not described. The distribution of occupations across the Holland types was unequal, ranging from 9 occupations in the Conventional category to 21 in the Social category. Beyond the placement of the Holland high point codes on the individual cards, it is unclear how the codes were to be utilized within the sorting procedure or within counseling in general. For example, the programmed materials encourage clients to "scan" the Holland codes. What precisely is involved in scanning or what is expected as a result is not clear. Only 12% of the occupations require only a high-school diploma or less, while 65% require a college degree or more. Consistent with the title, Dewey implied that the instrument applied equally to men as well as women. Again, how this was determined was not noted.

Dewey based her approach on the work of Tyler and Dolliver, but in calling her instrument the Non-Sexist Vocational Card Sort, she clearly intended to emphasize the nonsexist aspect of the instrument. In this regard Dewey noted that:

> The NSVCS is less sexist than traditional approaches to vocational counseling because (a) the same vocational alternatives are offered to both men and women, (b) the gender of the occupational titles has been neutralized, and (c) the process orientation of the technique allows the counselor to confront

and explore sex-role biases as such biases emerge in the counseling session. (p. 311)

Although the first two issues were relevant at the time when Dewey wrote her article, these concerns were eliminated by subsequent revisions of the most widely used commercially published instruments. However, there is some question about the actual effects of these alterations in terms of encouraging women to explore all of their available career alternatives. The remaining rationale for the use of the NSVCS is that the presence of a counselor will allow the issue of sex-role bias to be addressed as a part of the counseling session. This possibility is, however, dependent on the sensitivity and perceptiveness of the counselor and does not appear to be inherent in any particular procedure that is a part of the NSVCS. This rationale is also dependent on the assumption that counselors themselves are not sources of sex bias and that they are alert to and can deal effectively with sex bias as it occurs in the session. When clients take the self-directed version there are comments about sex bias in the accompanying materials. No studies on the effectiveness of this material were located. Overall, the importance and effects of the "nonsexist" aspects of the Dewey card sort are unclear.

The Missouri Occupational Card Sort

The Missouri Occupational Card Sort, College Form, by Krieshok, Hansen, and Johnston (1982), has 90 occupations, which are evenly distributed across the six Holland types. The incorporation of the Holland types into the task is rather vaguely described as a "step which could be included" (p. 10). About a quarter of the occupations require a high-school diploma, 63% require a college degree, and 12% more than a college degree. The MOCS assumes that a counselor will administer it. It is the only one of the commercially available sorts that does not have instructions so clients can take the instrument without the assistance of a counselor. Another difference is that in addition to ranking the top 10 *like* occupations the clients also rank order their bottom 10 *dislike* occupations. According to Dolliver, the MOCS occupation cards contain the most occupational information. Whether this information is of significance in the effects the task has on clients is not clear. No empirical studies that investigated or included the MOCS were located.

Occ-U-Sort/O-U-S

The Occ-U-Sort or O-U-S by Jones includes 60 occupational cards for each of three educational levels labeled *Plus 3 Level*, *Plus 4 Level*, and *Plus 5 Level*. The numbers refer to the General Educational Levels that are taken from the *Dictionary of Occupational Titles*. *Plus* in the titles indicates that some occupations from higher levels (of required educational background) are also included. The occupations are distributed equally across the six Holland types. In addition to the cards, a "self-guided booklet" is included to make the exploration experience self-directed. A specific approach to deriving a Holland code is provided for the client based on the occupations that are sorted as *might choose.* A Guide to Occupations contains 555 occupations that are organized according to Holland types, subdivided into worker trait groups, and assigned numbers according to the *Dictionary of Occupational Titles* and the *Guide for Occupational Exploration.*

In his review of the O-U-S, Dolliver (1981) questioned the strategy of not including occupations in which either sex predominated that was adopted by the O-U-S for addressing sex bias. Dolliver suggested that including some of these occupations might make sense because they represented some rather common occupations and their exclusion seemed a bit strange. Jones (1982) wrote a reaction to Dolliver's review that focused on this issue. In response to that reaction, Dolliver (1982) wrote yet another commentary. Neither author appeared to be noticeably persuaded by the other's perspective. Labeling the disagreement between Dolliver and Jones a controversy, Westbrook and Mastie (1982) wrote another review of the O-U-S provocatively titled, "Shall We Sort the Occ-U-Sort Into the Might-Choose, Would-Not-Choose, or Uncertain Pile?"

Westbrook and Mastie focused their concerns about the O-U-S on five basic issues. First, they stated that they were concerned that "the manual is misleading" (p. 249). They noted that the manual cites four studies under the heading "Occ-U-Sort as an Individual Career-Counseling Tool." They took issue with this title because they pointed out that, of the four studies describing the usefulness of card sorts, none used the O-U-S. They suggested that the O-U-S cannot be recommended until the necessary research is done. Second, they stated that the manual does not adequately support the claim that the O-U-S is effective as a "self-administered career-counseling experience" (p. 249). They suggested that more data on these issues need to be generated. Their third concern was that the data supporting the claim that the O-U-S assesses vocational interests were unclear and/or inadequate. Clarification and more data were called for. A fourth concern was whether the O-U-S codes were sufficiently dependable to serve as measures of vocational interests. Their fifth concern was that the manual's claims to have eliminated traditionally sex-linked job titles were simply inaccurate. Finally, they were concerned that the reading levels assigned to the cards were also inaccurate. They concluded that:

> The Occ-U-Sort is not at this time ready for serious use with students in a career counseling setting. Although the Occ-U-Sort appears to have considerable potential, the lack of empirical evidence to support its recommended uses means that it should be used for research purposes only until the necessary evidence is forthcoming. (p. 252)

Jones (1982) responded to the criticisms and concerns raised by West-brook and Mastie. He clarified the issues pertaining to reading level by noting that the actual occupational titles were not included in the determi-nation of the levels. Jones also responded to the charge that the manual had inaccurately implied that sex bias was attended to by eliminating tra-ditionally sex-linked job titles whereas titles like dental assistant, elemen-tary school teacher, and civil engineer remained. He cited the manual as stating, "To minimize the effect of sex bias, those occupations having strong sex-role stereotypes were excluded whenever possible" (p. 4).

These responses by Jones seemed responsive to only some of the con-cerns raised by the reviewers. They did clarify the concerns that were based on a lack of clarity or understanding. However, after citing the man-ual on the issue of sex bias, Jones concluded that, in minimizing the effects of sex bias, the O-U-S had succeeded "quite well considering the magnitude of the problem" (p. 255). It seems unclear whether Westbrook and Mastie or the careful reader would agree that the O-U-S had done "quite well" in responding to the issue of sex bias. In fact, the use of imprecise yet positive terms like *quite well* is at least one of the issues for which they took Jones and the manual to task. It does not seem difficult to imagine them asking what the term *quite well* means precisely and how it was determined that this term was an appropriate summation of the progress achieved in mini-mizing sex bias. It seems true that the indefinite and imprecise use of language does not help readers to determine what has actually been done with the O-U-S and what was found. In addition, Jones's responses were not directly responsive to some of the other criticisms and concerns raised by the reviewers. It is clear that Jones did not agree with many of the points raised by Westbrook and Mastie. It is less clear that his responses were consistently directed at clarifying the exact status, adequacy, and nature of the data gathered on the O-U-S.

Two additional reviews of the O-U-S appeared in the ninth edition of the *Mental Measurements Yearbook* (Mitchell, 1985). Cochran raised the interest-ing point that the method of calculating Holland types by using the primary and secondary codes of the occupations is biased because, although the primary codes are equally distributed across the types, the secondary codes of the occupations are not. He also noted that the requirement of selecting 12 occupations may bias the code because it may force clients to select occupations in which they have no real interest, but that are used in calculating the code. Consistent with other reviews, Cochran noted that "In general, the technical information presented in the Manual is inadequate" (p. 1077). In closing he noted that "The instrument offers much promise for career counseling. Unfortunately, as it stands, the measurement portion of the intervention is not suitable for research or practice" (p. 1077).

Crites (1985) noted, as did Westbrook and Mastie, that "the studies cited for it [i.e., the O-U-S] as an 'Individual Career-Counseling Tool' however, all pertain to other occupational card sorts. None pertains to the Occ-U-Sort" (p. 1078). Crites also raised basic questions about other data that were offered as support for the O-U-S. Beyond this, however, he raised an even more basic issue about whether the approaches to supporting the validity of the O-U-S were not simply misguided. According to Crites:

> The primary reason Tyler (1961) introduced the occupational card-sort was to explore the uniqueness of the individual's responses. These are given in the reasons for the card sorts; they are the source of data not provided by the SDS or interest inventories. Why not concentrate validation and interpretation on them? Otherwise research on the psychometric properties of Occ-U-Sort does not justify its use at this time, unless possibly as an adjunct to career counseling by an experienced counselor. This conclusion does not mean Occ-U-Sort has no promise. It does, but it needs to be validated differently in order to preserve and document its unique qualities. (pp. 1078–1079)

All of these reviews suggested that the database provided thus far for the O-U-S and presented in the manual contains inadequacies and, at the very least, that more data and clarification are needed. Crites agreed with that general assessment but raised the more intriguing question of whether the more or less conventional approach to gathering data, especially validity data, was not simply irrelevant to the nature of the vocational card sort task and its intended effects. Crites's statements on the issue of validity are reminiscent of the earlier comments of Tyler (1961) and Dolliver (1967) when they suggested that the vocational card sort represents a different type of instrument that is, in essence, an intervention. It appears that the approach to gathering validity data on vocational card sorts may need to be carefully reexamined.

The Vocational Exploration and Insight Kit

The Vocational Exploration and Insight Kit (VEIK) by Holland and his associates (1980) is really a combination of a Vocational Card Sort (VCS), the Self-Directed Search (SDS), and its instructional booklets, Understanding Yourself and Your Career, the Occupations Finder, an Action Plan Workbook, and the Counselor's Guide. The VCS consists of 84 occupations, equally divided over the six Holland types. About one quarter of the occupations require a high-school diploma or less, half require a college degree, and another quarter a postgraduate degree. The occupations are the same as those that are used in the SDS as well as in the Vocational Preference Inventory. The VEIK has, according to Dolliver (1981), "the greatest number and diversity of reflective questions for the client (e.g., In what occupation could I fulfill my hopes? and, In what occupation would I avoid my weaknesses?)" (p. 171). The client can also include occupations that are not on the cards. The VCS also contains, according to Takai and Holland (1979), "a specific step developed to confront a person with the role that sex, race, religion, or social class may have played in sorting occupational titles" (p. 313). Although the cards have only the occupational titles printed on them, the supplementary materials provide additional information that is relevant to career exploration and thinking about career choices and issues. Instructions are provided for computing a Holland code.

Reviews of the VEIK appeared in the ninth edition of the *Mental Measurements Yearbook* (Mitchell, 1985). Both reviewers seemed a bit unclear about the issues of reliability and validity as they apply to the VEIK. Daniels (1985) noted that "Evidence about the reliability and validity of the total program are not available, although such evidence for both the VCS and the SDS are available elsewhere" (p. 1675). He did not state where this evidence was available for the VCS, nor did he describe its exact nature. Tittle (1985) noted that "No reliability data are available for the VEIK. Two validity studies have compared the VEIK, the SDS, and the VPI-based VCS" (p. 1676). This latter statement makes it clear that, in referring to validity studies, Tittle was discussing what could also be classified as intervention or outcome studies. This issue has been previously referred to in discussing the validity of the card sort. There is some confusion about whether they are interventions or instruments that should have their items' reliability and validity assessed by using conventional means, that is, test–retest, split half, construct, or concurrent validity. For the VEIK, it seems clear that the package is meant to be an intervention for career counseling. Validity then, it can be argued, needs to be assessed in terms of whether the instrument or package performs or creates the effects that it states or suggests it should. Does it have validity as an intervention? It is important to note that it is far less clear how this determination of validity is to be made than it is when more conventional approaches to validity are considered. Considering the VCS as an embeddded component of the VEIK leaves it unclear what implications research results for the VEIK have for the VCS.

Both of the reviewers seemed generally positive about the VEIK. Both also suggested that more research was needed on the package. Daniels (1985) suggested that the VEIK was not significantly more helpful in expanding users' awareness than was the SDS alone. Tittle noted the same effect and cited the studies that led to that conclusion, namely, Takai and Holland (1979) and Talbot and Birk (1979). In addition, Tittle noted that:

The adaptation of VPI occupations to a card sort format and the particular questions included lack supporting data at present. Counselors following Holland's suggestion to take the VEIK themselves may well judge that only highly motivated and articulate clients are likely to complete this set of activities successfully. (p. 1676)

This latter point would appear to refer to the time required to complete the entire VEIK, which Dolliver stated is 3 to 4 hr. If, as it appears, research does seem to suggest that the total VEIK does not produce any differential additive treatment effects beyond those experienced by clients who take only the SDS, then very basic questions are raised about the advantages of the longer, more involving, and expensive VEIK. At the same time, there is also a question of whether the conclusions about the lack of effects for the VEIK are justified based on the limited empirical scrutiny it has received. To conclude that there are no treatment differences between interventions and then lose interest in and discard a treatment on this basis implies that the studies done have asked the right questions. Whether this has occurred for the VEIK is an issue that deserves consideration. Beyond this, the tendency to examine the VCS that is a part of the VEIK, as part of the total package, seems both natural in terms of the VEIK and confusing in terms of the VCS.

The Missouri Occupational Preference Inventory

The final commercially available vocational card sort was the Missouri Occupational Preference Inventory (MOPI), by Moore and Gysbers (with Pamela Carlson, 1980). The MOPI contains a total of 180 occupations, with 60 at each of three educational levels, requiring (a) a high-school education or less, (b) high school plus additional training, and (c) a college or post-graduate degree. The Holland types are not equally represented, nor are there equal numbers of occupations at each educational level. However, the MOPI includes more occupations at the lower educational level than does any other card sort. The Manual relates occupations to the DOT and illustrates how a Holland code can be determined based on the occupations chosen. In their recent book, *Career Counseling*, Gysbers and Moore (1987) devoted a chapter to occupational card sorts. They were quite concrete in their directions for using a card sort in career counseling and they focused on the specific approach used by the MOPI. It is not clear in this chapter that the MOPI is, in fact, quite different from the approaches taken by the other card sorts.

For example, after the client has sorted the cards into the three major groups, each individual card in the *like* pile is considered individually instead of as a part of a group of related occupations. The instructions, which are to be read or paraphrased, are as follows:

> In order to better consider the reasons (themes) for choosing certain occupational titles, begin by thinking about the first occupational card in the like pile. Explain the reason or reasons why you like it. Do this for each card in the pile. Make sure each reason is specific. (Moore & Gysbers, 1987, p. 139)

The counselor records the reasons beside each occupation. A slash mark is placed beside each reason on the Finding Themes work sheet each time a reason is repeated. When the client has gone through all of the *like* occupations, the *dislike* occupations are similarly addressed. The *undecided* occupations are also addressed individually and the reasons are tabulated. When this task is completed the reasons or themes are rank ordered, based on frequency, on the Understanding Themes worksheet. The *likes* are rank ordered first. Then the *dislikes* column is filled in, with attention to placing *dislikes* that are the opposite of the *likes* in the rank across the page. The same is done with the *undecided* column. Finally, those *likes* for which no opposites were noted are considered to determine what the opposite might be.

Then the client is asked to rank order the occupations using the *like* pile. The instructions, which are to be read or paraphrased, are:

Now that you know more about the reasons behind your occupational choices, rank-order them. Look at the cards in the like pile again. Decide which one would be your first choice, your second choice, and so on, for all the occupations that seem to be important to you. (p. 144)

The three-letter Holland codes of the occupations that are ranked are then used to derive a Holland code for the client. The authors use a weighted scoring system similar to that used as part of the SDS. A code is computed and checked, the Holland classification system is reviewed with the client, and the reasonableness of the code is discussed with the client. Finally, a worksheet entitled Your Career Information Summary is used to "help the client focus on what has been learned" (p. 146). There are five aspects:

1. The themes or the reasons for liking or disliking occupations are summarized.
2. The top five occupations are recorded.
3. The Holland codes are recorded.
4. The Holland code for the client is discussed.
5. A plan of action is formulated.

In the chapter on the occupational sorts, the authors seemed to suggest several central functions for which a counselor appears to be necessary. It is not clear how these functions are met when the task is self-directed. There are also several separate sheets to be completed. In Dolliver's review it is noted that the MOPI takes about ½ hour. The source for this estimate is unclear and, given the apparent complexity of the various operations, this sounds like an extremely conservative estimate of the time requirements for self-administering the MOPI. No studies on the MOPI were located, and

Gysbers and Moore cited no studies in their recent chapter. In addition, a recent letter from Dolliver (personal communication, 1988) quoted Gysbers as stating that he was not aware of any current research activity. Whether any research at all exists on this instrument is not clear. No reviews of the instrument in addition to the review by Dolliver (1981) were located.

Overall, the MOPI represents a different, if unexamined, approach to the card sort task. It is unclear whether the novel approach to examining the reasons for liking and disliking occupations leads to different effects or if the self-directed version is effective in examining the themes when clients take the MOPI by themselves. Although the total lack of research on this instrument suggests that the answers to such questions cannot be determined at present, potential users should at least be aware of the differences in the approach to the card sort that the MOPI represents.

Slaney's Vocational Card Sort

The final Vocational Card Sort to be discussed is not commercially available and has been used in a series of empirical studies of the VCS as a self-administered career intervention (Atanasoff & Slaney, 1980; Croteau & Slaney, 1994; Slaney, 1978, 1983; Slaney & Dickson, 1985; Slaney & Lewis, 1986; Slaney & MacKinnon-Slaney, 1986; Slaney & Slaney, 1981). Its origins can be clearly traced to the work of Dolliver and Tyler with a few alterations that are of interest. First, the Vocational Card Sort by Slaney included descriptions of the Holland types printed on 5×8 cards. Subjects were asked to rank order the cards according to how well each of the Holland types described them. From these rankings, subjects recorded their three-letter Holland codes This was, of course, a markedly different approach to getting the Holland types of the subjects than that used by any of the other instruments. These types were later used in making sense of the results of the VCS and, along with the Occupations Finder from the Self-Directed Search (SDS), to suggest additional occupations that the subjects might wish to explore. It was suggested, as part of the experimental procedure, that all permutations of the three-letter Holland codes be used in developing possible leads.

A small number of studies have investigated the rank ordering of the descriptions of the Holland types. Slaney (1978) derived three-letter Holland codes based on the rank-ordered Holland types done as part of the Vocational Card Sort and another set of three-letter codes taken from the Strong-Campbell Interest Inventory (SCII) for 84 undergraduate women. The agreement between the two codes varied considerably and appeared moderate overall. There were no statistically significant differences in the relationship of the rank-ordered themes and the SCII Holland themes to their respective second themes, the five highest basic interests, or the five highest occupational scales of the SCII. However, when the themes were related to three different measures of expressed vocational choices and college majors, the themes from the rank-ordered Holland types were found to be more highly related to expressed choices and significantly different from the relationships found for the SCII. Given the relationship between expressed choices and actual later choices, those findings are at least of interest and appear supportive of the ranking procedure.

Slaney (1978) had 32 undergraduate women, who were not in the comparative study, rank order the Holland themes. Three weeks later they returned and rank ordered the themes again. Spearman rhos, using all six themes, yielded a median rho of .83 and a mean rho of .84. Another sample of 42 undergraduate women was given the Vocational Preference Inventory and rank ordered the Holland themes as part of the VCS, in that order. The median Spearman rho was .66 and the mean rho was .56. Finally, a third sample of 30 undergraduate women rank ordered the Holland themes and 2 weeks later completed Holland's Self-Directed Search. The median Spearman rho was .77 and the mean rho was .69. Slaney concluded that while the measures of concurrent validity were not as highly related as might have been desirable, they did indicate that a substantial relationship existed between the rank-ordered Holland themes and other methods of deriving themes. A study by Harmon and Zytowski (1980) also found that when different sources were used for Holland codes, different instruments yielded different codes. Although there is no compelling rationale for preferring one of several possible sources for deriving Holland codes, the relationship between the rank-ordered codes and expressed choices does offer some support for the rank ordering procedure.

A study by Atanasoff and Slaney (1980) compared the three-letter Holland themes from the Vocational Card Sort with similar codes derived from the SDS and the SCII. The themes from the SDS and the VCS were both more highly related to the expressed choices of the subjects than were the themes of the SCII. The SDS and VCS were not significantly different from each other. Again, based on the importance of expressed vocational interests, these results seem supportive of the codes derived from rank ordering the descriptions of the Holland types. This seems particularly true given the wide use of the instruments used as a basis for comparison.

Slaney and Slaney (1981) compared the agreement of the Holland codes derived from the rank ordering of the Holland types with types derived from the SCII for 50 female and 50 male counseling center clients who requested career counseling. All clients had taken both the VCS and the SCII. The relationships between the two sets of three letter Holland codes varied a great deal but were generally moderate. Finally, Slaney and MacKinnon-Slaney (1986) studied 54 undergraduate females who requested career counseling at a university counseling center. Again all of the clients had taken both the VCS and the SCII. The sample was divided based on the agreement of the clients' expressed and inventoried choices, using the occupation on the SCII that had the highest standard score for the latter choice. Slaney and MacKinnon-Slaney found that clients with greater agreement between their expressed and inventoried interests had a stronger relationship between their rank-ordered Holland codes from the VCS and their expressed choices than did clients with low agreement. There were no differences between the SCII themes of clients in their relationship to expressed choices. It appeared that the higher agreement clients were better able to match their Holland personality types with their expressed choices through the rank ordering task than were the low-agreement clients. Given that high-agreement clients have been found to be more predictable in a number of studies, these results make intuitive sense and also seem to support the validity of the rank ordering of the Holland types as incorporated into the Vocational Card Sort. Although more research is clearly needed, the initial studies offer some support for rank ordering the Holland types as a part of the Vocational Card Sort. Given future support, one clear advantage of the rank-ordering task is that it encourages clients to think of themselves in holistic terms in relationship to the Holland types. These types can also be compared with the types that can be derived from the inspection of the specific occupations chosen on the VCS.

A second addition to the VCS that was made by Slaney (1978) was the incorporation of the Basic Interest categories from the SCII into the VCS. This was done as part of a series of studies that made comparisons between the VCS and the SCII. Again, only a few studies have examined the inclusion of the basic interests into the VCS. Slaney (1978) had subjects sort the basic interest categories into three groups: "I have a strong interest in these activities," "I have little or no interest in these activities," or "I dislike these activities." Slaney found that there was a clearer and more positive relationship between the basic interests of the SCII and those sorted as part of the VCS than there was, for example, for the occupations that were sorted and also listed on the SCII. Similar results were also found in Slaney and Slaney (1981). The greater similarity between the basic interest scales for the two instruments is quite probably related to the similarity of the methods of deriving the scale items for the SCII and expressed interests. The basic interest scales, in fact, resemble expressed interest scales. Although more recent studies of the VCS have dropped the sorting of the basic interests to reduce the total time needed, the use of the basic interests as a part of career exploration might be a particularly relevant exercise for younger students in junior high school or the lower high-school years. Thus far, however, the use of basic interests in career counseling has been largely unexamined.

The occupations used by Slaney were those that appeared on the printout of results of the SCII. This procedure was taken from Dolliver. However, Slaney (1981) added a descriptive pamphlet, "The Vocational Card Sort—Understanding Your Results." This pamphlet, first included in the Slaney (1983) study, reviewed the VCS and instructed clients in using Holland's Occupation Finder to locate occupations based on their rank-ordered Holland codes. Clients were also informed about the *Dictionary of Occupational Titles* and the *Occupational Outlook Handbook*. A particular effort is made to instruct clients on gender stereotyping and to encourage them to explore occupations that appeal to them separate from their sex-role stereotypes about those occupations. Other points of emphasis include ways of making sense of their final rank ordering of their career choices. Finally, "some next steps" to take in the exploration of career choices are presented. Some readings are also suggested, and the use of a career counselor is suggested if additional issues or questions need exploration. In the studies on the VCS, subjects or clients were given a copy of their record of their VCS results, a copy of the Occupations Finder, and a copy of the pamphlet "The Vocational Card Sort—Understanding Your Results." No specific studies of the effects of the pamphlet as a separate part of the VCS have been conducted.

The VCS used by Slaney contains some additions and permutations on the original card sort devised by Dolliver, but clearly the similarities outweigh the differences. The inclusion of the description of the Holland types and their rank ordering is an addition that has a number of implications. Certainly it presents an interesting task that can make the relationship of the Holland types to careers more involving and interesting for clients (as well as counselors). It also asks the client and the counselor to take a broad, holistic, integrative view of the client as a beginning step in considering career choices. With a counselor present, this task can get clients started in talking about themselves as whole persons and help them to focus on the importance of integrating themselves and their career possibilities.

Additional research is needed, but the study by Slaney and MacKinnon-Slaney (1986) suggested, logically enough, that clients whose expressed choices and inventoried choices were in agreement were better able to relate their Holland codes and their expressed choices. One implication of this finding is that low-agreement clients might productively spend more time thinking about who they are relative to the Holland types. This idea is reminiscent of a great deal of the conventional trait-factor theorizing on matching, which assumes a certain knowledge of self as a necessary precursor to informed matching. Additional research on the rank ordering of the Holland types would seem to be theoretically important as well as pragmatically useful. The inclusion of the Occupations Finder in relation to the rank-ordered Holland types also gives clients who take the VCS an additional important source of possible occupations to explore.

The inclusion of the basic interest category from the SCII was done as a part of the comparative studies with the SCII and the VCS as well as other instruments. Although the use of basic interests in career counseling seems like a potentially productive area of study, the basic interests are no longer included in the VCS because of the additional time required to sort them and their apparent limited relevance for most college and adult or reentry students. The explanatory booklet that has been developed for the VCS does seem like an important addition to the task, especially when the VCS is taken as a self-administered activity. It appears to add potentially useful information and it attempts to add cautionary notes about the importance of being aware of sex-role stereotyping in thinking about and selecting possible career choices. Although the information contained in the booklet seems helpful to clients, no data on the effects of this booklet have been gathered.

DESCRIPTION OF THE INSTRUMENT

Clients for Whom the Instrument Seems Most Appropriate

The flexibility of the vocational card sort technique makes it an appropriate career intervention for a broad variety of clients:

1. Undecided clients, particularly those who do not yet have a good sense of identity, as well as those who have not yet had an opportunity to explore the world of work.
2. Older clients who have the diversity of life and work experiences to draw upon.
3. Female clients who limit their career options to stereotypically feminine occupations.
4. Clients with psychopathology or handicaps—but the counselor must make the judgment about severity of pathology or level of comprehension.
5. Young clients working on self-assessment.
6. Intellectually oriented clients who like to control their own decision-making.
7. Clients for whom expressed and inventoried choices are not in agreement.

Undecided clients can be difficult to work with, especially when traditional testing does not add to their understanding of career choices. By using the vocational card sort technique, counselors can gain insight into how clients see themselves. Counselors can then note patterns of interests and abilities that make sense in relation to other biographical information (e.g., hobbies, extracurricular activities, courses that the client has enjoyed in school, family patterns, and ways of coping). The process allows the client to integrate self-knowledge with knowledge of occupations and, at the same time, allows the counselor to use clinical skills to further the integration process. The vocational card sort technique provides a productive intervention vehicle for both client and counselor, and offers the counselor an interactive treatment mode.

Older clients have varied life experiences that add to their understanding of who they are and how they see themselves in the work world. Many adults who are reconsidering careers have not had the time to think about turning aspirations into reality. The vocational card sort technique can help adult clients understand the process of career decision making, and yet assist them in considering alternatives in a realistic way. If the client is considering occupations that are not included in the occupation cards, the counselor can encourage the client to add those occupations, so that similarities and differences in all occupational preferences can be examined. Because vocational card sorts are very individual and dependent on the clinical skills of the counselor, the technique can be helpful with adult clients from all socioeconomic backgrounds: from executives terminated as a result of corporate acquisitions, to impoverished clients barely a step away from welfare.

Women clients may be hampered unwittingly in their career exploration by traditional values and stereotyped perspectives of occupations—even though it seems clear that nowadays very few jobs cannot be performed by either sex. Because gender is not mentioned on vocational card sorts, women clients do not have to be constrained by outdated conventions. In fact, as clients think out loud about the career selection process, counselors can reflect and explore values, stressing a developmental perspective. The developmental approach can take into consideration "what if" questions related to marriage, family, childrearing, divorce, and so forth. Female clients need the freedom to explore all occupations that fit their potential and interests; career choices can perhaps then be based on rational decision making and not internal or external sex biases (Slaney, 1983). Indeed, in a comparison of a vocational card sort technique and the Strong-Campbell Interest Inventory, women using the vocational card sort tended to select occupations that were less female dominated than did women using the SCII (Slaney & Slaney, 1981). The card sorting system seems to encourage women to consider a wide range of career options.

Clients who have physical or psychological handicaps sometimes feel unnecessarily limited in their career choices. By using the card sort technique in conjunction with clinical skills and judgment, counselors may gain insight into the impact of the disability on the vocational choice; they can monitor the effect of the disability on the client's self understanding and knowledge of occupations. Counselors can raise the issue of how clients might select a career differently if the handicap were not present. From an even more pragmatic perspective, clients with reading difficulties (because of learning disabilities) can be identified, and put at ease by the counselor. Thus the counselor can intervene to relax the client and to broaden the client's career horizons.

Young clients benefit from being in control of the vocational card sort process. It is easy for youngsters who do not have a clear understanding of their own identity to rely on a computer print out as "the voice of wisdom." Career counselors in the university setting often see clients who accept, without question, parental advice on the choice of a career or a major. However, because the first step of a card sort technique is the selection of the Holland code and an understanding of one's own vocational personality, clients immediately have a framework for understanding themselves as unique individuals—individuals with special configurations of personality traits. Some clients may feel that counselors have "magical" understanding and insight, because the self-selected Holland code makes so much sense and is easily grasped. The framework gives clients insight into the relationship between their own interests, abilities, and personality traits, and their occupational selections.

Intellectually oriented clients like to direct their own decision-making process. As the vocational card sort technique moves from self-knowledge to individual occupations, the client feels in control and understands the progression of events. The physical manipulation of the cards also places the client in control. Our observation has been that integration of self-knowledge and knowledge of occupations allows the decision-making process to build logically.

Clients for whom expressed choices differ from inventoried choices may not receive the confirmation hoped for (Slaney, 1978). By explaining the research on expressed versus inventoried choices, counselors can allay the fears that clients have when the inventory "says" that their interests are dissimilar to workers employed in a particular occupation. With the card sort technique, counselors can reassure clients that their career choices are either efficacious or perhaps in need of reexamination in light of personal or occupational variables.

Self-Directed Versus Counselor-Administered Versions

When using vocational card sorts, the counselor has two choices: (a) to monitor the client step by step, or (b) to provide the card sort in a self-directed manner, along with instructions (Slaney, 1978), and then process the results with the client later. The study by Moran (1991) provides a comparison of the effects of counselor-administered and self-administered versions of the Slaney VCS. Time and complexity of presenting issues will determine which method the counselor selects.

If the client is especially undecided or confused, the counselor may opt to facilitate the card sorting process in conjunction with clinical assessment strategies. As the client arranges and sorts the cards, the counselor asks the client to think out loud. By focusing on verbal and nonverbal behavior, the counselor can then clarify or intervene when appropriate. The thoughts elicited may be career oriented, personal, social, or family information. Thus the counselor can have some understanding of the client's thoughts and the way in which the client makes decisions.

Whether or not the client has a good sense of self, an understanding of occupations, or is undecided about career options, the counselor may assign the card sort technique as a counselor-free intervention. The process itself provides clarification for the client (Slaney, 1978). It also confirms the counselor's confidence that the client will resolve his or her own career choice issues, and focuses the answer to the problem on the client himself or herself. At a later session, the counselor can then question the client's perceptions of the process, as well as the outcome information furnished by the client. This is a less time-consuming procedure for the counselor, but not necessarily less clinically revealing.

ADMINISTERING VOCATIONAL CARD SORTS

Materials Needed

Vocational card sorts generally consist of three sets of cards, which can be used in conjunction with Directions for the Vocational Card Sort (Slaney, 1978), "The Vocational Card Sort—Understanding Your Results" (Slaney, 1981), and *The Occupation Finder* (Holland, 1985b). The cards are designed to be arranged and manipulated easily, making the career exploration task manageable for clients. Indeed, clients are in control as they sort the cards and monitor their own results, either with or without the direction of a counselor. If the process is counselor free, then clients will need response sheets, which automatically provide a carbon for the client and the original (because it is usually easier to read) for the counselor.

The first set of cards consists of six 5 × 8 cards labeled according to the Holland vocational personality types and containing a short description of each.

The second set of cards consists of 4 × 6 cards: The three category cards are labelled "I have a strong interest in these activities," "I have little or no interest in these activities," and "I dislike these activities." The remaining

23 cards have interest areas printed on them, such as Social Service, Religious Activities, Science, and Law or Politics.

The third set of cards consists of three 5 × 8 category cards and one hundred and seven 3 × 5 occupation cards. The category cards are labeled "Might choose," "In question," and "Would not choose." The occupation cards represent careers such as Reporter, Nursing Home Administrator, Carpenter, Dentist, Geographer, Secretary, and so forth.

Procedures

With a counselor-free version of a card sort, clients are instructed to read the pamphlet "Directions for the Vocational Card Sort" (Slaney, 1978). The directions indicate that clients should prepare for the vocational exploration task by focusing on themselves, so that they can react to a variety of activities and occupations and examine the reasons behind their reactions.

When the counselor administers the vocational card sort to a client, then the counselor should first focus on building a relationship with the client. The client must feel comfortable with the counselor—only then will the client feel free to provide all the necessary information related to the vocational exploration task. The vocational card sort technique fosters a holistic approach to career exploration.

In step 1, clients are instructed to read each of the six descriptions of the Holland vocational personality types and to arrange the descriptions in rank order, from most similar to their own personality to least similar. The ranking should then be recorded for later use.

In step 2, clients sort the activity cards into three piles, according to the category cards: "I have a strong interest in these activities," "I have little or no interest in these activities," and "I dislike these activities." The cards should be arranged relatively quickly. The client then focuses on the five activities in which he or she had the strongest interest and the five activities that he or she disliked the most. After these selections are recorded, the cards are put aside in their separate piles.

Step 3 instructs the client to look at the third set of cards and organize the occupations in groups: "Might choose," "In question," and "Would not choose."

The client then examines the "Would not choose" pile and arranges the cards into groups that logically go together, in terms of their relationship to each other. For example, people frequently see the occupations of dentist and doctor (physician) as related and group them together. When all the cards in the "Would not choose" pile are arranged into groups, then each group is labeled according to the client's perception of what the occupations have in common. The labels for the clusters may focus on values, aptitudes, fears, family concerns, socioeconomic status, educational concerns, money issues, and so forth. Clients are asked why they would not choose these occupations. Here the counselor can be particularly helpful by encouraging clients to be thoughtful about their responses. The groups and their labels should then be recorded.

Next, the client examines the "In question" pile. Are there any occupations in this group, that on second thought, the client might want to move to the "Would not choose" pile? Are there any that the client would like additional information about? Sources of information can be discussed later. Finally, the client is asked to state why these occupations are in question: How relevant is their status to the process of making a career choice? The client and counselor should keep notes on the process.

The client then examines the "Might choose" pile and arranges the cards into logically related groupings. When all the cards are sorted, the client is asked to give a label to each group and to think of reasons to explain why he or she might choose these occupations. Again groups and labels should be recorded.

From the occupations in the "Might choose" pile, the client is asked to select the 10 most preferred and to rank order them from most to least preferred. The client then examines the groups in which these 10 most preferred occupations reside, and looks for relationships, similarities, and differences. Each occupation can then be examined in light of "real world" issues facilitating or hampering the client from reaching his or her career goal. If the issues make a difference from either a positive or negative standpoint, that too should be noted, for later examination.

To be sure that nothing has been omitted, the client should review the list of preferred occupations to make sure that all occupations, whether on the cards or not, are on the list. Any occupation can be added and ranked accordingly.

After the client has completed the self-directed form of administration, he or she may be instructed to read "The Vocational Card Sort—Understanding Your Results" (Slaney, 1981). This pamphlet provides the client with information about the vocational exploration process, suggests sources of occupational information, and raises issues that the client may consider before seeing the counselor the next time.

Variations and Possibilities

Any number of variations on the sorting technique are available to the counselor—the counselor can be creative and imaginative in adapting the technique to meet the needs of the client.

The Holland vocational personality type cards are particularly useful for gaining insight into the client's personality and world. After having the client rank order the cards, the counselor may ask the client to point out the words and phrases on each card that are descriptive of him or her. This provides the counselor with additional information about the client. For example, if the client mentions that she enjoys being at the center of a group and taking leadership roles, the counselor can question further about prior experiences, positive and negative, related to that personality trait; or if the client mentions that he is a "people pleaser" the counselor can find out whether that occurs in family settings, work setting, or peer settings, and how the client feels about it.

With the Holland vocational personality type cards, the counselor can focus on self-acceptance, an important aspect of vocational exploration. Does the client like himself or herself? Which qualities would the client like to change? What do family members or friends say about these personality traits? What are the personality types of other family members and what does that do to relationships within the family? With this technique of vocational exploration, many personal and family issues become apparent, such as liking or disliking one's appearance, bulimia, family patterns of abuse, physiological symptoms related to stress, and so forth.

The Holland vocational personality types can also help clients explore why certain majors or college courses are a good fit and others a bad fit. The Holland types help to explain the paradigms, or world views of different fields of study (Kuhn, 1970). For example, if a student in computer science selects Social or Enterprising as the first theme in the rank ordering, then it is easy to explain how that particular paradigm may either be different from that student's predominating world view, or may take some extra work for that student to understand. Because the student rank orders all the Holland types, it becomes important to discuss how important each of the themes are to his or her personality. Most careers require multiple and diverse personality traits from just about all of the personality types, and most students can point out which of their own personality characteristics are associated with each type. The result for the student is a better understanding of himself or herself and a better understanding of different fields of study and careers.

The basic interest cards and the occupation cards can be sorted in many different ways. The counselor can instruct the client to arrange the cards according to different time periods: How would the client sort the cards today; how would the client have sorted the cards in high school. Different feeling modes provide another variation: When the client is feeling upbeat and positive, how would she sort the cards, in contrast with when feeling depressed. If there are strong parental or family pressures, the cards can be sorted according to how the client would arrange and label them, in contrast with how parents would sort and label. Clients with a physical handicap can be instructed to sort the cards as though the handicap were not an issue. Women may be asked to sort the cards as though they were men. Many variations of the sorting technique are possible, allowing the counselor to tailor the intervention to the perceived needs of the client.

For counselors in a university or college setting, the same sorting technique works with college majors. By dividing the available college majors into three groups (Might choose, In question, and Would not choose) and then providing labels for clusters, students can understand their interests in different majors and do some reality testing by taking courses (or browsing through books in the book store) in each of the Might choose majors. At the same time, the majors can be tied to the occupations and the ranking of the Holland vocational personality types. Because one college major provides the flexibility to enter several occupations—as well as graduate and professional school—the student can keep occupational options open until a choice is mandated at a later time.

MAKING SENSE OF THE INSTRUMENT

Constructs or Dimensions Assessed by the Instrument

For clients there are three obvious levels at which assessment of constructs occurs: (a) self-understanding of personality traits, (b) likes and dislikes of basic interests, and (c) likes and dislikes of occupations.

Because the first step of the vocational card sort technique is rank ordering the Holland types, clients usually have a better understanding of their own vocational personality (Slaney, 1978). This can be quite revealing for clients—and almost mystical—as they gain understanding of why certain occupations have appeal and others do not, and why certain courses or majors in school are more interesting for them than others. Strengths and weaknesses, which many clients take for granted, begin to make sense. Family issues and ways of coping can also be examined.

The second step and second level of assessment involves interest in broad categories of activities. What does the client like to do; what does the client dislike? These interests can then be meshed with the personality traits of the Holland types.

The third level of assessment relates to specific occupations. As the client divides occupations into clusters that seem interesting, and labels the clusters according to logical similarities, consistencies with the vocational personality type and preferred activities become apparent. By examining clusters of occupations that are not on the "Might choose" pile or are "In question," the client begins to understand some of the attitudes about occupations, as well as values that he or she holds. These attitudes and values can then be examined in light of developmental issues and other personal concerns.

Results

The results are produced as clients proceed with the task. Self-understanding occurs with each unit and level of exploration in a reasonable and organized way. Clients even report self-understanding, without counselor intervention (Slaney, 1978, 1983). No formal scoring procedure external to the client is needed.

The process of vocational exploration using a card sort technique provides results in and of itself. From the process, clients seem to have a better understanding of (a) their vocational personality, (b) their interests (both likes and dislikes), (c) the occupations that they like and dislike, and (d) their reasons for liking or disliking occupations.

Because the results are self-explanatory, when the counselor facilitates the process or goes over the recorded information with the client, he or she can focus on a holistic view of career counseling. By questioning the categories, groupings, and reasons, the counselor helps the client understand why certain choices seem more appropriate than others. The counselor may also encourage the client to keep all options open until additional information is obtained or a first choice is mandated.

Involvement of the Client in the Process

The client is the most important part of the vocational card sort technique. Results are produced by the client, monitored by the client, evaluated by the client, and used by the client without the assistance of a formal scoring procedure.

The counselor-free application of the card sort almost forces clients to be self-reliant and to make sense of the sorting procedure themselves. Although seeking help for their problems related to career choice, clients are shown that they have the capacity to find the answer to their own problems. The counselor-free application fosters independent decision making in a logical and organized manner.

Counselor-facilitated card sorting distributes the responsibility for problem solving to some degree to both the client and the counselor. Some clients become somewhat self-conscious as they sort the cards in front of the counselor. However, when counselors monitor the card sorting process, they can observe both verbal responses and nonverbal behavior. By facilitating the process, counselors are able to help clients focus on here-and-now issues of decision-making style, as well as historical and future concerns.

Immediacy of Feedback

Card sort techniques provide clients with immediate feedback. The client does not really need the counselor to interpret results and does not need to wait for a computer printout. The process provides results that are generally quite understandable to the client.

Lack of Technology

The lack of technology involved in the process of manipulating cards takes the mystery out of making career decisions. The process provides a logical and reasoned answer for the client. There is no instant voice of wisdom out of the computer printout telling the client what careers he or she is suited for. However, because feedback is immediate but not technological, clients are satisfied. Results come from the client's own efforts and readiness to find an answer to career choice issues.

EFFECTS AND INFLUENCE OF THE INSTRUMENT ON COUNSELORS

Importance of This Issue to Career Counseling

No issue is more important to our clients than their sense of identity—and that sense of identity is intimately connected with career choice. We invest time, energy, and ourselves in our careers—40 hours in a week, 2,000 hours in a year, and a hundred thousand hours or more in a life time. Career selection is of central concern to our clients.

Finding appropriate interventions for clients is not always easy. The card sort technique offers an alternative intervention that is focused on the individual client, is generated by the client, is not reliant on computer technology, and usually makes intuitive sense to the client.

Importance to Counselors in General

Card sort techniques are wonderfully counselor friendly. Because of the flexibility provided by the manipulation of the cards and the logical progression of the process, counselors can provide as much or as little input as seems appropriate.

The focus of the counselor–client interaction can be geared to any area of concern (family, personal, social, marital, aptitudes, values) that might help the client. Yet the card sorting process itself takes care of the assessment of the individual occupations and provides the client with an answer to his or her presenting problem of career indecision. The process leads to client understanding and not just another test-and-tell-'em method of career counseling.

Because the results are self-explanatory, the counselor does not need an intimate knowledge of test construction or statistics to help the client understand the results. Proficient clinical skills will add more to the process than will an understanding of standard scores or norms.

Anecdotal Experience and Prescriptions for Research

In the college or university career counseling center, undecided clients can be particularly difficult to deal with. Young college students do not have an appreciation for the free career counseling service that they receive, yet they are impatient to know what to major in. We have found that a combination of the card sort technique to assess careers and a similar process to assess college majors can provide interim answers and satisfaction for clients, in concert with reality testing by taking courses in different fields and reading about occupations. This format provides a productive and satisfying intervention for undecided clients whose expressed interests differ from their inventoried interests. These are the clients who otherwise tend to feel stranded with the unanswered questions.

Returning adult women students, who may select occupations on the basis of traditional female values, are also good candidates for the card sort technique. Research indicates that there are differences in cohort groups of reentry students: Women in their forties seem to select more female-dominated occupations than do women in their thirties or twenties (MacKinnon-Slaney, 1986). Married women tend to select more traditional occupations than either single or divorced women (MacKinnon-Slaney, Barber, & Slaney, 1988).

Because of these proclivities it makes sense to stimulate less stereotyped thinking on the part of reentry women. Because gender differences are not highlighted by the card sort process, adult women students seem to be less limited by thinking of occupations as being either "male" or "female." In our experience, these learned attitudes, powerful as they are for adults, seem to be muted by the card sort technique.

CASE EXAMPLE

Description of the Client

Susan was a 19-year-old first-semester college sophomore. She requested career counseling because she was not doing well in the classes that would prepare her for a career in veterinary medicine. She had been interested in veterinary medicine since her freshman year in high school and had worked part-time with a vet during her vacations. Her background was suburban. She described herself as being similar to her father, a computer hardware engineer who enjoyed a country atmosphere and animals.

Susan felt that her dreams had been shattered because her grade point average in college was barely passing—vet school was impossible. Her reasons for the poor grade point average centered on family matters, which had caused her a great deal of stress during her first year in college; she did not seem to want to elaborate further in the first session.

Because she had been interested in veterinary medicine for so long, Susan could hardly envisage alternative occupations. After being pressed to answer the Occupational Alternatives Question (Zener & Schnuelle, 1976), Susan offered dairy production, animal production, biology teacher, animal scientist, veterinary assistant, and veterinary medicine as her expressed choices. Because she still saw veterinary medicine as her first choice, even though reality testing was making that a questionable choice, Susan's level of indecision appeared to be between level 2 (first choice with alternatives) and level 3 (alternatives and no real first choice (Slaney, 1980).

Reasons for Using a Card Sort Technique with Susan

For Susan, the use of the vocational card sort technique seemed to make sense for a variety of reasons. Susan's expressed interest in veterinary medicine was of such long standing that any vocational interest inventory would be colored by that choice. Even if inventoried interests agreed with her expressed interests, other interests and abilities needed to be examined. And the nuances of animal science and dairy production were not usually found on an interest inventory. If Susan's interests were not confirmed by the inventory, then she would be discouraged by the results—leaving her more depressed than she already was.

There was something about Susan's manner that indicated some kind of personal problems or stresses that also might be affecting her at college. She had mentioned family concerns and a health problem that had never been fully resolved. The card sort technique offered the flexibility to explore careers issues, as well as personal and family issues to the extent that Susan desired.

Results and Effects

Susan rank ordered the Holland vocational personality type cards and discussed her own personality traits. First she selected the Realistic theme because that seemed to her to be the personality type most like her own. She noted that she preferred to deal with things rather than ideas or people. She enjoyed camping and her work with animals. The outdoors gave her peace of mind. She saw herself as being strong and having good physical skills (in high school she had been on the softball team). She indicated that she was practical and noted that she did have difficulty expressing her ideas and feelings to others. When asked to give an example of a situation in which she had trouble expressing her feelings, she said that there were some family matters during her senior year in high school that had caused her problems, but she did not elaborate.

The Investigative theme came second in Susan's ranking because she saw herself as interested in science, but neither creative nor original in that context. In high school she had always done very well in science; in fact the idea of veterinary medicine as a career had emerged in her sophomore year of high school and her teachers had encouraged her. She indicated that now in college she was not doing well in the sciences and was, in fact, only receiving good grades in biology. She particularly disliked college physics. Again she reiterated that she was not interested in work around people.

She selected the Conventional theme next because she was generally organized and did not seek leadership or power. She acknowledged that she did like to know what was expected of her, and could work well within a chain of command.

Susan's ranking of the last three themes was Social, Artistic, and Enterprising. The Social theme came next in her ranking because Susan saw herself as responsible, cheerful, and concerned with the welfare of others. She saw herself as being particularly concerned with her family because she was the oldest of three daughters. Her preference was not to be in the center of a group, but on the fringe. In high school she had been in the French club, the Honor Society, the school newspaper, and the biology club, but she had not played a central role in any of the groups. She described herself as not particularly popular, but able to get along well with others. She indicated again that she did not seek leadership—in fact even when thinking about being a vet, she wanted to be the assistant and not the vet in charge. Susan selected the Artistic theme next because she was sensitive and emotional, but not assertive about her own opinions and capabilities. She saw herself as having some creative tendencies and acknowledged that she was a very independent person. The Enterprising personality type was the one that was least in keeping with her personality. She knew that she did not like economics, sales, or the business fields.

It became clear that Susan's interest in animals might be related in some way to her disappointment in people. During the second session, she disclosed that family issues were complex. Her father was abusive, but it was for the good of the three daughters in the family; her mother, she said, "was a very nice, kind and gentle person" but unable to stand up for her daughters; Susan's younger sister had turned her father in to the police for child abuse, but the sister was a trouble maker; and so on. Susan's stomach problems had just about disappeared after one and a half years at college. The personal issues were overwhelming—the card sort technique provided a vehicle for those concerns to be placed alongside the career issues.

Career and family issues were foremost in Susan's thoughts. At least while Susan was away at school, family problems receded into the background a little. For Susan, resolving career goals and choice of college major could make an immediate difference in her feelings about herself, in the way she approached her college career, and in her view of her total life space.

Because of time limitations at the end of the school year, the basic interest cards were disregarded and Susan was asked by the counselor to sort the occupational cards. Many personal issues impinged on Susan's choice of career and major, so the counselor chose to facilitate the vocational card sort process.

Susan sorted the occupational cards into the three piles, "Would not choose," "In question," and "Might choose." After the "Would not choose" cards were sorted into clusters, Susan labelled the clusters: for example, (a) too much difficult science involved (medicine, dentistry, geology), (b) too confining (military and public official careers), (c) too much direct public service (executive housekeeper, food service, beautician), (d) no talent (artist, interior decorator), and (e) other people's theoretical money (investment, banking).

Next Susan examined the "In question" and "Might choose" piles. The "In question" cards were examined and moved to either the "Might choose" or "Would not choose" piles. Occupations that Susan wanted more information about were moved to a separate pile. Susan then examined the cards in her "Might choose" pile. She rank ordered the cards according to her interest in each occupation and added other occupations that were not listed on the cards (vet assistant, dairy production, animal production, and biology teacher were the occupations that interested her).

After categorizing the occupational cards that reinforced her interest in animals and biology, Susan turned to college majors. As she examined the possible majors at the university, and categorized them according to "Would not choose," "In question," and "Might choose," it became clear that animal science, dairy science, animal production, and even agronomy held some interest for Susan. After carefully examining these options in light of the labels from the "Would not choose" and "In question" card sorting, Susan found that her interests were confirmed. For Susan that information was comforting.

Interpretation

All her life, Susan had been playing a moderating role in her family between her sisters and her mother, between her mother and her father, and between her sisters and her father. So much of her energy had been channeled into family matters that she had not had time to realize that she had been focusing on everyone else's needs but her own. She had managed high school fairly easily under those circumstances, but college was a different matter.

Susan's call for help with career matters was also a call for help with life. She was relieved that counseling took a holistic approach to career issues and examined the personal and family concerns too. But her career plans were very important to her—this was something she could do for herself. She really did not want counseling to focus only on the personal issues. In fact, she felt that she could get personal counseling at any time, and already had, but the career issues were much more central to her well-being at this time in her life.

Evaluation by Client and Counselor

The card sorting technique allowed Susan to discuss all aspects of her life while she was concentrating on career issues. She was relieved to have her career interests confirmed and was quite willing to undertake homework assignments to discover more about kindred occupations: reading about careers, talking with faculty who could shed light on her areas of interest, talking to her friends to find out what they liked or did not like about their majors, joining student clubs related to majors that sounded interesting, and so forth. As a sophomore, Susan was beginning to panic about selecting a major, so she was eager to have concrete tasks to undertake in order to help her make a reasoned decision.

From the counselor's perspective, the card sort technique worked well. Susan had made a good beginning on the decision-making process. She had been able to see how personal and family problems impinged on her career decisions. She was now moving ahead to do some things for herself so that she could find her own niche in life, and her own identity as an individual separate from her family. The card sort had provided the vehicle.

RESEARCH ON THE VOCATIONAL CARD SORTS

This section examines the published research available on the vocational card sorts. The first published study located was a dissertation by Cooper (1976). She compared a Vocational Card Sort (VCS), which she based on Dewey's Non-Sexist VCS and adapted to be self-administered, with the then recently merged male and female forms of the SCII. Both were either given by themselves or preceded by the Auxiliary Information Material (AIM), which was a brief survey of myths and realities about men and women in the world of work. It was designed to increase awareness of the importance of the eventual career choice. Cooper also included a no-treatment control group. The general hypothesis was that the inclusion of the AIM would increase career salience and career exploration in college women. Cooper randomly distributed 120 undergraduate women to one of the five groups. The SCII groups received their results in the form of the interpretive report produced by NCS. The outcome measures were gathered 1 month after the treatment.

Cooper found that subjects who had taken the VCS were considering more occupational options, more nontraditional options, and were reading occupational information more than were the control group members. There were no differences between the groups on the proportion of nontraditional careers being considered. Only those subjects who had been exposed to the AIM were significantly more career salient than the control group members. The AIM had no effects on increasing career options or information seeking. The effects found for the AIM were mixed but somewhat promising. The results for the VCS were unexpected but seemed promising for expanding the number and type of the occupations being considered as well as the career exploration of college women. The authors did not speculate about the reasons for the differences between the VCS and the SCII.

Dolliver and Will (1977) did a 10-year follow-up of the 67 undergraduate subjects who had participated in Dolliver's dissertation research. Of the original 67, 46 had been clients seeking career counseling and 21 had had career counseling provided as part of a federally funded work–study program for students from low income families. There were 37 males and 30 females. A letter and questionnaire were sent to each subject who could be located. The questionnaire asked the subjects to record their present job, to select the SVIB occupational scale closest to that job, to record their level of job satisfaction, and to state whether they would be willing to fill out a current SCII. The subjects were also asked to sort the SVIB-M scale titles into the three VCS classifications (*like, indifferent, dislike*).

Thirty-seven respondents returned the questionnaire. An additional seven were contacted by phone, and the occupations of three more were established through the alumni office. Altogether, the current occupations of 47 subjects were determined, 28 males and 19 females; 35 had been counseling clients and 12 had been work–study students. The results, although complex, suggested to Dolliver and Will that the Tyler Vocational Card Sort was slightly more accurate than the SVIB in predicting occupations that were held 10 years later. Both were accurate for about 50% of the subjects. These and other results suggested that the results of the VCS were quite similar to the results of the widely used SVIB. Dolliver and Will (1977) suggested that the two instruments might have differential usefulness depending on the needs of the career client. They wrote:

> Measures of inventoried interests probably help orient clients to new occupational areas that had not previously been considered or to provide a confirmation of what had seemed an appropriate choice. Methods of expressed-interests measurement probably are helpful to clients who have considered a lot of occupational areas but have difficulty in narrowing their choices. Cognitively complex clients, especially, seem to benefit from the chance to sort out their ideas. Expressed-interests measures, by their nature, help the

client to take more seriously what they already know about their ideas, values, and goals. The TVCS and NSVCS both promote the clients' consideration of their reasons for being attracted to or repelled from occupations, an aspect of the method that could not be included in the present study. (p. 53)

In concluding their discussion section, Dolliver and Will suggested that counselors should use both an "expressed-vocational-interests method" and an inventory and make special note of the areas of agreement. This final suggestion was supported by a conclusion reached by Slaney and Russell (1981). Based on a review of the research comparing the predictive validity of expressed and inventoried vocational interests, they concluded that when expressed and inventoried interests are in agreement, predictive validity is higher than when they are not in agreement. The results of the Dolliver and Will study were quite supportive of the use of the vocational card sort in career counseling.

A study by Slaney (1978) was developed to compare the results and reactions of subjects who took both the VCS and the SCII. He had 84 undergraduate women, who were paid for participation, take both instruments. The subjects were screened to assure that they had not decided on a career choice. In the first session they were given a questionnaire and then asked to complete the SCII. Two weeks later they returned and took the VCS, which was self-administered. When they completed the VCS they were given the printout of their SCII results. After reading these results, they completed a questionnaire that compared the two instruments and were asked to return in 3 weeks. At this final session, the subjects filled out a final questionnaire, were asked for their reactions to the study, and were paid.

Slaney found moderate agreement between the two sets of Holland themes gathered from the two instruments. There was rather clear agreement between the basic interests of the two instruments and less clear agreement between the occupations as they were presented on the SCII printout and as they were sorted as part of the VCS. Slaney concluded that although there were generally statistically significant relationships between the corresponding Holland themes, basic interests, and occupations of the two instruments, the results of the instruments were not interchangeable for individual clients. He also found that the VCS Holland themes were not less consistent, as Holland defines consistency, than the SCII themes. The VCS themes were more highly related to expressed interests than were the themes of the SCII. The 12 bipolar items of a comparative questionnaire were specifically designed to measure differences between the two instruments based on the suggestions of Dolliver and Will quoted above. None of these differences was statistically significance.

A separate question asked subjects to identify which instrument they would recommend to a friend. One suggested neither, 76 (92%) suggested both, four suggested only the SCII, and three suggested only the VCS.

Finally, an open-ended question asked subjects to write comments that would compare the two instruments. These comments were combined for each instrument, and two raters were asked to summarize the comments they had read. The first rater, a female PhD, wrote the following:

> My overall impression was that the subjects found the instruments comple-
> mentary; the VCS was a more personal, thought-provoking experience but the
> computerized results of the SCII lent validity or provided a challenge to the
> personal evaluation. While the SCII was sometimes found boring, the VCS,
> because it questioned the reasons for choices, was more fun to take and kept
> interest alive.

The second rater, a male PhD, summarized the comments he had read as follows:

> The VCS seemed to stimulate more thinking and individual initiative, the SCII
> seemed to be regarded as more objective and having wider coverage. It was
> obvious that there is a great deal of individual variance in terms of how the
> two tests were perceived.

These comments of the raters do seem reminiscent of the earlier comments of Dolliver and Will that suggested that the VCS helps clients by encouraging them to think about their choices and, more specifically, their reasons for these choices.

The results of the study by Slaney seemed supportive of the inclusion of the Holland themes as rank ordered by the clients, as well as the relation of these themes to measures of expressed interests and college majors. The comparison of some of the psychometric aspects of the two instruments also seemed encouraging for the VCS. The generally positive evaluations of the instrument by the women who had taken both versions, as well as the summary of their comments on the two instruments, were also seen as positive support for continued investigation of the instrument. Taken to-gether, the results of this study suggested that the VCS held up quite well in comparison to the SCII. Given that the SCII was then, and continues to be, one of the most widely used inventories as well as one of the most carefully developed, these results were seen as encouraging.

Lawler (1979) investigated the effects of the Non-Sexist Vocational Card Sort and the Self-Directed Search when both were self-administered in their standard formats or were revised to conform to the requirements of the NIE Guidelines on Sex Bias and Sex Fairness. She also included an information-only group and a waiting-list control group. She studied 198 undergraduate women who were uncertain about their vocational futures and were inter-ested in participating in a study on career exploration. The women were randomly distributed to one of the six groups. Lawler found no differences based on whether the groups received the original or the revised versions of the instruments. There were also no statistically significant differences in the satisfaction with the various treatments or in the amount of vocational exploration that was reported or the vocational information that was requested. She did find that the NSVCS suggested a broader range of career alternatives to the participants than did the SDS. However, although the NSVCS suggested more nontraditional occupations to these women, there were no differences in the traditionality of the careers they were actually considering immediately following treatment and 2 weeks later. The fact that the NSVCS suggested more nontraditional choices is encouraging. The fact that the choices the women were actually considering were not affected is, of course, less encouraging. Lawler suggested that perhaps a lengthier treatment might have been more effective in influencing the actual choices of these women. Overall, the NSVCS suggested more nontraditional choices to these women and in other respects performed as well as the widely used Self-Directed Search. Although these results are not exciting, they were generally supportive of the card sort approach.

Two studies, one by Talbot and Birk (1979) and another by Takai and Holland (1979), investigated different aspects of the then new Vocational Exploration and Insight Kit (VEIK) by Holland and his associates. The VEIK contains the Self-Directed Search as well as a Vocational Card Sort (VCS) that was modified by Holland. The VCS, according to Talbot and Birk, consisted of 10 steps, which "instruct the user to sort occupational titles; explain tentative preferences and exclusions; confront the role that sex, race, social class, or religion may have played in the sorting process; and identify 'personal needs, hopes, talents, personal weaknesses, distasteful activities, and unpleasant roles or tasks' related to the user's occupational preferences" (p. 359).

Talbot and Birk assigned 103 undergraduate women to one of four groups: an SDS group, a VCS group, a VEIK group, or a control group. They found that subjects exposed to the SDS and the VEIK were considering significantly more occupations than the VCS or control groups. Later the authors noted that although the number of occupations being considered has been used in research with some frequency, its meaning is far from clear. They suggested that some subjects would probably be better served, for example, by having less choices as a result of treatment. Talbot and Birk also found no differences on a measure of client satisfaction with the treatments. Although some minor differences between the treatments were found, the expectation that the VEIK would surpass the effects of its component parts was not supported.

Takai and Holland assigned 252 high school girls to one of three treatments, an SDS group, a VCS group, or a VEIK group. Their study yielded even more disappointing findings than did Talbot and Birk's. Despite the expectation that the VEIK would exceed the VCS and the SDS in its effects on a variety of outcome measures, that was not found. Instead, it was found that the SDS had the highest means, although these were not statistically different, the VCS had the next highest means, and the VEIK, generally, had the lowest means. Some speculations were offered on the possible reasons for these results, for example, that a ceiling effect is quickly reached and additional treatments add nothing, or there may be an order effect. However, overall it was clear that the results for the more extensive VEIK were extremely disappointing. No other studies on the VEIK were located. In the present context it should be noted that the results of this study as well as the results of Talbot and Birk do add some support to the use of the card sort approach as a career intervention.

Jones and DeVault (1979) compared the Occ-U-Sort (O-U-S) and the SDS. They used 95 high-school students from a variety of training programs ranging from welding to advanced placement classes in Spanish. Half of the students took the O-U-S and the other half took the SDS. All took Holland's VPI and filled out a Satisfaction Opinionnaire. Jones and DeVault found one item on the Satisfaction Opinionnaire that favored the O-U-S. They did not, however, use multivariate analyses for the overall scale. The Holland codes derived from the SDS and the O-U-S did not differ significantly in their relationships to the Holland codes of the VPI. Both relationships were moderate. There were no differences in the number of errors made in calculating the Holland codes for each instrument. Jones and DeVault interpreted these results as indicating that the O-U-S had a lot of promise as a method of meeting the career development needs of students. They noted that the possible conclusions that could be derived from their study were qualified "by the limited scope of this investigation" (p. 340).

In a later study, Jones (1983) again compared the O-U-S and the SDS with 578 8th- and 10th-grade students from North Carolina. Although a few minor differences were found, several of these did not hold up after 3 weeks and, overall, the study was remarkable for the lack of differences, given the large number of subjects. The study also used a rather simplistic approach to the analyses of the results and failed to look for possible gender or race differences. The O-U-S did, however, appear to perform as well as the more widely used SDS on the dimensions measured.

Atanasoff and Slaney (1980) compared the effects of three counselor-free career interventions: the SDS, the interpretive format of the SCII, and the VCS. The subjects were 140 undergraduate women volunteers who were interested in career exploration and had not decided on a career choice. The women were randomly distributed to one of the treatment groups or to a no-treatment control group. The effects of treatment were measured 3 weeks after the subjects received the results from their particular intervention. Using a rather large number of outcome measures, Atanasoff and

Slaney found that the relationship between the Holland codes and expressed interests was significantly lower for the SCII than for the SDS and the VCS, which did not differ from each other. This result for the VCS and the SCII replicated the finding of Slaney (1978). All of the treatment-group members indicated that they understood the kinds of occupations suitable to their personalities better than did the control-group members. Beyond these results, most of the differences did not discriminate the treatment groups from the control group members. In addition, the few interaction effects that were found did not lead to unequivocal interpretations. It is interesting that the rank ordering of the Holland types in the VCS again seemed to be supported. Overall, however, the clearest findings were that the results of the three treatments were not strikingly different from each other. Given the widespread use of the SDS and the SCII, these results at least suggested that the effects of the lesser known VCS compared quite favorably with the effects of these instruments.

The next study in this series was by Slaney and Slaney (1981) and compared the results of the merged male and female form of the SCII and the VCS for 50 female and 50 male counseling center clients who had received career counseling at a university counseling center. There was moderate agreement between the Holland codes generated by the two instruments. Slightly less than three of the five highest basic interest scales for the two instruments overlapped, whereas for the five highest occupational scales slightly less than one overlapped for women and slightly more than one overlapped for men. For women, all of the five highest occupations suggested by the SCII were more stereotypically feminine than were the five highest occupations of the VCS. All of these results were statistically significant. For the men, there were no statistically significant differences in the sexual composition of the occupations suggested by the two instruments. These results were consistent with the results of Slaney (1978) for the relationships between the Holland codes, basic interests, and occupational scales of the SCII and the VCS. The results for the sexual composition of the occupations suggested by the two instruments were consistent with the findings of Cooper (1976), who also compared the SCII and another version of the VCS on this dimension. Given the amount of attention that was being directed toward expanding the career options of women, this result seemed to provide important support for the VCS, although the exact cause of these results was not clear.

Slaney (1983) blocked on three levels of career indecision and randomly distributed 180 undergraduate women (60 per indecision level) into a VCS or SCII treatment group or a control group. Using a large number of outcome measures, Slaney found few treatment differences, although three items of a satisfaction scale indicated that the SCII group members rated that intervention more positively than did the VCS group members. The means for both treatments were quite positive, however. There were also more judged changes in the career choices of the two treatment groups than occurred in the control group. For the VCS the greatest change took place at the most undecided level. For the SCII the changes were concentrated at the most undecided level but were also spread across the more decided levels more equally than occurred for the VCS. There were no differences between the treatments in the sexual composition of the occupations that the women were considering 3 weeks after treatment, no differences in vocational exploration, and no differences in satisfaction with career. Overall, there was much clearer and more consistent support for the importance of career indecision. The subjects who were most undecided showed the greatest change in their career choices and expressed the greatest need for additional vocational services, and the least satisfaction with their career choices.

The results of Slaney (1983) suggested that the level of career indecision of the subjects of career intervention studies was an important consideration for future research. This variable was clearly related to a variety of outcome measures in a convincingly consistent manner. The clarity of the treatment effects was less obvious. It is at least interesting to note that the differences in satisfaction with the two instruments were not found in the Slaney (1978) study where the women took both instruments or in that of Atanasoff and Slaney (1980). It is also interesting that the occupations being considered by the women 3 weeks after treatment were not less sexually stereotyped for the VCS group. This finding is inconsistent with the earlier results of Cooper but mirrors what was found by Lawler. Unfortunately, this study did not examine the occupations suggested to the subjects by the two instruments. However, even if the VCS suggested less stereotyped occupations, it is difficult to argue for the importance of this effect if the occupations actually considered do not differ. The finding that the SCII led to more changes in the decided subjects is even more intriguing. Atanasoff and Slaney in their 1980 study raised the possibility that the SCII, because it did not confirm the expressed choices of career decided subjects, may have led them to reexamine their choices even when those choices were perhaps appropriate. The present study did, in fact, find that SCII subjects who were decided changed more than did the decided subjects who received the VCS or were in the control group. None of the decided women in the control group changed, two women in the VCS group changed, and eight decided women in the SCII group changed. Although these numbers are not large and the case needs to be clearly labeled as a speculative one, the issues raised deserve further exploration.

Slaney and Dickson (1985) studied reentry women, that is, undergraduate women who were over the age of 30, who had responded to a mail survey ($N = 985$) and expressed a willingness to be involved in a study on career choice ($N = 526$). Slaney and Dickson blocked on level of career indecision, based on extreme scores (upper and lower 20% of the sample) on the Vocational Identity subscale of the My Vocational Situation scale (Holland, Daiger, & Power, 1980). For the undecided group 87% were willing to participate; for the decided group 35% were willing. For each level of indecision, reentry women were randomly distributed to either a VCS-only treatment group, a VCS-plus-videotape treatment group, or a control group. The videotape was included to attempt to encourage these women to consider more nontraditional careers. The videotape was "The Joy of Choosing" and was developed as a part of Project Born Free to "broaden the range of career options for both women and men" (Dege, Warsett, Hansen, & Miles-Novoa, 1980). There were about 20 women per cell and a total of 121 women completed the study. A follow-up was conducted 1 year after the original study, and over 84% of the women responded.

Outcomes were measured across a number of domains including career indecision, satisfaction with career choice, treatment satisfaction, vocational needs, the sexual composition of career choices, and career choice change. The only treatment effects found indicated that the women who had seen the videotape agreed more strongly than those who had not that they would recommend the treatment to a friend. They also agreed more strongly that the experience encouraged them to find information about occupations. Written comments from a number of the women suggested that they had responded positively to the VCS as well as the videotape. One woman wrote, "I particularly liked the 'Joy of Choosing.' My favorite gal . . . was the chemical engineer (an older lady). She will be among women I choose as a professional image." An undecided woman wrote, "In sorting the cards and really thinking about what I like to do, I was able to put more factors together and come up with a decision to research and probably commit to (the above) goals." Other undecided women also found the VCS helpful; for example, "This vocational planning experience helped me sort out my thoughts a little and gave me some ideas I hadn't thought of before." Another wrote, "Being part of this exploration in careers led me to really examine my wants and desires." Although the statements represented only a portion of the sample, they were almost entirely positive and supportive of the treatments.

As in Slaney (1983), the clearest effects were found for the variable of career indecision. The undecided women expressed a greater need for additional vocational services, were less satisfied with their career choices, and were clearly more undecided 2 weeks after treatment and 1 year after treatment. For the undecided women, indecision was reduced from pretest to posttest but unchanged from posttest to follow-up. They also had more changes in their career choices. For the satisfaction scale, undecided women agreed that they had clearer ideas about unsuitable occupations and that the experience encouraged them to find career information. They disagreed that the results of the experience had been confusing or unsatisfactory.

These results suggested that career indecision was not a transitory state for these reentry women. One year later the undecided women were still clearly undecided. The treatments for this group were not effective, and no spontaneous remission effects were in evidence. Although the possibility exists that these women were experiencing other life difficulties that made them particularly difficult to treat, they do represent a proportion of the reentry population that needs career counseling, will take the time to participate, and clearly need career interventions that attend to their states of career indecision. Minimal treatments, although appreciated by these women, were not adequate in dealing with the degree of career indecision that they were experiencing. It also was clear that the intervention to encourage the exploration of more nontraditional career choices did not have a clear effect on the career choices that these women were considering 2 weeks or 1 year after counseling. Although the effects of the VCS compared quite well with the effects of other interventions and did seem to influence the thought that at least some of these women were giving to their career choices, additional attention certainly seems to be needed for the growing population of reentry women. It is also clear, as it was in Slaney (1983), that career indecision is an extremely important and explanatory variable to include in future studies of interventions designed to increase career exploration.

Slaney and Lewis (1986) compared the effects of the SCII and the VCS using a different sample of career undecided reentry women. Level of indecision was assessed by the Occupational Alternatives Question (OAQ), which was the criterion measure used in Slaney (1983) for blocking on career indecision. A score of three on the OAQ indicates that a person has some alternative career choices but that there is no first choice. Women with this score in Slaney (1983) had shown the clearest and most dramatic responses to treatment, including career choice changes. Previous research has also linked this OAQ score to being undecided about a career choice (Slaney, 1980, 1983; Slaney & Dickson, 1985; Slaney, Stafford, & Russell, 1981). Slaney and Lewis (1986) used a score of three on the OAQ for selecting women. They randomly assigned 34 reentry women, who were undergraduate women over the age of 25, to either the VCS or the SCII. The study used a substantial number of outcome measures and included a 6-month follow-up. No statistically significant treatment differences were found on measures of vocational needs or on satisfaction with treatment at posttest. Three measures of career indecision were used and indicated that there were statistically significant reductions in career indecision for both groups 3 weeks after treatment but not from posttest to follow-up. Changes in career choices were not statistically significant, but post hoc inspection of the data indicated that 14 of the women (41%) had made substantive changes in their career choices, 7 from each group.

Overall, the results of the Slaney and Lewis study seem more supportive of both career interventions with reentry women who appeared to be appropriate candidates for career interventions. Both groups showed what can be considered positive treatment effects. Given that these women were rather clearly undecided and were also interested in being in a study on career exploration, it seems reasonable to suggest that becoming less career undecided equals a positive change. The generally high levels of satisfaction with both interventions are at least consistent with such an interpretation. However, a clear limitation of the study, which also limits the confidence that can be maintained in any interpretation, involves the lack of a control group. Still, these results do seem supportive of the two interventions for career undecided women. The fact that the differences in indecision that occurred after treatment were significant but the differences from posttest to follow-up were not seems to strengthen the argument that the treatments were related to the reductions in career indecision and the changes in career choices. Again, although the VCS compared quite well with the effects of the widely used SCII, the study, per se, provided no compelling rationale for preferring one treatment over the other.

Croteau and Slaney (1994), in an article based on Croteau's dissertation, compared 95 college men who were randomly assigned to an SCII treatment group or the VCS treatment group. The VCS was self-directed using Slaney's approach (Slaney, 1983). The SCII was interpreted using the individualized self-interpretive format. Croteau reasoned that the previous studies comparing the VCS and the SCII had not really looked for differences based on the possible differential effects that might be expected for each instrument. Croteau included a measure of Career Development Responsibility, an instrument that was seen as related to the Rotter Internal–External Locus of Control scale but specifically aimed at career development responsibility issues. The idea that Croteau attempted to measure was that the SCII might have greater appeal to men with external career development responsibility (who looked outside of themselves for making a career choice) in comparison with men with internal career development responsibility. He also reasoned that the VCS might be more likely to increase scores on the Career Decision Making Self-Efficacy Scale (Betz & Taylor, 1982). Neither hypothesis was supported by the data. Croteau did find that the immediate reactions to the interpretive results of the SCII were more positive than the immediate responses to the VCS. However, these differences faded over time, until at 2 weeks after each group had received the results of treatment there were no differences in the groups' reactions.

Croteau also had the subjects give written reactions to the two interventions. These reactions were then read and summarized by two experienced counselors. One counselor, an experienced female PhD in clinical psychology, seemed to suggest that the subjects who had taken the SCII reacted somewhat more positively than the VCS subjects. She noted that, "The vast majority of the responses . . . were very favorable to the Strong-Campbell." This same counselor began her comments on the VCS by stating that "Reactions to the Card Sort task were more varied than the reactions to the SCII." However, she also noted that "Many found the task (VCS) led them to want to get more information about particular jobs, and many commented that the task opened up new career choices that they had not previously considered." The second counselor, an experienced male counselor with an EdD in higher education, began his comments by stating that "The vast majority of respondents to the questionnaire thought positively about their experience with the VCS." His comments were more consistent with the comments made by the raters in Slaney (1978) and were more consistent with the expectations for the VCS. He wrote:

> For some, it provided new avenues to explore, gave them new insights about careers they hadn't considered and directed their thoughts in new directions. For others it helped them narrow down their focus. . . . Some just indicated that the experience was "easy," "different," "interesting," "fun." . . . There was the indication from some that it made them think about their values and what was important to them. (Croteau & Slaney, 1994, p. 259)

In commenting on the SCII, the second rater wrote:

> The Strong responses seemed to reflect a greater legitimacy once again because respondents interpreted specific careers as having been identified for themselves. They seemed more positively effusive about the SCII than the Card Sort. . . . There was less mention made of gaining insight about values, likes, and dislikes in the Strong. There seemed to be a greater focus among the responses to the Strong on specific career options and less on values and personal preferences. (Croteau & Slaney, 1994, p. 259)

Although it is not clear why there was not greater agreement between the raters, the comments of the second rater do seem consistent with the comments gathered earlier by Slaney (1978) and with the expectations of the study. Although this sort of support is well short of compelling, it is suggestive that the VCS makes clients think about the basis for their career decisions more than does the SCII. The other results of Croteau and Slaney (1994) suggest that for future studies that might examine this issue it will be important to consider the best time for gathering this sort of data.

Croteau's expectation of finding differential effects for the SCII and the VCS based on organismic variables, although a good idea, was not productive. Although possible reasons for this failure were examined, there was a very real question about whether the problem was with the measures used or the fact that the treatments were really not very discriminable to the subjects based on the dimensions of internal–external control and self-efficacy. Overall, the findings are consistent with the earlier studies that have compared the SCII and the VCS and found that, for the most part, the lack of treatment differences for the two interventions is much clearer than are the reasons for preferring one over the other based on the research.

Goldman (1995) took the study by Croteau and Slaney to task for using, or, from his perspective, misusing, the VCS. Goldman wrote, "It is a pity that the traditions of standardized testing, combined with the traditions of quantitative research methods lead people to transform this rich, projective, assessment-counseling procedure (i.e. the VCS) into just another test, with numbers as the bottom line" (p. 386). The "people" being referred to in this sentence were Croteau and Slaney. The astute reader will probably not be terribly surprised that these "people" disagreed with Goldman's perspective on their study. They stated their perspective in a rejoinder to Goldman (Slaney and Croteau, 1995). Interested readers are referred to this energetic but civil exchange to determine their own conclusions on the issues.

In their response to Goldman, Slaney and Croteau (1995) cited a dissertation by Moran (1991) as evidence that the counselor-administered VCS produced greater thoughtfulness in clients than the self-administered version. Moran compared the administration of the Slaney VCS by a counselor with the self-administered version by studying 82 women who had sought career counseling at the Career Development and Placement Service at Pennsylvania State University. Forty-two women received the counselor administered VCS and 40 women received the self-administered version. Moran blocked on career-decidedness and used a thought-listing procedure along with other career-relevant dependent measures. Both groups increased their scores on measures of career decidedness and career development. The counselor-administered group generated more reasons for their choices, had more positive and less negative thoughts after the intervention, were more satisfied with the intervention, and had more thoughts about the counseling. They also remembered more reasons for liking and disliking occupations. The self-administered group was more accurate in remembering their Holland codes. These results were seen as suggesting that the counselor administered group was more thoughtful and engaged in the intervention than the self-administered group. An interesting serendipitous finding that recalls the opening sections of this chapter was that the counselors in Moran's study frequently made favorable comments on the VCS. There were comments on "their increasing interest in and the engaging quality of . . . (the VCS) . . . and their surprise at the usefulness (of the VCS) in career counseling" (Moran, 1991). This last point, while based on the impressions of the investigator, is consistent with our experience and speculation that occurred earlier in this chapter. These results also provide a basis for interesting future studies.

EVALUATION AND FUTURE DIRECTIONS

Overall the research on vocational card sorts suggests that their effects on clients and subjects in intervention studies compare quite well with the effects of other widely used and carefully developed instruments. Whether this is encouraging for the card sorts, discouraging for all of the interventions considered, or somewhat encouraging for both may depend on one's perspective. Some effects do seem to be reliably measured, although the magnitude of those effects is not always impressive. Still, if these interventions are considered as only one part of the career counseling process, the results can be seen as encouraging. The link between the effects of treatment and the degree of career indecision being experienced by the client is a reasonable but important relationship for counselors and researchers to consider. The incorporation of the Holland types in Slaney's version of the card sort also seems like an interesting and promising addition, especially in relation to the research on expressed interests. The relationship of the rank-ordered Holland types to other aspects of the card sorts is also encouraging. Whether the reliability of these types as selected by clients holds up irrespective of career indecision is an interesting issue for future research.

Beyond the work just noted, it seems most accurate and conservative to say that overall relatively little research has been done on the vocational card sorts. For most versions of the card sort either very few or no studies at all have been done. It is also striking that of all the studies located, only Dolliver's original study and Moran's more recent dissertation involved a counselor in the administration of the card sort. Certainly Goldman (1983, 1995) has been clear in his opposition to making the card sort a self-administered treatment. He saw a clear need for a sensitive counselor to observe and interpret the reactions and responses of the client. Dolliver (personal communication, 1988), in writing about his original work with the TVCS, also seemed to agree on the need for a counselor. Our experience with the instrument lends support to this position. One important role for the counselor involves being aware of any possible limitations that clients may impose on themselves, especially if these are unrealistic and have an important influence on the careers being considered or excluded from consideration. In addition, in our experience, clients doing the VCS with counselors sometimes initially give rather simplistic responses when they are asked why they do or do not choose a particular group of occupations. The role of the counselor in encouraging more thoughtfulness in clients seems potentially important. Moran's dissertation examined the possibility of increased thoughtfulness, and her study added the most compelling support for the inclusion of a counselor thus far. Her results clearly indicate that clients do question or think about the reasons for their choices more energetically when the VCS is counselor administered. Methodologically it seems legitimate to argue that the exclusion of the counselor helped to clarify the effects of the instrument, separate from the effects of the counselor in the early research. However, it now seems appropriate to replicate and extend Moran's findings that the card sorts do produce differential effects when they are administered by a counselor. It is equally important to carefully explore what these effects are empirically. These are quite important directions for carefully conceived future research that have pragmatic implications for career counseling.

If one believes that a primary strength of the card sort resides in its ability to get clients to think about the reasons for their choices, then this becomes an important issue to study. A closely related issue is whether it can be demonstrated that the card sorts make clients more thoughtful about their actual career choices. To counselors who use the VCS, they do seem to have this effect. There are open-ended comments, especially in Slaney (1978), that seem to suggest that at least some clients and counselors see the card sorts as having this effect. Moran's dissertation appears to present a highly promising empirical demonstration of this effect. Additional demonstrations, perhaps using different dependent variable as well as both qualitative and quantitative approaches, seem called for at this point.

Another central issue that needs to be addressed through research is whether it can be demonstrated that the use of the card sort technique does, as we have suggested, actually increase the interest and involvement of counselors in career counseling. Moran's anecdotal report certainly seems suggestive on this issue and supportive of additional studies that would address a variety of related concerns. More specifically, a few studies might explore whether counselors who use the card sort feel more involved with their clients, like them better, and recall more about their interests, values, Holland types, career choices, and other aspects of their lives. Other related questions do not seem difficult to generate. We would, of course, suspect that the card sort would receive support, but these questions raise interesting possibilities for future exploration. Obvious comparisons would be with counselors who use the Strong, the SDS (Holland, 1985c), one of the many available computer programs, or any of a variety of other instruments or approaches. Similar issues could also be investigated from the perspective of clients. We would also predict that they would be more involved in the process of counseling, like their counselor and career counseling better, be more thoughtful about their choices, reveal more about themselves, miss fewer appointments, and remember their own career interests, values, Holland types, and career choices better than clients who received other interventions. These studies might also begin to explore the importance of the relationship in career counseling. The suggested studies would appear to be quite interesting to perform, and the results could have practical implications in terms of what effects are actually best achieved by the card sorts as well as the other approaches investigated.

Another issue that needs to be addressed through research concerns the reliability of the categories that clients use for the classification of the careers that they choose or reject as a part of the card sort. A related question would be whether this reliability is related to other career-relevant variables. The reliability of clients' final hierarchies of choices might also be studied, as well as the relationship of the rank-ordered Holland types to the career choices in relation to some other dimensions such as career indecision. For example, are the hierarchies of decided clients more stable than those of undecided clients? Are the relationships between the Holland types and career choices affected by degrees of career indecision? Other investigators have suggested that the number of categories used by clients might be related to the degree of career indecision, but thus far no studies have addressed this interesting and easily studied topic. The issue raised by several investigators about the validity of the instrument and how it should be studied also needs to be addressed. Some of the studies just suggested address the unique effects that the card sort may have on clients that might differentiate it from other instruments such as the SDS or the SII.

In summary, the vocational card sorts seem like a promising approach to include in career counselors' approaches to career interventions. At this point the enthusiasm and clinical or anecdotal support for the card sorts, from a number of sources, seems to outstrip the research investigations that have addressed this instrument. Indeed, the research has barely begun to investigate the effects of the card sort technique in career counseling. Whether future studies will provide data to support the effects that the card sorts appear to have on career clients is at this point an open question, although some early results seem promising. Several important and interesting questions have been raised here, and a substantial number of additional questions could have been generated. Whether the needed research will be conducted is, at present, unclear. These studies will involve a series of carefully developed investigations that will be expensive and difficult to carry out. The technique does at this point seem promising and worth the needed research effort. Hopefully, that effort will be forthcoming.

ACKNOWLEDGMENT

The authors express appreciation to Professor Paul R. Salomone for his careful and thoughtful comments on an earlier version of this chapter.

REFERENCES

Atanasoff, G. E., & Slaney, R. B. (1980). Three approaches to counselor-free career exploration among college women. *Journal of Counseling Psychology, 27,* 332–339.

Bartling, H. C., & Hood, A. B. (1981). An 11-year follow-up of measured interest and vocational choice. *Journal of Counseling Psychology, 28,* 27–35.

Betz, N. E., & Taylor, K. M. (1982). Concurrent validity of the Strong-Campbell Interest Inventory for graduate students in counseling. *Journal of Vocational Behavior, 29,* 626–635.

Birk, J. M., & Brooks, L. (1986). Required skills and training needs of recent counseling psychology graduates. *Journal of Counseling Psychology, 33,* 320–325.

Borgen, F. H., & Seling, M. J. (1978). Expressed and inventoried interests revisited: Perspicacity in the person. *Journal of Counseling Psychology, 25,* 536–543.

Cairo, P. C. (1982). Measured interests versus expressed interests as predictors of long-term occupational membership. *Journal of Vocational Behavior, 20,* 343–353.

Cochran, L. R. (1985). Review of Occ-U-Sort. In J. Mitchell, Jr. (Ed.), *The ninth mental measurements yearbook* (pp. 1076–1078). Lincoln, NE: Buros Institute of Mental Measurements.

Cooper, J. F. (1976). Comparative impact of the SCII and the Vocational Card Sort on career salience and career exploration of women. *Journal of Counseling Psychology, 23,* 348–352.

Crites, J. O. (1985). Review of Occ-U-Sort. In J. Mitchell, Jr. (Ed.), *The ninth mental measurements yearbook* (pp. 1077–1079). Lincoln, NE: Buros Institute of Mental Measurements.

Croteau, J. M., & Slaney, R. B. (1994). Two methods of exploring interests: A comparison of outcomes. *Career Development Quarterly, 42,* 252–261.

Daniels, M. H. (1985). Review of Vocational Exploration and Insight Kit. In J. Mitchell, Jr. (Ed.), *The ninth mental measurements yearbook* (pp. 1675–1676). Lincoln, NE: Buros Institute of Mental Measurements.

Dege, D., Warsett, S., Hansen, S. L., & Miles-Novoa, B. (1980). *Video viewers' guide no. 4: The joy of choosing.* Washington, DC: Office of Education.

Dewey, C. R. (1974). Exploring interests: A non-sexist method. *Personnel and Guidance Journal, 52,* 311–315.

Dolliver, R. H. (1966). *The relationship of certain variables to the amount of agreement in inventoried and expressed vocational interests.* Unpublished doctoral dissertation, Ohio State University.

Dolliver, R. H. (1967). An adaptation of the Tyler Vocational Card Sort. *Personnel and Guidance Journal, 45,* 916–920.

Dolliver, R. H. (1969). Strong Vocational Interest Blank versus expressed vocational interests: A review. *Psychological Bulletin, 72,* 95–107.

Dolliver, R. H. (1981). Test review: A review of five vocational card sorts. *Measurement and Evaluation in Guidance, 14,* 168–174.

Dolliver, R. H. (1982). Dolliver's response. *Measurement and Evaluation in Guidance, 15,* 170.

Dolliver, R. H., & Will, J. A. (1977). Ten-year follow-up of the Tyler Vocational Card Sort and the Strong Vocational Interest Blank. *Journal of Counseling Psychology, 24,* 48–54.

Fitzgerald, L. F., & Osipow, S. H. (1986). An occupational analysis of counseling psychology: How special is the specialty? *American Psychologist, 41,* 535–544.

Gade, E. M., & Soliah, D. (1975). Vocational Preference Inventory high point codes versus expressed choices as predictors of college major and career entry. *Journal of Counseling Psychology, 22,* 117–121.

Gelso, C. J., Prince, J., Cornfeld, J. L., Payne, A., Royalty, G., & Wiley, M. O. (1985). Quality of counselors' intake evaluations for clients with problems that are primarily vocational versus personal. *Journal of Counseling Psychology, 32,* 339–347.

Goldman, L. (1983). The Vocational Card Sort technique: A different view. *Measurement and Evaluation in Guidance, 16,* 107–109.

Goldman, L. (1995). Comment on Croteau and Slaney (1994). *Career Development Quarterly, 43,* 385–386.

Gottfredson, L. S. (1981). Circumscription and compromise: A developmental theory of occupational aspirations [Monograph]. *Journal of Counseling Psychology, 28,* 545–579.

Gottfredson, G. D., & Holland, J. L. (1975). Vocational choices of men and women: A comparison of predictors from the Self-Directed Search. *Journal of Counseling Psychology, 22,* 28–34.

Gysbers, N. C., & Moore, E. J. (1987). *Career counseling: Skills, and techniques for practitioner.* Englewood Cliffs, NJ: Prentice Hall.

Harmon, L. W., & Zytowski, D. G. (1980). Reliability of Holland codes across interest measures for adult females. *Journal of Counseling Psychology, 27,* 478–483.

Holland, J. L. (1985a). *Making vocational choices: A theory of vocational personalities and work environments* (2nd ed.). Englewood Cliffs, NJ: Prentice Hall.

Holland, J. L. (1985b). *The occupations finder.* Odessa, FL: Psychological Assessment Resources.

Holland, J. L. (1985c). *The Self-Directed Search: Professional manual—1985 edition.* Odessa, FL: Psychological Assessment Resources.

Holland, J. L., & Associates. (1980). *Counselor's guide to the Vocational Exploration and Insight Kit (VEIK).* Palo Alto, CA: Consulting Psychologists Press.

Holland, J. L., Daiger, D. C., & Power, P. G. (1980). *My vocational situation.* Palo Alto, CA: Consulting Psychologists Press.

Holland, J. L., & Gottfredson, G. D. (1975). Predictive value and psychological meaning of vocational aspirations. *Journal of Vocational Behavior, 6,* 349–363.

Holland, J. L., & Lutz, S. W. (1968). The predictive value of a student's choice of vocation. *Personnel and Guidance Journal, 46,* 428–434.

Jones, L. K. (1982). A reaction to Dolliver's review of the Occ-U-Sort. *Measurement and Evaluation in Guidance, 15,* 169.

Jones, L. K. (1983). A comparison of two self-directed career guidance instruments: Occu-Sort and Self-Directed Search. *School Counselor, 30,* 204–211.

Jones, L. K., & DeVault, R. M. (1979). Evaluation of a self-guided career exploration system: The Occu-Sort. *School Counselor, 26,* 334–341.

Krieshok, T. S., Hansen, R. N., & Johnston, J. A. (1982). *Missouri Occupational Card Sort manual (college form).* Career Planning and Placement Center, University of Missouri-Columbia, Columbia, MO.

Kuhn, T. S. (1970). *The structure of scientific revolutions* (2nd ed.). Chicago: University of Chicago Press.

Lawler, A. C. (1979). Career exploration with women using the Non-Sexist Vocational Card Sort and the Self-Directed Search. *Measurement and Evaluation in Guidance, 12,* 87–97.

MacKinnon-Slaney, F. (1986). Career indecision in reentry and undergraduate women. *Journal of College Student Personnel, 27,* 114–119.

MacKinnon-Slaney, F., Barber, S. L., & Slaney, R. B. (1988). Marital status as a mediating factor on the career aspirations of reentry women students. *Journal of College Student Development, 29,* 327–333.

Mitchell, J. V., Jr. (Ed.). (1985). *The ninth mental measurements yearbook* (Vols. I and II). Lincoln: University of Nebraska Press.

Moore, E. J., Gysbers, N. C., with Carlson, P. (1980). *Missouri Occupational Preference Inventory.* Columbia, MO: Human Systems Consultants, Inc.

Moran, W. J. (1991). *The effects of counselor versus self-administration of the Slaney Vocational Card Sort on the career-related thoughts and decision making of college students.* Unpublished doctoral dissertation, Pennsylvania State University.

O'Neil, J. M., & Magoon, T. M. (1977). The predictability of Holland's investigative personality type and consistency levels using the Self-Directed Search. *Journal of Vocational Behavior, 10,* 39–46.

Pinkney, J. W., & Jacobs, D. (1985). New counselors and personal interest in the task of career counseling. *Journal of Counseling Psychology, 32,* 454–457.

Rosenberg, M. (1957). *Occupations and values.* New York: Free Press.

Slaney, R. B. (1978). Expressed and inventoried vocational interests: A comparison of instruments. *Journal of Counseling Psychology, 25,* 520–529.

Slaney, R. B. (1980). Expressed vocational choice and vocational indecision. *Journal of Counseling Psychology, 27,* 122–129.

Slaney, R. B. (1981). *The Vocational Card Sort—Understanding your results.* Unpublished manuscript, available from R. B. Slaney, Department of Counseling and Educational Psychology, Pennsylvania State University, University Park, PA.

Slaney, R. B. (1983). Influence of career indecision on treatments exploring the vocational interests of college women. *Journal of Counseling Psychology, 30,* 55–63.

Slaney, R. B., & Croteau, J. M. (1995). Response to Goldman (1995). *Career Development Quarterly, 43,* 387–389.

Slaney, R. B., & Dickson, R. D. (1985). Relation of career indecision to career exploration with reentry women: A treatment and follow-up study. *Journal of Counseling Psychology, 32,* 355–362.

Slaney, R. B., & Lewis, E. T. (1986). Effects of career exploration on career undecided reentry women: An intervention and follow-up study. *Journal of Vocational Behavior, 28,* 97–109.

Slaney R. B., & MacKinnnon-Slaney, F. (1986). Relationship of expressed and inventoried vocational interests of female career counseling clients. *Career Development Quarterly, 34,* 24–33.

Slaney, R. B., Moran, W. J., & Wade, J. C. (1994). Vocational card sorts. In J. T. Kapes & M. J. Mastie (Eds.), *A counselor's guide to vocational guidance instruments* (3rd ed., pp. 347–360, 406–407). Alexandria, VA: National Career Development Association.

Slaney, R. B., & Russell, J. E. A. (1981). An investigation of different levels of agreement between expressed and inventoried vocational interests among college women. *Journal of Counseling Psychology, 28,* 221–228.

Slaney, R. B., & Russell, J. E. A. (1987). Perspectives on vocational behavior, 1986: A review. *Journal of Vocational Behavior, 31,* 111–173.

Slaney, R. B., & Slaney, F. M. (1981). A comparison of measures of expressed and inventoried interests among counseling center clients. *Journal of Counseling Psychology, 28,* 515–518.

Slaney, R. B., Stafford, M. J., & Russell, J. E. A. (1981). Career indecision in adult women: A comparative and descriptive study. *Journal of Vocational Behavior, 19,* 335–345.

Takai, R., & Holland, J. L. (1979). Comparison of the Vocational Card Sort, the SDS, and the Vocational Exploration and Insight Kit. *Vocational Guidance Quarterly, 27,* 312–318.

Talbot, D. B., & Birk, M. M. (1979). Does the vocational exploration and insight kit equal the sum of its parts?: A comparison study. *Journal of Counseling Psychology, 26,* 359–362.

Tittle, C. K. (1985). Review of Vocational Exploration and Insight Kit. In J. Mitchell, Jr. (Ed.), *The ninth mental measurements yearbook* (p. 1676). Lincoln, NE: Buros Institute of Mental Measurements.

Touchton, J. G., & Magoon, T. M. (1977). Occupational daydreams as predictors of vocational plans of college women. *Journal of Vocational Behavior, 10,* 156–166.

Tyler, L. E. (1961). Research explorations in the realm of choice. *Journal of Counseling Psychology, 8,* 195–201.

U.S. Department of Labor. (1979). *Guide for occupational exploration.* Washington, DC: U.S. Government Printing Office.

U.S. Department of Labor. (1991). *Dictionary of occupational titles* (4th ed. revised). Washington, DC: U.S. Government Printing Office.

Watkins, C. E., Jr., Lopez, F. G., Campbell, V. L., & Himmell, C. D. (1986). Contemporary counseling psychology: Results of a national survey. *Journal of Counseling Psychology, 33,* 301–309.

Westbrook, B. W., & Mastie, M. M. (1982). Shall we sort the Occu-U-Sort into the might-choose, would-not-choose, or uncertain pile? *Measurement and Evaluation in Guidance, 15,* 259–256.

Whitney, D. R. (1969). Predicting from expressed vocational choice: A review. *Personnel and Guidance Journal, 48,* 279–286.

Williams, S. K. (1978). The Vocational Card Sort: A tool for vocational exploration. *The Vocational Guidance Quarterly, 26,* 237–243.

Zener, T. B., & Schnuelle, L. (1976). Effects of the Self-Directed Search on high school students. *Journal of Counseling Psychology, 23,* 353–359.

Assessing Career
Decision Making

Mark L. Savickas

Northeastern Ohio Universities College of Medicine

Determining clients' readiness to make educational and vocational choices is the principal assessment task in comprehensive career counseling (Crites, 1974b; Super, 1983). This chapter begins with an explanation of this assertion. The bulk of the chapter describes three psychometric inventories, each of which is designed to measure different variables in the career decision-making process. The first scale, the Career Decision Scale (Osipow, Carney, Winer, Yanico, & Koschier, 1976), measures difficulties in making a career choice. The second scale, the Career Development Inventory (Super, Thompson, Lindeman, Jordaan, & Myers, 1981), measures adaptability for mastering career development tasks. The third scale, the Career Maturity Inventory (Crites, 1978b), measures dispositions for vocational decision making. Each scale's construction and development are described and its validity is considered. How psychologists may use the scales in counseling practice is discussed and then illustrated with a case example. The chapter concludes with an evaluation of career decision-making assessment in contemporary counseling practice.

CAREER CHOICE PROCESS

All too often career counselors have worked with clients only to find that they still cannot make a career choice. Counseling that leaves clients unable to choose a career usually deals with choice content, that is, the occupations that fit a client's interests and abilities. Counseling methods that match clients' interests and abilities to occupational positions work well for clients who are ready to make decisions. Decisive clients can use the results of interest inventories and aptitude tests to make realistic career choices. However, clients who are not ready to make decisions encounter difficulty when they try to make career choices. In fact, after discussing test results and occupational information, they become even more confused about their career choices because they have more data than they are ready to use.

Counselors who are sensitive to variations in clients' readiness to make career choices appreciate Crites's (1974b) distinction between the content and the process of vocational decision making. *Content* refers to which occupation a client should enter and thus focuses on the client's interests and abilities. *Process* refers to how a client arrives at an occupational choice and thus focuses on the client's decision-making concerns and coping responses. Crites used the analogy of an assembly line to describe the distinction. He likened career choice to the product and vocational decision making to production activities. Crites explicated the distinction between choice content and choice process in refining Super's (1955) model of vocational development. Crites' model charted two content dimensions and two process dimensions in the maturation of vocational decision making during adolescence (see Fig. 12.1). One content dimension, wisdom, deals with the development of fit between clients' occupational preferences and their interests, abilities, and experiences. The other content dimension, consistency, deals with the development of stability and coherence in clients' occupational preferences. The two process dimensions in Crites's model deal with the development of attitudes toward and competencies for vocational decision making. The decisional attitudes are dispositions that influence readiness to choose. The competencies refer to the information, comprehension, foresight, and problem solving required for rational decision making.

The classic matching model for career counseling focuses on the content dimensions of career choice (Bell, 1940; Williamson & Darley, 1937). Content-oriented counselors use matching methods such as aptitude tests to identify the occupational level at which a client can best function and interest inventories to identify the occupational field in which the client can find the most satisfaction. Counselors who use the matching model and methods in a pedestrian manner act as if all clients are ready to choose an occupation. Their behavior manifests a test-centered rather than client-centered approach and reflects the belief that all clients can be treated in the same way. For example, it is not uncommon for a student seeking vocational guidance at a college counseling center to be scheduled by the receptionist for an interest inventory prior to the initial appointment with a counselor. Nor is it unusual for a counselor to administer an interest inventory to an entire

MEASUREMENT OF VOCATIONAL MATURITY

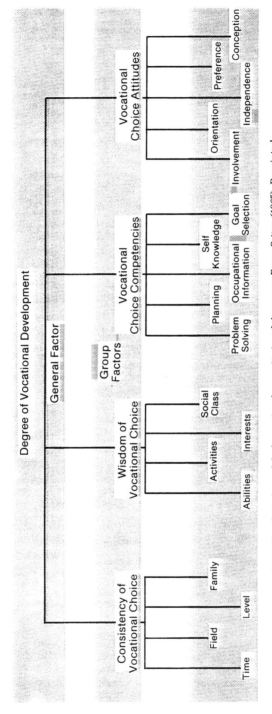

FIG. 12.1. Crites's model of vocational maturity in adolescence. From Crites (1965). Reprinted by permission.

high school class. Although this practice has been effective and efficient for clients who have been ready to make choices, at best it has been ineffective and inefficient for other clients. The piles of scored interest inventories taken by clients who never reappeared for an interpretation and the only partial success of group guidance with clients who have different career concerns reflect the inappropriateness of the matching model and methods for clients not ready to benefit from them.

To more effectively use the matching model and its content-oriented methods, experienced counselors view career choice as a process that develops over time. Typically, they conceptualize career choice as an adaptive process through which individuals meet and master social expectations (also called developmental tasks) to choose an occupation in which they can fulfill both the job demands and their own needs. The choice process begins with the task or social expectation that individuals orient themselves to work as a salient life role. This work salience or career orientation produces a "basic readiness" for vocational decision making, a readiness based on foresight, autonomy, and self-esteem (Super, Savickas, & Super, 1996). When career orientation reaches a critical threshold, people meet the task of crystallizing a career preference. Crystallization involves formulating a general preference for occupations within a particular field and at a particular level. The next task that they encounter is to convert their field and level preferences into specific choices. The specification task includes developing certainty about and comfort with one's occupational choice. The final task in the career choice process is to implement one's choice. Implementation as a developmental task means converting a choice into reality by preparing for and securing a position in the chosen occupation.

In practice, counselors may use the task sequence of orientation, crystallization, specification, and implementation to assess clients' degree of development and vary how they use the matching model and methods. To assess clients' progress in the career choice process, counselors identify the tasks that clients have mastered and are concerned about, the clients' difficulties in coping with the task of concern, and the clients' decision-making attitudes and competencies (Savickas, 1984). Based on this process assessment, counselors can decide whether or not to ask clients to respond to interest inventories and aptitude tests. Clients who do not show work-role commitment or a career orientation may not be mature enough for their interests to have meaning for career choice (Super, Savickas, & Super, 1996). They need life experiences or counseling to induce or strengthen the foresight, autonomy, and self-esteem that support the basic readiness for vocational decision making. If counselors do administer interest inventories to underdeveloped clients, then counselors should not interpret the results relative to clients' crystallizing preferences, specifying choices, or implementing plans. Instead, counselors should use the results to orient clients to the occupational structure in the world of work and to prepare them to investigate several career fields and clarify their work values.

In contrast to clients who are not oriented to career choice, clients who are more highly developed can derive personal meaning from the results of interest inventories and aptitude tests, especially if counselors interpret the scores (data) to them as information (meaning) that eases their coping with the tasks of crystallization, specification, or implementation. In particular, clients who face the crystallization task benefit from information that prompts them to explore several clusters of occupations in related fields and levels. Clients who face the specification task benefit from information that narrows their exploration to occupations in one field and level and helps them choose from among these occupational alternatives. Clients who face the implementation task benefit from information that helps them prepare for and secure positions in their chosen occupations. In short, counselors can assess clients' degree of development and then treat them in accordance with this assessment.

Even the architect of the matching model advised counselors to use developmental assessments to guide differential treatment of clients. In describing the goals of an initial career counseling interview, Parsons advised counselors to classify clients into one of two main classes.

First, those who have well-developed aptitudes and interest and a practical basis for a reasonable conclusion in respect to the choice of a vocation. Second, boys and girls with so little experience or manifestation of special aptitudes or interests that there is no basis yet for a wise decision. (1909/1967, p. 19)

Following Parsons's example, experienced counselors used interview techniques and clinical judgment to subjectively assess clients' development and select relevant counseling interventions. Early attempts to objectively assess clients' developmental readiness for career choice, such as the Interest Maturity scale of the Strong Vocational Interest Blank (Strong, 1943, Chap. 12), focused on the content of clients' interests. The marginal success of this approach led some counselors to focus on the structure of clients' interests such as "profile homogeneity" (Holland, 1966) or "interest patterning" (Super, 1955) as indices of readiness for decision making. As recently as 1982, Wigington (p. 179) reported a content-derived index of readiness for the Kuder Occupational Interest Survey: "Clients whose highest Occupation score and/or highest College Major score is below 50 would be viewed as less ready to participate in the career decision-making process."

Instead of deriving indices of readiness indirectly from interest inventories, Super (1955) suggested that counselors directly measure variables in the career choice process. After years of research and reflection that identified and defined the important variables in the career choice process, psychometricians devised objective inventories to directly measure these variables. Content-oriented researchers focused on "indecision" as "slow and complex rate of development" (Holland & Nichols, 1964, p. 33). They constructed measures of decidedness and difficulties in vocational decision making such as the Career Decision Scale (Osipow, Carney, Winer, Yanico, & Koschier, 1976), My Vocational Situation (Holland, Daiger, & Power, 1980), and the Vocational Decision Scale (Jones & Chenery, 1980). In contrast, process-oriented researchers focused on "career maturity" as readiness for vocational decision making (Super & Overstreet, 1960). They constructed measures of vocational development and career choice attitudes and competencies such as the Career Maturity Inventory (Crites, 1978b), the Career Development Inventory (Super et al., 1981), and Assessment of Career Decision Making (Harren, 1978). Counselors may use these indecision and career maturity scales to directly measure career choice process variables and differentially treat career counseling clients.

Although all of these scales measure career decision making, they differ in one fundamental way. The indecision scales address decision-making difficulties, whereas the career maturity scales address decision-making resources. Before comparing and contrasting the indecision and maturity approaches to process measurement, representative measures from each perspective are presented here in detail. Each of the next three sections in this chapter discusses one of the three most prominent career decision-making scales. These scales were selected for inclusion in this chapter because they were the only process measures that met three criteria: (a) sufficient research literature to judge their psychometric characteristics, (b) easy availability through commercial publishers or other means, and (c) adequate practitioner lore about appropriate use and clinical interpretation. The three scales that met the criteria are the Career Decision Scale (Osipow, Carney, Winer, Yanico, & Koschier, 1976), the Career Development Inventory (Super et al., 1981), and the Career Maturity Inventory (Crites, 1978b).

CAREER DECISION SCALE

For decades, researchers used just two categories—*decided* and *undecided*—to classify an individual's adaptation to the career choice process. They extensively investigated the personalities and situations of individuals who had been classified as undecided, yet they did not examine how these individuals engaged in vocational decision making (Osipow, 1983). In the mid-1970s, many researchers began to view adaptive status as a continuum of decidedness instead of a dichotomy between undecided and decided. They also became sensitive to the degree of closure among decided individuals and thus started to measure variation in choice satisfaction, choice certainty, commitment to a choice, and even choice implementation. Osipow, Carney, Winer, Yanico, and Koschier (1976) helped to popularize the process view of decidedness by providing a scale with which counselors could quickly survey high-school and college students' progress in making career choices. The Career Decision Scale (CDS) measures a person's career choice status and identifies difficulties that thwart career choice closure.

Development

The CDS originated as part of a proposed modular system for assisting clients with vocational indecision. Osipow, Winer, Koschier, and Yanico (1975) began by identifying separate components of indecision. They assumed that a finite number of relatively discrete problems thwart adaptation to the choice task. Although they have not written about the criteria used in selecting these problem behaviors, they explained that they identified the problems in their study of a model relating specific intervention strategies to distinct types of difficulties in the choice process (Osipow et al., 1975). Osipow and his colleagues considered problems they had encountered in their own experience with students as well as problems they found in examining records of students seeking career counseling. From these sources they compiled 14 problem behaviors that thwart progress in reaching closure on a career choice. They asserted that each of the 14 difficulties was a distinct antecedent of or unique reason for being undecided. The antecedents act as barriers to prevent adaptation to the choice task by thwarting progress along the decidedness continuum or by reducing satisfaction with, certainty about, and commitment to a choice that has been made. Because each antecedent differs from the other 13, an individual may experience several difficulties simultaneously or sequentially. People who experience more problems are expected to be more prone to indecision, to make slower progress in advancing along the decidedness continuum, and to be less satisfied with, certain about, and committed to choices they have made.

Each of the 14 types of indecision or reasons for being undecided were expressed in a descriptive item consisting of one to three statements. These 14 items were published originally as the Types Questionnaire (Osipow et al., 1975). Osipow and Carney revised the Types Questionnaire into the Scale of Vocational Indecision (see Osipow, Carney, & Barak, 1976, p. 237). This revision included five new items: Two items state additional explanations for indecision, an open-ended item allows respondents to describe unique sources of indecision, and two items measure certainty about career and major choices, respectively. Osipow, Carney, Winer, Yanico, and Koschier (1976) slightly revised the Vocational Indecision Scale and renamed it the Career Decision Scale (3rd rev.). Marathon Consulting and

Press published the Career Decision Scale from 1976 to 1987, when Psychological Assessment Resources assumed publication of the scale. More details about the early history of the CDS appeared in Winer (1992).

Description

The Career Decision Scale (CDS) was designed for high-school and college students and has been used successfully with women returning to college (Slaney, Stafford, & Russell, 1981). It also has been slightly modified for use with graduate students (Hartman, Utz, & Farnum, 1979) and medical students (Savickas, Alexander, Osipow, & Wolf, 1985). In fact, the CDS probably can be used with any individual crystallizing field and level preferences or specifying a career choice. Individuals can be given the CDS as a part of an intake process or a vocational appraisal test battery. Because it takes only 10 to 15 min to administer and is easy to understand and respond to, the CDS also can be used to survey large groups for screening purposes or to evaluate vocational interventions and career education programs.

The CDS is published in a four-page, 8½ × 11-inch booklet. The front page has lines for name, date of birth, age, grade, and sex, as well as instructions to respondents to indicate on a 4-point Likert scale how closely each item describes their thinking about career or educational choices. The response scale ranges from *exactly like me* (4) to *not at all like me* (1). Clients circle on the test booklet the appropriate number for each item. These ratings show how well each item corresponds to sources of clients' indecision.

Scale items appear on the inner two pages. The first two items compose the Certainty Scale. They state that one has already decided on a career (item 1) or a major (item 2) and that one feels comfortable with and knows how to implement that choice. Items 3 through 18 describe reasons for being undecided and compose the Indecision Scale. Item 19 asks clients to describe their unique difficulties if none of the 16 items describe them. Six lines are provided for written responses.

At the bottom of page 3, spaces are provided to record scores, identify a normative group, and indicate percentile ranks. Counselors compute the raw score for the Certainty Scale by summing the ratings for items 1 and 2. The scores can range from 2 to 8, with higher scores indicating greater certainty. They compute the Indecision Scale raw score by summing the ratings for items 3 through 18. The scores can range from 16 to 64, with higher scores indicating greater indecision. Item 19 is clinically interpreted. The manual presents four normative groups that can be used to convert raw scores to percentiles: high-school students ($N = 720$ males and 738 females); college students ($N = 225$ males and 192 females); adults seeking continuing education ($N = 81$); and women returning to college ($N = 67$). The back page of the booklet is blank.

Interpretation

To interpret a client's CDS scores, a counselor may begin by assessing the client's progress toward decidedness in general from the Certainty Scale score and then assess progress toward major and career choice in particular from the two item ratings. Based on experience, I have concluded that significant discrepancies between ratings for the two certainty items require further assessment. If major choice certainty exceeds career choice certainty by two or three points, then the counselor should investigate the possibility that the client has a plan without a clear goal. Often these clients have made pseudo-crystallized choices; that is, "they have not analyzed the essential elements and have not fully accepted the commitments entailed" (Ginzberg, Ginsburg, Axelrad, & Herma, 1951, p. 108). They may be implementing plans that reflect their parents' dreams rather than commitments to self-chosen goals that manifest their own vocational identities. If career choice certainty exceeds major choice certainty by two or three points, then the counselor should investigate the possibility that the client has a goal without a plan. For example, a high-school student may be certain about the goal of being a lawyer but not know, or eventually like, the activities required to become a lawyer. Often such clients have uninformed interests in choices that may be subject to change in light of new experience and information (Strong, 1943, p. 17).

After assessing the Certainty Scale results, counselors may look to the Indecision Scale score to assess degree of indecision, that is, number and intensity of difficulties in the decision-making process. Although the definition of high, average, and low indecision scores depends on the context, Osipow (1987) suggested that scores from the 16th to the 84th percentile be considered middle scores, with scores above the 84th percentile signifying high indecision and scores below the 16th percentile signifying low indecision. Counselors should expect the Indecision Scale score to oppose the Certainty Scale score because theoretically these variables associate inversely and empirically these scales correlate negatively. When both scores are either high or low, the counselor should investigate the possibility that the scores are invalid or that the client is quite unique. When the scores are valid, I have usually found that students with high certainty and high proneness to indecision feel very committed to a series of different choices over short time periods. In contrast, I have usually found that students with low certainty and low indecision feel very comfortable with being undecided and are not yet concerned about making a career choice. If certainty is high and indecision is low, then the counselor should hypothesize that the client may not need an intervention or, at least, that the client does not feel a need for assistance. Because combinations of middle scores on both scales are ambiguous, Osipow suggested that if this occurs counselors should further assess the client's vocational situation. If they need or want an intervention, these clients usually benefit from content-oriented career counseling. If certainty is low and indecision is high, then the counselor should hypothesize that the client would benefit from a process-oriented intervention.

When working with a client who scores low on the Certainty Scale and high on the Indecision Scale, the counselor examines the client's item ratings and considers any response to item 19. By studying the items that the client rated as most self-descriptive, the counselor can learn about the type and intensity of decision-making difficulties that the client experiences in trying to make career choices. With training and experience, a counselor can often discern a coherent pattern of decisional difficulties from the item ratings and then tentatively select a process intervention to address this pattern. To aid clinical judgment in pattern recognition, some counselors consider items in clusters based on factor analyses of the Indecision Scale.

Osipow, Carney, and Barak (1976) reported that four dimensions structure the Indecision Scale. Their factor analysis of 837 college students' responses to the 16 items produced four factors that explained 81.3% of the total variance. They did not report how much variance each orthogonal (uncorrelated) factor explained. They interpreted the factors as:

1. Avoidance of choice: nine items indicating choice anxiety and lack of structure and confidence in approaching vocational decision making.
2. External barriers: five items indicating the presence or perception of external barriers to a preferred choice and questions about alternative possibilities.
3. Approach-approach: two items indicating difficulty in deciding from among attractive alternatives.
4. Conflict: two items suggesting some kind of personal conflict about how to make a choice.

The items in these four factors total 18 rather than 16 because two items loaded on two factors.

Osipow, Carney, and Barak's (1976) conclusions about the factor-analytic results suggest that the items state 16 distinct manifest difficulties in decision making yet they reflect only four unique latent dimensions or basic types of indecision. Some counselors and researchers have taken this to mean that they could score the Indecision Scale for subscales to appraise the client across four major types of indecision. Osipow (1987, p. 7) warned CDS users that the instability of its factor structure does not warrant such a practice. His caution, which was shared by Allis (1984), Harmon (1985), Herman (1985), and Slaney (1985), is based on repeated failures to completely replicate the Indecision Scale factor structure. Kazin (1976), Slaney (1978), and Slaney, Palko-Nonemaker, and Alexander (1981) each replicated only the first factor, whereas Rogers and Westbrook (1983) replicated only the second and third factors.

One explanation for the failure to replicate the original factor-analytic results faults the scale items. The complexity of each item, according to Osipow, Carney, and Barak (1976), makes it subject to more than one answer. Recall that some of the items consist of two or three statements. In some cases statements within the same item are independent, so we cannot be sure exactly which statement evoked a respondent's rating. For example, item 7 describes intrapsychic confusion, interpersonal dependency, and an information deficit: "Until now, I haven't given much thought to choosing a career. I feel lost when I think about it because I haven't had many experiences in making decisions on my own and I don't have enough information to make a career decision right now." Although these elements may cohere in defining one type of indecision, they do not form an easily interpretable item in psychometric analyses. Slaney, Palko-Nonemaker, and Alexander (1981) hypothesized that this item complexity may cause the overlap and instability in the Indecision Scale factor structure.

Two other possible explanations for the failure to identify an invariant factor structure underlying the CDS were offered by Shimizu, Vondracek, Schulenberg, and Hostetler (1988): The structure of CDS indecision constructs varies at different levels of career maturity, and statistical–methodological artifacts attenuate the extent of factor similarity across the studies. In considering the latter possibility, they reasoned that the most serious problem in CDS factor-analytic studies was the selection of Varimax rotation procedures to produce orthogonal factors. To examine this hypothesis, they rotated each of the Varimax solutions presented in seven previous studies to Promax solutions, which produced oblique (correlated) factors. To compare the similarity of the correlated factors across the seven studies, they calculated congruence coefficients. From these comparisons, they concluded that "there are more similarities across the factor analytic studies than have been previously reported" (p. 218). They extended the generalizability of this conclusion with a new sample. Moreover, they suggested further research on four linearly independent subscales that represent the correlated factors in their two studies. They described the four subscales as (a) feelings of indecision, (b) relative decidedness yet desire for reinforcement and support, (c) classic approach–approach conflict, and (d) external and internal barriers to decision making. The underlying factor structure of the CDS continues to stir debate as shown by four articles in the winter 1994 issue of the *Journal of Career Assessment* (Osipow, 1994; Laplante, Coallier, Sabourin, & Martin, 1994; Schulenberg, Vondracek, & Shimizu, 1994; Shimizu, Vondracek, & Schulenberg, 1994).

Despite questions about the factor structure of the Indecision Scale, there is no doubt that it is multidimensional. However, almost all of the studies on the CDS used a single score as a unidimensional measure of decisional difficulties. The single best summary of these studies appears in the CDS manual.

Technical Information

The *Career Decision Scale Manual* (Osipow, 1987) is thorough and well organized. It summarized five factor-analytic studies of the Indecision Scale and cited reports of test–retest reliability at .90 and .82 for 2 weeks (Osipow, Carney, & Barak, 1976) and .70 for 6 weeks (Slaney, Palko-Nonemaker, & Alexander, 1981). An unpublished master's thesis not cited in the manual reported a 3-week test–retest reliability coefficient of .79 and an internal consistency coefficient of .91 (Williams-Phillips, 1983). Rogers and Westbrook (1983) reported an internal consistency coefficient of .88.

The manual presents different types of validity evidence in four sections. The first section discusses studies that compared demographic groups on the CDS and that related the CDS to other measures of career decision making. The second section reviews treatment studies indicating that the CDS is sensitive to pretest/posttest changes and is an effective outcome measure. The third section discusses studies that demonstrate how the CDS relates to personality variables such as locus of control and fear of success. The fourth and final section summarizes studies that relate the Indecision Scale to demographic variables. Four studies reported no significant sex differences, whereas two studies reported significant sex differences, one favoring females and the other favoring males. The only study that addressed ethnic or racial differences reported greater indecision in Blacks than in Whites.

A 1996 article by Osipow and Winer updated the technical manual in that it reviewed the major research findings concerning the CDS and discussed its use in program planning, gender and cross-cultural issues, and practice with special populations.

Reviews

In reviewing the CDS, Harmon (1994, p. 261) concluded that "if the user is looking for an overall measure of career indecision for use in counseling, evaluation, or research, there is probably no better measure." She concurred with Slaney (1985), who, in an earlier review, concluded that an impressive amount of research had been conducted in the early development of the CDS and that this research "provided substantial support for the reliability of the instrument and for its construct and concurrent validity" (p. 142). Three other reviewers were equally impressed by the CDS.

Harmon (1985) concluded that "the CDS is extremely well developed and researched for such a relatively new inventory" and highly recommended its use in career counseling and evaluation. Herman (1985) concluded that its "brevity, comprehensiveness, and extensive research support are important strengths of the inventory." Allis (1984) called support for its construct validity "impressive."

Research Directions

Each review of the CDS and many investigations of it have offered explicit suggestions for research to further develop the Indecision Scale. In sum, reviewers and researchers have called for:

1. Explication of the conceptual rationale for item selection.
2. Continuation of studies to define types of indecision, or patterns of vocational decision-making difficulties.
3. Development of subscales for the Indecision Scale that can be used in differential diagnosis of indecision types.
4. Extension of the inchoate work (e.g., Barak & Friedkes, 1981) on matching intervention methods and materials to types of indecision.
5. Initiation of research on written responses to item 19.
6. Examination of qualitative differences between male and female CDS responses (Hartman, Fuqua, & Jenkins, 1988).

Item revision is a potentially productive suggestion for future research (Harmon, 1994), but it requires a significantly greater commitment of time and resources than do the preceding suggestions. In the first published article dealing with the CDS, Osipow, Carney, and Barak (1976, p. 240) wrote that "because some of the items are complex and may be subject to more than one answer, the items may need further revision." Slaney, Palko-Nonemaker, and Alexander (1981) suggested that Osipow approach item revision by dividing the logically independent statements in complex items into separate items. Reducing the complexity of item statements and the corresponding ambiguity of item responses may produce a stable factor structure and thus facilitate definition of indecision types, construction of CDS indecision subscales, and development of differential diagnosis systematics. Osipow and his collaborators began the process of constructing a new measure of indecision by preparing a taxonomy of career decision-making problems (Gati, Krauss, & Osipow, 1996).

An alternative to simplifying items might be to revisit the original intent of the designers of the CDS. They sought to measure types of undecided students. If the CDS had been designed to be a quantitative measure of career indecision as a *trait*, then certainly its items should have been simpler. However, the CDS was constructed as a qualitative measure of *type* of undecided student. Although item complexity may reduce the reliability of a trait measure, it may increase the reliability of a type measure because types are defined by multiple traits. Preliminary evidence suggests that the CDS works well as a type indicator. Savickas and Jarjoura (1991) identified nine distinct types in a sample of 368 college students. Each of the nine types shared one or two problems that troubled their decision making. The types seemed more clear and coherent than the decisional difficulties identified by factor-analytic studies of CDS items.

Experimentation with refining the two Certainty Scale items could elaborate the CDS model of career choice status. Recall that the Certainty Scale represented an innovative and heuristic conception of status in adapting to the developmental tasks of career choice. Rather than categorizing choice status with the undecided–decided dichotomy, Osipow, Carney, and Barak (1976) conceptualized choice status as a continuous variable with levels of decidedness. Jones and Chenery (1980) demonstrated the merit of elaborating the conception of choice status from a univariate model (i.e., decidedness) into a multivariate model. They investigated four choice status subtypes created by combining the variables of decidedness and comfort with choice. Using the responses to two items of 224 college students in an introductory psychology class, they found that 70.4% were decided–comfortable, 17% undecided–uncomfortable, 3.2% undecided–comfortable, and 9.4% decided–uncomfortable. Each CDS Certainty Scale item combines statements about being decided, feeling comfortable with that choice, and knowing how to implement it. Dividing these statements into three separate items each for major and career choice could stimulate research on a differentiated model of career choice status, which might eventually systematically relate to a differentiated model of vocational decision-making difficulties. As a first step in this direction, Savickas, Carden, Toman, and Jarjoura (1992) conducted two studies in which they factor analyzed nine measures of career decidedness. They concluded that a single factor empirically defined choice status. Although the variety of words (e.g., decided, satisfied, certain, and comfortable) used in items to assess choice status connote multiple dimensions, empirically these words manifest a single latent dimension.

Rather than trying to make distinctions in choice status, researchers are probably best advised to ask questions about different choices rather than different dimensions of a particular choice. Their results strongly support the CDS Certainty Scale that inquires about certainty concerning choice of college major and career. If the CDS is revised, it might be useful to consider adding a third item to the Certainty Scale, so that the Scale measures choice satisfaction relative to academic major, career field, and occupation.

CAREER DEVELOPMENT INVENTORY

Super and his collaborators investigated the maturation of adolescents' coping repertoire for making the pre-vocational and vocational choices required by their school curricula. They conducted the longitudinal Career Pattern Study (Super & Overstreet, 1960) to determine which variables, in addition to socioeconomic status and intelligence, most affect vocational development in adolescents and young adults. The staff of the Career Pattern Study (CPS) postulated that vocational development occurs along five dimensions:

(1) Increasing orientation to vocational choice, (2) increasing amounts of vocational information and more comprehensive and detailed planning, (3) increasing consistency of vocational preferences, (4) the crystallization of traits relevant to vocational choices, and, consequently, (5) increasing wisdom of vocational preferences. (Super, 1955, p. 154)

They originally identified possible measures or indices of vocational maturity and grouped them into these five dimensions: orientation to choice, information about preferred occupation, consistency of preferences, crystallization of traits, and wisdom of preferences (Super, 1955, p. 161). Preliminary empirical work led them to add vocational independence as a sixth dimension and to group 20 indices into the six dimensions (Super, 1974, p. 12). They tested this six-dimensional model in the CPS. Their research eventually led them to construct a theoretical model of vocational maturity during adolescence (Super, 1974) that has five dimensions:

1. Planful attitudes toward life stages and tasks.
2. Attitudes toward exploration.
3. Educational and occupational information.
4. Knowledge of decision-making principles and practice.
5. Realism.

Although the variables that constitute these dimensions have been modified and refined (Super, 1983), the basic five dimensions in the theoretical model have remained unchanged.

Development

Super and his colleagues constructed the Career Development Inventory (CDI) to measure the first four dimensions of their theoretical model. They chose not to measure the realism dimension because the CPS realism measures did not interrelate with each other or correlate to other vocational maturity variables during adolescence. In this section, I briefly trace the development of the CDI from its two early predecessors through its three unpublished forms, before describing the published form in the next section. In 1969 Super and his collaborators devised a career development measure called the Student Questionnaire to evaluate a career education project (Myers, Lindeman, Thompson, & Patrick, 1975). It contained 87 items that had been validated in the CPS. They scored the items on six scales. In 1970, they expanded the Student Questionnaire to 216 items grouped into 13 scales and renamed it the Career Questionnaire. Factor analysis (Forrest, 1971) led to item reduction and rearrangement of the 13 scales into three basic scales that contained a total of first 93 and later 91 items. The three scales in Form I of the CDI (Super & Forrest, 1972) corresponded to the first four dimensions in Super's theoretical model of vocational maturity:

1. Scale A, Planning Orientation (33 items): concern with choice, specificity of planning, and self-estimated amount of occupational information

2. Scale B, Resources for Exploration (28 items): quality of the actually used and potentially usable resources for educational and occupational exploration

3. Scale C, Information and Decision Making (30 items): amount of educational and occupational information that a student has acquired, together with mastery of the use of information for sound decisions

Super and his collaborators expanded Form I of the CDI to more broadly measure knowledge of the world of work, assess specific types of occupational information, and diagnose cognitive awareness of career development tasks. They used Form II in laboratory research and then modified it to produce Form III, which they explicitly organized around a refined model of vocational maturity (Super & Thompson, 1979). Form III contained 191 items grouped into six scales:

1. Extent of Planning (30 items): similar to Form I, Scale A.

2. Use and Evaluation of Resources in Exploration (30 items): largely Form I, Scale B.

3. Career Decision Making (30 items, many new): principles and practice of decision making.

4. Career Development Information (30 items, many new): awareness of and concern with developmental tasks.

5. World of Work Information (30 items, many new): general occupational information.

6. Information about Preferred Occupation (41 new items): knowledge of occupational group selected by student as of interest.

Essentially, Form III used the Form I planning orientation (A) and exploration scales (B), split the decision-making and occupational information scale (C) into two scales and expanded each to 30 items, and added a scale to measure developmental task concern and a scale to measure specificity of information.

The test authors quickly concluded that Form III was too long because students required at least two 40-min class periods to respond to the 191 items. They returned to their original goal of devising a measure of career maturity that could be administered within one class period. Using factor analysis, they reduced the first three scales in Form III to 20 items each, combined the Career Development Information and World of Work Information scales into one 20-item scale, and reduced the Knowledge of Preferred Occupational Group scale from 41 to 40 items. Students require about 60 min to complete the 120 items, but by eliminating Knowledge of Preferred Occupational Group Scale, they can complete Form IV of the CDI in a 40-min class period.

Description

Super and his collaborators (1981) published this fourth version of the CDI in two forms: the Junior/Senior High School Form and the College and University Form. The forms are quite similar in that the authors slightly modified for the college form those high-school form items that deal with levels of educational and occupational options to make them more pertinent to college students. The CDI is sold as a reusable 16-page test booklet with separate, computer-scored answer sheets. The front page explains the purpose of the inventory and how to respond to the items on the answer sheet. It also explains that the inventory has two parts: Career Orientation, and Knowledge of Preferred Occupation.

Part I begins with Section A, Career Planning. This section measures extent of planning by asking about involvement in thinking about the future and in planning career-related high school and post-high school activities. Section B, Career Exploration, measures willingness to find and use good resources for career planning. Section C, Career Decision Making, measures ability to apply decision-making principles and methods to solve problems involving educational and occupational choices. Section D, World of Work Information, measures knowledge of types of occupations and ways to obtain and succeed in jobs.

Part II, Knowledge of Preferred Occupational Group, measures familiarity with the type of work that students say interests them most. Students select one personally preferred occupational group from 20 groups listed on the back of the IBM answer sheet. Then they answer 40 questions about the kinds of work in that field and the abilities, interests, values, and personal characteristics of workers in that field. The CDI manual states that Part II is most suitable for students in 11th and 12th grades who are about to enter the labor force and for college students who are about to declare a major. Younger students probably need take only Part I.

The CDI must be machine scored using differential item weights, which are not reported in the manual. Hand-scoring keys are unavailable. In addition to scores for the five scales, the computer scoring service provides three composite scores: Career Development Attitudes combines planning and exploration scores, Career Development Knowledge and Skills combines decision-making and world-of-work scores, and Career Orientation Total combines the planning, exploration, decision-making, and world-of-work scores. The composite scores offer increased reliability for individual interpretation because some of the basic scales have reported 3-week test–retest reliability in the low 60s.

The computer test report does not include raw scores. It provides only scale scores that have a mean of 100 and a standard deviation of 20. The basic scoring service offers four reports: (a) standard score and percentile on the five basic and three composite scales for individuals; (b) mean standard scores and standard deviations for the group; (c) percent of students selecting each alternative for the items in Part I; and (d) number and percentage of students in the group preferring each of the 20 occupational fields. The manual presents norms by sex for Grades 9 through 12 for each of the eight CDI scores based on the standardization group of 5,039 students, a nationwide but not demonstrably representative sample. The CDI authors advise users to compile local norms, a process facilitated by the reporting system when N is 100 or more.

Interpretation

Counselors use the CDI to measure students' readiness to cope with the developmental tasks of crystallizing, specifying, and implementing a career choice. Counselors and career educators can administer it within one high-school class period to obtain data for diagnosing individual career development attitudes and competencies, planning group guidance programs and career education curricula, and evaluating program outcomes. In addition, counselors can annually readminister the CDI to measure rate of career development and identify, for preventive interventions, those students who are regressing or maintaining rather than developing. After completing an individual diagnosis, group needs assessment, survey, or program evaluation, counselors may use the CDI data to plan individual counseling, structured learning programs, or exploration experiences.

To select an intervention, counselors begin by examining clients' scale scores to identify their assets and deficits. The CDI authors consider scores above the 75th percentile as strengths to build on and scores below the 25th percentile as weaknesses to remediate. They suggest interpretive hypotheses for each scale and illustrate their approach to interpretation with one case in the *User's Manual* (Thompson & Lindeman, 1981), three cases in the *Technical Manual* (Thompson & Lindeman, 1984), and three cases in an article on the Developmental Assessment and Counseling Model (Super, 1983). These illustrations demonstrate the logical order in which the CDI authors interpret the scales. This order follows the sequence of developmental task mastery. Fundamental to task mastery is awareness that one faces or will face a developmental task. Awareness precedes and prompts concern about and responsibility for task mastery.

Counselors look to scores on the Career Planning scale to assess clients' inclination to look ahead, take a planful approach, and involve themselves in career planning activities. A low score indicates that clients do not foresee their future in the world of work; therefore, they do not feel a need to acquaint themselves with or relate themselves to occupations. Often these clients display low work-role salience (Nevill & Super, 1988; Super & Nevill, 1984), either because they look forward to other life roles (e.g., homemaker) or because they do not look forward at all (Gordon, 1970). Clients who lack a future orientation typically need personal counseling to deal with their lack of optimism, goals, and achievement (Savickas, 1986; Whan & Savickas, 1998). Clients who only look forward to other life roles need to learn that they will probably work in the future. A counselor can facilitate both work salience and career orientation by teaching clients about the developmental tasks they face, the implications of ignoring these tasks, and the value of a planful approach in mastering the tasks. If clients' scores indicate a planful and responsible approach to developmental tasks, then the counselor considers clients' career exploration attitudes.

The Career Exploration scale score indicates inclination to use exploration opportunities and resources. It measures attitudes toward information sources and willingness to use and evaluate these sources. Low scores suggest that clients are not concerned with using good sources of data about the fields and levels of work. These clients should learn to distinguish between good and bad information sources and to appreciate how competent sources can facilitate their information gathering. Counselors help these clients increase their awareness of career exploration opportunities. If a client is inclined to use competent sources for career exploration, then the counselor assesses the information that the client has already acquired.

The World of Work Information scale score indicates knowledge about work, occupation, and career. Low scores indicate that clients need to learn about types of occupations, the mores of work, and career development tasks. They probably do not know much about the range of occupations available to them. Thus counselors encourage uninformed clients to survey a wide range of occupations and then explore the fields of work that they find interesting. High scores on this scale suggest that clients are sufficiently knowledgeable to apply occupational information to self and to begin crystallizing field and level preferences.

The Decision Making scale score indicates knowledge of the principles and practices of decision making. Low scores suggest that clients do not know what to consider in making choices. This means that clients are not ready to use the occupational information they have acquired for career planning. Counselors help these clients to understand sound principles of decision making and to apply these principles in matching self to occupations. High scores suggest that clients may be ready to make matching decisions. When decision-making knowledge is supported by an adequate fund of occupational information based on planful exploration, then clients are ready to make tentative career choices. Aptitude tests, interest inventories, and self-reports have meaning for these clients because they already know about the world of work and how to make vocational decisions. In other words, the client displays the dispositions and competencies needed to benefit from content-oriented career counseling.

The development of attitudes and competencies for task mastery does not follow the preceding sequence for some clients. In these cases, the counselor must rely on common sense and clinical experience to generate interpretive hypotheses. For example, if the Career Planning scale score is the only low scale score, then the counselor may want to determine if clients relate exploration and information to planning their own future. Or, if the Career Exploration scale score is the only low score, then the counselor may ask clients how they learned about occupations and developed decision-making skill.

Counselors do not need the Preferred Occupational Group scale to form these interpretive hypotheses; thus, it is not included in the Career Orientation Total score. Typically, counselors administer the Preferred Occupational Group scale only to students who are expected to be able to state a thoughtful preference for a career field. Ideally, these students have crystallized a preference for a group of occupations in a particular field and level of work and are beginning to specify a choice from among occupational alternatives in that group.

The Preferred Occupational Group scale score indicates knowledge about the occupational group of most interest to a client. Low scores suggest that clients do not possess accurate knowledge about their stated preferences. These clients need sharply focused exploration within their preferred field to generate and test specific career choices. The counselor must look at the four basic scales to determine if the client is ready for this focused exploration. Interpretation of high scores on the Preferred Occupational Group scale also requires relating the score to the other four basic scales. For example, a high Preferred Occupational Group score along with a low World of Work Information score means that clients know about the preferred field but not its place in the occupational structure. In these cases, the counselor should ask clients how they acquired this selective information and whether they have adequately examined other options. Often it is a case of premature closure, in which a client commits self to a parental preference or a glamorous preference. For example, some clients grow up in a family business (e.g., farming or medicine), learn about this one field in great detail, and specify a choice in this field without exploring other fields, perhaps because of parental pressure or financial incentives.

Technical Information

The CDI manual consists of two volumes and a supplement. The 27-page *User's Manual* (Thompson & Lindeman, 1981) presented the rationale, description of item content, administration instructions, scoring procedures, interpretation methods, and recommended uses. The 48-page *Technical Manual* (Thompson & Lindeman, 1984) presented the theory and research supporting the development of the CDI and detailed data on its psychometric characteristics. The 20-page *College and University Supplement* (Thompson & Lindeman, 1982) discussed psychometric characteristics of and normative data for that form. Savickas and Hartung (1996) published a literature review that systematically analyzed studies published from 1979 through 1995 that addressed the psychometric characteristics and uses of the CDI.

The manual appropriately cautions users about low test–retest reliabilities for the CDI scales (Career Planning, .79; Career Exploration, .73; Decision Making, .70; World of Work, .67; Preferred Occupation, .61) and encourages them to use the composite scales because of their greater reliability (Career Development Attitudes, .83; Career Development Knowledge, .83; and Career Orientation Total, .84). In light of their reliability, the authors instruct users in how to apply the standard error of measurement to interpret scale scores and score profiles.

The manual reports a respectable amount of validity evidence for an inventory published in 1981. However, Thompson and Lindeman (1981, p. 7) may have been overly enthusiastic when they wrote that much of the research on earlier forms of the CDI directly applies to the current form. The CDI possesses superior content validity because it explicitly operationalizes a model of career maturity that has been refined by four decades of programmatic research. Although the instrument's construct validity needs more empirical support, its factor structure and relations to age, grade, and school curricula provide an adequate base. In regard to criterion-related validity, Thompson and Lindeman (1984) cited three concurrent validity studies that showed the CDI related as expected to ability, work salience, and other career development measures.

In their review article, Savickas and Hartung (1996) concluded that the primary area for future research on the CDI should be its predictive validity. They were able to find only three studies that directly investigated the CDI's predictive validity. Two problems delayed research on this topic. The first problem involves the obvious difficulties typically encountered when trying to collect longitudinal data sets. The second problem, more particular to this topic, has been the confusion concerning criteria for predictive validity studies. Savickas (1993) evaluated the criteria used in 15 career development studies that focused on predictive validity. After identifying inappropriate criteria, he proposed that researchers use subsequent coping behaviors as the major criterion in predictive validity studies. Moreover, he urged that coping behaviors be operationally defined by indexes of (a) the realism, independence, and purpose of vocational behavior and (b) movement toward suitable career choices and viable occupational plans.

Reviews

The CDI's greatest strength derives from its articulation of a cogent model of career development (Pinkney & Bozik, 1994). Although the CDI is the culmination of 30 years of programmatic research on vocational behavior during adolescence, further research is needed to substantiate its tentatively established validity. While waiting for more validity research, CDI users are advised not to inadvertently apply research on earlier forms to the current form and not to overinterpret the scales by confusing the CDI's construct validity for criterion-related validity.

In a review based on the *User's Manual* (Thompson & Lindeman, 1981) and written before publication of the *Technical Manual* (Thompson & Lindeman, 1984), Hansen (1985) called for more reliability and validity research. In particular, she recommended criterion-related research to examine the CDI relative to occupational aspiration, career success, and job satisfaction. She concluded that the World of Work Information and Preferred Occupational Group scales were "sufficiently unreliable over short periods to warrant caution in their use" (p. 223). She also questioned the need for five scales in light of factor-analytic studies that show two factors accommodate the CDI—Career Development Attitudes and Career Development Knowledge. However, in a Rasch analysis of the psychometric characteristics of an Australian adaptation of the CDI, Punch and Sheridan (1985) reported that the two attitudinal scales (Career Planning and Career Exploration) do not constitute one dimension and should be considered as separate components of the CDI. Yet they did conclude, like Hansen, that the Decision Making and World of Work Information scales may represent one factor and added that the CDI authors may have erred in dividing Scale C of Form I into separate decision-making and information scales.

Research Directions

The CDI needs criterion-related research to firmly establish its validity and nomological network. In particular, researchers could refine the Developmental Assessment and Counseling Model (Super et al., 1996) by linking the CDI to variables commonly studied in developmental and personality psychology. To date, research on the CDI has been conducted in isolation from advances and debates in the behavioral sciences (Heath, 1976; Vondracek & Schulenberg, 1986). Linkages to this body of accumulated basic research would increase practitioners' understanding of career maturity and its facilitation. For example, researchers could relate the CDI variables to future orientation, causal attribution, and self-efficacy to learn if these personality variables determine career planning and exploration attitudes (Super et al., 1996).

Practitioners would also benefit from research on the interpretative hypotheses suggested for each CDI scale, especially as they pertain to minority and rural students (Pinkney & Bozik, 1994). Although the descriptive interpretations in the manual make sense, they await empirical confirmation. The interpretations of profile patterns also lack empirical support. For example, the interpretation that spiked Career Planning scale and Knowledge of Preferred Occupational Group scale scores reflect the premature closure or early fixation seems cogent but needs empirical confirmation. Validated decision rules for interpreting profiles could stimulate advances in differential treatment of clients.

Some revision of the CDI itself to increase scale reliabilities would strengthen confidence in scale and profile interpretation (Pinkney & Bozik, 1994). Attention should focus on increasing the reliability of the two cognitive scales and extending their divergence from measures of mental ability and educational achievement. The scale with the lowest reliability, Knowledge of Preferred Occupational Group, is quite innovative and may benefit from research to increase its reliability.

CAREER MATURITY INVENTORY ATTITUDE SCALE

The other prominent inventory which measures variables in the career choice process also evolved from the Career Pattern Study. In fact, the Career Maturity Inventory (CMI; Crites, 1978b) was the first paper-and-pencil measure of vocational development. Crites constructed the CMI to measure two dimensions in his model of vocational development, which appears in Fig. 12.1. He refined the original CPS model of vocational development by reorganizing and defining its dimensions. Crites accepted the Consistency of Vocational Choice and Wisdom of Vocational Preference dimensions and reorganized the other three dimensions into two dimensions. He proposed that the Orientation to Vocational Choice dimension, the Information and Planning dimension, and certain aspects of the Crystallization of Traits dimension (e.g., increasing independence) could be elaborated as several different kinds of career choice concepts and competencies, that is, attitudes and aptitudes for vocational decision making. Thus, the third and fourth dimensions in Crites's model were called Career Choice Attitudes and Career Choice Competencies. Crites (1965) defined *attitudes* as dispositional response tendencies that mediate both choice behaviors and competencies. He defined *competencies* as comprehension and problem-solving abilities that pertain to vocational decision making.

Development

Crites constructed and standardized the CMI to measure the attitude and competence dimensions in his vocational development model. The original form of the CMI was called the Vocational Development Inventory. It consisted of a Concept Test and a Competence Test. The Concept Test, which eventually became the CMI Attitude Scale, measured variables from the work of Ginzberg and Super: bases for choice, reliance on others in decision making, involvement in the choice process, planful daydreaming and fantasy, time perspective, and means–end cognizance. The Competence Test consisted of five subtests measuring variables that bear on decision making: self-appraisal, occupational information, goal selection, planning, and problem solving.

Although the Concept Test has gone through four research forms and two published forms, the Competence Test has not been developed beyond the original research edition, probably because of the excessive time required to administer it. Crites subsequently stopped working on the Competence Test and instead has been developing a new scale, the Career Readiness Inventory, to measure career choice competencies. The CMI Competence Test is not dealt with in this chapter.

The Concept Test consisted of self-descriptive statements about an individual's career choice attitudes and behaviors. Crites drew the subject matter from real life sources. He wrote a pool of 1,000 items based on attitudinal statements made by clients in vocational counseling over a 5-year period. To guide selection of items from the pool for inclusion in the scale, Crites wrote behavioral descriptions and literary definitions for five central concepts in vocational theory and research. The concepts and their definitions appear in Table 12.1.

Two experimental forms of the Concept Test consisted of the same 100 items written in two grammatical formats, first and third person. The two

TABLE 12.1
Variables in the CMI Attitude Scale, Screening Forms A-1 and A-2

Dimension	Definition	Sample Item
Involvement in the choice process	Extent to which individual is actively participating in the process of making a choice	"I seldom think about the job I want to enter."
Orientation toward work	Extent to which individual is task or pleasure oriented in his or her attitudes toward work and the values he or she places upon work	"Work is dull and unpleasant" and "Work is worthwhile mainly because it lets you buy the things you want."
Independence in decision making	Extent to which individual relies on others in the choice of an occupation	"I plan to follow the line of work my parents suggest."
Preference for vocational choice factors	Extent to which individual bases his or her choice on a particular factor	"Whether you are interested in a job is not as important as whether you can do the work."
Conceptions of the choice process	Extent to which individual has accurate or inaccurate conceptions about making an occupational choice	"A person can do any kind of work he wants as long as he tries hard."

Note. From Crites (1965). Copyright © 1965 by the American Psychological Association. Reprinted with permission.

test forms also differed in response format: true/false versus 5-point Likert scales. Crites administered the items to a stratified sample of 5th- through 12th-grade students with N varying from 500 to 1,000 in each grade. He wanted items that empirically differentiated among these criterion groups because he believed that any measure of a developmental variable must relate systematically to time (Crites, 1961). Of the 100 items used in Forms I and II, 86 items differentiated between grade level at or beyond the .01 level. Fifty of the 86 items related monotonically to grade (Crites, 1964, p. 332). Results also indicated that the two item formats and two response scales were essentially equal in differentiating power. He chose to retain both grammatical forms but to use only the less time-consuming true/false response scale in a 50-item revision of the original Vocational Development Inventory Concept Test that Crites (1971) named the Vocational Development Inventory Attitude Test. Crites published this form in 1973 and renamed it the Career Maturity Inventory Attitude Scale. The name change fit the then new emphasis on career education.

Crites referred to this 1973, 50-item version of the CMI Attitude Scale as the Screening Form (A-1) to distinguish it from a Counseling Form then being developed. In 1978, he published the Counseling Form (B-1) along with a revised screening form (A-2). Form A-2 differs only slightly from Form A-1.

SAVICKAS

Research indicated that two items needed to be keyed differently. One other item (number 46) was replaced with a new item. In addition, Crites reorganized the items to arrange identical scoring keys for forms A-1 and A-2. Crites constructed the Counseling Form to provide subscales that measure the career choice attitudes variables in his model of career maturity. However, the Counseling Form subscales do not correspond exactly to the variables listed in Table 12.1. Crites modified them in response to criticism that three of the variables reflected career choice content. He replaced the three variables that dealt with attitudes toward a career choice with three new variables that dealt with attitudes toward vocational decision making. Thus each of the five variables in the revised model, which are listed in Table 12.2, clearly pertains to the decisional process. Compromise replaced choice factors, and decisiveness replaced conception. Crites retained the variable named *orientation* but redefined it.

There is some confusion regarding the Orientation subscale in the Counseling Form (Stowe, 1985). The *Theory and Research Handbook* (Crites, 1978c, p. 10) mistakenly retained the original definition stated in Table 12.1. However, the items scored for it differ substantially from the orientation items in Form A-1. In Form A-1, items 7, 8, 14, 47, 24, 35, 4, and 9 measure orientation to intrinsic or extrinsic rewards in making a career choice. The items state that a job is important because it lets one make money, buy things, get ahead, and become famous. In Form B-1, the items measure orientation

TABLE 12.2
Variables in CMI Attitude Scale, Counseling Form B-1

Dimension	Definition	Sample Item
Decisiveness in career decision making	Extent to which an individual is definite about making a career choice	"I keep changing my occupational choice."
Involvement in career decision making	Extent to which individual is actively participating in the process of making a choice	"I'm not going to worry about choosing an occupation until I'm out of school."
Independence in career decision making	Extent to which an individual relies on others in the choice of an occupation	"I plan to follow the line of work my parents suggest."
Orientation to career decision making	Extent to which individual is familiar with and relates self to the career decision-making process	"I have little or no idea of what working will be like."
Compromise in career decision making	Extent to which individual is willing to compromise between needs and reality	"I spent a lot of time wishing I could do work I know I can never do."

Note. From Crites (1978c). Copyright © 1978 by McGraw-Hill, Inc. Reproduced by permission of CTB/McGraw-Hill.

to the decision-making process. They deal with how much one thinks about jobs, imagines self in a job, and thinks about preparing for a job. To correct the mistake in the *Handbook*, Savickas and Crites (1981) redefined orientation as the extent to which an individual is familiar with and relates self to the vocational decision-making process.

The 50 items in Form A-1 could not generate subscales to measure the new variables. To solve this problem, Crites added 25 items to the Screening Form A-2. He selected these items, after trying them out on a sample of 7,000 students, from 50 items drawn from the original 1,000-item pool. The empirical criterion for selecting these 25 items differed from the criterion used to select the 50 items in the Screening Form. Crites used a less restrictive definition of developmental phenomena based on conceptual refinements (Crites, 1974a, 1978c). The new criteria called for a systematic relation to grade but not necessarily a monotonic function. In the end, the 47 items in the five subscales used 28 items from Form A-2 and 19 new items.

Description

The Attitude Scale Screening Form (A-2) is published in an 8-page, 8½ × 11-inch booklet. The front page states the title and publishing information; the back page is blank. Page 2 explains the purpose of the inventory and page 3 explains how to answer the items and mark responses on the IBM answer sheet. The items appear on pages 4 through 7.

The Screening Form takes about 20 min to administer, and the Counseling Form takes about 30 min. Both forms have about a sixth-grade reading level. The manual gives clear instructions for individual administration and a script for group administration. The Attitude Scale resembles a survey questionnaire more than a test, so the administrator tells students to indicate their feelings about each item rather than attempt to discern the correct answer. The answer sheets can be scored by hand or computer. The Screening Form (A-2) yields only a total score. The Counseling Form (B-1) yields the screening scale total score and five subscale scores. The manual provides interpretive frequency distributions derived from 74,000 student scores collected between the fall of 1973 and spring of 1976. Counselors can use these distributions to convert Screening Form and Counseling Form scores to derived scores and percentiles for students in Grades 6 through 12. Nevertheless, Crites preferred that counselors compile and use local norms.

Interpretation

The Screening Form score is designed to indicate the maturity of a student's attitudes toward making a career choice. Higher scores indicate more mature attitudes and thus greater readiness to make a career choice. Crites likened readiness for career planning to reading readiness. Clients below a certain threshold of readiness are neither sufficiently mature nor properly disposed to make a realistic choice. These clients need to develop their attitudes more completely to reach the choice threshold. Unfortunately, the threshold point (i.e., raw score) at which attitudes are sufficiently developed to produce choice behavior and realistic career planning has not been empirically identified. Crites recommended that counselors consider students who score above the 25th percentile as progressing normally and suggested that counselors offer assistance to students who score in the bottom quartile because they may be delayed or impaired in their career development (Crites, 1978a, p. 32).

In interpreting Screening Form scores, counselors should remember that they represent the original five variables defined in Table 12.1, not the five variables measured by the Counseling Form subscales. It is worth noting that the majority of validity data for the Screening Form total score pertains to Form A-1. The screening scores for Forms A-2 and B-1 differ slightly from A-1 in that they contain one different item, score two items differently, and present the items in a different order. Nevertheless, it is probably safe to assume that the validity data for Form A-1 extends to Forms A-2 and B-1. In contrast to the screening score, the validity for use of the Counseling Form (B-1) subscales has not been firmly established. Only three validity studies have dealt with the subscales (Fouad & Keeley, 1992; Lopez-Baez, 1981; Stowe, 1985).

Teaching the Test Model

Instead of interpreting the subscale scores, many counselors interpret the items because they have content and criterion-related validity. In interpreting the items, counselors can draw on each item's conceptual rationale and empirical data. As rationally derived items, they have been linguistically explicated as part of a cogent theoretical model. Moreover, as empirically derived items, they have been operationally defined. This combination of theory and research makes CMI items especially suitable for interpretation to clients.

Crites (1974b) claimed that by discussing the items that they answered in the immature direction, clients can incorporate new ideas into their thinking and develop a more mature approach to vocational decision making. He recommended that counselors "teach the test" to clients in order to bring them up to the choice threshold. Simply stated, the logic for teaching the test is that the items state attitudes that the client should hold.

Some counselors "teach the test" by discussing the items that a client missed in the order in which the items appear in the Scale. Other counselors discuss all the items that a client missed within one subscale, then move in turn to items from another subscale until they have discussed all five subscales. This procedure allows counselors to use the subscale items to explain the five attitudinal variables and relate them to the client's decision making. A few counselors teach the test by organizing the five variables into two groups. Presenting the results in two large chunks helps some clients retain and apply the information. A logical grouping divides the scales into those that deal with planful concern about the future and those that deal with a sense of self-control over one's future.

A concerned approach to decision making is sustained by the attitudes Crites called orientation and involvement. *Orientation* items deal with the client's awareness of the vocational decision-making process. Clients with more mature attitudes usually seek to familiarize themselves with how people choose occupations and develop careers. Clients less inclined to orient themselves to how careers develop have vague and inaccurate notions about career choice. When pressed to make a career choice, they feel confused. These clients benefit from consciousness-raising counseling techniques (Skovholt & Hoenninger, 1974) that increase foresight and heighten awareness of career development tasks. When clients have a cognitive schema to sustain career dreams and occupational fantasies, they are ready to involve themselves in the decision-making process.

A client can be familiar with the choice process without getting involved in it. *Involvement* items address whether clients relate themselves to the process of making a choice and actively participate in it. Clients with more mature attitudes tend to think about alternative careers and try to relate their present behavior to future goals. Clients who are less inclined to get involved in the vocational decision-making process just do not worry about their future. Often, they prefer to enjoy the present and take life one day at a time. When pressed to make a career choice, they feel anxious. These clients benefit from counseling techniques that help them make their future "real" by populating it with anticipated events and goals that give it shape and substance (Oleksy-Ojikutu, 1986). Clients who are concerned about their futures are ready to take control of the vocational decision-making process.

A sense of control over vocational decision making is sustained by the attitudes Crites called independence, decisiveness, and compromise. *Independence* items deal with self-reliance in making career choices. Immature attitudes incline clients to depend on others to choose for them. *Decisiveness* items deal with commitment to making career choices. Immature attitudes incline clients to feel uncertain and to avoid committing themselves to making a choice. *Compromise* items deal with willingness to acknowledge and concede to the demands of reality. Immature attitudes incline clients to distort or deny aspects of reality that may limit or block their need fulfillment. To avoid anxiety or frustration, clients with immature compromise attitudes rigidly maintain their subjectivity rather than increase their objectivity.

Clients who incompletely develop or lack one or more of these attitudes usually display a dependent, uncertain, or rigid approach to career choice that leads to indecision. These clients typically benefit from behavioral counseling techniques (Woody, 1968) that increase their self-esteem and realism or develop their assertiveness and decisional skills. Clients disposed to independence, decisiveness, and compromise approach career choice with a sense of control because these attitudes facilitate self-reliant, confident, and realistic vocational decision making. Thus, they are ready for content-oriented career counseling.

As a transition to content-oriented assessment or counseling, a few counselors augment their discussions of career concern and control dispositions by discussing three more groups of items from the Attitude Scale. They base these item groups on three variables measured by the Screening Form: conception, orientation toward work, and preference for choice factors (see Table 12.1 for definitions).

To use an alliteration with "C," counselors can follow counseling about vocational decision-making *concern* and *control* with counseling about career *concepts, criteria,* and *choice bases.* Six items (5, 18, 21, 32, 41, and 68) in the Counseling Form deal with clients' conceptions of how to make a career choice. The counselor should try to disabuse clients of any misconceptions expressed in their responses to these items. Six items (6, 11, 26, 29, 47, and 50) deal with the criteria one imposes on making a choice. Originally these items were called orientation-toward-work items in that they referred to whether one sought intrinsic or extrinsic rewards from work. Savickas and Crites (1981) referred to these items as criterion items, that is, client's criteria for defining a good career choice. Counselors can use these items to identify clients who use power, prestige, or possessions as choice criteria and encourage them to consider the role of intrinsic rewards in producing job and life satisfaction.

After discussing a client's choice criteria, the counselor can use four items (2, 8, 17, and 35) to explain the intrinsic criteria on which one should base a career choice: needs, interests, abilities, and values. The counselor should try to convince clients to base their choices on a synthesis of these four factors because using any one factor alone can produce an incongruent career choice. Discussions of choice bases make a smooth transition to administration or interpretation of interest inventories and ability tests.

As noted earlier, critics argued persuasively that content-oriented elements confounded these three variables. Although they do not reflect the decision-making process itself, these variables do define important attitudes toward a career choice; therefore, they can be used validly in teaching the test. Furthermore, if a counselor discusses them after discussing the five attitudes toward the vocational decision-making process, then this discussion of attitudes toward a career choice makes a smooth transition to content-oriented assessment and counseling.

In summary, clients are ready for content-oriented assessment and counseling when they display concern for and a sense of control over the vocational decision-making process, hold an accurate conception of how to make a choice, identify intrinsic criteria for their choices, and want to base their choices on a synthesis of their needs, interests, abilities, and values.

Teaching the Test Materials and Methods

To help counselors interpret Attitude Scale items to clients, Crites (1973) wrote programmed instructional materials to use in teaching the test. For each item, he explained the rationale for the more mature responses. Crites and Savickas (1980) revised the Screening Form rationales based on feedback from counselors and their own experience in using the rationales. They also added rationales for the additional items in the Counseling Form. They suggested that counselors use a three-step cycle in discussing item rationales with a client: (a) nondirective exploration, (b) directive shaping, and (c) active learning. Different types of interviewing responses and goals define each phase in this item teaching cycle.

Nondirective Exploration. Counselors begin the cycle by reading an item that the client answered in the immature direction and asking the client to explain the reason for the chosen response. This sets the topic and begins the exploration of the client's outlook (Van Riper, 1974). For example, a counselor might say, "On item 54 you agreed that you would feel better if someone chose for you. What did you have in mind when you answered this question?" To draw out the client's attitude and to probe the beliefs, feelings, and behavioral tendencies associated with it, the counselor may use "nondirective" responses such as open questions, restatement of relevant content, reflection of feeling, silence, and clarification of meaning.

Directive Shaping. Having explored the client's outlook, the counselor actively uses responses that elicit and shape a more mature view (Flake, Roach, & Stenning, 1975). The counselor teaches the client the rationale for the item and uses values confrontation (Young, 1979) to create dissonance about immature attitudes toward vocational decision making. During the ensuing discussion the counselor may use responses such as instruction, persuasion, verbal modeling, storytelling, and reinforcement to help clients reduce the felt discrepancy by reconceptualizing their beliefs and developing new attitudes. Counselors use their expertness, trustworthiness, and attractiveness to block unproductive paths to dissonance reduction (e.g., discredit counselor, use counterpersuasion, devalue the issue, seek social support), and confirm client attitude change with encouragement and support (Strong, 1968).

Active Learning. When the client verbally expresses an improved outlook, the counselor encourages the client to translate it into goal directed vocational behavior. The counselor may use responses such as behavioral modeling, homework assignments, role playing, and feedback to guide instrumental learning. This completes the three phases in the item discussion cycle. Accordingly, the counselor moves to the next item that the client answered in the immature direction and repeats the cycle. In exploring the new item, the counselor listens to hear if the client has integrated and generalized pertinent insights that were learned in discussing a previous item. If the earlier learning has not generalized to the new item, then the counselor proceeds to the directive shaping and active learning steps.

After considering each item, the counselor usually summarizes what the client has learned and restates what the client will do to confirm and enact the new attitudes. The counselor may also draw from the client the implications that the new decisional attitudes have for choices the client is trying to make in interpersonal, family, or leisure roles. For example, the counselor might say, "I hear you now saying that it is important to make your own career choice. I wonder if you think it is okay to rely on people to make other kinds of choices for you?"

Teaching the Test Variations

A few counselors use the item discussion cycle without administering the CMI to clients. Unlike the test interpretation method, the test teaching method does not require that the client take the test. The counselor may just sit down with a client and begin to discuss the items by asking the client to verbally respond to the first item. If the client offers a mature response, the counselor reinforces it and moves to the next item. If the response shows an immature outlook, then the counselor begins the discussion cycle outlined earlier.

In addition to teaching the test to individual clients, counselors have used the item rationales in process-oriented career counseling groups. These groups do not address which occupational choice (content) is right for each group member, but instead deal with the approach to decision making (process) that is right for everyone in the group. Teaching the test works even more effectively when the counselor enlists group dynamics in the item discussion cycle. For example, those group members who have already developed a particular attitude receive reinforcement and serve as role models to other group members who are still developing that disposition. The group members can help the counselor confirm or contradict the thinking of a client as well as encourage the client to experiment with new attitudes and behaviors.

Although not widely used, other variants of teaching the test have been effective. Healy (1982, pp. 317–321) suggested that counselors reduce client errors and lessen anxiety associated with "instructional counseling" by teaching the concepts assessed by the scale before administering it and discussing incorrect answers. Savickas and Crites (1981) designed and field tested (Savickas, 1990) a course to teach the Counseling Form item rationales to high school students. A teachers' guide for the course includes detailed lesson plans, teaching tips, overhead transparencies, and student handouts. Freeman (1975) wrote and pilot tested 10 sociodramas to teach the Screening Form variables to students. The sociodramas are semistructured; an opening dialogue sets the problem and leaves the conclusion of the drama to the student actors. A community college placement center modified the item rationales for a series of "Dear Abby"-type articles in their newsletter for students. Other innovative ways of teaching the test probably will appear as more counselors use the item rationales.

Technical Information

Because of its extensive use in theoretical research and program evaluation, the Attitude Scale has a well-articulated nomological network and strong support for its validity. The large volume of research reflects the fact that the Attitude Scale was the first objective measure of career maturity and thus was widely used during the 1970s to evaluate career education programs and career counseling interventions. At least 1,000 studies involving the Attitude Scale have appeared as published journal articles or unpublished doctoral dissertations. To approach this voluminous literature, one should begin by reading Crites's (1971) monograph on the Attitude Scale and the *Theory and Research Handbook* (Crites, 1978c). After this introduction, the reader should review a Counseling Form validity study (Stowe, 1985) and several Screening Form validity studies (Alvi & Khan, 1982; Chodzinski & Randhawa, 1983; Fouad & Keeley, 1992; Hanna & Neely, 1978; Khan & Alvi, 1983; Neely & Hanna, 1977). So prepared, the reader is ready to consider critiques of the Attitude Scale.

Reviews

After hundreds of studies, four questions about the Attitude Scale's validity remain unanswered. The first question addresses the Attitude Scale's construct validity. Reviewers have disagreed with several decisions that Crites made in constructing the scale. Super (1969) and Katz (1978) criticized the operational definition and validity of the construct measured by the Attitude Scale because 43 of the 50 Screening Form (A-1) items were keyed false, that is, written to reflect what career maturity is not. Westbrook and Mastie (1973) expressed concern about the large number of items with low positive (<.30) and high negative biserial correlations with the total score. They argued that, even in a factorially complex instrument, all the items should relate positively to the total score. They wondered what the items with negative biserial correlations contribute to the principal construct measured by the scale. They also questioned whether the true/false response scale adequately reflects respondents' attitudes.

The second question addresses an aspect of the Attitude Scale's criterion-related validity. Hansen (1974) called for longitudinal studies to examine the Attitude Scale's predictive validity. Most of the available criterion-related validity data is concurrent. For example, Westbrook (1976) showed that students with higher Screening Form scores made more realistic vocational choices. Although a few longitudinal studies have been conducted (Collins, 1986; Herr, Good, McCloskey, & Weitz, 1982), we still do not know if students with higher Attitude Scale scores more accurately predict their future occupation or achieve greater job satisfaction and success. Researchers need to empirically investigate the assumption that career maturity during adolescence relates to career adaptability and work adjustment during adulthood.

The third question addresses the Attitude Scale's convergent and discriminant validity. Westbrook and Mastie (1973) questioned the Attitude Scale's convergent validity because it correlates more strongly with CDI cognitive scales than with CDI attitude scales. Researchers (Palmo & Lutz, 1983; Westbrook, 1982) also challenged the discriminant validity of the Attitude Scale because it correlates with measures of mental ability. Crites, Wallbrown, and Blaha (1985) countered these arguments, but the issue remains unresolved (Healy, 1994).

The fourth question addresses the Scale's validity for use. Hansen (1974) called for research to determine the usefulness of the Scale in career guidance. Katz (1978, p. 1563) expressed "reservations about the strong claims in the handbook and manual of categorical validity for various uses of the Scale in guidance," and Sorenson (1974) considered the validity data for the claimed uses unpersuasive. Zytowski (1978) faulted Crites for not using available data to distinguish the valid uses of the Scale. Cronbach's (1980) idea of validity for use should guide future studies of the diagnostic subscales in the Counseling Form.

Research Directions

At this time, the most pressing research need relative to the Attitude Scale is a literature review (Healy, 1994). The last literature review appeared in the *Theory and Research Handbook* (Crites, 1978c). A voluminous literature dealing with the CMI has appeared since 1975, the latest reference in the *Handbook* bibliography. A systematic synthesis of the accumulated evidence would allow theorists, researchers, and practitioners to make the fullest use of the varied information offered by the numerous studies. It might also help resolve the controversy surrounding the CMI Attitude Scale's relationship with intelligence (Crites et al., 1985; Westbrook, 1982).

The most pressing empirical research need is for studies of the validity of the five subscales. In order for these subscales to be helpful to counselors, their validity for use must be formally established. Research on interpreting the Attitude Scale should identify, if possible, the "threshold" of readiness to make a realistic career choice. It should also investigate the effect of teaching the test on career choice decidedness and realism. If teaching the test increases decidedness and realism, then investigators should examine the relative effectiveness of different instructional methods such as individual counseling, group counseling, programmed learning, and behavioral modeling.

After being overlooked for many years, measurement of career choice competencies is finally drawing the attention of CMI researchers. The major drawback in the Competence Tests has been the time required to administer them. Users of the Attitude Scale have rarely been wiling to ask clients to spend the two hours required to complete the five tests. To address this problem, Crites (1995) published a new form of the CMI that allows quick assessment of career choice competence. The original five subtests were eliminated and now each competence is represented by five items that, together, produce a total score ranging from 0 to 25. Testing time has also been reduced by changing from a multiple-choice format to an *agree* and *disagree* response format. Subscales were also eliminated from this version of the Attitude Scale, which uses the best 25 items from the prior version. In addition to eliminating subscales for both the Attitude Scale and the Competence Test, the revised CMI extends the applicability of the inventory to postsecondary students and employed adults by deleting items with content specific to students in Grades 5 through 12 (Crites & Savickas, 1996). Early validity studies for the revised CMI competence test produced encouraging results. Hopefully, the revised test will be a sensitive and specific measure of career choice competence, with minimal correlations to measures of intelligence.

USES OF THE MEASURES

This section deals with the selection and use of career decision-making measures. The first part compares and contrasts the three prominent measures and offers guidelines for their use. The second part discusses suggestions on how to interpret scores from process measures to clients. The third part presents a case that illustrates the use of process measures in career counseling.

The Measures Compared

In the introduction to this chapter, I noted that career decision-making scales measure either difficulties or resources. Having reviewed the three most prominent scales, we are now prepared to further distinguish the scales according to their various uses. Obviously the main distinction remains as stated in the introduction. The CDS deals with indecision, whereas the CDI and CMI deal with career maturity. More precisely, the CDS addresses adaptation to the tasks involved in developing a career choice. The CDS Certainty Scale helps counselors make a *differential diagnosis* of a client's decisional status, that is, degree of decidedness. The CDS Indecision Scale helps counselors assess the amount and variety of difficulties that delay clients' adaptation to career choice tasks. The CDI and CMI address not adaptation but adaptability, that is, the personal resources one can draw on to form behavioral responses to the vocational development tasks of crystallization, specification, and implementation. In particular, the CDI measures planning and exploration attitudes and informational and decisional competencies that people use to develop a realistic career choice. Counselors can use the CDI to make a *developmental diagnosis* of clients' readiness for coping with career choice tasks. In contrast, the CMI Attitude Scale measures attitudes toward career choice (Form A-2 or B-1 total score) and disposition for vocational decision making (Counseling Form B-1 subscales). Counselors can use the CMI to make a *decisional diagnosis* of clients' readiness to make realistic career choices. The differential, developmental, and decisional perspectives on the career choice process focus on distinct variables, yet the variables of difficulties, readiness, and dispositions may eventually be integrated into comprehensive career choice process measures (Jepsen & Prediger, 1981) and diagnostic classification schemes (Rounds & Tinsley, 1984, p. 156).

In addition to informing diagnosis for counseling, each of the career decision-making inventories discussed in this chapter has been used in evaluation, research, screening, and surveys. Each inventory has unique characteristics that make it likely to be selected for a particular purpose. This is most true with regard to research and evaluation.

The best documented use of the inventories is in research on treatment outcomes and evaluation of program effects. When selecting an inventory for program evaluation, evaluators should choose the one that most closely coincides with objectives of the program: the CDS to measure decisional status and difficulties, the CDI to measure developmental task mastery attitudes and competencies, and the CMI Attitude Scale to measure attitudes toward vocational decision making. Although this selection criterion seems obvious, some evaluators have overlooked it because the inventory titles describe in general, not in particular, what they measure. In selecting an inventory for a research study, investigators should choose the one that measures the variables being examined. An empirical comparison of the inventories reported by Jepsen and Prediger (1981) distinguished among the measures and can help researchers make a more informed choice. An article by Hilton (1974) offered suggestions on selecting an evaluation instrument and analyzing evaluation data.

Many counselors select the CDS and CMI Screening Form (A-2) to quickly screen large groups of students. The CMI Screening Form works particularly well with junior and senior high-school students. The CDS works better than the CMI with college students (Fretz & Leong, 1982) because it addresses major choice and has a higher ceiling. Students who are identified as needing assistance can be invited to orientation programs and career workshops or informed about opportunities for group guidance and individual counseling. Some college counselors have used the CDS to help students choose between personal and career development courses. They advise students with lower scores to take the personal development course first, whereas they advise students with higher scores to take only the career choice course.

When planning guidance programs and career education curricula, counselors can use career choice measures to survey students' needs. The CDI and CMI Counseling Form (B-1) are particularly useful in this regard. Because they each measure five variables, they provide multidimensional data as a basis for intervention design. With these data, counselors can design guidance programs and career education curricula to address the unique needs of the participants. Survey results can also be used to structure enrichment opportunities. For example, one college has administered the CDI to all incoming freshmen. At the first meeting with their academic advisors, students are given a booklet that explains their CDI results. The advisors engage students in "career conversations" to plan exploration experiences and select elective courses based upon CDI results. During the year, the counseling center staff invites students to different types of career development workshops based on their CDI profiles. The CDS (Savickas, Alexander, Jonas, & Wolf, 1986) and the CMI (Crites, 1978a) have been used similarly.

Using Process Assessments in Counseling

Several writers have discussed the use of career decision-making measures in counseling. The architects of the Developmental Assessment and Counseling Model viewed test interpretation as a prime counseling method. Super (1983) enjoined counselors to make CDI results "part of the active thinking of the client." In a book edited by Super, Jordaan (1974) used four case examples to discuss how interpreting CDI results can help clients "repair developmental deficits" and "build on strengths." In the same book, LoCascio (1974) described problems in using career decision-making measures with school dropouts and ethnic minorities, and Richardson (1974) discussed the use of these measures in counseling girls and young women. More recent case examples for using the CDI have been published by Niles and Usher (1993), Super (1990), and Super, Osborne, Walsh, Brown, and Niles (1992). Crites (1974b, 1981) asserted that counselors should use process measures to enhance clients' self-understanding and improve their thinking and problem solving as a foundation for future coping with career development tasks.

The writers seem to agree that the best counseling use of the measures involves focusing on developmental possibilities and discussing experiences that could facilitate clients' career development. Crites (1981) addressed how to meaningfully communicate this information to clients in an article on "integrative test interpretation." He suggested that counselors use the measures to focus on aspects of career development that are particularly difficult for the client, embed information from the results in discussions of these difficulties, respond to the clients' verbalizations rather than interpreting the profile, and attend to the client's decisions as opposed to the measurement instrument.

A Case Illustration

The following case illustrates one way of using career decision-making measures to improve a client's thinking about career choice, identify developmental possibilities, and select maturation experiences. A 20-year-old college student, dissatisfied with school, sought career counseling at the behest of a concerned friend. The student was about to successfully complete the third year of a 6-year accelerated program that led to bachelor of science and doctor of medicine degrees. However, as he was completing his first year in medical school, he experienced serious misgivings about his decision to become a physician. He felt uncomfortable with his classmates because they had different interests and lonely because school demands precluded time for old friends with similar interests. Although he passed every course, he claimed that it required tremendous willpower to study because he disliked the subject matter. In counseling, he wanted to reconsider his career choice of medicine, discuss his specialty choice within medicine (i.e., psychiatry versus family medicine), and identify career alternatives outside of medicine. After a brief intake interview, I told him that I wanted more data about the career difficulties he was experiencing, his resources for resolving these difficulties, and the pattern of his vocational interests. To provide more data, he agreed to take the CDS, CDI, and the

Jackson Vocational Interest Survey (JVIS; Jackson, 1977) during the next week and to return for counseling when they had been scored.

I assigned him the CDS to acquire specific information about the difficulties that were thwarting his adaptation to the task of specifying the details of his career choice with certainty and commitment. I assigned him the CDI to learn about the maturation of the attitudes and competencies that he would need to develop his career choice. I did not use the CMI with this client because I was more interested in his readiness for vocational development task coping in general rather than his disposition toward vocational decision making in particular. Based on the intake interview, he impressed me as having a pseudo-crystallized preference for medicine. CDI data are better suited than CMI data to objectively assess this subjective impression. For a case study that illustrates the use of the CMI, counselors may read the case of Karen as presented by Crites (1976).

In hand scoring the CDS, I determined that the client scored 3 points on the CDS Certainty Scale (i.e., 2 points for "only slightly like me" for major choice certainty plus 1 point for "not at all like me" for career choice certainty). The client scored 47 points on the CDS Indecision Scale. This raw score converted to the 99th percentile for decision-making difficulties among college students. In my experience, such an extreme score appears to mean that a person is in a state of career crisis and feels overwhelmed by career concerns. His response to the open-ended question (i.e., CDS item 19) coincided with this interpretation.

> I grew up in hospitals and it was "given" that I was going to be a doctor. I really don't know what a doctor does. It seems that one has to be "perfect" to be an M. D. Therefore, I can't be a good one. I am stuck. I still don't know what I would be good at, if anything. So, if I don't have medicine, I don't have anything. I am concerned and confused by everything.

The client rated five items as "4" or "exactly like me": CDS items 7, 8, 10, 13, and 14. I formed a composite statement of the client's salient decisional difficulties as stated in these items.

> I do not know what my abilities and interests are because I have not given much thought to my career choice until now. I feel lost and discouraged because I am not used to making my own decisions. Everything about choosing seems so uncertain but I want to be absolutely certain that I make the right choice. However, none of the careers I know about seem ideal for me so I need more information about careers.

After considering the CDS data, I turned to the CDI results to understand how the client's decisional difficulties may have developed and to begin to formulate ideas about what he could do to outgrow the difficulties. His percentile scores were career planning attitudes = 1, career exploration attitudes = 53, decision-making competence = 46, world-of-work information = 31, and knowledge of preferred occupation = 74. Two features of this CDI profile drew my attention. The first feature involved the Career Planning Scale (CP). By itself, the client's extremely low CP scale score indicated that he did not look ahead to foresee himself in the world of work nor involve himself in planning his future. The score coincided with his statement during the intake interview that he has trouble seeing himself as a competent physician. In relation to the Career Exploration, World of Work, and Decision Making scores, the CP score suggested that the client may be actively avoiding career planning in that he has not applied available exploration, comprehension, and problem-solving resources to relate himself to the world of work. The second CDI profile feature that drew my attention involved the Preferred Occupational Group Scale (PO). By itself, I was surprised that he had chosen Social Science Research as his preferred field and that he had a good fund of knowledge about this field. I wondered if he had explored occupations in this field. In relation to other CDI scales, I noted that PO exceeded his World of Work score. Apparently, he was somewhat naive about occupations in general but knew about occupations in social science research.

Next I considered the JVIS. The JVIS includes work-style scales along with more traditional interest scales. On work-style scales, the client scored low on independence, planfulness, and interpersonal confidence and high on stamina, job security, and accountability. On vocational interest scales, he scored "high," but not "very high," on life science, social science, medical service, mathematics, technical writing, and social service.

To me the data coincided with a diagnosis of pseudo-crystallized preference preventing specification of a choice with certainty and commitment. The CDS revealed difficulties in developing a clear and stable picture of talents, interests, and goals and difficulty in emotionally accepting a preference he was already implementing. The CDI revealed a naivete about occupations and a lack of involvement in planning his vocational future. The JVIS revealed an unfocused interest pattern and a disposition toward passively following rules rather than assertively choosing and planning his own behavior. As a group, his diffused vocational interests, occupational naivete, and passive work style seemed to explain his self-reported difficulty in specifying the details of his career choice with certainty and commitment. Moreover, as a group they formed a pattern that suggested that specification was not the problem but rather the symptom of an earlier problem. Based on the inventory data, I concluded that the client's career choice of physician was not holding up under pressures to perform in medical school and to elaborate a specialty choice because it followed from a pseudo-crystallized preference for a career in medicine. The preference seemed to be pseudo-crystallized in that he had failed to actively involve himself in the career choice process (CP score) and to analyze essential elements of his preference for medicine (PO score exceeded WW score). Furthermore, the JVIS work-style scores suggested the possibility that his preference for medicine might not have been a self-chosen goal. Instead, his preference might have resulted from the "interplay between the emotional needs of two persons—the individual making the choice and the individual who influences him" (Ginzberg et al., 1951, p. 110).

At our next meeting, I used the integrative interpretation approach described by Crites (1981) to present my assessment of the inventory scores. As recommended by Guardo (1975, 1977) in her writings on developmental existentialism, I used the client's vocational development pattern as a backdrop for understanding and appreciating his unique experiences and opinions. In discussing my assessment with him, I highlighted his developmental pattern to help him articulate the course, pace, and scope of his existential experiences. My goal for this session was to combine our perspectives on his experiences to identify problems in and opportunities for developing a realistic career choice.

After orienting him to this goal, I began the session by discussing his response to CPS item 19. During the discussion, the client orally elaborated his written response and described pervasive feelings of anxiety caused by his desire to be certain about and comfortable with his career choice. Next, we considered the CDS items that he rated as "4" by discussing my composite statement of his decisional difficulties. The student endorsed this statement as "him." He self-explored each of the four components in turn:

1. He lacked self-knowledge and planfulness because he had always passively succumbed to an aggressive father who demanded that he become a physician.
2. He lacked decision-making skill because he relied on his father's decisions.
3. He wanted to make the ideal choice because he saw the bitterness that had resulted from his father being trapped in the wrong career.
4. He lacked occupational information because of his early fixation on a career in medicine.

I used his self-disclosures about early fixation on medicine as a bridge to the CDI data. I informed him that the CDI indicated that his early fixation explained many of his current career concerns. To resolve these concerns, he might need to increase his foresight, deliberate more about the outcomes of his decisions, use daydreams to conceptualize himself in different kinds of work, explore several fields, and become more self-sufficient in decision making. I wove the JVIS work-style data into discussing the last idea. He agreed that he needed to take positive steps on his own behalf rather than passively accept his father's career commands. I did not mention the JVIS interest scores because they were not yet pertinent to the discussion. During the remainder of the session, I responded empathically to his anxiety about his future, fear of confronting his father, and disgust with himself for still making decisions like a child. We concluded the session with an agreement to meet again to design a plan to develop his autonomy and career choice.

During the planning session, we concentrated on two themes: transforming the client's relationship with his father, and developing his career choice. Because this case is presented to illustrate the use of career decision-making measures in counseling, and not interest inventory interpretation or counseling techniques, I only summarize the plan and its results. The client decelerated his movement through the accelerated BS/MD program by asking to spend 7 rather than 6 years in it. He used the extra year, at the end of his first year in medical school, to implement his growth plan. During this year he took no courses at the medical school while his classmates pursued full-time studies there. Instead, he (a) completed his BS requirements as a half-time student, (b) used electives in his BS curriculum to explore careers in clinical psychology, medical sociology, and journalism, (c) worked 20 hours per week for 6 months as a biochemistry laboratory technician, (d) "shadowed" a psychiatrist for a week, (e) spent the summer away from home working as an intern in a public health program, (f) participated in an assertiveness training course, (g) received short-term counseling to increase his self-esteem and reduce his obsessiveness, and (h) studied judo. These activities enhanced his self-esteem and his ability to make independent decisions. The activities also strained his relationship with his father, yet the client and his father both felt that their relationship was improving. At the end of this year, the client transferred to another university where he enrolled in a graduate program in epidemiology. He planned to become an epidemiologist and possibly teach at a medical school. On follow-up a year later, he reported success in and satisfaction with his graduate program as well as increased certainty about his career in epidemiology.

CONCLUSION

This chapter explained how some counselors view career choice as a sequence of developmental tasks from crystallizing field and level preferences, to specifying a choice, and then implementing that choice. Students must adapt to social expectations that they master these tasks in a viable and suitable manner. To facilitate task mastery, comprehensive career counseling deals with both the process of vocational decision making and the content of career choice.

Counselors begin comprehensive career counseling by making a differential diagnosis of the client's vocational decision-making status, that is, identifying the tasks that a client faces and the difficulties experienced. With clients who are ready to specify a choice, the counselor proceeds to assist the client by using content-oriented counseling methods and materials. For those clients who are not ready, the counselor makes a developmental diagnosis of the client's attitudes and competencies for mastering the tasks of crystallizing preferences and specifying choice. Furthermore, for those clients who need to develop the maturity to specify a choice, the counselor may make a decisional diagnosis of the client's disposition for vocational decision making.

Three scales that many counselors use to assess clients' career choice decision making were presented. The three scales may each be used to make all three of the diagnoses, yet each scale is especially useful for a particular assessment: the Career Decision Scale for differential diagnoses, the Career Development Inventory for developmental diagnoses, and the Career Maturity Inventory Attitude Scale for decisional diagnoses. The usefulness of each scale for a particular type of diagnosis probably explains counselors' practice of using the CDS to screen students for decision-making difficulties, the CDI to survey students for needs assessment in program development and evaluation, and the CMI to select students' individual counseling topics.

The instrument authors' ingenuity in theory construction, perseverance in instrument development, and leadership in research production have helped counselors expand occupational guidance to career counseling. In the future, research and reflection on the inventory's use in career counseling will probably result in new career decision-making instruments that measure a broader range of variables (Jepsen & Prediger, 1981), offer decision rules for diagnoses, and prescribe differential interventions for clients (Fretz & Leong, 1982; Rounds & Tinsley, 1984). The new instruments will build on the successes of the Career Decision Scale, Career Development Inventory, and Career Maturity Inventory.

REFERENCES

Allis, M. (1984). [Review of the *Career Decision Scale*]. *Measurement and Evaluation in Counseling and Development, 17,* 98–100.

Alvi, S. A., & Khan, S. B. (1982). A study of the criterion-related validity of Crites' Career Maturity Inventory. *Educational and Psychological Measurement, 42,* 1285–1288.

Barak, A., & Friedkes, R. (1981). The mediating effects of career indecision and subtypes on career counseling effectiveness. *Journal of Vocational Behavior, 20,* 120–128.

Bell, H. M. (1940). *Matching youth and jobs.* Washington, DC: American Council on Education.

Chodzinski, R. T., & Randhawa, B. R. (1983). Validity of Career Maturity Inventory. *Educational and Psychological Measurement, 43,* 1163–1172.

Collins, J. E. (1986). Career maturity as a predictor of job adaptation: A longitudinal study (Doctoral dissertation, Kent State University, 1985). *Dissertation Abstracts International, 47,* 357A.

Crites, J. O. (1961). A model for the measurement of vocational maturity. *Journal of Counseling Psychology, 8,* 255–259.

Crites, J. O. (1964). Proposals for a new criterion measure and research design. In H. Borow (Ed.), *Man in a world at work* (pp. 324–340). Boston: Houghton Mifflin.

Crites, J. O. (1965). Measurement of vocational maturity in adolescence: I. Attitude Scale of the Vocational Development Inventory. *Psychological Monographs, 79*(2, Whole No. 595).

Crites, J. O. (1971). *The maturity of vocational attitudes in adolescence.* Washington, DC: American Personnel and Guidance Association.

Crites, J. O. (1973). *Rationales for Career Maturity Inventory Attitude Scale (Form A-1) items.* Unpublished manuscript.

Crites, J. O. (1974a). Methodological issues in the measurement of career maturity. *Measurement and Evaluation in Guidance, 6,* 200–209.

Crites, J. O. (1974b). A reappraisal of vocational appraisal. *Vocational Guidance Quarterly, 22,* 272–279.

Crites, J. O. (1976). Carer counseling: A comprehensive approach. *Counseling Psychologist, 6,* 2–12.

Crites, J. O. (1978a). *Administration and Use Manual for the Career Maturity Inventory* (2nd ed.). Monterey, CA: CTB/McGraw-Hill.

Crites, J. O. (1978b). *The Career Maturity Inventory.* Monterey, CA: CTB/McGraw-Hill.

Crites, J. O. (1978c). *Theory and research handbook for the Career Maturity Inventory* (2nd ed.). Monterey, CA: CTB/McGraw-Hill.

Crites, J. O. (1981). Integrative test interpretation. In D. H. Montross & C. J. Shinkman (Eds.), *Career development in the 1980's: Theory and practice* (pp. 161–168). Springfield, IL: Charles C. Thomas.

Crites, J. O. (1995). *Career Maturity Inventory.* Clayden, NY: Careerwares:

Crites, J. O., & Savickas, M. L. (1980). *Rationales for Career Maturity Inventory Attitude Scale (Form B-1) items.* Unpublished manuscript.

Crites, J. O., & Savickas, M. L. (1996). Revision of the Career Maturity Inventory. *Journal of Career Assessment, 4,* 131–138.

Crites, J. O., Wallbrown, F. H., & Blaha, J. (1985). The Career Maturity Inventory: Myths and realities—A rejoinder to Westbrook, Cutts, Madison, and Arcia (1980). *Journal of Vocational Behavior, 26,* 221–238.

Cronbach, L. J. (1980). Validity on parole: How can we go straight? *New Directions for Testing and Measurement, 5,* 99–108.

Flake, M. H., Roach, A. J., Jr., & Stenning, W. F. (1975). Effects of short-term counseling on career maturity of tenth-grade students. *Journal of Vocational Behavior, 6,* 73–80.

Forrest, D. J. (1971). Construction and validation of an objective measure of vocational maturity for adolescents (Doctoral dissertation, Columbia University, Teachers College, 1971). *Dissertation Abstracts International, 32,* 3088A.

Fouad, N. A., & Keeley, T. J. (1992). The relationship between attitudinal and behavioral aspects of career maturity. *Career Development Quarterly, 40,* 257–271.

Freeman, M. (1975). A comparison of the relative effectiveness of two instructional methods for developing attitudinal dimensions of career maturity in adolescents (Doctoral dissertation, Kent State University, 1974). *Dissertation Abstracts International, 35,* 6583A.

Fretz, B. R., & Leong, F. T. L. (1982). Career development status as a predictor of career intervention outcomes. *Journal of Counseling Psychology, 29*, 388–393.

Gati, I., Krauss, M., & Osipow, S. H. (1996, August). *Taxonomy of career decision-making problems.* Paper presented at the annual meeting of the American Psychological Association, Toronto, Canada.

Ginzberg, E., Ginsburg, S. W., Axelrad, S., & Herma, J. L. (1951). *Occupational choice: An approach to a general theory.* New York: Columbia University Press.

Gordon, C. (1970). *Looking ahead: Self-conceptions, race, and family as determinants of adolescent orientation to achievement.* Washington, DC: American Sociological Association.

Guardo, C. J. (1975). The helping process as developmental existentialism. *Personnel and Guidance Journal, 53*, 493–499.

Guardo, C. J. (1977). Toward growth of adolescents. *Personnel and Guidance Journal, 55*, 237–241.

Hanna, G. S., & Neely, M. A. (1978). Discriminant validity of Career Maturity Inventory Scales in grade 9 students. *Educational and Psychological Measurement, 38*, 571–574.

Hansen, J. C. (1974). [Review of J. O. Crites, *Career Maturity Inventory*]. *Journal of Counseling Psychology, 21*, 168–172.

Hansen, J. C. (1985). [Review of *Career Development Inventory*]. *Measurement and Evaluation in Guidance, 17*, 220–224.

Harmon, L. W. (1985). [Review of *Career Decision Scale*]. In J. V. Mitchell, Jr. (Ed.), *The ninth mental measurements yearbook (1)* (p. 270). Lincoln: University of Nebraska Press.

Harmon, L. W. (1994). [Review of the *Career Decision Scale*]. In J. T. Kapes, M. M. Mastie, & E. A. Whitfield (Eds.), *A counselor's guide to career assessment instruments* (3rd ed., pp. 258–262). Alexandria, VA: National Career Development Association.

Harren, V. A. (1978). *Assessment of Career Decision Making: Counselor/instructor guide.* Unpublished manuscript, Southern Illinois University, Carbondale.

Hartman, B. W., Fuqua, D., & Jenkins, S. J. (1988). Multivariate generalizability analysis of three measures of career indecision. *Educational and Psychological Measurement, 48*, 61–68.

Hartman, B. W., Utz, P. W., & Farnum. S. O. (1979). Examining the reliability and validity of an adapted scale of educational-vocational undecidedness in a sample of graduate students. *Journal of Vocational Behavior, 15*, 224–230.

Healy, C. C. (1982). *Career development: Counseling through the life stages.* Boston: Allyn and Bacon.

Healy, C. C. (1994). [Review of the *Career Maturity Inventory*]. In J. T. Kapes, M. M. Mastie, & E. A. Whitfield (Eds.), *A counselor's guide to career assessment instruments* (3rd ed., pp. 268–272). Alexandria, VA: National Career Development Association.

Heath, D. H. (1976). Adolescent and adult predictors of vocational adaptation. *Journal of Vocational Behavior, 9*, 1–19.

Herman, D. O. (1985). [Review of *Career Decision Scale*]. In J. V. Mitchell, Jr. (Ed.), *The ninth mental measurements yearbook (1)* (pp. 270–271). Lincoln, NE: University of Nebraska Press.

Herr, E. L., Good, R. H. III, McCloskey, G., & Weitz, A. D. (1982). Secondary school curriculum and career behavior in young adults. *Journal of Vocational Behavior, 21*, 243–253.

Hilton, T. L. (1974). Using measures of vocational maturity in evaluation. In D. E. Super (Ed.), *Measuring vocational maturity for counseling and evaluation* (pp. 145–159). Washington, DC: National Vocational Guidance Association.

Holland, J. L. (1966). *The psychology of vocational choice.* Waltham, MA: Ginn & Company.

Holland, J. L., Daiger, D. C., & Power, P. G. (1980). *My vocational situation.* Palo Alto, CA: Consulting Psychologists Press.

Holland, J. L., & Nichols, R. C. (1964). The development and validation of an indecision scale: The natural history of a problem in basic research. *Journal of Counseling Psychology, 11*, 27–34.

Jackson, D. N. (1977). *Jackson Vocational Interest Survey.* Port Huron, MI: Research Psychologists Press.

Jepsen, D. A., & Prediger, D. J. (1981). Dimensions of adolescent career development: A multi-instrument analysis. *Journal of Vocational Behavior, 19*, 350–368.

Jones, L. K., & Chenery, M. F. (1980). Multiple subtypes among vocationally undecided college students: A model and assessment instrument. *Journal of Counseling Psychology, 27*, 469–477.

Jordaan, J. P. (1974). The use of vocational maturity instruments in counseling. In D. E. Super (Ed.), *Measuring vocational maturity for counseling and evaluation* (pp. 113–121). Washington, DC: National Vocational Guidance Association.

Katz, M. R. (1978). [Review of J. O. Crites, *Career Maturity Inventory*]. In O. K. Buros (Ed.), *The eighth mental measurement yearbook (2)* (pp. 1562–1565). Highland Park, NJ: Gryphon Press.

Kazin, R. I. (1976, August). *Educational/vocational indecision questionnaire: Replication of a factor analysis.* Paper presented at the meeting of the American Psychological Association, Washington, DC.

Khan, S. B., & Alvi, S. A. (1983). Educational, social, and psychological correlates of vocational maturity. *Journal of Vocational Behavior, 22*, 357–364.

Laplante, B., Coallier, J. C., Sabourin, S., & Martin, F. (1994). Dimensionality of the Career Decision Scale: Methodological, cross-cultural, and clinical issues. *Journal of Career Assessment, 2*, 19–28.

LoCascio, R. (1974). The vocational maturity of diverse groups: Theory and measurement. In D. E. Super (Ed.), *Measuring vocational maturity for counseling and evaluation* (pp. 123–133). Washington, DC: National Vocational Guidance Association.

Lopez-Baez, S. E. (1981). A study of career consciousness: Temporal experience and career maturity (Doctoral dissertation, Kent State University, 1980). *Dissertation Abstracts International, 41*, 3427A.

Myers, R. A., Lindeman, R. H., Thompson, A. S., & Patrick, T. A. (1975). Effects of educational and career exploration system on vocational maturity. *Journal of Vocational Behavior, 6*, 245–254.

Neely, M. A., & Hanna, G. S. (1977). A study of the concurrent validity of the Career Maturity Inventory. *Educational and Psychological Measurement, 37*, 1087–1090.

Nevill, D. D., & Super, D. E. (1988). Career maturity and commitment to work in university students. *Journal of Vocational Behavior, 32*, 139–151.

Niles, S. G., & Usher, C. H. (1993). Applying the Career Development Assessment and Counseling model to the case of Rosie. *Career Development Quarterly, 42*, 61–66.

Oleksy-Ojikutu, A. E. (1986). The career time-line: A vocational counseling tool. *Career Development Quarterly, 35*, 47–52.

Osipow, S. H. (1983). *Theories of career development* (3rd ed.). Englewood Cliffs, NJ: Prentice Hall.

Osipow, S. H. (1987). *Career Decision Scale manual.* Odessa, FL: Psychological Assessment Resources.

Osipow, S. H. (1994). The Career Decision Scale: How good does it have to be? *Journal of Career Assessment, 2*, 15–18.

Osipow, S. H., Carney, C. G., & Barak, A. (1976). A scale of educational-vocational undecidedness: A typological approach. *Journal of Vocational Behavior, 9*, 233–243.

Osipow, S. H., Carney, C. G., Winer, J. L., Yanico, B., & Koschier, M. (1976). *The Career Decision Scale* (3rd rev.). Columbus, OH: Marathon Consulting & Press and (1987) Odessa, FL: Psychological Assessment Resources.

Osipow, S. H., & Winer, J. L. (1996). The use of the Career Decision Scale in career assessment. *Journal of Career Assessment, 4*, 117–130.

Osipow, S. H., Winer, J. L., Koschier, M., & Yanico, B. (1975). A modular approach to self-counseling for vocational indecision using audio-cassettes. In L. Simpson (Ed.), *Audio-visual media in career development* (pp. 34–38). Bethlehem, PA: College Placement Council.

Palmo, A. J., & Lutz, J. G. (1983). The relationship of performance on the CMI to intelligence with disadvantaged youngsters. *Measurement and Evaluation in Guidance, 16*, 139–148.

Parsons, F. (1909/1967). *Choosing a vocation.* New York: Agathon Press.

Pinkney, J. W., & Bozik, C. M. (1994). Review of the Career Development Inventory. In J. T. Kapes, M. M. Mastie, & E. A. Whitfield (Eds.), *A counselor's guide to career assessment instruments* (3rd ed., pp. 263–267). Alexandria, VA: National Career Development Association.

Punch, K. F., & Sheridan, B. E. (1985). Some measurement characteristics of the Career Development Inventory. *Measurement and Evaluation in Guidance, 17,* 196–202.

Richardson, M. S. (1974). Vocational maturity in counseling girls and women. In D. E. Super (Ed.), *Measuring vocational maturity for counseling and evaluation* (pp. 135–143). Washington, DC: National Vocational Guidance Association.

Rogers, W. B., & Westbrook, B. W. (1983). Measuring career indecision among college students: Toward a valid approach for counseling practitioners and researchers. *Measurement and Evaluation in Guidance, 16,* 78–85.

Rounds, J. B., Jr., & Tinsley, H. E. A. (1984). Diagnosis and treatment of vocational problems. In S. D. Brown & R. W. Lent (Eds.), *Handbook of counseling psychology* (pp. 137–177). New York: Wiley & Sons.

Savickas, M. L. (1984). Career maturity: The construct and its assessment. *Vocational Guidance Quarterly, 32,* 222–231.

Savickas, M. L. (1986). Career time perspective in special populations. In E. A. Whitfield, H. W. Drier, & D. Hickey (Eds.), *Improving career development through counselor education programs* (pp. 57–62). Columbus, OH: Ohio Department of Education.

Savickas, M. L. (1990). The career decision-making course: Description and field test. *Career Development Quarterly, 38,* 275–284.

Savickas, M. L. (1993). Predictive validity criteria for career development measures. *Journal of Career Development, 1,* 93–104.

Savickas, M. L., Alexander, D. E., Jonas, A. P., & Wolf, F. M. (1986). Difficulties experienced by medical students in choosing a specialty. *Journal of Medical Education, 61,* 467–469.

Savickas, M. L., Alexander, D. E., Osipow, S. H., & Wolf, F. M. (1985). Measuring specialty indecision among career decided students. *Journal of Vocational Behavior, 27,* 356–367.

Savickas, M. L., Carden, A. D., Toman, S., & Jarjoura, D. (1992). Dimensions of career decidedness. *Measurement and Evaluation in Counseling and Development, 25,* 102–112.

Savickas, M. L., & Crites, J. O. (1981). *Career decision-making: Teaching the process.* Unpublished manuscript.

Savickas, M. L., & Hartung, P. J. (1996). The Career Development Inventory in review: Psychometric and research findings. *Journal of Career Assessment, 4,* 171–188.

Savickas, M. L., & Jarjoura, D. (1991). The Career Decision Scale as a type indicator. *Journal of Counseling Psychology, 38,* 85–90.

Schulenberg, J., Vondracek, F. W., & Shimizu, K. (1994). Convergence and obfuscation: A rejoinder to Osipow and to Laplante, Coallier, Sabourin, and Martin. *Journal of Career Assessment, 2,* 29–39.

Shimizu, K., Vondracek, F. W., & Schulenberg, J. (1994). Unidimensionality versus multidimensionality of the Career Decision Scale: A critique of Martin, Sabourin, Laplante, and Coallier. *Journal of Career Assessment, 2,* 1–14.

Shimizu, K., Vondracek, F. W., Schulenberg, J. E., & Hostetler, M. (1988). The factor structure of the Career Decision Scale: Similarities across selected studies. *Journal of Vocational Behavior, 32,* 213–225.

Skovholt, T. M., & Hoenninger, R. W. (1974). Guided fantasy in career counseling. *Personnel and Guidance Journal, 52,* 693–696.

Slaney, R. B. (1978). *Factor replication of the Career Decision Scale.* Unpublished data, Southern Illinois University, Carbondale, IL.

Slaney, R. B. (1985). [Review of S. H. Osipow, C. G. Carney, J. L. Winer, B. Yanico, & M. Koschier, *Career Decision Scale*]. In D. J. Keyser & R. C. Sweetland (Eds.), *Test critiques (2)* (pp. 138–143). Kansas City, MO: Test Corporation of America.

Slaney, R. B., Palko-Nonemaker, D., & Alexander, R. (1981). An investigation of two measures of career indecision. *Journal of Vocational Behavior, 18*, 92–103.

Slaney, R. B., Stafford, M. J., & Russell, J. E. A. (1981). Career indecision in adult women: A comparative and descriptive study. *Journal of Vocational Behavior, 19*, 335–345.

Sorenson, G. (1974). [Review of J. O. Crites, *Career Maturity Inventory*]. *Measurement and Evaluation in Guidance, 7*, 54–57.

Stowe, R. W. (1985). Convergent and discriminant validity of Crites' Career Maturity Inventory Attitude Scale, Counseling Form B-1. *Educational and Psychological Measurement, 45*, 763–770.

Strong, E. K. (1943). *Vocational interests of men and women.* Stanford, CA: Stanford University Press.

Strong, S. R. (1968). Counseling: An interpersonal influence process. *Journal of Counseling Psychology, 15*, 215–224.

Super, D. E. (1955). The dimensions and measurement of vocational maturity. *Teachers College Record, 57*, 151–163.

Super, D. E. (1969). Vocational development theory in 1988: How will it come about? *Counseling Psychologist, 1*, 9–14.

Super, D. E. (Ed.). (1974). *Measuring vocational maturity for counseling and evaluation.* Washington, DC: National Vocational Guidance Association.

Super, D. E. (1983). Assessment in career guidance: Toward truly developmental counseling. *Personnel and Guidance Journal, 61*, 555–562.

Super, D. E. (1990). A life-span, life-space to career development. In D. Brown, L. Brooks, & Associates (Eds.), *Career choice and development: Applying contemporary theories to practice* (2nd ed., pp. 197–261). San Francisco: Jossey-Bass.

Super, D. E., & Forrest, D. J. (1972). *Career Development Inventory, Form I: Preliminary manual* [Mimeo]. New York: Columbia University, Teachers College.

Super, D. E., & Nevill, D. D. (1984). Work role salience as a determinant of career maturity in high school students. *Journal of Vocational Behavior, 25*, 30–44.

Super, D. E., Osborne, W. L., Walsh, D. J., Brown, S. D., & Niles, S. G. (1992). Developmental career assessment and counseling: The C-DAC. *Journal of Counseling and Development, 71*, 74–80.

Super, D. E., & Overstreet, P. L. (1960). *The vocational maturity of ninth-grade boys.* New York: Teachers College Press.

Super, D. E., Savickas, M. L., & Super, C. M. (1996). The life-span, Life-space approach to careers. In D. Brown, L. Brooks, & Associates (Eds.), *Career choice and development: Applying contemporary theories to practice* (3rd ed., pp. 121–178). San Francisco: Jossey-Bass.

Super, D. E., & Thompson, A. S. (1979). A six-scale, two-factor measure of adolescent career or vocational maturity. *Vocational Guidance Quarterly, 28*, 6–15.

Super, D. E., Thompson, A. S., Lindeman, R. H., Jordaan, J. P., & Myers, R. A. (1981). *The Career Development Inventory.* Palo Alto, CA: Consulting Psychologists Press.

Thompson, A. S., & Lindeman, R. H. (1981). *Career Development Inventory: User's manual.* Palo Alto, CA: Consulting Psychologists Press.

Thompson, A. S., & Lindeman, R. H. (1982). *Career Development Inventory college and university form supplement to user's manual.* Palo Alto, CA: Consulting Psychologists Press.

Thompson, A. S., & Lindeman, R. H. (1984). *Career Development Inventory: Technical manual.* Palo Alto, CA: Consulting Psychologists Press.

Tinsley, H. E. A., & Tinsley, D. J. (1987). Use of factor analysis in counseling psychology research. *Journal of Counseling Psychology, 34*, 414–424.

Van Riper, B. W. (1974). From a clinical to a counseling process: Reversing the test appraisal process. *Measurement and Evaluation in Guidance, 7*, 24–30.

Vondracek, F. W., & Schulenberg, J. E. (1986). Carer development in adolescence: Some conceptual and intervention issues. *Vocational Guidance Quarterly, 34*, 247–254.

Westbrook, B. W. (1976). The relationship between vocational maturity and appropriateness of vocational choices of ninth-grade pupils. *Measurement and Evaluation in Guidance, 9,* 75–80.

Westbrook, B. W. (1982). Construct validation of career maturity measures. In J. D. Krumboltz & D. A. Hamel (Eds.), *Assessing career development* (pp. 66–112). Palo Alto, CA: Mayfield.

Westbrook, B. W., & Mastie, M. M. (1973). Three measures of vocational maturity: A beginning to know about. *Measurement and Evaluation in Guidance, 6,* 8–16.

Whan, K. M., & Savickas, M. L. (1998). Effectiveness of a career time perspective intervention. *Journal of Vocational Behavior, 52,* 106–119.

Wigington, J. H. (1982). Career maturity aspects of the Kuder Occupational Interest Survey. *Journal of Vocational Behavior, 20,* 175–179.

Williams-Phillips, L. J. (1983). *Five career decidedness scales: Reliability, validity, and factors.* Unpublished master's thesis, North Carolina State University, Raleigh.

Williamson, E. G., & Darley, J. G. (1937). *Student personnel work: An outline of clinical procedures.* New York: McGraw-Hill.

Winer, J. L. (1992). The early history of the Career Decision Scale. *Career Development Quarterly, 40,* 369–375.

Woody, R. H. (1968). Vocational counseling with behavioral techniques. *Vocational Guidance Quarterly, 17,* 97–103.

Young, R. A. (1979). The effects of value confrontation and reinforcement counseling on the career planning attitudes and behaviors of adolescent males. *Journal of Vocational Behavior, 15,* 1–11.

Zytowski, D. G. (1978). [Review of J. O. Crites, *Career Maturity Inventory*]. In O. K. Buros (Ed.), *The eighth mental measurement yearbook (2)* (pp. 1565–1567). Highland Park, NJ: Gryphon Press.

CONTEMPORARY ETHICAL
AND PROFESSIONAL ISSUES

13

Contemporary Issues in Testing Use

Nancy E. Betz
Ohio State University

The need for a consideration of contemporary issues in the use of tests in counseling is based on the fact that although tests have tremendous potential utility, they can also be misused. The misuse of tests may stem from characteristics of the test and/or the test user, and it is ultimately the responsibility of the test user to ensure that the test is of high quality and appropriate for use in the population intended. Because of the possibility of misuse of tests and test scores, psychologists and test specialists formulated ethical and professional standards designed to ensure that tests are used appropriately, effectively, and fairly.

First, many of the Ethical Principles of the American Psychological Association (APA, 1992) pertain to the use of psychological tests and assessments. Second, although a general set of ethical statements concerning test use is available, the American Psychological Association (APA), American Educational Research Association (AERA), and National Council on Measurement in Education (NCME) have formulated a much more specific set of professional standards by which the quality of psychological tests and assessments may be evaluated and by which the effectiveness and fairness of test use in specific situations may be judged.

In the first part of this chapter, ethical and professional considerations in the selection and use of psychological tests in counseling are described. The discussion contains sections on: (a) quality of tests and test materials, (b) test user competence, (c) protecting the rights of test takers, and (d) sources of information about tests.

Second, even though a test may be of generally high quality, there may be unique issues involved in using it with some type of clients. In particular, issues in the use of tests with racial/ethnic minorities, women, and cross-culturally are the subject of the second portion of this chapter.

ETHICAL AND PROFESSIONAL STANDARDS IN USING TESTS

Test Standards

The first and most fundamental consideration in using tests and assessments is that the tests be of high technical quality and accompanied by enough information for a test user to effectively evaluate, administer, use, and interpret the test. Concern about the quality of tests and accompanying test materials dates back to 1895, when the first APA committee on mental measurements was formed. In 1938, the first edition of Buros's *Mental Measurements Yearbook* appeared, providing extensive information about and reviews of the tests available at the time. In 1954, APA published its first set of *Technical Recommendations for Psychological Tests and Diagnostic Techniques*, providing initial guidelines concerning the evaluation of tests (e.g., validity, reliability, use of scales and norms) and stressing the importance of an informative manual accompanying a test. At about that same time (1954), the Technical Recommendations for Achievement Tests were published by the AERA and the NCME. By 1966, APA, AERA, and NCME were cooperating—the result was the 1966 *Standards for Educational and Psychological Measurement*.

Revisions of these standards were published in 1974 and 1985. The 1974 version was expanded to include a response to the 1970 EEOC Guidelines and other concerns of test misuse and bias and race and sex discrimination. The 1985 revision devotes complete chapters to clinical testing, testing in the schools, test use in counseling, employment testing, professional and occupational licensure and certification, program evaluation, and testing people who have handicapping conditions or who are linguistic minorities. These specialty uses are discussed later as appropriate, but the reader is referred to the 1985 *Standards for Educational and Psychological Testing* (AERA, APA, & NCME, 1985) for full details. The standards are currently being revised to reflect changes which have occurred in the last 10 years— the revision should be available in the year 2000.

Quality of Tests and Assessment Materials

A first major purpose of the test standards was to provide guidelines for the *quality* of tests and test materials. Standards for test quality must be observed by test developers in constructing the test, by test publishers before distributing the test, and by test users in evaluating and selecting tests. There are a number of dimensions along which test quality may be evaluated. In the 1985 version of the test standards (AERA, APA, & NCME, 1985), the following dimensions of quality may be addressed: (a) reliability and errors of measurement, (b) validity, (c) test development and revision, (d) scaling, norming, score comparability, and equating, and (e) test publication, technical manuals, and users' guides. The revision currently being completed will have similar sections: (1) validity; (2) reliability; (3) test development and revision; (4) scaling, norming, standards, and score comparability; (5) test and administration, scoring and reporting; and (6) test documents.

In general, high-quality tests are those for which evidence of both reliability and validity is available. Although methods of test construction and the accumulation of evidence for reliability and validity are beyond the scope of this chapter, a brief summary of the types of evidence needed is provided later. For more detailed information, see sources such as the Walsh and Betz (1995) *Tests and Assessment* and Dawis's (1987) article on scale construction in the *Journal of Counseling Psychology*. The reference volume *Responsible Test Use* (APA, 1993) provides a comprehensive list of textbooks in educational and psychological testing and assessment.

Reliability, the extent to which a test measures something in a consistent, stable manner, is assessed through such methods as internal consistency reliability, alternate or parallel forms, and test–retest reliability, also known as stability. With respect to reliability, several key points should be noted. First, there is no single reliability coefficient describing a test or scale; the values of obtained coefficients vary somewhat across studies using the same population, and with different research methodologies. A test is never said to "be reliable"–rather, we look for an accumulation of evidence supporting test reliability.

Tests to be used for applied purposes–that is, in counseling, selection, or placement–should consistently yield internal consistency reliability coefficients above .80 and, ideally, above .90. Tests for which internal consistency reliability coefficients are in the range of .70 to .80 may be used in research, but those with coefficients below .70 should be further refined before they are used in research, not to mention practice. Test–retest reliability, or stability, coefficients may be lower and still acceptable, particularly as the interval between testings lengthens. Although some researchers may contest these guidelines, the reality is that scales having reliability coefficients below about .70 are not measuring anything in a consistent manner–the information obtained from some of the items is not consistent with that yielded by other items purportedly measuring the same thing, and the information obtained on one testing is not necessarily the same information that will be yielded by testing an hour or a day later.

The test standards also emphasize that, if possible, the establishment of the reliability of the test should include all of the methods of studying reliability, that is, alternate forms, internal consistency, and test–retest stability. All of these methods of estimating reliability are important to supporting the test's reliability for applied purposes. In addition to evidence for reliability, information regarding the standard error of measurement should be reported in enough scope and detail to enable the test user to judge whether scores are sufficiently dependable for the intended uses of the test.

Along with evidence for its reliability, a test should be shown to possess validity for the intended uses. Validity refers to the extent to which the test actually measures what we intend it to measure. If scores from a test designed to measure career decision-making skills or career maturity actually correlate more highly with verbal ability or socioeconomic status than they do with other career-related variables, we would question the nature of the construct measured by our test. There are several different kinds of evidence pertinent to the establishment of a test's validity; the three basic types of validity evidence are construct validity, content validity, and criterion-related validity.

Construct validity, the most general validity concept, refers to a variety of evidence addressing the question, "Does the test measure the underlying construct or concept we intend it to measure?" Content validity refers to how well the particular sampling of items constituting the test represents the nature and scope of the domain of interest. Evidence for content validity includes expert judgements regarding the rational or logical relationship of an item to the content domain of interest. For example, the item "I enjoy planting flowers" has a clear logical relationship to the construct Artistic Interests but would have questionable relationship to, and thus content validity for, the construct Investigative Interests.

Finally, criterion-related validity is the degree to which test scores are related as predicted to criterion indices. The correlation between scholastic aptitude test scores and performance in college is an example of predictive validity evidence (because the predictor data are collected prior to the collection of the criterion data), whereas the relationship between Minnesota Multiphasic Personality Inventory (MMPI–2) scores and current *DSM–IV* diagnosis would be concurrent validity evidence (because predictor and criterion data are collected concurrently). The test standards emphasize that all three components of validity are important and that, ideally, evidence for a test's validity should include evidence from all three types of validity.

The third group of standards pertaining to test development requires that test developers use both expertise and care in their methods of test construction and that they revise their tests periodically to ensure that test content continues to be relevant and appropriate for the purposes for which the test is used. In addition, these standards specify that the test developers and publishers are responsible for the provision of a test manual describing the methods of construction and revision, data regarding reliability and validity, and normative and other information needed for effective and accurate test interpretation.

The fourth dimension of test quality pertains to the availability of scales, norms, and other means of interpreting test scores. Methods of scoring the test should be carefully described, and normative, criterion-referenced, or other methods of comparative interpretation of test scores should be provided. In addition, as new forms of a test are developed, information concerning methods of comparing or equating scores across forms may be necessary. The normative data provided should be clearly described in terms of the population from which they come and should be the same groups of people with whom the test is designed to be used.

Finally, standards regarding test publication, technical materials, and user guides emphasize the importance of published or at least widely available information about a test. Further, that information should provide a clear description of the extent to which and in what manner the test has met the other test standards; the information should be sufficient to allow the potential user to evaluate the quality and potential utility of the test. This complete information is best provided in a manual for the test; the manual should be revised as new data regarding the test's reliability, validity, norms, and use become available. Not only should test information be adequate to evaluate the test's quality, but it should provide detailed instructions for the administration and scoring of the test.

Ideally, these dimensions of test quality should be addressed before the test is distributed for use. More realistically, however, test manuals are expected to provide information by which the user can evaluate the extent to which the standards have been met, should mention areas in which technical support is lacking, and should describe the current research efforts that will increase the base of technical support for the quality of the instrument. Test manuals should also make it clear that extra caution in test use and interpretation is necessary in cases where there is as yet insufficient evidence supporting the test's quality. Also, tests not yet meeting quality standards should probably be reserved for needs for which there are no better alternative tests or assessment devices.

Finally, it should be emphasized that because test use occurs with a specific individual in a specific setting for a particular reason, the ultimate basis for judging the utility of a test is the good judgment, sound knowledge, and professional integrity of the counselor. Thus, the professional competence and integrity of the test user are the subject of the next section.

Test User Competence

No matter how good the test or assessment device, it is used, and can be *misused*, by a counseling practitioner. Recently a major new resource for the definition and explication of problems in test use, published by APA and entitled *Responsible Test Use: Case Studies for Assessing Human Behavior* (APA, 1993), became available. Two committees of the Joint Commission on Testing Practices (JCTP, a combined group representing APA, ACA, NCME, and other related organizations) were responsible for the preparation of the case book. It contains seven broad factors of test misuse (e.g., psychometric in knowledge), which contained 86 specific elements (considering errors of measurement of test score). The case book contains 78 case studies illustrating both the broad factors and the specific elements; in toto, the 78 case studies provide an excellent educational device for illustrating test misuse, through incompetence (including ignorance) and irresponsibility, versus competent, responsible test use.

The first two general categories of the case book, Training: General and Training: Professional Responsibility, pertain directly to the qualifications of test users (although all of the other five categories of misuse could also be attributed in some cases to lack of sufficient qualifications and/or knowledge). In essence, psychological tests are not toys—they can lead to dangerous misinterpretations if used by unqualified people. Thus, a major principle of the APA ethical code is that psychological knowledge and techniques, including tests, are used only by those qualified to use them and, conversely, that individuals practice only within the bounds of their own knowledge and competence. As related specifically to the use of tests, the principle states that psychologists who use test results have an understanding of "psychological or educational measurement, validation problems, and test research" (APA, 1981, p. 636).

Qualifications for test use vary according to the types of tests in question but, in general, are stricter with tests having greater potential for harm and misinterpretation. One of the earliest systems by which user qualifications were specified, provided by the first APA test standard (APA, 1954, pp. 146–148), classified tests according to three levels of complexity. *Level A* tests were those that could be administered, scored, and interpreted by responsible nonpsychologists who have carefully read the test manual and are familiar with the overall purposes of testing. Educational achievement tests would fall into this category.

Level B tests require technical knowledge of test construction and use and appropriate advanced coursework in psychology and related courses, for example, statistics, individual differences, and counseling. Vocational interest inventories, group intelligence and special aptitude tests, and some personality inventories are generally considered Level B tests. For example,

Consulting Psychologists Press limits purchase of such tests as the Strong Interest Inventory and State-Trait Anxiety Inventory to individuals who have completed university courses in tests and measurements or equivalent training. The Psychological Corporation requires a master's level degree in psychology or education or the equivalent, or membership in a professional organization requiring the necessary knowledge. The Differential Aptitude Tests are an example of a Level B test. Similar requirements for access to such tests as the Jackson Vocational Interest Inventory, Personality Research Form, and Jackson Personality Inventory are stated by their publisher, Research Psychologists Press.

Finally, *Level C* tests require an advanced degree in psychology or licensure as a psychologist and advanced training/supervised experience in the particular test. Level C tests generally include individually-administered intelligence tests and personality tests, for example, the Stanford-Binet, Wechsler Adult Intelligence Scale–Revised (WAIS–III), and Minnesota Multiphasic Personality Inventory–2 and California Psychological Inventory. Graduate students may be qualified to purchase and use Level B or Level C tests if they are being supervised in that work by someone who possesses the appropriate user qualifications.

In addition to user competence, there are several major principles of responsible, ethical test use. In the 1985 test standards, several of these principles are outlined. They include the following primary standards:

1. Test users should evaluate the available written information on the reliability and validity of the test for the uses intended.

2. When a test user makes a change in a test (e.g., in format, mode of administration, etc.), he or she should revalidate the test for the changed conditions.

3. When a test is to be used for a purpose for which it has not been previously validated, the user is responsible for providing evidence for validity.

4. Test users should accurately portray the relevance of a test to the assessment and decision-making process and should not use test scores to justify a decision that has been largely made on some other basis.

5. Test users should be alert to and avoid possible unintended consequences of test use, for example, the tendency of lay people to attribute surplus meaning or absolute "truth" to test scores.

6. Test users should not attempt to evaluate test takers whose special characteristics—for example, ages, handicapping conditions, linguistic, generational, or cultural backgrounds—are outside their range of academic training or supervised experience. If faced with such a request, the test user should seek consultation.

7. A test taker's score should not be accepted as a reflection of a lack of some type of ability without consideration of alternative explanations for the person's inability to perform well on that test.

Paralleling the guidelines in the APA Test Standards are the factors of responsible test use contained in the case book (APA, 1993). They are as follows:

1. Comprehensive assessment. Following up testing to get pertinent personal history data to integrate with test scores to enhance accuracy of interpretation.
2. Proper test use. Accepting the responsibility for competent use of the test; exercising appropriate quality control procedures over all aspects of test use.
3. Psychometric knowledge. Knowing and using correctly basic statistical principles of measurement (e.g., standard error of measurement, reliability, validity).
4. Maintaining integrity of test results. Correctly applying psychometric principles to the actual interpretation of test results; understanding the limitations of test scores.
5. Accuracy of scoring. Ensuring that all aspects of test scoring (e.g., recording, checking, correct reading of tables) are performed correctly.
6. Appropriate use of norms. Understanding and using different types of norms correctly, particularly in employment settings.
7. Interpretive feedback to clients. Providing correct interpretations of test scores to test takers.

It should be evident from the foregoing that a test user must be aware of possible misuses of tests and test scores, must be informed about both the psychometric quality and practical utility of a test, and must use tests with care, good judgment, and concern for the people being tested.

Protecting the Rights of Test Takers

Principle 5 of the APA ethical code and Chapter 16 of the Test Standards describe psychologists' obligations in maintaining the confidentiality of information obtained from individuals, through testing or any other formal or informal means of gathering information. The maintenance of confidentiality means protecting the individual's right to privacy and involves the principles of informed consent, constraints on the provision of individual information to other parties, and care in the storage and disposal of information.

The first responsibility of the test user is to minimize, as far as possible, the extent to which testing may invade a person's right to privacy. The extent to which the use of test constitutes an invasion of individual privacy is a complex issue with a number of considerations involved. It should be noted that test data are no more invasive of privacy than are other kinds of information obtained about people. With any kind of personal information, including test data, the use of the data should be characterized as far as possible by the principles of relevance and informed consent (Anastasi, 1982).

The concept of *relevance* means that test scores are collected and used only if they are relevant to some valid set of purposes—collecting a set of test scores for no other purpose than "curiosity" would constitute an unnecessary invasion of an individual's privacy. The principle of informed consent means that, as far as possible, the individual is informed concerning both the nature of the information collected and the purposes for which the information will be used. This principle does not imply that test takers (or their parents) necessarily have a right to information that would invalidate the use of the test or that is beyond the sophistication of the consumer, for example, test items or methods of scoring, but that the test taker is informed as fully as possible concerning the nature and uses of the test scores. See APA (1996) for further discussion of strategies for informing the test taker of purpose, use, and results of testing.

Although the principle of informed consent is intended to provide to the test taker at least some opportunity for choice in the matter of how much information to reveal and in the uses to which that information will be put, the extent to which the individual actually does have a choice varies across different situations. For a client in counseling, revealing personal information is important to the process of getting help; unwillingness to be open with the counselor or therapist may make treatment very difficult and client improvement less likely. As an extreme example, a client wishing help with vocational decision making who refused to talk about his or her vocational interests or take a vocational interest inventory would be very difficult for a counselor to help.

In essence, the issue of invasion of privacy means finding a compromise between the need for meaningful, relevant information to guide problem solving in counseling situations, and the individual's right to personal privacy and freedom of choice. This compromise is best achieved when respect for the individual is combined with sound professional judgment concerning the kinds of information needed for the purposes at hand.

Confidentiality issues pertain to decisions about access to test results on the part of those other than the original test user. For example, a psychologist may have given his or her client an MMPI-2, scores from which are later requested by another psychologist. Ethical and test standards mandate that, in general, the confidentiality of test results is to be protected by the original test user unless the test taker gives consent for test results to be provided to someone else. The original informed consent should have covered all intended test uses, and additional consent is necessary for any use beyond those originally agreed to. In the example given, the client would need to release his or her MMPI–2 scores to the second psychologist. For a more detailed discussion of issues involved in the disclosure of test data to third parties, see APA (1996) and *Strategies for coping with subpoenas or compelled testimony for test data* (APA Committee on Legal Issues, 1995).

An additional aspect of confidentiality involves the secure storage of test results and, when test results are too old to be useful, for the permanent disposal of test data. Keeping test results in places where they are accessible to anyone but the original test user is irresponsible, as is disposing of test scores in such a way that they could be easily retrieved by unauthorized individuals. The test user is also responsible for judgments concerning the continued utility of test results collected previously. According to the test standards, test scores should be kept in a person's file only as long as they serve a useful purpose.

Finally, test users must be aware of and respect copyright laws and other contractual obligations regarding tests. Disclosure of secure testing materials, including test items, test scoring, or test protocols, to unqualified persons may violate copyright laws and/or decrease the validity of the test. The case book (APA, 1993) gives examples of Rorschach cards being inadvertently shown on TV and being used in a university residence hall as a party game after being inappropriately distributed in a professor's class.

Sources of Information by Which to Evaluate Tests

Given the large amount of information needed by an informed, responsible user of psychological test data, it is fortunate that many sources of information are available. The most important source of information about a test is the test manual. Test manuals may be ordered from the test publisher, and information about the test publisher is available in Buros's *Mental Measurements Yearbook* series; the 13th ed. (Impara & Plake, 1998) is the most recent, or their *Tests in Print* series. The catalogs distributed by test publishers provide information about ordering test booklets, answer sheets, scoring keys, and other interpretive aids, as well as the manual itself. Many test publishers now make available several manuals, for example, a technical manual, a manual for administration and scoring, and an interpretive manual. A particularly noteworthy example of this is the comprehensive *Strong Interest Inventory applications and technical guide* (Harmon, Hansen, Borgen, & Hammer, 1994).

Beyond the test manual(s), test users should be familiar with the test reviews, as published periodically in the *Mental Measurements Yearbook* (MMY). Now in its 13th edition (Impara & Plake, 1998), the yearbook series provides descriptions of all published tests and reviews a number of tests in each edition. Because the MMY does not review every test in every edition, a potential user may need to go back to previous editions of the yearbook if the test in question is not reviewed in the most recent yearbook.

A similar review series is that provided by Pro-ed's *Tests* (Sweetland & Keyser, 1991), which is a description of available tests, and *Test Critiques* (Keyser & Sweetland, 1992), which publishes reviews of tests.

Other sources of information about tests are books on testing and test use. Books like this one and Walsh and Betz's (1995) *Tests and Assessments* are particularly useful because they provide interpretive information such as examples of test profiles and case studies. An important series entitled Advances in Vocational Psychology (edited by Walsh & Osipow and published by Lawrence Erlbaum Associates) includes several very helpful volumes, for example, *Volume I: The Assessment of Interests* (Walsh & Osipow, 1986) and *Volume II: The Assessment of Career-Decision Making* (Walsh & Osipow, 1988). Finally, many journals contain test reviews and articles about tests. Counselors using tests should closely monitor the articles in *Measurement and Evaluation in Counseling and Development, Journal of Career Assessment,* and *Educational and Psychological Measurement,* as well as those in such journals as the *Journal of Counseling Psychology, Journal of Vocational Behavior, Career Development Quarterly,* and the *Journal of Counseling and Development.*

Recently, professional societies and organizations have begun to sponsor the development of guidelines for specific uses or purposes. A joint committee of organizations, including the APA/AERA/NCME groups responsible for the original test standards, published the *Code of Fair Testing Practices in Education* (APA, 1988), and APA sponsored the publication of *Guidelines for Computer-Based Tests and Interpretations* (APA, 1986). The Society for Industrial and Organizational Psychology (SIOP) published the third edition of *Principles for the Validation and Use of Personnel Selection Procedures.* As test use becomes more widespread and technologically-sophisticated, continued attention to the development of relevant standards seems warranted.

Summary

The ethical and professional standards and guidelines for tests and test use are designed to ensure that tests and assessment devices themselves are of high technical, informative, and interpretive quality, and that they are used by qualified, knowledgeable, ethical people who care deeply about the rights and welfare of the individuals they serve. High-quality, effective, and fair test use is dependent on the quality of both the tests and the users. Even the highest quality test can be misused by an unqualified or careless person, and the most highly skilled test user in the world is ineffective without carefully developed, well-standardized, reliable, and valid tests. As test users, therefore, we are responsible for ensuring both our own competence and the quality of the tools we use. Ethical test use is knowledgeable, informed, careful, and critical test use.

USING TESTS WITH SPECIAL GROUPS

General Issues in Using Tests with Special Groups

A major recent focus within the counseling field has been whether or not traditional counseling methods are useful with women, racial/ethnic minorities, and other special groups of individuals. A parallel and a closely related concern within the more general field of mental measurement and individual differences has been fairness in testing. Although the issues regarding test use differ depending on the type of test involved (e.g., intelligence and aptitude tests, vocational interest inventories, personality inventories) and on the "special group" with which the test is to be used (e.g., women, racial and/or ethnic minorities, the disabled, etc.), there are some common bases for the concerns about special groups.

At the most fundamental level is the fact that tests are, at least to some extent, culture bound. It is difficult, if not impossible, to construct a test independently of a cultural context. For example, a test of verbal aptitude is constructed in a given language and is based on what may well be culture-specific item content. Even though test constructors may not purposely favor a given culture, it may be difficult to completely avoid this. Most intelligence and aptitude tests in use were constructed in the context of a Caucasian, middle-class value system. Thus, non-White or lower class examinees would possibly be less familiar with the test content than would examinees representing the White middle class. A picture of a deciduous tree on a picture vocabulary test of intelligence for children would be an unfair item for a Navaho child raised in the Arizona desert. An item representing a farm animal might be unfamiliar to an African American child raised in the inner city.

The issue of test item familiarity affects interest measurement as well as ability measurement. For example, basic dimensions of vocational interest have been measured using content differentially characteristic of the experiential backgrounds of males versus females. To ask a female whether she is interested in auto mechanics when she has never had the chance to experience activities related to it is an example of how item content can be gender biased. The use of sexist occupational titles (e.g., policeman, cleaning woman) or, as was the case in one inventory for children, pictures of Whites in higher status and Blacks in lower status occupations provide further examples of content bias.

Finally, when measuring dimensions of personality, cross-cultural differences in the perceived appropriateness of different behaviors may affect measurement. For example, the sometimes conflicting values of cooperation/community versus competition/individuality are differentially valued in different cultures. In some cultures—for example, the Japanese—assertiveness toward one's elders may be viewed as a sign of disrespect and therefore as highly inappropriate. In some cultures men are free to publicly express affection to other men, whereas in other cultures such displays would be frowned on. Different views of social appropriateness cannot help but influence self-reports of behavior and personality.

In addition to the cultural relativity of test item content is the nature of the standardization or norm groups. A basic principle of test interpretation is that test scores should be interpreted with reference to appropriate norm groups, that is, norm groups consisting of individuals comparable to the individual being tested. If norm groups are predominantly or totally White, the scores of a Black or Hispanic individual are of reduced interpretability. Similarly, using a test cross-culturally is unwise until both necessary translations of the test and collection of norms in the new population have been accomplished.

Thus, responsible test constructors and users no longer automatically assume the usefulness of a test for any examinee. Thanks to this widespread criticism of possible biases in test content and of the predominance of White middle-class individuals in norm groups, revisions in tests and collection of new, more diverse normative samples have occurred.

The following sections discuss issues in the use of tests and assessment devices with women, and with members of racial and/or ethnic minority groups and cross-culturally. In considering these issues it should be recalled, first of all, that assessment usually occurs with the framework of a counseling relationship, so no discussion of gender, racial/ethnic, and cross-cultural issues in assessment can be divorced from knowledge of those issues in counseling itself. Second, gender and racial/ethnic identity are not independent dimensions. Many women are also members of racial or ethnic minority groups, and vice versa. Thus, the use of separate sections for gender and ethnicity is somewhat artificial.

The vitally important issue of using ability tests in selection, especially with members of some racial minority groups, will receive less emphasis herein because this volume does not cover ability/aptitude tests. However, knowledge of this area of testing, and the associated issues, is important in counseling. A comprehensive review of ability, aptitude, and achievement tests and issues surrounding their use in selection is contained in Walsh and Betz (1995) and in many other general textbooks on psychological testing. Another very important resource helpful in ensuring fair and valid use of psychological tests across both groups and situations (e.g., selection) is the revision of the APA/AERA/NCME Test Standards which should be published by the publication of the present volume. These revised standards will have sections on fairness in testing and standards for different applications of testing, including educational testing and employment testing.

GENDER ISSUES IN TESTS AND ASSESSMENTS

A consideration of gender issues in tests and assessment is based most fundamentally on the existence and effects of two related yet distinct sociocultural processes, that of gender-related socialization and stereotyping, first, and, second, that of sexism, not only in society itself but in counseling and testing. Whole courses, and volumes, have been devoted to these topics, and it is impossible to adequately cover them in a single broadly focused chapter such as this one. It is assumed that the reader is familiar, or becomes so, with such foundational works as the American Psychological Association (1975) *Report of the Task Force on Sex Bias and Sex Role Stereotyping in Psychotherapeutic Practice*, Fitzgerald and Nutt's (1986) Division 17 "Principles Concerning the Counseling/Psychotherapy of Women: Rationale and Implementation," and Good, Gilbert, and Scher's (1990) "Guidelines for gender aware therapy," to name only a few. Excellent, comprehensive reviews of these issues as they affect counseling in general and career counseling in particular are provided in the volumes *Feminist Perspectives in Therapy* (Worell & Remer, 1992) and *Career Counseling for Women* (Walsh & Osipow, 1994) and in Brown and Forrest (1994), respectively. Matlin (1996) and others have written excellent textbooks on the psychology of women and gender roles, and Betz (1995) reviewed concepts and measures of gender role-related variables.

And most important for present purposes are recent works focusing specifically on assessment issues with women, for example, Hackett and Lonborg's (1994) chapter "Career assessment and counseling for women" in the Walsh and Osipow text *Career Counseling for Women* (1994), the 1993 special issue of the *Journal of Career Assessment* focusing on career assessment for women, and the chapter on feminist approaches to assessment in Worell and Remer (1992). The present section is intended to introduce some of the issues in assessment with women, but readers are referred to these more comprehensive, focused resources for a thorough grounding in these issues. Keeping these caveats in mind, this section provides an overview of gender issues in the use of aptitude and ability tests, vocational interest inventories, and personality assessments.

Gender Issues in Using Ability Tests

Although not covered in this volume, scholastic aptitude and ability tests are easily the most widely used psychological assessment devices in the country. Although it would be easy to find a U.S. citizen who has never taken either an interest inventory or a personality test, it would be difficult to find someone who had never taken an ability or aptitude test for selection or placement purposes. As reviewed by Walsh and Betz (1995), major scholastic aptitude tests include the Scholastic Aptitude Test (SAT), the American College Test (ACT) Assessment, and the Graduate Record Examination. Although these can be used in career counseling to help a student gauge his or her probabilities of acceptance to and/or success in a given educational institution or course of study, their most common use is in selection. To the extent that career psychologists and counselors can influence test use policies, knowledge of issues of gender (and racial) issues is crucial.

Also very useful in both selection and career counseling are *multiple aptitude batteries*, batteries providing measures of a number of different vocationally relevant aptitudes. Such batteries are designed to allow an assessment of the individuals' *patterns* of abilities, including both strengths and weaknesses. Among the well-known and widely used multiple aptitude batteries are the *General Aptitude Test Battery* (GATB), made available through the United States Employment Service and used primarily in the testing of adults; the Differential Aptitude Tests (DAT), used frequently in the testing of high-school students as well as adults; and the Armed Services Vocational Aptitude Battery, used in the classification and placement of recruits to armed services as well as in vocational counseling.

Historically, concerns about the use of ability tests with women (and minorities) have stemmed from their "adverse impact" on selection decisions, that is, the reality that lower scores on an aptitude test may result in fewer members of a group (e.g., women, African Americans) being selected for a given educational opportunity or job training program. As examples, lower total SAT scores (because of lower scores on SAT Mathematics) have led to fewer New York State Regents scholarship awards to females than males (Rosser, 1989). Similarly, lower scores on tests of mechanical aptitude could lead to fewer women being assigned to mechanics training programs in the Armed Services.

One approach to the problem of adverse impact was to investigate the possibility that tests were biased against some groups of individuals. As discussed in the literature (see Walsh & Betz, 1995 for a review), several types of bias can theoretically plague ability tests. *Content bias* can occur if a test contains content more familiar to one versus another group of examinees, in our case, males versus females. As an example, pictorial material that shows only White males and never females nor Blacks is biased, as would be test materials and pronouns always using the pronoun "he."

Test constructors have addressed the problem of content bias by obtaining expert judgments of the degree to which item content is culturally loaded and soliciting item contributions from test professionals representing other cultural groups. The construction of scholastic aptitude and

achievement tests is now done by panels of experts that include a representative balance of men and women, Whites, Blacks, Hispanics, and so on,
and members of higher versus lower socioeconomic status groups. These
panel members both contribute items and evaluate the item pool with the
objective of minimizing gender, race, cultural, and class bias. As examples
of how test constructors have addressed content bias problems, the 1980
revision of the DAT included balancing the number of male and female
figures depicted in the Mechanical Reasoning subtest and balancing the
number of male and female pronouns in the Language Usage subtest (see
Pennock-Roman, 1989).

The importance of item content was illustrated in a study by Betz and
Hackett (1983). They measured the perceived self-efficacy expectations of
college women and men with respect to a variety of math tasks and problems. There were 18 math tasks, 16 math-related college courses, and 18
math problems, or a total of 52 items. As predicted, males reported higher
expectations of self-efficacy on 49 of the 52 math-related items. There were
only 3 out of 52 items on which females reported higher expectations of
self-efficacy than males. Those three items were as follows: "Figure out how
much material to buy in order to make curtains," "Estimate your grocery
bill in your head as you pick up items," and "Calculate recipe quantities for
a dinner for 41 when the original recipe was for 12 people."

Given these data, one wonders what the effects would be of testing math
ability, as well as math self-efficacy, using a more balanced set of items. If
the sex differences in verbal ability (SAT) and self-efficacy expectations can
be eliminated or reversed by changing the gender content of the items, then
math ability measurement should also be examined. A similar conclusion
was made by Lunneborg and Lunneborg (1986) in their research exploring
the experiential bases for the development of spatial ability. They found
that self-estimated and objective spatial ability were highly related to childhood experiences from boys' (rather than girls) typical gender role experiences, for example, sports participation, using hand tools, and mechanical,
carpentry, and related activities.

A second major type of possible ability test bias is *selection bias*. Selection bias exists when a test has different predictive validity across groups
and is examined by comparing the regression lines obtained within different
groups of examinees. Recent research has strongly suggested that women's
college and graduate school performance are underpredicted by their aptitude test scores. In other words, a given SAT score predicts a higher college
grade-point average (GPA) for a female than a male student, even in math
and science courses. One of the results of this is that women get better
grades in college and graduate school than do men, even in science, mathematics, and engineering majors (Halpern, 1997; Rosser, 1989). Thus, women
are often rejected for admission or scholarships on the basis of test scores

that lead to higher predicted college GPAs than those of many of the men admitted or awarded scholarships. It is estimated that women earn college grades equivalent to those of men with combined SATs (V + M) 50–60 points higher (Rosser, 1989). Because of the underprediction of females' performance by aptitude test scores, several well-known universities no longer use them in admissions or financial aids decisions, relying instead on high-school grades. Thus, selection bias against women is clearly a problem needing to be addressed by policymakers.

In addition to the commonly studied forms of test bias, an even more fundamental problem is that referred to in the APA/AERA/NCME (1985) test standards, which reads as follows: "A test taker's score should not be accepted as a reflection of a lack of ability with respect to the characteristic being tested without alternative explanations for the test taker's inability to perform on that test at that time" (p. 43). One of the most basic reasons for "lack of ability" is lack of opportunity to learn or gain experience. Consider two students, each having scholastic aptitude scores at the 30th percentile, one of whom was well off and graduated from the top suburban high school in the state, and the other of whom was from a poor family and a substantially poorer (financially) inner-city school. Although these students have the same test scores, it would be reasonable to interpret them differently. Although we don't know if there are other factors that limited the suburban girl's intellectual development, we can assume that the background of the inner-city student was not conducive to the full development of her intellectual potential and that, given environmental enrichment, she may be able to do substantially better academically than her current test scores would indicate.

Although this example uses lower socioeconomic status to illustrate "educational deprivation," gender also leads to educational deprivation when girls are not encouraged to take courses in math, science, and technology or to gain experiences relevant to mechanical and other activities. If boys are encouraged to take "shop" courses in high school, and girls are encouraged to enroll in "home economics" or typing courses, gender differences in performance on tests of mechanical versus clerical aptitude (and, as discussed next, interests) should hardly be surprising. Similarly, the literature suggests that sex differences in math performance begin to appear only as girls stop taking math, and that the differences largely disappear when math background is controlled for or partialled out (see Betz & Fitzgerald, 1987, for an extensive review). Thus, lack of potential must not be inferred in the absence of ample opportunity to develop that potential.

Addressing the more fundamental problem of differential background experience can take at least two forms—one focusing on the test and the other focusing on the individual. Concerning the test, the availability of same-sex (or within-gender) norms provides a post hoc control for differential gender-related experiences, in that women are compared to others (women) who, presumably, have similar gender-role related socialization experiences. Within-gender norms allow scores that in a combined-sex norm group would be mediocre to "stand out" as possible avenues for further development or training.

An example of a multiple aptitude battery using same-sex norms is the Differential Aptitude Tests (DAT). The DAT are among the most widely used tests of multiple abilities. The battery is intended primarily for educational and vocational counseling with students in Grades 8–12, and with non-college-bound adults. Published by the Psychological Corporation, the DAT provides measures of verbal reasoning, numerical ability, abstract reasoning, clerical speed and accuracy, mechanical reasoning, space relations, spelling, and language usage (see Hattrup, 1995; Schmitt, 1995, for reviews). The DAT provides separate sex norms, because some of the tests reveal sizable sex differences (e.g., mechanical reasoning). In spite of concerns about the legality of using same-sex norms (see Adler, 1993), the publishers of the DAT argue that their use leads to less gender stereotyping in career choice. Considering the differential likelihood of mechanical training and experience in the backgrounds of males versus females, the greater fairness of same-sex norms becomes clear. Thus, preference in test usage, all other things being equal, should be given to tests whose developers have addressed gender issues in both test construction and revision and in the guidelines for use and interpretation contained in the test manual. Tests using same-sex norms provide counselors with the option of taking differential background experiences into account, using them as a stimulus for discussion of current competencies and future potential.

In addition to test developers' provision of same-sex norms, those using career assessment devices in counseling can use them in such a way as to stimulate new learning experiences for individuals. For example, young women need to be encouraged to continue math and science coursework throughout high school and, ideally, into the collegiate years (see Betz, 1997). Even if they do not end up choosing careers in science or engineering, math background is invaluable for most other career areas, especially at the graduate level (Sells, 1982). Goldman and Hewitt (1976) concluded that higher scores on the SAT Math subtest were the major explanation for the fact that more men than women pursue science majors. Because math coursework not only is necessary to the pursuit of collegiate science and engineering majors but is a major predictor of SAT–M performance, girls who continue in math will have the option to pursue science and engineering majors in college. This option is important, at least in part because 20% of science and engineering majors did not enter college with that intent (Office of Technology Assessment, 1989).

Another aspect of encouraging women (and men) to continue in math may be providing treatment for math anxiety. I recommend that treatment for math anxiety (or other forms of performance-related anxiety) be based on a self-efficacy (Bandura, 1986) model. A detailed discussion of the use of self-efficacy theory to guide career counseling interventions is provided by Betz (1992).

Thus, it should be clear that ability and aptitude tests should not be used without cognizance of the important role of background experience on test scores. And using such a framework, low scores can be seen as an opportunity to encourage learning experiences previously not available to the individual.

Gender Issues in the Use of Vocational Interest Inventories

From the standpoint of career counseling with women, the major source of adverse impact in using interest inventories stemmed from "sex restrictiveness" in these inventories. Although a review of the history of and issues regarding concerns about sex restrictiveness is beyond the scope of this chapter (but see Betz, 1993, and Walsh & Betz, 1995, for more extensive discussions), the problem of adverse impact in interest inventories resulted from their tendency to suggest, in one way or another, different occupations to men and women, with those suggested to women usually being fewer in number and including primarily traditionally female occupations. The extreme (and now corrected) examples of sex restrictiveness were separate and different forms of the Strong Vocational Interest Blank for men and women, earlier forms of the Kuder scales where women test takers received scores on only about one-third the number of occupations as did men, and sexist language in both inventory items and scale names (e.g., Policeman, Salesman, Cleaning Woman). In response to criticisms of sex bias (Association for Measurement and Evaluation in Guidance, 1977; Diamond, 1975), test publishers addressed the most blatant problems.

However, the problem of sex restrictiveness remains embedded in interest scales, for example, the Holland (1985, 1997) themes, composed of items differentially reflective of the experiences of males versus females (the items "I like to build things with wood" and "I like to take care of children" are illustrative). When raw or combined sex norms are used, females obtain higher mean scores on the Social, Artistic, and Conventional themes, and males obtain higher means on the Realistic, Investigative, and Enterprising themes (Gottfredson, Holland, & Gottfredson, 1975; Prediger & Hanson, 1976). Similar findings have resulted using the Vocational Interest Inventory (VII; Lunneborg, 1980, 1981), a measure of Roe's eight fields of occupational interest. High scores on the Social and Conventional themes suggest traditionally female educational and social welfare and office and clerical occupations. In contrast, females' lower scores on the Realistic, Investigative, and Enterprising themes result in less frequent suggestion of traditionally male professions—for example, medicine, engineering, and science—and of occupations in management and the skilled trades. Thus, socialized patterns of interest stemming from gender-stereotypic experiential backgrounds lead to interest inventory results that perpetuate females' overrepresentation in traditionally female occupations and their underrepresentation in occupations traditionally dominated by males.

As with ability tests, the problem of differential background can be addressed by focusing on the test and by focusing on the individual. The sex restrictiveness of interest inventory scores can be reduced through the use of same-sex normative scores and the use of sex-balanced items. Same-sex normative scores compare a person's scores on basic dimensions of vocational interest—for example, the Holland themes or the Basic Interest scales of the Strong Interest Inventory—to those of persons of the same sex. The use of same-sex norms increases the likelihood that the background socialization experiences of the comparison sample are more similar to those of the examinee, and this in turn tends to highlight interests that have developed in spite of the limiting effects of sex-role socialization.

The second approach to reducing sex restrictiveness in interest inventories is the use of sex-balanced item sets. A sex-balanced inventory scale—for example one of the Holland themes—would be constructed to include some items more likely to characterize male sex-role socialization and others more common in female socialization; the desired end result is interest scales on which the sexes obtain similar raw scores. The Unisex Edition of the ACT–IV (UNIACT; Lamb & Prediger, 1981) and the revised version of the Vocational Interest Inventory (VII, Lunneborg, 1980) are based on this strategy of scale construction, and both result in more equivalent distributions of scores across the six Holland themes (UNIACT) or Roe's eight fields (VII) for the two sexes. Thus, on the UNIACT, for example, the Realistic scale contains items pertaining to sewing and cooking, that is, content areas more often emphasized in the backgrounds of females, in addition to items more reflective of males' socialization experiences, for example, the skills learned in high-school shop courses.

In addition to structured interest inventories, Hackett and Lonborg (1994) suggest the advantages of using less structured assessment methods, such as vocational card sorts, values clarifications, and vocational life line exercises, in career counseling. These have the advantage of encouraging more active participation among clients and make it easy for the counselor to incorporate discussion of gender and cultural issues.

Regardless of which method of assessment is utilized, however, I suggest that their use with women be guided by exploratory versus confirmatory objectives and that interpretation be consistent with the "opportunity dominance" versus "socialization dominance" approach to interest inventories

(Cole & Hanson, 1975). The socialization dominance hypothesis suggests that stereotypic interest patterns are the result of durable gender-role socialization experiences and should not be tampered with. This approach implies that we should take a "laissez-faire" approach and leave people to go in the directions in which prior socialization experiences have led them. In contrast, the opportunity dominance hypothesis (Cole & Hanson, 1975) suggests that individuals can develop new interests if exposed to new learning experiences and, as a corollary, that we cannot accurately assess the potential for interest development if a person's previous learning experiences and opportunities have been limited in some way, for example, by gender-role socialization.

In other words, attempting to assess interest in science or carpentry or nature or cooking is premature if the person has not been exposed to background experiences in those areas. We can only conclude a lack of interest if the person has seriously tried the activity. It may be useful to again recall the APA Test Standard, mentioned in the previous section, concerning the danger of interpreting low test scores as indicative of a lack of ability prior to exhausting alternative explanations for the low scores. I would suggest that interpreting low scores on interest scales as indicative of lack of interest be deferred until alternative explanations such as lack of background exposure to the area have been considered and addressed. Rather, there seems no good reason why interests cannot be encouraged by suggesting further or, in some cases, initial opportunities for exploration. Most counselors would resist the suggestion that it is too late for them as individuals to develop new interests, so it would be inconsistent and unfair to endorse a view of clients, especially those 16 to 22 years old, as irrevocably limited by the shaping of gender-role socialization.

Thus, in addition to using same sex norms and/or sex-balanced interest inventory scales that allow counselors to be alert for areas in which the woman has developed interests in spite of gender role socialization, counselors have a responsibility to assist women in gaining experiences relevant to broadened career options. One of the career areas in which there will be most job openings and a shortage of White males to fill them is in the sciences, engineering, and technology (Betz, 1997).

Although we need much more research on how interests develop, one potentially useful conceptual approach is based on self-efficacy theory (Bandura, 1986; Betz, Borgen, & Harmon, 1996). As studied by Lapan, Boggs, and Morrill (1989) and Lent, Lopez, and Bieschke (1991, 1993), self-efficacy expectations are related to measured interests, and therefore increasing self-efficacy may increase level of interest. As mentioned earlier in this chapter, efficacy expectations are postulated to be increased by providing four types of information: (a) performance accomplishments, (b) observational learning or modeling, (c) anxiety management, and (d) verbal encouragement from others. Thus, educational programs or counseling interventions including one or more of these components (see Betz, 1992) may increase interests as well as self-efficacy. It should be noted that Hackett and Lonborg (1994), among others, recommend the usefulness for women of social learning theory approaches, of which self-efficacy theory is one example, because they are consistent with an approach involving remediation through counseling of gender-restrictive learning experiences.

To summarize, recommendations regarding facilitating broader experiences and adherence to an opportunity dominance hypothesis do not imply that we should tell women (or men) what to do. However, as discussed by Betz (1989), a major implication of the concept of the null environment for counselors and psychologists is that we have a responsibility to be "options restorers"—to be aware of how sexism and stereotyping reduce the viability or attractiveness of a given career option based solely on gender and to restore that option to our clients. So-called "free choice" is possible only in the context of viable, attractive options. As stated by Hackett and Lonborg (1994), "We argue that career counselors who fail to consider the adverse impact of gender-role socialization and differential life experiences in the interpretation of interest inventories and tests are merely unwitting accomplices of the status quo" (p. 56).

Issues in Personality Assessment with Women

As with other types of assessment, issues regarding the use of personality inventories with women clients can be based in the test itself, or in its interpretation and use. In comparison to developers of ability/achievement tests and vocational interest inventories, personality test developers have been less responsive to concerns of sex bias in their measures. Sex bias could enter at the item level if items on a given scale were associated more with the socialization experiences or expectations of one gender or the other. Likewise, interpretation and use of scores should include recognition that an individual's development is a joint function of genetic predisposition and learning experiences. Unfortunately, our learning experiences are often either enhanced or restricted because of our gender; thus, interpretation of a high score on a "negative" personality trait should include consideration of the degree to which positive learning experiences unrestricted by gender could help the client move toward a "healthier" personality.

In using personality measures with women, several recommendations can be made. The first one is that the counselor be aware of his or her "model of mental health" (e.g., see Matlin, 1993) and make sure that the model is the same for male and female clients. Groundbreaking research by the Brovermans (e.g., Broverman, Broverman, Clarkson, Rosenkrantz, & Vogel, 1970) suggested that mental health practitioners held different standards for the mental health of their male versus female clients. The ideal for male clients was similar to the ideal for the "healthy adult" and was closer to the stereotype of traditional masculinity, whereas the ideal for a female client was closer to the stereotype of traditional femininity but less similar to the description of a healthy adult.

Simplified, it was considered more acceptable for a woman than for a man to be passive, dependent, and so on. This research led to grave concerns about "the double standard of mental health," which was, in effect, a Catch 22 for women. Clinicians did not view traditional femininity as mentally healthy for "adults," yet they encouraged, or at least tolerated, this in their female clients. In fact, 25 years of research has now shown that the key elements of traditional masculinity, which is measured using adjectives such as *self-confident, active, independent, problem-solving,* and *poised,* and can be summarized by *Instrumentality,* are significantly related to other mental health indexes such as higher self-esteem, low levels of depression and anxiety, and greater ability to cope with stress. Traditional femininity, now more descriptively summarized as *expressiveness* and including characteristics like *emotionally expressive, affectionate, helpful, aware of others' feelings,* and *kind,* is not generally related to other mental health indexes. Thus, it is clear that the presence of traits associated with the traditional masculine role, that is, the characteristic of instrumentality, is generally facilitative of women's as well as men's mental health.

We can also discuss models of mental health using these concepts. The "normative" model of mental health (Rawlings & Carter, 1977) had a different, and stereotypic, standard for each sex—this was the implicit model suggested in the research of Broverman et al. (1970). An *androcentric* model is based on the assumption that we should all, male and female both, be encouraged to develop instrumentality. An *androgyny model* is based on the assumption (e.g., Bem, 1974) that because both instrumentality and expressiveness have positive features, psychological health and behavioral adaptability are facilitated by possession of both constellations of characteristics. Notice that regardless of whether the counselor prefers an androcentric or androgyny model of mental health, he or she uses the same model for both male and female clients, as use of different standards for the two sexes is inherently sexist.

A second general recommendation, discussed in detail by Worell and Remer (1992), requires counselors to attend to the environmental context of clients' lives in interpreting and treating so-called symptoms. For example, Briere (1984) and others noted the similarity in the symptomatology of adult survivors of childhood sexual abuse with the descriptions of the diagnostic criteria for Borderline Personality Disorder. Because of this, they and many others have urged increased emphasis on childhood sexual trauma in the etiology of this disorder and, consequently, as a focus of treatment.

A focus on the environmental context also makes it more likely that we will consider primary prevention strategies, that is, social and political changes that will make the world a healthier, less toxic place to live and thereby help people to be more psychologically healthy in the first place. Most basically, reducing the frequency and severity of violence against women could substantially reduce the frequency of mental health problems in women. In line with this increased emphasis, the *DSM–IV* (American Psychiatric Association, 1994) utilizes an Axis IV for Psychosocial and Environmental Problems that may affect the diagnosis, treatment, and prognosis of mental disorders. Examples of psychosocial and environmental problems include sexual or physical abuse, difficulty with acculturation, educational and/or occupational problems, poverty, homelessness, and/or inadequate health care.

A final recommendation is that counselors should be cautious when using diagnostic labels or systems such as the *DSM–IV*. As elaborated by Worell and Remer (1992), use of diagnostic labels can be plagued by sex-role stereotypes and/or by a tendency to "blame the victim" rather than also looking at the environmental contribution to the problem. The just mentioned case of Borderline Personality Disorder provides one example.

Another good example, which represents one of the most important diagnostic improvements in the last few years, has been the use of the diagnostic category of Posttraumatic Stress Disorder (PTSD) for survivors of rape, battering, and/or childhood sexual abuse. The PTSD label puts emphasis where it is deserved, that is, on the traumatic incident that has detrimentally affected the individual's mental health and functioning. We don't blame war veterans for their traumatization and, finally, have realized that neither should we blame abuse and violence survivors for their psychological distress.

Undue influence of sex-role stereotypes in diagnosis is also illustrated by differential diagnosis based on gender. For example, if the descriptors used in diagnostic categories elicit stereotypes of one gender versus the other, then they may also be differentially applied. For example, categories that use terms like *dependent* or *submissive* are more likely to be applied to females because these descriptors fit sexist stereotypes. Thus, counselors should be very careful not to accept or take for granted stereotypic but negative personality characteristics as suggested by tests. Again, it is essential to recall the emphasis of Hackett and Lonborg (1994) and many others on the usefulness of social learning theory. Things that have been learned through gender-role socialization can, like anything else, be unlearned or replaced with more adaptive, instrumental, healthy modes of behavior and functioning. Personality inventories do not have to be, in fact should *not* be, accepted as the individual's end point of development and functioning. They can also be used to suggest positive growth directions in female and male clients.

In summary, there are a number of important considerations in using assessment methods with women and girls. Counseling cannot fully help each individual achieve her maximum potential and fulfillment unless these issues are carefully and thoroughly considered by the psychologist or practitioner.

RACE/ETHNICITY IN TESTS AND ASSESSMENTS

Like the discussion of gender issues in using tests and assessments, issues regarding their use across racial and ethnic minority groups presume a more general knowledge of racial/ethnic issues in counseling itself. Although beyond the scope of this chapter, there are an increasing number of resources available to the psychologist/counselor.

For example, a chapter on racial, ethnic, and cultural variables in counseling (Atkinson & Thompson, 1992) and recent books by Pedersen, Draguus, Lonner, and Trimble (1996), Pope-Davis and Coleman (1996), and Ponterotto, Casas, Suzuki, and Alexander (1995) provide excellent basic resources in this area.

A number of special issues of journals have been devoted to issues in multicultural counseling. The April 1996 issue of *The Counseling Psychologist* was devoted to multicultural challenges in counseling, and the April 1994 issue of *Journal of Counseling Psychology* focused on race/ethnicity in counseling process and outcome. The September/October (1991) issue of the *Journal of Counseling and Development* focused on "Multiculturalism as a Fourth Force in Counseling" (Pedersen, 1991); the March 1991 issue of *Career Development Quarterly* concerned racial/ethnic minorities. The September 1993 special issue of the *Career Development Quarterly* (Savickas, 1993) concerned multicultural career counseling. An important article on career counseling with ethnic minority women was provided by Bingham and Ward (1996), and the April 1994 issue of the *Journal of Vocational Behavior* contained a special issue on the topic of racial identity and vocational behavior. Counselors should pay particular attention to work on multicultural counseling competencies (e.g., Coleman, 1996; Sodowsky, Taffe, Gutkin, & Wise, 1994) as a check of their own levels of knowledge and awareness of important issues and competencies.

In the area of test/assessment use per se, the last few years have been characterized by burgeoning interest in the use of tests and assessments with members of racial and ethnic minority groups. A few major sources for interested readers are the following: Geisinger's (1992) *Psychological Testing of Hispanics*, Leong and Gim-Chung's (1995) *Career Development and Vocational Behavior of Racial/Ethnic Minorities*, and Subich's (1996) article on diversity issues in career assessment. Special issues of the *Journal of Career Assessment* (summer 1994) and *Measurement and Evaluation in Counseling and Development* (July 1994) focused specifically on multicultural assessment. A special issue of the *American Psychologist*, on Intelligence and Life-long Learning (Sternberg, 1997) contained articles on the relevance of the construct of intelligence across race-ethnicity (Suzuki & Valencia, 1997) and cultures (Greenfield, 1997).

Assuming, then, a general familiarity with multicultural issues as they affect counseling theory and practice in toto, discussion of racial, ethnic, and cultural issues in assessment can be focused on several general issues, within which there may be specific considerations depending on the minority group concerned. In this connection, Helms (1994a, 1994b) and others pointed out the need to avoid use of the term *multicultural* in a way that obscures or prevents exploration of issues as they affect specific racial groups. Race, like gender, is itself a crucial individual differences variable that should be included in any research, as well as a specific focus of theory, assessment, and research. Thus, works such as Bowman (1995), Fouad (1995), Leong and Gim-Chung (1995), and Martin (1995), which specifically address career assessment with African Americans, Hispanics, Asian Americans, and American Indians, respectively, should form the basis of the counselors' knowledge.

General Issues in Test Use with Minority Groups

Probably the most important thing to realize when considering the use of tests and assessment devices with racially, ethnically, or culturally diverse individuals is that counseling and assessment occur within a cultural context that includes knowledge of and respect for the values of other cultures and also comfort with and knowledge of one's own values and ethnicity.

So what implications do race, ethnicity, and/or cultural context have for assessment? First, and most basically, most tests and assessment devices are provided in the English language. There are now translations of many major tests. For example, there are Hebrew, French, Canadian, Spanish, British, and Australian versions of the Strong Interest Inventory (Fouad, Harmon, & Hansen, 1994) and Canadian, Spanish, Vietnamese, and Braille versions of the Self-Directed Search (Holland, Fritzsche, & Powell, 1994).

Even if a client does speak English, his or her comfort with this language should not be assumed. For example, Martin (1995) noted that the extent to which an American Indian uses his or her native language, of which there are between 200 and 250, versus English will greatly influence decisions made in the assessment and intervention process. Similarly, many Asian Americans and Hispanics are bilingual, and English may be a second rather than a first language. Some African Americans, too, may have come most recently from the Caribbean. Thus, a cultural context requires the avoidance of ethnocentric assumptions regarding language use.

A second issue as basic as that of language is that tests and assessment devices are constructed and used within the context of a value system, whether made explicit or not. Most assessment methods used in the United States were developed by psychologists/test constructors most comfortable with a European–American, Caucasian middle-class value system, but not all examinees are familiar or comfortable with this value system.

For example, a value that differs across cultures is the greater emphasis on family and community orientation and the preference for cooperation among some members of racial and ethnic minority groups, versus the typical European–American orientations toward individualism and competition (Sue & Sue, 1990). Fouad (1995) wrote about the contrast between Hispanic and White middle-class U.S. values. In contrast to the latter group's belief in mastery over nature, future time orientation, emphasis on doing, and emphasis on the individual is Hispanics' emphasis (as a group) on living in harmony with nature, living in the present, emphasis on being rather than doing, and subordination of individual to group goals. Martin (1995) noted that, among American Indians, the home, family, and community are often more highly valued than jobs, career, or occupation. Leong and Gim-Chung (1995) summarized research suggesting that Asian Americans may be more likely to prefer extrinsic (e.g., security) to intrinsic (e.g., self-realization) work values and that they may be more conforming, externally oriented, and socially anxious. They discuss the Chinese values of respect for authority and submergence of individuality. Such value differences may potentially have import for the way in which people make life decisions. In both counseling and assessment, it is important to avoid automatic assumptions about what is "best" without incorporating into that consideration the culturally-specific values held by the individual.

In career assessment, Leong and Gim-Chung's (1995) and Fouad's (1995) discussions of possible cultural variations in such traditional variables as career maturity and vocational interests are relevant. For example, Leong and Gim-Chung suggest that Asian Americans may more often prefer "dependent" decision-making styles than do Anglo-Americans, but what our Eurocentric worldview calls "dependent" decision-making styles could be reconceptualized as a "collectivist orientation" in decision making. Thus, we must use caution when using measures of career maturity or career decision-making style. It should also be noted that our labeling of scales or variables themselves is a cultural construction in which the extent to which a group is described in more versus less favorable terms (e.g., collectivist orientation vs. dependent) is essentially arbitrary and, therefore, influenced by researchers' biases.

Unless the counselor has knowledge of other cultures, he or she may erroneously assume that all individuals share Western, Eurocentric values. A useful term coined by Sandra and Daryl Bem (1976) was that of *noncon-*

scious ideology, which refers to belief systems that are ingrained so deeply and subconsciously that we are not even aware that there are alternatives. The Bems' example is a fish that doesn't know that it lives in water. I have suggested elsewhere (Betz & Fitzgerald, 1995) that the Western value system has been a "nonconscious ideology" that is finally being challenged by the emergence of a cultural context in psychology.

Third, although a general knowledge of alternative value systems in other cultures is necessary, it is also important to avoid uniformity assumptions, that is, the assumption that all individuals of a given culture have the same values, goals, and experiences. The concept of individual differences is just as important when considering members of racial/ethnic minorities as with European–American clientele. Differences occur not only with one specific ethnic group but across groups generally lumped under one "ethnicity." For example, Fouad (1995) distinguished an *ethnic group* from a *racial group*, noting that the term *Hispanic* connotes an ethnic group whose members can be of many different races (White, Black, and indigenous native Americans). Country of origin varies from Mexico to countries in the Caribbean and Central and South America. Martin (1995) offered the striking statistic that among Native Americans there are some 509 nations, tribes, and Alaskan villages, each with its own traditions and, often, language. Leong and Gim-Chung (1995) noted the great variety even within members of one ethnic group—Chinese Americans have countries of origin ranging from the People's Republic of China to Taiwan to Malaysia and Singapore.

Martin (1991) provided a useful integration of the need for a cultural context without homogenizing: "Career counselors cannot approach [Indian] clients as a homogeneous group but must be keenly aware of individual differences while at the same time giving consideration to potential cultural influences" (p. 28). This statement can and probably should be applied to clients of any racial/ethnic minority group.

A fourth important issue is the nature of the normative group. Most frequently used tests were developed in largely Anglo-American middle-class samples, and consequently, their reliability, validity, and normative data are most appropriately applied to members of the original normative group. (This is less true of national achievement tests, for which the standardization samples are selected to be representative of a broad variety of school districts and to include large numbers of racial/ethnic minorities.)

There are two ways to address this issue of the ethnic diversity (or lack thereof) in the original development samples. The first, and most common, is to conduct additional research on the psychometric characteristics of the existing inventory or measure in additional groups not adequately represented initially. This approach is represented by, for example, Carter and Swanson's (1990) review of the use of the Strong Interest Inventory with African Americans or, more generally, Fouad and Spreda's (1995) review of research on the use of various interest inventories, including the Strong, Self-Directed Search (SDS), and Kuder Occupational Interest Survey (KOIS), with women and minority groups.

The other ultimately preferable approach is to incorporate members of racial/ethnic minority groups into the initial norming of an instrument. In the 1994 revision of the Strong Interest Inventory, for example, attempts were made to oversample members of racial minority groups in the new normative sample. By *oversampling* is meant making an attempt to obtain percentages of minority group members higher than those in the general population, with the ultimate objective of obtaining large enough representations to yield meaningful information. Although the attempt in the case of the Strong revision was not completely successful, primarily because racial and ethnic minority group members are overrepresented in some occupations and underrepresented in others, the result was a revised Strong with larger minority representation than any previous version of the Strong and, most likely, any other interest inventory. Even more importantly, the authors used this much larger minority development sample to conduct extensive comparisons of the scores of the various racial groups and to incorporate this research into the test manual (see Fouad, Harmon, & Hansen, 1994, in Harmon, Hansen, Borgen, & Hammer, 1994). Thus, users of the Strong Interest Inventory, for example, can now carefully evaluate the usefulness of the scales for clients of varying races/ethnicities.

In general, it can be stated at a minimum that the manual or accompanying materials for a test should contain a discussion of what is (or is not) known about the usefulness of a test with various racial or ethnic groups. If possible, normative data should be provided within race as well as within gender. Even better, test authors or others should conduct research examining the reliability and validity of a given test or measure in groups other than White Anglo-American. This research should be published in journal articles and/or, ideally, in the test manual.

It should be noted that there is cause for optimism in this regard. As discussed in Walsh and Betz (1995), both the construction and norming of aptitude and achievement tests now explicitly include representation across racial and socioeconomic status groups. There has been much progress in career assessment as well.

In addition to research evaluating the applicability of various measures or classes of measures for minority groups, Leong and Gim-Chung (1995) noted the need for research on Asians' attitudes toward and comfort with psychological testing, and this suggestion may be useful as well as with other racial/ethnic groups. For example, they noted that Asian Americans are more likely to live within authoritarian family and social systems and may thus be less likely to challenge the counselor's "authority" when the counselor assigns and/or interprets a test. Thus, not only the test itself but the whole process of test administration and interpretation needs to be considered within a cultural context.

Finally, many authors urge major changes in how the counselor uses assessment procedures in counseling. For example, Subich (1996) recommended a more collaborative model in using assessment devices in counseling. Integrating her suggestions concerning model issues with the work of Healy (1990) and displaying many similarities to feminist approaches (Hackett & Lonborg, 1994), Subich emphasized the importance to career counseling and assessment of collaborating more with clients, empowering them to take more active roles in their vocational development, and explicitly recognizing contextual concerns, for example, environmental barriers to career choices.

In addition to the examination of traditional assessment measures is the interview, which Hackett and Lonborg (1994) suggested be used to develop a "contextually-sensitive picture" (p. 200) of the client and the client's career-related concerns; although their chapter was addressed to the issue of career assessment with women, the importance of context, including race, ethnicity, gender, socioeconomic status (SES), and so on, applies to assessment and counseling with any client. As another example, Martin (1995) proposed a "Cultural and Contextual Guide for Planning Differential Assessment and Intervention with American Indians." This checklist included questions about language usage, cultural orientation, home community, family system, and communication styles.

Of possibly more general use are materials suggested by Ward and Bingham (1993), who proposed the use of a decision tree designed to help the counselor to decide when to consider racial or ethnic material. In the first step in assessment is the determination of whether a client is seeking career or personal counseling. If the client's questions have to do with career issues, then the counselor needs to assess the impact of culture (ethnicity), family influences, and finances. Ward and Bingham suggested that in some cases the examination of racial/ethnic issues may resolve the career issues, for example, by having the counselor challenge the client's beliefs that Black women can't be scientists or engineers.

Two final issues concern using tests in selection and the use of diagnostic categories. As reviewed in the previous section, the concept of *adverse impact* is the case when scores on an aptitude test result in fewer members of one group (gender or racial/ethnic) being selected for an educational or occupational opportunity in comparison to another group. In the case of minority groups, adverse impact has usually occurred when ability and aptitude tests are used in educational or job selection programs. The issues involved here are massive and complex and beyond the scope of the present chapter (but see Walsh & Betz, 1995). However, it can be said that the most crucial issues for counselors reading this chapter derive from the APA

Test Standard presented and discussed in the previous section on gender issues in using ability tests. As was discussed with women, the possibility that background experiences and opportunities have not facilitated the full development of an individual's (in this case one representing a racial or ethnic minority) intellectual potential should always be explored when ability test scores are low.

The revision of the *DSM–III*, now the *DSM–IV*, specifically included awareness of cultural diversity: "A clinician who is unfamiliar with the nuances of an individual's cultural frame of reference may incorrectly judge as psychopathology those normal variations in belief, behavior, or experience that are particular to the individual's culture" (American Psychiatric Association, 1994, p. xxiv).

Three types of information relative to cultural considerations have been included in the *DSM–IV*. These are: (a) discussion of cultural variations in the clinical presentations of disorder, (b) description of certain culture-bound syndromes not included in the regular *DSM–IV* classificatory system, and (c) an outline to assist the clinician in evaluating the cultural context of an individual. Thus, most diagnostic categories contain a section describing "specific culture, age, and gender features."

For example, the category "Depersonalization Disorder" mentions, under "Specific Culture Features," that voluntarily induced experiences of depersonalization form part of meditative or trance practices that are prevalent in many religions or cultures. These are not to be confused with or (worse) diagnosed as Depersonalization Disorder.

The *DSM–IV* provides an outline for the consideration of culture, which emphasizes assessment of: (a) cultural identity of the individual, (b) cultural explanations of the individual's illness, (c) cultural factors related to psychosocial environment, (d) cultural elements of the relationship between the individual and the clinician, and (e) overall cultural assessment for diagnosis and care (p. 844).

In summary, there is both tremendous need and tremendous opportunity in the area of using assessment devices with members of racial and ethnic minority groups. We need more information regarding the use of particular tests or inventories with particular minority groups; the most obvious kinds of information needed are relevant norms and evidence for reliability and validity. But we also need more attention to the whole concept and process itself, so that our work with members of racial/ethnic minority groups can be maximally helpful to them.

SUMMARY

This chapter has reviewed ethical and social issues concerning the use of tests in counseling. It is hoped that test users will become familiar with the uses, misuses, and limits of any test they are considering for use. An informed test user will be well on the way to ethical and socially responsible test use. Also important is further research on specific uses of tests, with, for example, ethnic minorities and individuals from other cultures. Counselors who use tests in their work should be continually alert to possible research hypotheses stemming from their actual counseling use of tests. Finally, respect for the individual and continuing awareness of the fact that tests are fallible sources of information (even if clients think they are infallible) are vital to ethical test use.

REFERENCES

Adler, L. L. (Ed.). (1993). *International handbook on gender roles*. Westport, CT: Greenwood.

American Educational Research Association, American Psychological Association, & National Council on Measurement in Education. (1985). *Standards for educational and psychological testing*. Washington, DC: American Psychological Association.

American Psychiatric Association. (1994). *Diagnostic and statistical manual of mental disorders* (4th ed.). Washington, DC: Author.

American Psychological Association. (1954). *Technical recommendations for psychological tests and diagnostic techniques*. Washington, DC: Author.

American Psychological Association. (1975). Report of the Task Force on Sex Bias and Sex-role Stereotyping in Psychotherapeutic Practice. *American Psychologist, 30*, 1169–1175.

American Psychological Association. (1981). Ethical principles of psychologists. *American Psychologist, 36*, 633–638.

American Psychological Association. (1986). *Guidelines for computer-based tests and interpretations*. Washington, DC: Author.

American Psychological Association. (1988). *Code of fair testing practices in education*. Washington, DC: Author.

American Psychological Association. (1992). Ethical principles of psychologists and code of conduct. *American Psychologist, 47*, 1597–1611.

American Psychological Association. (1993). *Responsible test use: Case studies for assessing human behavior*. Washington, DC: Author.

American Psychological Association Committee on Legal Issues. (1995). *Strategies for coping with subpoenas or compelled testimony for test data*. Washington, DC: American Psychological Association.

American Psychological Association. (1996). Statement on the disclosure of test data. *American Psychologist, 51*, 644–648.

Anatasi, A. (1982). *Psychological testing* (5th ed.). New York: Macmillan.

Association for Measurement and Evaluation in Guidance. Commission on Sex Bias in Measurement. (1977). A case history of change: A review of responses to the challenge of sex bias in interest inventories. *Measurement and Evaluation in Guidance, 10*, 148–152.

Atkinson, D. R., & Thompson, C. E. (1992). Racial, ethnic, and cultural variables in counseling. In S. D. Brown & R. W. Lent (Eds.), *Handbook of Counseling Psychology* (pp. 349–382). New York: Wiley.

Bandura, A. (1986). *Social foundations of thought and action*. Englewood Cliffs, NJ: Prentice Hall.

Bem, S. L. (1974). The measurement of psychological androgyny. *Journal of Consulting and Clinical Psychology, 47*, 155–162.

Bem, S. L., & Bem, D. J. (1976). Case study of a nonconscious ideology: Training the woman to know her place. In S. Cox (Ed.), *Female psychology* (pp. 180–191). Chicago: Science Research Associates.

Betz, N. (1989). The null environment and women's career development. *Counseling Psychologist, 17,* 136–144.

Betz, N. E. (1992). Counseling uses of career self-efficacy theory. *Career Development Quarterly, 41,* 22–26.

Betz, N. E. (1993). Issues in the use of ability and interest measures with women. *Journal of Career Assessment, 3,* 217–232.

Betz, N. E. (1995). Sex and gender as individual differences variables: New concepts and findings. In R. Dawis & D. Lubinski (Eds.), *Assessing individual differences in human behavior: New concepts, methods, and findings* (pp. 119–144). Palo Alto, CA: Consulting Psychologists Press.

Betz, N. (1997). What stops women and minorities from choosing and completing majors in science and engineering? In D. Johnson (Ed.), *Minorities and girls in school: Effects on achievement and performance* (pp. 105–140). Thousand Oaks, CA: Sage.

Betz, N., Borgen, F., & Harmon, L. (1996). *Skills Confidence Inventory: Applications and Technical Guide.* Palo Alto: Consulting Psychologists Press.

Betz, N. E., & Fitzgerald, L. F. (1987). *The career psychology of women.* New York: Academic Press.

Betz, N. E., & Fitzgerald, L. F. (1995). Career assessment and intervention with racial and ethnic minorities. In F. T. L. Leong (Ed.), *Career development of racial and ethnic minorities* (pp. 263–280). Hillsdale, NJ: Lawrence Erlbaum Associates.

Betz, N. E., & Hackett, G. (1983). The relationship of mathematics self-efficacy expectations to the selection of science-based college majors. *Journal of Vocational Behavior, 23,* 329–345.

Bingham, R., & Ward, C. (1996). Practical applications of career counseling with ethnic minority women. In M. L. Savickas & W. B. Walsh (Eds.), *Handbook of career counseling theory and practice* (pp. 291–314). Palo Alto, CA: Davies-Black.

Bowman, S. L. (1995). Career intervention strategies and assessment issues for African Americans. In F. L. Leong (Ed.), *Career development and vocational behavior of racial and ethnic minorities* (pp. 137–164). Mahwah, NJ: Lawrence Erlbaum Associates.

Briere, J. (1984, October). *The effects of childhood sexual abuse on psychological functioning: Defining a post-sexual-abuse syndrome.* Paper presented at Third National Conference on Sexual Victimization of Children, Washington, DC.

Broverman, I. K., Broverman, D., Clarkson, F. E., Rosenkrantz, P. S., & Vogel, S. (1970). Sex-role stereotypes and clinical judgments of mental health. *Journal of Consulting and Clinical Psychology, 34,* 1–7.

Brown, L., & Forrest, L. (1994). Feminism and career counseling. In W. B. Walsh & S. H. Osipow (Eds.), *Career counseling for women* (pp. 87–134). Hillsdale, NJ: Lawrence Erlbaum Associates.

Carter, R. T., & Swanson, J. L. (1990). The validity of the Strong Interest Inventory with Black Americans: A review of the literature. *Journal of Vocational Behavior, 36,* 195–209.

Cole, N. S., & Hanson, G. R. (1975). Impact of interest inventories on career choice. In E. E. Diamond (Ed.), *Issues of sex bias and sex fairness in career interest measurement* (pp. 10–25). Washington, DC: National Institute of Education.

Coleman, H. (1996). Portfolio assessment of multicultural counseling competency. *Counseling Psychologist, 24,* 216–229.

Conoley, J. C., & Impara, J. C. (1995). *Twelfth mental measurements yearbook.* Lincoln, NE: Buros Institute of Mental Measurements.

Dawis, R. V. (1987). Scale construction. *Journal of Counseling Psychology, 34,* 481–489.

Diamond, E. E. (1975). Guidelines for the assessment of sex bias and sex fairness in career interest inventories. *Measurement and Evaluation in Guidance, 8,* 7–11.

Fitzgerald, L. F., & Nutt, R. L. (1986). Principles concerning the counseling/psychotherapy of women: Rationale and implementation. *Counseling Psychologist, 14,* 180–216.

Fouad, N. (1995). Career behavior of Hispanics: Assessment and career intervention. In F. L. Leong (Ed.), *Career development and vocational behavior of racial and ethnic minorities* (pp. 165–192). Washington, DC: APA Office of Scientific Affairs.

Fouad, N. A., Harmon, L. W., & Hansen, J. C. (1994). Cross-cultural use of the Strong. In L. W. Harmon, J. C. Hansen, F. H. Borgen, & A. L. Hammer (Eds.), *Strong Interest Inventory: Applications and technical guide* (pp. 255–280). Palo Alto, CA: Consulting Psychologists Press.

Fouad, N. A., & Spreda, S. S. (1995). Use of interest inventories with special populations: Women and minority groups. *Journal of Career Assessment, 3*, 453–468.

Geisinger, K. (1992). *Psychological testing of Hispanics*. Washington, DC: APA.

Goldman, R. D., & Hewitt, B. N. (1976). The scholastic aptitude test "explains" why college men major in science more often than college women. *Journal of Counseling Psychology, 23*, 50–54.

Good, G. E., Gilbert, L. A., & Scher, M. (1990). Gender aware therapy: A synthesis of feminist therapy and knowledge about gender. *Journal of Counseling and Development, 68*, 376–380.

Gottfredson, G. D., Holland, J. L., & Gottfredson, L. S. (1975). The relation of vocational aspirations and assessments to employment reality. *Journal of Vocational Behavior, 7*, 135–148.

Greenfield, P. M. (1997). You can't take it with you: Why ability assessments don't cross cultures. *American Psychologist, 52*, 1115–1124.

Hackett, G., & Lonborg, S. D. (1994). Career assessment and counseling for women. In W. B. Walsh & S. H. Osipow (Eds.), *Career counseling for women* (pp. 43–85). Hillsdale, NJ: Lawrence Erlbaum Associates.

Halpern, D. (1997). Sex differences in intelligence: Implications for education. *American Psychologist, 52*, 1091–1102.

Harmon, L. W., Hansen, J. C., Borgen, F. H., & Hammer, A. L. (1994). *Strong Interest Inventory applications and technical guide*. Stanford, CA: Stanford University Press. Distributed by Consulting Psychologists Press.

Hattrup, K. Review of the Differential Aptitude Tests, Fifth Edition. In J. C. Conoley & J. C. Impara (Eds.), *Twelfth Mental Measurements Yearbook*. Lincoln, NE: Buros Institute.

Healy, C. C. (1990). Reforming career appraisals to meet the needs of clients in the 1990's. *Counseling Psychologist, 18*, 214–226.

Helms, J. E. (1994a). How multiculturalism obscures racial factors in the therapy process. *Journal of Counseling Psychology, 41*, 162–165.

Helms, J. E. (1994b). Racial identity and career assessment. *Journal of Career Assessment, 2*, 199–209.

Holland, J. L. (1997). *Making vocational choices: A theory of vocational personalities and work environments* (3rd ed.). Englewood Cliffs, NJ: Prentice Hall.

Holland, J. L. (1985). *Professional manual for the Self-Directed Search—1985 edition*. Odessa, FL: Psychological Assessment Resources.

Holland, J. L., Fritzsche, B. A., & Powell, A. B. (1994). *The Self-Directed Search (SDS): Technical manual*. Odessa, FL: Psychological Assessment Resources.

Impara, J. C., & Plake, B. S. (Eds.). (1998). *Thirteenth Mental Measurements Yearbook*. Lincoln, NE: Buros Institute.

Keyser, D. J., & Sweetland, R. C. (1992). *Test critiques* (Vol. IX). Austin, TX: Pro-ed.

Lamb, R. R., & Prediger, D. J. (1981). *Technical report for the unisex edition of the ACT interest inventory (UNIACT)*. Iowa City, IA: American College Testing Program.

Lapan, R. T., Boggs, K. R., & Morrill, W. H. (1989). Self-efficacy as a mediator of Investigative and Realistic themes on the SCII. *Journal of Counseling Psychology, 36*, 176–182.

Lent, R. W., Lopez, F. G., & Bieschke, K. J. (1991). Mathematics self-efficacy: Sources and relation to science-based career choice. *Journal of Counseling Psychology, 38*, 424–430.

Lent, R. W., Lopez, F. G., & Bieschke, K. J. (1993). Predicting mathematics-related choice and success behaviors: Test of an expanded social cognitive model. *Journal of Vocational Behavior, 42*, 223–236.

Leong, F. T. L. (Ed.). (1995). *Career development of racial and ethnic minorities.* Hillsdale, NJ: Lawrence Erlbaum Associates.

Leong, F. T. L., & Gim-Chung, R. H. (1995). Career assessment and intervention with Asian-Americans. In F. L. Leong (Ed.), *Career development and vocational behavior of racial and ethnic minorities* (pp. 193–226). Mahwah, NJ: Lawrence Erlbaum Associates.

Lunneborg, P. W. (1980). Reducing sex bias in interest measurement at the item level. *Journal of Vocational Behavior, 16,* 226–234.

Lunneborg, P. W. (1981). *The Vocational Interest Inventory manual.* Los Angeles: Western Psychological Services.

Lunneborg, P. W., & Lunneborg, C. E. (1986). Everyday Spatial Activities Test for studying differential experience and vocational behavior. *Journal of Vocational Behavior, 28,* 135–141.

Matlin, M. (1996). *Psychology of women* (3rd ed.). New York: Holt.

Martin, W. E., Jr. (1991). Career development and American Indians living on reservations: Cross cultural factors to consider. *Career Development Quarterly, 39,* 273–283.

Martin, W. E., Jr. (1995). Career development assessment and intervention strategies with American Indians. In F. L. Leong (Ed.), *Career development and vocational behavior of racial and ethnic minorities* (pp. 227–250). Mahwah, NJ: Lawrence Erlbaum Associates.

Matlin, M. M. (1993). *Psychology of women* (2nd ed.). New York: Holt, Rinehart, & Winston.

Office of Technology Assessment. (1989). *Higher education for science and engineering: A background paper.* Washington, DC: OTA, Congress of the United States.

Pedersen, P. B. (Ed.). (1991). Multiculturalism as a fourth force in counseling [Special issue]. *Journal of Counseling and Development, 70*(1).

Pedersen, P. B., Draguus, J. G., Lonner, W. J., & Trimble, J. E. (1996). *Counseling across cultures.* Thousand Oaks, CA: Sage.

Pennock-Roman, M. (1989). Review of Differential Aptitude Tests. In V. L. Willson (Ed.), *Academic achievement and aptitude testing* (pp. 124–133). Austin, TX: Pro-ed.

Ponterotto, J. G., Casas, J. M., Suzuki, L. A., & Alexander, C. M. (Eds.). (1995). *Handbook of multicultural counseling.* Thousand Oaks, CA: Sage.

Pope-Davis, D. P., & Coleman, H. L. K. (1996). *Multicultural counseling competence.* Thousand Oaks, CA: Sage.

Prediger, D. P., & Hanson, G. R. (1976). A theory of career applied to men and women: Analysis of implicit assumptions. *Journal of Vocational Behavior, 8,* 167–184.

Rawlings, E. I., & Carter, D. K. (1977). *Psychotherapy for women: Treatment toward equality.* Springfield: Charles C. Thomas.

Rosser, P. (1989). *The SAT gender gap.* Washington, DC: Center for Women Policy Studies.

Savickas, M. (Ed.). (1993). A symposium on multicultural career counseling. *Career Development Quarterly, 42, 3.*

Schmitt, N. (1995). Review of Differential Aptitude Tests, Fifth Edition. In J. L. Conoley & J. C. Impara (Eds.), *Twelfth Mental Measurements Yearbook.* Lincoln, NE: Buros Institute.

Sells, L. (1982). Leverage for equal opportunity through mastery of mathematics. In S. M. Humphreys (Ed.), *Women and minorities in science* (pp. 7–26). Boulder, CO: Westview Press.

Society for Industrial and Organizational Psychology, Inc. (1987). *Principles for the validation and use of personnel selection procedures* (3rd ed.). College Park, MD: Author.

Sodowsky, G. R., Taffe, R. C., Gutkin, T. B., & Wise, S. L. (1994). Development of the Multicultural Counseling Inventory: A self-report measure of multicultural competencies. *Journal of Counseling Psychology, 41,* 137–148.

Sternberg, R. J. (1997). Introduction to the special issue on Intelligence and lifelong learning. *American Psychologist, 52,* 1029.

Subich, L. (1996). Addressing diversity in the process of career assessment. In M. L. Savickas & W. B. Walsh (Eds.), *Handbook of career counseling theory and practice* (pp. 277–289). Palo Alto, CA: Davies-Black.

Sue, D. W., & Sue, D. (1990). *Counseling the culturally different: Theory and practice* (2nd ed.). New York: Wiley.

Suzuki, L. A., & Valencia, R. R. (1997). Race-ethnicity and measured intelligence: Educational implications. *American Psychologist, 52*, 1103–1114.

Sweetland, R. C., & Keyser, D. J. (1991). *Tests* (3rd ed.). Austin, TX: Pro-ed.

Walsh, W. B., & Betz, N. E. (1995). *Tests and assessment* (3rd ed.). Englewood Cliffs, NJ: Prentice Hall.

Walsh, W. B., & Osipow, S. H. (1986). *Advances in vocational psychology, Volume 1: The assessment of interests*. Hillsdale, NJ: Lawrence Erlbaum Associates.

Walsh, W. B., & Osipow, S. H. (1988). *Career decision-making*. Hillsdale, NJ: Lawrence Erlbaum Associates.

Walsh, W. B., & Osipow, S. H. (Eds.). (1994). *Career counseling for women*. Hillsdale, NJ: Lawrence Erlbaum Associates.

Ward, C. M., & Bingham, R. P. (1993). Career assessment of ethnic minority women. *Journal of Career Assessment, 1*, 246–257.

Worell, J., & Remer, P. (1992). *Feminist perspectives in therapy*. New York: John Wiley.

14

Computer Applications

James P. Sampson, Jr.
Florida State University

Computer applications in testing and assessment have now been in use for almost four decades. Experience with the application of this technology has resulted in the creation of a substantial body of knowledge. The goal of this chapter is to explore the potential benefits and problems associated with computer-assisted testing and assessment.

The chapter begins with a brief review of the historical development of computer-assisted testing and assessment, followed by a description of the state of the art. The necessity of keeping terminology related to computer applications congruent with actual professional practice is then examined and a rationale is presented for using computer technology to support the assessment process. The benefits associated with computer applications are explored in light of how appropriate use of technology may enhance: (a) the validity and reliability of testing and assessment, (b) client integration of assessment data in counseling, and (c) staff efficiency and cost-effectiveness. The problems associated with computer applications are then explored in light of how inappropriate use of technology may compromise (a) the validity and reliability of testing and assessment and (b) effective implementation of services. Finally, the future use of computer applications in testing and assessment is examined in terms of hardware developments, software developments, and professional practice.

EVOLUTION OF COMPUTER-ASSISTED TESTING AND ASSESSMENT

The use of computer applications in assessment began with quantitative features of the testing and assessment process and has now progressed to include many verbal features as well. Examples of early quantitative features included keyboard entry from existing answer sheets, optical scanning of specialized answer sheets, scoring of traditional paper-and-pencil tests, scores printed with scale labels, and graphic presentation of score profiles. With improvements over time in the cost-effectiveness of data processing, verbal features became available, such as the administration of test items and the development of narrative interpretive reports. As telecommunications improved, users could enter data and print reports at remote locations with scoring centralized in another location. The emergence of the personal computer provided substantial cost-effectiveness improvements and a shift in locus of control that brought test administration, scoring, profiling, and interpretive report generation into actual service delivery settings, as opposed to remote computer centers. Advancements in the integration of multimedia (first videotape and now videodisc, CD-I, and CD-ROM) technology with the computer have resulted in the presentation of generalized test interpretations directly to the client (Hansen, 1986, 1987; Sampson, 1983). Fowler and Butcher (1987) provided a comprehensive historical account of the evolution of computer-assisted psychological assessment.

State of the Art

The following is a description of state-of-the-art computer-assisted testing and assessment.

1. Test administration via keyboard input by the client from items presented on a computer display (with alternative input options available for clients with a physical disability), or client completion of a test answer sheet that is then optically scanned for computer input.
2. Test scoring via the computer.
3. Test score profile generation via the computer with profiles printed for the client and practitioner as appropriate.
4. Narrative interpretive report generation via the computer with reports printed for client and practitioner as appropriate (the narrative report may also include the test profile).
5. Multimedia-based generalized test interpretation provided to the client immediately following test administration.

Prior to test administration, computer-assisted instruction may be used to help clients understand (a) the role of assessment in the counseling and behavior change process and (b) the procedures to be involved in testing (Sampson, 1986a, 1990; Sampson, Kolodinsky, & Greeno, 1997).

Butcher (1995), Moreland (1987), Madsen (1986), and Roid and Gorsuch (1984) provided detailed descriptions of the specific options available for computer-assisted test administration, scoring, and report generation. Refer to Bridges (1988), Butcher (1987a), Krug (1993), Stoloff and Couch (1992), and Walz, Bleuer, and Maze (1989) for information on computer versions of specific tests. See Moreland (1990) for a description of the evolution of computer-assisted psychological testing.

Computer-Assisted Versus Computerized: Keeping Terminology Congruent with Recommended Practice

It appears that the terms *computer-assisted* and *computerized* are used with nearly the same frequency in describing the use of computer technology as an aspect of the assessment process (Sampson, 1987). Using *computerized* instead of *computer-assisted* may create problems because it may foster misunderstanding of the role of the computer in the testing and assessment process. Practitioners[1] who misunderstand the role of the computer may reject technology because they view the computer as performing inappropriate functions that lead to dehumanization or they are likely to view the computer as effective in performing functions not intended by the developer, such as compensating for a lack of professional skill. The former is likely to lead to underuse of the computer, the latter to misuse.

Using the term *computerized* implies that labor previously completed by humans is now completed by the computer; in essence, the testing and assessment process is now automated. The testing and assessment process is not, however, as automated as the term *computerized* implies. First, although a computer may actually administer individual items, the *APGA Policy Statement: Responsibilities of Users of Standardized Tests* (APGA, 1980) and the *Standards for Educational and Psychological Testing* (AERA, APA, & NCME, 1985) require that a trained professional be available for orientation, providing appropriate assistance, and observing the client in order to ensure the validity of the results. Second, although the computer often performs all scoring tasks, potential errors in optical scanning devices and scoring programs necessitate regular human intervention to evaluate the accuracy of test results. The verification of scoring accuracy of computer

---

[1]The term *practitioner* in this chapter refers to counselors, psychologists, and other mental health professionals who are qualified by virtue of their training and experience to engage in testing and assessment functions as one component of the counseling process.

applications has been included in the *Guidelines for Computer-Based Tests and Interpretations* (American Psychological Association, 1986), and the *Code of Ethics* (National Board for Certified Counselors, 1989). Third, even though a computer may generate a narrative test interpretation, the *Guidelines for Computer-Based Tests and Interpretations* (American Psychological Association, 1986, p. 12) state that the professional should judge the validity of computer-generated interpretive reports based on his or her "knowledge of the total context of testing and the test taker's performance and characteristics." Thus the term *computerized* is an inaccurate and potentially misleading depiction of the actual use of computer technology in the testing and assessment process.

The term *computer-assisted*, as used by Bleuer and Walz (1983), Walz (1984), and Loesch (1986), and *computer-as-assistant*, as used by Altemose and Williamson (1981), imply that the computer is being used to facilitate another more complex process. In this way the major emphasis is placed on testing and assessment, with the computer fulfilling a support role, improving, as opposed to replacing, the human element. This perspective is more likely to avoid practitioner or client underuse or misuse of computer applications. This perspective is also congruent with the professional standards described earlier.

RATIONALES FOR COMPUTER-ASSISTED TESTING AND ASSESSMENT

Both rationales for using computer technology to support the assessment process are directed toward improving the quality of counseling services. The first rationale focuses on assigning to humans and computers the tasks best suited to the respective capabilities of each. For example, computers are better at computational and repetitive instructional tasks, whereas practitioners are better at interpersonal tasks, such as helping clients understand how testing and assessment supports the counseling process, helping clients fully understand test results, and helping clients integrate the self-knowledge obtained in assessment into a broader plan for behavior change. See Sampson (1986b) for common assumptions about the use of computer applications in counseling.

The second rationale involves developing previously unavailable techniques that result in improved quality of test instruments and procedures. For example, adaptive devices allow disabled individuals to independently complete test items that previously would have required the assistance of an attendant (Burkhead & Sampson, 1985; Krug, 1987; Merrell, 1986; Sampson, 1983).

POTENTIAL BENEFITS ASSOCIATED WITH COMPUTER APPLICATIONS

The potential benefits of using computer applications in support of testing and assessment can be conceptualized into three general areas:

1. Enhanced validity and reliability (administration and scoring as well as test interpretation).
2. Enhanced client integration of assessment data in counseling.
3. Enhanced staff efficiency and cost-effectiveness.

Enhanced Validity and Reliability

Computer applications have the potential to enhance the validity and reliability of testing and assessment. This affects administration and scoring as well as interpretation.

Administration and Scoring. The greater degree of standardization inherent in computer functioning results in increased validity and reliability of test administration and scoring (Butcher, 1995; Denner, 1977; French, 1986; Hudson, Nurius, & Reisman, 1988). Test items and response sets are presented in the same way for each test taker, thus achieving more standardization than is available with paper and pencil tests. Krug (1987) noted that measurement errors are reduced because the computer can present very complex stimuli and maintain precise time limits for item presentation. Byers (1981) stated that in paper-and-pencil testing the test taker often errs by getting out of sync between the answer sheet and test item printed in a booklet. Because items are administered one at a time on the computer, extraneous errors of this type are eliminated. Erdman and Foster (1988) noted that receiving instructions from a computer tends to be less threatening than receiving instructions from a practitioner. Erdman and Foster also noted that the greater access afforded by computers, in comparison to access to practitioners, tended to result in a greater sense of client control. Furthermore, the rapid feedback available from computer-administered and -scored tests resulted in increased use of brief assessments (Flowers, Booraem, & Schwartz, 1993), as well as improved client attitudes toward testing (Byers, 1981) and counseling (Flowers et al., 1993).

Disabled individuals can now complete a test with only minimal assistance from staff members. The many adaptive devices that allow this flexibility grew out of the numerous computer options for data input (Burkhead & Sampson, 1985; Krug, 1987; Merrell, 1986; Sampson, 1983). Because staff members have a reduced opportunity to influence test administration, the results are more likely to be a valid representation of the disabled person's perceptions, knowledge, and behavior. In terms of test scoring accuracy, the computer is both faster (French, 1986; Hansen, 1977; Reardon & Loughead, 1988; Vansickle & Kapes, 1993) and more accurate in comparison to paper-and-pencil methods (French, 1986; Hansen, 1977).

Adaptive testing, ancillary data collection, and unobtrusive measures can also contribute to test validity. Adaptive testing can reduce administration time without compromising validity by only administering items that contribute to statistically valid results (Baskin, 1990; Green, 1991; Hofer & Green, 1985; Johnson, 1984; Johnson & Johnson, 1981; Roper, Ben-Porath, & Butcher, 1991; Space, 1981; Vale, 1981; Ward, 1984; Weiss & Vale, 1987). The computer can also collect data on the manner in which clients respond to items, as well as recording specific responses. These ancillary data, which can include random rapid response patterns, testee fatigue, and changes in response latencies for items comprising a specific scale, can be analyzed and included in CBTI reports in such a way that testing validity is improved (Baskin, 1990; Hofer & Green, 1985; Standing Committee on Test Standards, 1984; Stout, 1981). Computer-based unobtrusive measures may be especially important in improving the validity of self-report of sensitive data, such as alcohol-related behavior (Meier & Wick, 1991).

In addition to standardized tests, the computer can be used to effectively administer interviews and checklists. Nurius (1990a) categorized computer interviews as either broad-based interview schedules covering a range of topics, or content-specific interviews dealing with issues such as substance abuse, suicide risk, depression, marital problems, and mental status. Computer administration offers some important advantages over more traditional interviews. In comparison with human interviewers, the computer-assisted interviews provided more comprehensive and consistent topic coverage of important issues (Erdman, Klein, & Greist, 1985; Giannetti, 1987; Schwartz, 1984), generated less tension about evaluation (Canoune & Leyhe, 1985), and were less affected by time of day and interview sequencing (Slack & Slack, 1977). Clients were more honest in responding to the computer (Lucas, Mullins, Luna, & McInroy, 1977; Nurius, 1990a) and provided more information (Sawyer, Sarris, & Baghurst, 1991). Giannetti (1987) reported that clients reacted positively to computer-assisted interviews and that a majority of clients were capable of completing the computer-assisted interviews with minimal assistance. Levitan, Blouin, Navaro, and Hill (1991) found a computer-administered interview to provide valid diagnostic data.

Despite initial concerns that clients would perceive the use of computer technology as "impersonal" or "mechanistic" and react negatively to the computer, actual experience has shown that clients respond positively to both computer-assisted testing (Allen & Skinner, 1987; Byers, 1981; French & Beaumont, 1987; Johnson & Johnson; 1981; Nurius, 1990a, 1990b) and computer-assisted interviewing (Byrnes & Johnson, 1981; Giannetti, 1987; Lockshin & Romanczyk, 1986; Nurius, 1990b; Sawyer et al., 1991; Space, 1981; Stout, 1981). It is important to note, however, that clients do not always perceive computer use as a positive experience. Allen and Skinner (1987) reported that 5% of clients assigned to use a computer-assisted interview refused to complete the procedure. Cruickshank (1982) stated that nervous or highly stressed clients were less likely to accept the use of computer technology.

Test Interpretation. Computer-based test interpretation (CBTI) is designed to enhance the validity and reliability of testing by providing the practitioner with an expanded and consistent knowledge base to assist in the interpretation of the test data of an individual client. The knowledge base available to the practitioner is expanded as a function of the research data and clinical experience of other practitioners that is typically included in CBTI programs. Consistency in the knowledge base available for test interpretation is achieved as a function of the standardized nature of computer functioning. *Descriptive interpretations* typically include descriptive sentences related to specific scales (Roid & Gorsuch, 1984). Moreland (1987) stated that in descriptive interpretations, scales are interpreted independently of each other and are typically cryptic in nature. *Clinician-modeled interpretations (renowned clinician type)* are designed to replicate the interpretive judgments of a single clinician who has had the most experience with the test being used (Roid & Gorsuch, 1984). *Clinician-modeled interpretations (statistical model type)* are designed to replicate the interpretive judgments of a group of experienced clinicians by creating a statistically valid model that incorporates the best consensus possible among the experts (Roid & Gorsuch, 1984). *Clinical actuarial interpretations* are designed to provide "narrative descriptions and clinical hypotheses based on the clinical research findings for particular score patterns" (Roid & Gorsuch, 1984, p. 145). Lanyon (1987) categorized CBTI into three levels:

1. The *statement* level involves data-based descriptions.
2. The *narrative* level adds expert judgment in the sequencing of interpretive statements.
3. The *decision* level adds prediction of client behavior.

Karson and O'Dell (1987) provided an example of a clinician-modeled interpretation (renowned clinician type) for the Sixteen Personality Factor Questionnaire (16PF). Butcher (1995) provided a description of clinical actuarial interpretation of the Minnesota Multiphasic Personality Inventory–2 (MMPI–2). Fowler (1987) presented a detailed discussion of the factors involved in developing a valid CBTI system.

Used appropriately, CBTI serves in a consulting role, with the practitioner integrating data from a variety of sources in the creation of an assessment report (Butcher, 1995; Krug, 1987; Sampson, 1986b; Spielberger & Piotrowski, 1990). Butcher (1987b, p. 167) stated, "It is important that computerized interpretive reports be used only in an adjunct or 'advisory' way and not as the final word."

There are several potential benefits associated with using CBTI. First, CBTI "can usually provide a more comprehensive and objective summary of relevant test-based hypotheses than the clinical practitioner has the time and resources to develop" (Butcher, 1995, p. 78). Second, CBTI is not subject to interpreter bias or extraneous circumstances (Butcher, 1987c, 1995; Nurius, 1990a). Third, rapid data processing allows reports to be used in early counseling sessions (Butcher, 1995). Fourth, CBTI systems can be used by the practitioner to organize and systematically access the rapidly growing and often extensive data bases related to popular instruments (Krug, 1987). Fifth, CBTI systems can be easily updated as new research becomes available (Krug, 1987; Vale & Keller, 1987).

Enhanced Client Integration of Assessment Data in Counseling

Computer applications are intended to be used by qualified mental health professionals as one aspect of the psychotherapeutic process. In most cases the actual CBTI report is not given to the client. The tradition in career counseling, however, has been to provide interpretive reports directly to the client. The Interpretive Report for the Strong Interest Inventory (SII; Hammer & Grutter, 1994) is an example of a CBTI report designed for direct use by clients. The report is intended to synthesize the vast amount of interpretive data on the SII, providing the client with a basic understanding of the results, steps in the decision-making process, and suggested follow-up resources. This allows the practitioner to spend additional time exploring more complicated issues. The Self-Directed Search Form R (Holland, 1994) was created to be self-administered, scored, and interpreted. The Self-Directed Search Form R computer version (Reardon & PAR Staff, 1996) attempts to improve the administration, scoring, and interpretation process, as well as to extend the instrument by adding additional diagnostic and analytical components (Reardon, 1987; Reardon & PAR Staff, 1996). The client and the practitioner both potentially benefit by having information that is more reliable and more comprehensive. The client is also potentially better prepared for test interpretation. DISCOVER for Colleges and Adults (American College Testing Program, 1996) provides a self-assessment process, prior to searching for occupational alternatives. Clients have the option of either completing an online administration of the UNIACT Interest Inventory, or inputting scores for previously administered and scored instruments. This approach directly infuses assessment into the broader career counseling process.

Generalized test interpretations further integrate assessment data into the counseling process by adding video-based technology to test interpretation. "Clients who view a generalized interpretation of test results can improve their preparation for counseling by being aware of basic terminology, concepts, and the general nature of their scores" (Sampson, 1983, p. 294). A computer-controlled videodisc is used to embed the SII in a comprehensive career guidance system (Hansen, 1986, 1987). PATHFINDER (Interactive Videosystems, Inc., 1985) incorporated the SII into a four-step career exploration and decision-making process for individuals or groups.

Enhanced Staff Efficiency and Cost-Effectiveness

In comparison with traditional methods, computer-assisted testing and assessment tends to be more cost-effective (Butcher, 1987c; Byers, 1981; Byrnes & Johnson, 1981; Elwood, 1972; Hudson et al., 1988; Johnson & Johnson, 1981; Kaplan, Proditty, & Dover, 1991; Klinger, Miller, Johnson, & Williams, 1977; Nurius, 1990a; Space, 1981; Stout, 1981). Krug (1987) estimated that 15 to 50% of total testing time may be saved as a result of using computer technology. Baer, Brown-Beasley, Sorce, and Henriques (1993) found a computer-assisted interview administered via telephone to be valid, convenient, and cost-effective. Computer applications generally can improve the time utilization of support staff, and thus contribute to cost-effectiveness by increasing the number of tests and structured interviews that can be administered. Practitioners can also prepare for a test interpretation with a client or write a test report in a more timely manner.

Optical scanning or clerical staff input of item responses may result in the greatest cost-effectiveness when large numbers of tests are administered. Baskin (1990), Duthie (1984), Moreland (1987) and Space (1981) cautioned that online test administration reduces the availability of the computer to support other functions such as record keeping or word processing.

POTENTIAL PROBLEMS ASSOCIATED WITH COMPUTER APPLICATIONS

The potential problems of using computer applications in support of testing and assessment can be conceptualized into two general areas: (a) threats to validity and reliability (administration and scoring, test interpretation, ethical issues as well as ethical standards), and (b) ineffective implementation.

Threats to Validity and Reliability

Factors related to administration and scoring, test interpretation, and ethics have the potential to undermine the validity and reliability of the testing and assessment process.

Administration and Scoring. Although a number of studies have demonstrated the equivalence of results obtained from paper-and-pencil and computer-assisted administration (Beaumont & French, 1987; Booth-Kewley, Edwards, & Rosenfeld, 1992; Davis & Morse, 1991; Davis, Hoffman, Morse, & Luehr, 1992; Hansen, 1987; Kapes & Vansickle, 1992; Reardon & Loughead, 1988; Roper et al., 1991; Sawyer et al., 1991; Simola & Holden, 1992; Vansickle & Kapes, 1993; Wilson, Thompson & Wylie, 1982), other studies have shown that the difference in administration modalities affects the results obtained (Allred & Harris, 1984; Beaumont & French, 1987; Watson et al., 1990; Watson, Thomas, & Anderson, 1992). The validity of the testing and assessment process is compromised when the norms developed from paper-and-pencil administrations are applied to computer-assisted administrations, when in fact the method used may influence the results obtained (Duthie, 1984). In general, the existing literature suggests that traditional and computer administration tend to be equivalent more often than not (Hofer & Green, 1985; Moreland, 1987; Roid, 1984). The fact, however, that some data exist to the contrary suggests that each instrument needs to be examined individually to clearly establish equivalency and that blanket assumptions of equivalency are unwarranted (French, 1986). Hofer and Green (1985) provided guidelines for determining equivalency.

Another threat to validity and reliability involves scoring errors. Although it is true that computer-assisted testing has the potential to virtually eliminate scoring errors, it would be inappropriate to assume that this is automatically the case. Most (1987) stated, "The computer itself does not contribute error, but the complex nature of computer programming and the difficulty involved in reading computer programs or code makes it easy to make program errors which are difficult to find" (p. 377). Specific problems include incorrect weighting of items into scales, incorrect scoring of correctly weighted items, inaccurate algorithms, and cutting-scores that are so far apart that real differences are masked (Most, 1987). These problems are confounded by the common perceptions of the inherent credibility and infallibility of computers (Baskin, 1990; Ben-Porath & Butcher, 1986; Eberly & Cech, 1986; Elwork & Gutkin, 1985; Herr & Best, 1984; Hudson et al., 1988; Lister, 1970; Matarazzo, 1983; Turkington, 1984). It is often automatically assumed that if the output is computer generated, then it is necessarily accurate, when in fact this may not be true.

Computer administration of tests does not eliminate the need for professional involvement in the test administration process. Styles (1991) found that children and adolescents completing a computer-based measure of intellectual development experienced misunderstandings of instructions and items that required clarification from a professional. Styles also noted that impulsivity, general mood and demeanor, lack of concentration, and anxiety were potential threats to the validity of test results and required a trained observer who could intervene or at least incorporate these observations into an assessment report. Erdman and Foster (1988) noted that efforts to ensure that test takers are familiar with, and able to complete, a computer-assisted test may be particularly important for various client populations with limited computer experience.

Test Interpretation. Research validating CBTI has typically involved customer satisfaction studies and external criterion studies (Moreland, 1985). In one external criterion study, Eyde and Kowal (1987) found differences among MMPI CBTI reports from different software developers, as well as differences between the CBTI reports and the conclusion reached by a clinical interviewer. Eyde, Kowal, and Fishburne (1987) presented comparative data from seven MMPI CBTI reports that varied considerably in the type of output produced. Baskin (1990) noted that some CBTI reports contain obvious contradictory statements. Matarazzo (1986a) questioned the appropriateness of CBTI due to validity questions. Eyde and Kowal (1987) stated:

> Buyers should be aware of the limitations of computer products and remind themselves that computer output is only as good as the data behind the decision rules used to produce the interpretation. In the final analysis, these computer test interpretations cannot be expected to function as more than a signal to the test user regarding possible psychological problems or as corroboration of problems detected by other means (p. 407).

Butcher (1995) noted that the computer may be perceived as adding a level of scientific precision to test interpretation that is in fact unwarranted.

> Computerized psychological test results can lure individuals into feeling satisfied that they are finding out the most important and most accurate information about patients. However, the results provided by computers can be trivial, irrelevant, meaningless, or downright wrong. Keep in mind that one could program computers to generate nonsense syllables or horoscopes that have no empirical foundation or predictive value. Any report based on weak or meaningless data will be equally weak and meaningless (p. 91).

In a study of attitudes toward computer-based testing, Spielberger and Piotrowski (1990) found that although many practitioners found this technology useful in service delivery, CBTI narratives were a cause for concern. For a detailed analysis of the issue of CBTI validity see Erdman and Foster

(1988), Eyde (1987), Eyde and Kowal (1985, 1987), Eyde et al. (1987), Fowler and Butcher (1986), Matarazzo (1983, 1985, 1986a, 1986b, 1987), Moreland (1985), Murphy (1987), and Vale and Keller (1987).

Butcher (1995, p. 80) provided the following questions to consider in evaluating the adequacy of CBTI:

- Does the test on which the computer interpretation system is based have an adequate network of established validity research?
- Do the system developers have the requisite experience with the particular test(s) to provide reliable, valid information?
- Is there a sufficient amount of documentation available on the system of interest? Is there a published user's guide to explain the test and system variables?
- Is the system flexible enough to incorporate new information as it becomes available? How frequently is the system revised to incorporate new empirical data on the test?
- Was the interpretation system developed following the APA guidelines for computer-based tests?
- Do the reports contain a sufficient evaluation of potentially invalidating response conditions?
- How closely does the system conform to empirically validated test correlates? Is it possible to determine from the outputs whether the reports are consistent with interpretive strategies and information from published resources on the test?
- Does the company providing computer interpretation services have a qualified technical staff to deal with questions or problems?
- Are the reports sufficiently annotated to indicate appropriate cautions?

Farrell (1984) also provided specific criteria for determining when a CBTI system is ready for general use. The *Guidelines for Computer-Based Tests and Interpretations* (American Psychological Association, 1986), Conoley, Plake, and Kemmerer (1991), and Eyde et al. (1987) include similar evaluative criteria. In conducting validation research and preparing software reviews, it is essential that the purpose, theoretical basis, design assumptions, and formative analysis of the software serve as an evaluation standard (for examples of this type of literature see Baskin, 1990; Butcher, 1987b; Giannetti, 1987; Hansen, 1987; Krug, 1987; Reardon, 1987). Krug (1987) and Moreland (1985) presented additional suggestions for conducting CBTI validation studies.

The best way to improve the quality of CBTI reports is to exert economic pressure on developers and publishers. If practitioners consistently apply the evaluative criteria suggested by the *Guidelines for Computer-Based Tests and Interpretations* (American Psychological Association, 1986), Butcher

(1995), and Farrell (1984) as a condition of purchase, then the general quality of CBTI would gradually improve in response to market forces.

Ethical Issues. The potential for misuse of psychological testing has existed for some time (Ben-Porath & Butcher, 1986). The difficulties inherent in comprehending obtuse score profile forms, voluminous code books, and complicated decision rules previously served as an inherent deterrent to misuse of assessment instruments, such as the MMPI (Sampson, 1986b). These inherent deterrents have been removed with the advent of CBTI reports that explain the meaning of various test results in relatively clear unambiguous language. Practitioners may now erroneously conclude that CBTI systems can be used to "expand" the range of services they provide by offsetting their lack of training and experience. This type of misuse is likely to involve unqualified users—for example, individuals lacking training and experience in psychological assessment (Goodyear & Sinnett, 1984; Zachary & Pope, 1984)—and unsophisticated users, such as individuals who have general training in assessment but lack background in a specific test (Zachary & Pope, 1984). Meier and Geiger (1986) further explored the relationship between training issues and professional competence.

An issue related to the misuse just described involves practitioner dependence on computer-assisted testing and assessment. This author has previously stated (Sampson, 1986b):

> Practitioners who are confident of their skills and who wish to extend their abilities and the quality of the services that they provide will likely make good use of this technology. Practitioners who are inadequately trained, overworked, or unsure of their skills will be more likely to use this technology to compensate for their lack of training, time, or ability and, as a result, retard their growth as therapists and further detract from their self-concept as a competent counseling psychologist. It is also quite likely that the quality of services provided by such practitioners will be inadequate because of the inability of computer applications to compensate for the human aspects of the counseling process. (p. 571)

Expert and decision support systems (DSS) have the potential to improve the quality of CBTI or to exacerbate problems of practitioner dependence on technology. Expert systems and DSS provide an important opportunity to gain "second opinions" concerning the conclusions reached by a practitioner about the nature of client problems and potentially effective counseling strategies. Vale and Keller (1987, p. 66) stated that "An expert system is a knowledge-based reasoning program that emulates the work of a human expert to solve complex problems in a narrow domain." An important characteristic of an expert system is the capacity to interactively explain to the user the process used to reach a particular decision (Eyde, 1987; Waterman, 1986). As stated earlier, the computer serves a consulting function, with the practitioner having final responsibility for communicating test results (Butcher, 1987b; Krug, 1987; Sampson, 1986b). As expert systems and DSS become more sophisticated, there is a danger that practitioners will be even less willing to reach conclusions differing from systems that grow increasingly sophisticated and complicated. Butcher (1995, p. 91) noted that practitioners "who become overly enthralled with the marvels of computer-based test results may have difficulty questioning whether interpretations are appropriate or sufficiently tied to research." Conoley et al. (1991) observed that CBTI decision rules are often not communicated to the practitioner, which may encourage uninformed acceptance of computer-based interpretations. As CBTI systems become more complex, only highly trained practitioners would be capable of corroborating the judgments presented in the CBTI report. The insufficient information available about the programmed decision rules leaves less informed practitioners with the options of either trusting or rejecting the report.

Another important ethical issue involves the qualifications necessary for appropriate use of CBTI (Baskin, 1990; Butcher, 1987c, 1995; Eyde & Kowal, 1987; Fowler, 1987; Zachary & Pope, 1984). This issue is directly related to the broader question of who should have access to tests, irrespective of the type of technology in use. Proposals for revised standards have been formulated by Eyde, Moreland, Robertson, Primoff, and Most (1988) and Moreland, Eyde, Robertson, and Primoff (1995).

As with traditional paper-and-pencil testing and assessment, not all clients are capable of providing valid item responses or integrating assessment data into the counseling and behavior change process, due to cognitive, emotional, or neurological limitations. For example, an individual in crisis may not be able to adequately respond to items presented at the computer (Cruickshank, 1982; Johnson, Godin, & Bloomquist, 1981). George, Lankford, and Wilson (1992) found that computer anxiety resulted in elevated personality test scores, potentially confounding the results. Nurius (1990a), however, noted that computers have been successfully used with client groups that some practitioners would view as inappropriate candidates, such as acute psychiatric patients, individuals at risk of suicide, clients with profound handicaps, and clients with developmental disabilities. Use of computer-assisted testing and interviewing with client groups who may be likely to experience problems should proceed only under carefully monitored conditions until sufficient data accumulate on the validity of these applications.

Even if clients have the capabilities for completing a test or structured interview, they may have unrealistic expectations as to the potential power of the computer to provide absolute "answers" (Elwork & Gutkin, 1985; Eyde & Kowal, 1985; Lister, 1970). This particular issue is more problematic for computer-based than traditional assessment approaches. For these reasons, inadequate practitioner intervention may result in inappropriate clients using computer technology due to a lack of prescreening, and client inability to effectively and realistically integrate assessment data into the counseling and behavior change process.

Additional ethical issues having a potentially negative impact on the validity of testing in the broadest sense include the confidentiality of client records stored electronically (Butcher, 1995; French, 1986; Lister, 1970; Meier & Geiger, 1986; Sampson & Pyle, 1983; Sampson et al., 1997; Space, 1981), the lack of equality of access by all members of our society to computer technology (Elwork & Gutkin, 1985; Hofer & Green, 1985; Ibrahim, 1985, Sampson et al., 1997), and unauthorized duplication of copyrighted software (Butcher, 1987c; Fowler, 1987; French, 1986).

Erdman and Foster (1988) suggested that ethical problems may also result from failure to use available computer applications. "Failure to use a computer application that can assist the clinician in providing better care may itself be unethical" (pp. 80–81). What is needed is for practitioners to use valid and reliable software with appropriate clients in an effective manner. Various ethical standards, identified in the following section, have been proposed to clarify ethical issues associated with computer-assisted testing and assessment.

Ethical Standards. As a result of increased practitioner awareness of potential ethical problems, numerous computer-related ethical standards have been proposed and adopted. The most comprehensive standards proposed to date are the Guidelines for Computer-Based Tests and Interpretations (American Psychological Association, 1986). These standards include statements regarding the practitioner's responsibilities related to computer administration and interpretation of tests, as well as statements regarding the software developer's responsibilities related to the human factors, psychometric properties, classification, validity of computer interpretation, and review of computer applications. Prior to the publication of these guidelines, individual state psychological associations provided guidance on the appropriate use of computer applications in psychological assessment, such as the Guidelines for the Use of Computerized Testing Services (Colorado Psychological Association, 1982) and Principles for Dealing With Ethics Cases Involving Computerized Assessment (Ohio Psychological Association, 1983). The British Psychological Society (Standing Committee on Test Standards, 1984) made recommendations regarding the equivalence of computer-based and traditional testing and the staff qualifications necessary for using CBTI systems.

The ethical standards of the American Counseling Association (1995) and the Code of Ethics of the National Board for Certified Counselors (1997) include specific statements regarding the confidentiality of electronically stored data, the role of the counselor in relation to client use of a computer application, professional qualifications for CBTI use, equality of access to computer technology in counseling, and verification of the validity of CBTI systems. Ethical standards have also been proposed by Roid and Gorsuch (1984), Sampson and Pyle (1983), and Walker and Myrick (1985). In addition to ethical standards, standards of preparation need to include computer-related issues to increase the likelihood that entry level professionals will be competent in the use of computer technology (Sampson & Loesch, 1985). The 1994 revision of the *Accreditation Standards* of the Council for the Accreditation of Counseling and Related Educational Programs (1994) includes the requirement that counselors-in-training have the opportunity to obtain knowledge and skills related to computer technology in counseling and assessment.

The development of ethical standards represents a crucial step forward in maximizing the appropriate use of computer technology. The standards need regular review and revision as computer hardware and software evolve and as practitioners gain additional research data and service delivery experience. Mental health professionals need to develop the attitudes and skills alluded to in the standards during their initial training. These attitudes and skills then need to be reinforced by colleagues in professional practice and further supported by continuing professional education.

Ineffective Implementation

Staff resistance is a potential barrier to effective implementation of testing and assessment software (Space, 1981). Butcher (1986) stated:

> One salient roadblock to progress in the computerized assessment area is inertia among clinical practitioners when it comes to applying novel technology. Novelty and change are scary to many people. Many individuals are comfortable with the ways and methods they learned in graduate school and they resist change. (p. 7)

One of the primary factors contributing to staff resistance involves the lack of staff participation in decision making regarding hardware and software selection. This author has previously stated (Sampson, 1983, p. 297), "The potential benefits to be gained from a system that is theoretically sound are negated when, as a result of inadequate planning and implementation, professionals resist the use of such a system."

Hammer and Hile (1985) conceptualized practitioner resistance to computer applications as involving structural or process variables. Structural variables include:

1. Interaction of individuals with computers (cognitive style differences, perceptions of client resistance, efficacy questions, and value conflict).
2. Interaction among individuals as a result of automation (goal conflict, threats to power and status, and fears of evaluation).
3. Transactions with the environment (potential legal liability and ethical concerns).

Process variables include:

1. Initial involvement of end users.
2. Acquisition problems related to time and effort.
3. Time required for implementation.
4. Timing of implementation.
5. Training required.
6. Poor quality program documentation.
7. Value conflicts and organizational preparedness.

Experience in a variety of mental health settings has shown that poor staff support for computer applications is related to insufficient organizational readiness, lack of a planned change strategy, and an inadequate methodology for effectively dealing with staff concerns (Byrnes & Johnson, 1981). A lack of communication during implementation also generally results in reduced acceptance of computer applications (Johnson & Williams, 1980). The significant time investment necessary to implement computer technology and the confusing abundance of available software (Butcher, 1987c) also contribute. Allen and Skinner (1987) reported that staff acceptance of computer technology increases as a result of direct experience with computers.

It seems clear that a barrier to effective implementation of computer technology involves interpersonal dynamics and not issues directly related to hardware and software. Careful planning, group input in decision making, and a reasonable rate of change increase the likelihood of success. Alberts (1984), Pinkerton and Raffoul (1984), and Sampson (1984) provided specific suggestions for effective implementation of computer technology. Nurius (1990b) advocated improved computer literacy training in professional preparation programs as a key element in improving professional practice.

THE FUTURE

Hardware Developments

Butcher (1986) predicted that computer–human interaction by human voice will become the dominant method for test administration. In addition to the obvious advantages for persons with many physical disabilities, natural-language processing will likely make it easier for anxious clients to use the technology, as well as those clients with limited reading skills. Considerable research, however, will be necessary to equate voice and visually administered tests. Although, at present, the computer can realistically generate the sound of a human voice, it is not possible for the computer to "recognize" the human speech of several individuals at the speed of normal conversation. The complexity involved in understanding even a simple spoken sentence is enormous when the diversity of dialects, cultural influences, speech characteristics, and the multiple meanings of individual words are taken into account.

The presentation of items via video-based stimuli has been suggested for some time (Butcher, 1986; Green, 1991; Hofer & Green, 1985; Johnson, 1984; Nurius, 1990a, 1990b), although few such systems currently exist. The increasing availability of computers with multimedia capability may stimulate the development of this type of assessment. In addition to presenting items as text, a computer with multimedia capability allows the presentation of items in audio, visual, or combined audiovisual format. The test taker can hear an item being read as well as hear other relevant auditory stimuli. For example, an interest inventory item can be read to a test taker with sounds added that are typically associated with an occupation to provide additional stimuli for recall of self and occupational knowledge. This approach provides options for individuals with visual disabilities to complete an assessment without the potentially confounding effects of a reader. The test taker can also hear and view test stimuli. For example, an interest inventory item can show an individual in a generic office setting engaging in a specific work behavior. The gender, age, race, and ethnicity of the individual represented in the test item can be made to match the test taker in order to facilitate his or her analysis of interest congruence. This approach provides the test taker with additional auditory and visual data to clarify the meaning of items. Improved understanding of test items may lead to enhanced reliability and validity because the responses of the test taker are based on more reality-based data. Irvin and Walker (1994) presented reliability and validity evidence for a prototype videodisk-based assessment of children's social skills.

Booth (1991) noted that virtual reality offers additional opportunities for test administration. Using supplemental hardware worn by the individual, the computer can generate virtual environments that can be seen by the test taker and used to present assessment stimuli. For individuals now raised in a media-intense environment, such multimedia assessment methods may result in increased client motivation to complete various measures.

The use of multimedia applications in testing and assessment may, however, create problems. First, the high cost of developing and maintaining broadcast-quality media may increase development costs to such an extent that few clients and/or organizations could afford to use the resource.

Second, extraneous auditory and visual data may distract the test taker and limit information processing. For example, if the individual depicted in the video reminds the test taker of someone he or she dislikes, this may cause a biased reaction to the stimuli that would not have occurred with traditional assessment where the test taker generates perceptions from more neutral stimuli. Third, if auditory and visual stimuli reinforce occupational, gender, age, racial, or ethnic stereotypes, the test taker may react more to the stereotype than to the actual content of the situation depicted. Substantial investment in research and development activities will be necessary to maximize the benefits and minimize the limitations of applying multimedia to testing and assessment.

The current Internet and the future information highway offer additional options for delivering testing and assessment services. Potential options include: (a) orientation to the assessment provided via computer-assisted instruction; (b) completion of tests and assessment instruments between client sessions, with reports made immediately available to the practitioner; and (c) provision of generalized test interpretations to help prepare clients for subsequent sessions with a counselor. This approach has the advantages of enhancing access to CBTI software with the latest available clinical and research data and enhancing access to less frequently used psychological assessments when it is not cost-effective to prepurchase multiple test administrations. Potential problems, however, include: (a) confidentiality, (b) delivery of invalid information, (c) lack of necessary practitioner intervention, (d) misuse by inadequately trained or overworked counselors, (e) limited practitioner awareness of important location-specific counseling variables, (f) equality of access to computer resources, (g) inadequate privacy, and (h) delivery of services by individuals without appropriate credentials (Sampson et al., 1997).

Software Developments

Expert and decision support systems have the potential to make a significant impact in terms of the delivery of assessment services and the training of mental health professionals (Sampson, 1986c; Warzecha, 1991). Expert systems will likely be integrated into testing and assessment in three ways. First, new tests will be designed with expert system elements as an integral aspect of system design (e.g., Krug, 1987). Second, expert systems will be included as an integral aspect of the assessment components of computer-assisted career guidance systems (Ballantine, 1986). Third, instruments that are supported by extensive research databases, such as the MMPI, will gradually add expert system elements to existing computer-based test interpretations. Vale (1986) proposed a specific agenda for fully integrating expert systems into CBTI. Expert and decision support systems more fully provide for the consultant role envisioned for CBTI by Butcher (1987b) and Krug (1987). These systems can also be used as a powerful training resource by allowing professionals the opportunity to query the computer as to the rationale for a particular interpretive statement.

Testing and assessment are not isolated, but rather exist within the context of the counseling and behavior change process. An elegant computer-based test interpretation is ultimately useless if the client or the practitioner cannot apply the knowledge obtained. Multimedia-based generalized test interpretations (Hansen, 1986, 1987; Sampson, 1983, 1990) and computer-assisted instruction that provides the client with clarification of the role of assessment and the procedures involved in testing (Sampson, 1986a) can help the client make better use of testing and assessment data.

Professional Practice

The current literature generally reflects two basic positions on CBTI. One position tends to focus on the potential for CBTI to improve the validity and reliability of assessment. The variable quality of the "typical" traditional assessment by a practitioner is contrasted with the current and potential future quality of computer-assisted assessment. A second position tends to focus more on the present limitations of CBTI and the potential quality of traditional assessment services provided by competent practitioners. The issue of the quality of services provided by the average practitioner is just as important as the issue of the quality of current CBTI in deciding the extent to which computer technology should be used in the assessment process. An incompetent practitioner who prepares a substandard psychological assessment is likely to be no better or worse than an incompetent practitioner who misuses a CBTI report (with the possible exception that there may be greater uncritical acceptance of CBTI reports by unqualified professionals; Butcher, 1987c). The end result is poor-quality service in both cases. Similarly, quality assessment services can currently be provided by competent practitioners with or without computer assistance. The practitioner remains the key element in determining the quality of the assessment process, irrespective of the use of computer technology.

Computer-assisted testing research and development, including CBTI and Internet applications, should continue given the potential for this technology to improve services. At the same time, careful use of CBTI, multimedia, and the Internet in service delivery should proceed, monitored by practitioners who are aware of current standards and issues. In this way, actual practice can enrich the research and development process while at the same time making available the highest quality services possible. As a result of this potentially potent mixture of research, development, and practice, computer applications can evolve that will produce computer-assisted assessment services that will indeed surpass the skills of the current competent practitioner using traditional methods. Practitioners will then have the opportunity to more fully develop the therapeutic dimensions of testing and assessment.

CONCLUSION

In one sense, computer technology has had a profound impact on the testing and assessment process. Most popular instruments used by practitioners can now be administered and scored by computer, with many of these instruments having CBTI features. The computer is now an important design consideration in the creation of new tests. In another sense, however, little empirical evidence is available to suggest that the computer is being used on any widespread basis to do a better job of helping clients understand and apply personal data to the behavior change process.

Whether or not the computer actually helps practitioners to substantially improve the quality of the test administration, scoring, and interpretation process depends more on practitioner attitudes and skills in using this technology than on future advances in computer hardware and software. The discovery of fire by early humans would have been a meaningless footnote in history if something important had not been done to make effective use of what was then "new" technology.

ACKNOWLEDGMENTS

Appreciation is expressed to Rebecca E. Ryan-Jones and Shawn M. Herbert for their assistance with the literature review and to Shawn M. Herbert, Janet G. Lenz, Robert C. Reardon, and Sandra M. Sampson for their review of an initial draft of this chapter.

REFERENCES

Alberts, F. L. (1984). Microcomputers in clinical practice: Preparing and involving office personnel. In M. D. Schwartz (Ed.), *Using computers in clinical practice: Psychotherapy and mental health applications* (pp. 69–73). New York: Haworth Press.

Allen, B., & Skinner, H. A. (1987). Lifestyle assessment using microcomputers. In J. N. Butcher (Ed.), *Computerized psychological assessment: A practitioner's guide* (pp. 108–123). New York: Basic Books.

Allred, L. J., & Harris, W. G. (1984). *The non-equivalence of computerized and conventional administrations of the Adjective Checklist*. Unpublished manuscript, Johns Hopkins University, Department of Psychology, Baltimore, MD.

Altemose, J. R., & Williamson, K. B. (1981). Clinical judgment vs. the computer: Can the school psychologist be replaced by a machine? *Psychology in the Schools, 18*, 356–363.

American College Testing Program. (1996). DISCOVER for colleges and adults [Computer program]. Hunt Valley, MD: Author.

American Counseling Association. (1995). *Code of ethics and standards of practice*. Alexandria, VA: Author.

American Educational Research Association, American Psychological Association, & National Council on Measurement in Education. (1985). *Standards for educational and psychological testing*. Washington, DC: American Psychological Association.

American Personnel and Guidance Association. (1980). *APGA policy statement: Responsibilities of users of standardized tests*. Washington, DC: Author.

American Psychological Association. (1986). *Guidelines for computer-based tests and interpretations*. Washington, DC: Author.

Baer, L., Brown-Beasley, M. W., Sorce, J., & Henriques, A. I. (1993). Computer-assisted telephone administration of a structured interview for obsessive-compulsive disorder. *American Journal of Psychiatry, 150*, 1737–1738.

Ballantine, M. (1986). Computer-assisted careers guidance systems as decision support systems. *British Journal of Guidance and Counseling, 14*, 21–32.

Baskin, D. (Ed.). (1990). *Computer applications in psychiatry and psychology*. New York: Brunner/Mazel.

Beaumont, J. G., & French, C. F. (1987). A clinical field study of eight automated psychometric procedures: The Leicester/DHSS Project. *International Journal of Man-Machine Studies, 26*, 661–682.

Ben-Porath, Y. S., & Butcher, J. N. (1986). Computers in personality assessment: A brief past, an ebullient present and an expanding future. *Computers in Human Behavior, 2*, 167–182.

Bleuer, J., & Walz, G. R. (1983). *Counselors and computers*. Ann Arbor: ERIC/CAPS, University of Michigan.

Booth, J. (1991). The key to valid computer-based testing: The user interface. *European Review of Applied Psychology, 41*, 281–293.

Booth-Kewley, S., Edwards, J. E., & Rosenfeld, P. (1992). Impression management, social desirability, and computer administration of attitude questionnaires: Does the computer make a difference? *Journal of Applied Psychology, 77*, 562–566.

Bridges, M. (Ed.). (1988). *Guidance and counseling directory of microcomputer software* (Vols. 1 & 2). San Jose, CA: Department of Career/Vocational Education and Guidance, Santa Clara County Office of Education.

Burkhead, E. J., & Sampson, J. P., Jr. (1985). Computer-assisted assessment in support of the rehabilitation process. *Rehabilitation Counseling Bulletin, 28*, 262–274.

Butcher, J. N. (1986, August). Future directions in computerized psychological assessment procedures: The psychological clinic in the year 2001. In J. N. Butcher (Chair), *Future directions in computerized psychological assessment: Psychological clinics—Year 2000*. Symposium conducted at the meeting of the American Psychological Association, Washington, DC.

Butcher, J. N. (1987a). Commercially available computerized psychological software and services. In J. N. Butcher (Ed.), *Computerized psychological assessment: A practitioner's guide* (pp. 367–412). New York: Basic Books.

Butcher, J. N. (1987b). Computerized clinical and personality assessment using the MMPI. In J. N. Butcher (Ed.), *Computerized psychological assessment: A practitioner's guide* (pp. 161–197). New York: Basic Books.

Butcher, J. N. (1987c). The use of computers in psychological assessment: An overview of practices and issues. In J. N. Butcher (Ed.), *Computerized psychological assessment: A practitioner's guide* (pp. 3–14). New York: Basic Books.

Butcher, J. N. (1995). How to use computer-based reports. In J. N. Butcher (Ed.), *Clinical personality assessment: Practical approaches* (pp. 78–94). New York: Oxford University Press.

Byers, A. P. (1981). Psychological evaluation by means of an on-line computer. *Behavior Research Methods & Instrumentation, 13*, 585–587.

Byrnes, E., & Johnson, J. H. (1981). Change technology and the implementation of automation in mental health care settings. *Behavior Research Methods & Instrumentation, 13*, 573–580.

Canoune, H. L., & Leyhe, E. W. (1985). Human versus computer interviewing. *Journal of Personality Assessment, 49*, 103–106.

Colorado Psychological Association. (1982). *Guidelines for the use of computerized testing services.* Denver, CO: Author.

Conoley, C. W., Plake, B. S., & Kemmerer, B. E. (1991). Issues in computer-based test interpretive systems. *Computers in Human Behavior, 7*, 97–101.

Council for the Accreditation of Counseling and Related Educational Programs. (1994). *CACREP accreditation standards and procedures manual.* Alexandria, VA: Author.

Cruickshank, P. J. (1982). Patient stress and the computer in the consulting room. *Social Science and Medicine, 16*, 1371–1376.

Davis, L. J., Hoffmann, N. G., Morse, R. M., & Luehr, J. G. (1992). Substance use disorder diagnostic schedule (SUDDS): The equivalence and validity of a computer-administered and an interviewer-administered format. *Alcoholism Clinical and Experimental Research, 16*, 250–254.

Davis, L. J., & Morse, R. M. (1991). Self-administered alcoholism screening test: A comparison of conventional versus computer-administered formats. *Alcoholism Clinical and Experimental Research, 15*, 155–157.

Denner, S. (1977). Automated psychological testing. *British Journal of Social and Clinical Psychology, 16*, 175–179.

Duthie, B. (1984). A critical examination of computer-administered psychological tests. In M. D. Schwartz (Ed.), *Using computers in clinical practice: Psychotherapy and mental health applications* (pp. 135–139). New York: Haworth Press.

Eberly, C. G., & Cech, E. J. (1986). Integrating computer-assisted testing and assessment into the counseling process. *Measurement and Evaluation in Counseling and Development, 19*, 18–26.

Elwood, D. L. (1972). Test-retest reliability and cost analyses of automated face-to-face intelligence testing. *International Journal of Man-Machine Studies, 4*, 1–22.

Elwork, A., & Gutkin, T. B. (1985). The behavioral sciences in the computer age. *Computers and Human Behavior, 1*, 3–18.

Erdman, H. P., & Foster, S. W. (1988). Ethical issues in the use of computer-based assessment. In J. W. Murphy & J. T. Pardeck (Eds.), *Technology and human service delivery: Challenges and a critical perspective* (pp. 71–87). New York: Haworth Press.

Erdman, H. P., Klein, M. H., & Greist, J. H. (1985). Direct patient computer interviewing. *Journal of Consulting and Clinical Psychology, 53*, 760–773.

Eyde, L. D. (1987). Computerised psychological testing: An introduction. *Applied Psychology: An International Review, 36*(3/4), 223–235.

Eyde, L. D., & Kowal, D. M. (1985). Psychological decision support software for the public: Pros, cons, and guidelines. *Computers and Human Behavior, 1*, 321–336.

Eyde, L. D., & Kowal, D. M. (1987). Computerised test interpretation services: Ethical and professional concerns regarding U.S. producers and users. *Applied Psychology: An International Review, 36*(3/4), 401–417.

Eyde, L. D., Kowal, D. M., & Fishburne, F. J., Jr. (1987, September). Clinical implications of validity research on computer-based test interpretation of the MMPI. In A. D. Mangelsdorf (Chair), *Practical test user problems facing psychologists in private practice.* Symposium conducted at the meeting of the American Psychological Association, New York.

Eyde, L. D., Moreland, K. L., Robertson, G. J., Primoff, E. S., & Most, R. B. (1988). *Test user qualifications: A data-based approach to promoting good test use.* Washington, DC: Scientific Affairs Office, American Psychological Association.

Farrell, A. D. (1984). When is a computerized assessment system ready for distribution? Some standards for evaluation. In M. D. Schwartz (Ed.), *Using computers in clinical practice: Psychotherapy and mental health applications* (pp. 185–189). New York: Haworth Press.

Flowers, J. V., Booraem, C. D., & Schwartz, B. (1993). Impact of computerized rapid assessment instruments on counselors and client outcome. *Computers in Human Services, 10*(2), 9–18.

Fowler, R. D. (1987). Developing a computer-based test interpretation system. In J. N. Butcher (Ed.), *Computerized psychological assessment: A practitioner's guide* (pp. 50–63). New York: Basic Books.

Fowler, R. D., & Butcher, J. N. (1986). Critique of Matarazzo's views on computerized testing: All sigma and no meaning. *American Psychologist, 41*, 94–96.

Fowler, R. D., & Butcher, J. N. (1987). International applications of computer-based testing and interpretation. *Applied Psychology: An International Review, 36*(3/4), 419–429.

French, C. F. (1986). Microcomputers and psychometric assessment. *British Journal of Guidance and Counseling, 14*, 33–45.

French, C. F., & Beaumont, J. G. (1987). The reaction of psychiatric patients to computerized assessment. *British Journal of Clinical Psychology, 26*, 267–278.

George, C. E., Lankford, J. S., & Wilson, S. E. (1992). The effects of computerized versus paper-and-pencil administration on measures of negative affect. *Computers in Human Behavior, 8*, 203–209.

Giannetti, R. A. (1987). The GOLPH Psychological History: Response-contingent data acquisition and reporting. In J. N. Butcher (Ed.), *Computerized psychological assessment: A practitioner's guide* (pp. 124–144). New York: Basic Books.

Goodyear, R. K., & Sinnett, E. R. (1984). Current and emerging ethical issues for counseling psychologists. *Counseling Psychologist, 12*(3), 87–98.

Green, B. F. (1991). Computer-based adaptive testing in 1991. *Psychology & Marketing, 8*, 243–257.

Hammer, A. L., & Grutter, J. (1994). *Strong Interest Inventory interpretive report.* Palo Alto, CA: Consulting Psychologists Press.

Hammer, A. L., & Hile, M. G. (1985). Factors in clinicians' resistance to automation in mental health. *Computers in Human Services, 1*(3), 1–25.

Hansen, J. C. (1977). Evaluation of accuracy and consistency of machine scoring of the SCII. *Measurement and Evaluation in Guidance, 10*, 141–143.

Hansen, J. C. (1986). Computers and beyond in the decision-making process. *Measurement and Evaluation in Counseling and Development, 19*, 48–52.

Hansen, J. C. (1987). Computer-assisted interpretation of the Strong Interest Inventory. In J. N. Butcher (Ed.), *Computerized psychological assessment: A practitioner's guide* (pp. 292–321). New York: Basic Books.

Herr, E. L., & Best, P. (1984). Computer technology and counseling: The role of the profession. *Journal of Counseling and Development, 63*, 192–195.

Hofer, P. J., & Green, B. F. (1985). The challenge of competence and creativity in computerized psychological testing. *Journal of Consulting and Clinical Psychology, 53*, 826–838.

Holland, J. L. (1994). *Self-directed search.* Odessa, FL: Psychological Assessment Resources.

Hudson, W. W., Nurius, P. S., & Reisman, S. (1988). Computerized assessment instruments: Their promise and problems. In J. W. Murphy & J. T. Pardeck (Eds.), *Technology and human service delivery: Challenges and a critical perspective* (pp. 51–70). New York: Haworth.

Ibrahim, F. A. (1985). Human rights and ethical issues in the use of advanced technology. *Journal of Counseling and Development, 64*, 134–135.

Interactive Videosystems, Inc. (1985). *PATHFINDER: A career decision process.* Minneapolis, MN: Author.

Irvin, L. K., & Walker, H. M. (1994). Assessing children's social skills using video-based microcomputer technology. *Exceptional Children, 61*, 182–196.

Johnson, J. H. (1984). An overview of computerized testing. In M. D. Schwartz (Ed.), *Using computers in clinical practice: Psychotherapy and mental health applications* (pp. 131–133). New York: Haworth Press.

Johnson, J. H., Godin, S. W., & Bloomquist, M. L. (1981). Human factors engineering in computerized mental health care delivery. *Behavior Research Methods & Instrumentation, 13*, 425–429.

Johnson, J. H., & Johnson, K. N. (1981). Psychological considerations related to the development of computerized testing stations. *Behavior Research Methods & Instrumentation, 13*, 421–424.

Johnson, J. H., & Williams, T. A. (1980). Using on-line computer technology to improve service response and decision-making effectiveness in a mental health admitting system. In J. B. Sidowski, J. H. Johnson, & T. A. Williams (Eds.), *Technology in mental health care delivery systems* (pp. 237–249). Norwood, NJ: Ablex.

Kapes, J. T., & Vansickle, T. R. (1992). Comparing paper-pencil and computer-based versions of the Harrington–O'Shea Career Decision Making System. *Measurement and Evaluation in Counseling and Development, 25*, 5–13.

Kaplan, E., Proditty, S., & Dover, S. (1991). ComPsy: A modular-integrated answer to the differential demands of a computerized testing system. *European Review of Applied Psychology, 41*, 303–306.

Karson, S., & O'Dell, J. W. (1987). Computer-based interpretation of the 16PF: The Karson Clinical Report in contemporary practice. In J. N. Butcher (Ed.), *Computerized psychological assessment: A practitioner's guide* (pp. 198–217). New York: Basic Books.

Klinger, D. E., Miller, D. A. Johnson, J. H., & Williams, T. A. (1977). Process evaluation of an on-line computer-assisted unit for intake assessment of mental health patients. *Behavior Research Methods & Instrumentation, 9*, 110–116.

Krug, S. E. (1987). Microtrends: An orientation to computerized assessment. In J. N. Butcher (Ed.), *Computerized psychological assessment: A practitioner's guide* (pp. 15–25). New York: Basic Books.

Krug, S. E. (1993). *Psychware sourcebook* (4th ed.). Champaign, IL: MetriTech.

Lanyon, R. I. (1987). The validity of computer-based personality assessment products: Recommendations for the future. *Computers in Human Behavior, 3*, 225–238.

Levitan, R. D., Blouin, A. G., Navaro, J. R., & Hill, J. (1991). Validity of the computerized DIS for diagnosing psychiatric inpatients. *Canadian Journal of Psychiatry, 36*, 728–731.

Lister, C. (1970). Privacy and large-scale personal data systems. *Personnel and Guidance Journal, 49*, 207–211.

Lockshin, S., & Romanczyk, R. G. (1986). Assessment and diagnosis. In R. G. Romanczyk (Ed.), *Clinical utilization of microcomputer technology* (pp. 57–69). New York: Pergamon Press.

Loesch, L. C. (1986). Computer-assisted assessment: A reaction to Meier and Geiger. *Measurement and Evaluation in Counseling and Development, 19*, 35–37.

Lucas, R. W., Mullins, P. J., Luna, C. B. X., & McInroy, D. C. (1977). Psychiatrists and a computer as interrogators of patients with alcohol-related diseases: A comparison. *British Journal of Psychiatry, 131*, 160–167.

Madsen, D. H. (1986). Computer applications for test administration and scoring. *Measurement and Evaluation in Counseling and Development, 19*, 6–14.

Matarazzo, J. D. (1983, July). Computerized psychological testing. *Science, 221*, 323.

Matarazzo, J. D. (1985). Clinical psychological test interpretations by computer: Hardware outpaces software. *Computers in Human Behavior, 1*, 235–253.

Matarazzo, J. D. (1986a). Computerized clinical psychological test interpretation: Unvalidated plus all mean and no sigma. *American Psychologist, 41*, 14–25.

Matarazzo, J. D. (1986b). Response to Fowler and Butcher on Matarazzo. *American Psychologist, 41*, 96.

Matarazzo, J. D. (1987). Response to Murphy on Matarazzo. *American Psychologist, 42*, 193–194.

Meier, S. T., & Geiger, S. M. (1986). Implications of computer-assisted testing and assessment for professional practice and training. *Measurement and Evaluation in Counseling and Development, 19*, 29–34.

Meier, S. T., & Wick, M. T. (1991). Computer-based unobtrusive measurement: Potential supplements to reactive self-reports. *Professional Psychology Research and Practice, 22*, 410–412.

Merrell, K. W. (1986). Computer use in psychometric assessment: Evaluating benefits and potential problems. *Computers in Human Services, 1*(3), 59–67.

Moreland, K. L. (1985). Validation of computer-based test interpretations: Problems and prospects. *Journal of Consulting and Clinical Psychology, 53*, 816–825.

Moreland, K. L. (1987). Computerized psychological assessment: What's available. In J. N. Butcher (Ed.), *Computerized psychological assessment: A practitioner's guide* (pp. 26–49). New York: Basic Books.

Moreland, K. L. (1990). Some observations on computer-assisted psychological testing. *Journal of Personality Assessment, 55*, 820–823.

Moreland, K. L., Eyde, L. D., Robertson, G. J., & Primoff, E. S. (1995). Assessment of test user qualifications: A research-based measurement procedure. *American Psychologist, 50*, 14–23.

Most, R. (1987). Levels of error in computerized psychological inventories. *Applied Psychology: An International Review, 36*(3/4), 375–383.

Murphy, K. R. (1987). The accuracy of clinical versus computerized test interpretations. *American Psychologist, 42*, 192–193.

National Board for Certified Counselors. (1997). *Code of ethics.* Alexandria, VA: Author.

Nurius, P. S. (1990a). A review of automated assessment. *Computers in Human Services, 6*, 265–281.

Nurius, P. S. (1990b). Computer literacy in automated assessment: Challenges and future directions. *Computers in Human Services, 6*, 283–297.

Ohio Psychological Association. (1983). *Principles for dealing with ethics cases involving computerized assessment.* Columbus, OH: Author.

Pinkerton, G. L., & Raffoul, P. R. (1984). Professional colleagues: Confronting the attitudes of professionals toward microcomputers. In M. D. Schwartz (Ed.), *Using computers in clinical practice: Psychotherapy and mental health applications* (pp. 61–66). New York: Haworth Press.

Reardon, R. C. (1987). Development of the computer version of the Self-Directed Search. *Measurement and Evaluation in Counseling and Development, 20*, 62–67.

Reardon, R. C., & PAR Staff. (1996). Self-Directed Search Form R computer version [Computer program]. Odessa, FL: Psychological Assessment Resources.

Reardon, R. C., & Loughead, T. A. (1988). A comparison of paper–pencil and computer versions of the Self-Directed Search. *Journal of Counseling and Development, 67*, 249–252.

Roid, G. H. (1984). Computer technology in testing. In B. S. Plake & J. C. Witt (Eds.), *The future of testing: The Second Buros-Nebraska Symposium on Measurement and Testing* (pp.). Hillsdale, NJ: Lawrence Erlbaum Associates.

Roid, G. H., & Gorsuch, R. L. (1984). Development and clinical use of test-interpretive programs on microcomputers. In M. D. Schwartz (Ed.), *Using computers in clinical practice: Psychotherapy and mental health applications* (pp. 141–149). New York: Haworth Press.

Roper, B. L., Ben-Porath, Y. S., & Butcher, J. N. (1991). Comparability of computerized adaptive and conventional testing with the MMPI-2. *Journal of Personality Assessment, 57*, 278–290.

Sampson, J. P., Jr. (1983). Computer-assisted testing and assessment: Current status and implications for the future. *Measurement and Evaluation in Guidance, 15*(4), 293–299.

Sampson, J. P., Jr. (1984). Maximizing the effectiveness of computer applications in counseling and human development: The role of research and implementation strategies. *Journal of Counseling and Development, 63*, 187–191.

Sampson, J. P., Jr. (1986a). The use of computer-assisted instruction in support of psychotherapeutic processes. *Computers in Human Behavior, 2*, 1–19.

Sampson, J. P., Jr. (1986b). Computer technology and counseling psychology: Regression toward the machine? *Counseling Psychologist, 14*, 567–583.

Sampson, J. P., Jr. (1986c). Computer-assisted testing and assessment: Matching the tool to the task. *Measurement and Evaluation in Counseling and Development, 19*, 60–61.

Sampson, J. P., Jr. (1987). "Computer-assisted" or "computerized": What's in a name? *Journal of Counseling and Development, 66,* 116–118.

Sampson, J. P., Jr. (1990). Computer-assisted testing and the goals of counseling psychology. *Counseling Psychologist, 18,* 227–239.

Sampson, J. P., Jr., Kolodinsky, R. W., & Greeno, B. P. (1997). Counseling on the information highway: Future possibilities and potential problems. *Journal of Counseling and Development, 75,* 203–212.

Sampson, J. P., Jr., & Loesch, L. C. (1985). Computer preparation standards for counselors and human development specialists. *Journal of Counseling and Development, 64,* 31–33.

Sampson, J. P., Jr., & Pyle, K. R. (1983). Ethical issues involved with the use of computer-assisted counseling, testing and guidance systems. *Personnel and Guidance Journal, 61,* 283–287.

Sawyer, M. G., Sarris, A., & Baghurst, P. (1991). The use of a computer-assisted interview to administer the Child Behavior Checklist in a child psychiatry service. *Journal of the American Academy of Child and Adolescent Psychiatry, 30,* 674–681.

Schwartz, M. D. (1984). People in the organization: The effects of computer-mediated work on individuals and organizations (a review). In M. D. Schwartz (Ed.), *Using computers in clinical practice: Psychotherapy and mental health applications* (pp. 55–59). New York: Haworth Press.

Simola, S. K., & Holden, R. R. (1992). Equivalence of computerized and standard administration of the Piers–Harris Children's Self-Concept Scale. *Journal of Personality Assessment, 58,* 287–294.

Slack, W. V., & Slack, C. W. (1977). Talking to a computer about emotional problems: A comparative study. *Psychotherapy: Theory, Research and Practice, 14,* 156–164.

Space, L. G. (1981). The computer as psychometrician. *Behavior Research Methods & Instrumentation, 13,* 595–606.

Spielberger, C. D., & Piotrowski, C. (1990). Clinician's attitudes toward computer-based testing. *The Clinical Psychologist, 43,* 60–63.

Standing Committee on Test Standards. (1984). Note on the computerization of printed psychological tests and questionnaires. *Bulletin of the British Psychological Society, 37,* 416–417.

Stoloff, M. L., & Couch, J. V. (Eds.). (1992). *Computer use in psychology: A directory of software* (3rd ed.). Washington, DC: American Psychological Association.

Stout, R. L. (1981). New approaches to the design of computerized interviewing and testing systems. *Behavior Research Methods & Instrumentation, 13,* 436–442.

Styles, I. (1991). Clinical assessment and computerized testing. *International Journal of Man Machine Studies, 35,* 133–150.

Turkington, C. (1984). The growing use, and abuse, of computer testing. *APA Monitor, 15*(1), 7–26.

Vale, C. D. (1981). Design and implementation of a micro-computer based adaptive testing system. *Behavior Research Methods & Instrumentation, 13,* 399–406.

Vale, C. D. (1986, August). The computer technology of psychology in the year 2000. In J. N. Butcher (Chair), *Future directions in computerized psychological assessment: Psychological clinics—Year 2000.* Symposium conducted at the meeting of the American Psychological Association, Washington, DC.

Vale, C. D., & Keller, L. S. (1987). Developing expert computer systems to interpret psychological tests. In J. N. Butcher (Ed.), *Computerized psychological assessment: A practitioner's guide* (pp. 64–83). New York: Basic Books.

Vansickle, T. R., & Kapes, J. T. (1993). Comparing paper-pencil and computer-based versions of the Strong-Campbell Interest Inventory. *Computers in Human Behavior, 9,* 441–449.

Walker, N. W., & Myrick, C. C. (1985). Ethical considerations in the use of computers in psychological testing and assessment. *Journal of School Psychology, 23,* 51–57.

Walz, G. R. (1984). The computer: Counselor enhancement or eclipse? *CAPS Capsule,* No. 2.

Walz, G. R., Bleuer, J. C., & Maze, M. (Eds.). (1989). *Counseling software guide: A resource for the guidance and human development professions.* Alexandria, VA: American Association for Counseling and Development.

Ward, W. C. (1984). Using microcomputers to administer tests. *Educational Measurement: Issues and Practice, 3*(2), 16–20.

Warzecha, G. (1991). The challenge to psychological assessment from modern computer technology. *European Review of Applied Psychology, 41*, 213–220.

Waterman, D. A. (1986). *A guide to expert systems.* Reading, MA: Addison-Wesley.

Watson, C. G., Manifold, V., Klett, W. G., Brown, J., Thomas, D., & Anderson, D. (1990). Comparability of computer-and booklet-administered Minnesota Multiphasic Personality Inventories among primarily chemically dependent patients. *Psychological Assessment, 2*, 276–280.

Watson, C. G., Thomas, D., & Anderson, P. E. D. (1992). Do computer-administered Minnesota Multiphasic Personality Inventories underestimate booklet-based scores? *Journal of Clinical Psychology, 48*, 744–748.

Weiss, D. J., & Vale, C. D. (1987). Computerized adaptive testing for measuring abilities and other psychological variables. In J. N. Butcher (Ed.), *Computerized psychological assessment: A practitioner's guide* (pp. 325–343). New York: Basic Books.

Wilson, S. L., Thompson, J. A., & Wylie, G. (1982). Automated psychological testing for the severely physically handicapped. *International Journal of Man-Machine Studies, 17*, 291–296.

Zachary, R. A., & Pope, K. S. (1984). Legal and ethical issues in the clinical use of computerized testing. In M. D. Schwartz (Ed.), *Using computers in clinical practice: Psychotherapy and mental health applications* (pp. 151–164). New York: Haworth Press.

CONCLUSION

15

Some Final Thoughts About Using Tests and Assessment Procedures in Counseling

C. Edward Watkins, Jr.
University of North Texas

In this concluding chapter, I would like to provide some final thoughts about the use of tests and assessment procedures in counseling. This chapter presents 10 basic statements about the material considered in this book. Although there are numerous statements that could be made about the rich material the various contributors have provided, 10 integrative statements or postulates that I regard as particularly salient are put forth. The different statements, although quite fundamental, seem worthy of attention and consideration here; they consistently apply to most, if not all, of the reviewed instruments and procedures.

SOME POSTULATES ABOUT THE USE OF TESTS AND ASSESSMENT PROCEDURES IN COUNSELING

1. *The use of tests and assessment procedures in counseling should be guided by a model and method that considers both process and outcome variables.* Consistent with the material considered in Chapter 1, tests and assessment procedures should not be used in a random, purposeless, haphazard manner; instead, their use in counseling should be purposeful, with a goal, direction, and objective in view. To render the testing and assessment process most meaningful to counseling, counselors should follow some model or method of test/assessment use that informs their practice.

Such a model (like the model presented in Chap. 1) considers both process and outcome variables and provides the counselor with an overall perspective on how to use tests and assessment procedures and their place in the counseling process.

A model of test/assessment use takes into account such process and outcome variables as the purpose of assessment, client needs, the tests and assessment procedures available to provide the most useful information, the effective integration of test/assessment information into the counseling process, and means by which to maximize the benefit of test/assessment information to the client, among others. The model of test/assessment use, by considering these and other relevant variables, would provide direction to both the counselor's intrasession behavior (e.g., gauging a client's readiness to use the test information) and extrasession behavior (e.g., reviewing several tests to decide which one or ones would best meet the client's needs). An effective model of test/assessment use would seemingly apply to the various forms of assessment (e.g., personality, intellectual, vocational) in which the counselor may engage. Although providing directions, a good model is also a flexible schema that enables the counselor to accommodate to new information and needed changes.

2. *Tests and assessment procedures can be integrated into and can be facilitative of the counseling process.* If anything, the chapters in this book demonstrate that tests and assessment procedures can be facilitative of the counseling process; they can provide helpful information about client issues, stimulate client insights, confirm working hypotheses, and provide possible directions for clients to consider. Too often, it seems that tests and assessment procedures are not seen as valuable tools that can assist in the work of counseling. It also seems that, when used, they are often not integrated smoothly and effectively into the counseling process. Instead, they are used in a rather awkward and disjointed manner that may hinder rather than help the counselor and client.

In some work settings, it is not uncommon for clients to be given a battery of tests at the outset of counseling. Such a procedure can be very useful and provide much valuable information for the counseling relationship. Conversely, if such a procedure merely involves the routine administration of tests without appropriate follow-up or fails to actively involve clients in the assessment process (e.g., by not sharing test information with clients), the potential value of assessment for the counseling relationship remains unrealized. Similarly, if assessment is done only as an afterthought to the work of counseling, its potential value is again compromised. For tests and assessment procedures to be used most effectively, counselors must first realize that they can indeed be facilitative of the counseling process and then seriously focus on how best to integrate them into the work of counseling. The degree to which assessment instruments and information are useful to clients, in large part, depends on the counselor's effective utilization of them.

3. *Tests and assessment procedures are designed to be of benefit to the client and should be used accordingly.* The purpose of assessment is to assist the client in some way. Therefore, tests and assessment procedures should be seen as a means by which clients can be helped. The question for the counselor then becomes, "How might the use of tests and assessment procedures be of potential benefit to this client?" Before using them in counseling, this is a question counselors should always ask. It also is a question counselors may wish to directly pose to their clients as well.

Consistent with the focus on benefiting the client, the tests and assessment procedures reviewed throughout this book are considered to be aids or tools to stimulating personal development. They are thought of in terms of their facilitative, constructive potential. They are not regarded as static instruments (i.e., they do not merely reflect only the current status of the person, environment, etc.). Rather, they are regarded as process instruments. In other words, tests and assessment procedures are looked at for their ability not only to reflect the present but to give some means by which the future can be approached and considered.

4. *Tests and assessment procedures can be used to help individuals identify strengths, assets, and opportunities for growth.* If tests and assessment procedures are thought of in terms of their facilitative, constructive potential, how is this done? For one, as this postulate indicates, counselors approach tests and assessment procedures from a position of strength rather than weakness. That is, counselors use them to identify client strengths, assets, and opportunities for growth. Such an approach does not deny client weaknesses or deficiencies. Weaknesses or deficiencies are recognized, but counselors want to know how they can build on available strengths and assets to assist the client.

Perhaps a rather simplistic way of summarizing the preceding paragraph is that counselors, in using tests and assessment procedures, look for what is right with clients instead of what is wrong. Unfortunately, this approach is often seemingly misunderstood, being labeled as naive and uninformed about psychopathology. Such misunderstanding, however, is more often based on a lack of knowledge about counselors' conceptualization of assessment than otherwise. A focus on client strengths, assets, and constructive potentials, in both theory and practice, does not exist exclusive of client deficiencies and obstacles blocking growth. The approach to helping clients adopted by counselors evolves from a hygiological (health orientation; Super, 1955) rather than pathological (disease orientation) perspective. Counselors do not think of assessment as a method to identify what is "wrong" with the client. From the perspective adopted here, such a mind set is defeatist and unhelpful.

In reflecting on the rise and fall of psychodiagnosis, Cleveland (1976) seemed to capture well much of the thinking I am trying to communicate.

> Our test reports tend to emphasize pathology and to ignore assets, constructive characteristics, and healthy mechanisms used by the client. As testers, we must be as diligent in our search of test data for the positive features of a respondent's personality as we are in our invocation of pathology. Psychological test findings should serve as forecasts for useful and constructive potentials as well as for unfavorable portents. (p. 314)

5. *Tests can be used to enhance the functioning of well-adjusted or relatively well-adjusted individuals.* As indicated in the preface, the focus of this book has been on assessment of individuals characterized by such descriptors as well-functioning, relatively well-functioning, mild to moderately distressed, and non-psychiatrically disturbed. A not uncommon question, particularly with the current attitude prevailing in mental health care, is asked as follows: If individuals are functioning well or adequately, why do we then need to engage them in a assessment/counseling relationship? In answer to this question, the old adage, "If it ain't broke, don't fix it," is often invoked. From a purely cost-effectiveness perspective, this question and adage are highly appropriate and defensible. However, in terms of enhancing personal satisfaction and happiness, the previously asked question and adage may not be in the public's best interest.

Just as the poorly functioning client can benefit from a assessment/counseling process, the well-functioning client can also benefit from such a process. The chapters in this book, which largely focused on using tests with a non-psychiatrically disturbed clientele, illustrate this point well. Personality and vocational tests and related assessment methods (e.g., cognitive and behavioral methods) can all be used toward this end. Tests and related assessment methods, in being used with well-functioning or relatively well-functioning clients, can have a number of positive process and outcome effects: (a) provide insight into current behavioral patterns and thought processes; (b) narrow a seemingly vast field of possibilities to a manageable number; (c) provide life/career alternatives for consideration and review; (d) identify resources and abilities on which one can build; (e) identify areas needing further examination, analysis, or remediation; and (f) enhance self and life satisfaction. Thus, tests and assessment procedures indeed can be viably and very effectively used with a well-functioning or relatively well-functioning clientele. The benefits of assessment for such clients are many, with one important potential benefit being the development of even more and better life functioning for clients in counseling.

6. *Tests and assessment procedures provide a framework or schema for organizing, understanding, and integrating seemingly disparate types of infor-*

mation about clients. The tests and assessment procedures considered in Parts I and II are means by which various forms of information about clients can be organized. They bring a sense of coherence and order to what at first glance may seem to be irreconcilable pieces of data. They provide a framework or schema through which organization can occur. For example, each test scale can provide selected information on certain forms of behavior, affect, or aspects of personality. When different test scales of an instrument (e.g., the Minnesota Multiphasic Personality Inventory–2) are considered collectively, the configuration of scales can provide a comprehensive picture of the client's current functioning across a number of areas. Thus, test scales, when taken separately and collectively, provide a method for organizing, understanding, and integrating seemingly disparate types of information about clients.

In many of the tests and assessment procedures covered in this book, a higher order framework or schema is also used to organize the data. Such higher order schemas can be seen, for example, in Gough's cuboid model (Chap. 3), the concept of "types" in the Myers-Briggs Type Indicator (MBTI, Chap. 5), and the integration of Holland's type theory (Holland, 1985) into the use of the Strong Interest Inventory, Self-Directed Search, and vocational card sorts (Chaps. 7, 10, and 11, respectively). These higher order schemas provide a means of understanding assessment data at the macro level of analysis, whereas a test scale in and of itself provides a means of understanding data at a micro level of analysis. The higher order schemas are more molar and comprehensive in scope, whereas lower order schemas (i.e., test scales) are more molecular and specific in nature. Higher order and lower order schemas, although both potentially important when approached as independent sources of data, are really complementary forms of understanding, organizing, and integrating assessment information and are most meaningful when used as such.

7. *Tests and assessment procedures are multipurposed.* As is clear from these chapters, the tests and assessment procedures considered here can provide both counselor and client with rich information across a variety of areas. In considering the different information these tests and assessment procedures can provide, it also is important to regard them as multipurposed. In Parts I and II, we divided the test and assessment procedures into personality and vocational. But, as several of the contributors pointed out, some of the personality instruments can be useful in vocational counseling. For example, certain traits (Sixteen Personality Factor Questionnaire) or personality types (MBTI) may be more consistent with particular jobs or careers. Conversely, some of the vocational instruments can be useful in personal counseling (cf. Lowman, 1988). After all, Holland's theory of vocational types is a theory of personality types (see Holland, 1985). The counselor would do well to not exclusively consider a test or assesssment pro-

cedure (at least in terms of the ones covered here) as unidimensional and singular in focus. Instead, where appropriate, the counselor should consider the possible uses to which a test or assessment procedure can be put and its potential multipurposed, multidimensional nature.

If a test or assessment procedure is multipurposed and multidimensional in nature, then it follows that the counselor would also examine the multiclient and multisetting uses of it. For example, what are the different types of clients for which the test is appropriate and could be helpful? What are the different settings in which the assessment procedure could be viably used? The point here is not to consider a test or assessment procedure as serving all purposes for all clients, but to critically evaluate how it can assist certain types of clients who present with different types of issues and who come for counseling in different types of settings. These concerns relate back to point 1, the counselor's model or method for using tests and assessment procedures, and the material presented in Chapter 1.

8. *Counselors should be familiar with various tests and assessment procedures and, when appropriate, consider a multimethod approach to using them in counseling.* The use of tests or assessment procedures in combination with one another sometimes will be the best approach to obtaining the desired information for counseling. In considering the use of several in combination, the idea is not that "more is better." Instead, the question to be asked is as follows: Would two (or more) instruments complement one another in more effectively answering the questions that now present themselves in counseling? Again, the answer to such a question is guided by a model or method of assessment use and must be informed by the counselor's knowledge of the tests and assessment procedures being considered and how they would work together. The chapter by Savickas (Chap. 12), for example, provides a good illustration of how different instruments can be combined and used effectively.

If a multimethod approach to assessment is to be considered, then the counselor must have the requisite information available to evaluate this option. As indicated in the preceding paragraph, the counselor's knowledge base about the tests and assessmsent procedures is critical. Perhaps this goes without saying, but too often it seems that different assessment tools are used either separately or in conjunction with each other without the counselor possessing sufficient understanding of or knowledge about them. Any consideration of the multimethod approach must be solidly grounded in a critically informed perspective.

9. *Effective assessment use requires a sound knowledge base that is informed by contemporary assessment issues, test user guidelines and qualifications, and familiarity with the particular assessment methods being used.* This postulate and the preceding postulate are clearly interrelated. Effective assessment use is not a matter to be taken lightly, as the chapter by Betz (Chap. 13)

well illustrates. If tests and assessment procedures are to be used effectively, then there are a number of issues to which the user must be sensitive. A sound knowledge about ethical and professional standards in using tests/assessment procedures, reliability and validity of the assessment tools being used, and the qualifications needed to use them, among other areas, is critical to possess. Also, it is important to be knowledgeable about the concept of bias in testing and assessment and how this issue relates to women, racial/ethnic minorities, and cross-cultural applications.

If the counselor is to develop the knowledge base needed to use tests and assessment procedures effectively, then it pays to be ever mindful of the various sources that provide contemporary assessmsent information. These sources include the *Standards for Educational and Psychological Testing* (American Education Research Association, American Psychological Association, & National Council on Measurement in Education, 1985) and ethical principles that guide the practice of counselors and psychologists (American Association for Counseling and Development, 1988; American Psychological Association, 1992). Equally important are test reviews, which can be found in such sources as the *Mental Measurements Yearbook* and issues of the *Journal of Counseling and Development* and *Measurement and Evaluation in Counseling and Development*. Test reviews provide a valuable source of critical, evaluative information and their importance in appraising a test is well in evidence in several of the chapters presented here (e.g., see Slaney & MacKinnon-Slaney, Chap. 11; Savickas, Chap. 12). For other valuable sources of assessment information, the reader is referred back to the excellent chapter written by Betz. As mentioned in postulate 2, the degree to which assessment instruments and information are useful to clients largely depends on the counselor's effective utilization of them. In agreement with this statement, the effective utilization of assessment instruments and information largely depends on the soundness and thoroughness of the counselor's knowledge base about them.

10. *The computer-assisted testing and assessment services now available to the counselor represent an increasingly burgeoning technology, which should be approached favorably but with an awareness about the positive and negative features accompanying it.* The computer-assisted testing and assessment services now available for counselor use have mushroomed in growth in recent years. Indeed, the computer services available to the counselor have grown so rapidly that it is often difficult to remain abreast of contemporary developments. The counselor would do well, however, to be familiar with some of these developments because, as Sampson (Chap. 14) indicates, a number of benefits can accompany the use of computer-assisted assessment services. Some of these benefits, which include better integrating of assessment data into counseling, enhanced test reliability and validity, and the saving of counselor time, cut to the heart of some important assessment/counseling

issues and have the potential for rendering the assessment/counseling process more effective.

As Sampson further points out, just as there are potential benefits to the use of computer-assisted services in counseling, there are also potential problems. The potential problem areas he identifies—threats to test reliability and validity, and ineffective implementation—are by no means minor. The threats to test reliability and validity that Sampson mentions are certainly of concern and merit attention. As with much work in assessment and counseling, the problem area of ineffective implementation of computer services appears to be attitudinally based. Thus, the person—machine interface is and probably always will be an issue in the use of assessment services in counseling. With these limitations acknowledged, however, computer-assisted assessment services seemingly can contribute positively to the counseling experience. Counselors should become knowledgeable about these services but should be ever familiar with the potential benefits and problems that accompany them.

CONCLUSION

These 10 integrative, summative statements can be considered postulates about the use of tests and assessment procedures in counseling. Although quite fundamental and limited in scope, these postulates seem worthy of attention here because they provide some perspective on the material presented in this book. As has been evident in this chapter and preceding chapters, assessment is a complex process that involves such variables as forethought, planning, knowledge, and effective utilization. Assessment is not a haphazard, random process that can be done in a "quick and dirty" way. Like counseling, assessment requires a commitment on the parts of the counselor and client.

Although effective assessment use requires commitment and other variables as already mentioned, it is a process well worth the effort. The potential gains from using tests and assessment procedures in counseling far outweigh the effort invested. The chapters in this book attest again and again to the value of tests and assessment procedures and their many uses. The different chapter contributors have put together some highly valuable information on the state-of-the-art and state-of-the-science of the place of assessment in counseling. I hope that counselors may often find this information of value as they prepare to use tests and assessmsent procedures in counseling practice.

REFERENCES

American Association for Counseling and Development. (1988). Ethical standards of the American Association for Counseling and Development. *Journal of Counseling and Development, 67*, 4–8.

American Educational Research Association, American Psychological Association, & National Council on Measurement in Education. (1985). *Standards for educational and psychological testing*. Washington, DC: American Psychological Association.

American Psychological Association. (1992). Ethical principles of psychologists and code of conduct. *American Psychologist, 47,* 1597–1611.

Cleveland, S. E. (1976). Reflections on the rise and fall of psychodiagnosis. *Professional Psychology, 7,* 309–318.

Holland, J. L. (1985). *Making vocational choices: A theory of vocational personalities and work environments*. Englewood Cliffs, NJ: Prentice Hall.

Lowman, R. L. (1987). Occupational choice as a moderator of psychotherapeutic approach. *Psychotherapy, 24,* 801–808.

Super, D. E. (1955). Transition: From vocational guidance to counseling psychology. *Journal of Counseling Psychology, 2,* 3–9.

Author Index

557

Subject Index